CIRCULATING THE WORD OF GOD IN
MEDIEVAL AND EARLY MODERN EUROPE

SERMO

STUDIES ON PATRISTIC, MEDIEVAL, AND
REFORMATION SERMONS AND PREACHING

VOLUME 17

Editor

Regina D. Schiewer, *Katholische Universität Eichstätt-Ingolstadt*

Editorial Board

Roger Andersson, *Stockholms universitet*
Jussi Hanska, *Tampereen yliopisto (Tampere University)*
Thom Mertens, *Universiteit Antwerpen*
Franco Morenzoni, *Université de Genève*
Veronica O'Mara, *University of Leeds*
Anne Thayer, *Lancaster Theological Seminary*

Previously published volumes in this
series are listed at the back of the book.

Circulating the Word of God in Medieval and Early Modern Europe

Catholic Preaching and Preachers across
Manuscript and Print (c. 1450 to c. 1550)

Edited by
VERONICA O'MARA
and PATRICIA STOOP

BREPOLS

British Library Cataloguing in Publication Data
A catalogue record for this book is available from the British Library.

© 2022, Brepols Publishers n.v., Turnhout, Belgium.

All rights reserved. No part of this publication may be reproduced, stored in a retrieval system, or transmitted, in any form or by any means, electronic, mechanical, photocopying, recording, or otherwise without the prior permission of the publisher.

ISBN: 978-2-503-58515-4
E-ISBN: 978-2-503-58516-1
DOI: 10.1484/M.SERMO-EB.5.117718
ISSN: 1784–8806
e-ISSN: 2295–2764

Printed in the EU on acid-free paper.

D/2022/0095/151

Table of Contents

List of Illustrations   9

Acknowledgements   11

Abbreviations and Selected Online Resources   13

Introduction

**Circulating the Word of God in Medieval and Early
Modern Europe: Catholic Preaching and Preachers
across Manuscript and Print (*c.* 1450 to *c.* 1550)**
Veronica O'MARA and Patricia STOOP   17

England

**Books for Preaching and Preaching with Books:
Late Medieval Latin Printed Sermons and the
Witness of Thomas Swalwell of Durham Priory**
Anne T. THAYER   49

**The Early Printed Sermon in England
between 1483 and 1532: A Peculiar Phenomenon**
Veronica O'MARA   71

Scandinavia

**Preaching in Finland on the Eve of the Reformation
and Beyond: The Evidence from Manuscript and Print**
Jussi HANSKA

105

**Christiern Pedersen's *Alle Epistler oc Euangelia* (1515):
Reading a Catholic Text in the Danish Reformation**
Jonathan ADAMS

133

**The Word of God Purely Preached: Continuity and
Change in the Postils of the Swedish Reformation**
Christer PAHLMBLAD

161

Transylvania

**Latin Manuscript and Printed Sermons in
Late Medieval Transylvania (1470–1530)**
Adinel C. DINCĂ and Paula COTOI

187

Romance Regions

**Controversial Topics in the Sermons of Vicent Ferrer:
From Manuscripts to the Printing Press**
Oriol CATALÁN

223

**From Nicolas de Biard's *Summa de abstinentia*
to the Printed *Dictionarius pauperum*:
A Pastoral Compendium for Preachers**
Sophie DELMAS

257

**A Forgotten Italian Bestseller:
Ludovico Pittorio's *Omiliario quadragisimale***
Pietro DELCORNO

279

Germanic Lands

**The Neglected Carmelites: Evidence for their
Preaching Activities in Late Medieval Germany**
Ralf LÜTZELSCHWAB   313

**Johannes Kreutzer: A Preacher in Strasbourg and
Basel and his Work in Manuscript and Early Print**
Natalija GANINA   339

Instructio, correctio, **and** *reformatio*:
**Johannes Geiler von Kaysersberg
and the Transmission of his Sermons**   365
Rita VOLTMER

The Low Countries

**The Gouda Gospel Sermons: The Glosses of a Successful
Middle Dutch Pericope Collection (1477–1553)**
Thom MERTENS   411

**Diverging Perceptions: Johannes Tauler
in Sixteenth-Century Printed Editions**
Kees SCHEPERS   445

**Strategies of Publishing:
The Case of Franciscus Costerus**
Patricia STOOP   473

Indices   497

List of Illustrations

Figure 1.   Bernardino da Busti, *Rosarium sermonum predicabilium* (Lyon: Johannes Clein, 1502). Durham, Ushaw College Library, XVIII.B.4.24, fol. 88r.   59

Figure 2.   *Biblia Latina cum postillis Hugonis de Sancto Charo* ([Basel]: Johann Amerbach for Anton Koberger, 1502). Durham, Ushaw College Library, XVIII.B.3.10, fol. n. 6v.   64

Figure 3.   Map of Central Europe around 1500.   188

Figure 4.   Foundation Ceremony of the Universität Basel, 4 April 1460. First row, from left to right: Rector Georg von Andlau, an unknown cleric, Bishop Johann von Venningen, presumably Johannes Kreutzer, and Hans von Flachslanden. Register of the rector of the Universität Basel, 1 (1460–1567). Basel, Universitätsbibliothek, Cod. AN II 3, fol. 2v.   343

Figure 5.   Johannes Geiler von Kaysersberg, painted by Hans Burgkmair, the Elder, in 1490. München, Bayerische Staatsgemäldesammlungen, Inv.-Nr. 3568.   366

Figure 6.   Johannes Geiler von Kayersberg in the pulpit in Strasbourg Cathedral. Engraving in *Heilsame Predigt* (Strasbourg: Johannes Grüninger, 1513), fol. III verso (VD16 G 782; copy München, Bayerische Staatsbibliothek, Rar. 2241#Beibd.2).   376

Figure 7.   Title page of *Navicula fatuorum*, published by Jakob Otter (Strasbourg: Matthias Schürer, 1510) (VD16 ZV 6437; copy München, Bayerische Staatsbibliothek, 4 P.lat. 728).   382

10 LIST OF ILLUSTRATIONS

Figure 8. Title page of *Pilgerschaft*, published by Jakob Otter
(Basel: Adam Petri, 1512) (VD16 G 727;
copy München, Bayerische Staatsbibliothek,
Res/2 P.lat. 874). 388

Figure 9. Title page of the 1543 Köln edition of
Tauler's Works. Universiteit Antwerpen,
Ruusbroecgenootschap, 3112 A 3. 449

Figure 10. Table of Contents of the 1543 Köln edition
of Tauler's Works. Universiteit Antwerpen,
Ruusbroecgenootschap, 3112 A 3, fol. Aiv. 454

Figure 11. Title page of the 1565 edition of Tauler's Works,
printed in Franckfort (= Emden). Universiteit
Antwerpen, Ruusbroecgenootschap, 3116 B 10. 458

Figure 12. Portrait of Franciscus Costerus, designed by
Lucas Vorsterman I (1595–1675) in Antwerp in
1619. Engraving, *c.* 120 × 85 mm. Rijksmuseum
Amsterdam, RP–P–OB–33.098. 475

Figure 13. Title page of *Catholiicke sermoonen op de
evangelien van de sondaghen naer Sinxen tot den
Advent* (Antwerpen: Joachim Trognesius, 1598).
Universiteit Antwerpen, Ruusbroecgenootschap,
3048 A 1. 478

Figure 14. Beginning of the sermon preached by Costerus
in the church of Sint-Goedele in Brussels on
the Wednesday after Pentecost 1593. Brussel,
Koninklijke Bibliotheek, MS 614, fol. 10r. 487

Acknowledgements

Many of the essays in the present volume began life as papers given at a conference of the same title at the University of Hull on 25–27 March 2017. To these much revised essays some specially commissioned ones have been added. We are grateful to the speakers, chair persons, and audience who attended the original conference and made it such a memorable occasion for us all. We are similarly thankful both to the original and the new contributors for their enthusiasm for this project and for their hard work and diligence in thoroughly revising or preparing their essays for publication. We have all learnt much in the process of our collaboration. It has been heartening to have been part of such a co-operative exercise that has united scholars from the extremities of Europe to North America.

Research of the highest order cannot be carried out without the use of excellent libraries, manuscript repositories, rare book collections, and archival centres; it is a pleasure to acknowledge the many institutions listed in the essays below who granted access to their holdings. In particular we wish to thank those authorities and institutions who gave permission for the reproduction of images. In this regard Adinel Dincă and Paula Cotoi are thankful to Andrei Nacu for designing the map in their essay. Natalija Ganina wishes to express her thanks for permission to reproduce the image from Universität Basel, MS AN II 3. Kees Schepers acknowledges permission for the reproduction of images from the printed books (shelfmarks: 3112 A 3 and 3116 B 10) in the Heritage Library of the Ruusbroecgenootschap of Universiteit Antwerpen as does Patricia Stoop (shelfmark: 3048 A 1). Both of them wish to thank Erna van Looveren for her help in reproducing these images. Patricia Stoop also extends her gratitude to the Rijksmuseum in Amsterdam and the Koninklijke Bibliotheek in Brussels for allowing her to publish the portrait of Franciscus Costerus and the image from Brussel, Koninklijke Bibliotheek, MS 614. Anne Thayer is grateful to the Trustees of Ushaw College in Durham for permission to reproduce images from Ushaw College (XVIII.B.3.10 and XVIII.B.4.24) and to the kindness of the staff of Ushaw College Library and Palace Green Library, Durham University for facilitating this. The editor-in-chief of Artos, Magnus Åkerlund, has kindly granted permission for the publication here of a reworked, much abbreviated, and translated version of a previous essay in Swedish by Christer Pahlmblad. The editors wish to acknowledge permission from the Rare Book Collection of the Kislak Center for Special Collections, Rare Books and Manuscripts, University of Pennsylvania for the reproduction of the cover image. In addition, the contributors and the editors are especially cognisant of the debt they owe to their own university libraries, particularly the Brotherton Library of the University of Leeds and the library of the Ruusbroecgenootschap in Universiteit Antwerpen. Without such splendid resources much of the research and final checking for this volume could not have been carried out.

The editors are pleased to thank Jonathan Adams, David Bagchi, Stephan Borgehammar, and Robert J. Miles who generously offered wise advice and punctilious assistance at various points in the editing of this volume. We also extend our gratitude to Regina Schiewer, chair of the editorial board of SERMO: Studies on Patristic, Medieval, and Reformation Sermons and Preaching, and the other board members, and especially to the readers of this volume who made various perceptive comments that helped considerably towards its improvement. The superlative Guy Carney at Brepols (the embodiment of the perfect Publishing Manager) has continued to offer steadfast and kind help, and we are inestimably grateful to him. In addition, we are most appreciative of the skills of our diligent copy-editor, Anna Vergidou, and especially of our patient typesetter, Martine Maguire-Weltecke.

Despite the care taken by all, producing this complex volume of essays has been a challenge, and so we apologize in advance for any errors that may have crept in. But we editors have done our best to produce a worthy volume; we wish to thank each other for sharing the work in a spirit of good humour and kindness.

Veronica O'Mara and Patricia Stoop
30 January 2022

Abbreviations and Selected Online Resources

BSB-Ink Bayerische Staatsbibliotheek Inkunabeln (https://www.bsb-muenchen. de/sammlungen/historische-drucke/bestaende/inkunabeln/)

CA M. F. A. G. Campbell, *Annales de la typographie néerlandaise au 15e siècle: 1°–4° Supplement*, 4 vols ('s-Gravenhage: Nijhoff, 1878–1890; repr. 's-Gravenhage: Nijhoff, 1962)

EDIT16 Censimento nazionale delle edizioni italiane del XVI secolo (https://edit16.iccu.sbn.it)

EEBO Early English Books Online (www.proquest.com/eebo)

ESTC English Short Title Catalogue (estc.bl.uk)

Goff Frederick Richmond Goff, *Incunabula in American Libraries: A Third Census of Fifteenth-Century Books Recorded in North American Libraries* (New York: Bibliographical Society of America, 1964); *Incunabula in American Libraries: A Supplement to the Third Census of Fifteenth-Century Books Recorded in North American Collections (1964)*, ed. by Frederick Richmond Goff (New York: Bibliographical Society of America, 1972)

GW *Gesamtkatalog der Wiegendrucke*, ed. by the Kommission für den Gesamtkatalog der Wiegendrucke (Leipzig: Hiersemann, 1925–; Stuttgart: Hiersemann, 1978) (www.gesamtkatalogderwiegendrucke. de/GWEN.xhtml)

Hain Ludwig Hain, *Repertorium bibliographicum, in quo libri omnes ab arte typographica inventa usque ad annum MD. typis expressi ordine alphabetico vel simpliciter enumerantur vel adcuratius recensentur*, 2 vols (Stuttgart: Cotta, 1826–1838)

ISTC Incunabula Short Title Catalogue (https://data.cerl.org/istc/_search)

LN Lauritz Nielsen, *Dansk Bibliografi 1482–1600*, ed. by Erik Dal, 5 vols, rev. edn (København: Det Danske Sprog- og Litteraturselskab, 1996)

NK Wouter Nijhoff and M. E. Kronenberg, *Nederlandsche bibliographie van 1500 tot 1540*, 3 vols in 6 parts ('s-Gravenhage: Nijhoff, 1923–1971)

PiK Predigt im Kontext (pik.ku-eichstaett.de)

STC Short Title Catalogue: A. W. Pollard, and G. R. Redgrave, *A Short-Title Catalogue of Books Printed in England, Scotland, and Ireland, and of English Books Printed Abroad*, second edition revised and enlarged by W. A. Jackson, F. S. Ferguson, and Katherine F. Pantzer, 3 vols (London: The Bibliographical Society, 1976–1991); STC: Short Title Catalogue (revised at estc.bl.uk)

14 ABBREVIATIONS AND SELECTED ONLINE RESOURCES

STCV STCV: de bibliografie van het handgedrukte boek / Short Title Catalogus Flanders (www.stcv.be)

USTC Universal Short Title Catalogue (www.ustc.ac.uk)

VD Verzeichnis der Druck des 16. Jahrhunderts (www.bsb-muenchen. de/kompetenzzentren-und-landesweite-dienste/kompetenzzentren/vd-16/)

Biblia Sacra: Bibles Printed in the Netherlands and Belgium (www.bibliasacra.nl)

Bijbels digitaal (www.bijbelsdigitaal.nl)

Codices Fennici-project (www.codicesfennici.fi)

Douay-Rheims Bible (www.drbo.org)

15cBooktrade (15cbooktrade.ox.ac.uk)

Fragmenta membranea-collection (https://fragmenta.kansalliskirjasto.fi)

Kloosterlijst: beknopt overzicht van de Nederlandse kloosters tot 1800 (www2.fgw.vu.nl/oz/kloosterlijst)

Material Evidence in Incunabula (https://data.cerl.org)

Oxford Dictionary of National Biography (www.oxforddnb.com)

Introduction

VERONICA O'MARA and PATRICIA STOOP

Circulating the Word of God in Medieval and Early Modern Europe

Catholic Preaching and Preachers across Manuscript and Print (c. 1450 to c. 1550)

Introduction

From the earliest days of the Church transmitting the Word of God via preaching has been a central form of its ministry. Preachers sought to make the gospel known, understood, and applicable to people's lives; its transformative power was invoked for both individuals and communities. Preachers spoke with spiritual authority, shaping religious ideas, sensibilities, and experiences. The written preservation of the sermon developed at different rates throughout Europe and in varied languages and registers, with a continuous movement between Latin and the vernaculars. As valued texts, sermons have been collected in writing virtually as long as they have been preached. Monasteries became treasure houses of such manuscripts where patristic sermons were often read aloud at mealtimes. Their scriptoria copied and re-copied sermon collections that formed a central part of their growing libraries. The turn of the thirteenth century was a watershed in the history of preaching and sermon production in the West when there was a new zeal to imitate the life of the apostles, including their preaching, and members of mendicant orders, especially the Franciscans and Dominicans, became renowned preachers. The urban communities in which they ministered in the early 1200s experienced, what Carlo Delcorno has called, 'the importance and almost the intoxicating quality, as it were, of public discourse'.[1] As they developed, university centres became sites for the production and diffusion of preaching texts and their associated aids. Yet sermons were also written by humble parish clergy who either exerted themselves to compose their own material or relied on the numerous mainly Latin model collections that flooded Europe. By the late medieval and early modern periods preaching functioned as a means of mass communication, a sort of internet of its age.

---

1 Carlo Delcorno, 'Medieval Preaching in Italy (1200–1500)', in *The Sermon*, ed. by Beverly Mayne Kienzle, Typologie des sources du Moyen Âge occidental, 81–83 (Turnhout: Brepols, 2000), pp. 449–560 (p. 450).

Circulating the Word of God in Medieval and Early Modern Europe: Catholic Preaching and Preachers across Manuscript and Print (c. 1450 to c. 1550), ed. by Veronica O'Mara and Patricia Stoop, SERMO 17, (Turnhout: Brepols, 2022), pp. 17–45   BREPOLS ☙ PUBLISHERS   10.1484/M.SERMO-EB.5.130450

The sermon was a vehicle not only to purvey religious teaching but also a means to enable social cohesion, as well as to offset heretical leanings and to provide a bulwark against the spiritual or political enemy, whomsoever that might be. It both reflected and shaped European culture; it provided important parts of the mental equipment with which people processed the world; it informed them politically and socially. And, as the demand for more preaching continued to grow, the market for sermons and preachable material expanded. This need was satisfied in various ways and to varying degrees; there were surges in production at different points, be it in the mass produced manuscripts of Jacobus de Voragine's *Legenda aurea* that circulated to every area of Europe from the thirteenth century onwards to the publication of Johannes Herolt's printed *Sermones de tempore et de sanctis* that did likewise from the fifteenth century. There is no one pattern that unifies the whole of Europe, or even selected areas (such as the Germanic regions or the Romance languages). Neither can neat chronological classifications be made about developments. This is particularly the case with regard to the complicated transition from manuscript to print in the fifteenth century or for the part-movement from Catholicism to Protestantism in Europe from the first decades of the sixteenth century. It is for this reason that the essays in this volume deliberately concentrate on this time between the handwritten and the printed sermon, a period when not only the mode of production was changing but when the very purpose and meaning of preaching itself would soon alter in a Western Christian world that was becoming no longer completely Catholic.

We choose to focus on this liminal but important era that is a neglected one in sermon studies — as well as in other fields — and we make no apology for highlighting the word 'Catholic' in our title as it is fundamental to the explorations here, as we shall see. The topic is apt because no proper attention has been paid to the sermon's complex inter-relationship in manuscript and print over time. While there are numerous studies, both general and specific, concentrating on sermons in a particular language, others that focus on a prescribed period or that investigate an individual preacher, little attention has been given to the transitional era between manuscript and print or between Catholicism and Lutheranism or indeed to examine preaching in a comparative European perspective during this period.[2]

There are many informative disquisitions on the rise of print that have done much to inform us about this important technological development.[3]

---

2 For example, the foremost overview of individual language sermon studies in *The Sermon*, ed. by Kienzle, says little about printed material and does not extend much beyond 1500.

3 For instance (out of a large selection), Lucien Febvre and Henri-Jean Martin, *L'Apparition du livre*, L'Évolution de l'humanité, II, 8, iii (Paris: Michel, 1958); Rudolf Hirsch, *Printing, Selling and Reading, 1450–1550* (Wiesbaden: Harrassowitz, 1967); Elizabeth L. Eisenstein, *The Printing Press as an Agent of Change: Communications and Cultural Transformations in Early-Modern Europe*, 2 vols (Cambridge: Cambridge University Press, 1979), re-issued and

CIRCULATING THE WORD OF GOD IN MEDIEVAL AND EARLY MODERN EUROPE 19

Much has also been written about the growth, spread, and commercial imperatives of the early print industry in Europe that takes in both presses that have flourished and presses that have failed; other works have concentrated on printers or printing in particular languages or regions.[4] Yet, quite apart from the recent fevered concentration on Martin Luther (1483–1546),[5] sermons are usually incidental to such discussions and only occasionally get mentioned as examples of processes along the way, with a few noteworthy exceptions.[6]

---

abridged, without references but with images as *The Printing Revolution in Early Modern Europe* (Cambridge: Cambridge University Library, 1983); *Incunabula and Their Readers: Printing, Selling and Using Books in the Fifteenth Century*, ed. by Kristian Jensen (London: The British Library, 2003); *Geschreven en gedrukt: boekproductie van handschrift naar druk in de overgang van Middeleeuwen naar Moderne Tijd*, ed. by Herman Pleij, Joris Reynaert, and others (Gent: Academia Press, 2004); Andrew Pettegree, *The Book in the Renaissance* (New Haven: Yale University Press, 2011); Koen Goudriaan, 'The Church and the Market: Vernacular Religious Works and the Early Printing Press in the Low Countries, 1447–1540', 'The *Devotio moderna* and the Printing Press (*c.* 1475–1540)', and 'The Franciscans, the Laity and the Printing Press', in Koen Goudriaan, *Piety in Practice and Print: Essays on the Late Medieval Religious Landscape*, ed. by Anna Dlabačová and Ad Tervoort, ReLiC, Studies in Dutch Religious History, 4 (Hilversum: Verloren, 2016), pp. 240–56, 257–78, and 279–308; and *Printing R-Evolution and Society 1450–1500: Fifty Years that Changed Europe*, ed. by Christina Dondi, Studi di Storia, 13 (Venezia: Edizioni Ca'Foscari, 2020). Especially useful is the series of valuable books in Brill's Handpress World series starting with Andrew Pettegree, *The French Book and the European Book World*, Library of the Written Word, 1, The Handpress World, 1 (Leiden: Brill, 2007), with two of the more recent relevant volumes being *Print Culture and Peripheries in Early Modern Europe: A Contribution to the History of Printing and the Book Trade in Small European and Spanish Cities*, ed. by Benito Rial Costas, Library of the Written Word, 24, The Handpress World, 18 (Leiden: Brill, 2013); and Lotte Hellinga, *Incunabula in Transit: People and Trade*, Library of the Written Word, 62, The Handpress World, 47 (Leiden: Brill, 2018). See also Edit 16, ESTC, GW, ISTC, STC, STCV, and USTC, as well as *Material Evidence in Incunabula*, and *15cBooktrade*, which deal with provenance (all in the Abbreviations list and accessed 22 May 2021), in addition to dedicated journals such as the *Gutenberg Jahrbuch*.

4 For recent examples of the latter, again from a wide selection, see Christoph Reske, *Die Buchdrucker des 16. und 17. Jahrhunderts im deutschen Sprachgebiet: auf der Grundlage des gleichnamigen Werkes von Josef Benzing*, Beiträge zum Buch- und Bibliothekswesen, 51, 2nd edn (Wiesbaden: Harrassowitz, 2015); Catherine Kikuchi, *La Venise des livres: 1469–1530* (Cézeyrieu: Champ Vallon, 2018); and *Les Premiers imprimés français et la littérature de Bourgogne (1470–1550): Actes du colloque international tenu à l'Université du Littoral Côte d'Opale (Dunkerque)*, ed. by Jean Devaux, Matthieu Marchal, and Alexandra Vélissariou, Bibliothèque du XVe siècle, 86 (Paris: Honoré Champion, 2021).

5 Luther's perceived significance is summed up in the blurb on one of the many books and collections that appeared for the quincentenary: 'How an unheralded monk turned his small town into a centre of publishing, made himself the most famous man in Europe — and started the Protestant Reformation'; see Andrew Pettegree, *Brand Luther: 1517, Printing, and the Making of the Reformation* (New York: Penguin, 2015).

6 See in particular Miriam Usher Chrisman, *Lay Culture, Learned Culture: Books and Social Change in Strasbourg, 1480–1599* (New Haven: Yale University Press, 1982). There are, of course, a few studies that devote themselves to printing and sermons (or to mainly printed sermons), most notably for the early period, J. W. Blench, *Preaching in England in the Late Fifteenth and Sixteenth Centuries: A Study of English Sermons 1450–c. 1600* (Oxford: Blackwell,

There are even cases where such neglect is marked.[7] This is all the more surprising given the overall importance of sermon printing in the early period.[8]

Fewer in number are studies that concentrate on the interaction of manuscripts and print.[9] Mainly these tend to focus on handwritten additions to early printed books such as hand-coloured images or manuscript versions of printed works, with various examples of manuscript copies of printed texts of all genres extant throughout Europe, sometimes of exceptionally high quality.[10] It is rare to find studies of the actual relationship between the pre-printed manuscript text and the printed product, in part because little information is known about this.[11] Rarer still are studies that deal with manuscripts and early printed texts equally in all their complexity, something that we are hoping to address in the essays below as a whole.[12] In fact study of the sermon

---

1964); Larissa Taylor, *Soldiers of Christ: Preaching in Late Medieval and Reformation France* (New York: Oxford University Press, 1992); Larissa Juliet Taylor, 'Out of Print: The Decline of Catholic Printed Sermons in France, 1530–1560', in *Habent sua fata libelli / Books Have Their Own Destiny: Essays in Honor of Robert V. Schnucker*, ed. by Robin B. Barnes, Robert A. Kolb, and Paula L. Presley, Sixteenth Century Essays and Studies, 1 (Kirksville, MO: Truman State University Press, 1998), pp. 121–30; *Preachers and People in the Reformations and Early Modern Period*, ed. by Larissa Taylor, A New History of the Sermon, 2 (Leiden: Brill, 2001); Anne T. Thayer, *Penitence, Preaching and the Coming of the Reformation*, St Andrews Studies in Reformation History (Aldershot: Ashgate, 2002); and Emily Michelson, *The Pulpit and the Press in Reformation Italy*, I tatti studies in Italian renaissance history (Cambridge, MA: Harvard University Press, 2013). Studies on sermons in manuscript in Latin and the different vernaculars are far too numerous to list here, though a starting point is the 'Bibliography' compiled by George Ferzoco and Carolyn Muessig in *The Sermon*, ed. by Kienzle, pp. 19–142.

7 Two recent examples of this are Kathleen Tonry, *Agency and Intention in English Print, 1476–1526*, Texts and Transitions, 7 (Turnhout: Brepols, 2016) and Alexandra Da Costa, *Marketing English Books, 1476–1550: How Printers Changed Reading*, Oxford Studies in Medieval Literature and Culture (Oxford: Oxford University Press, 2020) where sermons barely rate a mention.

8 To take just one example, Chrisman, in *Lay Culture, Learned Culture*, notes that 'The heart of Catholic publication in Strasbourg from 1480 to 1499 was the printing of sermons, sermons of the great preachers of the past. Of the total of 770 Catholic books published, 192 (25 percent) were sermons, the majority printed before 1500' (p. 84).

9 See, for example, in general, David McKitterick, *Print, Manuscript and the Search for Order, 1450–1830* (Cambridge: Cambridge University Press, 2003) and *Books in Transition at the Time of Philip the Fair: Manuscripts and Printed Books in the Late Fifteenth and Early Sixteenth Century Low Countries*, ed. by Hanno Wijsman, Burgundica, 15 (Turnhout: Brepols, 2010). Individual studies such as Roberto Rusconi, 'Le prediche di Fra Girolamo da Ferrara: dai manoscritti al pulpito alle stampe', in *Una città e il suo profeta: Firenze di fronte al Savonarola*, ed. by Gian Carlo Garfagnini, Savonarola e Toscana, 15 (Firenze: SISMEL, 2001), pp. 201–34, that concentrate on the interaction of sermon manuscript and print are fairly rare overall.

10 Some particularly notable works were in the library of Rafael de Mercatellis (1437–1508), abbot and scholar and illegitimate son of Philip the Good, Duke of Burgundy (1396–1467), whose collection of some eighty books (a large part of which is now in Universiteitsbibliotheek Gent) was produced from 1479 to 1505.

11 An example is Lotte Hellinga, *Texts in Transit: Manuscript to Proof and Print in the Fifteenth Century*, Library of the Written Word, 38, The Handpress World, 29 (Leiden: Brill, 2014).

12 Better served chronologically and geographically are legendaries both in the manuscript and

is an ideal way to highlight continuities (and changes) in the period. As Falk Eisermann says, 'The historical term "revolution", I believe, turns out to be not too useful for characterizing a transitional process like the introduction of printing into European culture' going on to note that 'The sustainability and innovative power of the printing press, which would eventually turn out to be world-changing, only became evident decades, if not centuries, later'.[13]

While there are some laudable studies on the sermon in the later period, these have a tendency to overlook, dismiss, or even be surprised at the existence of medieval Catholic preaching. For instance, one commentator opens up her discussion by saying 'It is a well-established and only partly confounded myth that the English sermon was a product of the Protestant Reformation in England', but then sums up the earlier manuscript situation in a single sentence: 'In fact, sermons were an integral part of traditional religious life in fifteenth-century England, and sixteenth-century sermons built upon these foundations' followed by just another half page or so.[14] A researcher on German preaching alludes to how he had only in the last decade discovered his mistake when he had noted that he 'knew that "preaching and the German Reformation" was a Protestant phenomenon […]'.[15]

Although the argument about the printed sermon as a purely Protestant preserve, a topic of abiding interest among earlier scholars, is now questioned more seriously, the validation of Counter-Reformation or Catholic Reformation preaching can also serve to elide what had gone before.[16] Above all, scholarship on the sermon, like most research, either concentrates exclusively on what is deemed to be 'medieval' or, more usually, as we have seen, brushes this

---

later period; see, for example, the volumes in the series *Hagiographies: Histoire internationale de la littérature hagiographique latine et vernaculaire en Occident des origines à 1550*, ed. by Guy Philippart (I–V), Monique Goullet (VI–VII), and Michèle Gaillard and Monique Goullet (VIII), Corpus Christianorum Texts and Studies, 8 vols (Turnhout: Brepols, 1994–2020) or individual national studies such as Alison Knowles Frazier, *Possible Lives: Authors and Saints in Renaissance Italy* (New York: Colombia University Press, 2005), quite apart from the industrial quantities of books on Jacobus de Voragine's *Legenda aurea* and its dissemination, translation, and congeners in manuscript and print throughout Europe.

13 Falk Eisermann, 'A Golden Age? Monastic Printing Houses in the Fifteenth Century', in *Print Culture and Peripheries in Early Modern Europe*, ed. by Rial Costas, pp. 37–67 (p. 39).

14 Lucy Wooding, 'From Tudor Humanism to Reformation Preaching', in *The Oxford Handbook of the Early Modern Sermon*, ed. by Peter McCullough, Hugh Adlington, and Emma Rhatigan (Oxford: Oxford University Press, 2011), pp. 329–47 (p. 330).

15 John M. Frymire, *The Primacy of the Postils: Catholics, Protestants, and the Dissemination of Ideas in Early Modern Germany*, Studies in Medieval and Reformation Traditions, 147 (Leiden: Brill, 2010), pp. 1–2. This point is dealt with more fully in the essay by Jussi Hanska.

16 Frederick J. McGinness, *Right Thinking and Sacred Oratory in Counter-Reformation Rome* (Princeton: Princeton University Press, 1995); Bert Roest, 'Wat salmen met sulck volck maken? Franciscaanse stadspredikers en de verdediging van het katholicisme in Nederland, ca. 1520–1568', in *Stedelijk verleden in veelvoud: opstellen over laatmiddeleeuwse stadsgeschiedenis in de Nederlanden voor Dick de Boer*, ed. by Hanno Brand, Jeroen Benders, and Renée Nip, Middeleeuwse Studies en Bronnen, 134 (Hilversum: Verloren, 2011), pp. 245–58.

aside in favour of the 'early modern' period (however these are defined).[17] Yet as the English historian G. M. Trevelyan (1876–1962) once commented: '[Historical] periods are not facts. They are retrospective conceptions that we form about past events, useful to focus discussion but very often leading historical thought astray'.[18] The same may be said for literature; there is a difference between a chronological period and a cultural phenomenon. From an early modern perspective, the Middle Ages is always going to be downplayed, sandwiched as it is between the glories of classical antiquity and the heights of the Renaissance. Perhaps the best explanation of such attitudes is given by James Simpson in *Reform and Cultural Revolution*, a provocative if idiosyncratic book dealing with the period from 1350 to 1547 that has garnered its own critique:

> Sudden concentrations of cultural and political power both permit and necessitate an aggressive physical and ideological demolition of the 'old' order. Accordingly, such concentrations provoke cultural practices that stress the values of unity and novelty above all. The fact of a sudden historical break itself presupposes a large concentration of power. Thus the stress on unity: whereas the old order will be re-described as subject to a bedevilling complication of lines of authority, the new order will highlight a simple chain of command. A sudden, politically driven break in history will prize novelty because a new dispensation must legitimate itself, and must, therefore, re-describe the repudiated order as 'old' and depleted. These values of unity and novelty will inform all cultural practices, and especially architecture, historiography, jurisprudence, theology, philology, politics, painting, and literature.[19]

This entrenched medieval versus early modern divide has set up a number of simplistic binary oppositions that have coloured thinking about literature and history: scholasticism versus humanism; Latin versus the vernaculars; manuscript versus print; Catholicism versus Protestantism; religion versus the secular; nationalism versus internationalism, and so on. None of this is helped by the fact that there is a very imprecise correlation between what is meant by 'medieval' or 'early modern' in Europe. To take just one example, now that what used to be referred to as the Renaissance is called the 'early modern period', some scholars in England still claim that it begins in 1500 (or even 1485, the start of the Tudor reign) but its finish is dictated by whatever

---

17 A commendable exception to this is the collection *Preachers and People in the Reformations and Early Modern Period*, ed. by Taylor; although concentrating on the later period, in addition to general essays, the volume contains contributions on preaching respectively in France, Italy, Germany, Switzerland, England, Scandinavia, and the Low Countries at various points.

18 G. M. Trevelyan, *English Social History: A Survey of Six Centuries, Chaucer to Queen Victoria* (London: Longmans, Green and Company, 1944), p. 92.

19 James Simpson, *Reform and Cultural Revolution: 1350–1547*, The Oxford English Literary History, 2 (Oxford: Oxford University Press, 2002), p. 1.

approach is adopted to Reformation history. Whatever is claimed about the English Reformation beginning in 1534 with the Act of Supremacy that declared Henry VIII (1509–1547) as the head of the Church, there is no longer any consensus amongst early, revisionist or post-revisionist English historians about the end of what they would call the various 'reformations' or indeed their significance. At the extreme, what has been called the 'long reformation' may extend into the nineteenth century as the internecine struggles amongst Catholics, Lutherans, Protestants, Recusants, Calvinists, Puritans, Dissenters, Laudians, Anglicans, Evangelicals, and Tractarians for what Conrad Russell (focusing on the period between 1559 and 1625), calls 'the custody battle' for the English Church took a long time to work themselves out.[20]

Such complexities can be replicated throughout Europe where there is little agreement about the dating of literary periods or about assessments of Reformation/s.[21] Even in areas of geographical proximity, as in Scandinavian countries, influenced as they were by assorted political rule and the effect of external pressures, the date by which *the* Reformation may be said to have taken place is variable. Sweden's move to Lutheranism began early, in part helped by some direct contact with the teachings of Martin Luther: the preacher Olavus Petri (born in 1493 or 1497), one of the main proponents of the Swedish Reformation, studied in Wittenberg in the first decades of the sixteenth century. Denmark's shift to the new orthodoxies in some respects would appear to have been a more leisurely affair with monastic houses allowed to continue until their last inmates died, but this is not to overlook the decisive destruction of the Catholic past, particularly sermon manuscripts. Of course, in some European countries, such as Italy, the Reformation was never achieved at all, even if at the time there was some anxiety about it. As one critic comments, 'Italy never became a Protestant region, but in the mid-sixteenth century, the danger seemed grave and the outcome uncertain'.[22]

---

20 *England's Long Reformation 1500–1800*, ed. by Nicholas Tyacke, The Neale Colloquium in British History (London: UCL Press, 1998); Conrad Russell, *The Causes of the English Civil War*, The Ford Lectures Delivered in the University of Oxford, 1987–1988 (Oxford: Clarendon Press, 1990), p. 84.

21 The literature on the Reformation/s is clearly far too numerous to list here, but it may be noted that with regard to Martin Luther and preaching historiography has been somewhat dominated from the 1980s by the opposing views of Bernd Moeller, who was impressed by the conformity of printed Lutheran sermons with Luther's theology and that of Susan Karant-Nunn, who saw instead a rich heterogeneity.

22 Michelson, *The Pulpit and the Press in Reformation Italy*, p. 2. For a measured account of the different ways in which European countries were affected by the Reformation, see the essay by Anne T. Thayer, 'Ramifications of Late Medieval Preaching: Varied Receptivity to the Protestant Reformation', in *Preachers and People in the Reformations and Early Modern Period*, ed. by Taylor, pp. 359–86; she notes that with regard to printed penitential model sermon collections 'The places in which rigorist preaching was most popular tended to adopt the Reformation. Regions where absolutionist preaching was more prominent tended to remain Catholic' (p. 379).

In other regions the interlinked issues of periodization and Reformation are fundamental to later political developments, for example, the new Lutheran and Calvinist influences were the primary reason for the Dutch Revolt from Spain that led to a complicated history of an Eighty Years War.[23]

In many respects it is next to impossible to disentangle chronological periods like 'medieval' or 'early modern' or terms like 'Reformation'; each is used as a sort of verbal shorthand to pin down what are in effect moving targets. It is for such reasons that this book is given a time-frame that cuts across these permeable boundaries (as highlighted in the title) in the same way as it purposefully wishes to address the production of sermons in both manuscript and print across a broad swathe of Europe from the mid-fifteenth century to the mid-sixteenth century (and in some cases before and beyond these dates). And if there is more attention given in the essays to material in print than in manuscript, this just signals the direction of traffic at the time.

Our deliberate choice of 'Catholic' in the title serves two purposes. First, it is to stress that for the earlier period up to the advent of Martin Luther this is an historic fact. Secondly, our purpose is to trace the presence, importance, and development of Catholic sermons in particular parts of Europe from the end of the so-called Middle Ages. We do not attempt to supply a history of preaching in Europe in all its complexity for well over two centuries. We are not concerned with a re-telling of familiar narratives such as the rise of mendicant preaching in the Middle Ages, confessional movements from Catholicism to Protestantism, the importance of oppositional sermons in the Reformation, the spread of or reactions to new orthodoxies like Lutheranism or Calvinism, or the effects of the Council of Trent (1545–1563). We do not seek to overlook the value of such preaching or particularly the many ground-breaking studies in this scholarly field. We have no wish to ignore the numerous studies of Martin Luther, Jean Calvin (1509–1564), and so on, or the interesting complications and irreversible influences of the Lutheran Reformation for the whole of Europe.[24] What we *are* interested in is to follow the thread of Catholic preaching through the relevant centuries here without being distracted by what might be termed the interpellation of Lutheranism. This is not to forget that *the* Reformation took place or to argue that what may be termed Protestantism in general is not important (no more than Judaism or Islam or any other faith) or that Europe was wholly Catholic throughout this period, but to examine mainly Catholic preaching. To pretend otherwise would mislead readers of the volume: it is not about preachers or preaching in general but about a certain confessional type. To produce a book that

---

23 Judith Pollman, *Catholic Identity and the Revolt of the Netherlands, 1520–1635*, The Past & Present Book Series (Oxford: Oxford University Press, 2011).

24 For such discussions we would refer readers to the essays in *Preachers and People in the Reformations and Early Modern Period*, ed. by Taylor; see respectively, Thomas Worcester, 'Catholic Sermons', Beth Kreitzer, 'The Lutheran Sermon', and James Thomas Ford, 'Preaching in the Reformed Tradition', pp. 3–33, 35–63, and 65–88 and references therein.

addressed Catholic and Protestant preaching equally would have required a multi-volume work of long gestation and would inevitably have been dominated by the work of Martin Luther to the exclusion of some of the many anonymous preachers that are brought to light in the current volume. In following our remit we take account as and when necessary of occasions where Catholic preachers, traditions, or texts transitioned into Lutheran ones. This happens in the essays that focus on Scandinavia where each contributor either tangentially or in greater detail discusses this transitional period and in so doing highlights various important regional differences in the journey from Catholicism to Lutheranism, while one of the essays on the Low Countries demonstrates the way in which a Catholic medieval text was re-imagined for a Protestant readership. Like the other essays in the volume, these essays serve to show that for most Catholic preachers at the time, and even for those moving away from Catholicism, the religious outcome was far from fixed in a unified fashion but moved at its own pace. It is crucial also to recall that at the time 'Reform' did not just mean 'Reformation'; in general terms there had been a reform agenda (driven by various political motivations) during the time of the Fifth Lateran Council (1512–1517) even before Luther burst on the scene. We wish therefore to move away from the idea of the monolithic Reformation and deal not only with those preachers who were working in its shadow but also those for whom it did not exist, was a distant prospect, or was simply something to be worked around or ignored.[25]

Marking over 550 years since the first printed sermon collections (for example, Lilius Tifernas's edition of John Chrysostom's *Sermones de patientia in Job* published by Ulrich Zell in about 1467 in Cologne), the focus here is on sermons that were themselves altering dynamically in response to the new age of print, which long preceded any confessional divides. The present volume is therefore driven by the requirement not merely for sermon study in individual settings but for comparative research across particular chronological, geographical, and linguistic boundaries. Our aim in these essays is to move away from generalizing histories, by presenting research informed by innovative work by sermonists on manuscript and print in their individual areas. Effectively the emphasis here is on how Catholic preachers and Catholic preaching carried on in the period from the mid-fifteenth to the mid-sixteenth centuries. In order to do this, there is a need to strip away some of the earlier scholarly preconceptions, query contemporary comments, and — above all — to return to the original sources. Therefore all the essays

---

25 We are reminded of the comment by Larissa Taylor in *Soldiers of Christ* with regard to the French work she examines (1657 printed sermons comprising work by twenty-three preachers in forty-three collections and sixty-eight manuscript sermons in the period 1460–1560), 'Despite individual differences over certain matters, the theological formulations of all the pre-Tridentine Catholic preachers treated here are very similar, differing only in emphasis. Issues raised by the Protestants inevitably provoked discussion and response, but seldom caused a preacher to deviate from the accepted tenets of Catholic theology' (p. 83).

here are firmly grounded in an examination at first hand of archival documents, manuscripts, and early print. Little has been taken on trust; all materials have been investigated afresh. As appropriate, medieval library catalogues, account books, records, and even Church architecture, are investigated in an attempt to uncover what is known about certain aspects of preaching and preachers.

Rather than setting up the usual binary divides or envisaging the movement as necessarily always a forward one (for example, *from* manuscript *to* print), we highlight the linguistic complications, the textual inter-relationships, the confessional cross-currents, and the variations between public and private sermon dissemination operating at different rates and with variable effects throughout Europe. Each contributor, according to his or her own remit, freely crosses the so-called binary divide between the medieval and early modern, and presents the resultant research as he or she sees fit (for example, by laying out lists of early printed material according to the particular requirement of the essay). By examining case studies chosen from countries with contrasting manuscript and printing traditions (Denmark, England, Finland, France, Germany, Italy, the Low Countries, Romania, Spain, and Sweden), we aim to examine some of the main historical, literary, political, societal, and theological factors in the development of the sermon, which was itself in the process of changing formats, and sometimes languages, at a time of religious ferment from the advent of print to the death of Martin Luther. It is recognized, of course, that underlying the (modern-day) names of these countries are complex and intertwined political and linguistic histories. Yet to avoid an excess of historical explanation in this volume, we use the terms most readily understandable to current readers. For example, we refer to the country of Finland rather than to the easternmost part of Sweden (as it once was) and we avoid tortuous and politicised terms such as the Kalmar Union or the Spanish Netherlands in favour of Scandinavia and the Low Countries. This is not to forget the multiple border and organizational changes — frequently contested — that have taken place in Europe over the centuries. Searching questions underlie the various essays in order to cast light on different circumstances (sometimes overlapping, sometimes contradictory) in the varying languages and regions. For instance: What do we know about preaching activity, particularly from neglected regions or contexts, and about the preachers themselves? Which trends may be detected in different parts of Europe? What was the relative status of Latin versus the vernacular at different points and in different regions? How and where and by whom were sermons preserved? What may be discovered about the interaction of manuscript and print in sermon production? What evidence is there for links between the spoken and the printed Word? Why were certain collections of sermons, or work by particular preachers, selected for printing while others were ignored? Who was responsible for the dissemination of sermons in manuscript or print? What may be gleaned about the attitude of preachers to print? How were preachers' reputations made or lost? Is it possible to calibrate the range and varying purposes of sermons as written devotional material? How did sermon texts or aids to preaching develop over time? What evidence is there for the evolution of Catholic preaching during the Protestant Reformation? In such ways we hope to explain some of the differences in sermon content, delivery, printing, reading, and usage in Europe as it moved from medieval Christianity to early modern Catholicism. Our watchwords are continuity and change in all their variety. We are concerned with the negotiations that were made in such a theologically charged atmosphere between one format and another, one language and another, one congregation and another, one audience and another. In many cases what is said about sermons is also reflective of other tendencies in society at large. For instance, in Europe as a whole it is known that printing in Denmark, England, and Spain focused on the vernacular rather than Latin. It therefore comes as no surprise that printed sermons in these countries (to the extent that they exist) also tend to be in the vernacular.[26]

Effectively the interest here is on how preaching and preachers in different regions and different times and different milieux brought about the 'Circulation of the Word of God' (as they defined it depending on their individual persuasion); and how in turn this 'Circulation' was facilitated by the provision of handwritten or printed materials and how such texts (either in the vernaculars or Latin) continued to be used, altered, censored or cast aside. As noted by one scholar, 'Printing placed a mendicant preacher [or indeed any preacher] in direct competition with himself for the first time, and it forced the question of the value of the spoken word'.[27] Indeed, this weighing up of the relative merits of both is something that pre-occupied the age and continue to do for some time. Different preachers and different regions tackled such conundra (or had them tackled for them) in their own way, as we shall see. Throughout there are particularly obvious patterns, such as the prevalence of mendicant preaching from Finland to Transylvania, the general upsurge of printed sermons in the first decades of the sixteenth century, the spread of certain sermon collections, and the ubiquity of particular preachers, such as Vicent Ferrer, throughout much of Europe.[28] Yet the contrasts are equally compelling; for example, while most of the English manuscript sermons are parochial ones, most of those printed are episcopal, whereas in Italy it was not

---

26 In 10,000 consecutive items taken from the *Index Aureliensis*, the standard citation form for rare materials cataloguing, there is a marked difference between Latin and vernacular output. Of the books produced in Denmark and England only 11% of each were in Latin with Spain on 28% and Italy on 45% for Latin. All the other regions produced more Latin books to varying degrees in descending order: Bohemia (80%), the Swiss Confederation (77%), The Low Countries (67%), Hungary (66%), France (61%), and Germany (61%). See Andrew Pettegree and Matthew Hall, 'The Reformation and the Book: A Reconsideration', in Pettegree, *The French Book and the European Book World*, pp. 221–49, Figure 10.6 (p. 249).

27 Michelson, *The Pulpit and the Press in Reformation Italy*, p. 164.

28 For an analysis of the general patterns at work with regard to early printed sermons, see Thayer, *Penitence, Preaching and the Coming of the Reformation*.

unusual for lay men to produce sermons. And if there was an integrated and largely co-operative approach to the dissemination of one preacher's work (such as that of Johannes Geiler von Kaysersberg), in other regions (such as that of Dutch pericope sermons) there would seem to have no fixed agenda (at least at the ecclesiastical institutional level) about publication in print. Effectively, it is by such contrasts that illumination occurs. In other words, what we seek to do here is to provide a sort of bird's eye view that highlights different aspects of the preaching narrative over several centuries, by deliberately concentrating on a period of obvious transition and transformation and by asking some questions that have not been posed before, as well as highlighting factors that have not previously been considered.

Nothing less than a decades-long European study would attend properly to a thorough investigation of Catholic preaching during this period; what is presented here is merely a start to the process. No attempt is made at full coverage — something that would be impossible within a single volume in any case. Neither is it feasible to provide a case by case comparison in a Europe where it is estimated that, for instance, in Middle Dutch there are about 3,700 different sermons (or 11,000 duplicates) in excess of 550 manuscripts, compared with five surviving sermon manuscripts in medieval Danish.[29] So our aim is not to present a history of preaching in manuscript and print, even in the individual areas chosen. Most particularly we are not concerned with an overview of areas already well researched, for example, Dominican and Franciscan mendicant preaching, sermons emanating from Observant Reform movements in Germany, or studies of the superstar or notorious preachers such as Bernardino da Siena (1380–1444) or Girolamo Savonarola (1452–1498). Areas of Europe are omitted for various reasons (and not purely because full coverage is impossible). This may be because they have been addressed elsewhere as in French printed sermons.[30] Conversely it may be that there is little to be said either because of a pronounced tendency towards the part-preservation of the medieval past in much later manuscripts (as happens in Ireland) or because of late developments in the printing tradition or scant production therein.[31] Of course, in some cases the countries or regions included, such as Germany or Italy, could fill the whole volume so we have tried to keep a balance. This has resulted in a varied mix of material that should do much to provoke debate. The specially chosen contributors are experts in their fields and have been allowed to go their own way in examining what to them are the most interesting aspects of their individual language areas or historical situations. In seeking to discover more about the 'Circulation of

---

29 For details see the essays by Thom Mertens and Jonathan Adams.

30 Taylor, *Soldiers of Christ*.

31 For instance, of 10,000 consecutive items taken from the *Index Aureliensis*, only 1.7% of the total recorded editions belonged cumulatively to Denmark, Hungary, Ireland, Portugal, Scotland, and Sweden; see Pettegree and Hall, 'The Reformation and the Book: A Reconsideration', pp. 221–49, Figure 10.1 (p. 247).

the Word of God', our concern is to elicit what is special about a particular area or cleric. These essays, which are in dialogue with each other, are divided into geographical/linguistic sections organized along broadly chronological lines. Essentially they circulate from the peripheries of Europe to the centre, moving variously from areas where evidence is now scarce or hard to find to situations of thriving production, thereby providing a useful composite picture.

England, Scandinavia, Transylvania, Romance Regions, Germanic Lands, and The Low Countries

Rather than going down the well-trodden routes, the aim in these essays, as noted, is to open up new areas, to ask different questions, to ponder on problems not raised before, to explore honestly the gaps in our knowledge. For this reason we focus on neglected orders (the Carmelites), regions on the periphery of Europe that have not been explored before (Finland and Transylvania), and countries where there is little evidence of printed material (England), as well as exploring the continuities in particular forms, in this case Gospel preaching (the Low Countries). In the course of these essays attention is also given to the many practical impediments to textual survival and research activity that range from internal Carmelite governance, to numerous fires (such as the Great Fire of Turku in 1827) to previous Romanian governmental strictures to the perennial lack of evidence. Above all, in the essays the contributors seek to leave no stone unturned in trying to uncover whatever may be uncovered, as symbolized by the recovery of a long-forgotten preacher from the records: the Transylvanian parish priest Johannes Zeckel found at work on his sermon written in 1502 in his parish church in Ruşi for the celebration of St George.[32]

There is an ongoing and acute awareness of the vibrant contrasts between preachers in adjacent lands, even those under the same jurisdiction, for example, in the distinctive paths taken by Christiern Pedersen in Denmark, the Catholic who became a Lutheran, and the Swedish Petri brothers, Olavus and Laurentius, who were Lutherans working in a Catholic tradition. The contrasting fortunes and histories of other preachers are also worthy of note. For instance, Johannes Kreutzer, a famous preacher in his day whose sermons were never printed, largely disappeared from view, while the reputation of his fellow German, Johannes Geiler von Kaysersberg, hinged on the publication of his sermons a couple of years before his death. Yet, paradoxically, getting into print, even to the extent of being a bestseller from the early sixteenth to the seventeenth centuries, as in the case of the sermon writer Ludovico Pittorio, was insufficient for a lasting reputation, at least not one that endured into modern times. In these essays then much is done to debunk certain

---

32 For details, see the essay by Adinel C. Dincă and Paula Cotoi.

myths, for example, that Geiler was opposed to publication or that being well-known for centuries is a guarantee of critical longevity. Likewise attempts are made to disentangle changes between manuscript and manuscript and between manuscript and print, and the use thereof, whether this be among the producers of *distinctiones* in the thirteenth century (Nicolas de Biard), controversial preaching in the fifteenth (Vicent Ferrer), or texts produced in the sixteenth centuries (editions of Johannes Tauler, sermon preparation by Thomas Swalwell or texts from the lips or pen of Franciscus Costerus).

England

When parts of Europe were well advanced with Lutheran preaching, England (often an outlier in Europe) was witnessing what might be called the dying days of medieval Catholicism, not that it seemed like it at the time given the way that some clerics (secure in their Catholic strongholds) were still using the earlier theological stalwarts to help them in their own sermon production. Books of sermons had long been vital resources for preachers, but the advent of printing made them more widely available. Thomas Swalwell, a Benedictine monk of Durham Priory in north-east England who died in the very year in which the major dissolution of the monasteries took place (1539), serves as an example of a user of European model sermon collections and other works designed to support preaching. In the first part of this essay, 'Books for Preaching and Preaching with Books: Late Medieval Latin Printed Sermons and the Witness of Thomas Swalwell of Durham Priory', Anne T. Thayer surveys trends in the production of model sermon collections in the first century of printing. Over time, books tended toward smaller formats and lower cost. While some patristic authors' sermons were printed, the most popular collections were those of fairly contemporary mendicant authors. Many model sermon collections were in the scholastic style but works supporting the homily style were also available. Vernacular sermon collections became more popular, and such works were increasingly read by lay people in addition to active preachers. The books owned by the Durham Priory and those purchased by Swalwell himself generally reflect these trends. The second part of the essay examines Swalwell's marginalia as evidence of his use of printed resources in preparing to preach. The early printed *Rosarium sermonum predicabilium* by Bernardino da Busti (*c.* 1450–1513) provides material for a catechetical sermon in scholastic style on Christian faith. The Apostles' Creed provides foundational teaching; an interest in indulgences is prominent in the discussion of the forgiveness of sins. A possible homily for Palm Sunday for the Priory community emerges from Swalwell's marginalia in a Bible with commentary by Hugues de Saint-Cher (*c.* 1200–1263). Homiletic elaboration on the biblical text likely centred on the crucifixion, Joseph of Arimathea, Jesus's tomb as an image of religious life, and events surrounding the resurrection. Here then is a late preacher caught — thanks to Thayer's careful sifting of the evidence — in

CIRCULATING THE WORD OF GOD IN MEDIEVAL AND EARLY MODERN EUROPE   31

the very act of working between manuscript and print, the oral sermon and the literary text, and doing so in a way that exemplifies preaching methods throughout the Middle Ages.

In her essay, 'The Early Printed Sermon in England between 1483 and 1532: A Peculiar Phenomenon', Veronica O'Mara is faced with another challenge of reconstruction. She can easily account for Middle English sermons in manuscript: about 1480 extant unique texts that are almost exclusively anonymous and largely comprise parish sermons for the temporale. Similarly, there is little bother in simply listing the extant early printed sermons, both vernacular and Latin, largely because there are so few of them. Neither is there any difficulty about authorship as the vast majority are by known powerful episcopal figures or high-ranking clergy. Yet, having listed the texts and outlined something of the history of the preachers and the subject matter, she addresses the core of the problem. Not only is the number of surviving sermons very small, but their range is idiosyncratic. O'Mara demonstrates how these printed sermons have a fractured relationship with the manuscript tradition. Indeed, if the extant manuscript sermons had not survived, the available printed sermons would have given a very distorted picture of what medieval English preaching had been like. Having pondered on some general rationales for the printing of the sermons, she proceeds to focus on public preaching (at the famous sites of St Paul's Cross by St Paul's Cathedral and the Hospital of St Mary Bishopgate, commonly called St Mary Spital, in London) in an analysis of two manuscript sermons by Thomas Wimbledon in c. 1387 and Richard Alkerton in 1406 and two early printed sermons, by Richard Fitzjames and John Alcock, which were printed respectively in c. 1495–1496 and (first) probably in 1496. In so doing she makes an attempt to figure out what we know — or do not know — about why certain sermons were chosen (or sent forward) for publication, while many others lay neglected and forgotten about apart from sporadic mentions in the records.

Scandinavia

The first essay in the Scandinavia section focuses on an area on the periphery of Europe and one in which little is known about its sermon tradition. In 'Preaching in Finland on the Eve of the Reformation and Beyond: The Evidence from Manuscript and Print' Jussi Hanska notes how writing the history of preaching in Finland (a region considered part of eastern Sweden until 1809) in the lead up to the Reformation is a very difficult task for a number of reasons. Because of the lack of sources, he notes that there is an onus on the researcher to read closely the very few surviving books and manuscripts. In addition, it is necessary to reconstruct what has been lost due to wars, plunder, fires, and Reformation vandalism that destroyed masses of Catholic material. This means analysing all the references to preaching in the chronicles and other literary sources such as administrative acts, the surviving catalogues of the destroyed library of the Kungliga Akademien i Åbo (Royal Academy in Turku), inventories of the parish books from the early modern period, and even architectural evidence in the form of the external pulpits in medieval churches. The evidence collected here by these means (for the first time) — even if the number of surviving texts is minuscule — suggests that the situation of medieval preaching in Finland was not significantly different from Northern Europe in general. Indeed, despite some propaganda to the contrary, the situation changed very little after the Reformation and not necessarily for the better. In the first decades of the sixteenth century the impoverished parishes could not afford printed preaching materials and the level of clerical education declined due to the lack of funds. Indeed, the persistence of some Catholic customs for quite some time after the Reformation is also evident from the sources.

Despite all the difficulties, Hanska's diligent searches unearthed quite a wealth of information about preaching in medieval Finland, but no amount of investigation can reveal material from Denmark. Indeed, as a result of the wholesale destruction of the monastic past during the Reformation and the later abhorrence of medieval culture, there are just five surviving manuscripts and one early print that contain medieval vernacular Danish sermons. In 'Christiern Pedersen's *Alle Epistler oc Euangelia* (1515): Reading a Catholic Text in the Danish Reformation' Jonathan Adams considers the continued life of this print by the Danish scholar, humanist, and publisher Christiern Pedersen. He discusses this vernacular collection of Catholic miracle sermons, *Alle Epistler oc Euangelia*, after the Reformation by examining readers' annotations, underlinings, and deletions. These signs of usage show that the work continued to be read long after the Reformation as is also suggested by references to the book in other sixteenth- to eighteenth-century works. Some evidence points to a form of censorship where, for example, Latin is deleted and the Virgin Mary's name blotted out. Elsewhere, however, large sections of biblical Latin have been copied out and readers have added in the margin Latin translations of Danish words found in the text. Sometimes marginalia provide keywords to identify a passage, for example, a short piece by Pedersen on a folk tradition is marked with a reference to night-time sorcery. Such keywords can also express the reader's attitude to the text. It would seem that *Alle Epistler oc Euangelia* is evidence of a rather pragmatic approach to the Reformation whereby Catholic works were revised, adapted, and continued to be used long after the 1530s. In so doing, it fits the broader picture that emerges of the Danish Reformation whereby Catholic productions, such as church wall-paintings illustrating biblical stories, which were still considered beneficial to worshippers' spiritual growth and understanding of the faith, survived Lutheran censorship or destruction.

In contrast to Denmark, Sweden's drive towards Lutheranism seemed more pronounced, at least on the surface (though the opposite could also be argued as it did not receive a Church Order until 1571 whereas Denmark-Norway had received a Protestant Church Order in 1537/1539). In the sixteenth century five collections of sermons were printed in Sweden. Only two of these contain original Swedish texts: by two brothers. Olavus Petri (1493 or 1497–1552) and Laurentius Petri (1499–1573), with the former being responsible for *Een lijten postilla* (1530), and the latter for a sermon collection on the passion of Christ (1573). The other three consist of translations of German, Lutheran sermons. The contribution here considers these two Swedish collections in the light of the decision of the 1527 Diet in Västerås that the Word of God should be 'preached purely throughout the whole kingdom'. The decision has been interpreted as a Lutheran statement of the Diet, but in this essay, 'The Word of God Purely Preached: Continuity and Change in the Postils of the Swedish Reformation', Christer Pahlmblad shows that it should rather be understood as a formula acceptable both by those who wanted to remain true to the medieval Church and by the Lutheran reformers: 'purely' meant a sermon giving priority to the Word without the use of non-biblical material such as *miracula*. The priests of the medieval Church were compelled to translate the Gospel of the day and to comment on it by way of an *expositio evangelii*. A framework of catechetical texts surrounded the sermon in late medieval times. The Reformation retained this structure, reworked the texts, and informed them with Lutheran ideas. The old form became a vehicle for the new ideas. Two sermons from the postils demonstrate the consequences of the decision of the Diet. The essay also briefly discusses the ideal presented in the medieval and Lutheran sources of how priests ought to prepare their sermons and what can be discovered about the actual oral performance.

Transylvania

If questions abound with regard to various parts of Europe, this is even more the case with preaching in what is now Romania. While relations between the centre and the periphery within the European *Latinitas* have formed a frequently discussed topic of medieval studies in the course of the last decade, what is known about sermons in this area has largely been a *tabula rasa*. In their essay 'Latin Manuscript and Printed Sermons in Late Medieval Transylvania (1470–1530)', Adinel C. Dincă and Paula Cotoi suggest a fresh view of the aforementioned phenomenon, from the perspective of Latin sermon collections from late medieval Transylvania — the easternmost province of the Hungarian kingdom until 1526. Particularly after the accelerated spread of printed texts, sermons became the largest category of literary products owned, read, and even produced in the geographically peripheral province of Transylvania, thus reflecting perfectly the continuous and complex dynamic between the cultural middle points and their outskirts. In this essay the authors investigate, for the first time in historiography, the typology of both isolated sermons and sermon collections that can be found in this remote area of Latin Christianity, the interaction of printed text and manuscripts, and the motivations behind the preference for specific sermons: earlier traditions, university education abroad, or just local availability and price. This involves Dincă and Cotoi — *inter alia* — in an investigation into material in over a dozen manuscript and archival repositories throughout present-day Romania and beyond. They also seek to understand who owned and used these sermon collections and the role they played within the intellectual context of the region. With the help of details provided by medieval volumes containing sermons and other preaching material, they also try to determine in select cases the relationship between preacher and sermon, and how the texts were composed, organized, and delivered.

Romance Regions

The three essays in this section, respectively concentrating on Spain, France and its environs, and Italy, explore a wide range of material from different periods. The first essay is very concerned with transitions between manuscript and manuscript, and manuscript and print, and the critical misunderstandings that may arise in the process. Oriol Catalán in 'Controversial Topics in the Sermons of Vicent Ferrer: From Manuscripts to the Printing Press' argues that in spite of (or perhaps because of) the controversial topics that the Dominican friar Vicent Ferrer (1350–1419) dealt with in his preaching campaigns throughout large swathes of Europe his sermons gained enormous success during his lifetime and were later copied widely as well as being regularly printed during the fifteenth and sixteenth centuries. There are two main groups of editions: over fifty Latin costly editions with sermons for the liturgical year, and over fifteen cheap and modest Spanish editions that gather together sermons devoted to Doomsday and the Antichrist. However, there have been few comparisons made between the manuscript and early printed versions of Vicent Ferrer's sermons. Since the work of Sigismund Brettle, *San Vicente Ferrer und sein literarischer Nachlass* in 1924, the early modern Latin editions were considered to have faithfully followed a manuscript compilation (the so-called Toulouse Compilation) that purportedly silenced or censored controversial topics found in Ferrer's original sermons. This essay compares manuscript versions of some sermons containing controversial topics with their printed versions (mainly the editions of Köln 1485 and Valencia 1556). These topics concern social criticism, the coming of the Apocalypse, the Last Judgement, the birth of the Antichrist, Ferrer's support for the flagellant movement, and free will. Catalán analyses the changes and continuities in the context of the Reformation and the rise of prophecies in the Renaissance. He demonstrates that the purported 'censorship' or 'silencing' in early printed editions existed, but was not as important as previously thought, since compilers resorted to other manuscripts beyond the Toulouse Compilation so that they still included controversial arguments (sometimes displaced to sermons other than those in which the arguments originally appeared), even if to a lesser degree than in the manuscript versions.

We then turn towards the centre of Western Europe with an investigation into a genre that from the early medieval period onward was meant to help in sermon production. Sophie Delmas's essay, 'From Nicolas de Biard's *Summa de abstinentia* to the Printed *Dictionarius pauperum*: A Pastoral Compendium for Preachers', focuses on *distinctiones* that first appeared at the end of the twelfth century and were intended to be of enormous benefit to preachers throughout the medieval and early modern periods. From the thirteenth century onwards these collections of *distinctiones* were enriched by the addition of patristic quotations and *similitudines*; by the fourteenth century the numerous collections of *distinctiones* used by preachers were widely disseminated. The thirteenth-century Dominican preacher Nicolas de Biard left three works: a collection of biblical *Distinctiones*, the *Sermones de tempore et de sanctis*, and, less securely attributed, the *Summa de abstinentia*. At least 180 manuscripts of the *Summa de abstinentia* (produced by Nicolas de Biard between 1272 and 1288) were known at the end of the Middle Ages. This pastoral bestseller exists in over a dozen editions, for example, from Germany (Reutlingen, 1480; Köln, 1501, 1504, and 1505), Switzerland (Basel, 1481), the Netherlands (Deventer, 1484) and especially France (Vienne, 1481; Strasbourg, *c.* 1485, before 1487, 1516, and 1518; Paris, *c.* 1495–1497, 1498, 1512, and finally, 1530). These editions appear under the title *Dictionarius pauperum*. This contribution aims to clarify the relationship between the printed texts and manuscripts of the work. In so doing Delmas shows that the *Summa de abstinentia* is not a shortened version of the *Distinctiones*, as has long been believed; rather, it is part of a manual for preachers, which includes Nicolas de Biard's *Summa de abstinentia* and the *Quaestiones* of Johannes de Turrecremata (1388–1468).

Somewhat like Nicolas de Biard, little is known about the life of Ludovico Pittorio (*c.* 1452–*c.* 1525) beyond that contained in his own religious texts, written in prose and verse, both in Latin and in the vernacular. In his own day and beyond Pittorio's Lenten sermons were well-known and his reputation in early print tradition confirmed as demonstrated in Pietro Delcorno's essay, 'A Forgotten Italian Bestseller: Ludovico Pittorio's *Omiliario quadragisimale*'. But, unlike other preachers famous in their day, Pittorio has faded from history. Lenten sermon collections represent fascinating microcosms of late medieval religious culture, since they both reflected and constructed the religious knowledge of the time. Delcorno's contribution focuses on one of the most influential — and less studied — of these texts, namely the *Omiliario quadragisimale* written by Pittorio. This Lenten sermon collection originated from Pittorio's preaching to a lay confraternity in Ferrara and was published for the first time in 1506. In its printed format the *Omiliario* was dedicated to abbess Beatrice d'Este, abbess of Sant'Antonio in Polesine, a Benedictine monastery in the same city, and presented as spiritual nourishment for her nuns. The study of some of its sermons shows how Pittorio weaved basic exegesis, moral instruction, and an intense spiritual teaching into his sermons. Thanks to the accessibility of its vernacular language, the *Omiliario* became a religious bestseller, capable of addressing a differentiated readership composed of clerics, nuns, and lay people by providing them with reliable access to the Bible during the sixteenth century.

Germanic Lands

The section on Germanic Lands opens with what is possibly the most overlooked mendicant preaching order in the Middle Ages. In 'The Neglected Carmelites: Evidence for their Preaching Activities in Late Medieval Germany' Ralf Lützelschwab notes that Carmelites are the great unknown within Western monastic history. Even if the order struggled with its own migration history from the hills of Mount Carmel to Europe, for most Carmelites it was evident that had its members not chosen exile, they would not have survived. In Europe a *vita eremitica* was replaced by a *vita communis* in that preaching, hearing Confession, and dispensing sacraments were the new requirements of the day. Carmelites thereby followed the other mendicant orders in which sermons were part of the regular pastoral programme. As a result, there should be hundreds, even thousands of Carmelite sermons. Yet in Johann Schneyer's *Repertorium der lateinischen Sermones des Mittelalters für die Zeit von 1150–1350* only one sermon is noted. Lützelschwab shows how much material still exists more or less hidden in manuscripts or early printed books, but mostly quite easily traceable via new and/or digitized manuscript catalogues. In fact, Lützelschwab knows of about 200 sermons of Carmelite provenance generally belonging to the end of the fourteenth and the fifteenth centuries. His essay focuses on sermons and sermon collections, both in manuscript and print, shedding light on the importance of the Carmelites as preachers and directors in the order's provinces of *Alemania inferior* and *Alemania superior* or Lower and Upper Germany. To this end, the holdings of two important libraries in the Carmelite convents of Straubing (belonging to the order's province of Upper Germany) and Mainz (being part of the province of Lower Germany), their genesis, expansion, and fate are analysed with special attention given to pastoral works and sermons. Part of his investigation concerns a library catalogue from Straubing in 1414, together with a visitation protocol from Mainz written in 1434. These libraries collected and preserved books related to the order, as well as supporting pastoral activities both in the confessional and in the pulpit. The aim of the essay is to contribute to a better understanding of the richness of both convents' libraries and of the special role played by sermons. In the course of the essay some of the questions posed by Lützelschwab include: What does the presence or absence of sermon collections by Carmelite preachers tell us about the pastoral activities of the 'Brethren of Our Lady'? How did they fulfil their task as preachers and directors? And how did they shape the conscience of their flock?

With the next essay we turn from a neglected order to a neglected preacher. Whereas Vicent Ferrer, with his lasting reputation as a charismatic preacher, had travelled extensively on his European preaching campaigns delivering his sermons in Catalan, Castilian, and French, the preacher who is the subject of the next essay largely restricted himself to two major cities, albeit living quite a varied life. In 'Johannes Kreutzer: A Preacher in Strasbourg and Basel and his Work in Manuscript and Early Print' Natalija Ganina outlines how the works of the spiritual author and preacher, Johannes Kreutzer (*c.* 1424–1468) have remained unexplored until recently. Kreutzer was born in Guebwiller (Gebweiler) in Alsace and, having finished his studies in Erfurt, he became parish priest at the St. Lorenzaltar of Strasbourg Cathedral in 1454. Later he was one of the founding fathers of the university in Basel, which opened in 1460, and where he lectured in the theological faculty. A well-educated preacher, Kreutzer actively promoted the reform of the Upper Rhine nunneries and the implementation of strict observance, while becoming a Dominican himself in the latter years of his life. Yet despite this pedigree, without the scribal work of nuns in the Dominican convent of St. Nikolaus in undis, the Reuerinnenkloster St. Magdalena in Strasbourg, and the Clarissan convent in Pfullingen, none of Kreutzer's sermons would have been preserved for posterity. And in the absence of a single treatise, nothing would be known about him in print. As shown by Ganina, what is most typical of Kreutzer's surviving œuvre are spiritual allegorical treatises many of which are connected with significant aspects of the liturgical year. This opens up discussions about links between such treatises and sermon material. Kreutzer's only printed work is one of these treatises, which is analysed here. *Herbstmost I* was written for nuns who were his spiritual daughters; it combines features of a treatise, sermon, prayer, and a devotional exercise and was included in an anonymous compilation, *Betrachtung des Leidens Christi*, published in Basel by Nikolaus Lamparter in *c.* 1509.

If Johannes Kreutzer's reputation disappeared almost without trace, every effort was made during his lifetime to ensure that the same did not happen to Johannes Geiler von Kaysersberg who is considered one of the most important preachers of the late Middle Ages and the early modern period, with a surviving corpus of around 1300 sermons in various textual formats. The preaching event was considered a unique action towards spiritual enlightenment; for this very reason, the audience was concerned, as it were, with stabilizing the preacher's words in memory and on paper so as to make them repeatable through reading. Likewise, being a preacher of religious and political reform in the footsteps of Jean Gerson (1363–1429), Geiler was very interested in spreading his ideas in manuscript and print. In '*Instructio, correctio,* and *reformatio*: Johannes Geiler von Kaysersberg and the Transmission of his Sermons' Rita Voltmer shows that the argument about Geiler never having wished his sermons to be published is a mere hagiographical myth. On the contrary, the preacher maintained close contact with printers and thus published tracts based on his sermons. After 1500 his secretary, Jakob Otter, started to get Geiler's sermon journals into print. It was believed that the words of the famous doctor should not fall into oblivion. Already during his lifetime, manuscripts and prints became instruments for circulating observant and reformed religious knowledge. Moreover, Geiler wished his sermons to be preserved for future successors in the office and for the sake of other preachers. Voltmer shows that the Latin and vernacular prints, sometimes illustrated, were aimed at different recipients. Most surprisingly, Otter used manuscripts made by women religious to pad out sermon cycles from the cathedral. Printing Geiler's words became a fiercely embattled business between editors and printers, which did not last for long, since in 1522 Lutheran preaching started in the Cathedral in Strasbourg. Yet, despite such an illustrious pedigree, even today there is no full critical edition of Geiler's sermons.

The Low Countries

In the first contribution on preaching in the Low Countries, an area of Europe (like the Germanic Lands) for which an unquantifiable number of sermons in manuscript and print survives, Thom Mertens is on very firm ground as he is able to trace a particularly important sermon collection over time. In 'The Gouda Gospel Sermons: The Glosses of a Successful Middle Dutch Pericope Collection (1477–1553)' Mertens discusses a very successful Middle Dutch collection of Mass pericopes with sermons. He notes that the genre of pericope sermons is related to Bible translation, Bible commentary, and the sermon and that, including the Gouda Gospel Sermons, there are ten cycles of Middle Dutch pericope sermons, ranging from the thirteenth until the late fifteenth century. He analyses the form of the current collection, *Alle die epistelen ende ewangelien mitten sermonen vanden ghehelen jaere*, the form of the sermons, its authorship, and success. This consists of a temporale (197 occasions with fifty Sunday sermons) and a sanctorale (ninety-eight occasions, plus the Dedication of the Church with one sermon). The collection seems to have been composed for the printing press and it became the dominant form in which the Bible was read in the late medieval Low Countries in the decades around 1500. It was printed at least forty-one times in the years 1477–1553, and four manuscripts are extant, each of them supposedly copied from one of the prints. However, eventually, the collection did not survive the more severe views about reading the Bible in the vernacular that took root in the wake of the Council of Trent, the period that to a large extent marked a watershed in the history of Catholic preaching.

Ten years before the final publication of the Gouda Gospel Sermons the first edition of the sermons of the Dominican Johannes Tauler (1360–1361) was printed. In his contribution 'Diverging Perceptions: Johannes Tauler in Sixteenth-Century Printed Editions', Kees Schepers introduces and then compares two sixteenth-century editions of his works. Both editions purport to contain the *Opera omnia* of Tauler. Apart from the sermons for which he was famous, numerous texts in different genres were attributed to Tauler with which he had never before been associated. Only in hindsight do we know that these attributions are wrong. The two editions are different in that they aim respectively at a Catholic and a Protestant readership. The first sixteenth-century edition was published in Cologne in 1543, and edited by the enigmatic Petrus Noviomagus. This edition was part of an attempt to roll back the tide of Lutheranism by promoting authentic, 'Catholic' spirituality. It formed the starting point for the Europe-wide dissemination and fame of Tauler's works, especially achieved through their Latin translation by the Cologne Carthusian Laurentius Surius (1523–1578). The second edition, clearly a Dutch translation of the 1543 edition, was published in Emden in 1565, with a Protestant readership in mind. A brief comparison between both editions makes clear that the 1565 edition rigorously applies a series of adaptions intended to make the Catholic edition acceptable for a new, Protestant audience.

While the sermons of Tauler were being re-fashioned for those of a new confessional persuasion, a re-vitalized Catholic preaching had come on the scene in the form of the Jesuits. Founded as the Society of Jesus by Ignacio de Loyola (1491–1556) and his nine companions, it was approved in 1540 by Pope Paul III (1468–1549) in the bull *Regimini militantis ecclesiae* with its main remit as the establishment of humanist schools, missionary activity — and preaching. The Jesuit Franciscus Costerus (1532–1619) was an important pioneer of the Counter-Reformation in the Low Countries and his sermons have been preserved in both manuscript and print. The fact that Costerus's sermons circulated in both media raises issues about their authorship and dissemination as well as their readership. It also promotes questions about what effect these different kinds of publishing had on the extant sermons. In order to shed light on these topics, Patricia Stoop's essay, 'Strategies of Publishing: The Case of Franciscus Costerus', focuses on the earliest printed sermon collection, the *Catholijcke sermoonen op de evangelien van de sondaghen* (initially printed in Antwerp between 1598 and 1604), and the earliest manuscript, Brussel, Koninklijke Bibliotheek, MS 614, which contains sermons from the period between 11 June 1592 and the end of 1594. Her essay demonstrates that Costerus's printed sermons were mainly published to support the Catholic cause in the Low Countries and therefore served as a tool in the missionary offensive, for which the Jesuits are renowned. Being the result of Costerus's individual writing process, the transmitted texts have little or no relationship to the oral act of preaching. Instead, the printed sermon collections served as a treasure trove to make the true faith available to a Catholic audience. The handwritten sermons that were actually preached, on the other hand, show clear signs of Costerus's support of monastic life as well as the collaborative effort of women to save his sermons, at their own initiative, for the benefit of their devotion in a tradition extending back to the Middle Ages. Furthermore, the essay shows how the different strategies of publishing had an impact on the dissemination of the sermons. Whereas the sermons in the manuscript circulated among (groups of) women — both religious and lay — in the Brussels region, the printed sermons were disseminated widely and can be considered real bestsellers. Costerus's sermons thus show that early modern sermons in the Dutch vernacular, both in manuscript and print, build on a long existing, medieval tradition. Moreover, they demonstrate that sermons published in both media could easily exist and function next to one another, even a century and a half after the development of the printing press. This process evidentially provides a very meaningful example of the continuity and change that has been the hallmark of the essays in this volume.

Throughout the contributions here there are inevitably points of comparison and contrast and not just in the monumental disparity in the survival rate of manuscript and early printed sermons in the different vernaculars and in the vernaculars versus Latin. Occasionally one witnesses some of the varying attitudes among preachers to the new print medium. Apart from Johannes Geiler von Kaysersberg, who appeared to have been keen on the new technology — not surprising perhaps given that he came from the heart of the European printing industry — elsewhere there is evidence of a certain ambivalence. For example, Ludovico Pittorio goes out of his way in the dedicatory epistle to his *Omiliario* to stress that the initiative to publish was taken not by him but by someone probably connected with the confraternity of San Ludovico in Ferrara. This may or may not be evidence of an authorial modesty topos. But sometimes the reluctance appears to be genuine. One of the best examples of this occurs in John Fisher's 1526 anti-Luther sermon. In the six-page epistle that precedes the sermon Fisher justifies what would surely need no justification in Catholic circles at the time. He does so on the grounds that the subject matter is a serious one, and, most surprisingly of all, he states that it was very noisy when the sermon was originally delivered (in St Paul's Cathedral in London) and so it was best to have it printed so that people could read it for themselves.[33] And elsewhere there is even disavowal in that Christiern Pedersen later claimed to have regretted the publication of his sermons in 1515, most probably because of his new-found Lutheranism in a Denmark that had now left Catholicism behind. Whether or not such comments are evidence of humility or a drive towards encouraging sales is open to question, but it is interesting to see some of the comments put forward that show an apparent ambivalence towards print that lasts well into much of the early modern period whether sermons or not. Another factor here, of course, is that such highlighting of attitudes to print serves to ignore attitudes to manuscripts. What is evident from these essays is that sermons in manuscript continue to be important long after print was meant to have held sway. As mentioned in an early study of print, 'The transition from script to print was rarely dramatic' and 'The road from manuscript to print was continuous and broken'.[34]

Attention is also given here to other overlooked factors, with possibly one of the most important being the part played by nuns both in the patronage of preaching and the preservation of sermons. Without the scribal work of Clarissan, Dominican, and other nuns Johannes Kreutzer's sermons would

---

33 For full details see the essay by Veronica O'Mara.
34 Hirsch, *Printing, Selling and Reading, 1450–1550*, pp. 1 and 2.

CIRCULATING THE WORD OF GOD IN MEDIEVAL AND EARLY MODERN EUROPE

not have been preserved for posterity, while female religious also helped, via their copying, in the work of getting Johannes Geiler into print. With Ludovico Pittorio the link is even more public. In 1506 when Domenico Rococciola (*c.* 1440–1506) published Pittorio's second sermon collection, the *Omiliario quadragisimale*, he included a dedicatory letter addressed to Beatrice d'Este, the well-connected abbess of an important Benedictine convent in Ferrara; in this it was noted that the sermons were suitable as table readings during Lent. Indeed far beyond the medieval period certain nuns were very active in the preservation of texts, as shown in the work of the canonesses regular of the Augustinian convent of Jericho in Brussels to capture in manuscript form the sermons of the Jesuit Franciscus Costerus at a time when print was well established. In such ways it is demonstrable that the interaction of manuscript and print so evident when the printing press first came on the scene is a lasting feature of sermon production.

Above all, perhaps what is most notable in these essays is the 'flexibility' that is maintained by these Catholic preachers both with regard to new technologies and new confessional orthodoxies. Throughout there is a free interchange between manuscript and print, as need requires, and individual accommodations made depending on religious developments and historical or political circumstances. Taken as a whole the contributors here, while wedded to their own specialisms, do much to illuminate other areas — sometimes by design, sometimes by chance.

Circulating the Word of God in Medieval and Early Modern Europe: Catholic Preaching and Preachers across Manuscript and Print (c. 1450 to c. 1550) is therefore envisaged as a series of interlinked essays that will help provide a platform for future research. The international dimension of the contributions here provide a rich resource of material on sermons from a Europe that was experiencing a major shift from manuscript to print (and sometimes back) and to a greater or lesser extent from one confessional persuasion to another. The essays serve to show that, although we can broadly speak of 'European' preaching, such sermons are not monolithic but made up of a medley of influences that only truly emerge on close inspection of individual areas, and persons, when broad comparisons over large corpora in manuscript and print are made and so bring to light the unknown and the unexpected. This collection of essays should not only enlarge current sermon study but explore the wider cultural, literary, religious, and social impact as sermons became accessible in print. In this way connections are made with subjects of wider relevance in the period, for example, the shifting attitudes to preaching; variations in publishing traditions; negotiations between religious orthodoxies; and the cultivation of lay reading — which are all of major significance for later developments in Europe and so of broader scholarly interest.[35]

---

35 The editors are grateful to Anne T. Thayer who helped formulate a couple of paragraphs in this introduction and to David Bagchi and Pietro Delcorno for a few bibliographical

Bibliography

Blench, J. W., *Preaching in England in the Late Fifteenth and Sixteenth Centuries: A Study of English Sermons 1450–c. 1600* (Oxford: Blackwell, 1964)

Chrisman, Miriam Usher, *Lay Culture, Learned Culture: Books and Social Change in Strasbourg, 1480–1599* (New Haven: Yale University Press, 1982)

Da Costa, Alexandra, *Marketing English Books, 1476–1550: How Printers Changed Reading*, Oxford Studies in Medieval Literature and Culture (Oxford: Oxford University Press, 2020)

Delcorno, Carlo, 'Medieval Preaching in Italy (1200–1500)', in *The Sermon*, ed. by Beverly Mayne Kienzle, Typologie des sources du Moyen Âge occidental, 81–83 (Turnhout: Brepols, 2000), pp. 449–560

Devaux, Jean, Matthieu Marchal, and Alexandra Vélissariou, eds, *Les Premiers imprimés français et la littérature de Bourgogne (1470–1550): Actes du colloque international tenu à l'Université du Littoral Côte d'Opale (Dunkerque)*, Bibliothèque du xve siècle, 86 (Paris: Honoré Champion, 2021)

Dondi, Christina, *Printing R-Evolution and Society 1450–1500: Fifty Years that Changed Europe*, Studi di Storia, 13 (Venezia: Edizioni Ca'Foscari, 2020)

Eisenstein, Elizabeth L., *The Printing Press as an Agent of Change: Communications and Cultural Transformations in Early-Modern Europe*, 2 vols (Cambridge: Cambridge University Press, 1979)

Eisenstein, Elizabeth L., *The Printing Revolution in Early Modern Europe* (Cambridge: Cambridge University Library, 1983)

Eisermann, Falk, 'A Golden Age? Monastic Printing Houses in the Fifteenth Century', in *Print Culture and Peripheries in Early Modern Europe: A Contribution to the History of Printing and the Book Trade in Small European and Spanish Cities*, ed. by Benito Rial Costas, Library of the Written Word, 24, The Handpress World, 18 (Leiden: Brill, 2013), pp. 37–67

Febvre, Lucien, and Henri-Jean Martin, *L'Apparition du livre*, L'Évolution de l'humanité, II, 8, iii (Paris: Michel, 1958)

Ferzoco, George, and Carolyn Muessig, 'Bibliography', in *The Sermon*, ed. by Beverly Mayne Kienzle, Typologie des sources du Moyen Âge occidental, 81–83 (Turnhout: Brepols, 2000), pp. 19–142

Ford, James Thomas, 'Preaching in the Reformed Tradition', in *Preachers and People in the Reformations and Early Modern Period*, ed. by Larissa Taylor, A New History of the Sermon, 2 (Leiden: Brill, 2001), pp. 65–88

Frazier, Alison Knowles, *Possible Lives: Authors and Saints in Renaissance Italy* (New York: Colombia University Press, 2005)

Frymire, John M., *The Primacy of the Postils: Catholics, Protestants, and the Dissemination of Ideas in Early Modern Germany*, Studies in Medieval and Reformation Traditions, 147 (Leiden: Brill, 2010)

---

references, as well as to Jonathan Adams, Oriól Catalan, Ralf Lützelschwab, and Christer Pahlmblad for their helpful comments.

Goudriaan, Koen, 'The Church and the Market: Vernacular Religious Works and the Early Printing Press in the Low Countries, 1447–1540', 'The *Devotio moderna* and the Printing Press (*c.* 1475–1540)', and 'The Franciscans, the Laity and the Printing Press', in Koen Goudriaan, *Piety in Practice and Print: Essays on the Late Medieval Religious Landscape*, ed. by Anna Dlabačová and Ad Tervoort, ReLiC, Studies in Dutch Religious History, 4 (Hilversum: Verloren, 2016), pp. 240–56, 257–78, and 279–308

Hellinga, Lotte, *Incunabula in Transit: People and Trade*, Library of the Written Word, 62, The Handpress World, 47 (Leiden: Brill, 2018)

Hellinga, Lotte, *Texts in Transit: Manuscript to Proof and Print in the Fifteenth Century*, Library of the Written Word, 38, The Handpress World, 29 (Leiden: Brill, 2014)

Hirsch, Rudolf, *Printing, Selling and Reading, 1450–1550* (Wiesbaden: Harrassowitz, 1967)

Jensen, Kristian, ed., *Incunabula and Their Readers: Printing, Selling and Using Books in the Fifteenth Century* (London: The British Library, 2003)

Kienzle, Beverly Mayne, ed., *The Sermon*, Typologie des sources du Moyen Âge occidental, 81–83 (Turnhout: Brepols, 2000)

Kikuchi, Catherine, *La Venise des livres: 1469–1530* (Cézeyrieu: Champ Vallon, 2018)

Kreitzer, Beth, 'The Lutheran Sermon', in *Preachers and People in the Reformations and Early Modern Period*, ed. by Larissa Taylor, A New History of the Sermon, 2 (Leiden: Brill, 2001), pp. 35–63

McGinness, Frederick J., *Right Thinking and Sacred Oratory in Counter-Reformation Rome* (Princeton: Princeton University Press, 1995)

McKitterick, David, *Print, Manuscript and the Search for Order, 1450–1830* (Cambridge: Cambridge University Press, 2003)

Michelson, Emily, *The Pulpit and the Press in Reformation Italy*, I tatti studies in Italian renaissance history (Cambridge, MA: Harvard University Press, 2013)

Pettegree, Andrew, *The Book in the Renaissance* (New Haven: Yale University Press, 2011)

Pettegree, Andrew, *Brand Luther: 1517, Printing, and the Making of the Reformation* (New York: Penguin, 2015)

Pettegree, Andrew, *The French Book and the European Book World*, Library of the Written Word, I, The Handpress World, 1 (Leiden: Brill, 2007)

Pettegree, Andrew, and Matthew Hall, 'The Reformation and the Book: A Reconsideration', in Andrew Pettegree, *The French Book and the European Book World*, Library of the Written Word, 1, The Handpress World, 1 (Leiden: Brill, 2007), pp. 221–49

Philippart, Guy, eds, *Hagiographies: Histoire internationale de la littérature hagiographique latine et vernaculaire en Occident des origines à 1550* (I–V), Monique Goullet (VI–VII), and Michèle Gaillard and Monique Goullet (VIII), Corpus Christianorum Texts and Studies, 8 vols (Turnhout: Brepols, 1994–2020)

Pleij, Herman, Joris Reynaert, and others, eds, *Geschreven en gedrukt: boekproductie van handschrift naar druk in de overgang van Middeleeuwen naar Moderne Tijd* (Gent: Academia Press, 2004)

Pollman, Judith, *Catholic Identity and the Revolt of the Netherlands, 1520–1635*, The Past & Present Book Series (Oxford: Oxford University Press, 2011)

Reske, Christoph, *Die Buchdrucker des 16. und 17. Jahrhunderts im deutschen Sprachgebiet: auf der Grundlage des gleichnamigen Werkes von Josef Benzing*, Beiträge zum Buch- und Bibliothekswesen, 51, 2nd edn (Wiesbaden: Harrassowitz, 2015)

Rial Costas, Benito, ed., *Print Culture and Peripheries in Early Modern Europe: A Contribution to the History of Printing and the Book Trade in Small European and Spanish Cities*, Library of the Written Word, 24, The Handpress World, 18 (Leiden: Brill, 2013)

Roest, Bert, 'Wat salmen met sulck volck maken? Franciscaanse stadspredikers en de verdediging van het katholicisme in Nederland, ca. 1520–1568', in *Stedelijk verleden in veelvoud: opstellen over laatmiddeleeuwse stadsgeschiedenis in de Nederlanden voor Dick de Boer*, ed. by Hanno Brand, Jeroen Benders, and Renée Nip, Middeleeuwse Studies en Bronnen, 134 (Hilversum: Verloren, 2011), pp. 245–58

Rusconi, Roberto, 'Le prediche di Fra Girolamo da Ferrara: dai manoscritti al pulpito alle stampe', in *Una città e il suo profeta: Firenze di fronte al Savonarola*, ed. by Gian Carlo Garfagnini, Savonarola e Toscana, 15 (Firenze: SISMEL, 2001), pp. 201–34

Russell, Conrad Russell, *The Causes of the English Civil War*, The Ford Lectures Delivered in the University of Oxford, 1987–1988 (Oxford: Clarendon Press, 1990)

Simpson, James, *Reform and Cultural Revolution: 1350–1547*, The Oxford English Literary History, 2 (Oxford: Oxford University Press, 2002)

Taylor, Larissa Juliet, 'Out of Print: The Decline of Catholic Printed Sermons in France, 1530–1560', in *Habent sua fata libelli / Books Have Their Own Destiny: Essays in Honor of Robert V. Schnucker*, ed. by Robin B. Barnes, Robert A. Kolb, and Paula L. Presley, Sixteenth Century Essays & Studies, 1 (Kirksville, MO: Truman State University Press, 1998), pp. 121–30

Taylor, Larissa, ed., *Preachers and People in the Reformations and Early Modern Period*, A New History of the Sermon, 2 (Leiden: Brill, 2001)

Taylor, Larissa, *Soldiers of Christ: Preaching in Late Medieval and Reformation France* (New York: Oxford University Press, 1992)

Thayer, Anne T., *Penitence, Preaching and the Coming of the Reformation*, St Andrews Studies in Reformation History (Aldershot: Ashgate, 2002)

Thayer, Anne T., 'Ramifications of Late Medieval Preaching: Varied Receptivity to the Protestant Reformation', in *Preachers and People in the Reformations and Early Modern Period*, ed. by Larissa Taylor, A New History of the Sermon, 2 (Leiden: Brill, 2001), pp. 359–86

Tonry, Kathleen, *Agency and Intention in English Print, 1476–1526*, Texts and Transitions, 7 (Turnhout: Brepols, 2016)

Trevelyan, G. M., *English Social History: A Survey of Six Centuries, Chaucer to Queen Victoria* (London: Longmans, Green and Company, 1944)

Tyacke, Nicholas, ed., *England's Long Reformation 1500–1800*, The Neale Colloquium in British History (London: UCL Press, 1998)

Wijsman, Hanno, ed., *Books in Transition at the Time of Philip the Fair: Manuscripts and Printed Books in the Late Fifteenth and Early Sixteenth Century Low Countries*, Burgundica, 15 (Turnhout: Brepols, 2010)

Wooding, Lucy, 'From Tudor Humanism to Reformation Preaching', in *The Oxford Handbook of the Early Modern Sermon*, ed. by Peter McCullough, Hugh Adlington, and Emma Rhatigan (Oxford: Oxford University Press, 2011), pp. 329–47

Worcester, Thomas, 'Catholic Sermons', in *Preachers and People in the Reformations and Early Modern Period*, ed. by Larissa Taylor, A New History of the Sermon, 2 (Leiden: Brill, 2001), pp. 3–33

England

ANNE T. THAYER

Books for Preaching and Preaching with Books

Late Medieval Latin Printed Sermons and the Witness of Thomas Swalwell of Durham Priory

Medieval preachers often learned from books — books of sermons; guides to sermon composition and delivery; biblical commentaries; books of stories, themes, *distinctiones*, and so on. As literacy rose, the growing demand for books was increasingly met by printed books. Of course manuscripts did not disappear but continued to be used and produced. Yet printing made many kinds of literature available in unprecedented numbers, beginning with religious works. The printing of sermons was hailed from early on as a divine gift, one which, in the words of the German humanist and theologian Jakob Wimpfeling (1450–1528), 'makes it possible to propagate the correct doctrines of faith and morals throughout the world and in all languages [...]'.[1] From about 1470 on, printed model sermon collections quickly came to be representative of the popular sermon literature of the period. Significant trends may be discerned as sermon collections made the transition from manuscript to print. In the sixteenth century Protestants stressed the priority of the Word, and publication of sermon books and other materials for preachers only increased.

Model sermon collections both in manuscript but particularly in print were designed to support regular preaching, with *De tempore* collections providing sermons for Sundays and major feast days and *De sanctis* sermons for the feasts of the saints. The Lenten season was served by *Quadragesimale* collections. Such sermons could be preached more or less as they were written or printed, adapted to suit individual tastes and circumstances, or mined for themes, exempla, and authorities. The books themselves say they are for those

---

1 Cited in *Manifestations of Discontent in Germany on the Eve of the Reformation*, ed. by Gerald Strauss (Bloomington: Indiana University Press, 1971), p. 42; Aeneas Silvius and Jacob Wimpfeling, *Germania Enee Siluij* ([Strasbourg: Beck, 1515]), fol. Liij verso.

Anne T. Thayer (athayer@lancasterseminary.edu) is the Paul and Minnie Diefenderfer Professor of Mercersburg and Ecumenical Theology and Church History at Lancaster Theological Seminary.

Circulating the Word of God in Medieval and Early Modern Europe: Catholic Preaching and Preachers across Manuscript and Print (c. 1450 to c. 1550), ed. by Veronica O'Mara and Patricia Stoop, SERMO 17, (Turnhout: Brepols, 2022), pp. 49–69   BREPOLS ❧ PUBLISHERS   10.1484/M.SERMO-EB.5.130451

who need help preaching, in particular those preaching to the laity who are without extensive education or access to libraries. Model sermons do not tell us exactly what was preached in any given pulpit, but they convey the essence of what was considered worth preaching in a very usable form.[2]

In order to gain insight into how these books for preaching were actually used, we need additional evidence. Marginal notes made by preachers in their sermon books can help us see what they thought was useful or noteworthy and likely to be incorporated into their own sermons. Thomas Swalwell (d. 1539), monk in the Benedictine priory of Durham in north-east England, offers an illuminating example.[3] He had many books available to him, both in manuscript and in print, some purchased for his own use, some held in the Priory library. Books of sermons, as well as related materials such as biblical commentaries and collections of preachable materials, feature prominently. His abundant marginalia show him engaging books for preaching, preparing to preach from books.

Books for Preaching: Trends in Print

As printing began to impact the world of preachers and their books, what broad trends are discernible? Are they reflected in Thomas Swalwell's books? Although various kinds of books that supported preaching made the transition from manuscript to print, model sermon collections may be taken as exemplary of books for preaching in the period 1450–1550.[4] During the early decades of printing, there were no effective copyrights or printing privileges; printing decisions were largely made by printers in response to evidence of unsatisfied demand. When a sermon collection proved to be successful in print, it developed its own momentum and was printed repeatedly. Like most early printed books, sermon collections were printed on paper and sold without covers. The purchaser could put on a simple hard paper cover or have it bound in tooled leather, depending on available assets and the book's intended use. Indeed, the examination of bindings is a useful tool in assessing the history of particular volumes.

---

2 David L. d'Avray, *The Preaching of the Friars: Sermons Diffused from Paris before 1300* (Oxford: Clarendon Press, 1985), pp. 129, 259. D'Avray describes sermons as having a place in the history of ideas somewhere between the histories of creative thinkers and of popular beliefs.

3 On Thomas Swalwell, see A. J. Piper, 'Dr Thomas Swalwell, Monk of Durham, Archivist and Bibliophile (d. 1539)', in *Books and Collectors, 1200–1700: Essays Presented to Andrew Watson*, ed. by J. P. Carley and C. G. C. Tite (London: British Library, 1997), pp. 71–100. *Durham Liber Vitae: London, British Library, MS Cotton Domitian A.VII, Edition and Digital Facsimile with Introduction, Codicological, Prosopographical and Linguistic Commentary, and Indexes, including the Biographical Register of Durham Cathedral Priory (1083–1539)*, ed. by A. J. Piper, 3 vols (London: British Library, 2007), III, 393–96.

4 For a more detailed discussion of these trends, along with specific books and authors through 1520, see Anne T. Thayer, *Penitence, Preaching and the Coming of the Reformation*, St Andrews Studies in Reformation History (Aldershot: Ashgate, 2002), ch. 2, pp. 13–45.

Around 1470, when model sermon collections began to appear in large numbers in print, they were usually printed in folio volumes. Because of their large size, they were relatively expensive and non-portable. Many of these volumes would have been purchased by bishops, cathedral chapters, and religious houses for the purposes of training preachers and providing devotional reading. But as printed books quickly became less expensive and more widely available than manuscript ones, individual ownership outstripped that of institutions. Book prices tended to decrease even in a time of inflation for other products. It has been estimated that between 1470 and 1480 the price per printed page halved.[5] Increased printing in smaller formats also contributed to the affordability of popular sermon collections. By the sixteenth century, more and more quarto and octavo volumes were being produced. These smaller volumes suited the needs of those who worked away from fixed reading locations such as libraries and lecterns, often travelling and carrying their books with them. It also happened that some monastic libraries invested significantly in printed books, even duplicating texts that they already owned in manuscript. In England this is the case for Syon, Durham, Westminster, and elsewhere.[6] On occasion, Thomas Swalwell wrote the date and price of purchase in the front of his books. The earliest of these is a folio volume of Augustine's *Expositio Evangelii secundum Johannem*, purchased in 1503 for five shillings, a cost of 0.29 pence a folio. The latest of these is John of Salisbury's *Policraticus*, a quarto volume purchased in 1524 for 20 pence, a cost of 0.07 pence per folio.[7] In the decade, 1510–1519, the price Swalwell paid for folio books fluctuated between 0.21 pence and 0.35 pence per folio.

Among the first sermons to circulate in print were 'classics', those of patristic authors who had been studied and commented on in manuscript for centuries. For instance, John Chrysostom's *Homilies on Matthew* were printed in Strasbourg by 1466 and Leo the Great's *Sermons* by 1470 in Cologne.[8] Although Swalwell did not own these earliest editions, he did have access to the sermons in print of Chrysostom and Augustine, both in large folio volumes.[9] More contemporary authors soon came to the fore as printing

---

5   Konrad Haebler, *The Study of Incunabula*, trans. by Lucy Eugenia Osborne (New York: The Grollier Club, 1933), pp. 183–84; Rudolf Hirsch, *Printing, Selling and Reading, 1450–1550* (Wiesbaden: Harrassowitz, 1974), pp. 69–72.

6   Susan Powell, *The Birgittines of Syon Abbey: Preaching and Print*, Texts and Transitions, 11 (Turnhout: Brepols, 2017), p. 15.

7   Augustine, *Expositio Evangelii secundum Johannem* ([Basel: Johann Amerbach, not after 1491]), Durham, Durham Cathedral Library, ChapterLib Inc.45; John of Salisbury, *Policraticus* ([Paris]: Jehan Petit [1513]), Durham, Ushaw College Library, XVII.E.5.4.

8   Early editions: John Chrysostom, *Homiliae super Matthaeum* ([Strasbourg: Johann Mentelin], 1466 or earlier (Goff J–288)); Leo the Great, *Sermones* ([Germany (Köln?): Eponymous press, c. 1470] (Hain 10015/ Goff L–129)).

9   John Chrysostom, *Homilia* ([Basel: Apud inclytam germaniae (Johannes Frobenium), 1517]), Ushaw XVIII.C.5.10–11; Augustine, *Expositio Evangelii secundum Johannem* (see n. 7 for full bibliographical details).

developed. Not surprisingly, Franciscans and Dominicans, with their explicit vocation to preaching, led the way and provided international pathways for the dissemination of sermons and aids for preaching. Indeed, approximately two-thirds of the authors whose sermon collections were printed at least five times before the Protestant Reformation garnered much attention, that is, before 1521, were friars. Dominicans and Franciscans were nearly equally represented, although Franciscans produced a somewhat larger proportion of the individual sermon collections.[10] Their learning and expertise thus became widely available to other medieval clergy, both secular and religious. Swalwell, a Benedictine, annotated books by authors of many religious orders, but Franciscans dominated his sermon collections, including the *Sermones ad omnes status* by Guibert de Tournai (1200–1284), the *Decachordum christianum* by Marcus Vigerius (1446–1516), the *Gemma predicantium* by Nicolas Denyse (d. 1509), and the *Rosarium sermonum predicabilium* by Bernardino da Busti (*c.* 1450–1513).[11]

As suggested by Swalwell's volumes, readers of the expanding market, just starting to buy printed books of sermons, were especially interested in relatively recent works which were readily useful for contemporary preaching. Thus, it was the sermons of fifteenth- and early sixteenth-century friars that were most often printed across Europe. In many instances, there would have been fewer manuscripts of such authors available, adding to the attraction of print editions. All the mendicant authors with at least twenty-five printings of their sermon collections prior to the Reformation came from the fifteenth and sixteenth centuries. There is one exception to this contemporary dominance, Jacopo da Varazze. A Dominican from the thirteenth century, his sermons for Sundays, feasts of the saints, and Lent were all printed in multiple editions. Of course, he is most famous for the *Legenda aurea*, a collection almost entirely of saints lives readily adaptable for preaching. Jacopo da Varazze's works served as sources for many other authors of sermons.[12]

Between 1450 and 1520, there were two authors whose sermon collections were printed more often than those of other authors. These were the Italian Franciscan Roberto Caracciolo (*c.* 1425–1495) and the German Dominican Johannes Herolt (*c.* 1390–1468). Caracciolo was a very popular preacher in

---

10 Thayer, *Penitence, Preaching and the Coming of the Reformation*, p. 29.

11 Guibert de Tournai, *Sermones ad omnes status* (Lyon: Stephani Gueynard per magistrum Johannem de Uingle, [1511]), Durham, Durham Cathedral Library, ChapterLib P.IV.57; Marcus Vigerius, *Decachordum christianum* ([Fano]: Geršom Soncino, [1507]), Ushaw College Library, XVII.G.4.3; Nicolas Denyse, *Gemma Predicantium* (Paris: Peter Regnault for Peter Olivier, [1506]), Durham, Durham Cathedral Library, ChapterLib C.III.59; Bernardino da Busti, *Rosarium sermonum predicabilium* (Lyon: Johannes Clein, 1502), Durham, Ushaw College Library, XVIII.B.4.24.

12 See for example, Jacopo da Varazze, *Legenda aurea*, ed. by Giovanni Paolo Maggioni, Millenio medievale, 6 (Firenze: SISMEL, 1998).

Italy in the second half of the fifteenth century, called a 'second Paul'.[13] Six of his sermon collections were printed at least five times each.[14] The sermons were firmly grounded in his active preaching ministry; in rhetorically powerful passages, one can readily imagine the voice of the preacher. These sold well while he was alive and famous, but their reprinting dropped off significantly within a few years of his death. This decline may have been due to his passing out of the public eye, but may also have been due to a saturated market or changes in homiletic taste.[15]

Johannes Herolt was a well-known preacher in Nürnberg, an early printing centre. His popularity in print came largely from the far-reaching appeal of his *Sermones discipuli*. Herolt called the collection *Sermons of the Disciple* because, he says, he sought to offer simple rather than subtle sermons, in the manner of a disciple rather than that of a master. He claims that it is an 'opus perutile simplicibus curam animarum gerentibus' ['a very useful work for simple ones having the cure of souls'].[16] The collection is huge, with 164 *de tempore* and forty-eight *de sanctis* sermons, which were printed and sold together as well as separately. Herolt also put together a collection of exempla, arranged in alphabetical order by topic, and a compilation of the miracles of the Virgin for the use of preachers; these too were printed alone, together, and with the sermons.[17]

Like the *Sermones discipuli*, the bestsellers among late medieval printed sermon model collections were particularly useful reference books for the late medieval preachers, covering enough liturgical territory to serve the demand for regular, even weekly, preaching to the laity. Most frequently printed were

---

13   Steven J. McMichael, 'Roberto Caracciolo da Lecce and His Sermons on Muhammad and the Muslims (c. 1480)', in *Franciscans and Preaching: Every Miracle from the Beginning of the World Came about through Words*, ed. by Timothy J. Johnson, The Medieval Franciscans, 7 (Leiden: Brill, 2012), pp. 327–52 (p. 328).

14   *Quadragesimale de poenitentia, Sermones de adventu, Sermones de timore divinorum iudiciorum, Sermones de laudibus sanctorum, Sermones quadragesimales de peccatis*. See Thayer, *Penitence, Preaching and the Coming of the Reformation*, pp. 17–19.

15   There is a copy of Caracciolo's *Sermones Quadragesimales de poenitentia* (Strasbourg: [J. R. Grüninger], 1497) in the Durham Cathedral Library, ChapterLib Inc.4. This is not verifiably a book that was in Durham during Swalwell's lifetime, although this is a possibility since it was later in the library of Thomas Tempest, Baronet of Stella, along with other Priory books. See A. I. Doyle, 'The Library of Sir Thomas Tempest: Its Origins and Dispersal', in *Studies in Seventeenth-Century English Literature, History and Bibliography*, ed. by G. A. M. Janssens and F. G. A. M. Aarts (Amsterdam: Rodopi, 1984), pp. 83–93.

16   Johannes Herolt, OP, *Sermones discipuli de tempore et de sanctis unacum promptuario exemplorum* (Strasbourg: [Martin Flach], 1492), colophon.

17   As far as I know, there was not a copy of Herolt's sermons in the Durham Priory Library during Swalwell's time. Durham, Ushaw College Library currently holds two copies of the *Sermones discipuli de tempore et de sanctis unacum promptuario exemplorum* (Strasbourg: Martin Flach, 1503), Durham, Ushaw College Library, XVIII.C.3.13 and XVIII.C.3.14, suggesting that the collection was still considered valuable in Roman Catholic circles in the nineteenth century when they were donated.

de tempore et de sanctis collections. Collections of Sunday sermons were close behind, followed by *sermones quadragesimales.* Printed finding aids and instructions for adaptation made a volume more flexible and comprehensive. To take just one example, Bernardino da Busti's *Rosarium sermonum,* a Lenten collection and one of Swalwell's books, gives instruction to the preacher on how to use the collection. Just as the preacher has collected various 'flowers' from other writers, so the preacher should gather a little bouquet from this 'rosarium sermonum predicabilium' ['rose garden of preachable words']. The volume comes with an alphabetical table of topics, instructions on how to include material on the Virgin Mary in sermons, tables on how to adapt this collection for Sundays, feast days, and weekdays.[18] It is clear that even before the preacher preached, he could learn a great deal from a model sermon collection such as this.

Most of the mendicant preachers used what is known as the thematic, modern, university, or scholastic sermon style that had come into prominence in the early 1200s. These sermons were highly structured, often beginning with an introduction or protheme. At the heart of this style of preaching was the theme (a biblical or liturgical verse) and its division into the points to be made from or concerning it. These were often given as a rhyming series, aiding both preacher and hearer in remembering the sermon. The bulk of the sermon consisted of the confirmation, elaboration, and driving home of these points, especially by providing authorities, those scriptural and patristic citations and proofs of reason that confirm the points. Exempla often brought the message home. This style of preaching was used for all audiences. Among Swalwell's model sermon collections, Guibert de Tournai's *Sermones ad omnes status,* Nicolas Denyse's *Gemma predicantium,* and Bernardino da Busti's *Rosarium sermonum predicabilium* are in this style.

From the late Middle Ages into the early modern period, we also find a revival of an older style, the homily. This was the style of the early centuries of the Church and had been preserved in monastic settings. With the humanist return to biblical and early Christian sources, the homily came into new and popular use. The preacher took a biblical passage, a word or phrase or sentence at a time and offered commentary as he went along. He did not need to stay close to the text (homilies were replete with what may seem to be tangents or digressions), but the framework of the discourse was provided by the text. This style was increasingly advocated for preaching to the people.[19] Collections of homilies annotated by Swalwell include those of Chrysostom, Augustine,

---

18 Bernardino da Busti, *Rosarium sermonum predicabilium,* front matter.

19 Thomas Waleys, an English Dominican visiting Italy in the fourteenth century, noted that 'communiter quando praedicatur non clero sed populo, non accipitur breve themata, sed totum evangelium quod legitur in missa accipitur pro themate, et totum exponitur, et in eius expositione multa pulchra et devota dicuntur' ['often when preaching not to the clergy, but to the people, a short theme is not used, but the whole gospel which is read in the Mass is taken up as the theme and then explained in full, and in its exposition many beautiful

BOOKS FOR PREACHING AND PREACHING WITH BOOKS   55

and Bernard de Clairvaux.[20] Protestants tended to favour the homily as it foregrounded the fullness of the Biblical text.

Postils were commentaries designed to help preachers study and then explain the scriptures by providing commentary on the Gospel and Epistle lections for the liturgical year. This material might be all that an audience might receive, be included as a section in a thematic sermon, or be elaborated into a homily. The *Postilla Guillermi* dominated the market for such commentary, having about as many editions in print in its first fifty years as the Latin Bible and the *Legenda aurea*.[21] Its popularity was grounded in its stylistic adaptability and congeniality to a large theological spectrum of late medieval preachers.

By the middle of the sixteenth century the term *postilla* would be applied to model sermon collections themselves, especially in German territories. Luther's *Hauspostille* and *Kirchenpostille* guided Lutheran preaching. Catholics responded quickly and in kind to the Lutheran challenge via sermons, putting huge numbers of books for preachers on the market. Especially renowned were the postils of the Franciscan Johann Wild.[22] Similarly, the *First* and *Second Books of Homilies* (1547, 1562) came under mandatory use in the Church of England.[23]

As such history suggests, there was a significant trend toward more vernacular publication and localized popularity of printed sermon collections. By 1500 a rise in the incidence of regionally popular collections at the expense of international bestsellers was clear. These were often written by local authors, new preachers in a region such as Olivier Maillard (1430–1502) and Nicolas Denyse in France. In places where printing began somewhat later, such as England and Spain, more vernacular printing was done from the beginning.[24] This trend was furthered by the regional nature of sixteenth-century religious changes.

In a parallel trend, sermons were read by an increasing range of readers. In Italy Carlo Delcorno notes that the printed works of Caracciolo appear

---

    and devout things are said']. Cited in Anne T. Thayer, 'The *Postilla* of Guillermus and Late Medieval Popular Preaching', *Medieval Sermon Studies*, 48 (2004), 57–74 (p. 62).

20   The copy that Swalwell annotated of Bernard's sermons is now at Downside Abbey in Stratton-on-the Fosse in Somerset in south-west England; see Bernard de Clairvaux and Gilbert of Hoyland, *Sermones de tempore, de sanctis, et super cantica canticorum, etc.* (Paris: Jehan Petit, 1508), Stratton-on-the Fosse, Downside Abbey 18274.

21   This Guillermus was not the famous thirteenth-century bishop of Paris; some have suggested that he was Johannes Herolt, since these postils have certain parallels to his.

22   John M. Frymire, *The Primacy of the Postils: Catholics, Protestants, and the Dissemination of Ideas in Early Modern Germany*, Studies in Medieval and Reformation Traditions, 147 (Leiden: Brill, 2010).

23   *The First Book of Homilies* was authorized in 1542 and first printed in 1547; *The Second Book of Homilies* was first published in 1562–1563 and in an expanded edition in 1571.

24   See F. J. Norton, *Printing in Spain 1501–1520* (Cambridge: Cambridge University Press, 1966); Lotte Hellinga, *William Caxton and Early Printing in England* (London: British Library, 2010); *Print Culture and Peripheries in Early Modern Europe: A Contribution to the History of Printing and the Book Trade in Small European and Spanish Cities*, ed. by Benito Rial Costas, Library of the Written Word, 24, The Handpress World, 18 (Leiden: Brill, 2012).

in various private libraries where they would have been used for devotional reading.[25] The German humanist Johann Ulrich Surgant (*c.* 1450–1503) recommended the *Postilla* of Guillermus for laity who might 'hortare proximam ad viam veritatis secundum divinam scripturam' ['exhort one another in the way of truth according to the scriptures'].[26] Several volumes of recent essays have focused on reciprocity between sermons and devotional materials in England and Germany, highlighting the ways in which they were intended for spiritual reading and 're-oralizing', often in communal settings.[27] A number of the books that Swalwell annotated ended up in the household of one Thomas Tempest, a Catholic landowner who offered hospitality to monks leaving Durham Priory after the dissolution of the monasteries in 1539.[28] These were still in the family four generations later, and many eventually ended up in the nearby library of Ushaw College (established as a Catholic Seminary in 1808).

Preaching with Books: A Sermon

Although there are no extant sermons authored by Thomas Swalwell, we have good reason to believe that Swalwell was indeed a preacher. As early as 1277, there had been an indulgence for hearing monks preach in Durham city or cathedral.[29] *The Rites of Durham*, a late sixteenth-century text, nostalgically, even polemically, describing pre-Reformation practice in Durham, reports that a monk preached every Sunday afternoon at one o'clock in the cathedral's Galilee chapel for about two hours.[30] Swalwell's preaching career would

---

25 Carlo Delcorno, 'Medieval Preaching in Italy (1200–1500)', in *The Sermon*, ed. by Beverly Mayne Kienzle, Typologie des sources du Moyen Âge occidental, 81–83 (Turnhout: Brepols, 2000), pp. 449–560 (pp. 522–23).

26 Quoted in Marianne G. Briscoe, *Artes praedicandi*, Typologie des sources du Moyen Âge occidental, 61 (Turnhout: Brepols, 1992), p. 51. Commenting on the practices of his day, Surgant is clear that preaching belongs to clergy, but concedes that laypersons might exhort one another.

27 See, for example, *Die Predigt im Mittelalter zwischen Mündlichkiet, Bildlichkeit und Schrift-lichkeit: La Prédication au Moyen Âge entre oralité, visualité et écriture*, ed. by René Wetzel and Fabrice Flückiger, Medienwandel–Medienwechsel–Medienwissen, 13 (Zürich: Chronos, 2010) and *Preaching the Word in Manuscript and Print in Late Medieval England: Essays in Honour of Susan Powell*, ed. by Martha W. Driver and Veronica O'Mara, Sermo: Studies in Patristic, Medieval and Reformation Sermons and Preaching, 11 (Turnhout: Brepols, 2013).

28 Doyle, 'The Library of Sir Thomas Tempest'.

29 Durham, Durham Cathedral Muniments, 1.13.Pont.11.

30 *Rites of Durham: being a description of all the ancient monuments, rites, & customs belonging or being within the monastical church of Durham before the suppression (1539)*, ed. by J. T. Fowler, Surtees Society, 107 (Durham: Andrews & Co., 1903), p. 39. A newly published edition of the *Rites* stresses the pro-Catholic nature of the document: William Claxton, *The Rites of Durham*, ed. by Margaret Harvey and Lynda Rollason, Surtees Society, 226 (Woodbridge: The Boydell Press, 2020).

have started at Oxford[31] and continued in Durham, where he would have edified and exhorted the monks of the Priory, the people of the town, and mixed audiences at synods when presiding as the prior's official.[32] The many annotations in his books offer suggestive evidence for his homiletic practice in terms of both style and content, but his oral elaborations, the blending of authorities, examples and applications, and his rhetorical force must remain elusive. Most of his notes are topical, reflecting the content of the underlying text, but some are written as direct address to the reader and perhaps would ultimately be conveyed to the listening audience. Two examples will illustrate Swalwell's use of books in preparing to preach.

Bernardino da Busti put together his *Rosarium sermonum predicabilium*, printed in 1502, as he says, 'de varijs libris flosculos excerpendo' ['by excerpting choice flowers from various books'].[33] This collection of sermons is intended for Lenten catechetical preaching; it is in the scholastic style, offering its material in well-organized and frequently numbered series. By examining Swalwell's selective annotations, we may see him choosing his own 'flowers' from this rose garden. Bernardino's sermon thirteen takes Matthew 15. 28 as its theme, 'Mulier magna est fides tua fiat tibi sicut vis' ['Woman, great is your faith'].[34] This is a passage that comes up in the Benedictine lectionary for the Second Sunday in Lent, a time typically devoted to lay catechesis.[35]

Bernardino provides a sermon in three major divisions preceded by a protheme. This introduction centres on definitions of God, the focus of faith. The first major division is labelled 'de fidei diffinitione' ['on the definition of faith']. It names twelve ways faith can be accepted, describes faith as foundational for spiritual life, and then takes up the definition of faith given in Hebrews 11. 1, 'Fides est sperandarum subera rerum argumentum non apparentium' ['Faith is the assurance of things hoped for, the conviction of things not seen']. The second major division is 'de fidei declaratione' ['on the declaration of the faith'] and takes up the things that must be believed using the articles of the Apostles' Creed. It includes the story of the Creed's composition, scriptural support for each article, a long discussion of indulgences in conjunction with the forgiveness of sins, and concludes with the importance of learning the Creed. The third major division is called 'de fidei impeditione' ['on the impeding of the faith'] and takes up lust, avarice, and pride, three vices that hinder faith and lead to heresy.

---

31 R. Barrie Dobson, 'The Black Monks of Durham and Canterbury Colleges: Comparisons and Contrasts', in *Benedictines in Oxford*, ed. by Henry Wansbrough and Anthony Marett-Crosby (London: Darton, Longman and Todd, 1997), pp. 61–78 (p. 74).

32 Piper, 'Dr Thomas Swalwell', p. 86.

33 Bernardino da Busti, *Rosarium*, fol. 2r.

34 Bernardino da Busti, *Rosarium*, fols 84r–93r, for the Thursday after the First Sunday of Lent.

35 Matthew 15. 21–28; *Missale ad usum ecclesie westmonasteriensis*, ed. by John Wickham Legg, 3 vols (London: Harrison and Sons, 1891), I, col. 132.

Which passages does Swalwell select for his own use, judging by his annotations? In the protheme, he simply notes, 'quid deus' ['what God is'], as the text gives definitions such as 'bonum increatum omnem intellectum excedens' ['uncreated good exceeding all understanding'] and 'Credimus te esse quoddam summum bonum quo nihil maius cogitari potest' ['we believe you to be the highest good greater than which nothing can be thought'].[36] God is the focus of faith.

In Bernardino's first major division, Swalwell skips the twelve ways that faith is accepted, but comments on its foundational role. He writes, 'fides cur dicitur fundamentum omnis virtutum et edificij spiritualis' ['why faith is called the foundation of all virtues and of the spiritual edifice'] and 'exemplum quomodo est fundamentalis' ['exemplum of how it is fundamental'].[37] Here the text claims that faith is the ground of all virtues because one who believes that God exists and rewards the righteous hopes for eternal beatitude; similarly one abstains from sin out of fear of divine judgment. Just as everything has a first cause, so faith is the generative first cause of all the virtues. Faith is the first substance that ought to exist in the soul. As Hebrews 11. 1 is presented, Swalwell adds a few notes such as 'quomodo fides dicitur argumentum non apparencium' ['how faith is called the conviction of things unseen'],[38] 'infusio fidei' ['infusion of faith'], and 'de fide sancti ignatii' ['concerning the faith of St Ignatius']. This last note refers to the story of the early Church bishop and martyr upon whose heart Christ's name was said to have been found written in golden letters after his death.

Moving into the second major division of Bernardino's sermon, Swalwell briefly notes 'articulum unde dicitur, figura 12 apostolorum et 12 articulorum' ['why an article is so called, figure of the 12 apostles and of the 12 articles'], references to indivisible portions of truth and to the legend of the Creed's composition.[39] Like the twelve stones of the foundation wall of the city of Jerusalem, and like the twelve apostles, these articles constitute the foundation of the Church of God, reiterating the theme of the foundational nature of faith noted earlier. The explanation of the various articles would likely be the heart of a catechetical sermon. In keeping with his overall attention to scripture, Swalwell writes, underlines, and numbers, 'loca scripture in quibus fundantur articuli fidei' ['places in scripture on which the articles of the faith are founded'].[40] He also gives cross-references to other material which he might use in his preaching, including the *Rationale divinorum officiorum* of William Durandus and works of Bonaventura. As a well-educated preacher, he could elaborate at length.

---

36 Bernardino da Busti, *Rosarium*, fol. 84r–v.
37 Bernardino da Busti, *Rosarium*, fol. 85r.
38 Bernardino da Busti, *Rosarium*, fol. 85v.
39 Bernardino da Busti, *Rosarium*, fol. 86r.
40 Bernardino da Busti, *Rosarium*, fol. 86v.

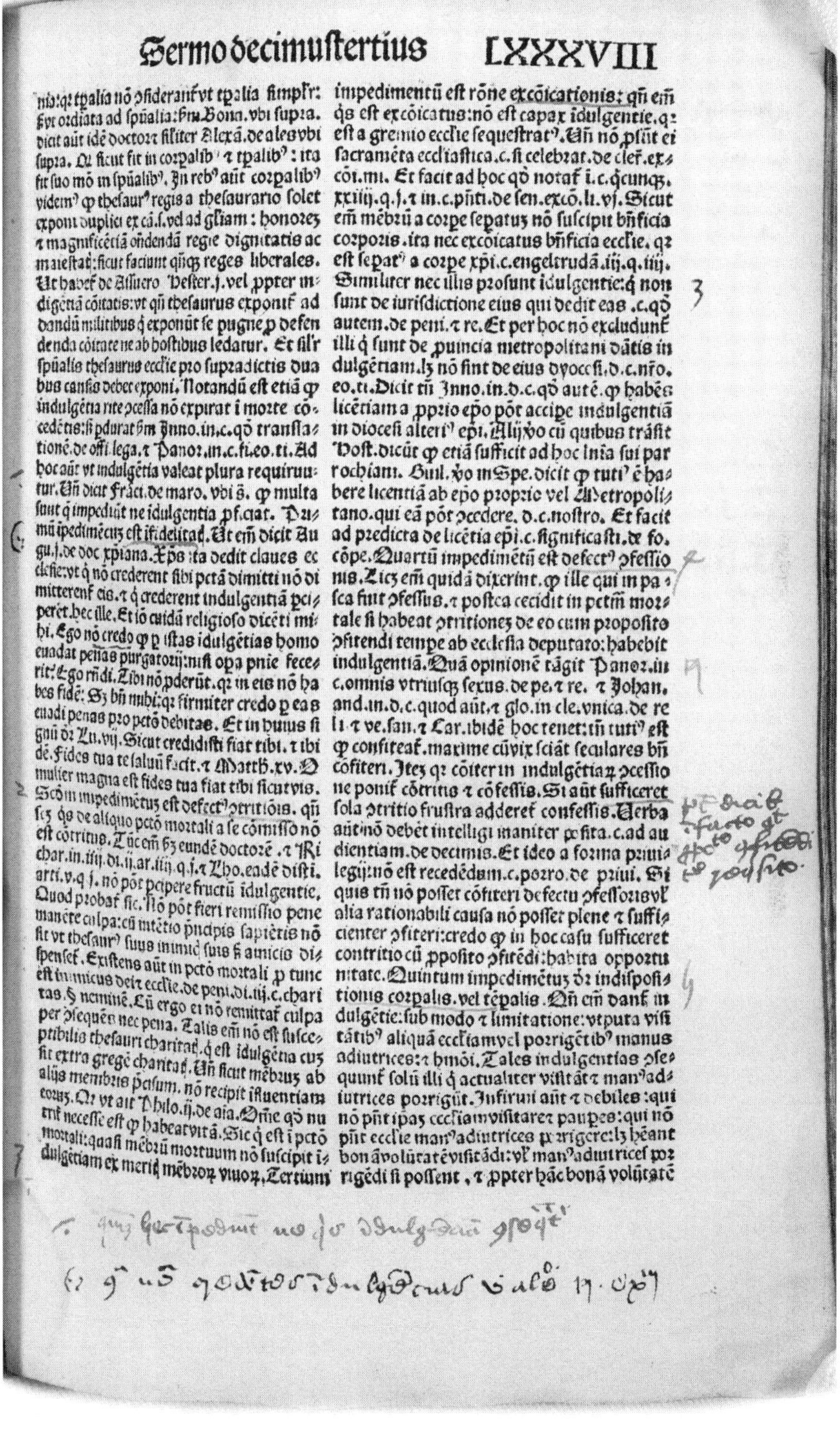

Sermo decimustertius   LXXXVIII

FIGURE 1. Bernardino da Busti, *Rosarium sermonum predicabilium*
(Lyon: Johannes Clein, 1502). Durham, Ushaw College Library, XVIII.B.4.24,
fol. 88r. Reproduced by kind permission of the Trustees of Ushaw College.

Bernardino spends a great deal of time on article eleven, the forgiveness of sins, much of which is devoted to indulgences. Swalwell's underlining and notes in this section show him tracking standard Church teaching: 'diffinitio indulgencia'; 'indulgencis includuntur in articulo xi°'; 'aut papa potest indulgencias dare' ['definition of indulgence; indulgences are included in article 11; whether the pope can give indulgences'].[41] Pastoral concerns are noted and lists are numbered: 'quinque hec impediunt ne quis indulgenciam consequitur'; 'quomodo indulgencie valent defunctis in purgatorio cum exemplo'; 'de dignitate indulgencie concesse beato francisco et de tercie honorij pape'; 'tercia hic bona sequuntur ex indulgencia' ['these five impede the working of an indulgence for someone; how indulgences avail for the dead in purgatory with exemplum; on the dignity of the indulgence granted to St Francis by Pope Honorius III; these three goods come from an indulgence'].[42] (See Figure 1).

Following this long digression, Bernardino's sermon returns to the twelfth article of the Creed, the resurrection of the dead. Swalwell has written, 'conclusio' ['conclusion'] next to 'Omnes ergo christiani debent symbolum apostolicum scire' ['Therefore all Christians ought to know the Apostles' Creed'], and an underlined reference to canon law asserting that the Creed and the Lord's Prayer are the most important texts for Christians to learn.[43] At the end of this section, Swalwell comments, 'ecce bene qualiter dives discebat pater noster' ['behold well how the rich man was able to learn the Lord's Prayer']. Here Bernardino tells a story about a merchant who learned the Lord's Prayer when a priest instructed his customers to give phrases of the prayer as their names.[44] Perhaps our preacher would use this story to goad his listeners to overcome any reluctance to memorization they might have.

Bernardino's third major section takes up what impedes faith. Swalwell makes fewer marginal notes here. Lust is unmarked. Avarice simply has, 'nota miraculum' ['note the miracle'], where the story by Alexander of Hales (1185–1245) is recorded about a man who was losing his fortune playing dice. He prayed to win and God answered his prayer! Pride too receives just one note, 'contra scire cupientem quod supra vires eius est et vide de contra curiositas in 2° parte f. 98' ['against those desiring to know what is beyond their power; see also against curiosity in part 2, folio 98'].[45]

Thus, Swalwell might have preached a catechetical sermon in which most of the material came from the first two major divisions of Bernardino's

---

41 Bernardino da Busti, *Rosarium*, fol. 87r.

42 Bernardino da Busti, *Rosarium*, fols 88r–90v.

43 Bernardino da Busti, *Rosarium*, fol. 91v.

44 Bernardino da Busti, *Rosarium*, fol. 91r.

45 Bernardino da Busti, *Rosarium*, fol. 92v. The whereabouts of Swalwell's copy of part 2 is no longer known; the copy now in Durham, Palace Green Library, Special Collections belonged to monk and then canon, John Tuting (*c.* 1527–*c.* 1559) who dated it in 1540. Bernardino da Busti, *Secunda pars Rosarii Bernardini de Bustis* ([Hagenau: Henricum Gran, impensis Johannis Rynman, 1503], Durham, Palace Green Library, Special Collections, SB+0046.

BOOKS FOR PREACHING AND PREACHING WITH BOOKS

sermon, enlivened by several exempla. The scriptural basis of the twelve articles of the Apostles' Creed would be presented. Indulgences would figure in his discussion of the forgiveness of sins; perhaps he might bring in the indulgences for visiting St Cuthbert's shrine in Durham along with, or instead of, the Franciscan examples that Bernardino gives.[46] He would likely end with an exhortation to learn the Creed and the Lord's Prayer as encapsulating the Christian faith, along with warnings against avarice and pride as impediments to faith and paths to heresy and infidelity.

Interestingly, Swalwell returned to this sermon later in his life when his handwriting was shakier, a transition that may be dated to 1533–1534.[47] He made additional notes, most notably in the discussion of indulgences. In the early days of the Reformation when indulgences became increasingly contentious, he may have sought additional material for his catechetical preaching, or preached a sermon devoted to indulgences, or he may simply have been shoring up his own understanding. The later set of notes suggests an interest in contemporary challenges to the practice of indulgences. For example, Bernardino asserts that faith is required for indulgences to work, and Swalwell writes, 'contra non credentes indulgentias valeo nota exemplum' ['I am strong against those not believing in indulgences, note the exemplum'].[48] Here Bernardino relates a story asserting that one must have faith in indulgences in order to escape the pains of purgatory by them; this is said to be taught in Luke 7, 'Sicut credidisti fiat tibi' ['Let it be done to you as you have believed'] and 'Fides tua te saluum facit' ['Your faith has made you well'].[49] But faith alone is insufficient; Swalwell also highlights Bernardino's claim that the conditions of indulgences have pastoral value and must be fulfilled.[50] Thus Swalwell seems to affirm established tradition as England heads into the Reformation.

Preaching with Books: A Homily

As noted earlier, the homily style was gaining in popularity as the sixteenth century progressed. Swalwell annotated a number of books that would well serve this mode of 'Circulating the Word of God', including *In Quatuor Euangelistas Ennarationes* by Denis the Carthusian (1402–1471) and the *Commentarii*

---

46 *Rites of Durham*, ed. by Fowler, pp. 155–56.

47 A. J. Piper, 'The Monks of Durham and Patterns of Activity in Old Age', in *The Church and Learning in Later Medieval Society: Essays in Honour of R. B. Dobson, Proceedings of the 1999 Harlaxton Symposium*, ed. by Caroline M. Barron and Jenny Stratford (Donington, UK: Shaun Tyas, 2002), pp. 51–63 (p. 60).

48 Bernardino da Busti, *Rosarium*, fol. 88r.

49 Bernardino da Busti, *Rosarium*, fol. 88r. Luke 7. 1–9 records the healing of the centurion's servant, as does Matthew 8. 5–13. Bernardino here cites Matthew 8. 13 as well as Luke 7. 50, while naming only Luke 7.

50 Bernardino da Busti, *Rosarium*, fol. 88v.

initiatorii in quatuor Euangelia, and *Quincuplex Psalterium* by Jacques Lefevre d'Etaples (1455–1536).[51] But perhaps pride of place would have gone to his seven-volume Bible with commentary by Hugues de Saint-Cher (*c.* 1200–1263), especially the volume on the Gospels.[52] The commentary interprets the text a word or phrase at a time, using the four senses of scripture and drawing on earlier interpretations. Swalwell's annotations are generally directed toward the commentary and often focus on the moral sense. There are a number of Gospel passages that receive targeted attention from Swalwell's pen, preceded and followed by clean text. These likely indicate preparation for a homily, especially when they line up with passages included in the Benedictine lectionary. One such passage is the end of the Gospel of Matthew where chapters 27 and 28 were designated for Palm Sunday. Swalwell's marginalia begin at Matthew 27. 30; the preceding sixteen pages receive just one comment. He continues to comment through 28. 15.[53] His notes highlight moral applications for a religious audience. Once during this portion, he writes 'nota religiose' ['note, religious one'], and twice he writes 'nota claustralis' ['note, cloistered ones'].[54] He makes two references to the importance of preaching well. The homily seems likely to have coalesced around the crucifixion, Joseph of Arimathea, Christ's burial in the tomb, and the morning of the resurrection. Swalwell indicates points to be made in each section as the preacher explains and applies to the text for his hearers.

Swalwell's annotations begin with the crucifixion. Swalwell writes, 'latrones — gentiles, judei' ['thieves — gentiles, Jews'], where Hugues explains that all of humanity was crucified with Jesus, Gentiles and Jews, those who repent and those who do not.[55] The three crosses at Golgotha are noted by Swalwell as 'crux carnis, spiritus, mundi' ['cross of the flesh, of the spirit, of the world'].[56] The text explains that each of these crosses has four branches. The cross of the flesh incorporates the four parts of discipline: vigils, abstinence, manual labour, and discipline. The cross of the world is contempt for the world. Its arms are consideration of the brevity and vanity of the world, disdain for temporal things, desire for eternal things, and meditation on the bitterness of death. The cross of the spirit is the imitation of Christ. Here Swalwell writes, '4^{or} brachia crucis' ['the four branches of the cross'].[57] These are obedience

---

51 Denis the Carthusian, *In Quatuor Euangelistas Ennarationes* (Köln: P. Quentell, 1532), Durham, Ushaw College Library, XVIII.B.6.10; Jacques Lefevre d'Etaples, *Commentarii initiatorii in quatuor Euangelia* ([Köln: Gottfried Hittorp, 1521]), Durham, Ushaw College Library, XVII.E.5.5; Jacques Lefevre d'Etaples, *Quincuplex Psalterium* (Paris: Ex chalcotypa Henrici Stephani, 1508–1509), York, York Minster Library, XI.G.4.

52 [*Biblia Latina cum postillis Hugonis de Sancto Charo*], vol. vi ([Basel]: Johann Amerbach for Anton Koberger, 1502), Durham, Ushaw College Library, XVIII.B.3.10.

53 *Biblia Latina,* fols n.4v–n.7v.

54 *Biblia Latina,* fol. n.6v.

55 *Biblia Latina,* fol. n.4v.

56 *Biblia Latina,* fol. n.4v.

57 *Biblia Latina,* fol. n.4v.

BOOKS FOR PREACHING AND PREACHING WITH BOOKS   63

to superiors, humility toward inferiors, kindness in prosperity, and patience in adversity. A skilled preacher could elaborate at length.

Swalwell then moves on to the figure of Joseph of Arimathea. As the commentary picks up the wording of Mark 15. 43, asserting that Joseph was a respected member of the council, Swalwell writes, 'quilibet christianus esset nobilis decuronius' ['every Christian ought to be a respected member of the council'].[58] Matthew notes that Joseph was rich, and Swalwell's underlining highlights that this means being rich in the gold of wisdom, the silver of eloquence, and the pearls of good works. At the same time, as a disciple of Jesus, one should be meek and humble of heart. One should also be from Arimathea, that is, keeping watch over those given into one's care. Joseph is granted Jesus's body and buries it in his own new stone tomb. Matthew says that Mary Magdalene and the other Mary were present. Swalwell writes, 'an 3 marie venerunt ad monumentum Christi' ['whether 3 Marys came to Christ's tomb'], indicating a discussion of the traditional representation of three Marys being present here and at the resurrection.[59]

Hugues then offers an interpretation of the burial of the shrouded Christ in Joseph's tomb, drawing a parallel to Christians receiving Christ's body in the Eucharist at Easter. Swalwell writes, 'quomodo quilibet reciperet corpus Christi' ['how anyone should receive the body of Christ'].[60] The text explains that just as Jesus was put in a clean winding cloth, so Christ ought to enter a clean conscience. Such a cloth/conscience is spun by thinking, deliberating, taking counsel; ordered by working; and woven by reworking and decorating.

The meaning of Christ's tomb is further elaborated in Hugues's commentary. The stone over its entrance is penitence which keeps Jesus in the believers by grace. The two Marys who visit the tomb illustrate contrition for evil deeds done and good ones not done. Here Swalwell writes in direct address, 'fac ut has habeas duas marias' ['act so that you have these two Marys'].[61] The text goes on to discuss various burials celebrated in church (baptism, penitence, and entry into religious life). Each has its own stone, seal, and guards. Next to the discussion of religious life, Swalwell writes 'nota religiose sepulturam tuam lapidem signaculium et custodes tuos' ['note, religious one, your burial, your stone, seal, and guards'].[62] Burial into the religious life is accomplished by handing oneself over to the abbot, as if entering a tomb. Rolling the stone over the entrance is undertaking obligation or vows. The tomb is sealed with tonsure and habit (see Figure 2). The guards are the novice master and the abbot or prior. Swalwell and his monastic brothers might

---

58 *Biblia Latina*, fol. n.6r.
59 *Biblia Latina*, fol. n.6r.
60 *Biblia Latina*, fol. n.6r.
61 *Biblia Latina*, fol. n.6r.
62 *Biblia Latina*, fol. n.6v.

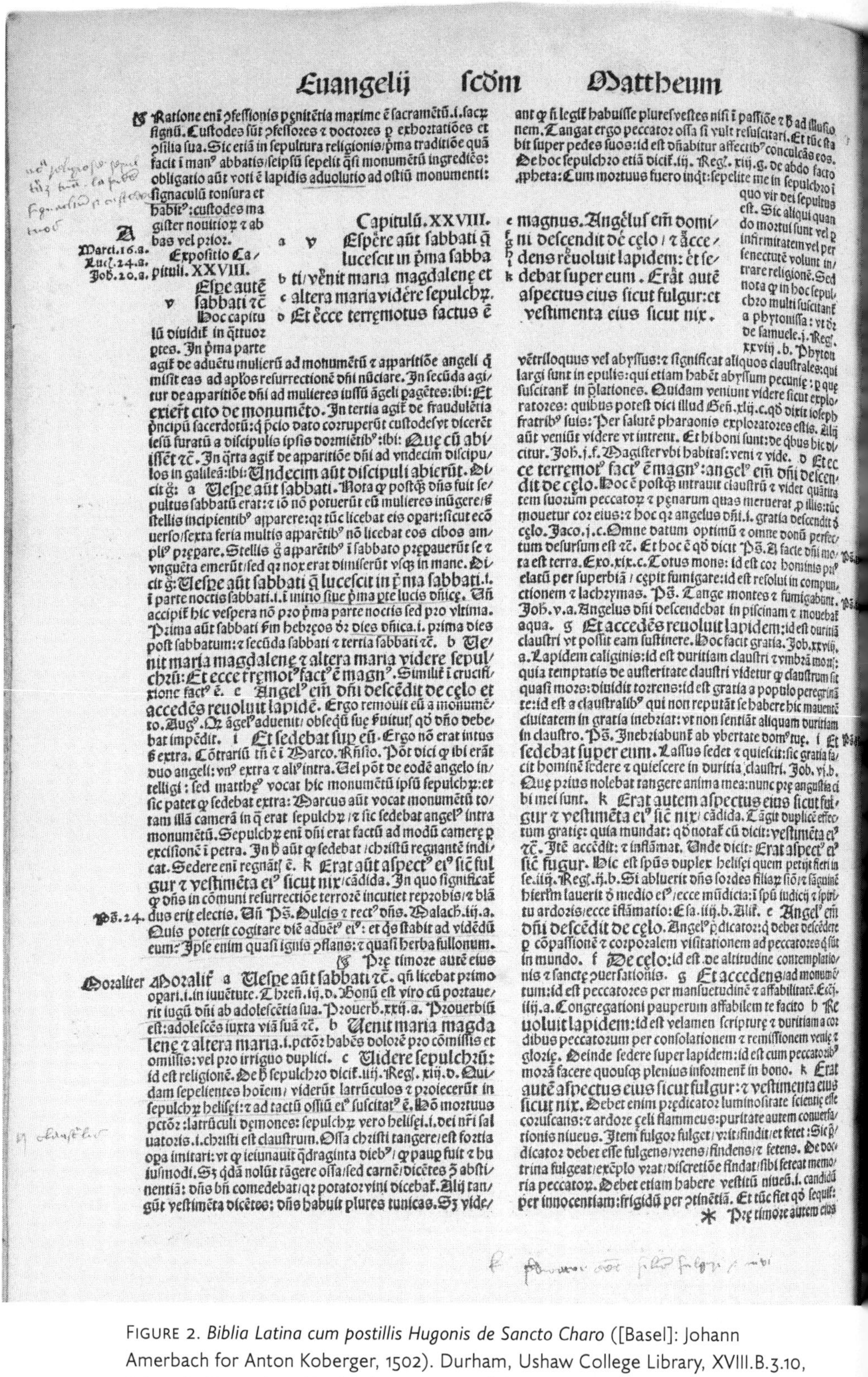

Euangelij scd̄m Mattheum

Capitulū. XXVIII.

Vespere aūt sabbati q̄ lucescit in p̄ma sabbati / venit maria magdalene et altera maria vidēre sepulchr̄. Et ecce terremotus factus ē magnus. Angelus em̄ domi/ni descendit dē celo / r̄ acce/dens reuoluit lapidem: et se/debat super eum. Erāt autē aspectus eius sicut fulgur: et vestimenta eius sicut nix.

FIGURE 2. *Biblia Latina cum postillis Hugonis de Sancto Charo* ([Basel]: Johann Amerbach for Anton Koberger, 1502). Durham, Ushaw College Library, XVIII.B.3.10, fol. n. 6v. Reproduced by kind permission of the Trustees of Ushaw College.

find both encouragement and exhortation here, with significant resonance to their own experience.

As the text turns to the morning of the resurrection, Swalwell writes, 'nota claustralis' ['note, cloistered ones'].[63] Here Jesus's tomb is once again compared to the religious life, a death that gives life, as the bones of Elisha revived a man thrown into his tomb in II Kings 13. 21. In this story the dead man is a sinner, the thieves are demons, the tomb is that of the true Elisha, that is, the cloister of Christ. Hugues compares the angel in white who spoke to the women who came to anoint Jesus's body to preachers, and Swalwell writes, 'predicatores essent similis fulgari et nivi' ['preachers are to be like lightning and snow'].[64] With respect to snow, the text claims that a preacher should be shining with the light of knowledge, enflamed with heavenly ardour, and living with snow-like purity. Like lightning, he should shine with doctrine, burn as an example, divide with discretion, and smell bad to himself with the memory of sins. Swalwell also includes cross-references to other works concerning whether or not Jesus arose in the middle of the night and how long he spent in the tomb, material Swalwell might choose to incorporate while preaching.[65] He has one more 'nota claustralis', where Hugues again says that the religious life is the tomb where Jesus lay. The head cloth and linen bands represent the monastic habit in which religious are buried; they are still buried while Jesus has risen.[66] Swalwell's final note on the resurrection story has to do with the bribe paid to the soldiers to say that Jesus's disciples stole the body. Again Swalwell notes the comparison to preachers. 'Quomodo quidam predicatores assimilanus custodibus mendacibus Christi corpus' ['How some preachers are like the guards lying about Christ's body']. Here Hugues criticizes mute preachers, likening them to the greedy dragon killed by eating the cakes of pitch, fat, and hair offered it in Daniel 14. 26.[67]

Thus, this putative homily moves through two chapters of Matthew, not explaining everything, but stopping to elaborate on items of interest and pertinence to a monastic audience whose ministry included preaching. Swalwell offers theology and biblical interpretation, exhortation to cruciform disciplines. Especially noteworthy is the repeated metaphor of the tomb of Christ as the religious life, an imitation of Christ in death leading to new life. As a preacher to other preachers, Swalwell stresses the importance of preaching well.

---

63 *Biblia Latina*, fol. n.6v.
64 *Biblia Latina*, fol. n.6v.
65 *Biblia Latina*, fol. n.7r.
66 *Biblia Latina*, fol. n.7r.
67 *Biblia Latina*, fol. n.7v.

Conclusion

Swalwell lived during the transition from manuscript to print and embraced the new technology eagerly. The books he annotated largely fit with the trends discerned as printed books increasingly supported the work of preaching. During his lifetime Swalwell and the Durham Priory purchased many printed books. He annotated some works of patristic sermons, but most of his sermon collections are from contemporary authors, especially Franciscans. His books offer finding aids, and Swalwell made his personal selections from the riches they offered. His marginalia suggest that he preached in both the scholastic sermon and homily styles. Swalwell exemplifies the large class of educated clergy in England in his day, but he is quite unusual in leaving behind so many traces of actual use in numerous books. He displays a commitment to preaching the Word, calling Christians to faith and Church leaders to live up to their responsibilities. Committed to the monastic life, Swalwell died in the autumn of 1539, just before the Priory was dissolved.

When the community was re-founded as a cathedral with the former prior becoming the first dean and former monks becoming the first canons, there was much continuity in available books for preaching and in actual preaching from books. Many books now in the Durham Cathedral Library were Priory books and bear the marginal notes of other monks. When Ushaw College was founded, the library received many donations of volumes formerly owned by the monks of the Priory. The current ongoing project to digitize the Durham Priory library draws on this continuity and seeks to virtually recreate the range of books available to Thomas Swalwell and his monastic brothers.[68]

---

68   Durham Priory Library Recreated [https://www.durhampriory.ac.uk/; accessed 21 June 2022].

Bibliography

Archives

Durham, Durham Cathedral Muniments, 1.13.Pont.11

Early Printed Works

This list includes shelf-marks and/or references to Goff and Hain as appropriate.

Aeneas Silvius and Jakob Wimpfeling, *Germania Enee Siluij* ([Strasbourg: Beck, 1515]), München, Bayerische Staatsbibliothek, 4 P.lat. 1174 b

Augustine, *Expositio Evangelii secundum Johannem* ([Basel: Johann Amerbach, not after 1491]), Durham, Durham Cathedral Library, ChapterLib Inc.45

Bernard de Clairvaux and Gilbert of Hoyland, *Sermones de tempore, de sanctis, et super cantica canticorum, etc.* (Paris: Jehan Petit, 1508), Stratton-on-the Fosse, Downside Abbey Library, 18274

Bernardino da Busti, *Rosarium sermonum predicabilium* (Lyon: Johannes Clein, 1502), Durham, Ushaw College Library, XVIII.B.4.24

Bernardino da Busti, *Secunda pars Rosarii Bernardini de Bustis* ([Hagenau: Henricum Gran, impensis Johannis Rynman, 1503]), Durham, Palace Green Library, Special Collections, SB+0046

[*Biblia Latina cum postillis Hugonis de Sancto Charo*], vol. VI ([Basel]: Johann Amerbach for Anton Koberger, 1502), Durham, Ushaw College Library, XVIII.B.3.10

Denis the Carthusian, *In Quatuor Euangelistas Ennarationes* (Köln: P. Quentell, 1532), Durham, Ushaw College Library, Ushaw XVIII.B.6.10

Guibert de Tournai, *Sermones ad omnes status* (Lyon: Stephani Gueynard per magistrum Johannem de Uingle, 1511), Durham Cathedral Library, ChapterLib P.IV.57

Jacques Lefevre d'Etaples, *Commentarii initiatorii in quatuor Euangelia* ([Köln: Gottfried Hittorp, 1521]), Durham, Ushaw College Library, Ushaw XVII.E.5.5

Jacques Lefevre d'Etaples, *Quincuplex Psalterium* (Paris: Ex chalcotypa Henrici Stephani, 1508–1509), York, York Minster Library XI.G.4

Johannes Herolt, *Sermones discipuli de tempore et de sanctis unacum promptuario exemplorum* (Strasbourg: [Martin Flach], 1492)

Johannes Herolt, *Sermones discipuli de tempore et de sanctis unacum promptuario exemplorum* (Strasbourg: Martin Flach, 1503), Durham, Ushaw College Library, XVIII.C.3.13 and XVIII.C.3.14

John Chrysostom, *Homilia* ([Basel: Apud inclytam germaniae (Johannes Frobenium), 1517]), Durham, Ushaw College Library, XVIII.C.5.10–11

John Chrysostom, *Homiliae super Matthaeum* ([Strasbourg: Johann Mentelin], 1466 or earlier), Goff J–288

John of Salisbury, *Policraticus* ([Paris]: Jehan Petit [1513]), Durham, Ushaw College Library, XVII.E.5.4

Leo the Great, *Sermones* ([Germany (Köln?): Eponymous press, *c.* 1470], Hain
10015/Goff L–129

Marcus Vigerius, *Decachordum christianum* ([Fano]: Geršom Soncino, [1507],
Durham, Ushaw College Library, XVII.G.4.3

Nicolas Denyse, *Gemma Predicantium* (Paris: Peter Regnault for Peter Olivier,
[1506]), Durham, Durham Cathedral Library, ChapterLib C.III.59

Roberto Caracciolo, *Sermones Quadragesimales de poenitentia* (Strasbourg: [J. R.
Grüninger], 1497), Durham, Durham Cathedral Library, ChapterLib Inc.4

Primary Sources

*Durham Liber Vitae: London, British Library, MS Cotton Domitian A.VII, Edition and
Digital Facsimile with Introduction, Codicological, Prosopographical and Linguistic
Commentary, and Indexes, including the Biographical Register of Durham Cathedral
Priory (1083–1539)*, ed. by A. J. Piper, 3 vols (London: British Library, 2007)

Jacopo da Varazze, *Legenda aurea*, ed. by Giovanni Paolo Maggioni, Millenio
medievale, 6 (Firenze: SISMEL, 1998)

Missale ad usum ecclesie westmonasteriensis, ed. by John Wickham Legg, 3 vols
(London: Harrison and Sons, 1891)

*Rites of Durham: being a description of all the ancient monuments, rites, & customs
belonging or being within the monastical church of Durham before the suppression
(1539)*, ed. by J. T. Fowler, Surtees Society, 107 (Durham: Andrews & Co., 1903)

William Claxton, *The Rites of Durham*, ed. by Margaret Harvey and Lynda
Rollason, Surtees Society, 226 (Woodbridge: The Boydell Press, 2020)

Secondary Studies

Briscoe, Marianne G., *Artes praedicandi*, Typologie des sources du Moyen Âge
occidental, 61 (Turnhout: Brepols, 1992)

d'Avray, David L., *The Preaching of the Friars: Sermons Diffused from Paris before 1300*
(Oxford: Clarendon Press, 1985)

Delcorno, Carlo, 'Medieval Preaching in Italy (1200–1500)', in *The Sermon*, ed. by
Beverly Mayne Kienzle, Typologie des sources du Moyen Âge occidental,
81–83 (Turnhout: Brepols, 2000), pp. 449–560

Dobson, R. Barrie, 'The Black Monks of Durham and Canterbury Colleges:
Comparisons and Contrasts', in *Benedictines in Oxford*, ed. by Henry
Wansbrough and Anthony Marett-Crosby (London: Darton, Longman and
Todd, 1997), pp. 61–78

Doyle, A. I., 'The Library of Sir Thomas Tempest: Its Origins and Dispersal', in
Studies in Seventeenth-Century English Literature, History and Bibliography,
ed. by G. A. M. Janssens and F. G. A. M. Aarts (Amsterdam: Rodopi, 1984),
pp. 83–93

Driver, Martha W., and Veronica O'Mara, eds, *Preaching the Word in Manuscript
and Print in Late Medieval England: Essays in Honour of Susan Powell*, Sermo:

Studies on Patristic, Medieval and Reformation Sermons and Preaching, 11 (Turnhout: Brepols, 2013)

Frymire, John M., *The Primacy of the Postils: Catholics, Protestants, and the Dissemination of Ideas in Early Modern Germany*, Studies in Medieval and Reformation Traditions, 147 (Leiden: Brill, 2010)

Haebler, Konrad, *The Study of Incunabula*, trans. by Lucy Eugenia Osborne (New York: The Grollier Club, 1933)

Hellinga, Lotte, *William Caxton and Early Printing in England* (London: British Library, 2010)

Hirsch, Rudolf, *Printing, Selling and Reading, 1450–1550* (Wiesbaden: Harrassowitz, 1974)

McMichael, Steven J., 'Roberto Caracciolo da Lecce and His Sermons on Muhammad and the Muslims (c. 1480)', in *Franciscans and Preaching: Every Miracle from the Beginning of the World Came about through Words*, ed. by Timothy J. Johnson, The Medieval Franciscans, 7 (Leiden: Brill, 2012), pp. 327–52

Norton F. J., *Printing in Spain 1501–1520* (Cambridge: Cambridge University Press, 1966)

Piper, A. J., 'Dr Thomas Swalwell, Monk of Durham, Archivist and Bibliophile (d. 1539)', in *Books and Collectors, 1200–1700: Essays Presented to Andrew Watson*, ed. by J. P. Carley and C. G. C. Tite (London: British Library, 1997), pp. 71–100

Piper, A. J., 'The Monks of Durham and Patterns of Activity in Old Age', in *The Church and Learning in Later Medieval Society: Essays in Honour of R. B. Dobson*, *Proceedings of the 1999 Harlaxton Symposium*, ed. by Caroline M. Barron and Jenny Stratford (Donington, UK: Shaun Tyas, 2002), pp. 51–63

Powell, Susan, *The Birgittines of Syon Abbey: Preaching and Print*, Texts and Transitions, 11 (Turnhout: Brepols, 2017)

Rial Costas, Benito, ed., *Print Culture and Peripheries in Early Modern Europe: A Contribution to the History of Printing and the Book Trade in Small European and Spanish Cities*, Library of the Written Word, 24, The Handpress World, 18 (Leiden: Brill, 2012)

Strauss, Gerald, ed., *Manifestations of Discontent in Germany on the Eve of the Reformation* (Bloomington: Indiana University Press, 1971)

Thayer, Anne T., *Penitence, Preaching and the Coming of the Reformation*, St Andrews Studies in Reformation History (Aldershot: Ashgate, 2002)

Thayer, Anne T., 'The *Postilla* of Guillermus and Late Medieval Popular Preaching', *Medieval Sermon Studies*, 48 (2004), 57–74

Wetzel, René, and Fabrice Flückiger, eds, *Die Predigt im Mittelalter zwischen Mündlichkeit, Bildlichkeit und Schriftlichkeit: La Prédication au Moyen Âge entre oralité, visualité et écriture*, Medienwandel–Medienwechsel–Medienwissen, 13 (Zürich: Chronos, 2010)

VERONICA O'MARA

The Early Printed Sermon in England between 1483 and 1532

A Peculiar Phenomenon

England's insular status — in all senses of the term — gave rise to certain peculiarities in the movement from the manuscript to the early printed sermon between 1483 and 1532. And the medieval English manuscript sermon up to the late fifteenth century also has its oddities and imponderables particularly when compared with other major European vernacular traditions.[1] Leaving aside the depredations of time and the ravages of history that will have been responsible for many losses, it is still possible to account for what survives of the Middle English prose sermon in manuscript. There are 1480 unique sermons extant in cycles or collections or as single sermons in one hundred and sixty-two manuscripts between the late thirteenth and the late fifteenth century.[2] Even considering a low population in medieval England and a largely rural society with fewer churches than in urbanized centres, this is a small quantity compared with regions such as Germany where huge numbers of sermons have been recorded,[3] albeit a treasure trove in comparison with what exists from Finland or Denmark.[4] The overwhelming majority of English sermons are anonymous short parochial ones for the major parts of the liturgical year with a special emphasis on Lent and Easter, albeit with little tangible evidence of sanctorale

---

1 There are, of course, differences in the development and survival patterns of all European sermons; for some of these, see *The Sermon*, ed. by Beverly Mayne Kienzle, Typologie des sources du Moyen Âge occidental, 81–83 (Turnhout: Brepols, 2000).

2 Veronica O'Mara and Suzanne Paul, *A Repertorium of Middle English Prose Sermons*, Sermo: Studies on Patristic, Medieval, and Reformation Sermons and Preaching, 1, 4 vols (Turnhout: Brepols, 2007).

3 Hans-Jochen Schiewer, 'German Sermons in the Middle Ages', in *The Sermon*, ed. by Kienzle, pp. 861–961.

4 See, for instance, Jussi Hanska's and Jonathan Adams's essays in this volume.

Veronica O'Mara (V. M.O'Mara@leeds.ac.uk) is Visiting Research Fellow in the Institute for Medieval Studies at the University of Leeds.

Circulating the Word of God in Medieval and Early Modern Europe: Catholic Preaching and Preachers across Manuscript and Print (c. 1450 to c. 1550), ed. by Veronica O'Mara and Patricia Stoop, SERMO 17, (Turnhout: Brepols, 2022), pp. 71–102   BREPOLS ⊛ PUBLISHERS   10.1484/M.SERMO-EB.5.130452

preaching.[5] The only exceptional texts include a handful of parliamentary sermons, a few sermons with reference to public affairs, a text that goes back to Old English traditions on Sunday observance, one addressed to nuns, and two major public sermons discussed below. There is also quite a number (largely unquantified) of anonymous Latin collections of sermons from England, as well as numerous names of notable preachers to whom extant sermons or sermon collections/cycles may be attached.[6]

In the early printed era there are both general and particular idiosyncrasies about the English situation. As is frequently noted, when printing came to England in 1476, it hardly compared with mainland Europe as it was confined largely to Westminster or London, with only limited and short-lived activity in places such as St Albans, Oxford, and Cambridge; England bore no relation to countries like Germany, Italy, or France where widespread printing was evident.[7] The total number of texts produced in England, let alone sermons, was miniscule: if one takes each decade from 1476 to 1536, the number of recorded works (irrespective of the various editions) for these years is as follows: 1476 (5); 1486 (7); 1496 (26); 1506 (31); 1516 (37); 1526 (48); and 1536 (48).[8] Not only was the establishment of printing first dependent on

---

5 This absence of sanctorale manuscripts is a complex issue; see V. M. O'Mara, 'Saints' Plays and Preaching: Theory and Practice in Late Middle English Sanctorale Sermons', *Leeds Studies in English: Essays in Honour of Peter Meredith*, n.s. 29 (1998), 257–74.

6 Siegfried Wenzel, *Latin Sermon Collections from Later Medieval England: Orthodox Preaching in the Age of Wyclif*, Cambridge Studies in Medieval Literature, 53 (Cambridge: Cambridge University Press, 2005).

7 Lotte Hellinga, 'Printing', in *The Cambridge History of the Book in Britain*, III: *1400–1557*, ed. by Lotte Hellinga and J. B. Trapp (Cambridge: Cambridge University Press, 1999), pp. 65–108; Andrew Pettegree, 'Printing and the Reformation: The English Exception', in *The French Book and the European Book World*, Library of the Written Word, 1, The Handpress World (Brill: Leiden, 2007), pp. 299–322; Lotte Hellinga, *William Caxton and Early Printing in England* (London: The British Library, 2010); Susan Powell, 'After Arundel but before Luther: The First Half-Century of Print', in *After Arundel: Religious Writing in Fifteenth-Century England*, ed. by Vincent Gillespie and Kantik Ghosh, Medieval Church Studies, 21 (Turnhout: Brepols, 2011), pp. 523–41; and *A Companion to the Early Printed Book in Britain, 1476–1558*, ed. by Vincent Gillespie and Susan Powell (Cambridge: Brewer, 2014) where every essay has something of value to offer.

8 A. W. Pollard and G. R. Redgrave, *A Short-Title Catalogue of Books Printed in England, Scotland, and Ireland, and of English Books Printed Abroad*, second edition, revised and enlarged by W. A. Jackson, F. S. Ferguson, and Katherine F. Pantzer, 3 vols (London: The Bibliographical Society, 1976–1991), II (1976), 331–40 (hereafter STC). For information (including dates and uniform titles), use has also been made of the *Catalogue of Books Printed in the XV*[th] *Century now in the British Library, Part XI: England* ('t-Goy-Houten: Hes & De Graaf, 2007); Lotte Hellinga, *Printing in England in the Fifteenth Century: E. Gordon Duff's Bibliography with Supplementary Descriptions, Chronologies and a Census of Copies* (London: The Bibliographical Society and The British Library, 2009); and the ESTC (English Short Title Catalogue), ISTC (Incunabula Short Title Catalogue), and USTC (Universal Short Title Catalogue) websites respectively at estc.bl.uk, https://data.cerl.org/istc/_search, and www.ustc.ac.uk [accessed 21 June 2022]. The texts are available on Early English Books Online (EEBO) at www.proquest.com/eebo [accessed 21 June 2022].

THE EARLY PRINTED SERMON IN ENGLAND BETWEEN 1483 AND 1532

foreign expertise, with Caxton (d. 1492) learning his trade in Cologne and Bruges, and his successors Wynkyn de Worde (d. 1535) and Richard Pynson (d. 1529) respectively hailing from the Low Countries and Normandy, but many of the books found in England in the first decades were imported from the major European centres.[9] England shared in just two of the major Latin sermon collections first produced in mainland Europe: Johannes Herolt's *Sermones discipuli de tempore et de sanctis* published by Julian Notary in 1510 (STC 13226) and Michael de Hungaria's *Eugatorium modus predicandi sermones. xiii. Michaelis de Hungaria [...]* printed by Richard Pynson possibly in 1510 (STC 17853).[10] In addition, in 1509 Richard Pynson had printed a translation into Latin of an Italian sermon by Girolamo Savonarola (1452–1498), *Sermo fratris Hieronymi de Ferraria in vigilia natiuitatis domini cora[m] fratris suis recitatus* (STC 21800).[11] The interest in Latin preaching was very limited in comparison to the rest of Europe, and little attempt was made either to print native Latin sermons. In the first decades of printing the English market was hardly flooded with sermons.[12] It has to be assumed that English preachers between the late fifteenth century and the early sixteenth century were largely making do with the manuscripts that they had always used.[13]

The story of the early printed sermon in England is a series of binary histories: an English and a Latin narrative; printing pre-Luther and post-Luther; a tradition that looks back to the Middle Ages and onward to the Renaissance. Depending on time and circumstances, any of these histories could coalesce. When English orthodox or mainstream sermons were printed, they simultaneously demonstrated a continuation of the medieval manuscript

---

9 Elizabeth Armstrong, 'English Purchases of Printed Books from the Continent 1465–1526', *The English Historical Review*, 94 (1979), 268–90; Paul Needham, 'Continental Printed Books Sold in Oxford, c. 1480–3: Two Trade Records', in *Incunabula: Studies in Fifteenth-Century Printed Books Presented to Lotte Hellinga*, ed. by Martin Davies (London: The British Library, 1999), pp. 243–70; and Margaret Lane Ford, 'Importation of Printed Books into England and Scotland', in *The Cambridge History of the Book in Britain*, III: 1400–1557, ed. by Lotte Hellinga and J. B. Trapp (Cambridge: Cambridge University Press, 1999), pp. 179–201.

10 See Anne T. Thayer, *Penitence, Preaching and the Coming of the Reformation*, St Andrews Studies in Reformation History (Aldershot: Ashgate, 2002), Table 2.8, pp. 36–37, where she accounts for thirty-five collections with ten editions or more between 1450 and 1520 available in the Empire, England, France, Italy, The Netherlands, and the Swiss Confederation; of these (apart from the *Festial*) England only had the two above, the lowest number by far of any of these regions.

11 I owe this reference to Susan Powell, 'After Arundel but before Luther', p. 535.

12 An exception to this is John Mirk's *Festial* that will be dealt with below.

13 This old-fashioned approach continued for some time; for instance, the Carmelite turned Protestant, John Bale (1495–1563), comments on how priests in the 1540s could still make use of the *Festial* and other Latin foreign printed collections; for full details, see Lucy Wooding, 'From Tudor Humanism to Reformation Preaching', in *The Oxford Handbook of the Early Modern Sermon*, ed. by Peter McCullough, Hugh Adlington, and Emma Rhatigan (Oxford: Oxford University Press, 2011), pp. 329–47 (p. 332).

74 VERONICA O'MARA

mores and a turning away from that tradition.[14] In textual terms it was as if many of the 1480 sermons above had never existed and in printing terms that preaching barely took place outside London, as we shall see.

In this investigation of early printed sermons in England a number of inter-related issues will be addressed, starting with what sermons were printed in the period between 1483 and 1532 (with a brief excursus on a sermon printed in 1540 and beyond) followed by some general considerations of this material. The focus will then turn to certain public sermons in manuscript and print and the relationship between those preached sermons and their printed equivalents. Finally, some overall comments will be offered about the selection criteria at work in the printing of sermons in England in the late fifteenth and early sixteenth centuries.[15]

The Early Printed Sermons

What was printed (listed in the Appendix and below) between 1483 and 1532 (and one example in 1540) demonstrates a fractured relationship between manuscript and print: of the major sermon cycles, collections or single sermons that existed in manuscript in England in the fifteenth century, only one cycle and one single sermon made it into print.

The only vernacular series published was the medieval bestseller, *The Festial* (a cycle of some seventy sermons for temporale and sanctorale) by the Austin canon, John Mirk. Its manuscript history outweighs all but the Wycliffite sermon cycle (294 sermons found in thirty-six manuscripts to a greater or lesser extent). *The Festial* is found in nineteen full, or nearly full, manuscript versions in two recensions, seventeen manuscripts containing

---

14 In this essay I am not concerned with the various printings of Wycliffite-related sermon and other material that took place mainly on the continent in the early sixteenth century; see Anne Hudson, *The Premature Reformation: Wycliffite Texts and Lollard History* (Oxford: Clarendon Press, 1988), especially pp. 483–94. I also omit the *Quattuor sermones*, first printed by William Caxton in 1483 and published alongside John Mirk's *Festial* from 1491 (STC 17959); these are not sermons but catechetical material cast in sermon form.

15 As will be shown below, 1532 effectively marks the end of medieval Catholic sermon printing. The concentration here will be on vernacular printed sermons as these can more readily be compared with manuscript sermons, but printed Latin sermons will also be included. Apart from incidental comment in the references here, the only sustained discussion of early printed sermons is still J. W. Blench, *Preaching in England in the Late Fifteenth and Sixteenth Centuries: A Study of English Sermons 1450–c. 1600* (Oxford: Blackwell, 1964), with some useful comment in Felicity Heal, 'The Bishops and the Printers: Henry VII to Elizabeth', in *The Prelate in England and Europe, 1300–1560*, ed. by Martin Heale (Woodbridge: York Medieval Press, 2014), pp. 142–69; see also *English Works of John Fisher, Bishop of Rochester: Sermons and Other Writings 1520 to 1535*, ed. by Cecilia A. Hatt (Oxford: Oxford University Press, 2002); John Fisher, *John Fisher's Court Sermons: Preaching for Lady Margaret, 1507–1509*, ed. by Cecilia A. Hatt (Oxford: Oxford University Press, 2021) and n. 63 below.

THE EARLY PRINTED SERMON IN ENGLAND BETWEEN 1483 AND 1532

variable amounts of the collection, four manuscripts with various material from a comprehensive revision, and four closely related manuscripts.[16] This popularity continued into the post-medieval period: it appeared twenty-five times between 1483 and 1532 (STC 17957–17975). It was first printed by Caxton at Westminster in 1483 (STC 17957), next (in a different version) at Oxford (previously attributed to Theodoric Rood and Thomas Hunte) in 1486/7 (STC 17958), and then again by Caxton in 1491 (STC 17959). Thereafter Caxton's second edition appears to have formed the model for all subsequent editions, which appeared with extraordinary rapidity. For instance, Richard Pynson produced two editions in 1493 (STC 17960–17961); both James Ravynell of Rouen (STC 17963) and Wolfgang Hopyl of Paris printed an edition in *c.* 1495 (STC 17964); while around 1499 there were no fewer than three separate editions by Wynkyn de Worde (STC 17967), Richard Pynson (STC 17866.5), and Julian Notary (STC 17968), plus one printed in Rouen by Martin Morin (STC 17966).

The only other extant sermon in Middle English that has a secure manuscript and a printed history is Thomas Wimbledon's sermon, preached at St Paul's Cross in *c.* 1387 that will be discussed further below. It survives in seventeen English and four Latin manuscripts, besides existing in an abbreviated version in a sermon cycle. Marketed with a new title, 'A sermon no lesse fruteful then famous', it is found in twenty-four early printed editions from 1540 to 1635 (STC 25823.3–25839) that were all printed in London. It is also included in the *Acts and Monuments* of John Foxe (1516–87) from 1563 onwards (STC 11122) and in three late works in 1731, 1738, and 1745.[17] There is then two halves to the circulation: manuscripts in the fifteenth century and print from the mid-sixteenth century.

Apart from the reprinting of the *Festial*, no sermons appeared between 1483 and 1491. Linked to the printed *Festial* tradition are the three sermons for the new feasts of the Visitation of the Virgin (2 July), the Transfiguration of the Lord (6 August), the Holy Name of Jesus (7 August), and the brief sermon-type instructional text, the *Hamus caritatis*. These were first annexed to the *Festial* in the 1491 edition (STC 17959) printed by Caxton. These feasts were not licensed by the Convocation of Canterbury until 1480, 1487, and 1488 respectively so the sermons, if they were ever preached before being printed, would date from around the same period. They would therefore class as 'new' sermons printed more or less contemporaneously. The sermons are anonymous, but their editor, Susan Powell, makes a case for an association between the *Hamus caritatis* and the work of Thomas Betson (d. 1516), the

---

16 John Mirk, *John Mirk's 'Festial'*, ed. by Susan Powell, Early English Text Society, o.s. 334–35 (Oxford: Oxford University Press, 2009–2011).

17 For full details, see Veronica O'Mara, 'Thinking Afresh about Thomas Wimbledon's Paul's Cross Sermon of *c.* 1387', *Leeds Studies in English: Essays in Honour of Oliver Pickering*, n.s. 41 (2010), 155–71, with a full listing on pp. 169–71.

librarian of the Birgittine Syon Abbey, and suggests a Syon provenance for the sermons, with one caveat addressed below.[18]

With three exceptions in the years 1508 to 1512 dealt with below, the only other published sermons are those by or attributed to bishops or future bishops. The episcopal figures whose work was printed were John Alcock (1430–1500), Richard Fitzjames (d. 1522), John Fisher (1469–1535), and John Longland (1473–1547). All these men were of national importance and Fisher was a scholar with a European reputation. Alcock was bishop of Ely (1486–1500) and so integrated into royal circles that he baptised Arthur (born in 1486), the first son of Henry VII (1485–1509). Fitzjames was warden of Merton College Oxford (1483–1507), chaplain to Henry VII from 1489, bishop of Rochester (1497–1503), later becoming Bishop of London from 1506. Fisher succeeded Fitzjames as bishop of Rochester (1504–1535) in addition to being the chancellor of the University of Cambridge from 1504. Longland was bishop of Lincoln (1521–1547) and the confessor of Henry VIII. Among them they covered the whole period of sermon printing from its advent up to the transition — or part transition — from a Catholic to a Protestant England.

In 1495/96–1501? there were six early printed Middle English single sermons and one in Latin, all printed by Wynkyn de Worde (with one exception): *Sermo die lune in ebdomada pasche* (STC 11024) was printed in c. 1495–1496; *Mons perfectionis* (STC 278–281) in 1496, 1497, and 1501 (all by de Worde), and in 1497–1498 (by Richard Pynson); a Sermon for the Boy Bishop (STC 282–283) in 1496 and c. 1497–1498; a Sermon on Luke VIII (STC 284–285.5) in 1496, c. 1496?, and 1501?; *Spousage of a Virgin* (STC 286–287) both in 1497–1498; and a Latin one, *Gallicantus* (STC 277) in 1498. *Sermo die lune in ebdomada pasche* is attributed to Richard Fitzjames and all the others are by or attributed to John Alcock.[19]

In the next decades the focus is almost entirely on John Fisher, an exemplar of episcopal probity and erudition who assisted his patron, Margaret Beaufort (1433–1509), the mother of Henry VII, in the foundation of Christ's College (1506) and St John's College Cambridge (1511). His most popular text was his work on the Psalms (STC 10902–10907) published in 1508, 1509, 1510, 1514?, 1519?, 1525, and 1529. His other sermons are on the death of Henry VII (d. 1509) found in two editions in 1509/10 (STC 10900–10901), and then in the same year a sermon for the Month's Mind of Margaret Beaufort (STC 10891). In the later half of his career Fisher helped counter the teachings of Luther,

---

18 *Three Sermons for 'Nova Festa', together with the 'Hamus Caritatis'*, ed. by Susan Powell, Middle English Texts, 37 (Heidelberg: Universitätsverlag Winter, 2007), pp. xxxi–xliv.

19 The evidence for Alcock's authorship of the Boy Bishop sermon is tenuous; see Veronica O'Mara, 'A Victorian Response to a Fifteenth-Century Incunabulum: The "Boy Bishop" Sermon and How it was First Edited', in *Preaching the Word in Manuscript and Print in Late Medieval England: Essays in Honour of Susan Powell*, ed. by Martha W. Driver and Veronica O'Mara, Sermo: Studies on Patristic, Medieval, and Reformation Sermons and Preaching, 11 (Turnhout: Brepols, 2013), pp. 351–90 (pp. 367–69).

THE EARLY PRINTED SERMON IN ENGLAND BETWEEN 1483 AND 1532   77

most memorably in his English Paul's Cross sermon given on 12 May 1521 at the burning of Luther's books and published in 1521 in Latin (STC 10898), as translated by Richard Pace, the Dean of St Paul's, and in 1521?, 1522?, and 1527 in English (STC 10894–10895). His sermon [Against Heretics] was published twice in 1526? and 1527? (STC 10892–10892.7). His [Two Fruitful Sermons] (STC 10909) were published in 1532, three years before he was martyred at the Tower of London on 19 May 1535 for his refusal to condone Henry VIII's (1509–1547) divorce from Katherine of Aragon (1509–1536) and to agree to the 1534 Act of Supremacy.

A few years after Fisher preached his sermons after the deaths of Henry VII and his mother, and before he moved to his anti-Lutheran printed sermons, there are three Latin works published by three preachers all with Cambridge connections. One is Stephen Baron (*fl.* 1508–1513), who may have been French; he was provincial of the Observant Franciscans and confessor to Henry VII. He preached fifteen sermons on the last things before the University of Cambridge, and these were published by De Worde after 1509 as *Sermones declamati coram alma vniversitatis Cantabrigiensi* [...] (STC 1497). Another is William Melton, a Cambridge humanist scholar and chancellor of York (1496–1528), who was responsible for *Sermo exhortatius cancellarij Eborum hijs qui ad sacros ordines petunt promoveri* (STC 17806) published by De Worde probably in 1510. Then probably also in 1510, the Dean of St Paul's Cathedral, and great humanist scholar, John Colet (1467–1519), gave his Address to Convocation that was published by Pynson in Latin probably in 1512 (STC 5545) and then published in English by Thomas Berthelet probably in 1530 (STC 5550) and 1531 (STC 5550.5). Then we return to the last of the bishops in this era, John Longland (a traditional preacher but a supporter of Henry VIII's divorce). For him *c.* 1527 was the year when he burst into print with his various Latin sermons on the Psalms published by Pynson (STC 16790–16793.5) and again in 1532 with two editions of his works by Robert Redman (STC 16791.5–16792).

This then is the sum total of early printed sermons in England up to 1532, hardly a thriving industry when set beside a vibrant sermon printing tradition in much of Western Europe. It is distinguished by a heavy emphasis on the vernacular that both looks backwards to traditional parochial sermon lore and forwards to more contemporary matters by university men used to moving in more public spheres.

General Considerations about the Early Printed Sermons

Taken at face value, the list above is a somewhat odd assortment. Apart from Mirk's *Festial* that links up directly with the manuscript tradition, if only these printed texts had survived (without the 1480 manuscript sermons), posterity would have gained a distorted view of what medieval English preaching had been like. Sermons at the institution of new feasts are unknown in Middle English manuscripts. Similarly, there is only one sermon in English addressed to nuns, as well as two short sermons in Latin, one sermon preserved in Latin that appears to have been preached in English, plus one imperfect early sixteenth-century English text that is an address by a chaplain or confessor to two nuns in the run-up to their profession.[20] Likewise, although preaching for the tradition of the Boy Bishop was well-known, the only text that survives in manuscript is one from 1558.[21] Finally, in the whole of the manuscript period there are just two surviving English sermons that were preached at the main public venues in the country, as we shall see.

Readers in the 1480s were first presented with a seamless continuity of the manuscript tradition in Mirk's printed *Festial* from 1483. And anyone who bought the 1486 Oxford edition would also have had images (woodcuts) for the first time. (In all the extant manuscripts only one has an illustration: an historiated initial of a preacher in a pulpit.[22]) In their printed *Festial* preachers, listeners or readers were given the usual ten to fifteen minutes of easy-to-follow sermons. Such people were on home territory in a tradition extending back to when the *Festial* was first composed in the late fourteenth century. The only difference was that literate lay people now also had Mirk's stories directly at their disposal.

A decade later in the 1490s readers in England were encountering new fare, all of which was rather random. First came the Mirk-like short and straightforward *Nova festa* series of 1491 while in the later 1490s readers could stretch their abilities by reading much longer texts and learning to grapple with more complex argumentation. Three works were aimed at religious orders. *Spousage of a Virgin* is a profession sermon for nuns, who we may assume were in Alcock's own diocese of Ely. *Gallicantus*, the only Latin text, and a play on Alcock's surname, was preached at a synod of the clergy at Barnwell outside Cambridge (also in Alcock's diocese). Calling this a sermon is somewhat of a misnomer; although it begins as such, it continues with thirteen chapters that outline the apostolic rule (from I Timothy 3. 2–6), specifying the behaviour required of clergy and it is followed by Alcock's constitutions. *Mons perfectionis* was addressed to the Carthusians at Coventry and is focused on the need to uphold the three vows of religious life. The Boy Bishop sermon, delivered at St Paul's Cathedral and focusing on the three ages of man, with its opening prayers for particular London clergy, was similarly a specialized type of sermon, albeit more outward facing than the others. In fact, of these new sermons in the period before 1500, only that by Fitzjames and Alcock's text on Luke VIII, which will be discussed below, may be said to have addressed the public at large. By the early decades of the sixteenth century the bulk

---

20 Described in V. M. O'Mara, 'Preaching to Nuns in Late Medieval England', in *Medieval Monastic Preaching*, ed. by Carolyn Muessig, Brill's Studies in Intellectual History, 90 (Leiden: Brill, 1998), pp. 93–119 (pp. 99–104 and 107–10).

21 O'Mara, 'A Victorian Response to a Fifteenth-Century Incunabulum', pp. 351–90 (p. 356 and n. 12).

22 Provided as the frontispiece to O'Mara and Paul, *A Repertorium of Middle English Prose Sermons*.

THE EARLY PRINTED SERMON IN ENGLAND BETWEEN 1483 AND 1532 79

of the new sermon material available was on the Psalms with the repeated editions of Fisher's sermons.

What is particularly noticeable about these early sermons is their variability of tone depending on language. In *Gallicantus* Alcock seeks to regulate the behaviour of the clergy. Equally censorious preachers were Melton and Colet who were part of a general call for clerical reform in the years running up to the Fifth Lateran Council (1512–1517). Melton's sermon concerns the quality of those entering holy orders and was meant to have been read to candidates in the period leading up to their ordination. The focus of Colet's hard-hitting sermon was episcopal reform. He advocated the selection of bishops purely on spiritual criteria and stressed the need for greater rigour in the examination of potential ordinands. Being in Latin these sermons were available only to a specialized readership, while none of the English sermons gave rise to anything controversial or any great cognisance of the Church at large. Especially unchallenging is Alcock's *Spousage of a Virgin* that presents a straightforward discussion of the stages of a nun's profession. Set in the tradition of the numerous virginity treatises produced for women in the Middle Ages, the context is that of a marriage ceremony where the incomparable groom is Christ.[23]

There may be a developing sense of the need for reform, with calls for increased clerical education, but this only occurs in the Latin sermons. Melton's and Colet's sermons published in 1510? and 1512 were unusually outspoken, but at this point they were in good company in arguing for the reform of the Church as it was a talking-point amongst the elite of Europe. Even if both were printed in England, the material was in Latin so there was no danger of such criticism becoming a rallying-cry for the masses, and it was not until 1530 that an English translation of Colet's sermon appeared. In the same way when Fisher entered the vexed debate about the identity of Mary Magdalene with the pamphlet *De unica Magdalena libri tres* published twice in 1510 by Josse Bade in Paris, he was entering into controversy as a major European figure; it was only proper for the purposes of wide dissemination that he turned to continental publishers — and that he did so in the universal language.[24]

The printed sermons (with the exception of Mirk and the *Nova festa*) may have been more sophisticated than much of what had gone before, but English was still only used for quotidian general matters that concerned the soul; Latin was largely for particular controversies that might involve the body politic. As far as sermons went, monoglot readers in England (most of the population) were largely protected from the contemporary theological controversies raging in Europe. Martin Luther may have pinned up his 95 Theses in 1517, but it took a while before England realised the danger, even

---

23 The sermon is described in O'Mara, 'Preaching to Nuns in Late Medieval England', pp. 104–07.
24 The Magdalene controversy is discussed in Richard Rex, *The Theology of John Fisher* (Cambridge: Cambridge University Press, 1991), pp. 65–77.

if Fisher's 1521 sermon at Paul's Cross was accompanied by book burning and ceremony. This serves again to stress the peculiarly English tenor of its Reformation; had Pope Clement VII (1523–1534) acceded to Henry VIII's request for an annulment from Katherine of Aragon, the Reformation, if it had ever succeeded, might have been considerably slower than it already was. In the event Henry's success in getting his way without papal authority changed not only the course of history, but also the development of the sermon. After his death in 1547, his son Edward VI (1547–1553), the most Protestant of the Tudor monarchs, set about making obligatory the rather inane *First Book of Homilies* in all English parish churches.

Why such clerical and mainly episcopal sermons were published — and most importantly — why only this somewhat amorphous range are the questions that will essentially occupy the rest of this essay. There are some straightforward general explanations, one of which must be simple availability; this would account for the printing of the *Festial* with its widespread manuscript transmission and why some of the better sermons in unique manuscripts never saw the light of day. The status of the bishop or other high-ranking cleric in the Church hierarchy must also be part of the answer. Most of the sermons were by eminent theological figures (some with important patrons), many of whom knew each other and who held or had occupied significant positions; and with the exception of Melton in York, they were largely local to London or its environs. Once local printers got used to printing the work of certain bishops, perhaps they just carried on printing whatever they had to hand.

Different narratives emerge when sermons in the two languages are studied. Various comments exist about the poor linguistic ability of English compositors; this has sometimes been used as the reason for the production of Latin material abroad. But again, this is only half the story. In the examples here we have seen that copies of Mirk's *Festial* were also printed abroad so this would imply that England had to resort to continental printers when there was insufficient capacity at home to cope with demand. Either that or canny continental competitors realised that there was quick money to be made from what was clearly a bestseller.

The fact that some of the sermons were preached near what had long been the centre of the book trade around St Paul's may also have been sufficient explanation to warrant publication.[25] It would have been simpler for printers to opt for what was near at hand rather than to have to traverse the country for other or better examples. Apart from the 1486 publication of the second edition of Mirk's *Festial* in Oxford and the translation by Richard Pace of

---

25 C. Paul Christianson, 'The Rise of London's Book-Trade', in *The Cambridge History of the Book in Britain*, III: *1400–1550*, ed. by Lotte Hellinga and J. B. Trapp (Cambridge: Cambridge University Press, 1999), pp. 128–47.

THE EARLY PRINTED SERMON IN ENGLAND BETWEEN 1483 AND 1532   81

Fisher's anti-Luther sermon published by Johannes Siberch of Cambridge in 1521, most of the sermons here were published in the capital.[26]

In sum, the putative reasons for the printing of these sermons are many and variable. Yet, though perfectly plausible rationales, these explanations are not the full story. There were certainly reasons for the printing of the various anti-Lutheran sermons by Fisher in the 1520s, but what is far more opaque is what motivated the publication of sermons in the period up to this period.[27] Therefore, the choice of sermons in public venues near the site of the printing industry around St Paul's Cathedral is one that merits further investigation.[28] To do so, I shall focus on the two interlinked and most important preaching venues in the country, Paul's Cross at St Paul's Cathedral and the Hospital of St Mary Bishopgate (commonly called St Mary Spital) in London, while attempting to show to what extent an English public sermon might have been printed either from the 'manuscript' era or later.

The Public Preaching Cross and the Vernacular Manuscript Sermon

As noted above, there are only two (extant) orthodox vernacular manuscript sermons that were preached at these aforementioned outdoor public venues.[29] The first of these was Thomas Wimbledon's sermon of *c.* 1387 that was preached at Paul's Cross and the second was Richard Alkerton's Easter Week sermon preached at St Mary Spital in 1406.

Much has been written about both public venues but, in brief, it may just be noted that St Paul's (itself an Anglo-Saxon foundation) had a long history as a place of assembly where bulls were published or malefactors cursed, with definite evidence of preaching from the fourteenth century. Donations were called for reparations to the preaching cross in 1387, while due to the efforts of Thomas Kempe (bishop of London between 1450 and 1489) a new cross was erected in the mid-fifteenth century. Although this cross was destroyed in 1643, it may be envisioned on the basis of John Gipkyn's diptych from *c.* 1616 and from 1878 excavations. The imposing cross would have been an octagonal

---

26   E. P. Goldschmidt, *The First Cambridge Press in its European Setting*, The Sandars Lectures in Bibliography, 1953 (Cambridge: Cambridge University Press, 1955) and *Siberch Celebrations, 1521–1971*, ed. by Brooke Crutchley (Cambridge: Cambridge University Press, 1971).

27   In Susan Powell, 'The Secular Clergy', in *A Companion to the Early Printed Book in Britain, 1476–1558*, ed. by Vincent Gillespie and Susan Powell (Cambridge: Brewer, 2014), pp. 150–75 (p. 159), it is argued that the public (English) sermons by Alcock and Fitzjames were printed at a time of some unrest in London. This view is not really convincing, partly on the grounds of sermon content and partly on the grounds of original delivery; see further n. 34.

28   Various sermons here were preached in the Cathedral itself, but I focus below on the preaching crosses as venues for exceptionally large sermon gatherings.

29   Radical Latin or unorthodox vernacular sermons would not have been printed in medieval England.

wooden roofed structure with open sides and stone steps leading up to it.[30] St Mary Spital was founded in 1197 on the east side of Bishopgate Street, but refounded in 1235 when the church was moved further east (around the area known as Spital Square). The house was under the auspices of Augustinian canons and by 1303 it had a community of twelve canons, five lay-brothers, and seven sisters to take care of the sick and needy. By the early decades of the sixteenth century the house was in a dire state and was suppressed in 1538. Although the Spital Cross, a walled enclosure containing a pulpit, was destroyed in the seventeenth century, the sermons continued to be preached in various London city churches into modern times.[31]

The history of preaching at Paul's Cross and St Mary Spital may be reconstructed from the account given in the *Survey of London* written in 1598 by John Stow (1525–1605). He refers to the 'laudable custome' whereby over Easter one sermon was to take place at Paul's Cross on Good Friday, and then three other sermons in the afternoons of Easter Monday to Easter Wednesday at St Mary Spital; these sermons were then to be summarized at Paul's Cross on Low Sunday or the First Sunday after Easter in addition to another sermon, with much spectacle at both venues:

> [...] the Maior, with his brethren the Aldermen were accustomed to bee present in their Violets at *Paules* on good Fryday, and in their Scarlets at the Spittle in the Holidayes, except Wednes[p. 168]day in violet, and the Maior with his brethren, on low sonday in scarlet, at *Paules* Crosse, continued vntill this day.[32]

>> [[...] the Mayor, with his brethren the Aldermen, were accustomed to be present in violet [robes] at Paul's on Good Friday and in their scarlet [robes] at the Spital on the holy days, except for Wednesday when [they were to be] in violet [robes], and the Mayor, with his brethren [were to be] in scarlet [robes] on Low Sunday at Paul's Cross, [and this custom] continues to this day].

According to Stow, the tradition had been instituted in 1398 and in 1488 a special house had been built in which the Mayor and the Aldermen could sit and listen to the sermon as it was preached at the pulpit cross in the churchyard of St Mary Spital; a gallery had been built for the same purpose

---

30 Millar Maclure, *The Paul's Cross Sermons, 1534–1642* (Toronto: University of Toronto Press, 1958), pp. 3–19 (especially pp. 4–6), and Mary Morrissey, *Politics and the Paul's Cross Sermons, 1558–1642* (Oxford: Oxford University Press, 2011), pp. 2–16 (especially pp. 8 and 12).

31 For full details of preaching at St Mary Spital, see *A Study and Edition of Selected Middle English Sermons: Richard Alkerton's Easter Week Sermon Preached at St Mary Spital in 1406, a Sermon on Sunday Observance, and a Nunnery Sermon for the Feast of the Assumption*, ed. by V. M. O'Mara, Leeds Texts and Monographs, n.s. 13 (Leeds: The School of English, 1994), pp. 32–38, with notes on pp. 52–53.

32 John Stow, *A Survey of London by John Stow Reprinted from the Text of 1603*, with introduction and notes by Charles Lethbridge Kingsford, 2 vols (Oxford: Clarendon Press, 1908), I, 167–68.

by the north choir aisle of St Paul's. Contemporary documentary evidence suggests that people thronged to the Spital sermons, encouraged perhaps by the indulgence granted by the pope in 1391 to all those who visited and gave alms to St Mary's Bishopgate at Christmas, Easter, and other great feasts.

Both venues also proved important for sermons that were printed. As noted, Wimbledon's sermon had a wide transmission in both English and Latin, and a long history in print, but not for the expected reasons. Alkerton's sermon, by contrast, is found only in one English manuscript, though it may have had wider dissemination; the one extant Latin manuscript is a translation apparently from another English version. All the known facts are incontrovertible: the history of Alkerton, his various clerical posts, and his public profile that included being a spokesman against Lollard heresy. Like Wimbledon's, Alkerton's text has a preoccupation with Doomsday and is altogether an engaging text, but one that was never printed, possibly for the sort of reasons outlined above (an early fifteenth-century sermon with restricted transmission). Even Alkerton's public status as a spokesman against the Lollard threat and as an appointee of Henry V (d. 1422) for a visitation to the Dominican convent of Dartford in Kent was insufficient to ensure his sermon's lasting reputation. Likewise, Wimbledon's sermon provides all the necessary contextual information: an author, a date, an occasion, a venue, and a thriving transmission. But, as has been discussed elsewhere, all but the identification of the venue is fraught with difficulty.[33]

In a sermon that lived on until the mid-eighteenth century Wimbledon concentrates on the question asked of the unjust steward in Luke 16. 2. Following an explication of the parable of the vineyard in Matthew 20. 1–9, he focuses on the workers divided into priests, knights, and labourers. In his questioning of these estates Wimbledon is most critical of the clergy and acerbic about the ruling classes, especially with regard to the corruption of legal processes and the exploitation of the poor by the rich. Yet the fact that he preached his lively sermon at Paul's Cross had nothing to do with the longevity of the sermon. No printer in the fifteenth century attempted to publish Wimbledon's sermon, even if they knew it existed. There is no evidence of a Wimbledon manuscript later than the mid-fifteenth century or of a printed text before *c*. 1540. It is far from clear to what extent medieval people regarded it as orthodox or not, as it occurs in orthodox and heterodox (or Wycliffite-related) manuscripts. Yet the printing of Wimbledon's sermon with its criticism of certain aspects of the medieval Church and its mistaken associations with John Wyclif had as much to do with the fact that in the Reformation period Wimbledon was seen as a spokesman for Protestantism as anything else. Indeed from 1540

---

33 For the complexities, see O'Mara, 'Thinking Afresh about Thomas Wimbledon's Paul's Cross Sermon of *c*. 1387'; see also Alexandra Walsham, 'Inventing the Lollard Past: The Afterlife of a Medieval Sermon in Early Modern England', *Journal of Ecclesiastical History*, 58 (2007), 628–55.

onwards a preface addressed 'To the Christian Reader' was added to each of the printed texts, with the clear purpose of demonstrating to the Protestant reader that criticism of the institution of the Catholic Church was justified given that such censure could be found in one of their own. It therefore became part of the vehement anti-Catholic drive of the sixteenth century, made most obvious by its incorporation into the greatest Protestant 'hagiographical text' of the them all, John Foxe's *Acts and Monuments*. This printing then was an aberration, as it were. But such idiosyncracies also applied to the fifteenth century, to which we shall now return.

The Public Preaching Cross and Incunabula

In the incunabula period there were two sermons that were preached respectively at Paul's Cross and St Mary Spital and subsequently printed; Alcock's sermon on Luke VIII and Fitzjames's sermon. It is estimated that Fitzjames's sermon was printed in *c.* 1495–1496 and Alcock's possibly first in 1496 with the former only printed once and the latter three times.[34] Neither makes the venue clear, but there is an internal reference to Paul's Cross in Alcock's sermon (c iiii verso) and the occasion helps provide verification for the Fitzjames venue. A concentration on these texts will help in discovering more about the decision-making process at work in sermon printing.[35]

Richard Fitzjames's sermon is on the theme 'Ipse Ihesus apropinquans ibat cum illis' from the second half of Luke 24. 15 where the disciples on the road to Emmaus encounter Christ. The occasion is provided as a title, 'Sermo in lune in ebdomada Pasche', beneath a woodcut showing three figures (including Jesus) dressed as pilgrims or travellers.[36] The only internal clue that it was preached at St Mary Spital is in this title; as an Easter Monday sermon (for which the reading is Luke 24. 13–35), it forms one of the series outlined by Stow. It would have been preached either on 20 April 1495 or 4 April 1496, as we shall see from later confirmatory evidence.[37] Having translated the theme, Fitzjames introduces the two main divisions: that Jesus approached humanity and that he walked with humanity so that ultimately he could bring mankind

---

34 Alcock's sermon is discussed in Paul Cavill, 'Preaching on Magna Carta at the End of the Fifteenth Century: John Alcock's Sermon at Paul's Cross', in *The Fifteenth Century xv: Writing, Records and Rhetoric*, ed. by Linda Clark (Woodbridge: Boydell & Brewer, 2017), pp. 169–90. He argues (p. 179) that the sermon was more likely to have been preached on 22 February 1495 than on 7 February 1496.

35 Reference is made to the online original texts at Early English Books Online (EEBO). The transcribed quotations below are presented with modern punctuation and capitalization as appropriate.

36 Edward Hodnett, *English Woodcuts, 1480–1535*, 1st edn 1935, reprinted with Additions and Corrections (Oxford: Oxford University Press, 1973), item 329, p. 148, and see also item 1469, p. 341.

37 See further below and n. 42.

THE EARLY PRINTED SERMON IN ENGLAND BETWEEN 1483 AND 1532

to eternal rest. He proceeds with his exordium by discussing three biblical figures all termed Jesus: the son of Nave (that is, Joshua), the son of Josedech, and the son of Sirach, with the first saving people through power, the second through obedience, and the third through wisdom, and all prefiguring Jesus Christ. Fitzjames intertwines his first set of three points in the exordium so that Jesus nears humanity by power, walks with mankind through obedience, and brings man to joy through wisdom. The first subdivision is then divided so that the approaching is done through the Creation, Christ's Birth, and Ministry. And then this first subdivision, Creation, is parted into three and the third subdivision in this range is itself divided, through a plethora of subdivisions. The text is rendered more perplexing by the number of biblical quotations and authorities. Fitzjames keeps up the momentum even though he is already at f. iv verso (in a text that finishes at g vi recto) before he turns to his second division; yet he brings the whole together at the end when he refers back to the three earlier figures of Jesus.

It is somewhat hard to tell what his central thesis is meant to be. There is no obvious social criticism, no direct exhortations for the congregation to stay on the straight path to salvation, and definitely no rebuke of any public ills. When he became bishop of London in 1506, Fitzjames had a reputation for being diligent against heresy, yet here his rebuke could not be milder, 'I woll ["will"] accuse no man' (dij verso). The only direct comment is 'Thenne, thou heretyk, how cannest thou excuse thyself?' (eij verso) ['Then, thou heretic, how can thou excuse thyself?'].

Alcock's sermon by contrast is more direct. Concentrating on the theme 'Ihesus clamabat: Qui aures habet audiendi, audiat' (Luke 8. 8), from the reading for Sexagesima Sunday (Luke 8. 4–15) — a less prestigious occasion than Easter Monday — he introduces the five proclamations made by Christ that provide the structure for his exordium. In outlining these proclamations he works through various biblical statements that when combined prefigure the seven sacraments. These sacraments then make a bridge between the introduction and the main text in the person of Mary who received all the sacraments except priesthood. The congregation is reminded that proclamations are only valid under the king's seal (that is, God in the Trinity). This prompts Alcock to meditate on the divisions of the diocese into parishes and religious orders. He avails himself of the opportunity to mention secular and religious clergy, albeit diplomatically praising both. Yet he firmly encourages the laity to avail of the services of their own parish church. Thereafter the metaphoric driver is provided by the idea of the chancery: if people wish to query a proclamation, they can resort to the chancery, either the king's chancery or the chancery of the Church headed by Christ. Alcock outlines how, as in the secular chancery, there are twelve masters, so God's chancery has its bishops, preachers, and so on. His argumentation involves him in a consideration of issues potentially contentious, such as the liberties of the Church where he invokes the idea of the *Magna Carta* (c iiii verso) and argues for clerical immunity from secular jurisdiction. Yet, in his consideration of the duties of the secular and religious authorities, Alcock manages to avoid anything too controversial, though he is firm on issues that could potentially give rise to heresy, such as the interpretation of the Eucharist: a person's duty is to accept the Church's teaching rather than to question.

Both sermons are of a completely different order from that of the populist Mirk with his ready exempla; they are more akin to learned Latin sermons in medieval manuscripts. Preachers in major public venues had an onus upon them not only to convince the faithful of the rectitude of their position, but also to show themselves to best advantage. Yet it is open to debate whether or not Fitzjames in particular might have been successful in this. Somewhat like the professor who forgets the academic inadequacies of his students and their wandering concentration, Fitzjames has a tendency to pile up biblical reference and patristic allusion in such a way that the main point is sometimes lost. Noticeable too, alongside the number of his subdivisions and subdivisions of subdivisions, is his sermon's length. It takes roughly two minutes to read a page of the printed text so the seventy-seven pages would equate with over two and a half hours. It is difficult to believe that the large congregation, with the Lord Mayor and the aldermen in their scarlet robes and the good and the great of London all set out in their finery, were captivated from start to finish.

Overall Fitzjames pays little attention to the fact that he is preaching to a listening audience. There are only a few occasions where he refers either to his own sermon or to the congregation. These include a reference to 'this poore collacion' (a ij recto), and 'poore sermon' (f. iv recto). Both just invoke the typical modesty topoi. Little is done to involve the audience, addressed once as 'maysters all' (f ij verso); for example, 'euery goode Crysten man here understondeth þat *verbum* is Ihesus Cryste' (c ij verso) ['every good man here understands that *verbum* is Jesus Christ'] presupposes a Latinity that not everyone might possess; if the aldermen present were capable of following, given a grammar school education, it is doubtful that their wives would have been. One of his comments is ironic under the circumstances; he says, 'Some men here present — ye, and not a fewe — woll perauenture muse why and to what entent I brynge in thys longe story of Ihesus Iosedech, the grete preest of the olde lawe' (b i verso) ['Some men here present — yes, and not [only] a few — will perhaps muse on why and for what purpose I bring in this long story about Jesus Josedech, the great priest of the Old Law']. He then attempts to answers his own question:

> Surely this is my cause, for syth al holy scripture is wryten for our erudicion after þe apostle (the xv chapytre to the Romayns), that we to whom trouthe is made open by Ihesu Cryste — as techeth Saynt Iohn in the fyrste chapytre — sholde lern obedience, lerne zele and diligence to the lawe of God, of thyse faders passyd in fygure; and agayn to take grete shame and conscyence whan we rede them to haue doon so zelously in Goddys cause and beholde ourself how neclygent we ben in the same. (b i verso)

THE EARLY PRINTED SERMON IN ENGLAND BETWEEN 1483 AND 1532   87

[Surely this is my reason, for since all holy Scripture is written for our erudition following the apostle (the 15 chapter to the Romans), that we to whom truth is made apparent by Jesus Christ — as St John teaches in the first chapter — should learn obedience, learn zeal and diligence to the law of God, by example of these late fathers; and again to have great shame and [a sense of] conscience when we read about them having behaved so zealously in God's purpose and [when] we see ourselves behave so negligently in the same respect].

Whether or not this explanation placated his putatively restive audience, it does much to illustrate Fitzjames's allusive style saturated with citation and quotation. That he does not learn the lesson of the dangers of wearing out his audience's patience is later made very clear when he notes 'To talke of all thyse sacramentes to þe purpose tyme woll not permitt I wote' (f. i recto) ['I know that time will not permit me to speak about all these sacraments for the purpose']. Yet this does not stop him spending another five pages on baptism, penance, and the sacrament of the altar.

By contrast, Alcock has a much firmer grasp of how to keep the attention of an audience; for a start, his sermon is considerably shorter, something in the region of an hour and a half. He keeps his congregation in mind throughout, addressing them as 'Frendes' on some thirty occasions, twice as 'Syres' and twice as 'Brethern'. While his quotations and references are also considerable, he does not lose sight of his main purpose. And he is not adverse to glossing the odd narrative for particular effect. For instance, when discussing the Eucharist, he tells the story of the disputatious Parisian doctor who was told that he should believe rather than debate (c ii verso), and when discussing the clergy uses a telling analogy: in the same way as the eye-ball is tenderly regarded by a person, so is priesthood by God (c iii verso). He even goes so far as to reminisce about a poem from his youth, by John Lydgate, a monk from Bury St Edmunds in the diocese of Ely (d viii verso).

These contrasts open up various issues. Were the original sermons written in Latin or English? Did preachers go into the pulpit with a prepared script in hand, a memorized text or merely notes? Were any *reportationes* made? Were the sermons written out afterwards for posterity, and if so, what sort of poetic licence was taken in terms of improvement or expansion? What happened between the delivery of the sermon and publication? And most important of all: were these sermons printed because they were preached at Paul's Cross and St Mary Spital or were they selected because of the status of the preacher — or both? Unfortunately, most of these questions are unanswerable. For example, we can only guess whether or not Fitzjames's original sermon was expanded later. Neither can we say if Fitzjames or Alcock read from a sermon text or used it merely as a prompt. The answer is ambiguous: there is evidence elsewhere for Fitzjames's penchant for reading sermons (and one cannot imagine such a convoluted work being committed to memory), yet Alcock's technique gives the impression of the preaching voice.[38]

And perhaps most significant of all: if my (modern) rather negative interpretation of the calibre of Fitzjames's sermon is correct, is this the reason why English publishers did not bother to print any more of his works whereas Alcock had a much more successful publishing career? Had Fitzjames's effort been so poorly received that he was never asked to preach again? Tempting as this hypothesis might be, it is not the case. First, there is solid evidence that Fitzjames was a frequent preacher, as we shall see. Secondly, there is another intriguing suggestion about the success of his preaching and his appearance in print. In her edition of the *Nova festa* sermons Susan Powell has pointed out the equivalence between the introduction to the sermon for the Holy Name and Fitzjames's use of the three figures of Jesus in his Spital sermon suggesting that, rather than being associated with Syon as she previously contends, this sermon could have been preached by Fitzjames to the Fraternity of the Holy Name on the relevant feast day in the Jesus Chapel in St Paul's Cathedral.[39] Given the striking nature of this analogy, it cannot be mere co-incidence. This Holy Name sermon is everything that his Spital sermon is not: short, pointed, effusive, with a string of *narraciones* — and it was printed. So Fitzjames *could* preach effectively and there is evidence elsewhere of his being congratulated for so doing.[40]

There are even more imponderables. Although much has been made above of the ease with which sermons preached at public venues such as Paul's Cross and St Mary Spital could lend themselves to print, the publishers make no mention of the venues in either edition here. There are also numerous public sermons by both preachers that were never printed. Alcock preached at the opening of parliament in 1472 and 1485, at his installation as bishop of Worcester in 1476, in Worcester, Gloucester, and Bristol during Henry VII's first progress in 1486, and at Great St Mary church in Cambridge in 1488.[41] Knowledge of Fitzjames's preaching career is even more extensive. He preached at Paul's Cross on no fewer than ten occasions: 13 September and 7 November 1490; 26 October 1494; 8 February and 8 November 1495; 6 November 1496; 19 November 1497; 11 November 1498; 11 February 1504; and 8 November 1506. On three occasions he preached at St Mary Spital: 20 April 1495, 4 April

---

38 Colet's comment about Fitzjames is reported by Erasmus, as noted in Cavill, 'Preaching on Magna Carta at the End of the Fifteenth Century', p. 174 and n. 43. In Alcock's case it is noticeable how he frequently inserts the word 'Frendes' into the midst of sentences in a very naturalistic manner.

39 *Three Sermons for 'Nova Festa'*, ed. by Powell, pp. xl–xliii.

40 Cavill, 'Preaching on Magna Carta at the End of the Fifteenth Century', cites the example of the court poet Bernard André declaring a sermon preached by Fitzjames on Sunday 31 October 1507 at Paul's Cross to be 'very wholesome' (*'saluberrimam'*) (p. 176 and n. 55).

41 For these, see Cavill, 'Preaching on Magna Carta at the End of the Fifteenth Century', p. 170, and references therein.

THE EARLY PRINTED SERMON IN ENGLAND BETWEEN 1483 AND 1532 89

1496, and 27 March 1497, thereby providing explicit proof of the venue for the printed sermon. In addition, he preached at the burial of Cardinal Morton at Canterbury on 26 September 1500, in Richmond at the marriage of Henry VII's daughter Margaret to James IV of Scotland (1488–1513) on 25 January 1502, and at the burial of the queen, Elizabeth of York (1486–1503) in Westminster on 11 February 1503.[42] Alongside these, he was said to have preached on ten occasions between 1491 and 1503 in his capacity as chaplain to Henry VII.[43] Moreover, there are also references to other sermons by Colet, Fisher, and Longland, as well as those by other preachers that were never printed and no longer survive. Over a long period Paul's Cross may have acted like a year-long factory for sermons on occasions solemn or contentious and as a necessary testing ground for Oxbridge theology students, yet only a tiny fraction of these are known about. Instead, texts like Alcock's profession sermon that could hardly have attracted a wide readership and only one out of the many by Fitzjames are some of the very few preserved in print. We are left then with a number of unanswered issues that beg the question: what do we really know about sermon publication in the first decades of the early printed era in England?

Known Information and Further Queries

While much of what can be gleaned about the external history of Middle English sermons in manuscript is supposition, the contextual matters of early printed texts are more certain. Sermons are identified with particular preachers and can facilitate more grounded comparative study. The authors here were important functionaries in ecclesiastical, political, regal or university governance. It is even possible to put faces to names: for example, the woodcut in Alcock's sermon *Gallicantus* is said to represent the preacher himself; in addition, there is as a manuscript image of Fitzjames, and an illustration of a bishop saying Mass that may be John Longland, quite apart from the well-known portrait of John Fisher by Hans Holbein the Younger (*c.* 1497/98–1543) and the bust of Colet after Pietro Torrigiano (1472–1528) from *c.* 1518.[44]

---

42 These are recorded in *Registrum Annalium Collegii Mertoniensis, 1483–1521*, ed. by H. E. Salter, Oxford Historical Society, 76 (Oxford: Clarendon Press, 1923), pp. 136, 140, 185, 187, 190, 194, 198, 203, 207, 216, 225, 247, 261, 273, 288, and 324.

43 These are noted in the entry on Fitzjames by S. Thomson in the *Oxford Dictionary of National Biography* [https://doi.org/10.1093/ref.odnb/9612; accessed 27 March 2021].

44 For Alcock, see Julie A. Smith, 'An Image of a Preaching Bishop in Late Medieval England: The 1498 Woodcut Portrait of Bishop John Alcock', *Viator: Medieval and Renaissance Studies*, 21 (1990), 301–22, with seventeen (unpaginated) Figures; see Figure 1 and also Figure 3. For the image of Fitzjames, see R. M. Thomson, *A Descriptive Catalogue of the Medieval Manuscripts of Merton College, Oxford* (Cambridge: Brewer, 2009), plate 16 (unpaginated). The image that may be Longland, in a missal owned by him, is opposite the title page in Margaret Bowker, *The Henrician Reformation: The Diocese of Lincoln under John Longland,*

Unlike the shadowy figures from manuscripts, such men were part of important networks and have traceable histories; they left documentary material in the form of registers or ordinances; they endowed grammar schools; they helped establish university colleges; they made wills; they bequeathed books; and they ensured their own reputations for posterity.

Likewise, the venue of the original sermon, even if not stated explicitly, can usually be fathomed. From such venues it is possible to estimate the extent and range of the congregation, whereas with most of the sermons in manuscript, much is guess-work. Similarly, it is usually known when the sermons were printed (though not when preached). Sometimes this can be very exact: for instance, in the case of Alcock's *Mons perfectionis* on 22 September 1496. Indeed, it is even possible to estimate in a few cases how long it took for the sermons to be printed. For instance, Norman Blake has worked out that 'if we can assume that the *Festial* was started as soon as the *Pilgrimage of the Soul* was completed, it was printed between 6 and 30 June [1483]. A book of 115 leaves with 38 lines per page was completed in 24 days'.[45] Sometimes direct evidence of the instigator of the sermon is given: Thomas Richard (Ricard/ Richards), the prior of the Charterhouse in Coventry, promoted the printing of *Gallicantus*, as noted in the colophon.

Yet there is still a host of matters about which little is known: the printed sermons' previous manuscript transmission (if any); their print runs; audience reaction; and primarily the selection criteria that first saw them printed. Although there had to have been manuscript copies of the printed sermons at some point, these are now virtually non-existent.[46] Even when manuscript copies exist, their relationship with the print is not always clear; for instance, the manuscript version of Fisher's text for the Month's Mind of Margaret Beaufort, though chronologically later than the printed text of 1509, may actually be closer to Fisher's original.[47] Nothing is known for definite about any print runs apart from De Worde's 1493 edition of the Mirk's *Festial* that ran to 600 copies, a sizeable number especially given that there were two editions of the text in that year.[48] Neither is there any known audience reactions to

---

1521–1547 (Cambridge: Cambridge University Press, 1981). The Fisher portrait is reproduced on the cover of Maria Dowling, *Fisher of Men: A Life of John Fisher, 1469–1535* (Basingstoke: Macmillan; New York: St Martin's Press, 1999) and for the Colet bust see the plaster cast NPG 4823 on the National Portrait Gallery website at npg.org.uk [accessed 28 January 2022].

45 N. F. Blake, *Caxton's Own Prose*, The Language Library (London: Deutsch, 1973), p. 19.

46 In general few manuscript exemplars of printed works exist; see Lotte Hellinga, *Texts in Transit: Manuscript to Proof and Print in the Fifteenth Century*, Library of the Written Word, 38, The Handpress World, 29 (Leiden: Brill, 2014).

47 The complexities of this are discussed in Veronica O'Mara, 'Unearthing the History of an Early Printed Sermon: John Fisher and St John's College, Cambridge', in *Middle English Manuscripts and Their Legacies: A Volume in Honour of Ian Doyle*, ed. by Corinne Saunders and Richard Lawrie, with Laurie Atkinson, Library of the Written Word, 102, The Manuscript World, 14 (Brill: 2022), pp. 212–33.

48 Henry R. Plomer, 'Two Lawsuits of Richard Pynson', *The Library: The Transactions of the*

THE EARLY PRINTED SERMON IN ENGLAND BETWEEN 1483 AND 1532 91

the sermons printed, apart from any sporadic contemporary annotation in the printed copies. And this leads to the final issue: the selection criteria.

In order to be printed, to have produced an interesting sermon was not enough or else Wimbledon's dramatic exercise would have been published in the fifteenth century rather than having to wait well over a century later when it emerged into print with its central message adapted for the good of the Protestant cause. It may have been, of course, that the very criticism of the clergy that endeared it to the reformers in the sixteenth century was what put off the fifteenth century printers or indeed the Church.[49] To have preached at major public venues or on prestigious occasions was no guarantee of getting into print, as witnessed by the various sermons alluded to above by Alcock and Fitzjames (and others) that were overlooked and so lost completely. Yet being an eminent cleric helped. Many of the preachers moved in the same circles focused on Cambridge or London: Alcock, like Fisher, founded a Cambridge College (Jesus); Melton was Fisher's tutor in Cambridge; Colet was Dean of St Paul's when Fitjames was bishop of London, and so forth. Clearly too to preach beyond the capital meant no great likelihood of publication, though there was a slightly higher prospect for those like Melton in York or Baron in Cambridge whose Latinate erudition and reforming zeal could appeal to others of a similar persuasion. A vernacular homilist whose work was confined to his local area had no hope of making it into print. As in modern times in England, the north/south divide held sway, unless one were as fortunate as John Mirk. Although writing in a neglected part of the country (Shropshire on the Welsh border), his work had become so successful in the Middle Ages that finding manuscripts was no trouble for a printer like Caxton who, as an astute business man, would have appreciated a tested success.[50] Yet, with this exception, English sermon printing was almost entirely focused on the metropolis. Unlike the manuscript era where there is plenty of evidence of preaching all over the country, with print only preaching in London counted — and very little at that.

Set in the context of an industry that had not quite formulated itself, the confused nature of the selection of sermon items for print in the early decades mirrored the somewhat uncertain choices being made elsewhere in the printing industry.[51] Medieval sermon printing mores would seem to have been rather haphazard. Despite claims for the agency and marketing capabilities of the industry, I am not sure that in its first decades in England the true importance

---

Bibliographical Society, 2nd series, 10 (1909), 115–33.

49 Another drawback would have been Wimbledon's precise dating for the end of the world, 1400, though that could have been omitted as it was in some of the manuscripts; see O'Mara, 'Thinking Afresh about Thomas Wimbledon's Paul's Cross Sermon of *c.* 1387', pp. 162–63.

50 The fact that Mirk's original composition dates probably from the late 1380s was no doubt overlooked (if it was known) given its widespread later manuscript dissemination.

51 This is not to overlook the fact that certain printers favoured particular categories of material; for example, Pynson was known for legal texts.

of sermon printing was grasped or that there was a concerted attitude either by Church or printer.[52] After the death of Caxton, who had an astute eye for commercial advantage, his successors appeared to lack direction so that there was a rather scattergun approach to the sermons printed. Even if it is argued that De Worde, for instance, favoured 'a wide variety of texts', this still does not answer for what sermons were printed.[53] Admittedly, the part played by the patronage of the regular and secular clergy together with the aristocracy and merchant bourgeoisie is imperfectly understood, though this could be influential, as it in the case of Margaret Beaufort and John Fisher.[54] In some rare cases a text could only have been printed with specific championing, with the best example here being the publication of the Savonarola sermon in 1509; at the beginning of the text it is noted that the translation (by Bartholomeus Gallus) was at the behest of John Young, rector of All Hallows church and Stephen Douce, master of Whittington College (of secular priests) in London.[55]

Yet the preachers themselves were hardly proactive in getting published. In the early period the most successful was Alcock but even his choices (if such they were) can be queried, and he had died by 1500. Admittedly, Fisher organized the printing of his sermon [Against Heretics] in 1526? and 1527?, but even then in the midst of a five-page appended epistle stressing the seriousness of the Lutheran threat he felt it necessary to justify the print with the rather odd comment on A iv recto (STC 10892): '[...] I haue put forth this sermon to be redde which for þe great noyse of þe peple within þe churche of Paules whan it was sayde myght nat be herde' ['I have produced this sermon to be read because it could not be heard when it was delivered owing to great noise in the church [cathedral] of Paul's']. As we have seen, there were also countless sermons preached at various venues that were never printed. Was this an oversight on the part of the printers, a sign that sermons (beyond the traditional like the *Festial*) did not sell well, or a general reluctance by preachers to make use of a technology devised for the written rather than the spoken word?[56] Perhaps the lay public preferred the hagiographical narratives found in Mirk and the

---

52 Kathleen Tonry, *Agency and Intention in English Print, 1476–1526*, Texts and Transitions, 7 (Turnhout: Brepols, 2016) and Alexandra Da Costa, *Marketing English Books: How Printers Changed Reading, 1476–1550*, Oxford Studies in Medieval Literature and Culture (Oxford: Oxford University Press, 2020) argue their cases stoutly, but pay no attention to sermons.

53 H. S. Bennett, *English Books and Readers, 1475–1557: Being a Study of the History of the Book Trade from Caxton to the Incorporation of the Stationers' Company*, 2nd edn (Cambridge: Cambridge University Press, 1969), p. 186.

54 A. S. G. Edwards and Carol M. Meale, 'The Marketing of Printed Books in Late Medieval England', *The Library: Transactions of the Bibliographical Society*, sixth series, 15 (1993), 95–124.

55 See further Powell, 'After Arundel and before Luther', pp. 535–36.

56 See Arnold Hunt, *The Art of Hearing: English Preachers and Their Audiences, 1590–1640*, Cambridge Studies in Early Modern British History (Cambridge: Cambridge University Press, 2010), ch. 3, 'From Pulpit to Print', pp. 117–86 (pp. 119–30), for ambivalence about print among preachers even into this later period.

THE EARLY PRINTED SERMON IN ENGLAND BETWEEN 1483 AND 1532   93

numerous other saints' lives from collections like the *Golden Legend* to single lives printed in the period rather than straightforward sermonizing. One churchman who might have made more of a difference was William Warham (d. 1532), bishop of London between 1502 and 1503 and afterwards archbishop of Canterbury. Warham had encouraged Longland in his printing activities.[57] But his appreciation of the print medium was hardly shared among his fellow bishops. For instance, while there were over a hundred editions of printed liturgical books brought out by reforming bishops all over Europe before 1501, there was only one English example, Archbishop Morton's patronage of the *Missale Saresberiense* in 1500 (STC 16173).[58] Morton's reluctance to use the print medium, in particular for sermons, may also have been owing to other reasons. In 1487 he had asked that any difficulties with regard to the Church should be communicated to him in private, nervous as he was by some of the radical sermons being preached at Paul's Cross.[59] Little is known in relation to printing about any continued impact of Archbishop Arundel's Constitutions of 1409 that had laid down what a preacher should or could not preach and there was no official attempt to monitor printing until the second half of the 1520s.[60] Yet it is noteworthy that between *c.* 1512 and 1521 nothing new was published. Perhaps in certain quarters there was a fear that print could be just too successful. Even a reforming cleric like Colet seemed disinclined towards publication, with only a single Latin sermon being printed so that knowledge of his œuvre depends mainly on reports by Desiderius Erasmus (1466/9–1536).[61] But these caveats still do not fully answer the reason why so few — and such a strange, if interesting, mixture — of sermons were published. One ends up falling back on putative rationales to do with patrons and their agendas and/or publishers and their imperatives), individual choice, historical event, and — if truth be told — sheer happenstance.

---

57 Bowker, *The Henrician Reformation*, pp. 11–12; Warham urges Longland 'that when ye preche moo[re] such sermons (as ye do many) that ye will continually putt them to prynte for the common prefecte' ['that when you preach more such sermons (as you preach many) that you will have them printed for the general good'] (p. 11). His comment about Longland's numerous sermons is well founded; as Bowker notes (p. 8), he preached extensively at Court between 1518 and 1521.

58 Natalia Nowakowska, 'From Strassburg to Trent: Bishops, Printing and Liturgical Reform in the Fifteenth Century', *Past and Present*, 213 (2011), 3–39.

59 Christopher Harper-Bill, 'Dean Colet's Convocation Sermon and the Pre-Reformation Church in England', in *The Impact of the English Reformation, 1500–1640*, ed. by Peter Marshall (London: Arnold, 1997), pp. 17–37 (p. 19 and n. 10, p. 33); this essay is reprinted from *History*, 73 (1988).

60 Discussed in Powell, 'After Arundel but before Luther'.

61 These are noted in the entry on Colet by J. B. Trapp in the *Oxford Dictionary of National Biography* [https://doi/org/10.1093/ref.odnb/5898; accessed 27 March 2021].

Conclusion

In the last years of the fifteenth century and the first decades of the sixteenth when any outright calls for reform were mainly seen to be a European issue, and England's own 'premature reformation' (the Lollard heresy) had largely been kept under control; controversy, for the moment, lay beyond England's shores. Indeed, it was not until the whole business of the circulation of God's Word was called into question through the arguments of Martin Luther, in conjunction with Henrician turmoil at home, that England finally woke up to the fact that the printing press could actually work as an agent of change, from whatever side that change was desired.

The year 1532 marks the last relevant date in medieval Catholic sermon printing before the 1534 Act of Supremacy declared Henry VIII head of the Church and so opened the way to successive waves of anti-Catholic, Catholic, Protestant, Puritan, non-conformist, evangelical, and Anglo-Catholic preaching that impelled religious controversy in England until the nineteenth century.[62] Fisher's anti-Lutheran sermons were in the vanguard of a glut of sermons. In essence it took longer for the effects of the Reformation to get going and particularly to play out in England than almost anywhere else in Europe, complicated as it was from the beginning by the personalized demands of Henry VIII, the theologically conservative Catholic who became England's first head of a Protestant Church. From the late 1520s onwards, England's insular status that had led to such idiosyncratic developments in sermon printing would hold no longer. If England's printed sermon past had largely seemed to lack direction and purpose (or at least any that can be deciphered), its future could not. The revolution started by its own king, combined with events in Europe, would eventually see to that, for good or ill.[63]

---

62 Debates about the impact of the Reformation (or rather 'Reformations') in England are extensive; a concise overview may be found in Peter Marshall, *Reformation England 1480–1642* (London: Arnold, 2003).

63 For some discussions of later developments, see Kenneth Carleton, *Bishops and Reform in the English Church, 1520–1559*, Studies in Modern British History (Woodbridge: Boydell, 2001), especially ch. 4, 'The Bishop and Preaching', pp. 81–98; Susan Wabuda, *Preaching during the English Reformation*, Cambridge Studies in Early Modern British History (Cambridge: Cambridge University Press, 2002); *The Oxford Handbook of the Early Modern Sermon*, ed. by Peter McCullough, Hugh Adlington, and Emma Rhatigan (Oxford: Oxford University Press, 2011); Morrissey, *Politics and the Paul's Cross Sermons, 1558–1642*; and *Paul's Cross and the Culture of Persuasion in England, 1520–1640*, ed. by Torrance Kirby and P. G. Stanwood, Studies in the History of Christian Traditions, 171 (Leiden: Brill, 2014). I am grateful to Susan Powell for incisive comments on an earlier draft of this essay.

Appendix: Early Printed Sermons between 1483 and 1532

These are set out by author in chronological order. Titles are given in accordance with the uniform titles in the English Short Title Catalogue (estc.bl.uk); where titles are missing, are very lengthy or opaque, a title is supplied in square brackets.

John Mirk

1483, 30 June: [*The Festial*] (Westminster: William Caxton) (STC 17957)

1486/7, 14 October or 19 March: [*Liber festivalis*] (Oxford: previously attributed to Theodoric Rood and Thomas Hunte) (STC 17958)

1491: *Incipit liber qui vocatur festialis* (Westminster: William Caxton) (STC 17959)

1492–1493: [*The Festial*] (London: Richard Pynson) (STC 17960)

1493: *Incipit liber qui vocatur festialis* (Westminster: Wynkyn de Worde) (STC 17962)

1493–1494?: *Liber festiualis* and *Quattuor sermones* (London: Richard Pynson) (STC 17961)

1495: [*Incipit liber qui vocatur ffestiualis*] (London: J. Rauyall) (STC 17963.5)

1495/6, 4 February: *Incipit liber qui vocatur festialis* (Rouen: James Ravynell) (STC 17963)

1495, 26 February: *Incipit liber qui vocatur festiualis* (Paris: Wolfgang Hopyl) (STC 17964)

1496: *Incipit liber (qui Festialis appelatur)* (Westminster: Wynkyn de Worde) (STC 17965)

1499, 22 June: *Incipit liber qui vocatur festiualis* (Rouen: Martin Morin) (STC 17966)

1499, 6 July: *Incipit liber qui vocatur festiualis* (London: Richard Pynson) (STC 17966.5)

1499: *Incipit liber qui Festialis appelatur* (Westminster: Wynkyn de Worde) (STC 17967)

1499/1500, 2 January: [*Liber festiualis*] (London: Julian Notary) (STC 17968)

1502, 10 July: [*Incipit liber qui vocatur ffestiualis*] (London: Richard Pynson) (STC 17969)

1506?: *Incipit liber qui vocatur festiualis* (London: Julian Notary) (STC 17970)

1506?: *Incipit liber qui vocatur festiualis* (London: Julian Notary) (STC 17970) [*sic*]

1507?: [*Incipit liber qui vocatur festialis*] (London: Richard Pynson) (STC 17970.5)

1508: *The festyuall* (London: Wynkyn de Worde) (STC 17971)

1511, 1 August: *The festyuall* (London: Wynkyn de Worde) (STC 17971.5)

c. 1512: [*Here begynneth the festyuall*] (London: Richard Fauques) (STC 17973)

1515, 5 May: *The festyuall* (London: Wynkyn de Worde) (STC 17972)

1519, 5 May: *The festyuall* (London: Wynkyn de Worde) (STC 17973.5)

1528, 5 November: *The festyuall* (London: Wynkyn de Worde) (STC 17974)

1532, 23 October: *The festyuall* (London: Wynkyn de Worde) (STC 17975)

Anonymous

Nova festa (sermons for the Visitation, Transfiguration, and the Holy Name, with the *Hamus caritatis*) 1491 (and following): see *The Festial* editions above from 1491

Richard Fitzjames

c. 1495–1496: *Sermo die lune in ebdomada pasche* (Westminster: Wynkyn de Worde) (STC 11024)

John Alcock

1496, 22 September: *Mons perfeccionis otherwyse in englysshe, the hyll of perfecc[i]on* (Westminster: Wynkyn de Worde) (STC 278)

1496: [*Sermon on Luke VIII*] (Westminster: Wynkyn de Worde) (STC 284)

c. 1496?: [*Sermon on Luke VIII*] (Westminster: Wynkyn de Worde) (STC 285)

late 1496? [May not be by Alcock]: *In die Innocencium sermo pro episcopo puerorum* [Boy Bishop Sermon] (Westminster: Wynkyn de Worde) (STC 282)

1497, 23 May: *Mons perfectionis, otherwyse in Englysshe, the hylle of perfeccyon* (Westminster: Wynkyn de Worde) (STC 279)

1497–1498: [*Mons perfectionis*] (London: Richard Pynson) (STC 280)

1497–1498: [*Desponsacio virginis xpristo. Spousage of a virgin to Christ*] (Westminster: Wynkyn de Worde) (STC 286)

1497–1498: [*Spousage of a Virgin to Christ*] (Westminster: Wynkyn de Worde) (STC 287)

c. 1497–1498: [May not be by Alcock]: *In die Innocenciu[m] s[er]mo pro episcopo puer[orum]* [Boy Bishop Sermon] (Westminster: Wynkyn de Worde) (STC 283)

1498: *Gallicantus Iohannis alcok epi Eliensis ad co[n]fratres suos curatos in sinodo apud Bernwell* (London: Richard Pynson) (STC 277)

1501: *Mons perfectionis, otherwyse in Englysshe, the hylle of perfeccyon* (London: Wynkyn de Worde) (STC 281)

1501?: [*Sermon on Luke VIII*] (London: Wynkyn de Worde) (STC 285.5)

John Fisher

1508, 16 June: [Penitential Psalms] (London: Wynkyn de Worde) (STC 10902)

1509: [Funeral of Henry VII] (London: Wynkyn de Worde (STC 10900)

1509, 12 June: [Penitential Psalms] (London: Wynkyn de Worde) (STC 10903)

1509 or 1510: [Funeral of Henry VII] (London: Wynkyn de Worde (STC 10901)

1509: [Month's Mind for Margaret Beaufort] (London: Wynkyn de Worde) (STC 10891)

1510, 7 August: [Penitential Psalms] (London: Wynkyn de Worde) (STC 10905)

1514? [dated 12 June 1509]: [Penitential Psalms] (London: Wynkyn de Worde) (STC 10903a)

1519? [dated 12 June 1509]: [Penitential Psalms] (London: Wynkyn de Worde) (STC 10904)

THE EARLY PRINTED SERMON IN ENGLAND BETWEEN 1483 AND 1532   97

1521: [Against Martin Luther, translated into Latin by Richard Pace] (Cambridge: Johannes Siberch) (STC 10898)

1521?: [Against Martin Luther] (London: Wynkyn de Worde) (STC 10894)

1522?: [Against Martin Luther] (London: Wynkyn de Worde) (STC 10894.5)

1525, 13 June: [Penitential Psalms] (London: Wynkyn de Worde) (STC 10906)

1526?: [Against Heretics at Quinquagesima] (London: Thomas Berthelet?) (STC 10892)

1526?: [Against Heretics at Quinquagesima] (London: Thomas Berthelet?) (STC 10892.4)

1527?: [Against Heretics at Quinquagesima] (London: Thomas Berthelet?) (STC 10892.7)

1527?: [Against Martin Luther] (London: Wynkyn de Worde) (STC 10895)

1529, 13 August: [Penitential Psalms] (London: Wynkyn de Worde) (STC 10907)

1532: [Two Fruitful Sermons] (London: W. Rastell (STC 10909)

Girolamo Savonarola

1509: *Sermo fratris Hieronymi de Ferraria in vigilia natiuitatis domini cora[m] fratris suis recitatus* (London: Richard Pynson) (STC 21800)

Stephen Baron

After 1509: *Sermones declamati cora[m] alma vniversitate Ca[n]tabrigie[n[si [...]* (London: Julian Notary) (STC 1497)

Johannes Herolt

1510, 22 June: *Sermones discipuli de tempore et de sanctis* (London: Julian Notary) (STC 13226)

Michael of Hungary

1510?: *Eugatorium modus p[re]dicandi sermones. xiii. Michaelis de Hungaria [...]* (London: Richard Pynson) (STC 17853)

William Melton

1510?: *Sermo exhortatius cancellarij Eborum hijs qui ad sacros ordines petunt promoveri* (London: Wynkyn de Worde) (STC 17806)

John Colet

1512?: *Oratio habita a D. Ioanne Colet decano Sancti Pauli ad clerum in conuocatione* (London: Richard Pynson) (STC 5545)

1530?: *The sermo[n] of doctor Colete, made to the conuocacion at Paulis* (London: Thomas Berthelet) (STC 5550)

1531?: *The sermon of doctor Colete, made to the conuocacion at Paulis* (London: Thomas Berthelet) (STC 5550.5)

John Longland

1527?: *Ioannis Longlondi Dei gratia Lincolnien[sis] Episcopi, tres conciones […]* (London: Richard Pynson) (STC 16790)

1527?: *[Psalmus sextus]* (s.l.: Richard Pynson) (STC 16793.5)

1527?: *Psalmus tricesi […]* (London: Richard Pynson) (STC 16793)

1527?: *Psalmus trisesimus [sic] septi. conciones […]* (London: Richard Pynson) (STC 16791)

1532, 28 May: *Psalmus quinquagesimus conciones […]* (London: Robert Redman) (STC 16791.5)

1532?: *Psalmus centesi […]* (London: Robert Redman?) (STC 16792)

Bibliography

Primary Sources

See Appendix above.

Blake, N. F., *Caxton's Own Prose*, The Language Library (London: Deutsch, 1973)

English Works of John Fisher, Bishop of Rochester: Sermons and Other Writings 1520 to 1535, ed. by Cecilia A. Hatt (Oxford: Oxford University Press, 2002)

John Fisher, *John Fisher's Court Sermons: Preaching for Lady Margaret, 1507–1509*, ed. by Cecilia A. Hatt (Oxford: Oxford University Press, 2021)

John Mirk, *John Mirk's 'Festial'*, ed. by Susan Powell, Early English Text Society, o.s. 334–35 (Oxford: Oxford University Press, 2009–2011)

John Stow, *A Survey of London by John Stow Reprinted from the Text of 1603*, with an introduction and notes by Charles Lethbridge Kingsford, 2 vols (Oxford: Clarendon Press, 1908)

Registrum Annalium Collegii Mertoniensis, 1483–1521, ed. by H. E. Salter, Oxford Historical Society, 76 (Oxford: Clarendon Press, 1923)

A Study and Edition of Selected Middle English Sermons: Richard Alkerton's Easter Week Sermon Preached at St Mary Spital in 1406, a Sermon on Sunday Observance, and a Nunnery Sermon for the Feast of the Assumption, ed. by V. M. O'Mara, Leeds Texts and Monographs, n.s. 13 (Leeds: The School of English, 1994)

Three Sermons for 'Nova Festa', together with the 'Hamus Caritatis', ed. by Susan Powell, Middle English Texts, 37 (Heidelberg: Universitätsverlag Winter, 2007)

Secondary Studies

Armstrong, Elizabeth, 'English Purchases of Printed Books from the Continent 1465–1526', *The English Historical Review*, 94 (1979), 268–90

Bennett, H. S., *English Books and Readers, 1475–1557: Being a Study of the History of the Book Trade from Caxton to the Incorporation of the Stationers' Company*, 2nd edn (Cambridge: Cambridge University Press, 1969)

Blench, J. W., *Preaching in England in the Late Fifteenth and Sixteenth Centuries: A Study of English Sermons 1450–c. 1600* (Oxford: Blackwell, 1964)

Bowker, Margaret, *The Henrician Reformation: The Diocese of Lincoln under John Longland, 1521–1547* (Cambridge: Cambridge University Press, 1981)

Carleton, Kenneth, *Bishops and Reform in the English Church, 1520–1559*, Studies in Modern British History (Woodbridge: Boydell, 2001)

Catalogue of Books Printed in the XVth Century now in the British Library, Part XI: England ('t Goy-Houten: Hes & De Graaf, 2007)

Cavill, Paul, 'Preaching on Magna Carta at the End of the Fifteenth Century: John Alcock's Sermon at Paul's Cross', in *The Fifteenth Century XV: Writing, Records and Rhetoric*, ed. by Linda Clark (Woodbridge: Boydell & Brewer, 2017), pp. 169–90

Christianson, C. Paul, 'The Rise of London's Book-Trade', in *The Cambridge History of the Book in Britain*, III: *1400–1557*, ed. by Lotte Hellinga and J. B. Trapp (Cambridge: Cambridge University Press, 1999), pp. 128–47

Crutchley, Brooke, ed., *Siberch Celebrations, 1521–1971* (Cambridge: Cambridge University Press, 1971)

Da Costa, Alexandra, *Marketing English Books: How Printers Changed Reading 1476–1550*, Oxford Studies in Medieval Literature and Culture (Oxford: Oxford University Press, 2020)

Dowling, Maria, *Fisher of Men: A Life of John Fisher, 1469–1535* (Basingstoke: Macmillan; New York: St Martin's Press, 1999)

Edwards, A. S. G., and Carol M. Meale, 'The Marketing of Printed Books in Late Medieval England', *The Library: Transactions of the Bibliographical Society*, sixth series, 15 (1993), 95–124

Ford, Margaret Lane, 'Importation of Printed Books into England and Scotland', in *The Cambridge History of the Book in Britain*, III: *1400–1557*, ed. by Lotte Hellinga and J. B. Trapp (Cambridge: Cambridge University Press, 1999), pp. 179–201

Gillespie, Vincent, and Susan Powell, eds, *A Companion to the Early Printed Book in Britain, 1476–1558* (Cambridge: Brewer, 2014)

Goldschmidt, E. P., *The First Cambridge Press in its European Setting*, The Sandars Lectures in Bibliography, 1953 (Cambridge: Cambridge University Press, 1955)

Harper-Bill, Christopher, 'Dean Colet's Convocation Sermon and the Pre-Reformation Church in England', in *The Impact of the English Reformation, 1500–1640*, ed. by Peter Marshall (London: Arnold, 1997), pp. 17–37

Heal, Felicity, 'The Bishops and the Printers: Henry VII to Elizabeth', in *The Prelate in England and Europe, 1300–1560*, ed. by Martin Heale (Woodbridge: York Medieval Press, 2014), pp. 142–69

Hellinga, Lotte, 'Printing', in *The Cambridge History of the Book in Britain*, III: *1400–1557*, ed. by Lotte Hellinga and J. B. Trapp (Cambridge: Cambridge University Press, 1999), pp. 65–108

Hellinga, Lotte, *Printing in England in the Fifteenth Century: E. Gordon Duff's Bibliography with Supplementary Descriptions, Chronologies and a Census of Copies* (London: The Bibliographical Society and The British Library, 2009)

Hellinga, Lotte, *Texts in Transit: Manuscript to Proof and Print in the Fifteenth Century*, Library of the Written Word, 38, The Handpress World, 29 (Leiden: Brill, 2014)

Hellinga, Lotte, *William Caxton and Early Printing in England* (London: The British Library, 2010)

Hodnett, Edward, *English Woodcuts, 1480–1535*, 1st edn 1935, reprinted with Additions and Corrections (Oxford: Oxford University Press, 1973)

Hudson, Anne, *The Premature Reformation: Wycliffite Texts and Lollard History* (Oxford: Clarendon Press, 1988)

Hunt, Arnold, *The Art of Hearing: English Preachers and Their Audiences, 1590–1640*, Cambridge Studies in Early Modern British History (Cambridge: Cambridge University Press, 2010)

Kienzle, Beverly Mayne, ed., *The Sermon*, Typologie des sources du Moyen Âge occidental, 81–83 (Turnhout: Brepols, 2000)

Kirby, Torrance, and P. G. Stanwood, eds, *Paul's Cross and the Culture of Persuasion in England, 1520–1640*, Studies in the History of Christian Traditions, 171 (Leiden: Brill, 2014)

Maclure, Millar, *The Paul's Cross Sermons, 1534–1642* (Toronto: University of Toronto Press, 1958)

Marshall, Peter, *Reformation England 1480–1642* (London: Arnold, 2003)

McCullough, Peter, Hugh Adlington, and Emma Rhatigan, eds, *The Oxford Handbook of the Early Modern Sermon* (Oxford: Oxford University Press, 2011)

Morrissey, Mary, *Politics and the Paul's Cross Sermons, 1558–1642* (Oxford: Oxford University Press, 2011)

Needham, Paul, 'Continental Printed Books Sold in Oxford, *c.* 1480–3: Two Trade Records', in *Incunabula: Studies in Fifteenth-Century Printed Books Presented to Lotte Hellinga*, ed. by Martin Davies (London: The British Library, 1999), pp. 243–70

Nowakowska, Natalia, 'From Strassburg to Trent: Bishops, Printing and Liturgical Reform in the Fifteenth Century', *Past and Present*, 213 (2011), 3–39

O'Mara, V. M., 'Preaching to Nuns in Late Medieval England', in *Medieval Monastic Preaching*, ed. by Carolyn Muessig, Brill's Studies in Intellectual History, 90 (Leiden: Brill, 1998), pp. 93–119

O'Mara, V. M., 'Saints' Plays and Preaching: Theory and Practice in Late Middle English Sanctorale Sermons', *Leeds Studies in English: Essays in Honour of Peter Meredith*, n.s. 29 (1998), 257–74

O'Mara, Veronica, 'Thinking Afresh about Thomas Wimbledon's Paul's Cross Sermon of *c.* 1387', *Leeds Studies in English: Essays in Honour of Oliver Pickering*, n.s. 41 (2010), 155–71

O'Mara, Veronica, 'Unearthing the History of an Early Printed Sermon: John Fisher and St John's College, Cambridge', in *Middle English Manuscripts and Their Legacies: A Volume in Honour of Ian Doyle*, ed. by Corinne Saunders and Richard Lawrie, with Laurie Atkinson, Library of the Written Word, 102, The Manuscript World, 14 (Brill: 2022), pp. 212–33

O'Mara, Veronica, 'A Victorian Response to a Fifteenth-Century Incunabulum: The "Boy Bishop" Sermon and How it was First Edited', in *Preaching the Word in Manuscript and Print in Late Medieval England: Essays in Honour of Susan Powell*, ed. by Martha W. Driver and Veronica O'Mara, Sermo: Studies on Patristic, Medieval, and Reformation Sermons and Preaching, 11 (Turnhout: Brepols, 2013), pp. 351–90

O'Mara, Veronica, and Suzanne Paul, *A Repertorium of Middle English Prose Sermons*, Sermo: Studies on Patristic, Medieval, and Reformation Sermons and Preaching, 1, 4 vols (Turnhout: Brepols, 2007)

Pettegree, Andrew, 'Printing and the Reformation: The English Exception', *The French Book and the European Book World*, Library of the Written World, 1, The Handpress World (Brill: Leiden, 2007), pp. 299–322

Plomer, Henry, 'Two Lawsuits of Richard Pynson', *The Library: The Transactions of the Bibliographical Society*, 2nd series, 10 (1909), 115–33

Pollard, A. W., and G. R. Redgrave, *A Short-Title Catalogue of Books Printed in England, Scotland, and Ireland, and of English Books Printed Abroad*, second edition, revised and enlarged by W. A. Jackson, F. S. Ferguson, and Katherine F. Pantzer, 3 vols (London: The Bibliographical Society, 1976–1991)

Powell, Susan, 'After Arundel but before Luther: The First Half-Century of Print', in *After Arundel: Religious Writing in Fifteenth-Century England*, ed. by Vincent Gillespie and Kantik Ghosh, Medieval Church Studies, 21 (Turnhout: Brepols, 2011), pp. 523–41

Powell, Susan, 'The Secular Clergy', in *A Companion to the Early Printed Book in Britain, 1476–1558*, ed. by Vincent Gillespie and Susan Powell (Cambridge: Brewer, 2014), pp. 150–75

Rex, Richard, *The Theology of John Fisher* (Cambridge: Cambridge University Press, 1991)

Schiewer, Hans-Jochen, 'German Sermons in the Middle Ages', in *The Sermon*, ed. by Beverly Mayne Kienzle, Typologie des sources du Moyen Âge occidental, 81–83 (Turnhout: Brepols, 2000), pp. 861–961

Smith, Julie A., 'An Image of a Preaching Bishop in Late Medieval England: The 1498 Woodcut Portrait of Bishop John Alcock', *Viator: Medieval and Renaissance Studies*, 21 (1990), 301–22

Thayer, Anne T., *Penitence, Preaching and the Coming of the Reformation*, St Andrews Studies in Reformation History (Aldershot: Ashgate, 2002)

Thomson, R. M., *A Descriptive Catalogue of the Medieval Manuscripts of Merton College, Oxford* (Cambridge: Brewer, 2009)

Tonry, Kathleen, *Agency and Intention in English Print, 1476–1526*, Texts and Transitions, 7 (Turnhout: Brepols, 2016)

Wabuda, Susan, *Preaching during the English Reformation*, Cambridge Studies in Early Modern British History (Cambridge: Cambridge University Press, 2002)

Walsham, Alexandra, 'Inventing the Lollard Past: The Afterlife of a Medieval Sermon in Early Modern England', *Journal of Ecclesiastical History*, 58 (2007), 628–55

Wenzel, Siegfried, *Latin Sermon Collections from Later Medieval England: Orthodox Preaching in the Age of Wyclif*, Cambridge Studies in Medieval Literature, 53 (Cambridge: Cambridge University Press, 2005)

Wooding, Lucy, 'From Tudor Humanism to Reformation Preaching', in *The Oxford Handbook of the Early Modern Sermon*, ed. by Peter McCullough, Hugh Adlington, and Emma Rhatigan (Oxford: Oxford University Press, 2011), pp. 329–47

Scandinavia

JUSSI HANSKA

Preaching in Finland on the Eve of the Reformation and Beyond

The Evidence from Manuscript and Print

Almost two decades ago the German historian Arnold Esch wrote an extremely interesting essay on the difficulties of researching the social and economic history of late medieval and renaissance Rome. He describes a situation where the number of surviving sources is scarce and — what is even worse — this not only means that there are fewer sources, but also that they have survived asymmetrically, which presents a distorted view of reality. With Esch's words in mind, medievalists also have to peer into the darkness.[1] To do this, they must find and make use of sources that modern historians would not consider worthy of time or trouble. One may say that a medievalist can be compared to a person trying to put together a puzzle of 10,000 pieces with just a few hundred surviving and without any cover picture to show how they should fit together. Even if it is difficult to think of a more pronounced difference than the one between late medieval Rome and late medieval Finland, Esch's insights are more than valid for the latter. In fact, the problems involved in studying the Finnish Middle Ages are in some respects even more difficult than those for medieval Rome where the scarcity of sources is more relative than absolute. There are numerous issues that make the study of the Finnish situation particularly challenging.

Finland had gradually become part of the Swedish kingdom during the twelfth and the thirteenth centuries, making up the easternmost outpost of Western Christianity. Most of present-day Finland belonged to the Catholic diocese of Turku (or Åbo in Swedish). The rest of Finland was inhabited by the Samì in the north and Russian Orthodox Carelians in the east.

---

1 Arnold Esch, 'Le fonti per la storia economica e sociale di Roma nel Rinascimento', in *Economia e società a Roma tra Medioevo e Rinascimento*, ed. by Anna Esposito and Luciano Palermo, Libri di Viella, 51 (Roma: Viella, 2005), pp. 1–32: 'Bisogna dunque sviluppare virtù che il medievista, rispetto al modernista, deve sviluppare comunque: il medievista deve vedere anche al buio' (p. 6).

Jussi Hanska (jussi.hanska@tuni.fi) is a Lecturer in History and Social and Religious Studies at Tampere University.

Circulating the Word of God in Medieval and Early Modern Europe: Catholic Preaching and Preachers across Manuscript and Print (c. 1450 to c. 1550), ed. by Veronica O'Mara and Patricia Stoop, SERMO 17, (Turnhout: Brepols, 2022), pp. 105–132   BREPOLS ✠ PUBLISHERS   10.1484/M.SERMO-EB.5.130453

The population in the coastal areas of western and south-western Finland were Swedish speakers whereas the rest of the population spoke Finnish. In towns, such as the cathedral town of Turku, the majority spoke Swedish but there was also a considerable minority of German-speaking merchants and artisans due to the intensive contacts of the merchant towns of the Hanseatic League. The diocese of Turku covered a wide geographical area, but only had about a hundred parishes and at most three hundred thousand people. Turku had some five thousand inhabitants, the other four towns Viipuri (Viborg), Rauma (Raumo), Ulvila (Ulfsby), and Naantali (Nådendal) were considerably smaller. Thus, the great majority of the population lived in rural areas. Being a border area meant that Finland enjoyed more than its share of wars and raids by the Russians and occasionally also by Danish pirates, quite apart from the ravages of fire that sometimes destroyed archives and manuscripts in its densely built medieval towns.[2]

Those manuscripts that managed to escape looters, fires, and general wear and tear were often lost during the Lutheran Reformation. The greatest reason for this was the so-called 'voutivandalismi' (bailiff vandalism). The Swedish king's bailiffs in Finland, who were in charge of collecting taxes, had to keep record books. In practice this meant notebooks made of paper with covers made of parchment. The bailiffs obtained this parchment by ripping apart medieval Catholic codices. More than 9000 folia of medieval manuscripts have been recovered from the account books dated between 1530 and 1630. These are now stored at the Suomen Kansalliskirjsto or Finnish National Library in Helsinki.[3] Compared to this, the number of manuscripts and early printed books is relatively small. There is only a handful of surviving medieval manuscripts and fewer than a hundred early printed books.

If the situation of surviving written material from medieval Finland in general is poor, it becomes even more dramatic when one looks at the sources for medieval preaching in Finland. Sermons and *praedicabilia* in general are only a small part of the surviving material and this makes the study of preaching in medieval Finland extremely difficult; one is forced to follow Esch's suggestion and try to search the most unlikely places to find even the smallest traces of homiletic culture preceding the Lutheran Reformation.

---

2 Tuomas Heikkilä, 'Kirjallistumisen jäljillä', in *Kirjallinen kulttuuri keskiajan Suomessa*, ed. by Tuomas Heikkilä, Historiallisia Tutkimuksia, 254 (Helsinki: Suomalaisen Kirjallisuuden Seura, 2010), pp. 11–61 (p. 46). Turku, the cathedral town, was destroyed or looted by enemies in 1318, 1396, 1509, and 1522. Furthermore, Turku was at least partly destroyed by major fires in 1429, 1464, 1473, 1491, 1523, 1537, 1546, 1549, 1552, 1565, 1569, sometime during the 1570s, and in 1593.

3 Heikkilä, 'Kirjallisuuden jäljillä', pp. 49–50. Today these 9319 folia from roughly 1500 different manuscripts have been digitized and are available on the *Fragmenta membranea*-collection of Kansalliskirjasto (the Finnish National Library): https://fragmenta.kansalliskirjasto.fi/ [accessed 21 June 2022].

PREACHING IN FINLAND ON THE EVE OF THE REFORMATION AND BEYOND

Trying to form a coherent general view of the situation on the basis of such limited material is challenging to say the least.

It does not help that the propaganda diffused during the Reformation period (*c.* 1530–1630) sought to give as grim an impression as possible of the *cura animarum* in general and preaching in particular at the end of the Catholic period. For example, Paulus Juusten (d. 1575), the second Lutheran bishop of Turku, paints a rather dark picture of the Catholic period in the preface to his *Postilla* (1570):

> Multi vestrum meminerunt, quod vigente adhuc apud nos idolatria papistica, sicut et in universo reliquo mundo, alebantur quidam sacerdotes, complures quibus adjuncti erant monachorum ordines in singulis fere civitatibus: horum omnium usus et officium maxime fuit ut praescriptum Psalmorum numerum, cum aliis cantiunculis quotidie decantarint: additis missis ad aras Sanctis mortuis consecratas […] Erant missae de Beata virgine, de corpore Christi, de quatuordecim adiutoribus, erant missae pro defunctis, et multae aliae, quarum non est numerus. Hae saepe ab illis recitabantur, qui ipsi unam periodum linguae latinae non intellexerunt […] Si lectio aliqua ex bibliis recitanda erat, id fiebat coram vulgo lingua non intelligibili. Conciones ad populum non fiebant, nisi tantum diebus dominicis et Sanctorum feriis: ne autem in illis habendis plures horae (inutiliter fortassis, prout illis videbatur) collocarentur, addebatur Epistola Dominicalis Evangelio aut prolixa aliqua legenda de Sanctis, quasi textus Evangelicus per se jejunam aliquam doctrinam contineret.[4]

> [Many of you will remember that when papistical idolatry still ruled in our land, as it did in the entire world, many priests were employed, most of them connected to monastic orders that were found in nearly every town, and whose only function was to chant daily the prescribed number of psalms and other chants. In addition to that they celebrated Masses in front of altars consecrated to dead saints […] There were Masses for the Blessed Virgin, on the body of Christ, for the Fourteen Holy Helpers; there were Masses for the dead and many others that cannot even be counted. These were often recited by men who barely understood any Latin themselves […] If there was any reading of the Bible in the presence of the people, it was done in a language they could not understand. There were no sermons for the people, unless on Sundays and saints' feast days and nor did they last many hours (which they perhaps thought would have been useless), and they added

---

4   Edited in K. G. Leinberg, 'Företalet till P. Iwstens Postilla', *Historiallinen Arkisto*, 19 (1905), 268–69. See also Simo Heininen, *Suomalaisen historian kirjoituksen synty: tutkimus Paavali Juustenin piispainkronikasta*, Suomen Kirkkohistoriallisen Seuran Tutkmuksia, 147 (Helsinki: Suomen Kirkkohistoriallinen Seura, 1989), pp. 23–24. As Heininen rightly observes, Juusten is merely repeating Lutheran standard topoi concerning Church life during the Catholic period.

Sunday's Epistle reading or prolix legends of the saints to the Gospel text as if the Gospel text alone lacked sufficient doctrinal material].

Neither does it help that the earlier historiography in Finland accepted this confessional propaganda with very little criticism. Henrik Gabriel Porthan, 'professor eloquentiae' at the Kungliga Akademien i Åbo (Royal Academy in Turku) published a study on early Finnish preaching in 1781. Porthan's view of the pre-Reformation sermons in Finland was rather bleak:

> Ut autem taceamus, raras eas saltim fuisse, certum fere videtur, non multum notitiae vel emolumenti ex illis ad auditores redundare potuisse: continebant enim prope nihil aliud, quam laudes Beatae Virginis, legendas sanctorum, atque alias tales ineptias; quae quam parum, vel potius nihil, ad veram salutis obtinendae rationem hominibus tradendam contulerint, quis non perspiciat ipsi quoque sacerdotes, in tanta versati sunt ignorantia, ut saepe nullam haberent lingvae latinae peritiam, adeoque e Scriptura Sacra nihil proficere possent; unde mirum videri debet nemini, ipsorum conciones jejunas atque inutiles fuisse.[5]

> [To say nothing else, there were very few of them and certainly it seems that the listeners did not get much information or benefit from them as they did not contain much other than praise of the Blessed Virgin, legends of the saints, and other such nonsense. They contributed very little, or more likely nothing at all as an attempt to lead people to true salvation. This was not noticed by the priests themselves, for they were in a such state of ignorance that often they did not have any command of Latin at all, and therefore they could not benefit from holy Scripture. Hence it should not come as a surprise to anyone that their sermons were simplistic in content and useless].

Porthan's evaluation was based on the above-mentioned prologue of Paulus Juusten and a limited number of other sources from Reformation times. Porthan, as a late eigthteenth-century historian, can be excused for underestimating medieval preaching. What is less excusable is the continuing historiographical tradition of accepting Lutheran reformers' anti-Catholic propaganda at face value when it comes to preaching. There is a well-established tradition among Reformation period scholars that — contrary to all the evidence — still takes the view that preaching was for the most part a Protestant phenomenon. John M. Frymire gives a striking example of this misunderstanding in his prologue to *The Primacy of the Postils*:

> Some ten years ago in the archives of the Congregation for the Doctrine of the Faith in Rome (aka The Inquisition and Index of Prohibited [p. 2] Books), I stumbled upon numerous sets of censorship protocols in which

---

5 Henrik Gabriel Porthan, *Historiola concionum sacrarum fennicarum* (Åbo: Frenckell, 1781), pp. 5–8.

the sources given the privilege of a purge blindsided me: these were German Catholic sermon collections; many of them were postils; and most had originally been published in the vernacular. Their translation into Latin not only guaranteed them an international audience, but also provided German books in a language that Roman censors could actually read. Having recently passed my Ph.D. comprehensive exams, I knew that 'preaching and the German Reformation' was a Protestant phenomenon. Did not Catholics, for their part, simply pour scorn upon the Evangelicals in polemical pamphlets that few wanted to print and fewer wanted to read? Was it not until the later sixteenth century, in the wake of the Council of Trent and especially during the Baroque period, that Catholic preaching really came into its own as an effective medium? Despite years of working in Germany, it was by accident and in Rome that I discovered a radical corrective to the long established conundrum of the German Catholic non-resistance to the Evangelicals in the pulpits, and one that came much earlier than the standard paradigms allowed.[6]

The remainder of this essay will seek to address head-on what underlies the sort of preconceptions in Frymire's comment by making a concerted attempt to uncover what evidence there is for preaching in Finland in the later Middle Ages as Europe moved from a manuscript to a print culture. Unlike many other regions in Europe, most notably Germany and the Low Countries, where examples of preaching activity is plentiful, for a complex mix of factors over several centuries that for Finland is very hard to find. In this essay we shall first examine what might loosely be called more direct evidence before moving on to indirect evidence gained from archival records and commentary, followed by a study of what manuscripts and early printed sermons actually survive in Finland (whether produced there or not), and end with a brief examination of the transition from Catholic to Lutheran preaching. In so doing we shall attempt to illuminate the ways in which the situation in Finland compares with — but largely contrasts to — the rest of Europe.

Direct Evidence

There are certain aspects about Finland that make it almost impossible to assume that there would not have been popular preaching there in the late medieval period. The most important of these is the presence of religious orders in the diocese of Turku. There were two Dominican convents in Turku and Viipuri; three Franciscan convents in Kökar, Rauma, and Viipuri; and finally there was the Birgittine monastery of Naantali. The preaching activities and indeed the

---

6 John M. Frymire, *The Primacy of the Postils: Catholics, Protestants, and the Dissemination of Ideas in Early Modern Germany*, Studies in Medieval and Reformation Traditions, 147 (Leiden: Brill, 2010), pp. 1–2.

primary role of preaching in both the Dominican and Franciscan apostolate is too well-known to require any further comment here. The Birgittine order and the preaching activities of the Birgittine brothers are less well-known to the wider scholarly community, but nevertheless well documented and studied.[7] It would be absurd to assume that the Dominicans and the Franciscans did not preach in Finland when they did so everywhere else. Furthermore, St Birgitta herself gave instruction for preaching to the lay people who came to Birgittine monasteries, sometimes from far away.[8] The Birgittine rule dictated that the brothers had to preach in the vernacular language at the monastery church every Sunday and at those feasts that had vigil days. There is no reason to imagine that this stipulation was not followed in Finland.

Moreover, one needs to take a look at the parish churches themselves, as they reveal some information concerning medieval preaching. Numerous late medieval Finnish stone churches include a structure that is called an exterior pulpit. There are twenty-three surviving exterior pulpits scattered throughout medieval churches in the Turku diocese.[9] These are staircases that end in small windows on the second floor walls that open to the church yard. The current assumption is that they were used to preach to the parishioners that were gathered in the church yard — a custom that was common in connection with all sorts of community meetings and especially during the yearly fairs and market days that were traditionally held on the day of a parish church's patronal feast.

---

7 On Birgittine preaching, see for example: Roger Andersson, *Postillor och predikan: en medeltida texttradition i filologisk och funktionell belysning*, Sällskapet Runica et Mediaevalia, Scripta minora, 1 (Stockholm: Runica et Mediaevalia, 1993); Stephan Borgehammar, 'Preaching to Pilgrims: Ad vincula Sermons at Vadstena Abbey', in *A Catalogue and Its Users: A Symposium on the Uppsala C Collection of Medieval Manuscripts*, ed. by Monica Hedlund, Acta Bibliothecae R. Universitatis Upsalensis, 34 (Uppsala: Almqvist & Wiksell, 1995), pp. 91–100; Roger Andersson, *Predikosamlingar i Vadstena klosterbibliotek: Vadstenabrödernas predikan*, Meddelanden, 1 (Uppsala: Uppsala universitet, Institutionen för klassiska språk, 1996); Roger Andersson, *De birgittinska ordensprästerna som traditionsförmedlare och folkfostrare*, Runica et Mediaevalia, Scripta minora, 4 (Stockholm: Sällskapet Runica et Mediaevalia, 2001); Monica Hedlund, 'The Use of Model Sermons at Vadstena: A Case Study', in *Constructing the Medieval Sermon*, ed. by Roger Andersson, Sermo: Studies on Patristic, Medieval, and Reformation Sermons and Preaching, 6 (Turnhout: Brepols, 2007), pp. 117–64.

8 Andersson, *De birgittinska ordensprästerna*, p. 25. Birgittine preaching in Finland is briefly dealt with by Marko Lamberg in his book on the first Finnish author, Jöns Budde, who was a monk in the monastery of Naantali. His information, however, is strictly based on what was known from the rule and the situation in Sweden; Marko Lamberg, *Jöns Budde: Birgittalaisveli ja hänen teoksensa*, Suomalaisen Kirjallisuuden Seuran Toimituksia, 1115 (Helsinki, Suomalaisen Kirjallisuuden Seura, 2007), p. 297.

9 Markus Hiekkanen, *The Stone Churches of the Medieval Diocese of Turku: A Systematic Classification and Chronology*, Suomen Muinaismuistoyhdistyksen Aikakauskirja, 101 (Helsinki: Suomen Muinaismuistoyhdistys, 1994), pp. 90–96. Hiekkanen points out that exterior pulpits appear to be rare in other countries. In addition to Finnish churches, there are only a few known churches in Sweden and Denmark with similar structures.

PREACHING IN FINLAND ON THE EVE OF THE REFORMATION AND BEYOND

Nevertheless, it needs to be stated that we do not have a single example of an original medieval sermon, either in Latin or in the vernacular, which was written in Finland. There are a few sermons — in fact very few — that may have been written in Finland, but none of them can be identified beyond any doubt as Finnish. A good example are the Latin sermons for the feast day of St Henry, the alleged first bishop of Turku and the patron saint of Finland.[10] Aarno Maliniemi has studied and edited thirty-one Latin sermons on St Henry, all surviving in the *C-samlingen* of Uppsala universitetsbibliotek.[11] All these sermon manuscripts came originally from the library of the Birgittine monastery of Vadstena (established sometime in the 1360s and consecrated in 1384). Some preachers remain unknown but others are known by name and we have further information on them in other sources such as the *Diarium Vadstenense*.[12] At least two of these preachers spent some time in the Birgittine house of Naantali, which was founded in 1442. Johannes Borquardi came to Finland in June 1446 and died there on 4 March 1447.[13] Clemens Petri (d. 1500) was sent to Finland to reform the Naantali monastery. He stayed in Finland for an unknown period of time between 1480 and 1484.[14] It is possible that some of Clemens Petri's sermons were originally delivered in Finland and, even if they were not, it is reasonable to assume that these two prolific preachers delivered sermons during their stay in Naantali. One could also speculate that some of Clemens Petri's sermons from that period found their way into his Latin model sermon collections.[15]

---

10 According to his legend, St Henry came originally from England. He came to Finland together with St Erik, the king of Sweden, to convert the Finns. He remained in the country and became the first bishop. St Henry was allegedly martyred by a pagan Finn around 1150. He was never officially canonized, but his cult was reasonably widely spread in Scandinavia. There is very little reliable evidence for his life and some scholars even doubt his existence.

11 *De S. Henrico episcopo et martyre: die mittelalterliche Literatur über den Apostel Finnlands.* II: *Legenda nova. Sermones*, ed. by Aarno Maliniemi, Suomen Kirkkohistoriallisen Seuran Tutkimuksia, 45 (Helsinki: Suomen Kirkkohistoriallinen Seura, 1942), II (only the second volume was published). On the manuscripts of the Uppsala C-collection, see Margarete Andersson-Schmitt and Monica Hedlund, *Mittelalterlichen Handschriften der Universitätsbibliothek Uppsala: Katalog über die C-Sammlung*, Acta Bibliothecae R. Universitatis Upsaliensis, 26, 8 vols (Stockholm: Almqvist & Wiksell, 1988–1995).

12 *Diarium Vadstenense: The Memorial Book of Vadstena Abbey*, ed. by Claes Gejrot, Studia Latina Stockholmensia, 33 (Stockholm: Almqvist & Wiksell, 1988) and *Vadstenadiariet: latinsk text med översättning och kommentar*, ed. by Claes Gejrot, Handlingar, 19 (Stockholm: Kungliga Samfundet för utgivande av handskrifter rörande Skandinaviens historia, 1996).

13 Andersson, *De birgittinska ordensprästerna som traditionsförmedlare och folkfostrare*, p. 209.

14 Roger Andersson, 'Översättaren som predikant: Clemens Petri och svenska språket', in *Dicit Scriptura: studier i C-samlingen tillägnade Monica Hedlund*, ed. by Sara Risberg, Sällskapet Runica et Mediaevalia, Scripta minora, 14 (Stockholm: Sällskapet Runica et Mediaevalia, 2006), pp. 149–64 (p. 152); *De S. Henrico episcopo et martyre*, ed. by Maliniemi, pp. 30–35 and 49–50.

15 There are two surviving model sermon collections by Clemens Petri; *de tempore* (Uppsala, Uppsala universitetsbibliotek, C-samlingen, MS C 321) and *de sanctis* (Uppsala, Uppsala universitetsbibliotek, C-samlingen MS C 308). Both these sermon collections are written

Maliniemi also published, in addition to sermons proper, the *Legenda nova* of St Henry of Finland written in Latin. He noticed that this legend is generically very close to the sermon genre: 'Die Form der Legende kommt derjenigen einer Predigt sehr nahe'; as Maliniemi points out, on the basis of internal evidence, this text was originally written by a Finnish Birgittine priest for the use of Turku cathedral.[16] On the basis of Maliniemi's views, Jesse Keskiaho has proposed that the *Legenda nova* was re-worked from a sermon.[17] However, for a scholar working in the field of medieval sermon studies it is quite clear that the *Legenda nova* does not structurally resemble a sermon and there is no real reason to suppose that it would have been based on a sermon or sermons. In fact, I present the *Legenda nova* here only as an example of the lengths to which scholars have gone to find some surviving evidence of Finnish medieval sermons.

Contemporary Sources on the Preaching and Preachers

In view of the lack of surviving sermons, one needs to look at other sources to find information about preachers and preaching during the latter half of the fifteenth century. Here one needs to consider that the same Reformation that destroyed most of the pre-Reformation Catholic literature also destroyed a good deal of the historical records. The surviving material concerning medieval Finland consists nearly exclusively of records concerning the ownership and sale of land and property. Such documents retained their value notwithstanding the Reformation.

Chronicles and annals reasonably common elsewhere in Europe are almost non-existent. There are few fragments from the fifteenth century. However, the *Catalogus et ordinaria successio episcoporum finlandensium* that was written during the Reformation period by the Lutheran bishop of Turku, Paulus Juusten, was partly based on earlier, mostly now lost, medieval historiographical works.[18] Unfortunately, Juusten is more concerned with the administrative achievements of the bishops. He has very little to say about preaching, and what he says is rather generic. His only mention of medieval preaching is his reference that Bishop Olavus Magni (1405–1460), who was

---

mostly in Latin but include here and there a few words or short passages in Swedish; Roger Andersson, 'Översättaren som predikant: Clemens Petri och svenska språket', pp. 150–51.

16   *De Sancto Henrico episcopo et martyre*, ed. by Maliniemi, pp. 4–5 (p. 5).

17   Jesse Keskiaho, 'Pappien koulutus ja Oppineen papiston kirjat', in *Kirjallinen kulttuuri keskiajan Suomessa*, ed. by Tuomas Heikkilä, Historiallisia Tutkimuksia, 254 (Helsinki: Suomalaisen Kirjallisuuden Seura, 2010), pp. 147–81 (p. 181).

18   Paulus Juusten, *Catalogus et ordinaria successio episcoporum finlandensium*, ed. by Simo Heininen (Helsinki: Societas Historiae Ecclesiastica Finlandiae, 1988). On Juusten's medieval sources, see Heininen, *Suomalaisen historian kirjoituksen synty*, pp. 32–92 (for the abbreviated German version, see pp. 128–29).

PREACHING IN FINLAND ON THE EVE OF THE REFORMATION AND BEYOND   113

consecrated in Rome during the holy year 1450: 'rhetor extitit facundissimus' ['was an eloquent orator'].[19] Searching through other documents and source publications produces almost as poor results. Any references to preaching are few and far between, and even those cases are not very solid or informative. For example, Bishop Olavus Magni gave a forty days' indulgence letter to the parish church of Rymättylä (Rimito in Swedish) in south-western Finland during his visitation tour in the autumn of 1450. In this letter he specifies that indulgence are given to those who (among other specified things) listen to sermons in the said church.[20] This does not necessarily imply that preaching for the parishioners would have been regular or even a common thing at Rymättylä church; it is more likely that the bishop was simply copying the standard formula of an indulgence letter.

More interesting is a document from the year 1448. In it, the general confessor of Vadstena monastery acknowledged receiving payments from certain books that had been sent to the Finnish daughter house of Naantali. Some of the books were sold to the Naantali monastery, but two of them were only loaned to be copied there and then to be returned to Vadstena. They were an unidentifiable exemplum collection and a sermon collection written by a certain Johannes Petri.[21] While the document does not specify who this Johannes Petri was, it is likely that he was one of the Vadstena brothers. In fact, the *Diarium Vadstenense* mentions that a certain brother Johannes Petri died in 1418. The *Diarium* mentions that this brother Johannes Petri 'Multa quoque bona reliquit in scriptis' ['left much good in writing'].[22] This document proves that the Birgittine brothers of the Naantali monastery took their preaching duties seriously, responsibilities that were explained in normative documents such as the *Regula Sancti Salvatoris* and the *Liber usuum* that guided the lives of the Birgittines.[23]

Furthermore, there is a short note in a Dominican general minister's *diarium* dated 15 June 1492 that a certain Brother Henricus Lelle (or Lolle) from the Dominican convent of Turku is given permission to stay with the bishop of Turku for the purpose of preaching: 'potest stare causa predicationis cum reverendissimo patre d. episcopo Ambuense' ['can stay with the most reverend Father, lord bishop of Turku, for the sake of preaching'].[24] A year

---

19 Juusten, *Catalogus et ordinaria successio episcoporum finlandensium*, p. 62.
20 *Finlands Medeltidsurkunder*, ed. by Reinhold Hausen, 8 vols (Helsinki: Finlands statsarkiv, 1910–1935), III (1921), no. 2854: '[...] similiter hii, qui processionibus fieri consuetis ante missas vel post missas et missis votiuis interfuerint ibique missas, predicationes ac alia diuina officia diurna uel nocturna audierint [...]' ['[...] similarly those, who participate in customary processions before or after Masses, or are present for votive Masses, Masses, preaching, or hear other Divine Offices in the day or night time [...]'].
21 *Finlands Medeltidsurkunder*, ed. by Hausen, VIII (1935), no. 6652.
22 *Diarium Vadstenense*, ed. by Gejrot, pp. 174–75.
23 Andersson, *Postillor och predikan*, pp. 194–204.
24 *Finlands Medeltidsurkunder*, ed. by Hausen, V (1928), no. 4413. The name of the diocese is misspelled, it should read Aboense. This was a common enough mistake as there were very

before this Brother Henricus Lelle had been given a letter of recommendation by the bishop. There he was entitled 'frater Henricus Lelle, in sacra pagina lector' that is, he was the Turku convent's lector and most probably a very well educated man.[25] This explains why the bishop would have wanted to have him accompany him as a preacher.

The Minister General's permission actually gave a stamp of approval to a pre-existing situation. It is known that two years earlier Henricus Lelle had followed bishop Magnus in his visitation tour. There is a document that shows how Bishop Magnus Stjernkors (1489–1500) consecrated the new cemetery of Lokalahti (Lokalax) church roughly 50 kilometres northeast of Turku. This document tells us that:

> Anno 1490 benedictum et consecratum est cimiterium in Lockalax ipso die Edwardi regis et martyris per reuerendum in Christo patrem et dominum, dominum Magnum Nicolai Serkelax, diuina et apostolice sedis gracia episcopum Aboensem, in honorem sancte trinitatis, passionis Christi et salvatoris necnon et in memoriam compassionis gloriosissime virginis Marie omniumque sanctorum et sancte Katharine virginis et martyris gloriose, in presentia plurimum de sua familia, clericorum et secularium, presertim magistri Pauli Lingonis, ecclesie Aboensis canonici, et parente eciam cancellario et fratre Henrico Lelle, lectoris sacre theologie qui primam missam tunc in eodem cimiterio cantando solenniter in presentia eiusdem reuerendi patris celebrauit et predicauit.[26]

> [In the year 1490 in the day of Edward the king and confessor, the new cemetery of Lokalahti was blessed and consecrated by the reverend father and lord in Christ, lord Magnus Nikolai Särkilahti, by divine and apostolic grace bishop of Turku, in honour of the Holy Trinity, the Passion of Christ the Saviour, and in memory of the compassion of the most glorious Virgin, all the saints, and the virgin and glorious martyr St Katherine, and in the presence of many members of the bishop's retinue, clerics and laymen, especially Master Paulus of Lingonis, canon of Turku cathedral, and also in the presence of [the bishop's] relative and chancellor Brother Henricus Lelle, reader of sacred theology, who solemnly celebrated the first Mass in that cemetery in the presence of the reverend father [the bishop] and preached].

The case of Henricus Lelle, however, only shows that preaching was actually carried out in the close vicinity of the bishop, either in the cathedral or during his visitation tours. It does not say anything about the situation in rural

---

few documents that dealt with the remote Turku diocese, and, consequently, its name was not as familiar as the names of bigger and more important dioceses for the scribes of the papal curia.

25 *Finlands Medeltidsurkunder*, ed. by Hausen v (1928), no. 4392.

26 *Finlands Medeltidsurkunder*, ed. by Hausen v (1928), no. 4333.

PREACHING IN FINLAND ON THE EVE OF THE REFORMATION AND BEYOND 115

parishes outside the cathedral town. The only source that actually mentions the sermons of the ordinary parish priests is the 1492 synodal statute of Bishop Magnus Stjernkors. It stipulates that:

> Preterea statuimus et ordinamus, quod quilibet curatorum per se vel per alium capellanum in qualibet dominica legat in wulgari ex ambone pater noster, aue Maria, credo et modum confitendi, sub pena sex marcarum tociens quociens, et quod habeat omnia predicta in wlgari conscripta, ita quod uniformiter semper doceat suos parrochianos ut facilius discant.[27]

> > [In addition, we stipulate that anyone in charge of the cure of souls, either personally or by a chaplain on each Sunday will read from the pulpit in the vernacular the *Pater noster*, the *Ave Maria*, the Creed, and the Form of Confession on pain of a fine of six marks for each occasion, and that they have all the above mentioned written down in the vernacular so that they can always teach them uniformly and thus make it easier for their parishioners to learn them].

This synodal statute follows the models known from the rest of Europe starting from John Pecham's famous Lambeth Constitutions of 1281 in England. It does not actually speak about preaching but rather of a catechetical instruction delivered from the pulpit. However, from the context it is clear that this instruction of the parishioners was meant to be carried out in connection with Sunday sermons, and it should be noted that 'in wulgari' in this context could mean either Swedish or Finnish depending on what was the generally spoken language in the parish.

Surviving Sermon Collections and *Praedicabilia*

Since, as seen above, the surviving direct source material does not allow us to form a coherent and integrated picture of preaching in medieval Finland, it is necessary to find other sources that provide us with indirect evidence of preaching. The best of these sources consists of surviving model sermon collections and other *praedicabilia*. The general logic here is that, taking into account the expensiveness of the books even after the spread of the use of paper and the development of print, they remained so pricey that one can easily suppose they were not copied or ordered just for aesthetic pleasure, but to be used. As the model sermon collections were mostly useful for priests writing their own sermons (and to a lesser extent as devotional reading), one

---

27 *Finlands Medeltidsurkunder*, ed. by Hausen, v (1928), nos 4415 and 4433. A mark in Finland equalled *c*. 210 grams of silver. However, one 'mark' as a monetary unit was not equal to one mark as a weight measurement. Some idea of the severity of the fine can be drawn from the fact that the very same year Bishop Magnus Stjernkors declared that the maximum annual wage of a chaplain was five marks.

can safely assume that if one can prove that a parish priest or a parish church owned a copy of such work, it was indeed used for preaching purposes.

A closer look at extant medieval literature from Finland shows that the surviving *praedicabilia* is indeed much richer than the narrative and documentary sources of preaching during the medieval Catholic period. However, before going into details an important methodological problem with these sources needs to be discussed. The provenance and history of these manuscripts, fragments, and early printed books is often poorly known and in many cases impossible to reconstruct. This is problematic because one cannot assume that a manuscript or a book found in the library registers in the nineteenth century was actually in Finland during the Middle Ages. It is a well-known fact that in the wars of the seventeenth century, that is, during Sweden's 'Stormaktstiden' or 'Great Power period', its armies plundered monasteries, castles, and bishops' palaces in central Europe and brought their booty back home. Some of these looting high-ranking officers came from Finland. A good example is the Swedish-speaking cavalry general Torsten Ståhlhandske (d. 1644) whose widow Christina Horn donated his looted book collection (consisting of 890 volumes) to the university library of the Kungliga Akademien of Turku in 1646.[28]

This brings us to a concrete example relevant for this study. In the collections of the Suomen Kansalliskirjasto in Helsinki, there is a manuscript C.ö.I. 1 that contains an anonymous collection of sermons for Sundays and saints (some of them by Jacopo da Varazze) and an abbreviated version of Jacopo da Varazze's *Legenda aurea*. This manuscript has been put together from several texts all written in Germany during the fifteenth century. The first folio of the manuscript informs us that before coming to the Suomen Kansalliskirjasto: 'Pöytis moderkyrcka tilhörig', that is, it belonged to the parish church of Pöytyä in south-west Finland.[29] As we still have the inventory books of the Pöytyä church, it is easy to find out that the manuscript was first mentioned in the inventory dated 17 April 1654 with the title 'Latinsk postilla'.[30] Leaving aside the question of whether one can automatically assume — as Ville Walta does in his description of this manuscript — that a general reference to a medieval postil automatically means that it is the same manuscript that is housed in the

---

28 Henrik Gabriel Porthan, *Historia Bibliothecae Regiae Academiae Aboënsis*, 25 vols (Åbo: Frenckell, 1771–1795), (1778), pp. 17–18. The facsimile is reprinted in Henrik Gabriel Porthan, *Henrici Gabrielis Porthan Opera omnia*, 13 vols (Turku: Porthan-Seura, 1939–2007), v (1974). Here one might also mention Queen Christina Vasa's library now housed in Biblioteca Apostolica Vaticana, codices reginenses which also consists partly of books looted in Germany during the Thirty Years War.

29 The description of the manuscript has been made by Ville Walta. The description and digital version of the manuscript is found on the pages of the *Codices Fennici*-project, which is executed under the auspices of the Suomalaisen Kirjallisuuden Seura [accessed 25 February 2021].

30 Pöytyä parish archive, inventories 1654–1759; see the digital archive of the Suomen Kansallisrkisto: http://digi.narc.fi/digi/view.ka?kuid=8246426 [accessed 25 February 2021].

Suomen Kansalliskirjasto today, one must ask when this manuscript actually came to Finland. As noted, it was written in Germany during the fifteenth century and most likely was still there towards the middle of the century as in the bindings there is a charter dated 1449 from Pope Nicholas V (1328–1330) concerning the city of Greifswald; we can also reasonably assume that it was in Pöytyä in the April of 1654 at the latest. However, what we cannot know for sure is if it found its way to Finland during the last years of the Middle Ages, perhaps with some of the Finnish students studying at the university in Greifswald, or was part of the booty of some officer of the Swedish army during the seventeenth–century wars (Greifswald was besieged and taken by the Swedish army in 1631 and belonged to Swedish Pomerania until 1815). For these reasons this manuscript cannot securely be used as evidence of preaching in medieval Finland.

The Suomen Kansalliskirjasto also has another surviving manuscript with two model sermon collections, namely MS C.ö.I.6. This manuscript includes the *Sermones de tempore et de sanctis* collection by the Dominican preacher Peregrinus de Oppeln (d. 1335) as well as sermons by his confrère Antonio Azaro Parmense (d. *c.* 1310). This manuscript was also originally written in Germany, but unlike the Pöytyä sermon collection, it has marginal notes written in Swedish during the late fifteenth or early sixteenth century.[31] These marginal notes make it highly likely that this manuscript was indeed used in Finland during the Middle Ages.

However, there is yet another sermon collection that was even more probably used in Finland during the medieval period, namely the copy of the so-called *Paratus postil* that is still found in the church archives of the Swedish-speaking parish of Rymättylä. It has not been possible to identify where and when this copy of the *Paratus postil* was printed as the title page as well as the first twenty-eight sermons are missing.[32] The postil — a *de tempore* collection — is bound together with a Psalter printed in Leipzig by Melchior Lotter (d. 1549) on 14 July 1505. This Psalter is mentioned in the oldest surviving inventory of the Rymättylä parish archives in 1821.[33]

---

31 The digitized manuscript is available at the website of the *Codices Fennici*-project [accessed 25 February 2021]. The description of the manuscript has been made by Ville Walta. The Swedish marginal notes are on fol. 22r–v. Peregrinus de Oppeln's sermon collection has been edited as Peregrinus de Oppeln, *Peregrini de Opole Sermones de tempore et de sanctis: e codicis manu scriptis primum*, ed. by Ryszard Tatarzyński, Studia 'Przegladu Tomistycnego', 1 (Warszawa: Instytut Tomistyczny, 1997). There is an extensive introduction to Friar Peregrinus and his literary work in Polish, German, and in Latin on pp. vii–cii. On Antonio Azaro Parmense and his sermon collection, see G. Meersseman, 'Le opere di fra Antonio Azaro Parmense', *Archivum Fratrum Praedicatorum*, 10 (1940), 20–47.

32 There are twenty-four printed editions between 1480 and 1517. See British Library, *Incunabula Short Title Collection*: https://data.cerl.org/istc/_search?query=paratus&size= 10&mode=default&from=20 [accessed 25 February 2021]. The fifteen editions available in digitized form have been checked, but none corresponds exactly with the Rymättylä book.

33 Rymättylä Parish Archive, inventories 1821–1891, digitized in the digital archive of the

However, the most important point is that there are several Swedish marginal notes in the *Paratus postil* written in a late fifteenth-century or early sixteenth-century hand. Some of the Swedish marginal notes are short commentaries on the text; others are Swedish translations of difficult Latin concepts, for example, in the second sermon on the Twelfth Sunday after Trinity the *Paratus postil* has: 'Non est speciosa laus in ore peccatoris'. On the side margin one reads the words 'speciosa höffwelighet' (that is, 'höflighet' in modern Swedish, which means 'suitable, good behaviour'). A few lines below the text says: '[…] oratio eius erit inexecrabilis'. And again one reads in the margin: 'inexecrabilis stakkeligh' (that is, 'styggt' which means 'nasty, ugly'). It does not seem to be too far fetched to assume that these translations in the margins were made to make it easier to use the *Paratus postil* when writing and delivering vernacular sermons in Swedish. Judging from the style of letters, it seems that the *Paratus postil* was printed in the 1480s or 1490s. This means that the Swedish language marginal notes were written at most twenty to twenty-five years after the book was printed and therefore it seems reasonable to assume that it was bought directly to a Swedish-speaking area, most likely to the parish of Rymättylä.[34]

Finally, one needs to take a closer look at the Suomen Kansalliskirjasto above mentioned fragment collection. These include fragments of several sermon and *praedicabilia* manuscripts that can be proved with reasonable certainty to have been in Finland during the Middle Ages.[35] In practice this means that those parchment leaves were used in bindings of bailiffs' accounts originating from Finland. These include, for example, folia from two different manuscripts of Jacopo da Varazze's Sunday sermon collection,[36] the Sunday sermons of the Dominican Jacques de Lausanne (d. 1321),[37] and parts of the sermon collection by the Franciscan Francesco d'Asti (active in the 1340s).[38] Furthermore this collection includes fragments of different *praedicabilia* manuscripts such as Jacopo da Varazze's *Legenda aurea*, collections of *distinctiones*, Nicolaus de Lyra's postils, Thomas Aquinas's *Catena aurea*, and so forth.

Here one may add a few words about early printed books and preaching in Finland. It is known that the first sermon collections in print had appeared by 1470 and from that time until the end of the Middle Ages the volume of

---

Suomen Kansallisarkisto: http://digi.narc.fi/digi/view.ka?kuid=8544045 [accessed 25 February 2021].

34 In 2009, when Rymättylä was incorporated into the neighbouring town of Naantali, it had fewer than six percent Swedish speakers, but during the Middle Ages the south-west coastal area of Finland was nearly exclusively Swedish speaking.

35 See the *Fragmenta membranea*-database of the Suomen Kansalliskirjasto mentioned in n. 3.

36 Johannes Baptist Schneyer, *Repertorium der lateinischen Sermones des Mittelalters für die Zeit von 1150–1350*, Beiträge zur Geschichte der Philosophie und Theologie des Mittelalters: Texte und Untersuchungen, 43, 11 vols (Münster: Aschendorffsche Verlagsbuchhandlung, 1969–1990), III (1971), 221–35.

37 Schneyer, *Repertorium der lateinischen Sermones des Mittelalters*, III (1971), 54–89.

38 Schneyer, *Repertorium der lateinischen Sermones des Mittelalters*, II (1970), 55–59.

PREACHING IN FINLAND ON THE EVE OF THE REFORMATION AND BEYOND 119

printed sermon collections, as indeed of all printed books, grew exponentially.[39] However, the situation in Finland, judging on the basis of surviving evidence, seems to be rather different. As we have seen in the case of Rymättylä parish, there are indeed a few extant early printed books from medieval Finland. Some of them are still in the parish archives; some at the Suomen Kansalliskirjasto and yet others in other public libraries. Yet, their numbers are rather small compared to the surviving manuscript fragments, albeit that sermon collections and *praedicabilia* are particularly well represented in these volumes. There are a few reasons for the relatively small number of surviving early printed books. First, they were in most cases printed on paper which does not last as well as parchment and, most of all, could not be used as cover material for bailiffs' account books and so were not 'preserved' in this way. Therefore a greater number of medieval printed books than parchment manuscript books have simply been lost. Secondly, in 1488 the bishop of Turku Konrad Bitz, ordered the printing of a rather expensive folio–sized *Missale* for the needs of his diocese. This was done to give more uniformity to the liturgy of the diocese. The purchase of the *Missale aboense* would have strained parish resources and perhaps distracted from the acquisition of sermon collections. The bishop used his authority to persuade his diocesan clergy to acquire the *Missale* for their respective parishes. He promised forty days of indulgence for all those who did so, and furthermore, it is easy to imagine that it would have been rather difficult for individual priests to decline the bishop's offer.[40] As the priests were practically forced to acquire the *Missale*, they probably had fewer resources to buy other books, given the poverty of some of the Finnish parishes.

Despite all this, there still remains a significant number of early printed model sermon collections in Finnish libraries and archives. The most significant collection, that is, the Suomen Kansalliskirjasto in Helsinki, includes copies of seventeen early printed model sermon collections (listed in the Appendix). Furthermore, there are also a few copies of other early printed *praedicabilia*, for example, four copies of Jacopo da Varazze's *Legenda aurea* (Venezia, 1493; Basel, 1493; Lyon, 1504; and Rouen, 1510).[41]

---

39 Anne T. Thayer, *Penitence, Preaching and the Coming of the Reformation*, St Andrews Studies in Reformation History (Aldershot: Ashgate, 2002), pp. 13–20; Frymire, *The Primacy of the Postils*, pp. 12–13.

40 Tuomas Heikkilä, 'Painoa sanalle: ensimmäiset Suomea varten painetut kirjat', in *Kirjallinen kulttuuri keskiajan Suomessa*, ed. by Tuomas Heikkilä, Historiallisia Tutkimuksia, 254 (Helsinki: Suomalaisen Kirjallisuuden Seura, 2010), pp. 353–62. *Missale aboense* was printed by Bartholomeus Ghotan in Lübeck, it survives in sixteen partial copies. Heikkilä estimates that circa 120 to 200 copies were originally printed, some on parchment, some on paper.

41 This information is gathered from Suomen Kansalliskirjasto electronic catalogue: https:// helsinki.primo.exlibrisgroup.com/discovery/search?vid=358UOH_INST:VU1&lang=en [accessed 25 February 2021]. Here it is important to remember that these volumes need to be inspected one by one to find possible evidence of their provenance (the library catalogue

120   JUSSI HANSKA

To sum up, a few manucsripts, a few dozen fragments of manuscripts, and a handful of early printed books give us an impression that there indeed was a certain number of *praedicabilia* available for the clergy of Turku diocese. However, it needs to be kept in mind that they most likely present only a small minority of the material that once existed and so does not allow us to estimate their relative numbers compared to other areas in medieval Europe.

Indirect Evidence

Above we have analysed surviving direct evidence concerning preaching and sermons in medieval Finland. It is possible to complete the picture by taking a look at some other indirect evidence largely beyond the medieval period. First, there is some information available in later sources, such as the archives of the parishes and some individual sources, concerning sermon collections and *praedicabilia* books and manuscripts that have not survived. Some manuscript books and early printed books managed to survive the vandalism of Gustav Vasa's (1496–1560) bailiffs and came to be appreciated by collectors during the seventeenth and eighteenth centuries. Some books found their way into private collections in Sweden and even abroad; others were bought or donated to the university library of the Kungliga Akademien in Turku. For example, according to the surviving inventory of 6 May 1630, the rural parish of Kokemäki in western Finland still owned a *Sermones de sanctis* and a *Catalogus sanctorum* in octavo. The rector of the parish, Simon Cardiaster, donated these two manuscripts to the university library on 27 December 1651. The *Sermones de sanctis* collection was returned to Kokemäki because it appears again in the inventory of 1680 but after that all trace of it disappeared.[42] The fate of the *Catalogus sanctorum* was much more grim. The city of Turku burned down nearly *in extenso* in the great fire of 1827. This fire destroyed the university library completely and all of its holdings. The Turku fire also meant that the major part of surviving Finnish medieval manuscripts was lost, although we still have partial catalogues of the library that give us some indication of what was lost.[43]

---

does not include any information in this respect). It is very likely that at least in some cases these books have come to Finland only after the Middle Ages.

42   Tapio Salminen, *Joki ja sen väki: kokemäen ja Harjavallan historia jääkaudesta 1860-luvulle*, Kokemäen ja Harjavallan historia, I:1 (Jyväskylä: Kokemäen ja Harjavallan seurakunnat ja kaupungit, 2007), p. 282.

43   *Bibliotheca Academiae Aboensis sive elenchus quo non modo certus scriptorum et librorum cujusque facultatis numeratus ordine alphabetico continetur, sed etiam ex quo initio, quibus incrementis, quorumve liberalitate et munificentia bibliotheca haec academica, ad tantam, qua nunc est, excrevit molem, paucis indicatur* (Åbo: Typographica academica, 1655). Digitized: https://www.doria.fi/bitstream/handle/10024/119801/Bibliotheca_Academiae_Aboensis_ sive_elenchus_quo_non_modo_ce.pdf?sequence=1&isAllowed=y [accessed 21 June 2022]. Most of the books in the catalogue are from the post-Reformation period, but there were

PREACHING IN FINLAND ON THE EVE OF THE REFORMATION AND BEYOND   121

Another place to search for information concerning lost medieval material are the inventory books of the parish churches. By the end of the Middle Ages the diocese of Turku had approximately one hundred parishes and roughly thirty chapels that eventually became independent parishes in modern times. Nearly all of them have surviving inventories, the oldest ones dating from the first decades of the seventeenth century. Most of these inventories provide information concerning books owned by the parish. Some of them are reasonably detailed; others use generic expressions such as the short notice one finds in the inventories of 1774 from Tammela parish church: 'Legenda monachorum in folio'.[44] An exceptional number of medieval books, both manuscripts and fragments of manuscripts, from Tammela parish have survived: fragments of a gradual, an antiphonary, and a copy of the *Missale aboense* (printed in 1488) are all now stored at the Suomen Kansalliskirjasto in Helsinki.[45] One can legitimately doubt the expertise of an eighteenth-century priest who wrote the inventory with regard to the proper identification of some medieval text; moreover, it is hardly possible that the book referred to can be any of the surviving Tammela books or fragments. However, it is possible to speculate what it might have been. First of all, one should not pay any attention to the word 'monachorum' as all the medieval books and

---

a few manucripts and early printed books by medieval authors such as Nicolaus de Lyra, Thomas Aquinas, Robert Holcot, and so on. Furthermore, this catalogue predates the period of bibliophilic interest in medieval books and manuscripts and therefore it is plausible that the number of such volumes increased between the printing of the catalogue and the great fire of 1827. We get some further information from the history of the library of the Kungliga Akademien i Åbo published by its librarian (1772–1777), Professor Henrik Gabriel Porthan, in twenty-five *fasciculi* published between 1771 and 1795. Porthan tells us that during the 1650s fourteen different rural parishes and their clergy donated thirty-five books (presumably medieval manuscripts and early printed books) to the library. He also gives a description of manuscripts and early printed books. Among these he mentions manuscripts: Gregory the Great, *Moralia in Job* and Raymund Peñaforte, *Summa de penitentia* as well as several printed model sermon collections and other volumes useful for preachers: Birgitta of Sweden's *Revelationes* (printed in 1492 in Lübeck), Antonino da Firenze's *Confessionale* (Memming, 1483), (Pseudo-)Thomas Aquinas, *Tractatus solennis de arte et vero modo predicandi* (printed in 1483 no mention of the place), Roberto Caracciolo da Lecce, *Sermones de laudibus sanctorum* (Venezia, 1490), François de Mayronnes, *Sermones quadragesimales* (Venezia, 1491), Vicent Ferrer, *Tractatus de vita et instructione pie in Christo vivere volentium* (Magdeburg, 1494), Angelo Carletti di Chivasso, *Summa angelica de casibus conscientie* (Strasbourg, 1495), Johannes Herolt, *Liber de eruditione Christi fidelium* (Köln, 1496), Jacopo da Varazze, *Lombardica historia* (Nürnberg, 1501), Petrus Comestor, *Historia Scolastica* (Strasbourg, 1503); Henrik Gabriel Porthan, *Historia bibliothecae regiae academiae Aboensis*, 25 vols (Åbo: Frenckell, 1771–1795), II (1772), 26–27; XI (1783), 156–57, and XV (1785), 227–29.

44 Tammela Parish Archive, Inventories 1774–1855, p. 7, digitized in the digital archive of the Suomen Kansallisarkisto: http://digi.narc.fi/digi/view.ka?kuid=6705941 [accessed 25 February 2021].

45 Jesse Keskiaho, 'Seurakuntien ja seurakuntapappien kirjat', in *Kirjallinen kulttuuri keskiajan Suomessa*, ed. by Tuomas Heikkilä, Historiallisia Tutkimuksia, 254 (Helsinki: Suomalaisen Kirjallisuuden Seura, 2010), pp. 265–67.

manuscript in parish inventories were generally described 'möncke böcker' ['monk books']. Considering that it is a printed book and that the title seems to refer to saints' legends, it is perhaps not too far-fetched to assume that it was Jacopo da Varazze's *Legenda aurea* that was available in numerous folio-size editions. While it has not been possible here to research systematically all the inventories of the parish archives, the above-mentioned cases of Kokemäki and Tammela parishes clearly indicate that they may provide us with further indirect evidence of pre-Reformation preaching in Finland.

The Lutheran Reformation and Preaching in Finland

As we have seen previously, the first generation of Reformation commentators in Finland, Mikael Agricola and Paulus Juusten, did not give us a very flattering picture of preaching at the end of the medieval period. The implicit — and sometimes explicit — message of the reformers was that things were now generally better than they had been during the Catholic period, and especially when it came to preaching. This invites us to assume that the quantity and quality of the preaching must have improved after the Reformation. If that is true, one would expect to see some evidence of such an improvement in the form of more frequent mentions of preachers and sermons, new homiletic works and postils in print, and signs of popular devotion to evangelical preaching of the Word of God. In practice none of this happened.

Paulus Juusten's Chronicle has not a word to say about evangelical preaching during the first decades of the Reformation era. He only mentions that his predecessor, Mikael Agricola, preached at Turku as well as during Bishop Martinus Skytte's visitation tours. Even this mention actually tells more about Catholic and Lutheran preaching as it took place before Agricola was sent to study in Wittenberg and was seriously exposed to Luther and his new learning.[46] Agricola came to Turku in 1528 and thus encountered the preaching and teaching of the Lutheran priest and schoolmaster Petrus Särkilax. However, Särkilax died the following year and therefore one cannot know how seriously he influenced Agricola. Mikael Agricola was ordained by Bishop Martinus Skytte who was not Lutheran but rather a Catholic bishop who was not that keen on the Lutheran Reformation, but did not consider it wise to stand against King Gustaf Vasa's Church politics. One may doubt that Bishop Skytte would have ordained anyone who was militantly Lutheran, not to mention promoting such a person as his chancellor. Agricola's preaching, alluded to by Juusten, took place between his ordination in 1530 and his departure for Wittenberg in 1536.[47] One can assume that at the time Agricola's Lutheranism was very mild, if it existed at all.

---

46 Juusten, *Catalogus et ordinaria successio episcoporum finlandensium*, p. 74.
47 Simo Heininen, *Mikael Agricola: Elämä ja teokset* (Helsinki: Edita, 2007), pp. 45–47.

After his return from Wittenberg, Agricola had certainly internalized Lutheran doctrines, otherwise Martin Luther and Philipp Melanchthon would hardly have provided him with letters of recommendation for King Gustav. Undoubtedly, Agricola did preach in Turku and as a bishop during his visitation tours to parishes in the Åland archipelago in 1544, and to the northern parishes of the diocese in 1555.[48] However, Agricola's literary activities had very little to do with preaching. Between 1543 and 1552 he published nine books in the Finnish vernacular.[49] These did not include postils or any other *praedicabilia* which is rather surprising considering the traditional view of the importance of vernacular preaching for the reformers.

Furthermore, Agricola's own view of evangelical preaching in Finland two decades into the Reformation was rather pessimistic. He writes in the prologue to his vernacular translation of the Psalter (1551):

Wai eike se pappein wirca ole?
Studera, saarnaa ia rucole.
Hwij häpie, se wähä quin kirioitetan,
haruoin se sarnatan eli luetan.
Quingas wastat sen Herran domios,
ettes aighas culutat laiskuos.
Oij sine surckia locasecki,
etkös neite mieleses ecke
Haiseua raato oleuas,
ia matoin eues cooltuas?
Ios sine sis wircas hitas teet,
niin carta cuhungas wiimein ieet.

> [Isn't it the duty of a priest
> to study, preach and pray?
> Woe! It is a shame how little is written,
> how rarely it is preached and read out aloud.
> How will you answer at the Lord's Judgement Day
> if you spend your time in idleness?
> Oh you miserable bag of dirt!
> Don't you understand
> that you are just a stinking corpse
> and food for worms once you die?
> If you do your duties half-heartedly,
> you will have to fear where you will spend your eternity].[50]

---

48 Juusten, *Catalogus et ordinaria successio episcoporum finlandensium*, p. 77.

49 Heininen, *Mikael Agricola*, p. 156. Agricola wrote an ABC-book (1543), a Prayer Book (1544), a Finnish translation of the New Testament (1548), a Handbook for Baptism and other Sacraments (1549), a Finnish Mass (1549), a tractate on the Passion of Christ (1549), and a Psalter (1551).

50 This poem is quoted in Heininen, *Mikael Agricola*, pp. 311–12. The translation is my own.

There is no doubt that Agricola is addressing his readers, that is, his contemporary Finnish priests, and not their Catholic predecessors. Allowing for the normal rhetorical exaggeration typical of such prologues, one still gets the impression that the Finnish priests' zeal in their duties in general, and especially when it came to preaching, left much to be desired. There was very little to help priests in their preaching activities. During the first hundred years of the Reformation period there were no printed Finnish language *postillae* available for the parish priests. The first Finnish postil was written by Bishop Paulus Juusten in 1570. This postil, however, was never printed. The library of the Kungliga Akademien in Turku purchased Juusten's autograph copy in 1738. This manuscript was destroyed in the great fire of Turku in 1827 and no other manuscripts are known to have existed.[51] (The first Finnish language postil or collection of sermons for the Sundays of the Church year, which was actually printed came out in two volumes in 1621 and 1625 respectively — nearly a hundred years after the beginning of the Reformation in the Swedish realm. This postil, quoting heavily from German fifteenth-and sixteenth-century Lutheran postils, was also written by a bishop of Turku, Ericus Erici Sorolainen (d. 1625).[52])

Fortunately, Juusten's prologue was copied before the fire and so survives. In it, he produces a more optimistic view of his contemporary clergy than Agricola had written two decades earlier. Juusten had to admit that the Mass had lost much of its ornateness and worldly pomp, but — he added — otherwise things are better. Sermons are preached in towns daily and on Sundays and feast days there are three sermons a day![53] However, Juusten does not tell us anything about the situation in rural parishes where more than 95 percent of the faithful lived The difference in Agricola's and Juusten's testimonies seems to imply that by the 1570s Turku diocese was slowly starting to recover from the religious and economic shock of the Lutheran Reformation. However, one must not jump to conclusions on the basis of two sources, both of a polemical nature.

The Slow Reformation and the Continuity of Catholicism

There are two significant reasons why the evangelical preaching revolution never happened. First, the Reformation in Finland happened very slowly indeed. It began in the 1520s when the first Lutheran-minded clergymen started to work and preach at the cathedral town of Turku, and during the following decade when the Church ceremonies also began to adopt the new

---

51 Simo Heininen, *Agricolan perintö: Paulus Juustenin elämä* (Helsinki: Edita, 2012), p. 144.
52 Erkki Kouri, *Saksalaisen käyttökirjallisuuden vaikutus Suomessa 1600-luvulla: Ericus Ericin postillan lähteet*, Suomen Kirkkohistoriallisen Seuran Toimituksia, 129 (Helsinki: Suomen Kirkkohistoriallinen Seura, 1984), p. 20. For a resumé in German, see pp. 293–307.
53 Heininen, *Agricolan perintö*, p. 148.

Lutheran features in the rural parishes. However, these changes in Finland were cautious and slow. In fact, it could be claimed that the Reformation was truly only carried out in Finland in 1599 when Gustaf Vasa's son Duke Karl of Södermanland (later King Karl IX, 1604–1611), triumphed over the Catholic King Sigismund (1592–1599) in southern Sweden and also conquered Finland from the noblemen loyal to the king. Pro-Catholic clergy left the country and in 1617, as the so-called Lutheran orthodoxy became gradually more and more intolerant, the Catholic faith was banned on pain of death.[54] While it is questionable when the Reformation actually happened in Finland, it certainly was far from being established fully by Luther's death in 1546.

The sources for the attitudes of the Finnish clergy towards the Reformation during the early decades of the Lutheran era are very scarce. However, there are some sources that shed some light on the situation further away from the bishop's seat at Turku. In 1554, that is, roughly two decades after the Reformation really started in Sweden, the Swedish priest Hans Pauli Montanus was imprisoned at Hämeenlinna castle in Finland because of his religious disobedience. Montanus's public practice of Catholicism annoyed Gustaf Vasa and led to his imprisonment. In Hämeenlinna castle Hans Pauli found sympathizers, including the bailiff of the castle. Therefore, he was able to get his hands on writing materials and to write a *postilla* for the whole year in two volumes. His books had been confiscated by the king's officials, but he found local help and was able to borrow material from the vicinity of the castle. Most likely those books came from the surrounding parishes. When Johan III became king in 1568, Hans Pauli was released and was able to return to Sweden. He ended up working as a chaplain for the nuns that still resided in Vadstena Abbey. Therefore his Postil became part of the Vadstena library and from there it was removed to Uppsala universitetsbibliotek where it is still housed.[55] Hans Pauli's Postil is not the most glorious example of the genre, but what is interesting is that he gives a list of his source books, that is, the books he managed to borrow from the vicinity of Hämeenlinna castle. In addition to patristic works that could have been acceptable to the Lutheran ecclesiastical authorities such as Augustine, Ambrose, and Gregory the Great, we also have the Sunday sermon collection by the Dominican Ugo da Prato that most certainly was not material that any Lutheran bishop would have accepted for priests of his diocese.[56]

---

54 Jyrki Knuutila, 'Resistance to the Reformation in 16th-Century Finland', in *Lived Religion and the Long Reformation in Northern Europe c. 1300–1700*, ed. by Sari Katajala-Peltomaa and Raisa Maria Toivo, Studies in Medieval and Reformation Traditions, 206 (Leiden: Brill, 2016), pp. 255–73 (pp. 256 and 271).

55 Magnus Nyman, *Förlorarnas historia: katolskt liv i Sverige från Gustav Vasa till drottning Kristina* (Stockholm: Veritas, 2002), pp. 121–25.

56 Hans Pauli Montanus, *Postilla*, Tomus I, Uppsala universitetsbibliotek, MS C 41a, fol. 3r. The manuscript is available at the website of the *Codices Fennici*-project [accessed 25 February 2021]. On Ugo da Prato, see Thomas Kaeppeli, *Scriptores ordinis praedicatorum medii aevi*, 4 vols (Roma: Istituto Storico Domenicano, 1970–1993), II (1975), 258–60.

126 JUSSI HANSKA

The fact that Ugo da Prato's Sunday sermon collection was still available in one of the parishes around Hämeenlinna castle not only provides us with one more clue about the *praedicabilia* that existed in pre-Reformation Finland, but it also gives us the impression that not all Finnish priests were ready to renounce Catholicism even in the 1550s. Indeed, there are some indications that not all the priests were particularly happy with the new situation. As late as 1573, Bishop Paulus Juusten saw it necessary to exhort the priests of his diocese to suffer poverty, not to despise their calling or to think that they had been forsaken by God, and — most of all — not to leave their posts.[57]

Another interesting source concerning the situation in Finland is the Jesuit Antonio Possevino's report in 1580 to Pope Gregory XIII concerning the situation in the Swedish realm. Possevino writes that King Johan III had decided to reintroduce the Catholic faith and that there would not be any great problem in reconverting people as they already are, especially in Götaland (the southernmost part of medieval Sweden) and in Finland, inclined towards the old religion and love the old order and ceremonies.[58] It is clear that Possevino was overly optimistic and perhaps also exaggerating on purpose to please his lord and master. However, it is interesting that Götaland and Finland are mentioned as more inclined towards Catholicism than the rest of Sweden. From the point of view of Lutheran preaching during the Reformation era if, as it seems, there were priests who still held either open or secret Catholic sympathies, then one must assume that they were not particularly keen on preaching God's Word in pure evangelical fashion in accordance with resolutions at the Diet of Västerås in 1527 as the demanded by Lutheran reformers. In fact, it is possible that simultaneously with the new Lutheran preaching there continued some remnants of Catholic preaching for some time.

Gustaf Vasa's Plundering of the Church

The second reason for the lack of the revolution in preaching was materialistic. The Reformation in Sweden and hence in Finland meant economic disaster for the Church. The loss of property and revenues made it very difficult for the Church to organize the education of the clergy and, moreover, to attract capable young men to a clerical career. Serving the Chuch did not guarantee a comfortable life anymore, but rather an everyday battle to make

---

Ugo's *Sermones de tempore super evangelia et epistolas* was printed sixteen times before 1520 and it is most likely that the edition Johannes Pauli was using was one of these early printed books rather than a manuscript.

57 Knuutila, 'Resistance to the Reformation in 16th-Century Finland', p. 266.

58 Quoted in Nyman, *Förlorarnas historia*, p. 66: 'Ne si vede grande difficoltà alla riduttione de populi […] altra parte i populi sono inclinata alla religione antica, et massima in Gothia, et in Finlandia, et sono amatori della vecchia disciplina et ceremonie'.

PREACHING IN FINLAND ON THE EVE OF THE REFORMATION AND BEYOND 127

ends meet. Furthermore, depriving the Church of its property and political power meant also that the Church's prestige, authority, and even credibility in the eyes of the parishioners collapsed. The Church did not provide rural parishioners with blessings for their fields and did not guarantee the help of Christ and the saints against famine, torrential rain, floods, frost, and the other hardships that threatened their daily lives. Therefore, the parishioners no longer found themselves obliged to support the Church any more than they were forced to do by royal tax collectors. They saw that the taxes that used to go to the Church, the local parish, and for the benefit of the sick and poor, now ended up in the bottomless chests of the king far away in Sweden.[59] Gustav Vasa's confiscations hit the Church hard. During the 1540s the clergy of the cathedral town of Turku lost three-quarters of its income and the rural clergy roughly half of theirs. This radical change in economic conditions made it difficult to send students to foreign universities and for the clergy to buy the necessary books to help them with their preaching duties. The few remaining resources had to be allocated to the liturgical books that the king's decision to unify liturgy in the whole of Sweden demanded. Mikael Agricola wrote on 11 December 1543 to Gustav Vasa's chancellor Georg Norman and complained about the low quality of his students at Turku cathedral school. He stated that some vicious person had disseminated a false rumour among the people that priests' income would be totally withdrawn by the Crown. In reality, the rumour was perfectly true and well-informed. Therefore, smaller and smaller numbers of young men came to study to enter a clerical career.[60]

Conclusion

Most of the preaching materials from the Catholic Middle Ages in Finland have disappeared through natural causes, fires, or as a result of post-Reformation vandalism. Therefore, it is extremely difficult to establish what preaching in medieval Finland was like. At the current state of research we know of two surviving model sermon collections in manuscript (by Clemens Petri), fewer than fifty early printed sermon collections or other preaching aids, and a few dozen fragments of parchment ripped from *praedicabilia* manuscripts and re-used as covers of bailifs' account books. In many cases it is not absolutely certain that these sermon manuscripts and books were in Finland during the Middle Ages. It is possible that they were bought and brought to the country by individual collectors or belonged to the booty brought home by the Swedish armies during the wars of the seventeenth century. This material can be complemented by a handful of mentions concerning preaching in chronicles and other surviving written documents. Furthermore, there

---

59 Knuutila, 'Resistance to the Reformation in 16th-Century Finland', p. 262.
60 Heininen, *Mikael Agricola*, p. 107.

is indirect evidence of medieval sermon materials and preaching. A few mentions of medieval manuscripts and early printed books are found in the seventeenth- and eighteenth-century parish inventories.

The quantity and quality of these surviving sources do not allow us to conclude how common a practice preaching was in medieval Finland. However, it does prove that there was some preaching and that at least some priests saw it as important to obtain model sermon collections and other *praedicabilia* literature for that purpose. Furthermore, the small amount of surviving material needs to be seen in proportion to the fact that, as noted previously, the diocese of Turku, even if it covered a wide geographical area, only had about a hundred parishes and at most 300,000 people living in it. Taking into account the small number of parishes and scarce population, the surviving sources and indirect evidence presented above seem to suggest perhaps that the quantity of preaching was not so different from many parts of the rest of Europe.

The Reformation in Finland was carried out over an extended period of time. The first Lutheran bishops provided a rather pessimistic and propagandistic picture of Church life in general and preaching in particular during the Catholic period. However, in the light of current research the situation does not seem to have been that hopeless, and it certainly did not improve with the Lutheran Reformation. On the contrary, it seems that the educational level of the clergy dropped and preaching was not particular common, especially during the first decades of the Lutheran period. During the seventeenth century things began to improve and the Church recuperated from the economic damages of the Reformation.

Despite the difficulties of lacking or destroyed sources, this essay shows that it has been possible to re-construct and present a picture of medieval and early modern preaching, sermon manuscripts, and printed sermon collections in Finland by using indirect sources in a creative manner. The puzzle has been put together and the picture is recognizable even if the majority of the pieces have been lost.

Appendix: Early Printed Model Sermon Collections from the Suomen Kansalliskirjasto in Helsinki

[see n. 41].

Albertus Magnus, *Sermones de tempore et de sanctis* (Ulm, c. 1478–1480)

Antonio da Bitonto, *Sermones dominicales per totum annum* (Venezia, 1492)

Antonio da Bitonto, *Sermones de epistolas dominicales et quadragesimales* (Venezia, 1496)

Antonio da Vercelli, *Sermones quadragesimales de xii mirabilibus fidei excellentiis* (Venezia, 1492)

Bernard de Clairvaux, *Sermones de tempore et de sanctis* (Venezia, 1495)

Bernardino da Busti, *Mariale* (Milano, 1493)

Guillaume Peyraut, *Sermones de tempore et de sanctis* (Tübingen, 1499)

Jacopo da Varazze, *Sermones quadragesimales, de tempore et de sanctis* (Venezia, 1497; three volumes)

Johannes de Verden, *Dormi secure de tempore* (Basel, before 1484)

Leonardo da Udine, *Sermones de sanctis* (Köln, 1473)

Leonardo da Udine, *Sermones quadragesimales de legibus* (Venezia, 1473)

Leonardo da Udine, *Sermones floridi de tempore* (Lyon, 1496)

Meffreth, *Sermones de tempore et de sanctis sive Hortulus reginae* (Nürnberg, 1487)

Pseudo-Pierre de Palude, *Sermones thesauri novi de tempore* (Strasbourg, 1497)

Roberto Caracciolo, *Sermones quadragesimales de poenitentia* (Basel, 1475, and Venezia, 1482)

Ugo da Prato, *Sermones de sanctis* (Heidelberg, 1485)

Vicent Ferrer, *Sermones de tempore et de sanctis, tom. 2 pars aestivalis* (Nürnberg, 1492)

Bibliography

Manuscripts

Uppsala, Uppsala universitetsbibliotek, MS C 41a

Primary Sources

Bibliotheca Academiae Aboensis sive elenchus quo non modo certus scriptorum et librorum cujusque facultatis numeratus ordine alphabetico continetur, sed etiam ex quo initio, quibus incrementis, quorumve liberalitate et munificentia bibliotheca haec academica, ad tantam, qua nunc est, excrevit molem, paucis indicatur (Åbo: Typographica academica, 1655)

De S. Henrico episcopo et martyre: die mittelalterliche Literatur über den Apostel Finnlands. II: *Legenda nova. Sermones*, ed. by Aarno Maliniemi, Suomen Kirkkohistoriallisen Seuran Tutkimuksia, 45 (Helsinki: Suomen Kirkkohistoriallinen Seura, 1942), II

Diarium Vadstenense: The Memorial Book of Vadstena Abbey, ed. by Claes Gejrot, Studia Latina Stockholmensia, 33 (Stockholm: Almqvist & Wiksell, 1988)

Finlands Medeltidsurkunder, ed. by Reinhold Hausen, 8 vols (Helsinki: Finlands statsarkiv, 1910–1935)

Henrik Gabriel Porthan, *Henrici Gabrielis Porthan Opera omnia*, 13 vols (Turku: Porthan-Seura, 1939–2007)

Henrik Gabriel Porthan, *Historia Bibliothecae Regiae Academiae Aboënsis*, 25 vols (Åbo: Frenckell, 1771–1795)

Henrik Gabriel Porthan, *Historiola concionum sacrarum fennicarum* (Åbo: Frenckell, 1781)

Peregrinus de Oppeln, *Peregrini de Opole Sermones de tempore et de sanctis: e codicis manu scriptis primum*, ed. by Richardus Tatarzyński, Studia 'Przegladu Tomistycnego', 1 (Warszawa: Instytut Tomistyczny, 1997)

Vadstenadiariet: latinsk text med översättning och kommentar, ed. by Claes Gejrot, Handlingar, 19 (Stockholm: Kungliga Samfundet för utgivande av handskrifter rörande Skandinaviens historia, 1996)

Secondary Studies

Andersson, Roger, *De birgittinska ordensprästerna som traditionsförmedlare och folkfostrare*, Runica et Mediaevalia, Scripta minora, 4 (Stockholm: Sällskapet Runica et Mediaevalia, 2001)

Andersson, Roger, 'Översättaren som predikant: Clemens Petri och svenska språket', in *Dicit Scriptura: studier i C-samlingen tillägnade Monica Hedlund*, ed. by Sara Risberg, Sällskapet Runica et Mediaevalia, Scripta minora, 14 (Stockholm: Sällskapet Runica et Mediaevalia, 2006), pp. 149–64

Andersson, Roger, *Postillor och predikan: en medeltida texttradition i filologisk och funktionell belysning*, Sällskapet Runica et Mediaevalia, Scripta minora, 1 (Stockholm: Runica et Mediaevalia, 1993)

Andersson, Roger, *Predikosamlingar i Vadstena klosterbibliotek: Vadstenabrödernas predikan*, Meddelanden, 1 (Uppsala: Uppsala universitet, Institutionen för klassiska språk, 1996)

Andersson-Schmitt, Margarete, and Monica Hedlund, *Mittelalterlichen Handschriften der Universitätsbibliothek Uppsala: Katalog über die C-Sammlung*, Acta Bibliothecae R. Universitatis Upsaliensis, 26, 8 vols (Stockholm: Almqvist & Wiksell, 1988–1995)

Borgehammar, Stephan, 'Preaching to Pilgrims: Ad vincula Sermons at Vadstena Abbey', in *A Catalogue and Its Users: A Symposium on the Uppsala C Collection of Medieval Manuscripts*, ed. by Monica Hedlund, Acta Bibliothecae R. Universitatis Upsalensis, 34 (Uppsala: Almqvist & Wiksell, 1995), pp. 91–100

Esch, Arnold, 'Le fonti per la storia economica e sociale di Roma nel Rinascimento', in *Economia e società a Roma tra Medioevo e Rinascimento*, ed. by Anna Esposito and Luciano Palermo, Libri di Viella, 51 (Roma: Viella, 2005), pp. 1–32

Frymire, John M., *The Primacy of the Postils: Catholics, Protestants, and the Dissemination of Ideas in Early Modern Germany*, Studies in Medieval and Reformation Traditions, 147 (Leiden: Brill, 2010)

Hedlund, Monica, 'The Use of Model Sermons at Vadstena: A Case Study', in *Constructing the Medieval Sermon*, ed. by Roger Andersson, Sermo: Studies on Patristic, Medieval, and Reformation Sermons and Preaching, 6 (Turnhout: Brepols, 2007), pp. 117–64

Heikkilä, Tuomas, 'Kirjallistumisen jäljillä', in *Kirjallinen kulttuuri keskiajan Suomessa*, ed. by Tuomas Heikkilä, Historiallisia Tutkimuksia, 254 (Helsinki: Suomalaisen Kirjallisuuden Seura, 2010), pp. 11–61

Heikkilä, Tuomas, 'Painoa sanalle: ensimmäiset Suomea varten painetut kirjat', in *Kirjallinen kulttuuri keskiajan Suomessa*, ed. by Tuomas Heikkilä, Historiallisia Tutkimuksia, 254 (Helsinki: Suomalaisen Kirjallisuuden Seura, 2010), pp. 350–66

Heininen, Simo, *Agricolan perintö: Paulus Juustenin elämä* (Helsinki: Edita, 2012)

Heininen, Simo, *Mikael Agricola: Elämä ja teokset* (Helsinki: Edita, 2007)

Heininen, Simo, *Suomalaisen historian kirjoituksen synty: tutkimus Paavali Juustenin piispainkronikasta*, Suomen Kirkkohistoriallisen Seuran Tutkmuksia, 147 (Helsinki: Suomen Kirkkohistoriallinen Seura, 1989)

Hiekkanen, Markus, *The Stone Churches of the Medieval Diocese of Turku: A Systematic Classification and Chronology*, Suomen Muinaismuistoyhdistyksen Aikakauskirja, 101 (Helsinki: Suomen Muinaismuistoyhdistys, 1994)

Juusten, Paulus, *Catalogus et ordinaria successio episcoporum finlandensium*, ed. by Simo Heininen (Helsinki: Societas Historiae Ecclesiastica Finlandiae, 1988)

Kaeppeli, Thomas, *Scriptores ordinis praedicatorum medii aevi*, 4 vols (Roma: Istituto Storico Domenicano, 1970–1993)

Keskiaho, Jesse, 'Pappien koulutus ja Oppineen papiston kirjat', in *Kirjallinen kulttuuri keskiajan Suomessa*, ed. by Tuomas Heikkilä, Historiallisia Tutkimuksia, 254 (Helsinki: Suomalaisen Kirjallisuuden Seura, 2010), pp. 147–81

Keskiaho, Jesse, 'Seurakuntien ja seurakuntapappien kirjat', in *Kirjallinen kulttuuri keskiajan Suomessa*, ed. Tuomas Heikkilä, Historiallisia Tutkimuksia, 254 (Helsinki: Suomalaisen Kirjallisuuden Seura, 2010), pp. 256–67

Knuutila, Jyrki, 'Resistance to the Reformation in 16th-Century Finland', in *Lived Religion and the Long Reformation in Northern Europe c. 1300–1700*, ed. by Sari Katajala-Peltomaa and Raisa Maria Toivo, Studies in Medieval and Reformation Traditions, 206 (Leiden: Brill, 2016), pp. 255–73

Kouri, Erkki, *Saksalaisen käyttökirjallisuuden vaikutus Suomessa 1600-luvulla: Ericus Ericin postillan lähteet*, Suomen Kirkkohistoriallisen Seuran Toimituksia, 129 (Helsinki: Suomen Kirkkohistoriallinen Seura, 1984)

Lamberg, Marko, *Jöns Budde: Birgittalaisveli ja hänen teoksensa*, Suomalaisen Kirjallisuuden Seuran Toimituksia, 1115 (Helsinki: Suomalaisen Kirjallisuuden Seura, 2007)

Leinberg, K. G., 'Företalet till P. Iwstens Postilla', *Historiallinen Arkisto*, 19 (1905), 268–69

Meersseman, G., 'Le opere di fra Antonio Azaro Parmense', *Archivum Fratrum Praedicatorum*, 10 (1940), 20–47

Nyman, Magnus, *Förlorarnas historia: katolskt liv i Sverige från Gustav Vasa till drottning Kristina* (Stockholm: Veritas, 2002)

Salminen, Tapio, *Joki ja sen väki: kokemäen ja Harjavallan historia jääkaudesta 1860-luvulle*, Kokemäen ja Harjavallan historia, I:1 (Jyväskylä: Kokemäen ja Harjavallan seurakunnat ja kaupungit, 2007)

Schneyer, Johannes Baptist, *Repertorium der lateinischen Sermones des Mittelalters für die Zeit von 1150–1350*, Beiträge zur Geschichte der Philosophie und Theologie des Mittelalters: Texte und Untersuchungen, 43, 11 vols (Münster: Aschendorffsche Verlagsbuchhandlung, 1969–1990)

Thayer, Anne T., *Penitence, Preaching and the Coming of the Reformation*, St Andrews Studies in Reformation History (Aldershot: Ashgate, 2002)

JONATHAN ADAMS

Christiern Pedersen's
Alle Epistler oc Euangelia (1515)

Reading a Catholic Text in the Danish Reformation

Medieval Danish Vernacular Sermons

The extant corpus of medieval vernacular manuscripts and early prints from Denmark has been shaped and, it must be said, decimated by a series of events and ideologies that have had calamitous consequences for the preservation of Old Danish literature. The destruction of Catholic works during and after the Reformation, the numerous fires that ravaged libraries and collections (not least the Great Fire of Copenhagen in 1728 that destroyed the university library), the tastes and whims of collectors and their skill (or lack thereof) in care and conservation have all left a mark. The nemesis of medieval religious literature in this part of the world was, of course, the Lutheran Reformation. In 1536 Christian III (1503–1559) came to power after a successful coup and immediately set about pushing through the Reformation and making Lutheranism the official religion in Denmark. Saints, relics, fast days and feasts, celibacy, Confession, Latin liturgy, and the Divine Office — all that was part and parcel of late medieval devotion — were swept away overnight. However, nuns and monks were, for the most part, allowed to stay in their convents and monasteries: only when the last sister or brother died did the house go to the Crown. Similarly, priests could keep their churches until they passed away. Thus, the Reformation in Denmark is often viewed as a 'bloodless', gentle affair that liberated the kingdom from the 'folly of *papisteri*' with little serious opposition and that introduced worship in the mother tongue with the Bible at its core.[1] Although little human blood was shed, destructive violence

---

1 Of course this interpretation completely ignores the fact that events were not quite as benign in other parts of the kingdom. For example, in Iceland there was significant opposition to the king's efforts to make the country Protestant. Only when Jón Árason, the Catholic bishop of Hólar, was executed along with his two sons in 1550 was the country converted. Although 'arcane' Latin was removed from the liturgy, Danish, rather than their mother tongue, came

> **Jonathan Adams** (jonathan.adams@gu.se) is a Researcher in the Department of Historical Studies at the University of Gothenburg.

Circulating the Word of God in Medieval and Early Modern Europe: Catholic Preaching and Preachers across Manuscript and Print (c. 1450 to c. 1550), ed. by Veronica O'Mara and Patricia Stoop, SERMO 17, (Turnhout: Brepols, 2022), pp. 133–160   BREPOLS ❧ PUBLISHERS   10.1484/M.SERMO-EB.5.130454

was wrought against the material and intellectual culture and accoutrements of the now rejected faith. As Latin was no longer of use in the Church and religious works in both Latin and the vernacular contained Catholic teachings and 'errors', manuscripts, along with relics and religious art, such as church wall-paintings, statues, and stained-glass windows, were destroyed in the years after the Reformation.[2] Monastic and cathedral libraries were scattered to the four winds and their manuscripts' parchment folios were cut up and used in book bindings, as fire-lighters and cloths for cleaning out gun-barrels, as cartridges for fireworks and rockets, or simply thrown into the street.[3] A revealing eye-witness account by Kristen Sørensen Testrup (1685–1761) of the sale of Viborg Cathedral's large wooden trunks in 1700–1702 provides us with an insight into what probably was not an exceptional fate for hundreds of medieval documents:

> I Viborg Dom-kirke var i min tiid et Capel ganske fuldt af Jernbundne Munke-kister, som laae fulde af breve. Disße Kister stode stablede oven paa hinanden til op imod Hvælvingen, Men da den bekendte Biskop Deichman Engang fik i sinde at selge samme Capel til et begravelse, bleve disße Kister udrÿddede, og solte til tieneste folk og deslige, som væltede brevene deraf udenfor Kirke-Dören, hvor de blev nedtraad og ved en stor Skyl-Regn flöd bort i gader og rendestenen; Mig kom deraf siden nogle for ögen, som en Person i Viborg ongefæhr havde optaget, hvoraf kunde sees, at i disße Kister var eÿ alene Munkebreve, Regenskaber og andre Documenter [...] Jeg kom og over en gammel Closter-bog in folio, som var skrevet meget || curieus paa Pergament i Form af en Calender, hvor alle Helgens navne vare skrevne med röt eller anden farve, og et stort Rum jmellem hver, for derhos at tegne, hvilke afdöde paa den Dag skulde siunges mesße for, og hvad de derfor havde givet til Closteret, samt hvor de laae i Kirken begravet, alt paa de tiiders usle latin [...] For i samme bog var og

---

to be imposed upon the Faroe Islanders and Norwegians as their language of worship. This had huge consequences for the development of Faroese and Norwegian in the centuries to follow.

2 However, it should be noted that in many churches, wall paintings, as long as they were biblical or purely decorative — and not of saints, legends, or popes — were not whitewashed; their useful didactic purpose was recognized. Surprisingly, there are some cases of wall-paintings of saints that date from after the Reformation, for example: St Laurence ('sanctus larense') in Auning Church, Jutland, painted according to the inscription in 1562, and St Christopher in Gørløse Church, Sjælland, painted in 1550–1560. Other wall paintings were renovated in the years following the Reformation, for example, the paintings in Estruplund Church, Jutland, were improved according to an inscription on the chancel arch in 1542. Indeed, it would seem that a great deal of the whitewashing of church walls was due more to a change in aesthetic or a lack of funding or interest in renovation than to anti-Catholic zeal.

3 On the destruction and remains of medieval Danish book collections, see Lauritz Nielsen, *Danmarks Middelalderlige Haandskrifter: en sammenfattende boghistorisk Oversigt* (København: Gyldendal, 1937), pp. 163–81.

CHRISTIERN PEDERSEN'S *ALLE EPISTLER OC EUANGELIA* (1515)

giort nogle Statuta, hvor iblant at de eÿ maatte spytte i Choret, Denne bog tilligemed flere Documenter og Antiqviteter bekom Prof. Arnas Magnus[4] af mig i Aaret 1720, hvor de maaskee blev öde i Kiöbenhafns brand.[5]

[During my lifetime there was a chapel in Viborg Cathedral filled with iron-clad 'monk chests' that were full of letters. These chests stood stacked up on top of each other into the vaulted ceiling, but when the well-known Bishop Deichmann got it into his head to sell this very chapel for a burial [plot], these chests were cleared out and sold to servants and the like, who tipped out the letters right outside the church-door where they were trodden upon and carried into the streets and gutters by a shower of rain. Of these, I later saw some that a person in Viborg had picked up by chance, from which it could be seen that these chests did not just contain monkish letters, accounts, and documents [...] I also came across an old monastic book in folio which was written on parchment in a most curious manner in the form of a calendar where all the saints' names were written in red or another colour with a large space between them in order there to note for which deceased person a Mass should be sung on that day and what they had given to the monastery in return for this as well as where they lay buried in the church, everything in the dreadful Latin of that age [...] At the beginning, in the same book, were also written some *statuta*, among which it was not allowed to spit in the choir. I gave Prof. Árni Magnússon this book along with several other documents and antiquities in the year 1720: they were probably destroyed in the fire of Copenhagen].

It will come as no surprise then that the Reformation and the subsequent centuries' abhorrence of medieval culture had far-reaching consequences for the preservation of Old Danish sermons. Today, we have just five manuscripts and one early print that contain medieval vernacular Danish sermons: isolated sermons or fragments in København, Den Arnamagnæanske Samling, MS AM 783 4°, fols 263r–268v;[6] København, Den Arnamagnæanske Samling,

---

4 Árni Magnússon (1663–1730) was an Icelandic–Danish scholar and collector of manuscripts. Although his house burnt down in the Great Fire of 1728 and he lost all of his printed books, he did manage to save most of his manuscript collection. Today these manuscripts form the bulk of Den Arnamagnæanske Samling in Copenhagen.

5 Unpublished manuscript: Christen (Kristen) Sørensen Testrup, *Om Klostrene i Viborg Stift* (1746) in København, Det Kongelige Bibliotek, Additamenta 75 fol., pp. 1–2.

6 The manuscript is from *c.* 1500, possibly Jutlandic in origin, and contains devotional works by several authors: Heinrich Seuse, *Horologium divinae* (fols 1r–145v); Thomas à Kempis, *De imitatione Christi* (fols 150r–262r); Pseudo-Bonaventura, *Stimulus amoris* (fols 271r–311v); St Gregory, *Tractatus* (fols 311v–327r), and Bonaventura, *Viginti quinque memoria* (fols 327v–346v). There are two short sermon texts: 1. Conclusion of a sermon (fol. 263r), and 2. Sermon on property (fols 263r–268v, 'Aff eydom').

136   JONATHAN ADAMS

MS AM 76 8°, fols 128r–142v;[7] Wien, Österreichische Nationalbibliothek, MS 13013, fols 54ra–vb, 56vb–57va;[8] sermon cycle collections in København, Det Kongelige Bibliotek, MS GKS 1390 4°;[9] and Uppsala, Universitetsbibliotek, MS C 56;[10] and a printed sermon cycle in Christiern Pedersen, *Alle Epistler oc Euangelia som lesiss alle Søndage om aared, sameledis Iule dag Paaske dagh, Pingetz dag. meth deriss vdtydning oc glose oc eth Iertegen till huer dag meth flere artickle som alle menniske nyttelige ere* (Paris: Jodocus Badius Ascensius [Josse Bade], 1515).[11] Compared to even our closest neighbour Sweden, this

---

7   The manuscript is a theological handbook, possibly from the Birgittine monastery in Maribo, from *c.* 1465–75 that contains songs, poems, visions, and the like, as well as *Lucidarius* (fols 32r–91v), and finally, after a long introductory address, five sermons in Old Danish: 1. Sermon for First Sunday in Advent, Genesis 49. 10 (fols 129v–133r); 2. Sermon for Christmas Day, Isaiah 9. 6 (fols 133r–138r); 3. Sermon for the Feast of the Circumcision, Luke 2. 21 (fol. 138r–v, incomplete); 4. Sermon for the Nativity of Our Lady, Song of Songs 6. 9 (fols 138v–141v), and 5. Sermon on Corpus Christi, 1 Corinthians 11. 28 (fols 141v–142v). See Roger Andersson, *Postillor och predikan: en medeltida texttradition i filologisk belysning*, Sällskapet Runica et Mediævalia: Scriptora minora, 1 (Stockholm: Sällskapet Runica et Mediævalia, 1993), pp. 157–65; and *A Danish Teacher's Manual of the Mid-Fifteenth Century (Cod. AM 76,8°)*, ed. by Sigurd Kroon and others, Kungl. Vitterhets historie och antikvitets akademien, Skrifter utgivna av Vetenskapssocieteten i Lund, 85, 96, 2 vols (Lund: Lund University Press, 1993–2008), I (1993), 510–69; II (2008), 61–64.
8   A compilation of various religious texts (according to fol. 1r once belonging to the Carthusians of Erfurt), including Hussite works, with three Old Danish sermons: 1. Sermon on Marriage, Genesis 2. 24 (fol. 54ra–b); 2. Sermon on Tithing, Genesis 14. 17–20 (fol. 54rb–vb), and 3. Sermon for Easter Sunday, Psalm 117. 24 (fols 54vb–57va). See *Displaced Texts: An Old Swedish Birgittine Revelation in Copenhagen, GkS 1154 fol. and Three Sermons in Vienna, Cod. Vind. 13013*, ed. by Jonathan Adams, Samlingar utgivna av Svenska fornskriftsällskapet, Serie 3: Smärre texter och undersökningar, 4 (Uppsala: Swedish Science Press, 2008), pp. 36–80.
9   The manuscript comprises a sermon collection, translated from Swedish, from *c.* 1450–1500 that contains sermons and Gospel readings from Advent to Good Friday; see *Dansk Klosterlæsning fra Middelalderen I*, ed. by Carl Joakim Brandt, 3 vols (København: Selskabet for Danmarks Kirkehistorie, 1858–1865), III (1865); Britta Olrik Frederiksen, 'Et forsøg til dateringen af det gammeldanske postilhåndskrift GKS 1390 4to', in *Oppa Swänzsko oc Oppa Dansko: Studien zum Altostnordischen*, ed. by Harry Perridon and Arend Quak, Amsterdamer Beiträge zur älteren Germanistik, 62 (Leiden: Brill, 2006), pp. 151–206.
10 This fifteenth-century manuscript from the Premonstratensian monastery in Bækkeskov/Bäckaskog, Skåne, contains nearly a hundred sermons with Birgittine influence. The sermons cover a large part of the liturgical calendar. See *Svenska medeltids-postillor efter gamla handskrifter*, ed. by Gustaf E. Klemming and others, Samlingar utgivna av Svenska fornskriftsällskapet, Serie 1: Svenska skrifter, 23, 8 vols (Stockholm: Norstedt, 1879–1983), III (1893); Johannes Brøndum-Nielsen, *Fra Skaanes Senmiddelalder: den skaanske Postille fra Bekkaskough*, Festskrift udgivet af Københavns Universitet (København: Københavns Universitet, 1959); Andersson, *Postillor och predikan*, pp. 67–70, 148–55.
11 The title of Pedersen's work translates as 'All the Epistles and Gospels that are read every Sunday during the year including Christmas, Easter, Pentecost, with their expositions and glosses and a miracle for each day with several divisions that are of use to people'. See *Christiern Pedersens Danske Skrifter*, ed. by C. J. Brandt and R. Th. Fenger, 5 vols (København: Gyldendal, 1850–1856), I, (1850); II (1851), 1–270; Carl Joakim Brandt, *Om Lunde-Kanniken Christiern Pedersen og hans Skrifter* (København: Gad, 1882), pp. 60–81.

CHRISTIERN PEDERSEN'S *ALLE EPISTLER OC EUANGELIA* (1515)   137

is a very small number of works, and some of these manuscripts appear to be translated or at least derive from Swedish versions.[12] This may suggest that the extant sermons — just a small pool of derivative material — are not particularly interesting or worth further investigation. Yet nothing could be further from the truth, not least because the corpus contains a true diamond: Pedersen's *Alle Epistler oc Euangelia* from 1515, a collection that is without counterpart elsewhere in medieval Scandinavia. This was the largest printed work in Danish at its time of publication and it contains sermons that cover the entire liturgical year divided into winter and summer cycles. With its miracle tales (*jærtegn*), the work found a readership that lasted well beyond the Reformation and into the eighteenth century.[13]

In this essay I shall describe Pedersen's life and works and investigate the afterlife of *Alle Epistler oc Euangelia* by looking at the deletions, additions, and other marginalia or 'paratext' found in the nine copies of the work housed in the Det Kongelige Bibliotek (Royal Library) in Copenhagen. In this way, I hope to cast some light onto how medieval Catholic sermon traditions persisted into early modern Protestant religious life in Denmark.

Christiern Pedersen: His Life and Works

Christiern Pedersen[14] was born *c.* 1480 on the island of Sjælland, probably in Helsingør, and he attended school in Roskilde, where according to what he later wrote, he did not even learn proper Latin.[15] Between 1496 and 1498, he studied at the University of Greifswald where he took his bachelor degree.[16] In 1505 he is mentioned as a canon at Lund Cathedral in Skåne (which was part

---

12 For an introduction to the Swedish sermon material, see Andersson, *Postillor och predikan*.

13 In Denmark, the work is usually referred to as *Jærtegnspostillen* 'the miracle sermon collection' (from the words *jærtegn* 'miracle tale' and *postillen* 'the postil').

14 On Pedersen's life, see Brandt, *Om Lunde-Kanniken*; *Om urtevand: Malmö 1534. Faksimiledition med en efterskrift*, ed. by Bengt Holmström (Malmö: Föreningen Malmö stadsbiblioteks vänner, 1986), pp. 1–15; Jens Anker Jørgensen, *Humanisten Christiern Pedersen: en præsentation* (København: Reitzel, 2007).

15 'Men ieg nøddis till saa vel som alle andre danske At læse Alexandrum / puerilia Donatum Peder laale / Composita verborum / caser oc andet saadant skarn Aff huilke mand kan aldrig lære eller komme til ret fwndamente till ath forstaa dicte eller scriffue nogen god reth Latine / eller forstaa Huad andre gode klercke / Poeter och Historici haffue før screffuit och dicted vdi forme tid' ['But like all other Danes I had to read Alexander of Villedieu and the trivialities of Donatus, Peder Laale, *Composita verba*, cases [?] and other such rubbish from which one can never learn or gain a good enough foundation to understand poems or write good correct Latin or understand what other good clerics, poets, and historians have written before or composed in earlier times'], *Om børn ath holde till Scole och Studium Och ath skicke gode Scolemestere till dem*, fol. f. 2r (*Christiern Pedersens Danske Skrifter*, ed. by Brandt and Fenger, IV (1854), 505). On Pedersen's descriptions of his experiences at school, see Brandt, *Om Lunde-Kanniken*, pp. 10–17.

16 Holmström, *Om urtevand*, p. 1.

of Denmark until the Treaty of Roskilde in 1658) where he was attached to the cathedral's altar of the Three Kings and as *vicarius perpetuus* at the altar of St Christopher. Between 1507 and 1515 he was deployed to Paris by the cathedral to study at the university, and during his time there he took a master's degree in *artes liberales* and also published several books: Latin–Danish dictionary (*Vocabularium ad usum dacorum*, 1510 [LN 216]);[17] Saxo Grammaticus's *Gesta Danorum* (*Danorum Regum heroumque historiæ*, 1514 [LN 240]); a book of hours (*Vor froe tider*, 1514 [LN 212]);[18] a book on the Mass (*I denne bog leriss at Hore messe*, 1514 [LN 206]);[19] the Latin schoolbook *Puerilia et Facetus* (*Incipiunt puerilia Iuuenibus multum vtilia*, 1514 [LN 223]);[20] his collection of miracle sermons (*Alle Epistler oc Euangelia*, 1515 [LN 208]),[21] and an edition of Peder Laale's collection of proverbs (*Parabolæ*, 1515 [LN 122]).[22] With the exception of the *Vocabularium* that was printed by Jean Barbier (*fl.* 1502–1516), all these works came off the press of the famous Flemish pioneer of printing Jodocus Badius Ascensius (1462–1535) who had established a printing shop in Paris in 1503. These early prints comprise important monuments in Danish literary history, not least as Pedersen's Saxo edition is now the oldest known complete copy (the original manuscript is lost) and, as mentioned above, his *Alle Epistler oc Euangelia* with its 204 folios was at the time the largest book ever printed in Danish.

After his sojourn in Paris, Pedersen returned to Denmark and his position as canon at Lund Cathedral. We know that in April 1524 he received a ten-year indulgence at Lund Cathedral and so apparently was still a faithful Catholic at this time, and, indeed, his writings up to this point do not show any reservations about the Church's teaching on indulgences.[23] His return to Denmark coincided with a period of friction between Christian II (1481–1559) and burghers on the one hand and the nobility and aristocratic clergy on the other. Pedersen, however, had long been a friend of the king and so when, in 1523, after a series of failed reforms and uprisings against him, Christian II was forced into exile in the Low Countries, Pedersen kept in contact with

---

17 LN = the entry number in Lauritz Nielsen, *Dansk Bibliografi 1482–1600*, ed. by Erik Dal, rev. edn, 5 vols (København: Det Danske Sprog- og Litteraturselskab, 1996). Pedersen's *Vocabularium ad usum dacorum* was reprinted in Cologne by Heinrich Quentell's sons in 1514 (LN 217); edited by Henrik Smith and reprinted in Leipzig by Melchior Lotter in 1518 (LN 218).

18 Edited by Henrik Smith and reprinted in Leipzig by Melchior Lotter in 1517 (LN 213).

19 Edited by Henrik Smith and reprinted in Leipzig by Melchior Lotter in 1517 (LN 207).

20 See J. Paludan, 'En middelalderlig Skolebog', *Nordisk Tidskrift for Filologi*, n.s. 10 (1890–1892), 83–88.

21 Edited by Henrik Smith and reprinted in Leipzig by Melchior Lotter in 1518 (LN 209).

22 On Pedersen's prints from this period in Paris, see Christian Bruun, *Aarsberetninger og Meddelelser fra Det Store Kongelige Bibliothek*, 1: *1864–1869* (København: Gyldendal, 1870), pp. 200–11, 219–20, 231–39.

23 *Acta Pontificum Danica: Pavelige Aktstykker vedrørende Danmark*, ed. by Alfred Krarup and Johannes Lindbæk, 7 vols (København: Gad, 1904–1943), VI (1915), 431–32, no. 4978.

CHRISTIERN PEDERSEN'S *ALLE EPISTLER OC EUANGELIA* (1515)

him. The canon continued to support the king which caused some friction between himself and the Cathedral authorities, and when in 1525 he joined a failed uprising against the nobility in Skåne, he was stripped of his office and excommunicated. Pedersen left Denmark and for the next five years was a member of the king's court in exile in Lier near Antwerp. During this time, and under the influence of the king, he became a Lutheran. In 1529 he published a translation of the New Testament (*Det Ny Testamente* [LN 271]) with the printer Willem Vorsterman in Antwerp.[24] In 1531 he published a whole series of translations and adaptations of some of Luther's shorter works with the same printer: *Huorledis huert Christet menniske skal bere sit kaarss* (LN 146: a translation of Martin Luther, *Sermon von Kreuz und Leiden eines rechten Christenmenschen*);[25] *Huorledis huert menniske skal betencke Herris dod oc pine* (LN 147: a translation of Martin Luther, *Sermon von der Betrachtung des heiligen Leidens Christi*); *Om børn ath holde till Scole* (LN 155: a reworking of Martin Luther, *An die Ratsherren aller Städte deutschen Landes, daß sie christliche Schulen aufrichten und halten sollen*); and *Om vaar Herris dod oc pine* (LN 158: an adaption of parts of Martin Luther, *Betbüchlein*)[26] — as well as *En Christelig bogh Om merckelige sporsmaall och swar* (LN 22: a translation of Martin Luther, *Ein trostlich Disputation auf Frag und Antwort gestellet*), *Den rette vey till Hiemmerigis Rige* (LN 215: a compilation of *inter alia*: Martin Luther, *Kurze Form der Zehn Gebote, Auslegung des Vaterunsers für die einfältigen Laien, Kurzer Begriff und Ordnung aller vorgeschriebenen Bitten*, and *Ave Maria*),[27] and *Dauidz psaltere* (LN 53: a Danish translation based on Latin and Luther's translation). Presumably, these works were intended for use in Denmark once Christian II regained the throne and introduced a reformation of the Church. However, the exiled king's campaign failed again and he was defeated and imprisoned for the next twenty-seven years. Pedersen was somewhat more fortunate. The new king, Frederik I (1471–1533), who was sympathetic to the Lutheran cause, pardoned him and allowed him to settle in Malmö in 1532 where he married a widow, Else Jacobsdatter, in 1534. They had a daughter, Anna, in 1539, but Else died during the birth.

Pedersen continued his career as translator, editor, and publisher in Malmö. On Johannes Hoochstraten's printing press he published a few

---

24 Reprinted by Vorsterman in 1531 (LN 272).
25 See Eva Louise Lillie, 'Imitatio Christi: om Christiern Pedersens "Huorledis huert Christet menniske skal bere sit kaarss"', *Iconographisk Post: Nordisk tidskrift för ikonografi*, 4 (1995), 44–53.
26 Reprinted later that same year by Vorsterman (LN 159).
27 This work was translated into Scots English by John Gau as *The richt vay to the Kingdome of heuine* and printed by Johannes Hoochstraten in Malmö in 1533 (LN 214), after which copies were to be smuggled to Scotland. Gau's translation is quoted no fewer than 222 times in the *Oxford English Dictionary* and was the first Scottish book written on the side of the reformers. See Philipp Marshall Mitchell, 'The English Imprints of Denmark', *Fund og Forskning*, 5 (1958), 34–61 (pp. 34–36).

more Lutheran texts as well as non-religious works: *Hundrede och halffierde sindz tiwe merkelige och ret Christelige sporsmaall met deris Suar* (1533, LN 5: a translation of Johann Agricola, *130 gemeine Fragestücke für die jungen Kinder in der deutschen Mädchenschule zu Eisleben*, 1528); a psalter, the title page of which is lost (1533, LN 237); two medical handbooks: *En nottelig Legebog* (1533, LN 210); *Om Urte Uand* (1534, LN 211); and two fictional, historical works: *Keyser Karlls Magnus Kronicke* (1534, LN 117) and *Kong Olger Danskis Kronicke* (1534, LN 118). After yet again backing Christian II in another failed Danish uprising against the king, Pedersen was forced to stop his printing activities for good and moved to Helsinge, a small town in northern Sjælland, where he spent his final years in relative obscurity, passing away in January 1554. Two years after his death, Pedersen's son-in-law published his translation of Aesop's fables *Esopi leffnit oc nogle hans fabel som vore udsette aff Gredske paa latine oc aff latine paa tydske* (Malmö: Oluff Ulricksen, LN 1671).

Christiern Pedersen, often referred to as Denmark's first Renaissance humanist, is a fascinating figure who lived through one of the most transformative periods of Danish history and who himself was transformed from a traditional Catholic canon to a leading Lutheran figure in the Danish Reformation. Indeed, he is the only Danish intellectual whose writing career extends beyond the religious schism of the early sixteenth century. He is thus a rather interesting case, a Dane who wrote and published religious works both before and after converting to Lutheranism and whose oeuvre thus reflects the ideologies and beliefs from both sides of the Reformation (from the period 1510–1518 on the one hand and 1529–1534 on the other). While many of his earlier religious works fell into obscurity after the introduction of Lutheranism, his *Alle Epistler oc Euangelia* continued to be a popular work that was read long after new forms of preaching and sermons had been established.

Alle Epistler oc Euangelia

Pedersen's *Alle Epistler oc Euangelia* is in praise and honour of

> Den alsommectiste Gwd Jomfrw Marie oc alle gwdz helghen i hiemmerigiss rige till loff oc ære Alle enfoldige Danske folk som icke forstaa latine till nøtte oc salighed Ere alle Epistler och Ewangelia som læsiss alle søndage vdsette paa danske met deriss vtydninger oc i Jerteghen til hwert aff dem At de som icke latine forstaa Mue nw selffue læse paa danske hworlediss de rettelige leffue skwlle effter gwdz budord som stonde i dem Och fonge siden effter deriss død den ewindelige glæde for vden ende.[28]

---

28 *Alle Epistler oc Euangelia*, 1515, fol. i verso (*Christiern Pedersens Danske Skrifter*, ed. by Brandt and Fenger, I (1850), xiii). In the transcriptions, the following editorial principles have been followed:

CHRISTIERN PEDERSEN'S *ALLE EPISTLER OC EUANGELIA* (1515)   141

[God Almighty, the Virgin Mary, and all of God's saints in heaven and for the use and salvation of all simple Danes who do not understand Latin. All the Epistles and Gospels that are read on Sundays are translated into Danish with their expositions and a miracle tale for each of them, so that those who do not understand Latin can now read themselves in Danish how they should live correctly in accordance with God's commandments as are in them and then after their death receive eternal joy without end].

Pedersen's introduction explains why he has translated the texts into Danish and ends with the following argument, a familiar medieval trope for justifying vernacular translation:

Sancte Hanss apostel oc euangelista oc *Sanctus* Lucas screffue till greken euangelia paa grekiske ath the skwlde dem vel forstonde *Sanctus* Mattheus screff ewangelia paa ebraiske til dem som talede ebraiske maall Sancte Pouild apostel screff epistler paa grekiske och ebraiske till dem som talede saadanne maall Hagde nogen aff dem screffuit euangelia till d<an>marckiss Righe Da hagde han dem visselighe screffuit paa ret danske saa alle det forstondet hagde thii hwert menniske bør ath kwnde dem paa sit egeth maall Jnghen skal tro ath de ere helligere paa eth twngemaall en paa eth andet De ere saa gode paa danske oc tydske som de ere paa latine naar de ellerss reth vdtydiss Thii kand inth*et* vfornymstigt eller awendzfulth menniske rettelige sige ath det er ilde giort eller wbeque*m*meligt At vdsette dem paa danske Men ingen kand bliffue salig for vden dem och den hellige tro.[29]

[St John the Apostle and Evangelist and St Luke wrote the Gospels for the Greeks in Greek so that they would understand them clearly. St Matthew wrote the Gospels in Hebrew for those who spoke Hebrew. St Paul the Apostle wrote Epistles in Greek and Hebrew for those who spoke such languages. If any of them had written the Gospels

---

Abbreviations:	All abbreviations have been expanded and placed in italics.
Punctuation:	The punctuation of the original is followed. The virgule appears as /.
Supplied text:	Text that is missing in the original and has been supplied by the editor has been placed in angle brackets <>.
Damage:	Text that is missing in the original due to damage has been placed in square brackets []. If it is not possible to supply the missing text, the assumed number of missing letters are marked with a hyphen, for example: [---] means three unknown letters are missing due to damage.
Breaks:	A page break is marked by two vertical lines || and a line break by a single vertical line |.
Deletion:	Text that has been deleted by a reader is marked by crossing out.
Insertions:	Handwritten additions above the line made by a reader have been marked using \/.

29 *Alle Epistler oc Euangelia*, 1515, fol. i verso (*Christiern Pedersens Danske Skrifter*, ed. by Brandt and Fenger, I (1850), xiv).

for the Kingdom of Denmark, then he would certainly have written in proper Danish so that everyone had understood it, because every person ought to know them in his own language. No one must think that they are more holy in one language than another. They are as good in Danish and German as they are in Latin when they have otherwise been correctly expounded. Thus, no irrational or hateful person can justifiably say that it is bad or improper to translate them into Danish. But no one can be saved without them and the Holy Faith].

This introduction clearly places Pedersen in the tradition of humanism with its interest in the original languages of the Bible and translation into the vernacular. This justification for translating all the readings into Danish is followed by tables of contents and then a short section on the importance of remembering the suffering of Christ ('Om vor herriss piness ihukommelse'). After this begins the main part: the texts of every Sunday and holy day in the Church year from the First Sunday in Advent to the Twenty-Fifth Sunday after Trinity. The schedule for each day varies slightly, but for most of the year it is the same: First, the day's readings from the Epistles of Paul and the Gospels. Both are reproduced in Danish in Pedersen's own translation. Then follows the exposition, which runs through the Gospel text sentence by sentence, often repeating Scripture, either both in Latin and Danish or just in Danish. The interpretation of the text is full of references to various religious authorities. Finally comes a portent, a tale about a sign from God, confirming the message of the sermon. Usually it is a miracle, but it can also be a rather mundane, everyday event used to make the message concrete with ordinary people exemplifying morality.

As far as Pedersen's sources for his sermon collection are concerned, the two most noticeable influences are from the late fifteenth century. The scholars Carl Joakim Brandt and Johan Jensen have both shown that the exposition part of each sermon follows the *Postilla super epistolas et evangelia* by Guillermus Parisiensis (1437–1485) rather closely, which in turn makes much use of Ugo da Prato (*c.* 1262–1322), Nicolas de Gorran (*c.* 1232–1295), and Nicolaus de Lyra (*c.* 1270–1349).[30] The miracle tales are all taken from the compilation by the Dominican Johannes Herolt (*c.* 1390–1468), *Sermones discipuli de tempore et de sanctis cum promptuario exemplorum et miraculis Beate Virginis Marie*. This popular work was printed at least forty-five times between 1474 and 1500.[31]

The sermon collection's readers were mainly to be found in Denmark, but we also know that it was read in Sweden, Norway, and Iceland. For example, when, in 1525, King Gustav Vasa of Sweden ordered Johannes Magnus

---

30 Brandt, *Om Lunde-Kanniken*, p. 62; Johan R. M. Jensen, 'Christiern Pedersen Jærtegnspostil: Mellem Middelalder og Reformation', in *Mentalitet & Historie: Om fortidige forestillingsverdener*, ed. by Charlotte Appel, Peter Henningsen, and Nils Hybel (Ebeltoft: Skippershoved, 2002), pp. 25–49 (p. 32).

31 Jensen, 'Christiern Pedersen Jærtegnspostil', p. 32.

CHRISTIERN PEDERSEN'S *ALLE EPISTLER OC EUANGELIA* (1515)

(1488–1544), the last functioning Catholic archbishop in Sweden, to make available a Swedish translation of the New Testament for the enlightenment of his subjects, there were numerous protests from Swedish clerics. The most vociferous was Hans Brask (1464–1538), archbishop in Linköping, who insisted there was no need for a translation as the Gospels for the entire year were already readily available in Danish. He argued that the affinity between Danish and Swedish, given that the two languages are mutually intelligible, meant that the work could be used to advantage in Sweden. Magnus must have been referring to *Alle Epistler oc Euangelia*, as the only other Danish New Testament around at the time was Christian II's New Testament, a Lutheran, and therefore heretical translation largely undertaken by Hans Mikkelsen and published in 1524.[32] There are also two manuscript fragments in Den Arnamagnæanske Samling in Copenhagen from between 1520 and 1540 that each contain an independent Icelandic translation of the work (AM 238 XXIX fol. and AM 696 XVII 4°). In Norway, Bishop Eiler Hagerup of Trondheim was given a copy of *Alle Epistler oc Euangelia* as a present while visiting Telemark in 1786.[33]

The sermon collection is mentioned several times by the Dano-Norwegian writer, playwright, and philosopher Ludvig Holberg (1684–1754), albeit rather disparagingly. For example, in the poem *Peder Paars*, we read about a priest who was learned and a good preacher, but who did not own a Bible; instead he used *Alle Epistler oc Euangelia*:

> Vor Præst er meget lærd, hand præker, døber vel,
> Ey nogen andet kand ham sige paamed Skiel.
> Hand ingen Bibel har, men herlige Postiller
> Med Kaaberstycker i, hand læser uden Briller
> I Kircken af en Bog, en gammel lærd Postil,
> Som *Jertegns heder, slig en Bog er aldrig til.
> Den handler ickun om sandfærdige Mirakler,
> Og trøster, styrcker dem, som udi Troen vakler,
>
> *Mand veed udi hvilcken Credit Jertegns Postil var udi gamle Dage,
> da der var stor Overtroe blant Folck.[34]

> [Our priest is very learned, he preaches and baptizes well
> No one can say anything else about him
> He has no Bible, but marvellous postils
> With copperplates, he reads without glasses
> In the church from a book, an old learned postil
> That is called *Miracles, there is no other such book.

---

32 *Thette ere thet Noye testamenth paa danske ret effter latinen vdsatthe* (Leipzig: Melchior Lotter, 1524); see LN 270.

33 Brandt, *Om Lunde-Kanniken*, pp. 79–80.

34 *Peder Paars, Poema Heroico-comicum*, Book 1, Song 2.

It is just about true miracles,

And it consoles, strengthens those who are stumbling in their faith.

*It is known in which high regard the Book of Miracle Sermons was held in days of yore when people were very superstitious].

His play *Mester Gert Westphaler eller Den meget talende Barbeer* from 1723 contains a diatribe about the Prophet Muhammad in which he describes the Qur'an as being nearly four times thicker than *Alle Epistler oc Euangelia*: 'Sat Christne Folk paa Spid, stegte og aad dem op, hvor hand kom, og med det Blod, som hand tappede af dem, skrev Alcoranen, en stor Bog, fast fire gange saa tyck, som Jertegns Postill' ['[Muhammad] placed Christians on skewers, roasted them and gobbled them up wherever he went, and with the blood that he drained from them, he wrote *Alcoran*, a large book, nearly four times as thick as *Jærtegnspostillen*'].[35] By this point, the book had become a joke, a gauge for formidable thickness and, presumably, mendacity.

In the preface to his New Testament translation (1531) Pedersen distanced himself from his sermon collection:

> Ieg bekender her oc selff min store vildfarelse som ieg vaar før vdi / den tid ieg lod sette de Iertegen oc fabel i de || andre bøger i Paris (som menniskene haffue opdictet och drøme<t>) At man skulle leffue som de helgene giorde / oc der met faartiene Hiemmerige / oc met deris egne gode gerninger Hwilket dog er løgn oc vildfarelse / Thi at Christus haffuer all ene giort fyllest for vaare synder / oc fortient oss Hiemmerigis Rige met sin død oc pine / Thi beder ieg alle / ath i lade samme Jertegen oc fabel hen fare / och setter ingen tro eller loffue til dem / Men bliffuer all eniste stadelige oc fast hoss Gudz egne sande ord oc Euangelia Oc lader ingen drage eder fra dem met andre falske lerdomme / Gud vere benedidet til euig tid Som drog mig aff min vildfarelse aff sin miskundhed Oc vnte mig sin naade til at lære oc forstaa sine ord oc Euangelia bedre en ieg giorde førre i min blindhed.[36]

> [I myself hereby also confess my great error that I previously made when I had the miracles and fables (which people had made up and dreamt) printed in the other books in Paris that one should live as the saints did and thus earn heaven also by means of their own deeds. These are lies and error because Christ alone has atoned for our sins and made us worthy of heaven through his death and suffering. Thus I beg everyone to let these very miracles and fables pass them by and place no faith or honour in them, but remain solely constant and firm to God's own true words and the Gospels. And let no-one draw you from them with false teachings. May God be blessed for all eternity

---

35 *Mester Gert Westphaler eller Den meget talende Barneer*, 1723, Act 4, Scene 11.

36 'Det nye Testamente', fol. a6 recto–verso (*Christiern Pedersens Danske Skrifter*, ed. by Brandt and Fenger, III (1852), x).

CHRISTIERN PEDERSEN'S *ALLE EPISTLER OC EUANGELIA* (1515)   145

who through his loving kindness drew me out of my error and gave me his mercy to learn and understand his words and Gospels better than I had before in my blindness].

Yet despite the author himself expressing scorn for his work, his sermon collection continued to be read and known. In fact, a particularly peculiar feature of Christiern Pedersen's prints is the popularity and longevity of his *Alle Epistler oc Euangelia* in certain Protestant circles during the last couple of centuries, most notable among Grundtvigian intellectuals, who saw Pedersen as a particularly clear-sighted writer, a man before his time.[37] With the blossoming of the Danish National-Romantic movement in the first half of the nineteenth century, *Alle Epistler oc Euangelia* was framed as a monument to the national spirit and the pre-conversion Pedersen is re-baptized and rehabilitated.

> [...] et af de herligste Mindesmærker om dansk Sandheds-Kjærlighed, Kristendom og Veltalenhed, som Historien kjender, og den er det især som beviser, hvad Danmarks opvaagnende historiske Aand alt den Gang havde i Sinde. At Lærdommen i denne Bog ej er aldeles ren, og at de Prædikenerne vedhængte Jærtegn indeholde meget fabelagtigt, følger ej alene af den Omstændighed, at Chr. Pedersen var ingen Luther; men ogsaa af den Magt, indgrode Vildfarelser en Stund øve selv over Reformatorer som Luther. At derimod Bogen er skreven af Medynk over Folket, der, som det hedder, vel sjælden fik Prædiken at høre; at den véd at forsvare Bibelens Oversættelse paa dansk med den lysende Grund: at Folk maa kjende det Ord, der skal dømme dem.[38]

> [[...] one of the most wonderful monuments of Danish love of truth, Christianity, and eloquence, that history has ever known, and it is particularly that, that shows what Denmark's awakening historical spirit had in mind. That the teaching in this book is not completely pure, and that the miracle stories appended to the sermons contain much make-believe is not just a result of the fact that Christiern Pedersen was no Luther, but also of the power that engrained delusions exercise even over Reformers such as Luther. That the book is written out of

---

37 Nikolaj Frederik Severin Grundtvig (1783–1872), considered alongside Søren Aabye Kierkegaard (1813–1855), as the foremost Danish theologian in the nineteenth century, started a reforming movement in Danish Lutheranism in 1824. This movement (Grundtvigianism) led to an increased understanding of the Church and the sacraments. Grundtvig became preacher at the Vartov Hospital from 1839 onwards and in 1861 was given the title of 'Bishop'; he was also an expert in the study of Old English and Old Norse literature and was active in the establishment of Folk High Schools in Denmark. His manuscripts are housed in Det Kongelige Bibliotek in Copenhagen. For further information, see Arthur Macdonald Allchin, *N. F. S. Grundtvig: An Introduction to his Life and Work* (Aarhus: Aarhus University Press, 2015).

38 Nikolaj F. S. Grundtvig, *Danne-Virke: Et Tids-skrift*, 1 (1816), 339–40.

pity for the people who, as it says, but rarely heard a sermon; that it defended the translation of the Bible into Danish with the shining reason: that people must know the word that they shall be judged by].

He was in essence always a Protestant filled with the 'Danish love of truth'. Indeed, when all of Pedersen's writings were published as a five-volume collected edition in the middle of the nineteenth century, it was a group of Grundtvigians who stood behind the project.

Perhaps even more peculiarly, *Alle Epistler oc Euangelia* is still praised in current Danish research for introducing vernacular preaching into Denmark (!): it is still quite normal in Denmark to hear that (until Pedersen) all medieval preaching was in Latin. For example, historian Henrik Horstbøll writes about Pedersen: '[...] og samtidig introducerede han en ny genre, der havde en stor fremtid for sig — den folkesproglige postil [...]' ['and at the same time he introduced a new genre, that had a great future ahead of it, the vernacular sermon collection'].[39]

Marginalia, Deletions, Additions, and Substitutions

Given the long life of Pedersen's sermon collection, its many readers must have left traces on the extant copies of the work. Today, there are in all twenty-five surviving copies of *Alle Epistler oc Euangelia* — twelve from the 1515 printing and thirteen from 1518. I have investigated the five copies from Paris 1515 (LN 208) and the four from Leipzig 1518 (LN 209) that are kept at Det Kongelige Bibliotek in Copenhagen (here referred to by the letters A–I) in order to explore traces of usage by readers in the form of deletions and additions.[40]

Repository	Shelfmark	Year	Copy
København, Det Kongelige Bibliotek	LN 208, ex. 1	1515	A
København, Det Kongelige Bibliotek	LN 208, ex. 2	1515	B

---

39 Henrik Horstbøll, *Menigmands medie: det folkelige bogtryk i Danmark 1500–1840* (København: Det Kongelige Bibliotek, 1999), p. 236.

40 These copies were selected for study as they are available online and are therefore easily accessible to readers who may wish to check the annotations for themselves and/or take this investigation further; see www.kb.dk. My references to foliation follows that of Pedersen in the copies themselves. To mark the point in the printed text where readers' comments have been or most likely were intended to be inserted, I use the symbol ↓. Comments seem to have been made by multiple readers. For information about the library's acquisition of the copies, see Bruun, *Aarsberetninger*, pp. 235–36. Of the other sixteen extant copies, four can be found in Denmark (Aarhus, Horsens, and Odense), and the remainder in various European cities: Germany (Stuttgart), Norway (Trondheim and Oslo), and Sweden (Lund, Stockholm, and Uppsala).

CHRISTIERN PEDERSEN'S *ALLE EPISTLER OC EUANGELIA* (1515)   147

Repository	Shelfmark	Year	Copy
København, Det Kongelige Bibliotek	LN 208, ex. 3[41]	1515	C
København, Det Kongelige Bibliotek	LN 208, ex. 4	1515	D
København, Det Kongelige Bibliotek	LN 208, ex. 5	1515	E
København, Det Kongelige Bibliotek	LN 209, ex. 1	1518	F
København, Det Kongelige Bibliotek	LN 209, ex. 2	1518	G
København, Det Kongelige Bibliotek	LN 209, ex. 3[42]	1518	H
København, Det Kongelige Bibliotek	LN 209, ex. 4	1518	I

The books are rather large, with 204 folios in the Paris edition and 185 folios in the Leipzig edition, and as they are packed with miracle stories, tales about saints, and texts praising the Virgin, one might expect the indignation and horror of a post-Reformation Danish reader to be aroused by such material. However, the signs of use from the late sixteenth and seventeenth centuries point in different and conflicting directions.

The vast majority of pages in all the copies are untorn and clean (thumb prints aside) and several do not have signs of revisions even if they have all clearly been used. Copies B, F, and G are particularly clean and A has by far the greatest quantity of paratext. In two of the copies (C and I) pages are missing. However, rather than leave it at that, the owners or users have carefully copied out the missing text and bound it into the original print. In C, we can see that eight print-pages of the sermon for Good Friday are missing (fols 105r–108v) and part of the sermons for the Twenty-Second (with a miracle tale) and Twenty-Third Sunday after Trinity (fol. 299r–v). Again, someone has carefully written them by hand and bound them into the book even mimicking the use of large illuminated capitals. In I, a missing folio comprising part of the contents page and the beginning of the text on the Passion (fol. a5) has been copied out and added to the book. Of course it is impossible to know whether this was done out of antiquarian interest or pious fervour, but for these readers at least, the book was something valuable that should be preserved in its entirety.

Ex libris comments usually occur on the frontispiece or at the very end of the copies on flysheets and covers. With the exception of just a few interlinear scribblings (for example, H, fols 56v and 59r), all the additions are in the margins. Among banalities, there are several occurrences of 1) pen trials using letters from the alphabet; 2) copies of the text; 3) personal names, 4) comments on the day's weather, or 5) even short poems in Danish and German:

---

41 Formerly, København, Det Kongelige Bibliotek, Hielmstierne 19 fol.
42 Formerly, København, Det Kongelige Bibliotek, Hielmstierne 20 fol.

1. Pen trials

C, fol. 53v	*left margin*	a series of pen strokes
C, fol. 80r	*right margin*	letters of the alphabet and a doodle

2. Copying the text

D, fol. 80v	*above the heading*		
		'Udtydningen her paa'	Udtÿdningen her paa
		[The exposition of this]	[The exposition of this]

3. Personal names

G, fol. 83r	*top margin*	NICOLAVS
H, fol. 59r	*right margin*	powell lauritssøn

4. The day's weather

A, fol. 47r	*bottom margin*	Den dag Anno 16[--] Tordnes och lius[es] dett Engang Møgit
		[On this day in 16-- there is thunder and at once much lightning].

5. Poems / ditties

A, fol. 172v	*next to a miracle about an angry woman*	Quinde de erre well fromme, dog icke alle, men somme
		[Women, they are certainly pious, though not all, but some].
E, fol. 115r	*bottom margin*	[---]t ist allein der gelobene Heltt, Suß iß der kein gelouen in der Weltt
		[Christ(?) alone is the promised hero, Sweetness(?) is promised to no-one in this world].

With approximately forty-two lines on each page, the volume of ink is substantial and readers have taken various approaches to creating aids for navigating the text. As we might expect, there are numerous occurrences of 'NB', 'Nota', and 'Nota bene' written in the margins. There are also *maniculae* or pointing hands, for example in E (fols 40r, 50v, 53v, 75v, and 197v) that mark parts of the text that the reader found to be particularly important. Underlining is also commonly used to draw attention to certain words, phrases, or entire sections. The ruling often runs through the text itself, and in some cases it may be an attempt to delete the words rather than highlight them. For example, in A, fol. 6v, the Danish translations of quotations from Augustine, Isaiah, Chrysostom, Albertus Magnus, and Bernard de Clairvaux have all been 'struck through' by underlining: yet alongside these rulings we find 'Nota' written in

CHRISTIERN PEDERSEN'S *ALLE EPISTLER OC EUANGELIA* (1515)

the margin, which suggests that this mid-height underlining is highlighting rather than deletion. However, later in the same copy, quotations in Latin have been consistently ruled through (as also, though less frequently, have the names of the authorities in the margin); for example, fol. 53r:

Ieronim*us*   Sanctus Ieronimus oc siger ~~Non memini me legisse mala morte mortuum quie liberter opera pietatis exercuit~~ Ieg dragiss icke til minde ath iegh nogen tiid haffuer leest at den fick vkristelig død som gerne giorde miskundelighe gerninger

[Jerome]   [St Jerome also says ~~Non memini me legisse mala morte mortuum quie libenter opera pietatis exercuit~~ I cannot recall that I have ever read that whoever performs acts of loving kindness receives an unchristian death].

Are these rulings deletions that assisted a reader who was reading aloud and might inadvertently read out some Latin during a sermon 'performance'? Or are they quite the opposite: markings that are intended to highlight the Latin? It is difficult to tell, but it is the result of a sort of censorship that is not complete censorship: the new religious directives are followed, but the words remain visible for anyone who wishes to see them or speak them.

A few initials have been coloured in C (for example, fols 111v 'S', and 113r 'A'). Also in C, several sermons have had pause markings inserted into the day's reading (a red down-stroke), for example, fols 83v–84r and 102r–v, which strongly suggests that these sermons were prepared to be read aloud. However, due to the nature of the marking, it is not possible to determine whether these were made before or after the Reformation. Further evidence of preparing the sermons for reading aloud is the addition of concluding formulas:

B, fol. 12v *Printed text*	*User's note (concluding doxology)*
Och engen tiid skall vere hannwm long met hwilke han forwerffue kan den euighe salighed ↓ ~~Her om finde~~ wii et exempell oc iertegen saa lydendiss	huilkit giffue oss gud fad*er* wed sinn Sønn Jhesum Christum wor h[erre] Amen
[And no time shall be long for him with which he can obtain eternal bliss ↓ ~~About this~~ we find an exemplum and miracle that goes like this ...]	[May God the Father give us this through his son Jesus Christ our Lord, Amen].

It looks as though this addition is meant to mark the end of the sermon as the introduction to the *exempell* ('About this [...]') has been crossed out, so the following edifying story of the ascetic woman in Brabant was not to be read.

150   JONATHAN ADAMS

In the same copy, another addition of a concluding formula appears:

B, fol. 97v   *Printed text*   *User's note (concluding formula)*

Naar nogen dette retthelige betencke vil da   Der till Giffue oss gud fader sinn node
offuer vinder han lettelige alle onde fristelser och Bistandt med Iesum Christum
och legemenss begærelser ↓   wor herre Amen

[When someone considers this correctly,   [May God the Father give his mercy
then he will easily conquer evil temptations   and support through Jesus Christ our
and bodily desires. ↓]   Lord for this. Amen].

And in H:

H, fol. 178v   *Printed text*   *User's note (concluding formula)*

Der han dette hørde da gruede hannem   Det vnde oss gud fader vid sin
swarlige thii omwende han sin leffnid och   elskelig søn Jesum Christum vor
fick eth gaat endeligt Amen ↓   herre oc frelsere Amen

[When he heard this he was overcome with   [May God the Father grant us this
regret, so he turned around his life and   through his beloved son Jesus Christ
received a good end. Amen ↓]   our Lord and Saviour. Amen].

All three of these added formulas focus on Jesus Christ as the means by which
God the Father grants his mercy.

Comprehension has been eased in some copies by the readers correcting
mistakes in the printed text. For example, a missing word has been inserted in A:

A, fols 41v–42r   *Printed text*   *User's note (correction)*

iosep kom till bage igen och hagde mange iøder meth   omskæris
sig som skwlle følge barnid till templen den tiid det
skulle ↓

[Joseph returned and had many Jews with him who   [be circumcised].
were to accompany the child to the Temple when he
was to ↓]

Sometimes a Danish word is glossed with a more contemporary or recognizable
term:

A, fol. 7r   *Printed text*   *User's note (gloss)*

offuerdadige och dolle menniske ↓   Det ere offuerflødige oc praalende Men

[overconfident and arrogant people ↓]   [That is superficial and boastful men].

C, fol. 12v   *Printed text*   *User's note (gloss)*

Thii ~~torffue~~ ↓ i icke haffue omhw   tøræ

[because you do not need/   [dare]
dare ↓ to have consideration]

CHRISTIERN PEDERSEN'S *ALLE EPISTLER OC EUANGELIA* (1515)   151

In E, a reader has gone through the entire text correcting typographical errors and older forms. For example:

E, fol. 23v	biudet>budet	E, fol. 31r	hagge>hagde
E, fol. 24v	naat>naar	E, fol. 32r	Sancte halss>Sancte hanss
E, fol. 25r	hestelige>hastelige	E, fol. 33r	Egiptem>Egipten
E, fol. 27r	baware>beware	E, fol. 35v	ebbe>eble

Navigation and comprehension of the text has also been eased by the insertion of keywords and summaries of key points in the margins. Examples in Danish include:

A, fol. 10r	*Printed text*	*User's note (keyword)*
	Saa giorde oc lucifer mod vor herre som vor offuer hannum thi skød han hannum nederste ned i heluediss aff grwnd	Lucifers Hoff
	[Thus Lucifer also did this to our Lord who is superior to him. So he shot him down into the deepest abyss of hell]	[the court of Lucifer]

A, fol. 33r	*Printed text*	*User's note (keyword)*
	Disse Ord sagde Christus till Jøderne, daa han wor 33 aar gam[mel]	Jerusalems Ødel[æggelse]
	[Christ said these words to the Jews when he was thirty-three years old]	[the destruction of Jerusalem]

Similarly, a short piece by Pedersen on a folk tradition is marked in the margin with 'Troldom som brugis Nat' ['sorcery used in the night-time'] (A, fol. 21r) and a section on souls in hell is marked with the keyword 'Syele dag' ['Soul-day'] (H, fol. 135r). A miracle story about a nun who ran away from a convent is simply marked 'skøge' ['harlot'] (E, fol. 20v).

Sometimes the printed text has been marked by underlining and/or numbering with an additional marginal note:

A, fol. 5v	*Printed text*	*User's note (keyword)*
	Først gaff han ¹gud fader sin siel ²Jøderne sit legeme ³iomfrw marie sancte hanss. ⁴apostlene forfølning oc modgong her i verden ⁵Røffueren paradiss ⁶Alle syndere som icke ville gøre penitentz helwede. ⁷cristne menniske som haffue anger och ruelse for deriss synder korsset	Christi testament, paa Korszitt er
	[First he gave 1. God the Father his soul, 2. the Jews his body, 3. the Virgin Mary, St John, 4. the apostles persecution and adversity here in the world, 5. the thief paradise, 6. all sinners who do not want to do penance hell, 7. Christians who have remorse and repentance for their sins the Cross]	[Christ's testament on the Cross is]

152   JONATHAN ADAMS

Notably, the marginal notes are sometimes in Latin:

| A, fol. 6v | *Printed text* | *User's note (keyword)* |

Naar i se figen træ blomsterss oc fonge løff da vide i
visselighe effter natwrenss løff ath sommeren snarlige
komme skal Saa mwe i oc visselighe vide ath den yderste
strenge domme dag komme skal snarlighe naar i saadan
tegen paa hiemmelen i haffuit oc paa iorden set haffue

Similitudinem hanc
pronuntiavit Christus
suis discipulis

[When you see the fig tree flower and get leaves, then you
know for sure according to the laws of nature that summer
is soon approaching. So can you also know that the final
severe Day of Judgement is soon approaching when you
have seen such signs in the sky, in the sea, and on earth].

[Christ declared this
comparison to his
disciples]

| A, fol. 29r | *Printed text* | *User's note (keyword)* |

Det vor en megtig swar stad i huilken der vor ganske
megen almue

Historia de siuitate

[There was a very large city in which quite a lot of
common people lived]

[Story of a city]

| A, fol. 79r | *Printed text* | *User's note (keyword)* |

~~Da drog wor herriss billede som hengde paa det hellige
korss sine hender aff naglene oc stoppede fingrene i
sine ørn saa alle men~~niske saa det obenbarlige som der
til stede waare

Miraculum magnum

[~~Then our Lord's image that was hanging on the Holy
Cross pulled his hands off the nails and stuck his
fingers in his ears, so that every~~one who was present
could clearly see it].

[A great miracle]

The vernacular text can be annotated with a numbered summary in Latin in
the margin (the ordering is muddled):

| A, fol. 10r | *Printed text* | *User's note (keyword)* |

Her skal hwer merke at wii gerne anamme fire honde
personer Først ¹vor konge oc herre ²Vore slectinge
Dem som haffue forskyldet ³noget got aff oss Oc vore
⁴serdeliss venner

(4) 1. REX | 2. Amici | 3.
Cognati | 4. illi qui prest:
n | beneuol: v | bona f

[Here we should each notice that we happily receive
four types of people: First, 1. our king and lord, 2. our
relatives, 3. those who have deserved something
from us and 4. our special friends]

[(4) 1. KING | 2. Friends |
3. Relatives | 4. Those
who stand out(?) | kind |
good]

In addition to these, often rather learned, summaries in Latin, we find other
additions of a scriptural or liturgical nature. Biblical quotations and references

CHRISTIERN PEDERSEN'S *ALLE EPISTLER OC EUANGELIA* (1515)

are added; for example, A, fol. 71r: 'Math*eus* xi capt.'. The Latin terms for the names of the Sundays have been added in most of the headings in C. Even entire readings have been written out in Latin in D: fols 1v (Matthew 21); 6v (Luke 21); 10r (Matthew 11); 198r (Matthew 18), and 199v (Matthew 13). These handwritten notes that refer to or comment on the text in Latin point to a more scholarly readership who used *Alle Epistler oc Euangelia* for biblical study, which runs counter to Pedersen's original intentions of an audience. Furthermore, although learned Protestants were perfectly *au fait* with Latin, particularly the international Neo-Latin of science and scholarship, such an emphasis on writing out the Bible in Latin could point to a more traditional, pre-Reformation appreciation, if not endorsement, of the Latin Bible as a source of liturgy and spiritual nourishment and, indeed, of the Latin language itself as a channel for devotion.

There are a few occurrences of prayers inserted by users next to or beneath the sermons. In G, fol. 41v left margin, alongside a story about Jesus giving a blind man his sight again, there is the handwritten exhortation: 'Gud beuare oss fra [d]iefflen' ['May God protect us from the devil']. In H, fol. 8v bottom margin, there is a longer prayer blotted out in smudged red ink: 'myn Siel nu loffue Herren / Huad i mig er hans hellige Naffn / sin godhed rundelig giffuer / thi skalt du altid tacke hamnen din Synd haffuer' ['May my soul praise the Lord, his holy name is within me, liberally giving its goodness, thus you should always thank him who has your sin']. There are many other marginalia in H that have been blotted out which unfortunately makes them very difficult to read now. They are in both Danish and Low German; for example, fol. 4v: 'Herr Jesu Christ† Min hopning steit vp erden / ick weth dat du min Tröster / bis [...]' ['Lord Jesus Christ, my hope stands on the earth. I know that you are my consoler'].[43]

There are a few occasions where text has been added to Pedersen's words without any clear 'theological' intent:

A, fol. 21r	*Printed text*	*User's note (addition)*
	Siette maade ath gud som er rigest han er verden fattigst At gode oc fattige ydmyge me*n*niske skulle bliffue rige til ewig tiid met hannwm i hie*m*merige ↓	Oc dermed trøste sig i deriis fattigdom her j werdenn
	[The sixth way: that he is richest to God who is poorest to the world; that good and poor, humble people shall be rich for all eternity with him in heaven].	[And thus are consoled in their poverty here in the world]

---

43 According to the *ex libris* on the frontispiece ('Fredericu*s* Canuti possideo An*n*o 1601 pastor i*n* Quers'), this copy of *Alle Epistler oc Euangelia* once belonged to Frederik Knudsen who was pastor in Kværs Church from 1572. Kværs, near Gråsten, Southern Jutland, lies in what was, and to some extent still is, a multilingual border region with speakers of Danish, Low German, High German, and South Jutlandic (*sønderjysk*). It is not unlikely that these Low German annotations can be traced back to the time the copy was in Southern Jutland.

154   JONATHAN ADAMS

All this suggests a rather neutral or positive reaction to *Alle Epistler oc Euangelia*, an interest and acceptance of the book's contents and continued use of the material for preaching, reading, and study. However, there is evidence of a more critical anti-Catholic nature, but this is surprisingly rare. We find 1) deletions; 2) comments, and 3) substitutions. These traces of usage usually concern the miracle tales and they are by far most frequent in A, where the word 'iertegn' ['miracle tale, portent'] has sometimes even been changed to 'historia' ['story'].

The only noteworthy deletion in this context is B, fol. 160v, where a paragraph describing the Virgin Mary as the greatest of all the saints and the Queen of Heaven has been crossed out with diagonal strokes.[44] There are several marginal comments about the sermons, however, that clearly demonstrate disapproval:

A, fol. vr *Printed text*	*User's note (comment)*
A miracle story in which Mary rescues men drowning at sea	Miraculum falsum [False miracle]

A, fol. 8v *Printed text*	*User's note (comment)*
A miracle story in which Mary intercedes to save a soul	Si credere fas est [If it is right to believe this]

A, fol. 36r *Printed text*	*User's note (comment)*
A sermon for the Day of the Innocents ends: Der kommer ingen tid om aaret saa mange helghen paa i dag vden al eniste paa alle helgeniss dag ~~Thii ville wii alle fly til dem i dag met~~ ~~waare gudelige bøner at de ville foruerffue oss naade aff gud oc hiemmerigiss rige effter døden~~	icke vill Ieg
[There is no other time of year when there are so many saints on one day except for All Saints' Day. ~~So we shall all flee to them this day with our divine prayers so that they will obtain God's mercy and the kingdom of heaven after death for us~~].	[I will not]

A, fol. 67v *Printed text*	*User's note (comment)*
A miracle tale where Mary saves some drowning sailors.	Si credere fas est[45]

---

44   There are some small deletions in C, fol. 158r, but they appear to be more stylistic than theological: 'Saa bør oc oss hwor som behoff gøriss ath woghe wort liff for wor ieffn cristenss gaffn och salighedz skyld Hwo som haffuer verdenss rigdom och seer sin ieffn cristen lyde nødh paa legemenss vegne met hunger swlt tørst frost kwld for nøgenhedz skyld [...]'; ['So wherever there is need we should direct our lives for the sake of our fellow Christian's benefit and bliss. Whoever has the riches of the earth and sees his fellow Christian suffer bodily need through starvation, hunger, thirst, frost, cold because of nakedness [...]'.

45   Next to the title of this miracle tale, a user has also written 'Papistrii' ['Popery'].

CHRISTIERN PEDERSEN'S *ALLE EPISTLER OC EUANGELIA* (1515)

A, fol. 76v *Printed text*	*User's note (comment)*
A miracle tale where Mary saves the soul of a virgin.	Si chredere fa[s] est

A, fol. 101v *Printed text*	*User's note (comment)*
A deceased man appears in a vision.	Fictum est [This is fiction]

G, 138v *Printed text*	*User's note (comment)*
A description of souls in Limbo: Den tiidh denne fattighe mand døde da førde gudz engle hannem i abrahamss skødh. Der wor ned till de hellige forfedre som vaare i heluediss forborg thii dette skede før vor herre tolde sin død och pine oc frelste dem aff samme mørck.	Negatur nec unum verbum de hoc Limbo Patrum in S. Scripturâ legitur
[When this poor man died, God's angels accompanied him to the lap of Abraham who was down with the Holy Fathers in the forecourt to hell as this happened before our Lord suffered and died his death and saved them from this very darkness].	[We say no. There is not one word to read about the Limbo of the Fathers in the Holy Scripture].

There are also a couple of places where the text has been deleted and a more 'appropriate' word or phrase written above the line. In this way the reader removed Catholic content:

A, fol. 29r   *Printed text with reader's substitution*

da gik denne Paulus for Sancte Staffens altere i hanss cappel oc fald ydmygelige paa knæ oc bad inderlige till ~~hanwm~~ \gud/ met eth stadigt hob oc tro at han skulle foruerffue hannum sin helbrede igen ~~aff gud~~ [...] Saa loffuede de alle gwdh som da der till stede waare for den store naade han giorde met syndige menniske ~~for Sancti Staffens bøn skyld~~ \ved sin krafft/.

[Then this Paul went before St Stephen's altar in his chapel and humbly fell onto his knees and prayed fervently to ~~him~~ \God/ with a constant hope and belief that he would obtain for him his health ~~from God~~ [...] Then all those who were present praised God for the great mercy he showed to the sinful man ~~on account on St Stephen's prayer~~ \through his power/].

A, fol. 101v   *Printed text with reader's substitution*

Thii skulle alle menniske scriffte alle deriss synder och engen tye eller dølye aff dem for ~~deriss scrifftefader~~ \Gud/

[Thus should all people confess their sins and not conceal or hide any of them from their ~~father confessors~~ \God/].

It is noteworthy that the text is not deleted or torn out, but merely 're-categorized' with a comment. In this example, a bailiff in the tale has been replaced by a merchant:

B, fol. 176v	Eth Iertegen om en streng oc onder ~~fogedh~~ \Kiøbmand/
	Vi læse at det vaar en onder oc wmilder ~~foged~~ \Kiøbmand/
	som tog en ko fra en fattig encke [...]
	[A miracle tale about a strict and evil ~~bailiff~~ \merchant/
	We read that there was an evil and unkind ~~bailiff~~ \merchant/
	who took a cow from a poor widow [...]]

It may be possible that this is somehow a reflection of a new social order and an alliance between the State and Church. The sermon describes a wicked state official or bailiff who, in spite of her desperate pleas, takes a cow off a poor widow who is subsequently unable to feed herself or her children. The official dies shortly afterwards and ends up in hell where he receives unbearably harsh torture at the hands of one particular devil who informs him that he is being extra cruel because of the way the official treated the widow. Perhaps the connection in sixteenth-century Denmark between Church and State where the Lutheran Church became inseparably entwined in the state apparatus meant that an edifying story about a cruel state representative causing a widow to starve and therefore being tormented in hell was unthinkable to this reader; and the character was changed to a merchant, a much more likely and less politically charged figure of the wicked man.

Conclusion

All the various copies show signs of having continued to be read into the early modern period, and some even of being used for preaching, but generally they have not been subject to Protestant revisions. This is quite remarkable as even the book's writer, Christiern Pedersen, distanced himself from the work after his conversion, advising people to steer clear of such miracle stories and 'lies'.[46] Only A has extensive signs of attempts to remove or deny Catholic content; G has just one instance; none of the other copies has such amendments, apart from B's deletion of the paragraph on the Virgin Mary. So, what was it about *Alle Epistler oc Euangelia* that meant it continued to be read after the Reformation? And why might it have had such a positive reception, even among Protestants? Most importantly, it contains stories from the life of Jesus written in an entertaining and engaging manner, and such biblical reading has always been popular. We might have expected it to fall out of use after the publication in 1550 of the authorized and official Christian III's Bible, but this Bible was expensive and rather grand and never became popular reading. The miracle stories, if treated as nothing more than tall tales, may have been acceptable for reading in the privacy of one's own home for their entertainment value. Moreover, it would seem that the book also continued

---

46 See above and also his comments on his previous 'blindness' in *Den rette vej til Hiemmerigis Rige* (*Christiern Pedersens Danske Skrifter*, ed. by Brandt and Fenger, IV (1854), 214).

to be used for preaching or reading aloud. The many learned comments in Latin (copies A, C, and D) also suggest that the work was used for studying the stories of the Bible and their lessons.

The period after the Reformation in Denmark was characterized by pragmatism; so, monastic orders could live out their natural lives, 'harmless' wall paintings were not covered under layers of whitewash, and, so it would seem, Christiern Pedersen's book of miracle sermons continued to be read and studied. The annotations in the copies investigated here show that readers did not take seriously the miracles and the doctrines they often aimed to prove, and if we put these aspects of the book to one side, the book of sermons does not contain much that is theological harmful, but, for want of anything better, does contain plenty that can develop and nurture a good Christian.

Pedersen himself when he published his book seems to have been aware that the miracle stories would become popular reading material; he included in the contents pages a special index of the miracles found in the book. Of course, another sign of its instant popularity is the fact that it was printed again three years after the first edition, and, indeed, the fact that twenty-five copies of the miracle-sermon collection have survived is also testament to its widespread high regard. It is, of course, precisely these miracle stories that attract the ire of the reader in A.

Pedersen's reputation is also important to consider. His books from after his conversion were immensely popular and as Lutheranism took hold in Denmark, these publications constituted the written guides for the new Lutheran state and way of life that Denmark adopted. The breadth of their influence is quite astonishing and often subtle. For example, a woodcut illustrating the Crucifixion from his 1531 *Om vaar Herris død oc pine*, a translation of one of Luther's works, was copied precisely as a wall-painting in Sulsted Church in Jutland seventeen years after its publication. Pedersen, unlike many of his contemporaries, was able to redeem himself — religiously if not politically — through his conversion to Lutheranism, and perhaps this redemption also applied to his entire book production. In spite of his own protests, his *Alle Epistler oc Euangelia* preserved an air of respectability through its author's reputation, and even though it was no longer authorized for use by the new Church, it continued to thrive as a cheaper, more folksy and entertaining alternative to the Lutheran Bible translation of 1550.

Clearly, it was not loved by everyone, but *Alle Epistler oc Euangelia* did have readers after the Reformation, who read it for pleasure and enlightenment, or, it would appear, who used it critically, adapting the contents to suit the new articles of faith, as a book for preaching, edifying reading, and scholarship. It is quite a remarkable story of survival against the odds. One might indeed call it a book miracle.

158   JONATHAN ADAMS

Bibliography

Manuscripts

København, Den Arnamagnæanske Samling, MS AM 238 XXIX fol.
København, Den Arnamagnæanske Samling, MS AM 696 XVII 4°
København, Den Arnamagnæanske Samling, MS AM 783 4°
København, Den Arnamagnæanske Samling, MS AM 76 8°
København, Det Kongelige Bibliotek, MS Additamenta 75 fol.
København, Det Kongelige Bibliotek, MS GKS 1390 4°
Uppsala, Universitetsbibliotek, MS C 56
Wien, Österreichische Nationalbibliothek, MS 13013

Early Printed Works

Christiern Pedersen, *Alle Epistler oc Euangelia som lesiss alle Søndage om aared, sameledis Iule dag Paaske dagh, Pingetz dag. meth deriss vdtydning oc glose oc eth Iertegen till huer dag meth flere artickle som alle menniske nyttelige ere* (Paris: Jodocus Badius Ascensius, 1515)
Christiern Pedersen, *Alle Epistler oc Euangelia som lesiss alle Søndage om aared, sameledis Iule dag Paaske dagh, Pingetz dag. meth deriss vdtydning oc glose oc eth Iertegen till huer dag meth flere artickle som alle menniske nyttelige ere*, ed. by Henrik Smith (Leipzig: Melchior Lotter, 1518)
Christiern Pedersen, *En nottelig Legebog* (Malmö: [Johannes Hoochstraten], 1533)
Christiern Pedersen, *I denne bog leriss at Hore messe* (Paris: [Jodocus Badius Ascensius], 1514)
[Christiern Pedersen], *I denne bog leriss at Hore messe*, ed. by Henrik Smith (Leipzig: Melchior Lotter, 1517)
Christiern Pedersen, *Keyser Karlls Magnus Kronicke* (Malmö: [Johannes Hoochstraten], 1534)
Christiern Pedersen, *Kong Olger Danskis Kronicke* (Malmö: [Johannes Hoochstraten], 1534)
Christiern Pedersen, 'The Malmö Psalter' [the title page is lost] (Malmö: [Johannes Hoochstraten], 1533)
Christiern Pedersen, *Om Urte Uand* (Malmö: [Johannes Hoochstraten], 1534)
[Christiern Pedersen], *The richt vay to the Kingdome of heuine*, trans. by John Gau (Malmö: Johannes Hoochstraten, 1533)
Christiern Pedersen, *Vocabularium ad usum dacorum* (Paris: Jean Barbier, 1510)
Christiern Pedersen, *Vocabularium ad usum dacorum* (Köln: Heinrich Quentell's sons, 1514)
Christiern Pedersen, *Vocabularium ad usum dacorum*, ed. by Henrik Smith (Leipzig: Melchior Lotter, 1518)
[Christiern Pedersen], *Vor froe tider* (Paris: [Jodocus Badius Ascensius], 1514)
[Christiern Pedersen], *Vor froe tider*, ed. by Henrik Smith (Leipzig: Melchior Lotter, 1517)

CHRISTIERN PEDERSEN'S *ALLE EPISTLER OC EUANGELIA* (1515)   159

Christiern Pedersen, trans., *Dauidz psaltere* (Antwerpen: Willem Vorsterman, 1531)
Christiern Pedersen, trans., *Det Ny Testamente* (Antwerpen: Willem Vorsterman, 1529)
Christiern Pedersen, trans., *Det Ny Testamente* (Antwerpen: [Willem Vorsterman], 1531)
Christiern Pedersen, trans., *Den rette vey till Hiemmerigis Rige* (Antwerpen: [Willem Vorsterman], 1531)
Christiern Pedersen, trans., *En Christelig bogh Om merckelige sporsmaall och swar* (Antwerpen: [Willem Vorsterman], 1531)
Christiern Pedersen, trans., *Esopi leffnit oc nogle hans fabel som vore udsette aff Gredske paa latine oc aff latine paa tydske* (Malmö: Oluff Ulricksen, 1556)
Christiern Pedersen, trans., *Incipiunt puerilia Iuuenibus multum vtilia* (Paris: Jodocus Badius Ascensius, *c.* 1514)
[Hans Mikkelsen, trans.], *Thette ere thet Noye testamenth paa danske ret effter latinen vdsatthe* (Leipzig: Melchior Lotter, 1524)
[Johannes Agricola], *Hundrede och halffierde sindz tiwe merkelige och ret Christelige sporsmaall met deris Suar*, trans. by Christiern Pedersen (Malmö: [Johannes Hoochstraten], 1533)
[Martin Luther], *Huorledis huert Christet menniske skal bere sit kaarss*, trans. by Christiern Pedersen (Antwerpen: [Willem Vorsterman], 1531)
[Martin Luther], *Huorledis huert menniske skal betencke Herris dod oc pine*, trans. by Christiern Pedersen (Antwerpen: [Willem Vorsterman], 1531)
[Martin Luther], *Om børn ath holde till Scole*, trans. by Christiern Pedersen (Antwerpen: [Willem Vorsterman], 1531)
[Martin Luther], *Om vaar Herris dod oc pine*, trans. by Christiern Pedersen (Antwerpen: [Willem Vorsterman], 1531)
[Martin Luther], *Om vaar Herris dod oc pine*, trans. by Christiern Pedersen (Antwerpen: [Willem Vorsterman], 1531 [repr.])
Peder Laale, *Parabolæ*, ed. by Christiern Pedersen (Paris: Jodocus Badius Ascensius, 1515)
[Saxo Grammaticus], *Danorum Regum heroumque historiæ*, ed. by Christiern Pedersen (Paris: Jodocus Badius Ascensius, 1514)

Primary Sources

Acta Pontificum Danica: Pavelige Aktstykker vedrørende Danmark, ed. by Alfred Krarup and Johannes Lindbæk, 7 vols (København: Gad, 1904–1943)
Christiern Pedersen, *Christiern Pedersens Danske Skrifter*, ed. by C. J. Brandt and R. Th. Fenger, 5 vols (København: Gyldendal, 1850–1856)
A Danish Teacher's Manual of the Mid-Fifteenth Century (Cod. AM 76,8º), ed. by Sigurd Kroon and others, Kungl. Vitterhets historie och antikvitets akademien, Skrifter utgivna av Vetenskapssocieteten i Lund, 85, 96, 2 vols (Lund: Lund University Press, 1993–2008)
Dansk Klosterlæsning fra Middelalderen I, ed. by Carl Joakim Brandt, 3 vols (København: Selskabet for Danmarks Kirkehistorie, 1858–1865)
Displaced Texts: An Old Swedish Birgittine Revelation in Copenhagen, GkS 1154 fol. and Three Sermons in Vienna, Cod. Vind. 13013, ed. by Jonathan Adams,

160   JONATHAN ADAMS

Samlingar utgivna av Svenska fornskriftsällskapet, Serie 3: Smärre texter och
undersökningar, 4 (Uppsala: Swedish Science Press, 2008)
Om urtevand: Malmö 1534. Faksimiledition med en efterskrift, ed. by Bengt
Holmström (Malmö: Föreningen Malmö stadsbiblioteks vänner, 1986)
Svenska medeltids-postillor efter gamla handskrifter, ed. by Gustaf E. Klemming and
others, Samlingar utgivna av Svenska fornskriftsällskapet, Serie 1: Svenska
skrifter, 23, 8 vols (Stockholm: Norstedt, 1879–1983)

Secondary Studies

Allchin, Arthur Macdonald, *N. F. S. Grundtvig: An Introduction to his Life and Work*
(Aarhus: Aarhus University Press, 2015)
Andersson, Roger, *Postillor och predikan: en medeltida texttradition i filologisk
belysning*, Sällskapet Runica et Mediævalia: Scriptora minora, 1 (Stockholm:
Sällskapet Runica et Mediævalia, 1993)
Brandt, Carl Joakim, *Om Lunde-Kanniken Christiern Pedersen og hans Skrifter*
(København: Gad, 1882)
Brøndum-Nielsen, Johannes, *Fra Skaanes Senmiddelalder: Den skaanske Postille
fra Bekkaskough*, Festskrift udgivet af Københavns Universitet (København:
Københavns Universitet, 1959)
Bruun, Christian, *Aarsberetninger og Meddelelser fra Det Store Kongelige Bibliothek*,
1: *1864–1869* (København: Gyldendal, 1870)
Frederiksen, Britta Olrik, 'Et forsøg til dateringen af det gammeldanske postil-
håndskrift GKS 1390 4to', in *Oppa Swänzsko oc Oppa Dansko: Studien zum
Altostnordischen*, ed. by Harry Perridon and Arend Quak, Amsterdamer
Beiträge zur älteren Germanistik, 62 (Leiden: Brill, 2006), pp. 151–206
Grundtvig, Nikolaj F. S., *Danne-Virke: Et Tids-skrift*, 1 (1816)
Horstbøll, Henrik, *Menigmands medie: Det folkelige bogtryk i Danmark 1500–1840*
(København: Det Kongelige Bibliotek, 1999)
Jensen, Johan R. M., 'Christiern Pedersen Jærtegnspostil: Mellem Middelalder og
Reformation', in *Mentalitet & Historie: Om fortidige forestillingsverdener*, ed. by
Charlotte Appel, Peter Henningsen, and Nils Hybel (Ebeltoft: Skippershoved,
2002), pp. 25–49
Jørgensen, Jens Anker, *Humanisten Christiern Pedersen: En præsentation* (Køben-
havn: Reitzel, 2007)
Lillie, Eva Louise, 'Imitatio Christi: Om Christiern Pedersens "Huorledis huert
Christet menniske skal bere sit kaarss"', *Iconographisk Post: Nordisk tidskrift för
ikonografi*, 4 (1995), 44–53
Mitchell, Philipp Marshall, 'The English Imprints of Denmark', *Fund og Forskning*,
5 (1958), 34–61
Nielsen, Lauritz, *Danmarks Middelalderlige Haandskrifter: En sammenfattende
boghistorisk Oversigt* (København: Gyldendal, 1937)
Nielsen, Lauritz, *Dansk Bibliografi 1482–1600*, ed. by Erik Dal, rev. edn, 5 vols
(København: Det Danske Sprog- og Litteraturselskab, 1996)
Paludan, J., 'En middelalderlig Skolebog', *Nordisk Tidskrift for Filologi*, n.s. 10
(1890–1892), 83–88

CHRISTER PAHLMBLAD

The Word of God Purely Preached

Continuity and Change in the Postils of the Swedish Reformation

In the foreword to his 1566 treatise *Om kyrkio stadgar och ceremonier* Archbishop Laurentius Petri reminds his readers that 'God's pure Word' was first publicly proclaimed, both orally and in writing, forty-six years earlier by his brother Olavus Petri and other right-minded persons.[1] This is the victorious party's interpretation of how the Swedish, royally supported, Reformation came about and what its foremost weapon was. However, Laurentius also admits that there was broad popular resistance to the changes: 'thet war största hopenom emoot och swårliga förtretzligit' ['it was against the will of the majority and sorely vexed them']. The indignation of the people was directed against 'Predicarenar, som genom Gudz ord sådant hade kommit till wäga' ['the preachers who had brought such things about by means of God's Word'], and he was held to be best who 'mest orckade ropa Lutheraner, Kettare, troospillare, Gudzförrädhare' ['most strongly cried Lutherans, heretics, faith-spoilers, God-betrayers']. In the agrarian, sparsely populated country, where ninety-five percent of the inhabitants were peasants who lived, worked, and died in their native parishes, there was little enthusiasm for innovation in religious matters. The organization of the Church, its legal framework, and the medieval liturgy remained basically intact for the first two decades following the year 1520, which is when the Reformation project had begun, if we are to believe Laurentius Petri.

Olavus and Laurentius Petri, the sons of a smith from the town of Örebro in the province of Närke (some 200 kilometres west of Stockholm), were the two foremost proponents of the Swedish Lutheran Reformation. Olavus, the older brother, was born in 1493 or 1497.[2] In the latter part of the 1510s

---

1 Laurentius Petri, *Om kyrkio stadgar och ceremonier, hurudana och huilka man vthi een christeligh församling bruka må eller ey* (Wittenberg: M. Simon Gronenberg, 1587), fols 1r–2v. The manuscript is from 1566 but was first printed in 1587 in Wittenberg by Abraham Andreæ Angermannus.
2 The year 1493 stems from the longer autobiography which probably is a fabrication by Nils

Christer Pahlmblad (christer.pahlmblad@ctr.lu.se) is Reader in Practical Theology in the Centre for Theology and Religious Studies at Lund University.

Circulating the Word of God in Medieval and Early Modern Europe: Catholic Preaching and Preachers across Manuscript and Print (c. 1450 to c. 1550), ed. by Veronica O'Mara and Patricia Stoop, SERMO 17, (Turnhout: Brepols, 2022), pp. 161–184   BREPOLS ❧ PUBLISHERS   10.1484/M.SERMO-EB.5.130455

he studied in Wittenberg, where he became a master in 1518. Martin Luther was probably one of his teachers. His return to Sweden and ordination as a deacon in the cathedral of Strängnäs in 1520 is the event alluded to by his brother Laurentius in the opening quotation. Olavus was made chancellor to the bishop and preacher at the cathedral. The Lutheran character of his sermons was noted by his fellow canons.[3] In 1524 he became secretary to the town council of Stockholm and preacher at the town church, St Nicholai (present-day Storkyrkan). He took part in the production of the Swedish New Testament, printed in 1526, and published around 1530 a series of books that came to determine the liturgical development of the Church of Sweden right up until the middle of the twentieth century, the most important being the reformed Order of Mass in 1531. Only in 1539 was he ordained a priest by the bishop of Strängnäs. He became rector of St Nicholai in 1543 and died in 1552.[4]

His younger brother Laurentius Petri was born in 1499. He enrolled in the university in Wittenberg in 1527. After his return to Sweden he worked as a school master in Uppsala from 1530. In August of the following year he was elected archbishop. He wrote extensively in defence of the liturgical reforms and of the Lutheran theology of the Eucharist. His most important contribution to the development of the Reformation in Sweden is the publication in 1571, with royal approval, of *Then swenska kyrkoordningen*. He died in 1573. He had then been archbishop for forty-two years under three kings and had established himself as the foremost guarantor of the Swedish Reformation.[5]

The two brothers each published one postil, or sermon collection. None of their sermons survives in manuscript form — indeed, almost no manuscript sermons remain from the sixteenth century.

Rabenius (1648–1717), known for his imaginative counterfeiting of historical documents, see Olavus Petri, *Samlade skrifter af Olavus Petri*, ed. by Bengt Hesselman, 4 vols (Uppsala: Sveriges kristliga studentrörelse, 1914–1917), IV (1917), 560.

3   In a letter from Nicolaus Benedicti, canon at the Strängnäs cathedral, to Hans Brask, the bishop of Linköping; see Hans Brask, *Latinsk korrespondens 1523*, ed. by Hedda Roll, Acta Universitatis Stockholmiensis, Studia Latina Stockholmiensia, 19 (Stockholm: Almqvist & Wiksell, 1973), pp. 75–76.

4   On the biography of Olavus Petri, see Christer Gardemeister, *Den suveräne Guden: en studie i Olavus Petris teologi*, Studia Theologica Lundensia, 43 (Lund: Lund University Press, 1989), pp. 7–16; Gunnar T. Westin, 'Olavus Petri', in *Svenskt biografiskt lexikon* (Stockholm: Svenskt biografiskt lexikon, 1918–), 28 (1992–1994), 151–66. On his theology, see primarily Sven Ingebrand, *Olavus Petris reformatoriska åskådning*, Acta Universitatis Upsaliensis, Studia Doctrinae Christianae Upsaliensia, 1 (Lund: Gleerups, 1964), and Gardemeister, *Den suveräne Guden*.

5   On the biography of Laurentius Petri, see Olle Hellström, 'Laurentius Petri', in *Svenskt biografiskt lexikon* (Stockholm: Svenskt biografiskt lexikon, 1918–), 22 (1977–1979), 376–85. On his theology, see Bo Ahlberg, *Laurentius Petris nattvardsuppfattning*, Studia Theologica Lundensia, 26 (Lund: Gleerups, 1964), Rémi Kick, *Tel un navire sur la mer dechaînée: la communauté chrétienne dans l'œuvre de Laurentius Petri, archevêque d'Uppsala (1531–1573)*, Studia Theologica Lundensia, 52 (Lund: Lund University Press, 1997), and Christer Pahlmblad, 'Laurentius Petri, gudstjänstbruken och sakramentsfromheten', in *Laurentius Petri och svenskt gudstjänstliv*, Årsbok för svenskt gudstjänstliv, 79 (2004), 120–49.

The Postils

Six postils were published in Swedish during the Reformation period. The first was printed in 1528 with the title *En nyttog postilla*.[6] It contained twenty-seven sermons from the summer section of Martin Luther's *Kirchenpostille*, published in 1526, translated and revised by Olavus Petri, probably in collaboration with another prominent early reformer in Sweden, the archdeacon Laurentius Andreæ.[7] The reason why only these few sermons were translated was, according to the foreword, partly that they were difficult to understand, partly that they now and then treated abuses, which could scandalize 'weak' readers. They were in other words too polemical for the Swedish situation. But omissions apart, the translation is true to its model.[8] The foreword promised a new postil on the Gospels for the whole year, one that everyone could understand and no one would be offended by. This promise was fulfilled by Olavus Petri's *Een lijten postilla* of 1530.[9] This Postil is in several ways connected with the provincial synod of Örebro in 1529. The foreword states that prelates and other honourable men had approved the publication, probably in the context of that synod. Furthermore, the synod had decided that all priests should begin and end their sermons in a similar way — formulas for this are found in the Postil.[10]

In 1555 Laurentius Petri printed a Postil with translated German sermons,[11] primarily from the *Kinderpostille* (1546) by Veit Dietrich, but also from Luther's sermon collections.[12] This Postil, too, contains brief texts that can begin and conclude a sermon. Only in 1573 did Laurentius Petri publish a collection

---

6   *En nyttog postilla ofuer någhor fåå euangelia aff sommardelen, ther man må tagha jtt sätt och grund aff huru all euangelia som här icke insatt äre vthlägias och forclaras skole* (Stockholm: [Kungl. tryckeriet], 1528); Olavus Petri, *Samlade skrifter af Olavus Petri*, ed. by Hesselman, II (1915), 1–310.

7   Ingebrand, *Olavus Petris reformatoriska åskådning*, p. 41.

8   Ingebrand, *Olavus Petris reformatoriska åskådning*, p. 41.

9   Olavus Petri, *Een lijten postilla offuer all euangelia som om söndaghanar läsen warda offuer heela året, ther til och offuer the euangelia som på the nampnkunnogasta höghtijder om året warda läsen, och en lijten cathechismus eller vnderuisning, på the stycke som en christen lerdom mest påhenger* (Stockholm: Claes Pederson, 1530); Olavus Petri, *Samlade skrifter af Olavus Petri*, ed. by Hesselman, III (1916), 1–470. An unaltered reprint was produced in Lübeck in 1537, with a variant edition in 1538; see Isak Collijn, *Sveriges bibliografi intill år 1600*, 3 vols (Uppsala: Svenska litteratursällskapet 1927–1938), II (1927–1931), 53–60.

10 Olavus Petri, *Samlade skrifter af Olavus Petri*, ed. by Hesselman, III (1916), 9–10 and 467–70 respectively.

11 The Postil consists of four parts: Advent to Easter Eve, Easter Day to Advent, Saints' days, and a part containing some general Gospels (Stockholm: Amund Laurentzson, 1555); reprinted in Stockholm in 1641; see Collijn, *Sveriges bibliografi intill år 1600*, II (1927–1931), 219.

12 H. B. Hammar, 'Studier i evangelisk predikan i Sverige under reformationstidevarvet' (unpublished licentiate dissertation, Lund University, 1939), pp. 54–62. See, however, Ahlberg, *Laurentius Petris nattvardsuppfattning*, pp. 22–23 n. 4. The sermons by Luther had been thoroughly revised already in the German edition used by Laurentius Petri; H. B. Hammar, 'Reformationstidens predikan i Sverige', in *Reformationen i Norden: kontinuitet och förnyelse*, ed. by Carl-Gustaf Andrén, Skrifter utgitt av Nordiskt institut för kyrkohistorisk forskning, 3 (Lund: Gleerups, 1973), pp. 263–80 (p. 269).

164   CHRISTER PAHLMBLAD

written by himself, titled *Öffuer historien om wårs Herras Jesu Christi werdigha pino och dödh*.[13]

The Swedish publisher Petrus Johannis Gothus printed a Postil on the Gospels in Rostock in 1597/98. It contained German sermons translated into Swedish without any obvious revisions.[14] No postils were published in Finnish for the priests in the dioceses of Åbo (Turku) and Viborg during the sixteenth century.

The Postils of 1530 and 1573 are thus the only collections of vernacular sermons composed and printed in Sweden in the sixteenth century. Two sermons with a similar theme taken from these will be compared below: the Easter Day sermon from Olavus's Postil and Laurentius's last Passion sermon — on the grave of Jesus — which also treats the events of Easter Day.

'The Pure Word of God'

In Laurentius Petri's description of events in and immediately after 1520 he uses a phrase that was central to the Reformation: 'the pure Word of God'. Here it has become a stock phrase, a kind of confessional formula referring to a Lutheran understanding of Scripture. The expression appears in the negotiations preceding the decisions made at the Diet of Västerås in 1527. In the actual decision or 'recess' it appears as a petition made by the representatives to the king, 'att Gudz ord motte allestadz i rikit renliga predicat varde' ['that the Word of God may everywhere in the Kingdom be purely preached'].[15]

The expression was used by the reformers to legitimize the changes they were introducing. According to Laurentius Petri, the decision that 'reena Gudz ordh och Ewangelium [skulle] predikes kringh om alt Landett' ['that God's pure Word and Gospel should be preached everywhere in the country'] also entails 'alt thett som Ewangelij Predikan fölier' ['everything that comes with the preaching of the Gospel'], that is 'förandringar och reformacier [...] efter Ewangelij sinne och meningh' ['changes and reforms [...] according to the sense and meaning of the Gospel'].[16] In the Minutes of the Diet, however, the

---

13   *Öffuer historien om wårs Herras Jesu Christi werdigha pino och dödh, någhra eenfalligha sermoner eller predicaner* (Stockholm: Amund Laurentzson, 1573); reprinted in Rostock in 1609. Hammar, 'Studier i evangelisk predikan', pp. 65–66; Hammar, 'Reformationstidens predikan', p. 271.

14   *Postilla ther inne aff hwart och ett söndags euangelium, etc. warder tagen een besynnerlig lära tröst, och förmaning, eller warning, medh widhengda böön til hwart euangelium sampt några merkeliga sententier aff scrifftenne, och aff kyrkionnes lärarom, sammandragne och vthgångne aff Petro Johannis Gotho medh sine egna bekåstning* (Rostock: [Staffan Möllman], 1597–1598); see Hammar, 'Reformationstidens predikan', p. 273.

15   *Svenska riksdagsakter jämte andra handlingar som höra till statsförfattningens historia*, ed. by Emil Hildebrand and Oscar Alin (I–II), and Emil Hildebrand (III), 3 vols (Stockholm: Nordstedts, 1887–1890), I (1887), 86 (hereafter *Svenska riksdagsakter*).

16   Laurentius Petri's explanation in 1533 of the 'recess and ordinance', that is the decisions of the

expressions 'the pure Word of God' and 'purely preach God's Word' hardly have this confessional sense. Such expressions were compatible with different views about the faith and life of the Church and functioned as the common denominator of the various parties at the Diet.

In fact, in their replies to the royal proposition presented at the Diet, the councillors and nobility as well as the peasants required adherence to 'goda, gambla christeliga sidvenior' ['good, old Christian customs'],[17] that is, that the practices of the medieval Church — its liturgy, rituals, monasteries et cetera — should be maintained in compliance with the Church's own legal order, which had been honoured by previous kings and was cherished by the majority of Swedish citizens — so dear to them, in fact, that changes were cause for revolt.[18] To abide by 'good, old Christian customs' was clearly not seen by them as incompatible with the 'pure' preaching of the Word of God. Therefore, 'the pure Word of God' and 'purely preach God's Word' cannot have been understood by all participants as referring to the Lutheran opinion.

Nevertheless, although 'the pure Word of God' was not yet a confessional formula in 1527 it did imply a quite specific requirement, one that was partly at odds with medieval ideas about proper sermon content. The background of the requirement was 'biblical humanism', a movement embraced by reformists who wanted to stay true to the medieval Church and Lutheran reformers alike, causing them to raise similar demands for the primacy of the Bible in preaching. The reply of the councillors and nobility contains a clarification to this effect. In their opinion, priests should preach the pure Word of God and not 'oviss järteken, menniskio dict och fabel, som her til dags mykit skedt är' ['uncertain miracles, human inventions and fables, which hitherto has been very common'].[19]

We find the same interpretation in a letter sent by Gustav Vasa in 1528 to the clergy in Finland: it had been agreed in Västerås 'att kring om hela rijkit skal predicas reena gudz ordt och euangelium, och låtas til baka onyttug squaller, owiss iertekne, fabuler och menniske dict' ['that God's pure Word and

---

Diet of 1527 and the concomitant royal proclamation; see *Handlingar till Sverges reformations- och kyrkohistoria under konung Gustaf I*, ed. by P. E. Thyselius, 2 vols (Stockholm: Bagges, 1841–1845), I (1841–1842), 82.

17 On the meaning of the phrase and its background in the conflicts around the Kalmar Union in the fifteenth century, see Christer Pahlmblad, 'Fyra reformationstida påskpredikningar', in *Svensk påskpredikan genom tiderna*, ed. by Christer Pahlmblad and Sven-Åke Selander (Skellefteå: Artos, 2010), pp. 47–90 (pp. 49–51).

18 See the dissenters' pronouncements of 1529, *Sveriges traktater med främmande magter jemte andra dit hörande handlingar*, ed. by Olof Simon Rydberg, 14 vols (Stockholm: Nordstedts, 1877–1934), III (1895), 357–58: King Gustav Vasa is accused of having broken the oath that he should protect the Church and its persons. Instead he had destroyed the worship of the Church and expelled bishops and prelates. On the revolts during the reign of Gustav Vasa, see Martin Berntsson, *Mässan och armborstet: uppror och reformation i Sverige 1525–1544* (Skellefteå: Artos, 2010).

19 *Svenska riksdagsakter*, I (1887), 78.

166   CHRISTER PAHLMBLAD

Gospel shall be preached all over the kingdom and useless rumours, dubious miracles, fables, and human inventions be restrained'].[20] In the opinion of Laurentius Petri, a bad practice had arisen whereby priests preached little or nothing from God's Word, or 'förmängde thett medh falsk Jerteekn, Fabuler, och Menniskiors stadgar, Så att tå man nu begynte åhter Predika rene Gudz ordh och Euangelium, syntes thett mangom wara sälsindt, och kallade thett ena nya troo' ['mixed it with false miracles, fables, and human laws, so that when God's pure Word and Gospel once more began to be preached, it seemed strange to many and was called a new faith'].[21] The reference here is quite specific. What is meant are the homiletic tools of the medieval preacher: exempla, miracle stories, saints' legends and quotations from authorities such as Church Fathers and classical authors — the stuff that was used in sermons in order to support the argument, explain biblical passages in accordance with ecclesiastical tradition, and help the audience to remember what had been said.

The Diet of Västerås, then, decided that all priests in the kingdom should expound and explain the Word of God alone, without the use of such extra-biblical texts, because they might arrogate the authority of the divine revelation or risk distorting the meaning of the Bible or simply could be considered superstitious.[22] The provincial synod of Örebro in 1529 confirmed the decision. The priests, it said, were bound to 'förkunna, uthspridha och fremia Gudz ord' ['proclaim, spread and further God's Word']. In all churches of the kingdom,

---

20   *Konung Gustaf den förstes registratur*, ed. by Joh. Ax. Almquist and others, 29 vols (Stockholm: Nordstedts, 1861–1916), V (1871), 155–56. A similar criticism of late medieval preaching had been raised in 1525 during the Diet of Rendsburg (in the duchy of Slesvig-Holsten, Denmark): the priests preached fables and not the Gospel; at the Diet of Kiel in 1526 the priests were required to expound the Gospel 'rätt [...] utan fabler' ['rightly [...] without fables']; see Hjalmar Holmquist, *Svenska kyrkans historia* (Stockholm: Svenska kyrkans diakonistyrelse, 1933), III:1, 126; *Den danske Kirkes Historie*, ed. by Hal Koch and others, 8 vols (København: Gyldendal, 1950–1966), III (1965), 292–93; P. G. Lindhardt, 'Reformationen i Norden i komparativ belysning', in *Reformationen i Norden: kontinuitet och förnyelse*, ed. by Carl-Gustaf Andrén, Skrifter utgitt av Nordiskt institut för kyrkohistorisk forskning, 3 (Lund: Gleerups, 1973), pp. 19–27 (p. 14).

21   *Handlingar till Sverges reformations- och kyrkohistoria*, pp. 81–82; see also *Den svenska kyrkoordningen 1571 jämte studier kring tillkomst, innehåll och användning*, ed. by Sven Kjöllerström (Lund: Håkan Ohlsson, 1971), p. 24.

22   This very specific meaning of 'rena','renliga', 'oförmängt', 'klara' ['pure', 'purely', 'without admixture', 'clear'] et cetera has not been sufficiently recognized in previous research. See, for example, Knut B. Westman, *Reformationens genombrottsår i Sverige* (Stockholm: Svenska kyrkans diakonistyrelse, 1918), pp. 416 and 421; Holmquist, *Svenska kyrkans historia*, III:1, 15–16; Yngve Brilioth, *Predikans historia: Olaus Petri-föreläsningar hållna vid Uppsala universitet*, 2nd edn (Lund: Gleerups, 1962), pp. 170–71. These authors tended to understand expressions such as 'God's pure Word' as referring more generally to the Word of God as the 'highest norm'. The most outspoken proponent of this view was Sven Kjöllerström, who consequently (and quite wrongly) concluded that the reformers prevailed over the other parties at the Diet of 1527 and succeeded in forcing a decision where 'sola scriptura' was the only norm, although the king had wanted a compromise. Sven Kjöllerström, 'Västerås ordinantia', *Scandia: tidskrift för historisk forskning*, 26 (1960), pp. 41–89 (pp. 85–86).

THE WORD OF GOD PURELY PREACHED   167

the Word should 'rent och oförmängdt predikat varda' ['be preached purely and without admixture'].[23] These decisions applied to all priests, those who adhered to the old faith and the received customs just as much as those who with the aid of Lutheran ideas wished to reform the Church. Likewise, it was this readership — the entire clergy of the kingdom — that Olavus Petri had in mind when he published his Postil in 1530.

The Structure and Liturgical Setting of Preaching

The overall structure of the sermons in Olavus Petri's 1530 Postil is simple. The Gospel text is quoted from the 1526 translation of the New Testament. Then follows what Olavus Petri consistently refers to in the Postil as the 'meaning' of the Gospel, more precisely 'the simple meaning' or 'the meaning of the text simply rendered'. In one place he describes this part of the sermon as 'korteliga löpa texten offuer' ['briefly run over the text'].[24]

Olavus Petri can also talk of the Gospel text and its 'meaning' as 'Evangelium medh sijn vthlegning' ['the Gospel with its exposition']. He insists that there must always be such an exposition or explanation of the meaning of the text.[25] This is not a pious desire on his part, but a reference to the duties of parish clergy as laid down in medieval ecclesiastical legislation. At Mass on every Sunday and public holiday, after the Gospel and the Creed had been sung in Latin at the altar, priests were obliged to translate the Gospel text while standing at the pulpit — *de ambone* is the medieval term — and to explain it by means of what medieval sources usually call an *expositio evangelii*.[26] The sermons in Olavus Petri's Postil thus begin with such an *expositio*, whose purpose is to clarify the 'simple meaning' of the Gospel text, that is, the *sensus historicus* or *sensus literalis*. The second part of the sermon — the sermon proper — almost always begins in the following manner: 'Nw wilie wi, käre wener, tilsee hwad lärdom oss giffuin warder' ['Now, dear friends, let us see what knowledge is

---

23 *Svenska riksdagsakter*, I (1887), 118–19.
24 Olavus Petri, *Samlade skrifter af Olavus Petri*, ed. by Hesselman, III (1916), 17, 21, 30, passim. The expression is found in the sermon for the anniversary of the dedication of a church, p. 359.
25 Olavus Petri, *Samlade skrifter af Olavus Petri*, ed. by Hesselman, III (1916), 415.
26 See Christer Pahlmblad, *Mässa på svenska: den reformatoriska mässan i Sverige mot den senmedeltida bakgrunden*, Bibliotheca Theologiæ Practicæ, 60 (Lund: Arcus, 1998), pp. 98–105. See also Anne Riising, *Danmarks middelalderlige prædiken* (København: Gad, 1969), p. 21 n. 58; Sven-Erik Pernler, 'Predikan ad populum under svensk medeltid: till frågan om sockenprästernas predikoskyldighet', in *Predikohistoriska perspektiv: studier tillägnade Åke Andrén*, ed. by Alf Härdelin, Skrifter utgivna av Svenska Kyrkohistoriska Föreningen, 2, n.s. 35 (Stockholm: SkeabVerbum, 1982), pp. 73–94 (p. 76); H. Leith Spencer, *English Preaching in the Late Middle Ages* (Oxford: Clarendon Press, 1993), pp. 254–55 and 351 as well as pp. 257 and 262; and Roger Andersson and Stephan Borgehammar, 'The Preaching of the Birgittine Friars at Vadstena Abbey (*ca* 1380–1515)', in *Revue Mabillon: revue internationale d'histoire et de littérature religieuses*, n. s. 8 (69), (1997), 209–36 (pp. 229–30).

given us']. 'Knowledge' is here to be understood as the application of the Gospel text to the Christian's spiritual life. The sermons in the Postil regularly end with a brief *votum*, frequently followed by a doxological formula.

The same sermon structure is found also in Christiern Pedersen's pre-Reformation Danish Postil (1515).[27] Here, too, each sermon begins with a translation of the Gospel and an *expositio evangelii*. The text is expounded verse by verse and each comment is supported by an extract from Scripture or a Church Father or some other ecclesiastical authority. Christiern Pedersen (*c.* 1480–1554) calls the *expositio* 'vdtydningen' ['the interpretation'] or 'glosen' ['the gloss']. As a rule, he fetches his *expositiones* from well-known medieval Bible commentaries.[28] For the period from the First Sunday of Advent to the Eleventh Sunday after Trinity a sermon follows, while the remaining Sundays only have enough material for parish priests to fulfil their legal duty: a translation and brief explanation of the day's Gospel text.

There is, then, a significant difference between the Danish and the Swedish Postil: while Christiern Pedersen's Gospel commentaries and sermons are based on quotations from Church Fathers and other ecclesiastically approved authors in the medieval manner, such references are completely absent from Olavus Petri's Postil — as are of course every trace of the illustrative stories and miracles that the Danish pre-Reformation Postil provides for each Sunday, therefore commonly referred to as *Jærtegnspostilen* (in Danish) or *Järteckenspostillan* (in Swedish), that is, *the Miracle Postil*. The absence of extra-biblical material in the Swedish Postil demonstrates the intention of the decision at the Diet of Västerås in 1527: the Word of God was to be 'purely preached' throughout the kingdom. Sermons should convey the words of the Bible, not 'fables and human inventions'.

Olavus Petri's Postil takes it for granted that sermons are always preceded by an *invocatio divini auxilii*, a prayer for divine aid. An example of such an

---

27 Christiern Pedersen, *Christiern Pedersens Danske Skrifter*, ed. by C. J. Brandt and R. Th. Fenger, 5 vols (København: Gyldendal, 1850–1856), I–II; for a discussion of Christiern Pedersen's work, see the essay by Jonathan Adams in the current volume. A German example, a Roman Catholic text from 1570, states that the priest after the *invocatio divini auxilii* should pronounce the *thema* of the sermon and thereafter translate the Gospel text, briefly comment upon it and then, in one or two points, treat some aspect of the faith; see Anton Beck, *Kirchliche Studien und Quellen* (Amberg: Böes, 1903), p. 353.

28 Mostly from the *Postilla super epistolas et euangelia de tempore et de sanctis et pro defunctis* attributed to Guillermus Parisiensis, which in turn draws on material from the Bible commentaries of Nicolaus de Lyra and other sources; see Riising, *Danmarks middelalderlige prædiken*, pp. 44 and 482–90. Compare also the Gospel commentaries in *Studium Upsalense: Specimens of the Oldest Lecture Notes Taken in the Mediaeval University of Uppsala*, ed. by Anders Piltz, Acta Universitatis Upsaliensis. Skrifter rörande Uppsala universitet C, Organisation och historia, 36 (Uppsala: [Uppsala universitet], 1977), pp. 60–62 and pp. 170–202; the commentaries were delivered as lectures at the University of Uppsala in the late fifteenth century: the form of the academic lecture on scripture and this part of the medieval sermon is the same. Both are *expositiones*, running commentaries verse by verse.

THE WORD OF GOD PURELY PREACHED 169

invocation is, as mentioned, given in the Postil. It consists of a greeting followed by an exhortation to pray that God, the heavenly Father, might grant a correct understanding of his holy Word, and that the Word might be confirmed in the hearts of preacher and audience alike, so that they not only hear it but also do what it requires. The audience is then called upon to kneel and pray the Lord's Prayer. A *votum* follows, a wish that God may send his Holy Spirit and enable all those present to heed the Word and will of God. The Gospel text is recited and the sermon begins. All of this is in basic accordance with medieval practice.[29] Moreover, it gave rise to a standard way of beginning sermons, with an exordium followed by a silent Lord's Prayer, which was to characterize Swedish preaching for centuries. In accordance with medieval tradition, the Postil also states that the act of preaching should conclude with intercessions and a confession of sins and gives an example of how this may be done.

The framework of preaching that is presupposed in the Postil of 1530 accords well with what we know of public preaching at Mass on Sundays and public holidays in late medieval Sweden. Such preaching was performed in a liturgical setting that remained the same throughout the sixteenth century. The following may be taken as a fair synopsis (italicized words refer to content found in sources other than Olavus Petri's Postil):

Introduction with invocatio divini auxilii

> The Lord's Prayer
>
> Votum

Translation of the day's Gospel

Sermon:

> Explanation of the Gospel text (expositio evangelii)
>
> The sermon proper
>
> Concluding votum and doxology

Liturgical conclusion in the vernacular:

> *Announcements (for example, of upcoming days of obligation), followed by* intercessions, in the form of a series of exhortations to prayer
>
> *The Lord's Prayer, collect*

---

29 Detached examples of such sermon introductions are found in, for example, *Svenska medeltidspostillor*, Samlingar utgivna av Svenska fornskriftsällskapet, serie 1, Svenska skrifter, 23: I–VIII, I–III (1879–1894), ed. by Gustaf Edvard Klemming; IV–V (1905–1910), ed. by Robert Geete; VI–VIII (1974–1983), ed. by Bertil Ejder (Uppsala: Svenska fornskriftsällskapet, 1879–1983), VI, 128–29, and in *A Danish Teacher's Manual of the Mid-Fifteenth Century (Cod. AM 76,8°)*, ed. by Sigurd Kroon and others, Kungl. Vitterhets historie och antikvitets akademien, Skrifter utgivna av Vetenskapssocieteten i Lund, 85, 96, 2 vols (Lund: Lund University Press, 1993–2008), I (1993), 510–11. See further Pahlmblad, *Mässa på svenska*, pp. 93–94 with nn. 3 and 4.

The Apostles' Creed
Confession of sins
Exhortations to works of mercy and almsgiving, et cetera.[30]

If the late medieval clergy fulfilled their duties according to the legal require-ments of the Church, then their congregations received a basic knowledge of the Gospel stories. As indicated above, catechetical instruction took place in immediate connection with the sermon: the traditional catechetical texts — the Apostles' Creed, the Lord's Prayer, the *Ave Maria* and the Ten Commandments — were pronounced by the congregation *docente sacerdote*, 'taught by the priest', which is to say that they were dictated by the priest in the vernacular and repeated by the congregation, one sentence at a time. The occasion for controlling each individual's knowledge of the faith was the sacrament of Confession: sufficient knowledge was a prerequisite for absolution, and absolution was in turn a prerequisite for Communion.[31]

Olavus Petri's Postil presupposes this system of instruction. As previously mentioned, it addresses itself to all the clergy. At the time of its publication, and for most of the 1530s, the clergy in Sweden was quite unaffected by Reformation views. The *Sitz im Leben* of the Postil, then, is the unaltered medieval Latin Mass and the received modes of instruction at Mass. The form of the sermons in the Postil, the liturgical comments sometimes found at the beginning of a sermon, the catechetical texts in the appendix (the Apostles' Creed, the Lord's Prayer, the *Ave Maria* and the Ten Commandments in Swedish), the intercessions and the Form of Confession given as an adjunct to the Postil's sermons — all this was familiar to the medieval clergy who were its intended users. However, although the forms were well established, the content of the sermons, prayers, and confession of sins conveys Olavus Petri's Lutheran views. The old forms were made the primary vehicle of the new ideology.

In the course of the sixteenth century an attempt was made to strengthen the catechetical character of preaching itself. The first half-hour of the sermon should, according to a statute of 1561, be spent on preaching the catechism,

---

30 The structure outlined here is the one that appears to have established itself generally after the Reformation, as indicated by Laurentius Petri's Postil of 1555, *Den svenska kyrkoordningen 1571*, and the seventeenth-century Swedish Mass in *Handbook, ther vthi är författadt, huruledes gudztiensten medh christelighe ceremonier och kyrkiosedher, vthi wåra swenska församblingar skal bliffua hållin och förhandladt* (Uppsala: Eskil Matzson, 1614). For a Danish example, see for instance, *Malmø-Salmebogen 1533: faksimiledition*, ed. by John Kroon (Malmö: Dansk-Skånsk Förening, 1967), fols 71v–74r. The Swedish and Danish traditions reflect the German as found in, for example, *Die kleineren althochdeutschen Sprachdenkmäler*, ed. by Elias von Steinmeyer (Berlin: Weidmannsche Buchhandlung, 1916), pp. 357–61 (twelfth century), and Beck, *Kirchliche Studien und Quellen*, pp. 274–81 (Regensburg, *c.* 1500); see Pahlmblad, *Mässa på svenska*, pp. 113–65.
31 For Swedish, English, and German examples of this practice, see Pahlmblad, *Mässa på svenska*, pp. 143–52.

THE WORD OF GOD PURELY PREACHED   171

the second half on explaining the Gospel.[32] To what extent this was fulfilled we cannot know, but that the inculcation of doctrine became an increasingly important part of preaching during the latter half of the century is clear, as indicated also by the translations of German Postils.

Olavus Petri's Easter Sermon in *Een lijten postilla*

The expositio in Olavus Petri's Postil of the Gospel for Easter Day, from Mark 16, begins with the statement that the text is clear enough in itself but that there are nevertheless a few things to consider. Olavus Petri explains the Jewish way of reckoning days from the preceding evening and that 'the first day' refers to Sunday. On this day the three women came to the grave in order to anoint Jesus's body, 'epter som plägsidh war ibland iudarne, at när nogher merkelig man dödh war pleghade the smöria hans lekamen medh welluchtande crydder' ['since it was a custom among the Jews that when some prominent man was dead, they would anoint his body with fragrant spices']. The rest of the *expositio* retells the Gospel text, so that a congregation might at Mass in fact hear the day's Gospel thrice, the third time paraphrased and augmented with commentary.[33]

The transition from *expositio* to *sermo* occurs with the following words: 'Och thetta är nw korteligha meningen j texten. Nw wilie wij och, käre wener, tilsee hwad lärdom oss giffuin warder j Jesu Christi vpstondilse. Och är oss först merkiandes [...]' ['And this is now briefly the meaning of the text. Now, dear friends, we also want to see what knowledge is given us in the resurrection of Jesus Christ. And first we should note [...]']. In medieval Swedish-language sermons similar expressions are used throughout in order to describe the purpose of the sermon: it is for 'andelikin kennedom' ['spiritual knowledge'], and several things 'är märkiande' ['are to be noted'].[34]

The sermon treats two themes: the general meaning of Christ's resurrection and its meaning for the individual Christian. The first theme is developed in the form of a paradox: death serves our good, it says, because through Christ's death and resurrection death has become 'en rätt ingong til lijffuet' ['a right entry into life']. Therefore, it is not harmful for us to die but wholesome, for

---

32 *Svenska förarbeten till kyrkoordningen av år 1571*, ed. by Sven Kjöllerström, Samlingar och studier till Svenska kyrkans historia, 2 (Stockholm: Svenska kyrkans diakonistyrelse, 1940), p. 73.

33 Olavus Petri, *Samlade skrifter af Olavus Petri*, ed. by Hesselman, III (1916), 172–74. The Gospel reading that was chanted from the altar was to be recited again at the beginning of the sermon. This principle was maintained throughout the sixteenth century, even though the language of the Mass and its readings was changed from Latin to Swedish; see *Den svenska kyrkoordningen 1571*, ed. by Kjöllerström, pp. 40–41, and Pahlmblad, *Mässa på svenska*, pp. 97–99.

34 Olavus Petri, *Samlade skrifter af Olavus Petri*, ed. by Hesselman, III (1916), 174; *Svenska medeltidspostillor*, 23:1, passim.

when we die, we begin rightly to live. The devil is forced to serve us, and his evil intention is foiled, for where he meant to harm us, he instead gained us; through sorrow and grief our Old Adam and sinful desires are killed and wiped out. Christ's death and resurrection have earned all this for us. In the second part of the sermon, Olavus Petri applies this to the individual by proclaiming the consequences of Christ's resurrection for the Christian life: just as Christ died and was buried but rose again and can no more die, so are we who believe empowered 'til at dödha och nidhertryckia wor gambla Adam, thet är wort syndigha wäsende medh sin onda begierelse' ['to kill and suppress our Old Adam, that is, our sinful nature with its evil desire']. We also receive 'macht til at vppstå til itt nytt rätferdigt och helight leffuerne' ['the power of rising up to a new just and holy life'].[35]

An exhortation follows, based on this proclamation. No one can partake of this resurrection to eternal life who has not with his Old Adam first died in Christ and then risen with Christ to a just life. Therefore 'we' must always kill the Old Adam and the evil inclination we are born with, as well as the evil ways that follow from it, and thank him through whose power we can do this. As St Paul says: we are dead to sin and live for God through Christ (Romans 6. 11). After this quotation there follows a more detailed explanation of what this 'killing' of evil means: if we are dead to sin, then we shall also flee sin and instead 'leffua efter gudz sinne, och öffua oss vthi the ting som thet nyia leffuernet tillydher, som är j kerleek, barmhertigheet, kyscheet, tolamood, ödhmiwkheet' ['live according to God's will and train ourselves in the things that pertain to the new life, which are in love, mercy, chastity, patience, humility'] and live in friendship with every man. Such a life belongs to those who have risen to new life with Christ and who with him will rise to eternal life on the last day, 'hwilket oss allom vnne gud wor himmelske fadher, sich til loff och prijs j ewigh tijdh AMEN' ['which may God, our heavenly Father, grant us all, to his own praise and glory forever. Amen'].[36]

Only twice does Olavus Petri quote the Bible overtly in support of his presentation. His dependence on Scripture is, however, more intricate than that. Romans 6. 1–14 is in fact paradigmatic for the whole second part of the sermon. Like St Paul, Olavus Petri does not speak of this life of the resurrection as primarily belonging to the future. It is to be lived now. The exhortatory section likewise corresponds to St Paul's insistence that the limbs of the body should not be used for evil but as instruments of righteousness (Romans 6. 13). The way this is expounded in the sermon is reminiscent of medieval lists of vices and virtues, but here we do not find the 'seven deadly sins', the 'works of mercy', the 'cardinal virtues' or any of the other medieval catechetical categories. The model is rather the Pauline exhortations.

---

35 Olavus Petri, *Samlade skrifter af Olavus Petri*, ed. by Hesselman, III (1916), 174–76.
36 Olavus Petri, *Samlade skrifter af Olavus Petri*, ed. by Hesselman, III (1916), 176–77.

THE WORD OF GOD PURELY PREACHED   173

In Romans 6 the application of the resurrection of Christ to the life of the Christian is tied to baptism. This connection is not explicit in Olavus Petri's Easter Day sermon, but it is in the air. There are striking similarities to the fourth main section of Luther's *Kleine Katechismus*: baptism indicates that the Old Adam in us should by daily contrition be drowned and that a new man should daily arise 'der jn gerechtigkeyt vnd reynigkeit vor Got ewigklich leb' ['to live before God in righteousness and purity forever'].[37] Or, as it says in the revised version of Luther's *Große Katechismus* that Olavus Petri added to *Een lijten postilla*: the baptised persons shall, by participation in all the good things that Christ has acquired by his death, 'dö medh honom ifrå det syndogha wäsendet [...] och the skola begynna föra itt nyt liffuerne epter gudz helga budh och wilia' ['die with him from the sinful life [...] and they shall begin to live a new life according to God's holy commandments and will'].[38] In Luther's *Kleine Katechismus*, too, this assertion is followed by a quotation of Romans 6. 4.

Faith in Christ is a central point in the sermon, even though few words are said about it. The person realizing the seriousness of sin begins to fear God and flees to Christ. Through faith in him God's Spirit is given, by whose aid 'we who believe in Christ' are empowered to kill Old Adam. But the most striking trait of the sermon is perhaps its strong emphasis on the connection between Christ's resurrection and life in this world. The believer, who has risen to new life in Christ, must here in this world practise 'the ting som thet nyia leffuernet tillyder' ['those things that belong to the new life']. Olavus Petri primarily applies the resurrection of Christ to the present life; the resurrection of the body is in his view the fulfilment of that which through faith and with the aid of the Spirit has already begun in 'the resurrection life' of holiness and righteousness in this world. The meaning of death and resurrection with Christ is thus not primarily a future conformity with Christ in one's own death and resurrection, but a present imitation of Christ. For the believer, God's law therefore remains in force according to Olavus Petri. Not only does it reveal sin, which in Lutheran theology is called the second use of the Law; by faith a person receives a new 'power' to fulfil God's demands as expressed in the Law. This is in fact a characteristic of Olavus Petri's theology: he strongly emphasizes what would later be called the *usus tertius in renatis*, or third use of the Law.[39]

The language of the Postil is inclusive throughout. Olavus Petri prefers to speak about 'we', never about himself. Nor are there any references to the author's subjective experience. The translations of Martin Luther's sermons

---

37 Martin Luther, 'Der kleine Katechismus', in *D. Martin Luthers Werke: kritische Gesamt-ausgabe*, 109 vols (Weimar: Herman Böhlau / Herman Böhlau Nachfolger, 1883–2009), III: 1, 241–63 (p. 257).

38 Olavus Petri, *Samlade skrifter af Olavus Petri*, ed. by Hesselman, III (1916), 462.

39 Ingebrand, *Olavus Petris reformatoriska åskådning*, pp. 243–45 and pp. 282–84.

174 CHRISTER PAHLMBLAD

in the Postil of 1528 are illustrative in this respect. Wherever Luther writes in the first or second person, the translation changes it to the third person.[40] This is so consistent that it must be regarded as programmatic. God's Word should be 'purely preached' also in the sense that the Word and not the preacher comes to the fore.

The way the audience is addressed seems normal for this period: 'Kära wener' ['Dear friends']. It is certainly not unique to Olavus Petri. In medieval German sermons we find 'Mein viel Lieben', in the Latin sermons from Vadstena Abbey it is always 'Karissimi', and in the medieval Swedish-language sermons we find now and again, 'Mine kära wäner' ['My dear friends'].[41] Several other expressions in the sermons are also 'medieval' in the sense that they were widely used by late medieval clergy, for instance, 'oss til lärdom' ['for our knowledge'], 'är oss först märkiandes' ['we should first note'] and, more fully as the introduction of a division, 'J thesse helgo läst märkias siw ting nytteligen til kennedom. Först [...] Annantidh [...] Tridhie [...]' ['In this holy Gospel one notes seven things that are useful to know. The first [...] Secondly [...] The third [...]'], et cetera.[42] The *votum* that ends the sermon is likewise familiar from medieval preaching. Olavus Petri's sermons have a simple form and use verbal expressions that were familiar to everyone. But whereas the structure of the sermon and many of its details stand in self-evident continuity with 'the Middle Ages', its content is quite reformatory and bears the unmistakable stamp of Olavus Petri's own theology.

Laurentius Petri's Sermons on the Passion (1573)

Laurentius Petri's Postil on the Passion of Christ contains twenty sermons.[43] Each has a title, for example, 'Then XVIII. Sermonen. Om mörkret, Jesu roop, torst och endtligha affskedh' ['Sermon XVIII. On the Darkness, the Cry of Jesus, His Thirst and Final Farewell']. The titles are unpretentious and simply serve the purpose of indicating the content of the sermon as related to the story of the Passion. The pericopes are taken from *Passio. Wårs herres Jhesu Christi pina, aff alla euangelisterna vthdraghen*, in other words, *Passio. The Suffering of Our Lord Jesus Christ, Composed from all the Gospels*, that is,

---

40 Ingebrand, *Olavus Petris reformatoriska åskådning*, p. 41.
41 *Altdeutsche Predigten*, I: *Texte*, ed. by Anton E. Schönbach (Graz: Verlagsbuchhandlung Styria, 1886), passim. In the sermons from Vadstena, for example, Uppsala, Uppsala universitetsbibliothek, MS C 303, fol. 283r, MS C 304, fol. 71r, MS C 311, fol. 160r; *Svenska medeltidspostillor*, 23:1–5, passim.
42 *Svenska medeltidspostillor*, 23:1, passim.
43 On the Postil, see Hammar, 'Studier i evangelisk predikan', pp. 64–65; Brilioth, *Predikans historia*, p. 180; Ahlberg, *Laurentius Petris nattvardsuppfattning*, pp. 165–66 and n. 1, and Hammar, 'Reformationstidens predikan', p. 271.

THE WORD OF GOD PURELY PREACHED   175

the Gospel harmony that was printed in at least eleven editions during the sixteenth century, the first being published in 1544.[44]

The twenty sermons sort the material of the passion story under a number of themes, but each sermon is in turn made up of separate sections that treat only one or a few verses. Thus the above-mentioned eighteenth sermon consists of six sections: the darkness at the sixth hour; Christ's cry of 'My God, my God' at the ninth hour; Christ's thirst and the drink of vinegar; the comment 'Let us see if Elijah comes to take him down'; 'It is fulfilled'; and the moment when Christ gave up his spirit. Each of the twenty sermons is roughly fifteen pages long, the format of the book being octavo. The Postil as a whole thus consists of a running commentary on the story of the Passion. Each single sermon has the character of a homily, working its way sentence by sentence through the text. In this way, each section becomes relatively independent. Here, too, there exists a Danish parallel: Hans Tausen's Postil of 1539. The sermons in this Postil also take the form of homilies, expounding the biblical text sentence by sentence.[45]

As in a medieval homily, Laurentius Petri's exposition is supported by biblical quotations that confirm or illumine it. In the last sermon he refers to fourteen passages from the Old Testament (including two from deuterocanonical books) and thirteen from the New (of which five are from the Gospels, one from Acts and the rest from the Epistles).[46] Church Fathers are sometimes adduced, but the regular use of Church Fathers and other ecclesiastical authors in order to support interpretations, typical of the Middle Ages, is absent in Laurentius Petri.[47] By contrast, Laurentius Petri in his theological works quite frequently quotes Church Fathers and other authorities, often with a crowning, confirmatory quotation from Martin Luther or some other Reformation theologian.

The proclamation of God's Word still reflects the decisions of Västerås 1527 and Örebro 1529: it must be preached 'purely' or 'without admixture'. As we have seen, Laurentius Petri argued in his explanation of the decision at the Diet of Västerås for the reformers' interpretation of the phrase 'God's pure Word' and strongly emphasized the primacy of Scripture.[48] This has not

---

44 On the various editions, see Collijn, *Sveriges bibliografi intill år 1600*.

45 Hans Tausen, *Hans Tausens Postil*, ed. by Bjørn Kornerup, Facsimile, Det Danske Sprog- och Litteraturselskab (København: Levin & Munksgaard, 1934), passim. When the Postil was printed, Hans Tausen was a priest at the cathedral of Roskilde; in 1542 he was appointed bishop of Ribe.

46 A leaf is missing in Lund University Library's copy of the Postil; the number of biblical quotations may thus be somewhat greater.

47 See *Den svenska kyrkoordningen 1571*, ed. by Kjöllerström, p. 27. Hammar, 'Studier i evangelisk predikan', p. 167. Hammar, 'Reformationstidens predikan', pp. 278–80.

48 On Laurentius Petri's exegetical principles, see Ahlberg, *Laurentius Petris nattvardsuppfattning*, pp. 39–52. On Laurentius Petri's relation to the tradition of the Church, see Bo Ahlberg, 'Laurentius Petri och traditionen', *Kyrkohistorisk årsskrift* (1963), 145–99, and Ahlberg, *Laurentius Petris nattvardsuppfattning*, pp. 27–32.

176 CHRISTER PAHLMBLAD

prevented him from referring in one of the Postil's sermons to martyrs and their legends, which, however, is in line with the usage recommended by the Swedish reformers in some of their own documents: saints' legends are not to be preached on, nor may they be used as arguments in the interpretation of Scripture, but it is permissible to quote passages 'uthur then helige mans lefuerne, som them kan wara till godo och någon förbättring' ['out of the holy man's life that can be of some benefit and improvement to them']. The sermon itself must be an exposition of the Gospel, not of Church Fathers, legends, and other things.[49]

Interestingly enough, Laurentius Petri sometimes also accepts an allegorical interpretation of the biblical text: thus Christ's vestments, which the soldiers at the cross divided among themselves, can according to him be interpreted as *bona ecclesiastica*, the property of the Church, with which the poor are clothed and fed. The soldiers, on the other hand, represent those who 'Kyrkionnes äghodelar rappa och byta emellan sigh, och dräpa medh hunger Christum vthi sina fattiga' ['steal and share among themselves the property of the Church and kill Christ in the poor with hunger'].[50]

The twentieth and last sermon has the title 'Om wårs Herras begraffning' ['On the Burial of Our Lord'].[51] Human graves, says Laurentius Petri, are outwardly adorned but inwardly mere putrefaction. With Christ's grave and burial it was different. His grave had no outward decoration but within contained a true adornment: Christ's body, which not only was without sin,

---

49 Laurentius Petri, *Öffuer historien om wårs Herras Jesu Christi werdigha pino och dödh*, fol. A 7r–v. *Svenska förarbeten*, ed. by Kjöllerström, p. 72 (a statute concerning sermons, 1561); *Den svenska kyrkoordningen 1571*, ed. by Kjöllerström, pp. 34–35.
50 Laurentius Petri, *Öffuer historien om wårs Herras Jesu Christi werdigha pino och dödh*, fol. j 7r. On Laurentius Petri's view of preaching and how to prepare sermons, see Laurentius Petri, 'Hypotiposes, sive breves subiectiones, pro formandis moribus ministrorum verbi Dei, in variis suae functionis partibus obeundis, clero diocesis Upsaliensis propositae, in synodo anno Christi 1566 celebrata: authore Laurentio, Episcopo Upsaliensi', in *Skrifter och handlingar til uplysning i swenska kyrko och reformations historien*, ed. by Uno von Troil, 5 vols (Uppsala: [Johan Edman], 1790–1791), IV (1791), 221–68 (pp. 221–34); Laurentius Petri's handwritten proposal for a new Church order in *Laurentius Petris handskrivna kyrkoordning av år 1561*, ed. by Emil Färnström, Samlingar och studier till Svenska kyrkans historia, 34 (Stockholm: Svenska kyrkans diakonistyrelse, 1956), pp. 43–53; *Den svenska kyrkoordningen 1571*, ed. by Kjöllerström, pp. 23–34. Here he writes about Bible study as a prerequisite for preaching, how to prepare a manuscript, the proper use of language, the oral presentation, the use of authorities, the use of postils, how to quote the Bible in support of an argument, preaching method, and so forth. He also urges the diligent study of Melanchthon's *Loci communes*, probably referring to Eric Falck, *Een kort vnderwijsning om några aff the förnemligaste articlar j then christeligha läron, stelt på spörsmål, för eenfalligha landz prester och andra som predica skola* (Stockholm: Amund Laurentzson, 1558), a translation and revision of Johann Spangenberg's compendium on *Loci* entitled *Margarita theologica*; thus *Den svenska kyrkoordningen 1571*, ed. by Kjöllerström, p. 29. 'Hypotiposes' is a revised extract from Laurentius Petri's proposal for a new Church order.
51 Laurentius Petri, *Öffuer historien om wårs Herras Jesu Christi werdigha pino och dödh*, fols q 1v–r 10r.

THE WORD OF GOD PURELY PREACHED 177

vthan war ock thär til så heligh och dyrbara, at hela werlden war genom honom återlöst, hwarföre han icke heller kunde förrotna såsom i psalmen står, 'Tu, HERre, skalt icke öffuergiffua mijn siel i heluetet, och icke tilstädja att tin helge förwarder'.[52]

> [but was also in addition so holy and precious that the whole world was redeemed through him, wherefore he neither could putrefy, as the Psalm (16. 10) says: 'Thou, Lord, shalt not abandon my soul in hell nor allow thy holy one to see corruption'].

Moreover, says Laurentius Petri, Christ adorned his grave with his powerful and glorious resurrection. By his resurrection he has become Lord over heaven and earth. He lives now not for himself, but

> han är vpstånden och leffuer för oss alla som på honom troo, thet är, wij leffue j honom, lika som ock wij sampt medh wåra synder äre med honom korsfeste och döde. Efter som Paulus betyghar, 'Jag är korsfest med Christo oc leffuer nu, dock icke iagh vthan Christus i migh'. Jtem, 'wij äre begraffne medh honom genom dopet j dödhen'.[53]

>> [he is risen and lives for all of us who believe in him, that is: we live in him, just as we together with our sins are crucified with him and dead. As Paul affirms (Galatians 2. 12–20): 'I am crucified with Christ and live now, yet not I, but Christ in me'. Item (Romans 6. 4): 'we are buried with him through baptism in death'].

After Christ's death, grave, and resurrection have been connected with the faithful in this manner, the sermon proceeds to an application. That which has been buried with Christ through baptism must not be dug up anew. That which Christ has hallowed must not once more be profaned and contaminated by us. If sin, which was buried with Christ, is revived again in us here in this world, it will lead to eternal death. Therefore 'we', who have the spirit of his elect children, shall daily kill the deeds of the flesh through him. By doing so we prove that we are dead and buried as far as sins are concerned and live a new righteous life. For to this life, says Laurentius Petri, we have risen 'with Christ and in Christ' through renewal by the Holy Spirit.

The proclamation of Christ's death, burial, and resurrection thus causes Laurentius Petri, just like his brother Olavus, to refer to Romans 6. In contrast to his brother, he does so by speaking about baptism as the believer's death, burial, and resurrection with Christ; and in an attempt at comprehensiveness he also mentions the sacrament of the altar as a confirmation of this life in communion with Christ. The dynamic and immediate connection between Christ's resurrection and the believer's life in this world that we found in Olavus Petri is lacking here. The emphasis in Laurentius Petri is rather on

---

52 Laurentius Petri, *Öffuer historien om wårs Herras Jesu Christi werdigha pino och dödh*, fols r 4v–r 5r.
53 Laurentius Petri, *Öffuer historien om wårs Herras Jesu Christi werdigha pino och dödh*, fol. r 5v.

178   CHRISTER PAHLMBLAD

Christ's resurrection as a return to sovereignty, and on the Christian as crucified with Christ and recipient of the new life in him through sacraments and faith. The decisive factor is faith for the realization of a life lived in Christ. The application that follows consists of warnings and admonitions. The two brothers have this in common, that they include themselves among the addressees of the sermon. Speech in the first person-singular is avoided and subjective experiences are excluded.

Laurentius Petri can occasionally, as noted above, use the Church Fathers in his passion sermons.[54] Quotations of ancient authors such as Horace, Seneca, and Cicero are fairly common in medieval sermons. Laurentius Petri can refer to them in his theological writings and he is not averse to quoting them in sermons, if it is done sparingly.[55] They have, he says, written about morals based on their experience, but Scripture teaches more reliably.[56]

The style of Laurentius Petri is often heavy and cumbersome. The sermons can hardly have been pronounced in that manner. It is not a spoken word. The Postil is desk-work, written as an aid for preachers. In an afterword Laurentius Petri writes: 'thetta haffuer iagh giordt effter mijn ringa gåffuo, meer til at öffua mig sielff j thetta saligha och nödhtorfftigha ärendet, än androm, som thetta bätter kunna göra, något förescriffua' ['this I have done according to my modest gift, more to exercise myself in this blessed and necessary task than to prescribe something for others who can do it better'].[57]

Were the Sermons in the Postils Ever Preached?

We cannot know for certain whether the sermons presented here were ever really preached. The accessible character of the sermons in Olavus Petri's Postil of 1530 suggests that at least some of them were in fact pronounced in some form or another. When the Postil was published, Olavus Petri had been active as a preacher in Strängnäs and Stockholm for ten years. He is likely to have had manuscript sermons that he could use in order to compose *Een lijten postilla*, and to that extent its contents may reflect his own preaching.

Henrik Schück, a Swedish historian of literature, characterizes Olavus Petri's sermons as providing an almost childishly simple exposition of the Gospel. At the same time Schück admires the efficiency of their style: it is dry and sober, yet has what he calls an 'enfaldens poesi' ['poetry of simplicity'].[58] Other scholars, too, have been struck by the simple character of these

---

54 On the use of the Church Fathers in Swedish sixteenth-century preaching, see Hammar, 'Studier i evangelisk predikan', pp. 165–82.

55 For example, in Laurentius Petri, 'Hypotiposes', pp. 224, 225, §§ 9 and 12.

56 Laurentius Petri, 'Hypotiposes', p. 227, § 16.

57 Laurentius Petri, *Öffuer historien om wårs Herras Jesu Christi werdigha pino och dödh*, fol. r 7r.

58 Henrik Schück and Karl Warburg, *Illustrerad svensk litteraturhistoria*, I, 5 vols (Stockholm: Geber, 1911–1916), I (1911), 269.

THE WORD OF GOD PURELY PREACHED   179

sermons. The Church historian Hjalmar Holmquist calls the expositions of the Gospels that precede the sermons an almost naïve explanatory paraphrase of the text.[59] Yngve Brilioth, a theologian with homiletics as one of his main fields of research, sees in Olavus Petri's Postil a literary artist dressed up in an unpretentious clarity, which makes the Postil one of the great monuments in the history of the Swedish language.[60] Brilioth thinks, however, that the Postil is a repertorium for preachers and hardly represents Olavus Petri's own preaching style. But cannot the very simplicity and accessibility of the Postil's sermons be seen as evidence that they reflect *the preacher* Olavus Petri? If one wants to present a message that is perceived as a novelty, it is hardly a disadvantage if one is able to make oneself understood.

It seems clear that neither of the Postils treated here was intended to be recited verbally. Laurentius Petri explicitly disapproves of preachers who are so bound to their postils that they neglect to study Scripture. The postil should be 'een hielp och lijka som een inleedning til sakena' ['an aid and a kind of introduction to the matter'], not a substitute for the preacher's own work.[61] It can be tolerated for a time that inexperienced priests recite sermons from a postil. But the normal state of affairs, according to Laurentius Petri, is that a preacher memorizes the subject and the development of a carefully thought-out sermon. The elaborated manuscript is a *formula concionis*, a model for preaching. Its function is that of a memory aid. The sermon is to be delivered from memory, not from a page.[62] This is also the way in which the Latin sermon manuscripts from Vadstena Abbey were transformed into vernacular preaching. That process can be studied in some detail thanks to the Latin-and-Swedish notes taken down by a person in Vadstena who was listening to vernacular sermons based on some of the preserved Latin manuscripts.[63]

The intention of Olavus Petri was likewise not that the sermons in his Postil should be read out exactly as written; but if this was nevertheless done it might, he thought, still be fruitful, since they were so easy to understand.[64] The fact that Olavus Petri provided his Postil with a subject index indicates that he envisaged other, more creative ways of using it.[65]

In other words: even if the Postils were indeed compiled from manuscripts that Olavus Petri or Laurentius Petri had used in preparation for their own preaching, their preached sermons did not consist in the recitation of such

---

59 Holmquist, *Svenska kyrkans historia*, III:1, 205–06.
60 Brilioth, *Predikans historia*, p. 177.
61 Laurentius Petri, 'Hypotiposes', p. 224, § 10. *Den svenska kyrkoordningen 1571*, ed. by Kjöllerström, p. 28.
62 Laurentius Petri, 'Hypotiposes', pp. 225–26, §§ 12–13, and p. 231, § 28.
63 See Håkan Hallberg, *Acho Johannis scribens, prædicans, auditus. Två vadstenapredikningar i två versioner*, Vadstenabrödernas predikan. Meddelanden, 4 (Uppsala: [Dept. of Classical Philology], 1997).
64 Olavus Petri, *Samlade skrifter af Olavus Petri*, ed. by Hesselman, III (1916), 5.
65 Olavus Petri, *Samlade skrifter af Olavus Petri*, ed. by Hesselman, III (1916), 10–12.

180 CHRISTER PAHLMBLAD

manuscripts — they most likely did not even bring a manuscript to the place where a sermon was to be held. This cautions us against reading the sermons in the postils as if they directly reflect *the preaching* of their authors.

We do know, however, based on notes, underlined words and crossed-out sections in preserved copies of the postils, that they have been used precisely in the way that the reformers regarded as less appropriate. There even exist handwritten copies of sermons in the Postils that incorporate only slight revisions of the original text.[66] Theory and reality are often poles apart. It goes without saying that priests now and then read straight out of the postils.[67] Their sermons have then indeed been preached as printed — but only after they were printed, by people other than their authors.[68]

---

66 Hammar, 'Studier i evangelisk predikan', pp. 99–103, 196–209.

67 Priests have bought and borrowed postils. When Laurentius Petri in his speech to the clergy in 1566 expresses his disapproval of priests' dependence on postils, he points out that this applies regardless of whether they are in Latin or in Swedish. It may be that he here also had unprinted postils in mind, even medieval ones, since in 1566 only two postils in Swedish had been printed. The Church Order of Johan III, *Nova Ordinantia*, 1575, cautions against foreign postils that are circulating. *Nova Ordinantia* in *Kyrko-ordningar och förslag dertill före 1686*, 4 vols, Handlingar rörande Sveriges historia, andra serien (Stockholm: Nordstedts, 1872–1920), I (1872), 181–351 (p. 199). On the dependence of Swedish preaching on German, see Hammar, 'Studier i evangelisk predikan', pp. 104–20, and Hammar, 'Reformationstidens predikan', pp. 273–76.

68 This contribution is a shortened and reworked version of Christer Pahlmblad, 'Fyra reformationstida påskpredikningar', in *Svensk påskpredikan genom tiderna*, ed. by Christer Pahlmblad and Sven-Åke Selander (Skellefteå: Artos, 2010), pp. 47–91. Professor Stephan Borgehammar has kindly translated the Swedish text.

Bibliography

Manuscripts

Uppsala, Uppsala universitetsbibliothek, MS C 303
Uppsala, Uppsala universitetsbibliothek, MS C 304
Uppsala, Uppsala universitetsbibliothek, MS C 311

Early Printed Works

En nyttog postilla ofuer någhor fåå euangelia aff sommardelen, ther man må tagha jtt sätt och grund aff huru all euangelia som här icke insatt äre vthlägias och forclaras skole (Stockholm: [Kungl. tryckeriet], 1528)

Eric Falck, *Een kort vnderwijsning om några aff the förnemligaste articlar j then christeligha läron, stelt på spörsmål, för eenfalligha landz prester och andra som predica skola* (Stockholm: Amund Laurentzson, 1558)

Handbook, ther vthi är författadt, huruledes gudztiensten medh christelighe ceremonier och kyrkiosedher, vthi wåra swenska församblingar skal bliffua hållin och förhandladt (Uppsala: Eskil Matzson, 1614)

Laurentius Petri, *Öffuer historien om wårs Herras Jesu Christi werdigha pino och dödh, någhra eenfalligha sermoner eller predicaner* (Stockholm: Amund Laurentszson, 1573)

Laurentius Petri, *Om kyrkio stadgar och ceremonier, hurudana och huilka man vthi een christeligh församling bruka må eller ey* (Wittenberg: M. Simon Gronenberg, 1587)

Laurentius Petri, *Postilla*, 4 vols (Stockholm: Amund Laurentzon, 1555)

Olavus Petri, *Een lijten postilla offuer all euangelia som om söndaghanar läsen warda offuer heela året, ther til och offuer the euangelia som på the nampnkunnogasta högh-tijder om året warda läsen, och en lijten cathechismus eller vnderuisning, på the stycke som en christen lerdom mest påhenger* (Stockholm: Claes Pederson, 1530)

Postilla ther inne aff hwart och ett söndags euangelium, etc. warder tagen een besynnerlig lära tröst, och förmaning, eller warning, medh widhengda böön til hwart euangelium sampt några merkeliga sententier aff scrifftenne, och aff kyrkionnes lärarom, sammandragne och vthgångne aff Petro Johannis Gotho medh sine egna bekåstning (Rostock: [Staffan Möllman], 1597–1598)

Primary Sources

Altdeutsche Predigten, I: *Texte*, ed. by Anton E. Schönbach (Graz: Verlagsbuchhandlung Styria, 1886)

Christiern Pedersen, *Christiern Pedersens Danske Skrifter*, ed. by C. J. Brandt and R. Th. Fenger, 5 vols (København: Gyldendal, 1850–1856)

A Danish Teacher's Manual of the Mid-Fifteenth Century (Cod. AM 76,8°), ed. by Sigurd Kroon and others, Kungl. Vitterhets historie och antikvitets akademien, Skrifter utgivna av Vetenskapssocieteten i Lund, 85, 96, 2 vols (Lund: Lund University Press, 1993–2008)

Den svenska kyrkoordningen 1571 jämte studier kring tillkomst, innehåll och användning, ed. by Sven Kjöllerström (Lund: Håkan Ohlsson, 1971)

182   CHRISTER PAHLMBLAD

Handlingar till Sverges reformations- och kyrkohistoria under konung Gustaf I, ed. by
P. E. Thyselius, 2 vols (Stockholm: Bagges, 1841–1845)

Hans Brask, *Latinsk korrespondens 1523*, ed. by Hedda Roll, Acta Universitatis
Stockholmiensis, Studia Latina Stockholmiensia, 19 (Stockholm: Almqvist &
Wiksell, 1973)

Hans Tausen, *Hans Tausens Postil*, ed. by Bjørn Kornerup, Facsimile, Det Danske
Sprog- och Litteraturselskab (København: Levin & Munksgaard, 1934)

Die kleineren althochdeutschen Sprachdenkmäler, ed. by Elias von Steinmeyer
(Berlin: Weidmannsche Buchhandlung, 1916)

Konung Gustaf den förstes registratur, ed. by Joh. Ax. Almquist and others, 29 vols
(Stockholm: Nordstedt, 1861–1916)

Kyrko-ordningar och förslag dertill före 1686, Handlingar rörande Sveriges historia,
andra serien, 4 vols (Stockholm: Nordstedts, 1872–1920)

Laurentius Petri, 'Hypotiposes, sive breves subiectiones, pro formandis moribus
ministrorum verbi Dei, in variis suae functionis partibus obeundis, clero
diocesis Upsaliensis propositae, in synodo anno Christi 1566 celebrata: authore
Laurentio, Episcopo Upsaliensi', in *Skrifter och handlingar til uplysning i swenska
kyrko och reformations historien*, ed. by Uno von Troil, 5 vols (Uppsala: [Johan
Edman], 1790–1791), IV (1791), 221–68

Laurentius Petris handskrivna kyrkoordning av år 1561, ed. by Emil Färnström,
Samlingar och studier till Svenska kyrkans historia, 34 (Stockholm: Svenska
kyrkans diakonistyrelse, 1956)

Malmø-Salmebogen 1533: faksimiledition, ed. by John Kroon (Malmö: Dansk-Skånsk
Förening, 1967)

Martin Luther, 'Der kleine Katechismus', in *D. Martin Luthers Werke: kritische
Gesamtausgabe*, 109 vols (Weimar: Herman Böhlau / Herman Böhlau
Nachfolger, 1883–2009), XXX: 1, 241–63

Olavus Petri, *Samlade skrifter af Olavus Petri*, ed. by Bengt Hesselman, 4 vols
(Uppsala: Sveriges kristliga studentrörelse, 1914–1917)

*Studium Upsalense: Specimens of the Oldest Lecture Notes Taken in the Mediaeval
University of Uppsala*, ed. by Anders Piltz, Acta Universitatis Upsaliensis:
skrifter rörande Uppsala universitet, C. Organisation och historia, 36 (Uppsala:
[Uppsala universitet], 1977)

Svenska förarbeten till kyrkoordningen av år 1571, ed. by Sven Kjöllerström, Samlingar
och studier till Svenska kyrkans historia, 2 (Stockholm: Svenska kyrkans
diakonistyrelse, 1940)

Svenska medeltidspostillor, Samlingar utgivna av Svenska fornskriftsällskapet, serie 1,
Svenska skrifter, 23: I–VIII, I–III (1879–1894), ed. by Gustaf Edvard Klemming;
IV–V (1905–1910), ed. by Robert Geete; VI–VIII (1974–1983), ed. by Bertil
Ejder (Uppsala: Svenska fornskriftsällskapet, 1879–1983)

Svenska riksdagsakter jämte andra handlingar som höra till statsförfattningens historia,
ed. by Emil Hildebrand and Oscar Alin (I–II), and Emil Hildebrand (III), 3 vols
(Stockholm: Nordstedts, 1887–1890)

Sveriges traktater med främmande magter jemte andra dit hörande handlingar, ed. by
Olof Simon Rydberg, 14 vols (Stockholm: Nordstedts, 1877–1934)

Secondary Studies

Ahlberg, Bo, 'Laurentius Petri och traditionen', *Kyrkohistorisk årsskrift* (1963), 145–99

Ahlberg, Bo, *Laurentius Petris nattvardsuppfattning*, Studia Theologica Lundensia, 26 (Lund: Gleerups, 1964)

Andersson, Roger, and Stephan Borgehammar, 'The Preaching of the Birgittine Friars at Vadstena Abbey (*ca* 1380–1515)', *Revue Mabillon: revue internationale d'histoire et de littérature religieuses*, n.s. 8 (69) (1997), 209–36

Beck, Anton, *Kirchliche Studien und Quellen* (Amberg: Böes, 1903)

Berntsson, Martin, *Mässan och armborstet: uppror och reformation i Sverige 1525–1544* (Skellefteå: Artos, 2010)

Borgehammar, Stephan, 'Svensk senmedeltida påskpredikan: tre exempel', in *Svensk påskpredikan genom tiderna*, ed. by Christer Pahlmblad and Sven-Åke Selander (Skellefteå: Artos, 2010), pp. 9–46

Brilioth, Yngve, *Predikans historia: Olaus Petri-föreläsningar hållna vid Uppsala universitet*, 2nd edn (Lund: Gleerups, 1962)

Collijn, Isak, *Sveriges bibliografi intill år 1600*, 3 vols (Uppsala: Svenska litteratursällskapet, 1927–1938)

Gardemeister, Christer, *Den suveräne Guden: en studie i Olavus Petris teologi*, Studia Theologica Lundensia, 43 (Lund: Lund University Press, 1989)

Hallberg, Håkan, *Acho Johannis scribens, prædicans, auditus: två vadstenapredikningar i två versioner*, Vadstenabrödernas predikan. Meddelanden, 4 (Uppsala: [Dept. of Classical Philology], 1997)

Hammar, H. B., 'Reformationstidens predikan i Sverige', in *Reformationen i Norden: kontinuitet och förnyelse*, ed. by Carl-Gustaf Andrén, Skrifter utgitt av Nordiskt institut för kyrkohistorisk forskning, 3 (Lund: Gleerups, 1973), pp. 263–80

Hammar, H. B., 'Studier i evangelisk predikan i Sverige under reformations-tidevarvet' (unpublished licentiate dissertation, Lund University, 1939)

Hellström, Olle, 'Laurentius Petri', in *Svenskt biografiskt lexikon* (Stockholm: Svenskt biografiskt lexikon, 1918–), 22 (1977–1979), 376–85

Holmquist, Hjalmar, *Svenska kyrkans historia*, III:1–2 (Stockholm: Svenska kyrkans diakonistyrelse, 1933)

Ingebrand, Sven, *Olavus Petris reformatoriska åskådning*, Acta Universitatis Upsaliensis, Studia Doctrinae Christianae Upsaliensia, 1 (Lund: Gleerups, 1964)

Kick, Rémi, *Tel un navire sur la mer dechaînée: la communauté chrétienne dans l'œuvre de Laurentius Petri, archevêque d'Uppsala (1531–1573)*, Studia Theologica Lundensia, 52 (Lund: Lund University Press, 1997)

Kjöllerström, Sven, 'Västerås ordinantia', *Scandia: tidskrift för historisk forskning*, 26 (1960), 41–98

Koch, Hal, and others, eds, *Den danske Kirkes Historie*, 8 vols (København: Gyldendal, 1950–1966)

Lindhardt, P. G., 'Reformationen i Norden i komparativ belysning', in *Reformationen i Norden: kontinuitet och förnyelse*, ed. by Carl-Gustaf Andrén, Skrifter utgitt av Nordiskt institut för kyrkohistorisk forskning, 3 (Lund: Gleerups, 1973), pp. 9–27

Pahlmblad, Christer, 'Fyra reformationstida påskpredikningar', in *Svensk påskpredikan genom tiderna*, ed. by Christer Pahlmblad and Sven-Åke Selander (Skellefteå: Artos, 2010), pp. 47–90

Pahlmblad, Christer, 'Laurentius Petri, gudstjänstbruken och sakraments-fromheten', in *Laurentius Petri och svenskt gudstjänstliv*, Årsbok för svenskt gudstjänstliv, 79 (2004), 120–49

Pahlmblad, Christer, *Mässa på svenska: den reformatoriska mässan i Sverige mot den senmedeltida bakgrunden*, Bibliotheca Theologiae Practicae, 60 (Lund: Arcus, 1998)

Pernler, Sven-Erik, 'Predikan ad populum under svensk medeltid: till frågan om sockenprästernas predikoskyldighet', in *Predikohistoriska perspektiv: studier tillägnade Åke Andrén*, ed. by Alf Härdelin, Skrifter utgivna av Svenska kyrkohistoriska föreningen, 2, n.s. 35 (Stockholm: SkeabVerbum, 1982), pp. 73–94

Riising, Anne, *Danmarks middelalderlige prædiken* (København: Gad, 1969)

Schück, Henrik, and Karl Warburg, *Illustrerad svensk litteraturhistoria*, 5 vols (Stockholm: Geber, 1911–1916)

Spencer, H. Leith, *English Preaching in the Late Middle Ages* (Oxford: Clarendon Press, 1993)

Westin, Gunnar T., 'Olavus Petri', in *Svenskt biografiskt lexikon* (Stockholm: Svenskt biografiskt lexikon, 1918–), 28 (1992–1994), 151–66

Westman, Knut B., *Reformationens genombrottsår i Sverige* (Stockholm: Svenska kyrkans diakonistyrelse, 1918)

Transylvania

ADINEL C. DINCĂ and PAULA COTOI

Latin Manuscript and Printed Sermons in Late Medieval Transylvania (1470–1530)

Transylvanian Context

The province known today as Transylvania,[1] part of the Romanian state since 1918, has a complex cultural, social, and political history: a voivodeship (or duchy in medieval western terms) situated during the Middle Ages on the easternmost borderland of the territories ruled by the Hungarian Crown,[2] it has been inhabited by Eastern-rite Christians (Romanians or Vlachs) together with Hungarian-speaking (including Szeklers) and German-speaking members of the Latin Church.[3] Beyond its linguistic and ethnic aspects, this regional diversity was further enhanced by the mid-sixteenth century religious Reformation, which additionally divided the Catholic population among Protestant branches (Lutheran, Calvinist, and Unitarian), whereas the majority of Romanians preserved their Orthodox faith. Moreover, the inner tension generated on the medieval Transylvanian communities by the ethnic and denominational particularities — which gave rise to various narratives of alterity — was doubled by the outer threat of the Ottomans, whose enmity over more than a century culminated in 1526 with the dismantling

---

1   Ioan-Aurel Pop, *Romanians and Hungarians from the 9th to the 14th Century: The Genesis of the Transylvanian Medieval State* (Cluj-Napoca: Center for Transylvanian Studies, 1996); Ioan-Aurel Pop and Thomas Nägler, *The History of Transylvania (until 1541)* (Cluj-Napoca: Center for Transylvanian Studies, 2005); Ioan-Aurel Pop, Thomas Nägler, and András Magyari, *The History of Transylvania (from 1541 to 1711)* (Cluj-Napoca: Center for Transylvanian Studies, 2009).

2   Pál Engel, *The Realm of St Stephen: A History of Medieval Hungary 895–1526* (London: Tauris, 2001); Nora Berend, Przemyslaw Urbanczyk, and Przemyslaw Wiszewski, *Central Europe in the High Middle Ages: Bohemia, Hungary and Poland c. 900–c. 1300*, Cambridge Medieval Textbooks (Cambridge: Cambridge University Press, 2013).

3   Cristian Daniel, 'Bridging the Gap: The Ecclesiological Landscape of Transylvania Seen Through the Comparative Lens', *New Europe College Yearbook*, 10 (2010), 51–84.

> **Adinel C. Dincă** (adinel.dinca@ubbcluj.ro) is Associate Professor at Babeș-Bolyai University, Cluj-Napoca, and Associated Researcher of the 'George Barițiu' History Institute of the Romanian Academy.
>
> **Paula Cotoi** (paula.cotoi@bcucluj.ro) is a Special Collections Librarian at 'Lucian Blaga' Central University Library in Cluj-Napoca.

Circulating the Word of God in Medieval and Early Modern Europe: Catholic Preaching and Preachers across Manuscript and Print (c. 1450 to c. 1550), ed. by Veronica O'Mara and Patricia Stoop, SERMO 17, (Turnhout: Brepols, 2022), pp. 187–220   BREPOLS ❧ PUBLISHERS   10.1484/M.SERMO-EB.5.130456

Figure 3. Map of Central Europe around 1500. © Andrei Nacu, Sibiu, Romania.

of the Hungarian Kingdom.[4] The multi-layered character of this peripheral society, yet in continuous connection with the European cultural centres,[5] has shaped the uneven local reception and evolution of literacy: the organized structures of the Catholic bishopric (the so-called diocese of Transylvania)[6] and the prosperous urban settings have favoured the circulation of Latin (and later vernacular) religious texts; at the same time the rural parts inhabited by Romanians preserved the Old Church Slavonic liturgical tradition and the Cyrillic script up to the nineteenth century. The medieval ecclesiastical landscape of the province was also moulded by the active monastic (Benedictine,

---

4 Cosmin Popa-Gorjanu, 'Transylvanian Identities in the Middle Ages', in *Identitats: reunió científica, XIV Curs d'Estiu Comtat d'Urgell, celebrat a Balaguer els dies 1, 2 i 3 de juliol de 2009*, ed. by Flocel Sabaté (Lleida: Pagès, 2012), pp. 175–90; Irina Mastan, 'Urban Identity and Historical Discourse in a Frontier City. Case Study: Brașov during the 16th and 17th Centuries', *Prace Historyczne*, 141 (2014), 15–35; Florian Kührer-Wielach, 'Siebenbürgen als administrative Einheit und diskursives Konzept', in *Das Südosteuropa der Regionen*, ed. by Oliver Jens Schmitt and Michael Metzeltin (Wien: Verlag der Österreichischen Akademie der Wissenschaften, 2015), pp. 349–409.
5 Ioan Drăgan and others, *A Century in the History of Transylvania: The Late Crusades, Humanism, Church Union and Social Mobility at the End of the Middle Ages (1387–1490)* (Cluj-Napoca: Center for Transylvanian Studies, 2008).
6 Adinel C. Dincă, *Instituția episcopală latină în Transilvania medievală (sec. XI/XII–XIV)* (Cluj-Napoca: Argonaut, 2017).

Cistercian) and mendicant (Dominican, Franciscan, Augustinian) orders, the latter having settled their convents in Transylvanian cities and market-towns, expanding their missionary work even across the Carpathian Mountains, into the neighbouring, Romanian-inhabited principalities of Wallachia and Moldavia.[7] However, by the late sixteenth century Catholic significance would gradually fade in the newly-created and Protestant-dominated Principality of Transylvania (1570–1711), where Hungarian and German slowly took over from Latin as administrative and liturgical languages, while Romanian remained disconnected from the government and predominantly part of the local oral culture, despite isolated efforts at constructing a literary language around liturgical texts.[8]

What we know about sermons and preaching in late medieval (1470–1530) Transylvania is limited to a handful of collateral remarks in literary histories[9] or to an even smaller number of mentions in articles concerning the history of the Church in the pre-Reformation period.[10] Few studies have directly concerned collections of texts used for pastoral activities in the Middle Ages.[11] Even fewer have discussed sources that were indeed produced and/or used in Transylvania, and not purchased later out of bibliophile passion.[12] It is therefore fair to state that in the case of Transylvania the activity of preaching and the textual material which supported it form a research field that still awaits

---

7   Claudia-Florentina Dobre, *Mendicants in Moldavia: Mission in an Orthodox Land* (Daun: Aurel, 2009); Mihai-D. Grigore, 'The Space of Power: State Consolidation by Means of Religious Policy in the Danube Principalities in the Fourteenth to Sixteenth Centuries', *Acta Poloniae Historica*, 116 (2017), 35–56.

8   Nicolae Cartojan, *Istoria literaturii române vechi* (București: Ed. Fundației Culturale Române, 1996); Gheorghe Chivu, 'Scrisul religios, componentă definitorie a culturii vechi românești', *Dacoromania*, 17 (2012), 54–67.

9   Joachim Wittstock and Stefan Sienerth, *Die deutsche Literatur Siebenbürgens: von den Anfängen bis 1848* (München: Südostdeutsches Kulturwerk, 1997), I: *Mittelalter, Humanismus, Barock*; *Lexikon der regionalen Literaturgeschichte des Mittelalters: Ungarn und Rumänien*, ed. by Cora Dietl and Anna-Lena Liebermann (Berlin: Akademie, 2015).

10 For example, Maria Crăciun, 'Mendicant Piety and the Saxon Community of Transylvania c. 1450–1550', in *Communities of Devotion: Religious Orders and Society in East Central Europe, 1450–1800*, ed. by Maria Crăciun and Elaine Fulton (Farnham: Ashgate, 2011), pp. 29–70.

11 Edit Madas, 'A Dominican Sermon Collection', *Budapest Review of Books*, 5 (1996), 193–99; Edit Madas, *Középkori prédikációirodalmunk történetéből: a kezdetektől a XIV. század elejéig* (Debrecen: Kossuth Egyetemi Kiadó, 2002).

12 Andreas Scheiner, 'Zur geschichtlichen Wertung des Mediascher Predigtbuchs', in *Beiträge zur Geschichte der Ev. Kirche A.B. in Siebenbürgen: Bischof d. Friedrich Teutsch, dem Meister sächsischer Volks- u. Kirchengeschichte, zum 70. Geburtstage am 16. September 1922* (Hermannstadt: Michaelis, 1922), pp. 46–58; Adolf Schullerus, 'Das Mediascher Predigtbuch', *Archiv des Vereins für Siebenbürgische Landeskunde*, 41 (1923), 5–296; Karl Reinerth, 'Wer war der Verfasser des sogenannten Mediascher Predigtbuches?', *Korrespondenzblatt des Arbeitskreises für Siebenbürgische Landeskunde*, 1 (1971), 75–83; Balázs J. Nemes, 'Das "Mediascher Predigtbuch": Miszelle zu einem Plenar mit Perikopen in deutsch-lateinischer Mischsprache aus Siebenbürgen am Vorabend der Reformation', *Zeitschrift für Siebenbürgische Landeskunde*, 38 (2015), 31–36.

investigation. The absence of previous scholarly interest regarding preaching and sermons must be understood within a larger cultural and intellectual context. While the beginning of modern scholarship in east-central Europe around 1900 witnessed an evident preference for medieval written sources issued by chancery institutions, perceived as more reliable testimonies of a past that preserved old political and social roots, the communist state ideology (c. 1947–1989), both in Romania and Hungary — the two countries preoccupied with the historical development of the Transylvanian cultural landscape — displayed an open adversity towards any form of investigation regarding the medieval Church and religion.[13] The direct consequence of these distinctive cultural-political evolutions, here only very briefly described, was an almost complete lack of engagement with manuscripts and printed books as a source for medieval and early modern studies while scholarly editing projects of chancery-issued documents are still ongoing.[14] A general catalogue of incunabula from Romanian libraries and archives was published in 2007,[15] and the very first attempt to count and describe briefly all the medieval manuscripts in Latin preserved in domestic collections was successfully completed only in 2018.[16] As for the sixteenth-century book, we do not yet have a similar evaluation, as many of the collections in the country have not been catalogued at all.

In the absence of such vital tools, solid research on sermon literature and preaching activity in late medieval Transylvania has been immensely obstructed. There is yet another important observation to be made in the context of discussing Transylvanian preaching and its textual evidence. An important proportion of the books, either printed or handwritten, available now in the custody of various libraries or archives in Romania reached their current locations under post-medieval circumstances. Schools of the Counter-Reformation, starting with the late sixteenth century such as Jesuit gymnasia throughout Transylvania or antiquarian bibliophilic acquisitions around 1800, gathered a written patrimony, which shares nothing with the local, medieval past (just as elsewhere in many parts of Europe). Therefore, the initial task of every academic endeavour currently dealing with old books from Romanian holdings is to establish accurately the material evidence and its links with domestic Transylvanian use and/or production.

And finally, there is a third contextual element to be considered. Medieval preaching overall, as an expression of complex communication processes,

---

13 Carmen Florea, 'Is there a Future for Medieval Studies in Romania?', *Annual of Medieval Studies at CEU*, 15 (2009), 279–87.

14 Adrian Papahagi and Adinel C. Dincă, 'Latin Palaeography and Codicology in Romania', *Chôra: Revue d'Études Anciennes et Médiévales*, 5 (2007), 159–86.

15 For the incunabula, see Elena-Maria Schatz and Robertina Stoica, *Catalogul colectiv al incunabulelor din România* (Bucureşti: CIMEC–Institutul de Memorie Culturală, 2007).

16 Adrian Papahagi and Adinel C. Dincă, *Manuscrisele medievale occidentale din România: Census* (Iaşi: Polirom, 2018).

remains influenced in Transylvania, the most eastern province of Hungary, by the active expansion of literate mentality, a slow process, strictly circumscribed and limited to several societal terms and conditions. The peripheral position of the land within Latin Christianity imposed not only a time lag of approximately a hundred to one hundred and fifty years in comparison to Western Europe, but also certain typical solutions, like the predominance of the pragmatic, institutional, and ecclesiastical character of literate behaviour as well as receptivity, rather than originality and creativity.[17] Orality holds its ground for a very long time, even in elevated strata of society and in crucial contexts such as legal matters, the more so as the written vernacular starts gradually to play a more important role only after the Protestant Reformation. Before the religious challenges of the mid-sixteenth century, the knowledge bearers and multipliers of the written forms of communication are the German colonists of the land, the so-called 'Transylvanian Saxons', who progressively started to build a network of urban settlements located favourably along important commercial routes, under the protection of royal privileges. In the long run, in this climate of economic prosperity, social development and cultural transformation started to thrive, the foundation of Central European universities after the middle of the fourteenth century boosting the formation of an intellectual elite in Transylvania. Today's medieval textual heritage of this part of the former Catholic world is therefore almost exclusively written in Latin and linked to this 'Saxon' population and to its administrative institutions, either ecclesiastical or secular. From the perspective of our current discussion, but also for the general proliferation of written communication and literate mentality in Transylvania, the crucial role was played by the parish clergy and parochial structures of the German settlements (followed by the mendicant orders, especially the Dominicans and Franciscans), the very first group of intellectuals of the land, shaped by the late medieval university and adapted to the local requirements.

In an oversimplified but nonetheless accurate manner, one can describe medieval book history in this part of the Latin world as a phenomenon that evolved simultaneously according to three central factors: German urban society, the parish church, and university education. In terms of chronological progression, the pinnacle of book culture in late medieval Transylvania should be sought in the last quarter of the fifteenth century and around 1500. The true impact of printing technology, translated into an increased availability

---

17 The close relationship between secular literacy and the ecclesiastical environment in Transylvania is highlighted by Adinel C. Dincă in 'Medieval Literacy in Transylvania: Selective Evidence from the Parish Church', *Transylvanian Review*, 1 (2015), 109–21; 'Scrieri autografe în Transilvania medievală: de la cele mai timpurii mărturii, până în secolul al XVI-lea', in *Autographa et signaturae Transilvaniae (sec. XIV–XVII)*, ed. by Susana Andea, Avram Andea, and Adinel Dincă (Cluj-Napoca: Argonaut, 2015), pp. 11–85; and 'Urban Literacy in Medieval Transylvania' in *Between Public and Private: Writing Praxis in Transylvania during the XIII–XVII Centuries*, ed. by Susana Andea (Cluj-Napoca: Argonaut, 2016), pp. 71–186.

of texts, including sermons, favoured the formation of private or institutional (small) libraries, together with the very first signs of local, specialized book commerce or manual illumination. Anticipating some of the final thoughts of the present essay, the overlapping of manuscripts and printed books of the generation that witnessed the turn of the sixteenth century can be regarded as a highlight of Transylvanian cultural and religious life, with sermon literature as an active vector in the process of deeper integration or 'bringing up to date' of local realities into the larger, continental stream of ideas.

Manuscripts

The source material at our disposal is not overwhelming, unlike in the larger libraries throughout the continent, especially in the Western, Southern, and Central European regions. However, the smaller number of books or isolated textual units (especially where manuscript transmission is concerned) should always be regarded within the context of the previous preliminary remarks. The definite figures for surviving books still available in this south-eastern periphery of Europe bear no comparison with the very dynamic cultural centres, with prosperous nearby universities, with thriving urban settlements, the long established and uninterrupted activity of monastic or religious orders, an early and lively written engagement in the vernacular, all combined in a diverse and intensive book production. The Transylvanian periphery can make a compelling subject for comparisons with other regions situated at the margin of the Latin medieval world, like the Northern realms of the Scandinavian Peninsula.[18]

From a little over one hundred medieval manuscripts that can now be linked with solid evidence to the region under discussion, preserved in Romania or abroad, around one third or thirty-four codices more precisely contain either exclusively or at least predominantly various sermon-related writings. Other theological or liturgical manuscripts bear different annotations that may indicate attempts to copy or draft smaller texts designed for preaching. Tomes of this sort can be found in Sibiu, the former 'Transylvanian Saxon' administrative and ecclesiastical capital situated in the centre of present-day Romania, at various institutions: nineteen volumes at Biblioteca Muzeului Național Brukenthal (the Library of the Brukenthal National Museum),[19] another four at Arhiva Centrală a Bisericii Evanghelice C. A. din România

---

18 See Anna Adamska, 'Intersections: Medieval East Central Europe from the Perspective of Literacy and Communication', in *Medieval East Central Europe in a Comparative Perspective: From Frontier Zones to Lands in Focus*, ed. by Gerhard Jaritz and Katalin Szende (London: Routledge, 2016), pp. 225–38.

19 Papahagi and Dincă, *Census*, nos 450, 459, 461, 463, 465–66, 468–71, 473, 477, 479, 481, 485, 487, 490, 496–97.

(ZAEKR) (the Central Archive of the Lutheran Church in Romania),[20] and one more in the local branch of Arhivele Naţionale ale României (the Romanian National Archives).[21] Situated only a few kilometres away from Sibiu, the small town of Cisnădie is an important place on the map of literacy in late medieval Transylvania. In the archive of the former parish church dedicated to St Walpurgis, which is now Lutheran, there are still twelve manuscripts preserved, with seven of them forming a strong body of pastoral literature.[22] Beside this accumulation of homiletic texts in or around the city of Sibiu, handwritten preaching compilations copied in Transylvania can be found in the Saxon towns of Mediaş[23] and Braşov,[24] and also in the Biblioteka Jagiellońska in Krákow.[25] For some of the texts mentioned here it is difficult or even impossible to establish the exact historical context of use. However, for the majority it may be inferred that they have circulated within the mendicant or parochial environment, sometimes changing owners, from the private hands of secular clergy or laypeople into the possession of the friars.

This rather sketchy picture regarding the presence and distribution of sermon literature in late medieval Transylvania may be focussed a little if one takes into consideration the sundry documentary witnesses available. The most important one by far is the so-called *Matricula Plebaniae Cibiniensis*, a churchwarden's account book recording valuable goods, belongings, and financial matters of St Mary's parish church in Sibiu, beginning in the last quarter of the fourteenth century.[26] This inventory also records, on several occasions, books owned by the parish, the most impressive list being the one compiled in 1442. This extensive description of the church *libraria* mentions 154

---

20 Papahagi and Dincă, *Census*, nos 419, 421–22.
21 Papahagi and Dincă, *Census*, no. 428.
22 Papahagi and Dincă, *Census*, nos 346–48, 352–54, 357.
23 Papahagi and Dincă, *Census*, no. 399.
24 For a fragment mentioned in the academic literature, now presumably lost, see Papahagi and Dincă, *Census*, Annex, no. vi.
25 Kraków, Biblioteka Jagiellońska, Uniwersytet Jagielloński W Kraków, MS 2332.
26 Alba Iulia, Biblioteca Naţională a României, Biblioteca Batthyaneum, MS II.135. The research history of *Matricula* was considered of utmost importance from a linguistic perspective, especially over the last two centuries: Anton Kurz, 'Die ältesten deutschen Sprachdenkmale und die bis jetzt bekannte älteste Handschrift der Sachsen in Siebenbürgen, mitgetheilt aus dem Original-Fragment einer auf Pergament geschriebenen Hermannstädter Kirchenmatrikel des xiv. und späterer Jahrhundert', *Serapeum*, 16 (1848), 193–200; Friedrich Müller, *Deutsche Sprachdenkmäler aus Siebenbürgen: aus schriftlichen Quellen des zwölften bis sechzehnten Jahrhunderts* (Hermannstadt: Steinhaussen, 1864), pp. 16–21, and 32–34; Gustav Seiwert, 'Das älteste Hermannstädter Kirchenbuch', *Archiv des Vereins für Siebenbürgische Landeskunde*, 11 (1874), 323–410 (including the list of books on pp. 348–50); Elemér Varjú, 'A gyulafejérvári Batthyány-könyvtár', *Magyar Könyvszemle*, 7 (1899), 134–75, 209–43, and 329–45; 8 (1900), 17–55, 131–69, 228–50, and 337–61; 9 (1901), 24–52, and 256–79; Robert Szentiványi, *Catalogus concinnus librorum manuscriptorum Bibliothecae Batthyanyanae* (Szeged: Bibliotheca Universitatis Szegediensis, 1958), pp. 158–69, no. 294 (including a transcription and an attempt to identify works and authors).

'titles', of which some thirty are overtly labelled as *sermones, postilla, homili(a)e*, or *de tempore/sanctis, quadragesimales*, et cetera. In the typically condensed manner of medieval library catalogues the references to some works are quite blurred (*liber de quodlibet, pastoralia et libellus Gregorii*, et cetera) and could possibly augment the number of preaching texts. If we added writings on moral or mystical theology and history (*Gesta Romanorum*, for example) that were usually incorporated in the auxiliary body of preaching aids, we would get close to the one-third ratio of sermon texts that have survived. However, as surprisingly well endowed as it may appear, the Sibiu parish library, according to the status quo described in 1442, seems to be the result of an 'historical accident', not the direct consequence of a gradual accumulation. It is likely that the previous holdings of the local Dominican convent had been incorporated in or shortly after 1438, due to the intentional dismantling of the friary buildings, situated outside the city walls, an act conducted by the municipal administration out of fear of the besieging Ottoman Turks. Regardless of their initial location, the booklist from 1442, from which only a few volumes are still extant, recreates the most complex and vivid corpus of sermon collections in Late Medieval Transylvania in the pre-printing age.

Another churchwarden's account book gives us additional information, this time concerning a small rural parish, by no means comparable with the quasi-episcopal church in Sibiu.[27] This financial and administrative informal record of the parish of Jelna, a German village in the northern part of Transylvania, covers the period between 1455 and 1571, witnessing also the adherence of the community to the Lutheran confession in the early 1540s. Along with several mentions of liturgical books, on fol. 42v of the unpublished source,[28] an unskilled hand reluctantly notes (around 1512) that: 'Dominus Martinus habet bibliam magnam, Discipulum, [followed by illegible text], Passionale, Sermones autori antiquas [*sic!*], Historia cum "In principio", Postillam' ['Master Martin owns a large Bible, and the volumes: Disciple [followed by illegible text], Passion, Sermons of ancient authors, History starting with "In the beginning", Postil'], and then: 'Dominus Felix [habet], Vincencium, Jacobus de Voragine, Peregrinus, Postilla, Lombardica, Rubricam' ['Master Felix owns: Vincent, Jacobus de Voragine, Peregrine, Postil, Lombard, Rubrica']. Although uncertain, Felix and Martinus may have been members of the parish clergy, either the *predicator*, mentioned already in 1508, the *scolaris* (schoolteacher), or the chaplain of the St Leonhardus chapel.[29] This joint preaching library, which quite likely combines manuscript (the so-called 'old sermons') and printed sermons, is indeed noteworthy, especially for a small church that

---

27 Sibiu, Serviciul Județean al Arhivelor Naționale, Colecția 'Brukenthal', MS B. 268.

28 An edition of this account book is now at an advanced stage of development, *The Rural Parish in Late Medieval Transylvania: Churchwardens' Accounts of Jelna (1455–1570)*, ed. by Adinel C. Dincă (forthcoming).

29 Fol. 34r: '[...] in presentia domini plebani et domini Simonis, predicatoris in Zolna [...]' ['in the presence of the parish priest and of master Simon, the preacher in Jelna'].

does not seem to have had more than a dozen books at any given time, even after the Reformation.

Wills too may provide important insights into the presence, circulation, and provenance of sermon texts in pre-Reformation Transylvania. For example, a draft of the last will and testament[30] of Nicholaus, *presbyter de Yegerdorff, Olomucensis diocesis*, residing in the Benedictine abbey of Cluj-Mănăştur (today part of the city of Cluj-Napoca) stipulates in 1435 that the Moravian clerk bequeaths to the monastery ('cenobium') where he was living, besides a cross and a chalice (both of gilded silver), three books ('simulcum tribus voluminibus librorum'): 'postille Conradi super ewangeliis dominicalibus, ac alter de Gestis Romanorum, et tercius nova legenda de passione sanctorum per anni circulum' ['the postils of Conrad on the Sunday Gospels, and another one on the Deeds of the Romans, and the third one about the new legend on the passion of the saints throughout the entire year'].[31]

As a matter of fact, it can be assumed that most of the materials relating to preaching were produced outside Transylvania and entered the land randomly, according to personal interest and opportunity, not through a programmed approach or institutional policy. Perhaps a slightly different situation should be taken into consideration for the religious orders, especially for the Dominicans, in the age of the printed book, as will be discussed below.

The Southern German regions seem to be the most likely source of handwritten sermons, at least for parish libraries such as Cisnădie (whose manuscripts are now in the archive of the local Lutheran church) and Sebeş (whose manuscripts are now in Sibiu).[32] One of the earliest sermons surviving from medieval Transylvania is in a late thirteenth century manuscript of French origin (produced at the university of Paris?) that bears an ownership mark of the Cistercian Abbey from Cârţa, and refers to the *Quattuor Libri Sententiarum* of Petrus Lombardus (*c.* 1096–1160).[33] This is one of the few

---

30 1435.II.18. Budapest, Magyar Nemzeti Levéltár, Diplomatikai Levéltár, no. 36897. https://archives.hungaricana.hu/en/charters/view/140813/?pg=0&bbox=1115%2C–2018%2C2170%2C–1711; accessed 10 June 2022].

31 Géza Entz, *Erdély építészete a 14–16. században* (Kolozsvár: Az Erdélyi Múzeum-Egyesület Kiadása, 1994), p. 329.

32 Respectively Cisnădie, Biserica Evanghelică C. A., Oficiul Parohial, MS D. 27; Papahagi and Dincă, *Census*, no. 353 (*Sermones dominicales*, and so on) mentioning the Franconian city of Nürnberg, fol. 196r: 'liber magistri Conradi Mullner de Nurenberge' ['The book belongs to master Conrad Mullner of Nuremberg'], and Sibiu, Arhiva Centrală a Bisericii Evanghelice C. A. din România (ZAEKR), MS 601–C–28; Papahagi and Dincă, *Census*, no. 422, colophon: '[…] per manus Johannis Girlatii de Wienna' ['by the hand of John Girlatii of Vienna'] (fol. 186r); '[…] expliciunt sermones dominicales totius anni scripti per manus Michaelis de Bern […]' ['here end the Sunday sermons for the entire year, written by the hand of Michael of Bern'] (fol. 307v).

33 Sibiu, Biblioteca Muzeului Naţional Brukenthal, MS 660; Papahagi and Dincă, *Census*, no. 471, fol. 3r: 'Introitus in quattuor libro sententiarum. In nova signa et immuta mirabilia. 36 Ecclesiastici' ['Introduction to the four books of sentences. Renew thy signs, and work new miracles. Ecclesiasticus 36'].

texts that are relevant to the present topic and is not dated to the usual period from the early fifteenth to the early sixteenth century.

There are, however, several collections of sermons copied locally, in Transylvania. Some unspecified sermons of Jacobus de Voragine (*c.* 1230–1298) were copied in Brașov in 1427, although, unfortunately, the extensive fragment that documented the existence of the manuscript now seems to be lost.[34] Fully preserved instead is Albertus de Padua's (1282–1328) *Postilla*, a work which was copied around 1429 by Anthonius from Mediaș, who had clerical offices in various churches in Transylvania (Codlea and Moșna).[35] From a different manuscript note in the same *opus* we learn that Anthonius died in 1442 and was in fact *predicator*, although he always described himself with a general term, *sacerdos*. So, the copyist of the sermons authored by the Augustinian theologian of the early fourteenth century was the prime beneficiary and the reason behind the effort was a pragmatic one, to have his own copy of the work. Around the same time, an anonymous scribe from Sibiu, most likely working for the parish church (perhaps, he was also a preacher), was transcribing several texts for preaching purposes. The core of the bulky volume, however, consisted of sermons and smaller works of university theologians, like Robert Holcot (1290–1349), and Henricus de Langenstein (*c.* 1325–1397), highly regarded at the universities of Prague and Vienna, two main points of attraction for Transylvanian students. Strongly linked to the university milieu and especially with the Austrian place of higher education was Petrus Nowag (d. 1456), eventually a highly esteemed bishop of Wrocław. It is usually overlooked that Petrus, also professor of Canon Law in Vienna, started his ecclesiastical career in Transylvania, roughly from 1429 to 1434 as *plebanus* in Lechința, a small village in the north of the province, but an important parish, as the place was associated many times with the vicars of the Transylvanian bishops. During his stay in Transylvania he wrote down sermons in his own hand to inspire his parishioners or for the episcopal synods, as we learn from a manuscript now preserved in the Biblioteka Jagiellońska in Krákow.[36]

Similarly drafted (for private use, informally written in the form of autographs) were the sermons compiled in MS 657 from the Biblioteca Muzeului Național Brukenthal in Sibiu, by Johannes Zeckel, a parish priest in the nearby village of Ruși, around 1502 and the so-called 'Mediascher Predigtbuch'.[37] The

---

34 Papahagi and Dincă, *Census*, Annex, no. vi: 'Explicit liber sermonum de tempore Jacobi de Voragine terminatus per manus Nicolai de vetere ciuitate feria sexta ante palmarum Anno domini M°cccc°xxvii, etc.' ['Here ends Jacobus de Voragine's book of the *de tempore* sermons, completed by the hand of Nicholas from the Old City, on the Friday before the Palm Sunday of the year of our Lord 1427 et cetera'].

35 Sibiu, Biblioteca Muzeului Național Brukenthal, MS 647; Papahagi and Dincă, *Census*, no. 465.

36 Kraków, Biblioteka Jagiellońska, Uniwersytet Jagielloński W Kraków, MS 2332, fols 346v, 357r–v, 363r–v, 370v–371v, 375r–v, 381r, 439v, 464r.

37 Sibiu, Biblioteca Muzeului Național Brukenthal, MS 657; Papahagi and Dincă, *Census*, no. 470: 'Hunc sermonem colegi feci in ecclesia mea in festo Sancti Georgii, ego Johannes

LATIN MANUSCRIPT AND PRINTED SERMONS IN LATE MEDIEVAL TRANSYLVANIA

latter is somehow different in comparison with the previous Latin works, linked predominantly with parochial contexts. It was copied around 1535–1536 by an unprofessional, occasional, scribe, probably in the environment of the Franciscan convent in the Transylvanian village of Albeşti, being also the only preaching compilation that contains German texts, besides Latin passages.

Early Printed Sermons

These two Transylvanian texts mentioned above from the first half of the sixteenth century, although handwritten, were much indebted to printed works, a medium already dominant by then within the Catholic world. Some 180 Latin pastoral works published between *c.* 1470 and 1530 have been identified so far in Transylvanian libraries hosting extensive collections of early printed books.[38] Among them, only thirty-five to forty volumes are undoubtedly related to medieval Transylvania, as documented mostly through ownership notes.

Zekel anno 1502' ['I, John Zekel, compiled and composed this sermon in my church on the feast day of St George in the year 1502'] (fol. 6r) and 'Hunc sermonem ego Joannes Zekel feci et colegi predicauique dominica Cibinii' ['I, John Zekel, composed, compiled, and preached this sermon on Sunday in Sibiu'] (fol. 212r); and Mediaş, Biserica Evanghelică C. A., MS (no shelfmark), *Sermones de tempore, de sanctis, de communis sanctorum*; Papahagi and Dincă, *Census*, no. 399.

38   The institutions covered by this research are: Biblioteca Muzeului Naţional Brukenthal, Biblioteca Teleki-Bolyai, Târgu Mureş, Biblioteca Centrală Universitară 'Lucian Blaga' (BCU), Cluj-Napoca, as well as the book collection of Muzeul Secuiesc al Ciucului, Miercurea Ciuc, and a smaller local library from Sighişoara, Biblioteca Municipală 'Zaharia Boiu'. Although the richest collection is held by the Batthyaneum Library in Alba Iulia, increasing the number of printed sermon collections by approximately fifty copies, it was not included in our survey, since it holds mostly books acquired abroad by its bibliophile founder, in the eighteenth century. Included in this estimation is also the source material newly discussed by Adrian Papahagi, 'The Incunabula of the Dominicans from Bistriţa at the Central Piarist Library in Budapest', *Philobiblon: Transylvanian Journal of Multidisciplinary Research in Humanities*, 22/2 (2017), 51–66, by Adinel C. Dincă, regarding Franciscan convents from Braşov and Albeşti, near Mediaş (unpublished paper) or pertaining to the Dominican friars in Cluj-Napoca; we would like to thank Gyöngyi Bíró for allowing us to consult her unpublished work regarding the nineteen incunabula preserved today in Arhiva Parohiei Romano-Catolice Sfântul Mihail din Cluj-Napoca. Three more incunabula were identified in the archive of the Evangelical Church at Cisnădie (former St Walpurgis), Inv. 1355: Guido de Monte Rocherii, *Manipulus curatorum* (Strasbourg: Printer of the 'Legenda aurea', 30 August 1483), bound together with *Gesta Romanorum* (Strasbourg: Printer of the 'Vitas Patrum', *c.* 1484/1486); sine signatura: Rainerius de Pisis, *Pantheologia, sive Summa universae theologiae* (Venezia: Hermannus Liechtenstein, 12 September 1486); sine signatura: Nicolaus de Lyra, *Postilla litteralis in vetus et novum testamentum, mit Expositiones prologorum von Guilelmus Brito, Additiones ad Postillam Nicolai de Lyra von Paulus Burgensis und Replicae contra Burgensem von Matthias Doering*, parts 1–2 (Genesis–Psalmi; Proverbia– Apocalypsis)], (Nürnberg, *c.* 1481), I; see also Adinel C. Dincă, 'The University and the Parish: The Medieval Books from Heltau/Cisnădie', *Philobiblon: Transylvanian Journal of Multidisciplinary Research in Humanities*, 24 (2019), 337–52.

However, an additional group of fifty-six volumes bear proof of their presence in the region in the second half of the sixteenth and during the seventeenth centuries, most of them displaying material evidence that indicate a possible circulation and use in Transylvania. Those books currently preserved in the Biblioteca Muzeului Național Brukenthal in Sibiu and in Muzeul Secuiesc al Ciucului (the Szekler Museum in Miercurea Ciuc) (thirty-eight works) are especially likely to have had an earlier reception in the aforementioned region, given the fact that at the very core of these libraries stand book accumulations that evolved locally. For approximately sixty other works there is not enough research yet undertaken to allow us to establish their medieval or early modern history. Some of these books bear no signs of use or their ownership marks are quite vague, mentioning only names that may not be identified as yet, or are illegible due to the precarious state of preservation, or the existing handwritten notes have been regrettably deleted by subsequent users.

Because the first Transylvanian printing press (in Sibiu) may only be attested around 1525,[39] all the volumes relevant for this discussion were imported.[40] As for the places of printing, one may notice the remarkable prevalence of the centres within the Holy Roman Empire (such as Strasbourg, Nürnberg, Speyer, Basel, Reutlingen, Augsburg, and Köln), with Venezia and Lyon as noteworthy exceptions. Partly determined by the fact that the Holy Roman Empire with its numerous printing presses dominated the market and by the large number of sermon collections printed in the centres listed above,[41] the Transylvanian situation was also influenced by the traditional trade routes and intellectual contacts existing between this region and Central Europe.[42]

---

39 Zsolt Simon, 'Primele tipărituri din Transilvania (Sibiu, 1525)', *Anuarul Institutului de Istorie 'G. Barițiu' din Cluj-Napoca*, 46 (2007), 89–106.

40 Attila Verók, 'Das Buch als Repräsentationsmittel bei den Siebenbürger Sachsen', *Zeitschrift für Siebenbürghische Landeskunde*, 39 (2016), 91–99, especially p. 93. For a survey concerning possible import routes for printed texts in Transylvania, as well as some details on the local book trade, see Adinel C. Dincă, 'La Transilvania nel commercio europeo di libri intorno al 1500: stampe veneziane nella Sibiu (Cibinium — Nagyszeben — Hermannstadt) medievale', a paper presented at the international conference 'I Convegno Sismed della medievistica italiana', 14–16 June 2018, Bertinoro (Forlì-Cesena), Italy, and published in *I Convegno della medievistica italiana: Bertinoro (Forlì-Cesena), 14–16 giugno 2018* (Roma: Open Archive di Reti Medievali, 2019), pp. 580–99.

41 The statistics provided by Anne Thayer present Strasbourg as the second producer of sermon collections, while Nürnberg and Basel were also important; see Anne T. Thayer, *Penitence, Preaching and the Coming of the Reformation*, St Andrews Studies in Reformation History (Aldershot: Ashgate, 2002), pp. 32–34. Regarding Strasbourg, Miriam Chrisman emphasizes that sermon collections represented a quarter of the books printed there; see Miriam Usher Chrisman, *Lay Culture, Learned Culture: Books and Social Change in Strasbourg (1480–1599)* (New Haven: Yale University Press, 1982), pp. 84–85.

42 On the trade routes, see Samuil Goldenberg, 'Der Handel Transsilvaniens vom 14. bis zum 17. Jahrhundert', *Scripta Mercaturae*, 11 (1977), 4–24; on the intellectual contacts, see Andrea Fara, 'I sassoni di Transilvania nelle Universita d'Europa tra XIV e XVI secolo', *Annuario dell'Instituto Romeno di Cultura e Ricerca Umanistica di Venezia*, 8 (2016), 119–33.

In particular the larger urban settlements inhabited by the above mentioned 'Transylvanian Saxons' were important hubs on the trade routes between Western Europe and the Ottoman Empire, and as such closely connected to the German territories.[43]

The chronology of printing may also offer some interesting information. The earliest pertinent anthology of sermons evidenced in Transylvania was printed in 1473,[44] while the latest one was published in 1533.[45] The number of incunabula, however, far exceeds the number of *cinquecentine*, the ninth decade of the fifteenth century being the best represented. The situation is not surprising. The analyses carried out in this respect have revealed that the last decades of the fifteenth century constituted the pinnacle; after 1500, and especially after 1520, the printing of sermon anthologies experienced a marked decrease.[46] A more nuanced picture regarding the reception of homiletic

---

That the general geographical distribution of the printing of sermon collections was not the single determining factor is also suggested by the fact that the leading position of Lyon and the significant number of sermons printed in Venice are not entirely reflected by the Transylvanian situation; see, for example, Thayer, *Penitence, Preaching and the Coming of the Reformation*, pp. 32–34.

43 The German provenance of the early printed books from Transylvania is sometimes documented by administrative records, such as the episode from 1533, when the town magistrate of Brașov paid 10 florins to Luca Plecker, *predicator huius civitatis*, for buying and bringing home books 'from Germany' ('Ex quartali corporis Christi domini senatus dederunt in subsidium librorum e Germania advehendorum emendorumque, domino Lucae Plecker predicatori huius civitatis flor. 10' ['The members of the city council gave from the revenues of the Corpus Christi neighbourhood 10 florins to Luke Plecker, preacher of the same town, as a subsidy for buying and bringing books from Germany'], quoted from *Quellen zur Geschichte der Stadt Kronstadt in Siebenbürgen, Rechnungen aus dem Archiv der Stadt Kronstadt*, II *(1526–1540)* (Kronstadt: Albrecht & Zillich, 1889), p. 294. Ownership marks can reveal the place from where a book was brought, as in the case of a priest from Dobârca (a village 35 kilometres away from Sibiu), who bought a volume of the works of St. Jerome in Vienna which was printed in Basel in 1516, Sibiu, Biblioteca Muzeului Național Brukenthal, V. III. 160: 'Liber hic cum ceteris Heronimi libris pertinet ad me, Georgium presbiterum Doborkanum, emptus autem unacum reliquis per me idem, Vienne Austrie. Anno domini 1525'. The best way to track the provenance of late fifteenth-early sixteenth century books now in Romania is provided by the analysis of the material details, such as the binding. Especially in the Brukenthal Library, many books either printed or hand-copied have been transmitted with their original bindings (late fourteenth to early sixteenth century). However, this detail has not been exploited by the scholarship yet.

44 Sibiu, Biblioteca Muzeului Național Brukenthal, Inc. 68: Leonardo da Udine, *Sermones aurei de sanctis* (Köln: Ulrich Zell, 1473); Veturia Jugăreanu, *Catalogul colecției de incunabule* (Sibiu: Biblioteca Muzeului Brukenthal, 1969), no. 356.

45 Sighișoara, Biblioteca Municipală 'Zaharia Boiu', F. 90: Johannes Eck, *Quinta pars operum Iohannis Eckii, contra Lutherum et alios declamatoria, continet Homilias de Tempore, Sanctis ac Sacramentis* (Augsburg: Alexander Weißenhorn, 1533).

46 Thayer, *Penitence, Preaching and the Coming of the Reformation*, pp. 27–29; Larissa Taylor argues that such a decrease should not be interpreted as a sign of lower preaching activity itself, but rather it can be explained through the incapacity of an already saturated market to absorb new prints of this kind, following the great number of incunabula comprising sermons, which themselves overlapped a previous corpus of manuscripts; see Larissa Taylor,

literature in Transylvania can be achieved by surveying the times when relevant collections appeared in the land. Such an approach is tentative, as clear evidence in this matter is not always available. Regardless of such caveats, the bulk of the data gathered indicates the last decade of the fifteenth century and the first years of the sixteenth century as the time of concentrated acquisitions. Between the date of printing and that mentioned by an ownership or contextual annotation from Transylvania there is usually a gap varying from four to thirty-two years, with a single exception when the year coincides (1533).[47] Hence, it seems that the peripheral, Transylvanian, reception of the newest preaching tools happened with a certain, but not very long delay, explicable by the features of the book trade during the first age of printing, the distances for distribution, and the travel possibilities for individuals, underlining at the same time the desire of people living on the outskirts of the Latin world to acquire new pastoral tools. In addition, as production no longer responded to a well-defined demand, sometimes a book stock needed more time to get into the public eye and find its way onto the shelves.[48] Another aspect worth mentioning is the presence of sixteenth-century annotations, even from the 1530–1540s, on copies printed in the fifteenth century, proof that incunabula continued to be used, making the acquisition of newer books less imperative.

Notes written on the pages of printed sermons point to some twenty different localities, both urban and rural, though unevenly distributed throughout the region. Predictably, the southern part, controlled by prosperous and active German towns and more developed rural surrounding areas, joined by other urban settlements inhabited by the German colonists, like Cluj and Bistrița, show the utmost density.[49] A second accumulation of preaching texts comes from the eastern area of the province, the so-called Szeklerland.[50]

Ownership of Printed Collections

Looking more closely at the profile of owners or users of printed sermon collections, the picture is unsurprisingly dominated by the mendicant orders, well-known both for their culture of learning and for assuming the mission of spreading the Word of God through preaching. According to the existing

---

'Out of Print: The Decline of Catholic Printed Sermons in France, 1530–1560', in *Habent sua fata libelli / Books Have Their Own Destiny: Essays in Honor of Robert V. Schnucker*, ed. by Robin B. Barnes, Robert A. Kolb, and Paula L. Presley, Sixteenth Century Essays & Studies, 1 (Kirksville, MO: Truman State University Press, 1998), pp. 121–30.

47 See n. 74.

48 Andrew Pettegree, *The Book in the Renaissance* (New Haven: Yale University Press, 2011), pp. 65–78; Peter Zahn, 'Die Endabrechnung über den Druck der Schedelschen Weltchronik 1493 vom Juni 1509', *Gutenberg Jahrbuch*, 66 (1991), 177–213.

49 Laurențiu Rădvan, *At Europe's Borders: Medieval Towns in the Romanian Principalities* (Leiden: Brill, 2010), pp. 81–84.

50 Engel, *The Realm of St Stephen*, pp. 115–17.

source material, four main focal points can be demarcated, each deriving from individual late medieval libraries pertaining to mendicant convents from Sibiu, Cluj-Napoca, Bistriţa, and Şumuleu-Ciuc, with the first three being Dominican and the fourth Franciscan.

More than fifty percent of the printed volumes that have survived in Transylvania were part of Dominican holdings.[51] Their impressively consistent presence as users of preaching materials is very much owed to Conventul Sfintei Cruci or the Convent of the Holy Cross in Sibiu, which possessed at least eight printed sermon collections. Another eighteen homiletic works kept in the Brukenthal Library — previously part of the library of the Lutheran Gymnasium of the same town (today Colegiul Naţional Samuel von Brukenthal), the institution which gathered all medieval ecclesiastical book collections of Sibiu in the context of the Reformation[52] — may come from the same convent.[53] A second compact group of printed sermons, five books (from a total of eleven still extant), belonged to the Dominican convent of the Holy Cross in Bistriţa.[54] Printed during the eighth and the beginning of the ninth decade of the fifteenth century (1473–1485), they are among the earliest copies to have reached Transylvania, one featuring handwritten additions of a homiletic nature.[55] The evaluation of the early printed books that originated from the Dominican friary in Cluj is not yet complete, but the rather large collection of nineteen volumes comprises two sermon anthologies[56] that could have been used for preaching alongside other theological *corpora* from the same library, works authored by famous names in the field

---

51 Mária Lupescu-Makó, 'The Book Culture of the Dominican Order in Transylvania', *Philobiblon: Transylvanian Journal of Multidisciplinary Research in Humanities*, 22/1 (2017), 187–204.

52 Friedrich Müller, 'Die Incunabeln der Hermannstädter Capellenbibliothek', *Archiv des Vereins für Siebenbürgische Landeskunde*, 14 (1877), I. Lieferung 1460–1490, 293–358, and II. Lieferung 1491–1500, 489–543.

53 The aforementioned volumes also have their covers or edges marked in hot iron with the coat of arms of Sibiu, a distinctive sign that according to recent research is likely to point precisely toward the books of the Dominican collection, a book-historical quirk that can only be encountered in Sibiu. See Adinel C. Dincă, '"Biblioteca oraşului Sibiu" în evul mediu: câteva consideraţii pe marginea unei confuzii istoriografice', in *Cluj — Kolozsvár — Klausenburg 700: várostörténeti tanulmányok = studii de istorie urbană*, coordinated by Mária Lupescu-Makó and others (Cluj-Napoca: Erdélyi Múzeum Egyesület, 2018), pp. 431–36.

54 Papahagi, 'The Incunabula of the Dominicans from Bistriţa', see especially the Appendix: 'Handlist of Incunabula of Transylvanian Provenance at the Central Piarist Library, Budapest: A. Incunabula from Bistriţa', pp. 61–62.

55 Papahagi, 'The Incunabula of the Dominicans from Bistriţa', pp. 57–58.

56 St Michael's Roman-Catholic Parish Church in Cluj-Napoca, Ambrosius de Spiera, *Quadragesimale de floribus sapientiae*, ed. by Marcus Venetus (Venezia: Antonius de Stanchis de Valentia, Jacobus Britannicus et socii, 24 March 1481); Bonaventura, S: *Opuscula*. Octavianus de Martinis: *Oratio in vitam et merita S. Bonaventurae*. Johannes Franciscus de Pavinis: *Relatio circa canonizationem Bonaventurae*. Robertus [Caracciolo?]: *Sermo de laudibus Bonaventurae*. Sixtus IV: *Bulla canonizationis* (Strasbourg: [Printer of the 1483 Jordanus von Quedlinburg (Georg Husner)], 1495).

of homiletic literature, such as Jean Gerson. These supplementary 'titles' would considerably enhance the pastoral library of the Dominicans in Cluj at the end of the Middle Ages.

The order of the Friars Minor is not entirely missing from the list of Transylvanian owners of sermon collections, although the books displaying traces of use in a Franciscan milieu are numerically smaller. It is not the case with the library of the convent in Şumuleu-Ciuc, an exceptional context, due to its almost uninterrupted existence from the fifteenth century until the present day. A consistent part of its medieval and early modern book stock is currently preserved in the Muzeul Secuiesc al Ciucului or Szekler Museum of Miercurea Ciuc. Among the early printed compilations, more than forty are homiletic works, but ownership marks reveal that not all of them belonged to the Friars Minor of this convent during the Middle Ages. While an important number of books seems to have arrived here during the late sixteenth and seventeenth century (perhaps rescued from other friaries or parishes affected by the Protestant Reformation), there are also a few sermon collections bearing fifteenth- or sixteenth-century handwritten annotations, revealing book gifts to the 'fratribus in Schik'.[57] Other preaching materials — sermonaries (that is, collections of sermons) and preaching aids alike — are in a precarious state of conservation, as a consequence of the fact that they were hidden in order to be saved from confiscation by communist authorities after the order was dissolved in 1949, and only retrieved in 1980 and 1985.[58]

Besides these relatively well-known examples, Transylvanian sermon literature is rather scattered, institutions and individuals being usually represented by a single volume or, in better circumstances, up to three pertinent works. For instance, other Dominican convents with a discrete appearance in local book history are in Braşov and Alba Iulia. The books of the Dominicans in Braşov — a fairly large collection, according to an inventory from 1575 — were integrated after the Reformation into the library of the Lutheran Gymnasium (today Colegiul Naţional Johannes Honterus)[59] only to be destroyed in the Great Fire of 1689, with the exception of a handful of fortunate cases, such as a sermon collection by Bernard de Clairvaux (Speyer, c. 1481–1482),[60] and of the second part of *Sermones de tempore et de sanctis*, attributed to Vicent

---

57 Erzsebet Mukenhaupt, *A Csíksomlyói Ferences Könyvtár Kincsei* (Budapest: Balassi, 1999), no. II. 51, no. II. 69, no. II. 1.

58 Schatz and Stoica, *Catalogul colectiv al incunabulelor din România*, pp. 30–31; Mukenhaupt, *A Csíksomlyói Ferences Könyvtár Kincsei*, pp. 13–15.

59 Julius Groß, 'Zur ältesten Geschichte der Kronstädter Gymnasialbibliothek', *Archiv des Vereins für Siebenbürgische Landeskunde*, 21 (1887), pp. 591–708.

60 Miercurea Ciuc, Muzeul Secuiesc al Ciucului/Csíki Székely Múzeum, Inv. 6243; Schatz and Stoica, *Catalogul colectiv al incunabulelor din România*, B-43. Bernardus Claravallensis (Sanctus), *Sermones de tempore et de sanctis et de diversis* (Speyer: Peter Drach, post 31 August 1481, *non post* 1482).

Ferrer (Köln, 1487).[61] The book ownership of the Dominicans from Alba Iulia was virtually unknown until recently, when a volume currently preserved in the Biblioteca Centrală Universitară 'Lucian Blaga' in Cluj-Napoca, *Sermones quadragesimales Pomerii* by Pelbartus de Themeswar (Haguenau: Henrich Gran, 1501), came to light.[62] An extensive annotation reveals: 'Liber sum fratris Petri de Vasarhel et propinavit michi dominus Petrus Teremi de Coloswar pro anima domini Gervasii, sacerdotis de eadem civitate, pertinet ad conventum albagiulensem quia et ego filius sum istius conventus 1532 die Marie virginis' ['This book belongs to brother Peter of Târgu Mureş and it was handed over to me by Peter Teremi of Cluj for the soul of Gervase, priest of the same city. It is in the possession of the convent in Alba Iulia, as I am also a son of this convent. 1532, the day of the Virgin Mary']. Another note explains which friary is being referred to, mentioning 'Conventus Albegywlense ordinis predicatorum' ['The Alba Iulia convent of the Order of Friars Preachers']. Similarly, four other homiletic works come from three convents of the Friars Minor, either Observant or Conventual, in Cluj,[63] Braşov,[64] and Mediaş.[65]

Alongside the mendicants, secular churches and their clergy were theoretically much interested in owning this kind of literature. However, only isolated evidence indicates the existence of printed books in the possession of churches.[66] Such scarce and scattered evidence would rather suggest a disregard

---

61 Miercurea Ciuc, Muzeul Secuiesc al Ciucului/Csíki Székely Múzeum, Inv. 6218; Schatz and Stoica, *Catalogul colectiv al incunabulelor din România*, F–7. Vicent Ferrer, *Sermones de tempore et de sanctis* (Köln: Heinrich Quentell, 1487).

62 Cluj-Napoca, Biblioteca Centrală Universitară 'Lucian Blaga', Colecția de carte veche maghiară, BMV 46.

63 Târgu-Mureş, Biblioteca Teleki-Bolyai, 0671; *Catalogus Incunabulorum Bib. Teleki*, no. 35: *Sermones thesauri novi de sanctis* (Strasbourg: Martin Flach, 1488), 'Conventus Colosvariensis ad plateam Lupi 1512 Fratrum minorum de observantia' ['The Cluj convent of the Observant Friars Minor, on the Wolf's street, 1512']. Additional evidence in Csapodi Csaba, Csapodiné Gárdonyi Klára, *Bibliotheca Hungarica: kódexek és nyomtatott könyvek Magyarországon 1526*, Kötet 1 (Budapest: MTAK 1988), no. 1116: *Sermones dominicales Biga salutis intitulatus* of the Hungarian Observant Osualdus de Lasko: 'Liber Conuentus Coloswariensis fratrum minorum observantium, iam ad Johannem plebanum de Carasna residentem pertinet' ['The book belongs to the convent of the Observant Friars Minor in Cluj, now owned by John, resident parish priest in Crasna'].

64 Dej, Conventul Franciscan, Inc. C. 197: Angelus de Clavasio, *Summa angelica de casibus conscientiae*. Hieronymus Tornieli (Speyer: [Peter Drach], 1488): 'Johanniß Flasbart capellanus Braschow 1500' ['John Flasbart, chaplain in Braşov 1500'], Béla Baráth, 'Ösnyomtatványok a Székelyföldön és Délerdélyben', *Erdélyi Tudósító*, 21 (1942), p. 31.

65 Sibiu, Biblioteca Muzeului Național Brukenthal, Inc. 38; Jugăreanu, *Catalogul*, no. 236: Pelbartus de Themeswar, *Sermones Pomerii quadragesimales* (Haguenau: Heinrich Gran, 10 November 1499): 'Istud quadragesimale deputatum est pro communi usu fratrum in Megges degentium per reverendum P. V. [?] quod nullus usui suo audeat eciam per alium usurpare'. ['This book of Lent sermons was assigned by the reverend father vicar for the common use of the friars living in Mediaş, so that nobody should dare to usurp it for his own or even for someone else's use'].

66 Sibiu, Biblioteca Muzeului Național Brukenthal, Inc. 50; Jugăreanu, *Catalogul*, no. 74:

for preaching tasks. Still, there are quite a few examples of homiletic works pertaining to parish priests themselves, as part of some small private collections. This is interesting considering that the quality of pastoral performance was still determined around 1500 by personal involvement and the dedication of individual parochial clergy rather than by a higher policy of the Church. A few examples given in this respect will suffice: Sigismundus, parish priest in the Saxon village of Apoldul de Jos, possessed a work of the Dominican Leonardo da Udine (d. 1470) comprising sermons for the feasts of saints.[67] Additionally, a copy of Bernardinus de Senis's *Sermones de evangelio eterno* bears the note: 'Liber Doctoris Blasii Insule Christiane plebani manu propria' ['The book belongs to the doctor Blasii, parish priest in Cristian. [Written] in his own hand'],[68] with the same priest writing a similar autograph annotation on the pages of the three volumes of the *Speculum historiale* compiled by Vincent de Beauvais, a work that was previously owned by Johannes, parish priest in Brateiu, who bought it himself in 1476.[69] Similarly, a copy of *Donatus moralisatus* authored by Jean Gerson seems to have been used by Martinus Huet,[70] a clerk with a long and successful career, parish priest in the area of Sibiu, and later dean of the local chapter, an important owner of several books, as well. A comparable case is that of Matheus of Rupea (parish priest in the Saxon

---

Nicolaus de Lyra, *Biblia latina cum postillis Nicolai de Lyra*, 4 vols (Nürnberg: Anton Koberger 3 December 1487): 'Liber ecclesie et dotis in Kysselk'['The book belongs to Şeica Mică church and its patrimony']; Inc. 113; Jugăreanu, *Catalogul*, no. 282: *Speculum exemplorum* (Strasbourg: Printer of Jordanus von Quedlinburg, 4 December 1495): 'Liber ecclesie oppida czeydinensis'['The book belongs to the church of the town of Codlea']; Inc. 102; Jugăreanu, *Catalogul*, no. 162: Gregorius I Papa, *Moralia* (Basel: Bertold Ruppel, before 1468).

67 Sibiu, Biblioteca Muzeului Naţional Brukenthal, Inc. 229; Jugăreanu, *Catalogul*, no. 356: Leonardo da Udine, *Sermones aurei de sanctis* (Köln: Ulrich Zell, 1473): 'Iste liber est conventus Cibiniensis ad sanctam crucem ordinis fratrum predicatorum de libris domini Sigismundi plebani de Appoldia Inferiore'. ['This book belongs to the convent of the Holy Cross of the order of the Friars Preachers in Sibiu, from among the books of Sigismund, parish priest in Apoldu de Jos'].

68 Sibiu, Biblioteca Muzeului Naţional Brukenthal, Inc. 253; Jugăreanu, *Catalogul*, no. 68: Bernardinus de Senis, *Sermones de evangelio eterno* (Basel: Johann Amerbach, 1489).

69 Sibiu, Biblioteca Muzeului Naţional Brukenthal, Inc. 290; Jugăreanu, *Catalogul*, no. 376: Vincentius Bellovacensis, *Speculum historiale* (s.l.: s.n., 1474), 3 vols: 'Liber doctoris Blasii Insulensis manu propria, Emptus per dominum Johannem plebanum in Parathya anno MCCCC 76' ['The book belongs to doctor Blasii from Cristian. Written in his own hand. Bought by John, parish priest in Brateiu, in the year 1476'] (although not a sermon collection, this history of the world is counted among the popular medieval preaching aids).

70 Sibiu, Biblioteca Muzeului Naţional Brukenthal, Inc. 130; Jugăreanu, *Catalogul*, no. 154: Johannes Gerson, *Donatus moralisatus seu per allegoria traductus* (Augsburg: Günther Zainer, 1472): 'Liber Martini Decretorum doctor prepositi sanctis Sigismundi de Buda et plebani in rihonfalwa 1531' ['The book of Martin, doctor in canon law, provost of St Sigismund in Buda and parish priest in Richiş, 1531']. Gustav Gündisch, 'Die Bibliothek des Sachsengrafen Albert Huet: 1537–1607', *Korrespondenzblatt des Arbeitskreises für Siebenbürgische Landeskunde*, 4 (1974), 32–51.

village of Dealul Frumos), who had a consistent private library known because of his will, mentioning among other volumes two sermon collections.[71] In addition, two copies of *Postillae in epistolas et evangelia* attributed to Guillelmus Parisiensis (1437–1485) also reached Transylvania. One of them, printed in 1512, belonged to a certain Leonardus, priest in Sântana de Mureş,[72] while the other recorded the names of three priests, all of them active in the area inhabited by Szeklers: Nicholaus, parish priest in Mojna, Georgius, in Ulieş, and another Georgius, priest in Daia.[73] Finally, a volume already mentioned here, with homilies written by Johannes Eck and printed in 1533, was used by Zacharias, parish priest of the Saxon communities of Velţ and Senereuş.[74]

It cannot be ignored that lay people from Transylvania — mostly men, though we also find some remarkable mentions of women — formed a third category of owners of sermons. The various documentary contexts suggest that this group was neither small, nor uneducated. Analysing this specific complex evidence, it has been convincingly argued that this surprising form of book ownership appears only in contexts of pious donations,[75] suggesting strongly that the laity used such printed compilations as expressions of devotion, as elements within a salvation strategy, and perhaps also as a means of social representation.[76] There is also the parallel phenomenon of clerical donation of pastoral texts in printed form, books usually being given by owners from

---

71 Karl Fabricius, 'Geschichtliche Nebenarbeiten. III: das Testament des Schönberger Plebans Mattheus von Reps aus dem Jahre 1502', *Archiv des Vereins für Siebenbürgische Landeskunde*, 12 (1875), 373–78.

72 Târgu-Mureş, Biblioteca Teleki-Bolyai, 0594; Mihály Spielmann-Sebestyén, Balázs Lajos, Hedvig Ambrus, and Ovidia Mesaroş, *Catalogus Librorum Sedecimo Saeculo Impressorum Bibliothecae Teleki-Bolyai Novum Forum Siculorum* (Târgu-Mureş: Lyra, 2001), G99: Guillelmus Parisiensis, *Postillae majores in Epistolas et Euangelia totius anni* (Basel: Johann Froben, 1512): 'Sum Leonardi, presbiterii de Maros Zenth Anna'.

73 Târgu-Mureş, Biblioteca Teleki-Bolyai, 0533; *Catalogus Librorum Sedecimo Saeculo Impressorum Bibliothecae Teleki-Bolyai Novum Forum Siculorum*, G100: Guillelmus Parisiensis, *Postille sive expositiones epistolarum et euangeliorum tam dominicalium quam serialium ... unacum quaestionibus super euangeliis* (Lyon: Simon Vincent, 1515): 'Georgy ersyty, presbitery de kanyad, Liber iste [...] Nicolaus de [...]anad, plebani de Musna, Liber Georgy, presbitery de Dalya anno 1545 etc' ['The book of George Ersyty, presbyter of Kanyad. This book [...] Nicholas from [...] parish priest in Muşna. The book belongs to George, presbyter of Daia, in the year 1545'].

74 Sighişoara, Biblioteca Municipală 'Zaharia Boiu', F. 90: Johannes Eck, *Quinta pars operum Iohannis Eckii, contra Lutherum et alios declamatoria, continet Homilias de Tempore, Sanctis ac Sacramentis* (Augsburg: Alexander Weißenhorn, 1533): 'Liber ille pertinent ad Zacharia de Czyueress 1533, Ego Zacharia plebanus in Velcz, Zacharia in parochum electus in Czynaweress summa cum penitudine Anno 1548' ['This book pertains to Zachary of Senereuş, 1533. I, Zachary, parish priest in Velţ. Zachary, elected as parish priest in Seneruş [...] in 1548'].

75 A thorough analysis of all the examples is available in Paula Cotoi, 'Book as Object of Lay Devotion in Late Medieval Transylvania', *Studia Universitatis Babeş-Bolyai: Historia*, 66 (2021), 27–42.

76 Attila Verók, 'Das Buch als Repräsentationsmittel bei des Siebenbürger Sachsen', pp. 91–99.

within the ecclesiastical personnel in secular churches to the religious orders, or more rarely to fellow priests or parishes.[77] This observation leads us to one final remark about pastoral literature existing in Transylvania, on the periphery of Latin Europe. In examining the manuscript annotations from this batch of thirty-five sermon anthologies with local use a total of fifty owners may be listed (mendicants included), thus broadening the picture of their reception. This enhanced circulation of books relevant for our subject may also be confirmed in the case of manuscripts.

Preliminary Assessment

Many of the works clearly attested in late medieval Transylvania, either printed or in manuscript form, are sermon anthologies designed to offer models and resources for preachers, arranged thematically, while copies of *postillae* or homilies occur relatively rarely. This remark, however, is based on the current state of research on surviving volumes, even though medieval records mention the existence and use of such preaching texts. With regard to the liturgical time they were meant to cover, there is an equal share of texts *de tempore et de sanctis, quadragesimales*, and *de sanctis*. In comparison to the aforementioned categories of *de sanctis* and *quadragesimales*, the smaller number of printed sermons *de tempore* seems unusual as this last category was remarkably present on the market with the greatest number of editions.[78]

As a general remark, due to the overall pragmatic orientation of literate behaviour throughout the region, the pastoral literature used in medieval Transylvania was naturally concerned with what Anne Thayer defines as 'routine preaching', serving the needs of those who addressed the laity and not elevated audiences or more sophisticated contexts.[79] Such a judgement may be applied especially to the period around 1500, when a definitive prevalence of the mendicant orders cannot be questioned, and even the secular clergy seems to relate to the preaching of the friars. For the earlier time, in the first half of the fifteenth century, university sermons and pastoral care filtered through higher theological education, as promoted by the Viennese professors, played an important role in the intellectual life in Transylvania. The large

---

77 For example, Sibiu, Biblioteca Muzeului Național Brukenthal, Inc. 162; Jugăreanu, *Catalogul*, no. 116: Conradus de Brundelsheim, *Sermones de sanctis* (Reutlingen: Michael Greyff, before 1478): 'Iste liber est conventus Cibiniensis ordinis fratrum predicatorum ad sanctam crucem legatus testamentaliter per venerabilem virum dominum Martinum de Corona magistrum arcium et protunc predicatorem Cibiniensem Anno domini 1490' ['This book was bequeathed in a will to the convent of the order of the Friars Preachers in Sibiu, dedicated to the Holy Cross, by the reverend man Martin of Brașov, master of arts and at that time preacher in Sibiu, 1490'].

78 Thayer, *Penitence, Preaching and the Coming of the Reformation*, pp. 20–21.

79 Thayer, *Penitence, Preaching and the Coming of the Reformation*, p. 24.

anthology of preaching texts and moral-theological treatises — specifically thought to be used for drafting sermons — copied in Sibiu in 1432–1433, as well as the intensive reception of Nicholaus de Dinkelsbühl as a theologian and author of sermons,[80] all mirror the influence of the Austrian university on the formation and activity of the parish clergy in Transylvania. Sermons on the subject *De bono sacerdote*, widespread in the region, suit well the sermon written by the previously mentioned Petrus Nowag for the episcopal synod in 1434, a piece concerned with the reform of the secular clergy. It should not be overlooked that interesting phenomena such as the establishment of an intellectual elite or the emergence of a new type of spiritual shepherd in Transylvania from the late fourteenth to the mid-fifteenth century have no other means of documentation (or only vague, collateral sources), apart from the surviving corpus of sermons copied or used locally.

The range of authors is larger in the age of printing, and follows closely the thematic profile described earlier, including the most popular names of printed volumes of model sermons. It is not easy to detect a clear preference for one personality or another, but *Thesaurus novus*, attributed to Petrus de Palude (*c.* 1275–1342), must have been widespread, with seven exemplars out of the thirty-five pastoral volumes under review here. A consistent presence can also be identified in the case of Guillelmus Parisiensis with his versatile volumes of *Postilla super epistolas et evangelia*,[81] and the Dominican Leonardo da Udine. They are followed by other authors whose writings were repeatedly edited during the first decades of printing, such as Nicolaus de Lyra (*c.* 1270–1349), Pelbartus de Themeswar (*c.* 1435–1504), Johannes Herolt (*c.* 1390–1468), Roberto Caracciolo da Lecce (*c.* 1425–1495), Vicent Ferrer (1350–1419), Petrus Blesensis de Lutrea (*c.* 1130–*c.* 1211), Bernardinus de Senis (1380–1444), Conradus de Brundelsheim (d. 1321), Johannes Gritsch (*c.* 1420–*c.* 1470), Johannes Nider (*c.* 1436–1495), Osualdus de Lasko (*c.* 1450–1511), and Albertus Magnus (1193–1280). Even though his name is linked to a single volume whose local, late medieval circulation is absolutely certain, it is worth mentioning the presence of Johannes Eck (1486–1543),[82] the author of some collections of homilies written in the effervescent cultural and religious context of the theological controversies triggered at the dawn of the Reformation.

Manuscript or printed sermon texts sometimes worked together. For example, a hagiographic work regarding the Hungarian saints, *Legendae Sanctorum Regni Hungarie*, the treatise discussing the benefits of holy water

---

80 Adinel C. Dincă, 'Reading Nicholas of Dinkelsbühl in Medieval Transylvania: Surviving Texts and Historical Contexts', in *Nicholas of Dinkelsbühl and the Sentences at Vienna in the Early xv[th] Century*, ed. by Monica Brînzei (Turnhout: Brepols, 2015), pp. 5–23.

81 Anne T. Thayer, 'The *Postilla* of Guillermus and Late Medieval Popular Preaching', *Medieval Sermon Studies*, 48 (2004), 57–74.

82 Paula Cotoi, 'Sermon Collections of Johannes Eck in Transylvanian Libraries', *Studia Universitatis Babeş-Bolyai: Historia*, 62 (2017), 11–22, especially pp. 16–17.

of Johannes de Turrecremata, and another one authored by Jacobus de Clusa (1381–1465), *Tractatus de apparitionibus animarum post exitum earum a corporibus*, were all bound together and included in the same volume with a manuscript consisting of *Expositio Symboli Apostolorum* by Nicholaus de Graetz (d. 1444), and *Sermones dominicales*.[83] Therefore, the composite volume is by itself a small library, gathering various works of different genres, all having the potential to serve as *materia predicabilis*.

On other occasions, print, as a medium of textual reception, influenced the manual preparation of special sermons. This is the way the previously mentioned parish priest Johannes Zeckel drafted two pastoral texts, one of the rare situations when we can learn that a sermon was delivered, and under what circumstances. The most important source of inspiration for the Transylvanian pastor seems to have been, at least in part, the *Sermones de laudibus sanctorum* written by the Franciscan Roberto Caracciolo da Lecce, one of the most famous Italian preachers of his time.[84] Two sermons of this Friar Minor were used by Zeckel, although not in the exact wording, but rather as inspiration: *Sermo septimus de iocundissima nativitate salvatoris nostri domini iesu Christi, filii Dei et Virginis gloriose* (fols 1r, 3r–v, and 4r)[85] and *Sermo LI. De Sancto Georgio* (fols 6r–7r).[86] Other homiletic fragments from the pen of

---

83   Sibiu, Biblioteca Muzeului Național Brukenthal, MS 650, colligate with Inc. 61, 62, 63. See Papahagi and Dincă, *Census*, no. 468; Jugăreanu, *Catalogul*, no. 205, 353.

84   For the Hungarian reception of the Franciscan's work see Cecilia Tóthne Radó, *Robertus Caracciolus OFM prédikációs segédkönyveinek magyarországi felhasználása* (unpublished doctoral dissertation, Budapest: Pázmány Péter University, 2014).

85   fol. 1r [inc.]: 'Annuncio vobis gaudium magnum quod natus est hodie saluator mundi Luce 20 et in Evangelio occurentis solempnitatis. Sonuit vox leticie in terra nostra, vox exultationis advenit, auditum est verbum suave omni iocunditate repletum. Ihesus Christus, filius dei in Bethlehem Iude der virgine natus est. Iubilate deo omnes homines mundi et laudate' ['I announce to you a great joy that the saviour of the world is born today, Luke 2, and in the Gospel with the occurring celebration. The voice of joy sounds in our land, the voice of exaltation arrives, heard is the word filled with all sweet joy. Jesus Christ, Son of God, was born in Bethlehem of Judea from a virgin. Celebrate and praise God, all you people of the world!']; fol. 2r: 'Cum iocunditate nativitatem Sancte Marie celebremus ut ipsa intercedit pro nobis ad dominum Ihesum Christum. Ista sunt verba ecclesie et merito assumentur' ['Let us celebrate the birth of the Holy Mary with joy for she intercedes for us with our Lord Jesus Christ. These are the words of the Church and they should be observed'].

86   Sibiu, Biblioteca Muzeului Național Brukenthal, MS 657, fol. 7r: 'Fortis fuit in bello scribuntur hec verba originaliter Ecclesiastici xlvj c. Licet hec verba de Zosue dicantur ad literam qui alius dicitur Ihesus Naue, successor Moyse in prophetis qui fuit magnus secundum nomen suum, maximus in salute dei electorum expungnare insurgentes hostes, ut consequeretur hereditatem Israhel. Quam gloriam adeptus est in tollendo manus suas et iactando contra ciuitates rompheas'. ['These are the words written in the beginning of the Book of Ecclesiasticus 46. 1. Joshua the son of Nun was valiant in war, and was the successor of Moses in prophecies: who according to his name was made great for the saving of God's elect, to take vengeance of the enemies that rose up against them, that he might give Israel their inheritance. What great glory he secured, by lifting up his hands and throwing his spears against the cities'].

Johannes Zeckel have left little room for interpretation: a sermon dedicated to the Virgin Mary *Congaudent angelorum* starts with the sequence 'Qua gloria in celis ista virgo colitur, que Domino celi prebuit hospitium corporis, Hec sunt verba ecclesie' ['With glory in the heavens this virgin is revered, who has given the Lord a corporeal lodging. These are the words of the Church']. It thus supports the traditional significance of St Mary's cult in Sibiu.[87]

The partial or full pages, which were penned directly by the parish priest Johannes Zeckel, offer an unfortunately rare example of pre-Reformation preaching and at the same time an insight into the 'workshop' of a preacher in Transylvania.[88] Thus, one learns that one sermon was written in 1502 in his parish church in Ruși for the celebration of St George: 'Hunc sermonem colegi (*sic*) et feci in ecclesia mea, in festo Sancti Georgii, ego Ioannes Zeckel anno 1502' ['I, John Zekel, compiled and composed this sermon in my church on the feast day of St George in the year 1502']['89] and another, this time without any temporal indication, was delivered in Sibiu 'Hunc sermonem ego Joannes Zeckel feci et collegi predicatque dominicam Cibinii' ['I, John Zekel, composed, compiled, and preached this sermon on Sunday in Sibiu'].[90] Neither of the two *sermones* was randomly selected. While the latter sermon of the village pastor, which was datable around 1502, was given before the clergy or the laity of the capital city, and accordingly dedicated to the patron (*de benefactore*),[91] the other one performed in the rural surroundings of Ruși had a different theme. The patron saint of this small village parish was St George, therefore this sermon had a special meaning, especially since it was in the Franciscan tradition of the fifteenth century: the martial virtues of the former Roman soldier were particularly emphasized and praised in the context of the contemporary Ottoman danger.[92] No less indicative seems the more extensive and well-crafted text unit on fols 8r–9v, in which the dominant role of clerics in society is dealt with boldly.[93]

---

87 Carmen Florea, 'Identitate urbană și patronaj marian în evul mediu târziu', *Studia Universitatis Cibiniensis: Series Historica*, 5 (2008), 59–81.

88 Additional insight in Adinel C. Dincă, 'Dorfkirche und Schriftlichkeit in Siebenbürgen um 1500', in *Common Man, Society and Religion in the 16th Century: Piety, Morality and Discipline in the Carpathian Basin / Gemeiner Mann, Gesellschaft und Religion im 16. Jahrhundert: Frömmigkeit, Moral und Sozialdisziplinierung im Karpatenbogen*, ed. by Ulrich A. Wien (Göttingen: Vandenhoeck & Ruprecht, 2021), pp. 39–54.

89 Sibiu, Biblioteca Muzeului Național Brukenthal, MS 657, fol. 7r.

90 Sibiu, Biblioteca Muzeului Național Brukenthal, MS 657, fol. 212r.

91 Inc.: 'Accipiens septem panem gratias agens' ['Taking the seven loaves, giving thanks'] (Mark 8. 6). 'Commune proverbium est quod arbori aqua habetur umbra detur' ['It is common knowledge that watered trees cast a shadow'].

92 Steven J. McMichael, 'Roberto Caracciolo da Lecce and His Sermons on Muhammad and the Muslims (*c.* 1480)', *Franciscans and Preaching: Every Miracle from the Beginning*, ed. by Timothy Johnson (Leiden: Brill, 2012), pp. 327–52.

93 fol. 8r: 'Ita tanta est dignitas sacerdotum quod absolute super principes terre' ['So great is the dignity of priests which is above that of the princes of the earth']; fol. 9r: 'Tercio dico quod

Conclusion

Following the incentive and optimistic advice of Père Louis Jacques Bataillon OP (d. 2009) four decades ago, this essay maps in a pioneering manner the terrain for future academic scrutiny, acting not only as a stepping stone but also widening the field of study to encompass the newly disclosed religious, social, and cultural perspectives.[94] In trying to reclaim the time lapse that continues to dominate the centre-periphery relationship, the main objective is to draw the general lines of evolution regarding the Latin manuscript and printed sermons in late medieval Transylvania as an opening for further research. A rather descriptive and source-based approach could not be avoided at this point, considering the traditional lack of interest in Romania for Latin preaching and the relevant texts, as they were received, copied, and, perhaps, performed in one of the peripheries of medieval *Latinitas*. The prevalence of the model sermon collections extant in late medieval Transylvania, either printed or hand copied, does not allow for surprising results. Sermons were an instrument of *cura animarum*, and their delivery was a routine activity. And yet, widespread pastoral anthologies for 'universal' use, found in Transylvanian late medieval contexts, are not dull and repetitive constructions, but illuminate the integrative function of pastoral-theological thinking in the pre-Reformation Church, according to the description of David d'Avray: 'it was precisely the detachment of the context from any immediate social context that enabled them to "travel"'.[95] Such standardized sermon collections emphasize the effort of the educated elements from a region on the periphery to align to the intellectual streams from Western and Central European cultural centres. Observations of this nature should nonetheless not be extended to the entire Transylvanian territory. The administrative and religious privileged territory of the Saxons constitute the core of pastoral literature and preaching performance in late medieval Transylvania, due to the locally existing prerequisites in favour of an advanced literate behaviour. Even at this stage of investigation there is compelling proof that pastoral literature mirrored the social development of the German colonists' settlements, towards the predominance of the urban, commercial, and entrepreneurial ruling classes, with a clear devotional pattern,[96] hence the welcoming attitude regarding the mendicant orders. Internal circulation of sermon texts and transfer of ownership does not

---

potestas sacerdotum apparet esse maxima' ['Thirdly I say that the power of priests appears to be the greatest'].

94 Louis Jacques Bataillon, 'Approaches to the Study of Medieval Sermons', *Leeds Studies in English*, 11 (1980), 11–35, p. 30.

95 David L. d'Avray, *The Preaching of the Friars: Sermons Diffused from Paris before 1300* (Oxford: Oxford University Press, 1985), p. 158.

96 Konrad Gündisch, *Das Patriziat Siebenbürgischer Städte im Mittelalter* (Köln: Böhlau, 1993); Carmen Florea, 'Women and Mendicant Orders in Late Medieval Transylvania', *Studia Universitatis Babeş-Bolyai: Historia*, 56 (2011), 67–87; Maria Crăciun, 'Communities

suggest a competing preaching between parish churches and friaries, quite the opposite. The Dominicans in Brașov, for example, allowed the secular clergy to have access to their books, serving as a para-parochial structure, and parish priests donated their sermon collections to the mendicants.[97] Additionally, a good coverage of smaller, rural settlements, may be noticed, so that the preaching activity of the parish clergy supplemented and complemented that of the mendicant orders.

Scholastic and university sermons are not absent from medieval Transylvania; they can still be traced, even if in significantly smaller numbers. These texts record interesting intellectual processes like the (relatively) early contact with higher education abroad, or the struggle to impose a 'modern' vision on pastoral care.[98] Our few examples from the 1420s and 1430s highlight a thriving attention towards preaching and it should be seen as a direct, mature consequence of the university foundations in Central Europe (Prague, Vienna, or Krákow), places in close contact with the Transylvanian commercial cities along the Carpathians.[99] Therefore, the type of sermon, the preaching circles, and the social-intellectual context of delivery reflect in our historical setting the evolution of audience, mainly urban laity and diocesan or regional clergy, stressing once more that the meaning of a given sermon is better valued with the help of additional sources and contextual elements.[100]

There are very few performance indicators available, as seen in the afore-mentioned example of Johannes Zeckel in 1502, and yet a closer look at the texts reveal the continuous dialogue between textual fixity and oral delivery.[101] In fact, a deeper textual interpretation of the available sermons, as well as a closer look at the fragments of manuscript and printed book scattered in great numbers throughout all the Romanian library and archival institutions would be a way to carry on the investigation of the sermon literature introduced to pre-modern Transylvania, in order to recover the textual patrimony available

---

of Devotion: The Saxons in Early Modern Transylvania', *Studia Universitatis Babeș-Bolyai: Historia*, 58 (2013), 156–95.

97 *Urkundenbuch zur Geschichte der Deutschen in Siebenbürgen: 1458–1473*, ed. by Gustav Gündisch (București: Editura Academiei Române, 1981), VI, 103–04, no. 3256 from 1461.VI.15.

98 Ernst Haberkern, *Die 'Wiener Schule' der Pastoraltheologie im 14. und 15. Jahrhundert: Entstehung, Konstituenten, literarische Wirkung*, Göppinger Arbeiten zu Germanistik, 712, 2 vols (Göppingen: Kümmerle, 2003), p. 67. See also *Kirchliche Reformimpulse des 14./15. Jahrhunderts in Ostmitteleuropa*, ed. by Winfried Eberhard and Franz Machilek (Köln: Böhlau, 2006).

99 Katalin Szende, 'Towns and Urban Networks in the Carpathian Basin between the Eleventh and the Early Sixteenth Centuries', in *The Art of Medieval Hungary*, ed. by Xavier Barral i Altet, and others (Roma: Viella, 2018), pp. 65–81.

100 Anne T. Thayer, 'The Medieval Sermon: Text, Performance and Insight', in *Understanding Medieval Primary Sources: Using Historical Sources to Discover Medieval Europe*, ed. by Joel Thomas Rosenthal (London: Routledge, 2012), pp. 43–58, here pp. 43–44.

101 Paula Cotoi, 'Predica medievală între oralitate și scris: abordări metodologice și perspective transilvănene', *Anuarul Institutului de Istorie 'G. Barițiu' din Cluj-Napoca, Supplement*, 58 (2019), 159–74.

before the last quarter of the fourteenth century, to add new information for later times, and to better evaluate the connections with supporting texts, as theology, law, and pragmatic aids for pastoral offices,[102] all extant in medieval libraries in Transylvania. Such a complex approach, requiring time and human resources, as well as support from the international academic community, would stress the central role played by the sermons within the literary landscape at the periphery of the medieval Latin commonwealth.[103]

---

102 'Introduction', in *The Sermon*, ed. by Beverly Mayne Kienzle, Typologie des sources du Moyen Âge occidental, 81–83 (Turnhout: Brepols, 2000), pp. 147–50.

103 The research for this essay was supported by a grant from the Romanian National Authority for Scientific Research, CNDI–UEFISCDI, project PN–III–P4–ID–PCCF–2016–0064: 'Nașterea elitei intelectuale in Europa Centrală: Formarea profesorilor la Universitatea din Viena (1389–1450)/The Rise of an Intellectual Elite in Central Europe: Making Professors at the University of Vienna, 1389–1450'.

Bibliography

Archival Repositories Consulted

Alba Iulia, Biblioteca Naţională a României, Biblioteca Batthyaneum
Budapest, Magyar Nemzeti Levéltár
Cisnădie, Biserica Evanghelică C. A., Oficiul Parohial
Cluj-Napoca, Arhiva Parohiei Romano-Catolice Sfântul Mihail
Cluj-Napoca, Biblioteca Centrală Universitară 'Lucian Blaga'
Dej, Conventul Franciscan
Kraków, Biblioteka Jagiellońska, Uniwersytet Jagielloński W Kraków
Miercurea Ciuc, Muzeul Secuiesc al Ciucului/Csíki Székely Múzeum
Sibiu, Arhiva Centrală a Bisericii Evanghelice C. A. din România
Sibiu, Biblioteca Muzeului Naţional Brukenthal
Sibiu, Serviciul Judeţean al Arhivelor Naţionale
Sighişoara, Biblioteca Municipală 'Zaharia Boiu'
Târgu-Mureş, Biblioteca Teleki-Bolyai

Manuscripts

Alba Iulia, Biblioteca Naţională a României, Biblioteca Batthyaneum, MS II.135
Budapest, Magyar Nemzeti Levéltár, Diplomatikai Levéltár, no. 36897
Cisnădie, Biserica Evanghelică C. A., Oficiul Parohial, MS D. 27
Kraków, Biblioteka Jagiellońska, Uniwersytet Jagielloński W Kraków, MS 2332
Mediaş, Biserica Evanghelică C. A., MS (no shelfmark)
Sibiu, Arhiva Centrală a Bisericii Evanghelice C. A. din România (ZAEKR),
     MS 601–C–28
Sibiu, Biblioteca Muzeului Naţional Brukenthal, MS 647
Sibiu, Biblioteca Muzeului Naţional Brukenthal, MS 650, colligate with Inc. 61, 62, 63
Sibiu, Biblioteca Muzeului Naţional Brukenthal, MS 657
Sibiu, Biblioteca Muzeului Naţional Brukenthal, MS 660
Sibiu, Serviciul Judeţean al Arhivelor Naţionale, Colecţia 'Brukenthal', MS B. 268

Early Printed Works

Cisnădie, Biserica Evanghelică C. A., Oficiul Parohial, Inv. 1355: *Gesta Romanorum*
     (Strasbourg: Printer of the 'Vitas Patrum', *c.* 1484/1486) [ISTC ig00287000;
     GW 10892]
Cisnădie, Biserica Evanghelică C. A., Oficiul Parohial, Inv. 1355: Guido de Monte
     Rocherii, *Manipulus curatorum* (Strasbourg: Printer of the 'Legenda aurea', 30
     August 1483) [ISTC ig00586000; GW 11814]
Cisnădie, Biserica Evanghelică C. A., Oficiul Parohial, sine Signatura: Nicolaus
     de Lyra, *Postilla litteralis in vetus et novum testamentum, mit Expositiones
     prologorum von Guilelmus Brito, Additiones ad Postillam Nicolai de Lyra von
     Paulus Burgensis und Replicae contra Burgensem von Matthias Doering*, parts

1–2 (Genesis — Psalmi; Proverbia — Apocalypsis)] (Nürnberg, *c.* 1481)
[ISTC in00135000; BSB-Ink N-114; GW M26513]

Cisnădie, Biserica Evanghelică C. A., Oficiul Parohial, sine Signatura: Rainerius de Pisis, *Pantheologia, sive Summa universae theologiae* (Venezia: Hermannus Liechtenstein, 12 September 1486) [ISTC ir00010000; BSB-Ink R-6; GW M36944]

Cluj-Napoca, Arhiva Parohiei Romano-Catolice Sfântul Mihail, Ambrosius de Spiera, *Quadragesimale de floribus sapientiae*, ed. by Marcus Venetus (Venezia: Antonius de Stanchis de Valentia, Jacobus Britannicus et socii, 24 March 1481) [ISTC is00679000]

Cluj-Napoca, Arhiva Parohiei Romano-Catolice Sfântul Mihail, Bonaventura, S: *Opuscula*. Octavianus de Martinis: *Oratio in vitam et merita S. Bonaventurae.* Johannes Franciscus de Pavinis: *Relatio circa canonizationem Bonaventurae.* Robertus [Caracciolo?]: *Sermo de laudibus Bonaventurae.* Sixtus IV: *Bulla canonizationis* (Strasbourg: [Printer of the 1483 Jordanus von Quedlinburg (Georg Husner)], 1495) [ISTC ib00928000]

Cluj-Napoca, Biblioteca Centrală Universitară 'Lucian Blaga', Colecția de carte veche maghiară, BMV 46: Pelbartus de Themeswar, *Sermones quadragesimales Pomerii* (Haguenau: Henrich Gran, 1501)

Dej, Conventul Franciscan, Inc. C. 197: Angelus de Clavasio, *Summa angelica de casibus conscientiae*: Hieronymus Tornieli (Speyer: [Peter Drach], 1488) [ISTC ia00716000]

Miercurea Ciuc, Muzeul Secuiesc al Ciucului /Csíki Székely Múzeum, Inv. 6218: Ferrerius, Vincentius, *Sermones de tempore et de sanctis* (Köln: Heinrich Quentell, 1487) [ISTC if00130000]

Miercurea Ciuc, Muzeul Secuiesc al Ciucului /Csíki Székely Múzeum, Inv. 6243: Bernardus Claravallensis (Sanctus), *Sermones de tempore et de sanctis et de diversis* (Speyer: Peter Drach, post 31 August 1481, not post 1482) [ISTC ib00437000]

Sibiu, Biblioteca Muzeului Național Brukenthal, Inc. 38: Pelbartus de Themeswar, *Sermones Pomerii quadragesimales* (Haguenau: Heinrich Gran, 10 November 1499) [ISTC ip00255500]

Sibiu, Biblioteca Muzeului Național Brukenthal, Inc. 50: Nicolaus de Lyra, *Biblia latina cum postillis Nicolai de Lyra*, 4 vols (Nürnberg: Anton Koberger, 3 December 1487) [ISTC ib00614000]

Sibiu, Biblioteca Muzeului Național Brukenthal, Inc. 68: Leonardo da Udine, *Sermones aurei de sanctis* (Köln: Ulrich Zell, 1473) [ISTC il00151000]

Sibiu, Biblioteca Muzeului Național Brukenthal, Inc. 102: Gregorius I Papa, *Moralia* (Basel: Bertold Ruppel, before 1468) [ISTC ig00427200]

Sibiu, Biblioteca Muzeului Național Brukenthal, Inc. 113: *Speculum exemplorum* (Strasbourg: Printer of Jordanus von Quedlinburg, 4 December 1495) [ISTC is00655000]

Sibiu, Biblioteca Muzeului Național Brukenthal, Inc. 130: Johannes Gerson, *Donatus moralisatus seu per allegoria traductus* (Augsburg: Günther Zainer, 1472) [ISTC ig00221000]

Sibiu, Biblioteca Muzeului Naţional Brukenthal, Inc. 162: Conradus de Brundels-heim, *Sermones de sanctis* (Reutlingen: Michael Greyff, before 1478) [ISTC is00585000]

Sibiu, Biblioteca Muzeului Naţional Brukenthal, Inc. 229: Leonardo da Udine, *Sermones aurei de sanctis* (Köln: Ulrich Zell, 1473) [ISTC il00151000]

Sibiu, Biblioteca Muzeului Naţional Brukenthal, Inc. 253: Bernardinus de Senis, *Sermones de evangelio eterno* (Basel: Johann Amerbach, 1489) [ISTC ib00349000]

Sibiu, Biblioteca Muzeului Naţional Brukenthal, Inc. 290: Vincentius Bellovacensis, *Speculum historiale* (s.l.: s.n., 1474), 3 vols

Sibiu, Biblioteca Muzeului Naţional Brukenthal, V. III. 160: Hieronymus, *Omnium operum divi Eusebii Hieronymi* (Basel, 1516)

Sighişoara, Biblioteca Municipală 'Zaharia Boiu', F. 90: Johannes Eck, *Quinta pars operum Iohannis Eckii, contra Lutherum et alios declamatoria, continet Homilias de Tempore, Sanctis ac Sacramentis* (Augsburg: Alexander Weißenhorn, 1533)

Târgu Mureş, Biblioteca Teleki-Bolyai, 0533: Guillelmus Parisiensis, *Postille sive expositiones epistolarum et euangeliorum tam dominicalium quam serialium […] unacum quaestionibus super euangeliis* (Lyon: Simon Vincent, 1515)

Târgu Mureş, Biblioteca Teleki-Bolyai, 0594: Guillelmus Parisiensis, *Postillae majores in Epistolas et Euangelia totius anni* (Basel: Johann Froben, 1512)

Târgu-Mureş, Biblioteca Teleki-Bolyai, 0671: *Sermones thesauri novi de Sanctis* (Strasbourg: Martin Flach, 1488) [ISTC ip00513000]

Primary Sources

Quellen zur Geschichte der Stadt Kronstadt in Siebenbürgen, Rechnungen aus dem Archiv der Stadt Kronstadt, Band II (1526–1540) (Kronstadt: Albrecht & Zillich, 1889)

Urkundenbuch zur Geschichte der Deutschen in Siebenbürgen: 1458–1473, ed. by Gustav Gündisch (Bucureşti: Editura Academiei Române, 1981), VI

Secondary Studies

Adamska, Anna, 'Intersections: Medieval East Central Europe from the Perspective of Literacy and Communication', in *Medieval East Central Europe in a Comparative Perspective: From Frontier Zones to Lands in Focus*, ed. by Gerhard Jaritz and Katalin Szende (London: Routledge, 2016), pp. 225–38

Baráth, Béla, 'Ösnyomtatványok a Székelyföldön és Délerdélyben', *Erdélyi Tudósító*, 21 (1942), 31

Bataillon, Louis Jacques, 'Approaches to the Study of Medieval Sermons', *Leeds Studies in English*, 11 (1980), 11–35

Berend, Nora, Przemyslaw Urbanczyk, and Przemyslaw Wiszewski, *Central Europe in the High Middle Ages: Bohemia, Hungary and Poland c. 900–c. 1300* (Cambridge: Cambridge University Press, 2013)

Cartojan, Nicolae, *Istoria literaturii române vechi* (București: Ed. Fundației Culturale Române, 1996)

Chivu, Gheorghe, 'Scrisul religios, componentă definitorie a culturii vechi românești', *Dacoromania*, 17 (2012), 54–67

Chrisman, Miriam Usher, *Lay Culture, Learned Culture: Books and Social Change in Strasbourg (1480–1599)* (New Haven: Yale University Press, 1982)

Cotoi, Paula, 'Book as Object of Lay Devotion in Late Medieval Transylvania', *Studia Universitatis Babeș-Bolyai: Historia*, 66 (2021), 27–42

Cotoi, Paula, 'Predica medievală între oralitate și scris: abordări metodologice și perspective transilvănene', *Anuarul Institutului de Istorie 'G. Barițiu' din Cluj-Napoca, Supplement*, 58 (2019), 159–74

Cotoi, Paula, 'Sermon Collections of Johannes Eck in Transylvanian Libraries', *Studia Universitatis Babeș-Bolyai: Historia*, 62 (2017), 11–22

Crăciun, Maria, 'Communities of Devotion: The Saxons in Early Modern Transylvania', *Studia Universitatis Babeș-Bolyai: Historia*, 58 (2013), 156–95

Crăciun, Maria, 'Mendicant Piety and the Saxon Community of Transylvania c. 1450–1550', in *Communities of Devotion: Religious Orders and Society in East Central Europe, 1450–1800*, ed. by Maria Crăciun and Elaine Fulton (Farnham: Ashgate, 2011), pp. 29–70

Csapodi, Csaba, and Klára Csapodiné Gárdonyi, *Bibliotheca Hungarica: kódexek és nyomtatott könyvek Magyarországon 1526*, Kötet I (Budapest: MTAK, 1988)

d'Avray, David L., *The Preaching of the Friars: Sermons Diffused from Paris before 1300* (Oxford: Oxford University Press, 1985)

Daniel, Cristian, 'Bridging the Gap: The Ecclesiological Landscape of Transylvania Seen Through the Comparative Lens', *New Europe College Yearbook*, 10 (2010), 51–84

Dietl, Cora, and Anna-Lena Liebermann, eds, *Lexikon der regionalen Literaturgeschichte des Mittelalters: Ungarn und Rumänien* (Berlin: Akademie, 2015)

Dincă, Adinel C., '"Biblioteca orașului Sibiu" în evul mediu: câteva considerații pe marginea unei confuzii istoriografice', in *Cluj — Kolozsvár — Klausenburg 700: várostörténeti tanulmányok = studii de istorie urbană*, coordinated by Mária Lupescu-Makó and others (Cluj-Napoca: Erdélyi Múzeum Egyesület, 2018), pp. 431–36

Dincă, Adinel C., 'Dorfkirche und Schriftlichkeit in Siebenbürgen um 1500', in *Common Man, Society and Religion in the 16th Century: Piety, Morality and Discipline in the Carpathian Basin / Gemeiner Mann, Gesellschaft und Religion im 16. Jahrhundert: Frömmigkeit, Moral und Sozialdisziplinierung im Karpatenbogen*, ed. by Ulrich A. Wien (Göttingen: Vandenhoeck & Ruprecht, 2021), 39–54

Dincă, Adinel C., *Instituția episcopală latină în Transilvania medievală (sec. XI/XII–XIV)* (Cluj-Napoca: Argonaut, 2017)

Dincă, Adinel C., 'Medieval Literacy in Transylvania: Selective Evidence from the Parish Church', *Transylvanian Review*, 1 (2015), 109–21

Dincă, Adinel C., 'Reading Nicholas of Dinkelsbühl in Medieval Transylvania: Surviving Texts and Historical Contexts', in *Nicholas of Dinkelsbühl and the*

Sentences at Vienna in the Early XVth Century, ed. by Monica Brînzei (Turnhout: Brepols, 2015), pp. 5–23

Dincă, Adinel C., *The Rural Parish in Late Medieval Transylvania: Churchwardens' Accounts of Jelna (1455–1570)* (2023, forthcoming)

Dincă, Adinel C., 'Scrieri autografe în Transilvania medievală: de la cele mai timpurii mărturii, până în secolul al XVI-lea', in *Autographa et signaturae Transilvaniae (sec. XIV–XVII)*, ed. by Susana Andea, Avram Andea, and Adinel Dincă (Cluj-Napoca: Argonaut, 2015), pp. 11–85

Dincă, Adinel C., 'La Transilvania nel commercio europeo di libri intorno al 1500: stampe veneziane nella Sibiu (Cibinium — Nagyszeben — Hermannstadt) medievale', in *I Convegno della medievistica italiana, Bertinoro (Forlì-Cesena), 14–16 giugno 2018* (Roma: Open Archive di Reti Medievali, 2019), pp. 580–99

Dincă, Adinel C., 'The University and the Parish: The Medieval Books from Heltau/Cisnădie', *Philobiblon: Transylvanian Journal of Multidisciplinary Research in Humanities*, 24 (2019), 337–52

Dincă, Adinel C., 'Urban Literacy in Medieval Transylvania', in *Between Public and Private: Writing Praxis in Transylvania during the XIII–XVII Centuries*, ed. by Susana Andea (Cluj-Napoca: Argonaut, 2016), pp. 71–186

Dobre, Claudia-Florentina, *Mendicants in Moldavia: Mission in an Orthodox Land* (Daun: Aurel, 2009)

Drăgan, Ioan, and others, *A Century in the History of Transylvania: The Late Crusades, Humanism, Church Union and Social Mobility at the End of the Middle Ages (1387–1490)* (Cluj-Napoca: Center for Transylvanian Studies, 2008)

Eberhard, Winfried, and Franz Machilek, eds, *Kirchliche Reformimpulse des 14./15. Jahrhunderts in Ostmitteleuropa* (Köln: Böhlau, 2006)

Engel, Pál, *The Realm of St Stephen: A History of Medieval Hungary 895–1526* (London: Tauris, 2001)

Entz, Géza, *Erdély építészete a 14–16. században* (Kolozsvár: Az Erdélyi Múzeum-Egyesület Kiadása, 1994)

Fabricius, Karl, 'Geschichtliche Nebenarbeiten, III: das Testament des Schönberger Plebans Mattheus von Reps aus dem Jahre 1502', *Archiv des Vereins für Siebenbürgische Landeskunde*, 12 (1875), 373–78

Fara, Andrea, 'I sassoni di Transilvania nelle Universita d'Europa tra XIV e XVI secolo', *Annuario dell'Instituto Romeno di Cultura e Ricerca Umanistica di Venezia*, 8 (2016), 119–33

Florea, Carmen, 'Identitate urbană și patronaj marian în evul mediu târziu', *Studia Universitatis Cibiniensis: Historica*, 5 (2008), 59–81

Florea, Carmen, 'Is there a Future for Medieval Studies in Romania?', *Annual of Medieval Studies at CEU*, 15 (2009), 279–87

Florea, Carmen, 'Women and Mendicant Orders in Late Medieval Transylvania', *Studia Universitatis Babeș-Bolyai: Historia*, 56 (2011), 67–87

Goldenberg, Samuil, 'Der Handel Transsilvaniens vom 14. bis zum 17. Jahrhundert', *Scripta Mercaturae*, 11 (1977), 4–24

Grigore, Mihai-D., 'The Space of Power: State Consolidation by Means of Religious Policy in the Danube Principalities in the Fourteenth to Sixteenth Centuries', *Acta Poloniae Historica*, 116 (2017), 35–56

Groß, Julius, 'Zur ältesten Geschichte der Kronstädter Gymnasialbibliothek', *Archiv des Vereins für Siebenbürgische Landeskunde*, 21 (1887), 591–708

Gündisch, Gustav, 'Die Bibliothek des Sachsengrafen Albert Huet: 1537–1607', *Korrespondenzblatt des Arbeitskreises für Siebenbürgische Landeskunde*, 4 (1974), 32–51

Gündisch, Konrad, *Das Patriziat Siebenbürgischer Städte im Mittelalter* (Köln: Böhlau, 1993)

Haberkern, Ernst, *Die 'Wiener Schule' der Pastoraltheologie im 14. Und 15. Jahrhundert: Entstehung, Konstituenten, literarische Wirkung*, Göppinger Arbeiten zu Germanistik, 712, 2 vols (Göppingen: Kümmerle, 2003)

Jugăreanu, Veturia, *Catalogul colecţiei de incunabule* (Sibiu: Biblioteca Muzeului Brukenthal, 1969)

Kienzle, Beverly Mayne, ed., *The Sermon*, Typologie des sources du Moyen Âge occidental, 81–83 (Turnhout: Brepols, 2000)

Kührer-Wielach, Florian, 'Siebenbürgen als administrative Einheit und diskursives Konzept', in *Das Südosteuropa der Regionen*, ed. by Oliver Jens Schmitt and Michael Metzeltin (Wien: Verlag der Österreichischen Akademie der Wissenschaften, 2015), pp. 349–409

Kurz, Anton, 'Die ältesten deutschen Sprachdenkmale und die bis jetzt bekannte älteste Handschrift der Sachsen in Siebenbürgen, mitgetheilt aus dem Original-Fragment einer auf Pergament geschriebenen Hermannstädter Kirchenmatrikel des XIV. und späterer Jahrhundert', *Serapeum*, 16 (1848), 193–200

Lupescu-Makó, Mária, 'The Book Culture of the Dominican Order in Transylvania', *Philobiblon: Transylvanian Journal of Multidisciplinary Research in Humanities*, 22/1 (2017), 187–204

Madas, Edit, 'A Dominican Sermon Collection', *Budapest Review of Books*, 5 (1996), 193–99

Madas, Edit, *Középkori prédikációirodalmunk történetéből: a kezdetektől a XIV. század elejéig* (Debrecen: Kossuth Egyetemi Kiadó, 2002)

Mastan, Irina, 'Urban Identity and Historical Discourse in a Frontier City. Case Study: Braşov during the 16th and 17th Centuries', *Prace Historyczne*, 141 (2014), 15–35

McMichael, Steven J., 'Roberto Caracciolo da Lecce and His Sermons on Muhammad and the Muslims (*c.* 1480)', *Franciscans and Preaching: Every Miracle from the Beginning*, ed. by Timothy Johnson (Leiden: Brill, 2012), pp. 327–52

Mukenhaupt, Erzsebet, *A Csíksomlyói Ferences Könyvtár Kincsei* (Budapest: Balassi, 1999)

Müller, Friedrich, *Deutsche Sprachdenkmäler aus Siebenbürgen: aus schriftlichen Quellen des zwölften bis sechzehnten Jahrhunderts* (Hermannstadt: Steinhaussen, 1864)

Müller, Friedrich, 'Die Incunabeln der Hermannstädter Capellenbibliothek', *Archiv des Vereins für Siebenbürgische Landeskunde*, 14 (1877), 293–358 and 489–543

Nemes, Balázs J., 'Das "Mediascher Predigtbuch": Miszelle zu einem Plenar mit Perikopen in deutsch-lateinischer Mischsprache aus Siebenbürgen am Vorabend der Reformation', *Zeitschrift für Siebenbürgische Landeskunde*, 38 (2015), 31–36

Papahagi, Adrian, 'The Incunabula of the Dominicans from Bistriţa at the Central Piarist Library in Budapest', *Philobiblon: Transylvanian Journal of Multidisciplinary Research in Humanities*, 22/2 (2017), 51–66

Papahagi, Adrian, and Adinel C. Dincă, 'Latin Palaeography and Codicology in Romania', *Chôra: Revue d'Études Anciennes et Médiévales*, 5 (2007), 159–86

Papahagi, Adrian, and Adinel C. Dincă, *Manuscrisele medievale occidentale din România: Census* (Iaşi: Polirom, 2018)

Pettegree, Andrew, *The Book in the Renaissance* (New Haven: Yale University Press, 2011)

Pop, Ioan-Aurel, *Romanians and Hungarians from the 9th to the 14th Century: The Genesis of the Transylvanian Medieval State* (Cluj-Napoca: Center for Transylvanian Studies, 1996)

Pop, Ioan-Aurel, and Thomas Nägler, *The History of Transylvania (until 1541)* (Cluj-Napoca: Center for Transylvanian Studies, 2005)

Pop, Ioan-Aurel, Thomas Nägler, and András Magyari, *The History of Transylvania (from 1541 to 1711)* (Cluj-Napoca: Center for Transylvanian Studies, 2009)

Popa-Gorjanu, Cosmin, 'Transylvanian Identities in the Middle Ages', in *Identitats: reunió científica: XIV Curs d'Estiu Comtat d'Urgell, celebrat a Balaguer els dies 1, 2 I 3 de juliol de 2009*, ed. by Flocel Sabaté (Lleida: Pagès, 2012), pp. 175–90

Rădvan, Laurenţiu, *At Europe's Borders: Medieval Towns in the Romanian Principalities* (Leiden: Brill, 2010)

Reinerth, Karl, 'Wer war der Verfasser des sogenannten Mediascher Predigtbuches?', *Korrespondenzblatt des Arbeitskreises für Siebenbürgische Landeskunde*, 1 (1971), 75–83

Schatz, Elena-Maria, and Robertina Stoica, *Catalogul colectiv al incunabulelor din România*, (Bucureşti: CIMEC — Institutul de Memorie Culturală, 2007)

Scheiner, Andreas, 'Zur geschichtlichen Wertung des Mediascher Predigtbuchs', in *Beiträge zur Geschichte der Ev. Kirche A.B. in Siebenbürgen: Bischof d. Friedrich Teutsch, dem Meister sächsischer Volks- u. Kirchengeschichte, zum 70. Geburtstage am 16. September 1922* (Hermannstadt: F. Michaelis, 1922), pp. 46–58

Schullerus, Adolf, 'Das Mediascher Predigtbuch', *Archiv des Vereins für Siebenbürgische Landeskunde*, 41 (1923), 5–296

Seiwert, Gustav, 'Das älteste Hermannstädter Kirchenbuch', *Archiv des Vereins für Siebenbürgische Landeskunde*, 11 (1874), 323–410

Simon, Zsolt, 'Primele tipărituri din Transilvania (Sibiu, 1525)', *Anuarul Institutului de Istorie 'G. Bariţiu' din Cluj-Napoca*, 46 (2007), 89–106

Spielmann-Sebestyén, Mihály, Balázs Lajos, Hedvig Ambrus, and Ovidia Mesaroş, *Catalogus Librorum Sedecimo Saeculo Impressorum Bibliothecae Teleki-Bolyai Novum Forum Siculorum* (Târgu-Mureş: Lyra, 2001)

Szende, Katalin, 'Towns and Urban Networks in the Carpathian Basin between the Eleventh and the Early Sixteenth Centuries', in *The Art of Medieval Hungary*, ed. by Xavier Barral i Altet, and others (Roma: Viella, 2018), pp. 65–81

Szentiványi, Robert, *Catalogus concinnus librorum manuscriptorum Bibliothecae Batthyanyanae* (Szeged: Bibliotheca Universitatis Szegediensis, 1958)

Taylor, Larissa Juliet, 'Out of Print: The Decline of Catholic Printed Sermons in France, 1530–1560', in *Habent sua fata libelli / Books Have Their Own Destiny: Essays in Honor of Robert V. Schnucker*, ed. by Robin Bruce Barnes, Robert A. Kolb, and Paula L. Presley, Sixteenth Century Essays & Studies, 1 (Kirksville, MO: Truman State University Press, 1998), pp. 121–30

Thayer, Anne T., 'The Medieval Sermon: Text, Performance and Insight', in *Understanding Medieval Primary Sources: Using Historical Sources to Discover Medieval Europe*, ed. by Joel Thomas Rosenthal (London: Routledge, 2012), pp. 43–58

Thayer, Anne T., *Penitence, Preaching and the Coming of the Reformation*, St Andrews Studies in Reformation History (Aldershot: Ashgate, 2002)

Thayer, Anne T., 'The *Postilla* of Guillermus and Late Medieval Popular Preaching', *Medieval Sermon Studies*, 48 (2004), 57–74

Tóthne Radó, Cecilia, *Robertus Caracciolus OFM prédikációs segédkönyveinek magyarországi felhasználása* (unpublished doctoral dissertation, Budapest: Pázmány Péter University, 2014)

Varjú, Elemér, 'A gyulafejérvári Batthyány-könyvtár', *Magyar Könyvszemle*, 7 (1899), 134–75, 209–43, 329–45; 8 (1900), 17–55, 131–69, 228–50, 337–61; 9 (1901), 24–52, 256–79

Verók, Attila, 'Das Buch als Repräsentationsmittel bei den Siebenbürger Sachsen', *Zeitschrift für Siebenbürgische Landeskunde*, 39 (2016), 91–99

Wittstock, Joachim, and Stefan Sienerth, *Die deutsche Literatur Siebenbürgens: von den Anfängen bis 1848* (München: Südostdeutsches Kulturwerk, 1997), I: *Mittelalter, Humanismus, Barock*

Zahn, Peter, 'Die Endabrechnung über den Druck der Schedelschen Weltchronik 1493 vom Juni 1509', *Gutenberg Jahrbuch*, 66 (1991), 177–213

Romance Regions

ORIOL CATALÁN

Controversial Topics in the Sermons of Vicent Ferrer

From Manuscripts to the Printing Press

Vicent Ferrer (1350–1419), a Dominican friar, doctor of theology, and a charismatic preacher, was an influential character in the Aragonese and Castilian royal families as well as in the papal court of Pope Benedict XIII (1394–1417). His most important preaching campaigns began in 1399, after being healed from a disease that put his life at risk and having had several visions in which God asked him to start a new life as a wandering preacher — in which he gained tremendous success.[1] A retinue of friars, clerics, and lay men followed him during his campaigns, which reached Switzerland, and France, as well as Aragon and Castile. He delivered his sermons in the local languages of Catalan, Castilian, and French, and many of them were transcribed by what might be called stenographers and then circulated in different manuscripts. According to the main index of his sermons, there are more than 900 extant sermons by Vicent Ferrer.[2]

He was indeed a very successful preacher. His preaching style was full of narration and very well adapted to the laity in its use of colloquial language, exempla, the lives of saints, and humour. The fact that he engaged with highly controversial topics (mainly the existence of the Antichrist, the Apocalypse, and the Last Judgement), sometimes voicing opinions that were not according to the official doctrine of the Church, made him well-known in Western Christianity. In spite of his occasional controversial preaching, he was canonized in 1455 by Callixtus III (1455–1458), who was born, like Vicent himself, in the Kingdom of Valencia.

---

1 The number of books devoted to Vicent Ferrer is overwhelming. Cited below are some references that may serve as introduction to the topic. For Vicent Ferrer's biography, see Philip Daileader, *Saint Vincent Ferrer, His World and Life: Religion and Society in Late Medieval Europe*, The New Middle Ages (New York: Palgrave Macmillan, 2016).

2 Josep Perarnau, 'Aportació a un inventari de sermons de sant Vicenç Ferrer: temes bíblics, títols i divisions esquemàtiques', *Arxiu de Textos Catalans Antics*, 18 (1999), 479–811.

> **Oriol Catalán** (oriol.catalan@upf.edu) is a Teacher in the Ostelea Tourism Management School at the University of Lleida.

Circulating the Word of God in Medieval and Early Modern Europe: Catholic Preaching and Preachers across Manuscript and Print (c. 1450 to c. 1550), ed. by Veronica O'Mara and Patricia Stoop, SERMO 17, (Turnhout: Brepols, 2022), pp. 223–256 BREPOLS ✠ PUBLISHERS 10.1484/M.SERMO-EB.5.130457

After a long period of publishing and analysing sermons by the Dominican Vicent Ferrer, scholars have recently begun to discuss the reception of his life and miracles between the fifteenth and the twentieth centuries. According to first impressions, a 'bewildering array of portrayals' appear, and 'the fifteenth-century Vincent Ferrer jostles with the multiple Vincents of later centuries.'[3] However, not much research has actually been carried out into the changes in Vicent Ferrer's sermons in the early printed era. This essay intends to be a preliminary investigation into these changes by comparing the handwritten and early printed versions of some sermons by Vicent Ferrer in order to attempt to differentiate what might be termed the original message of the saint from the layers superimposed or eliminated in later centuries.[4]

Vicent Ferrer: Manuscripts and Prints

The changes made over time in the manuscripts of Vicent Ferrer's sermons are known in broad terms.[5] The first group of extant manuscripts contain schematic sermons made out of the notes (*reportationes*) taken by stenographers who copied (more or less literally) the preacher's words.[6] The preacher might also take part in the process of an 'edition' of the text. These manuscripts follow the preacher's actual preaching during a certain period of time, sometimes with missing sermons or periods with no preaching delivered or copied, so that they roughly follow the liturgical order. They do not contain sermons for the full liturgical year, and the *de sanctis* and *de tempore* sermons are often mixed.

A second group of manuscripts collects full sermons (not schematic sermons) from a specific period in the order they were delivered.[7] Fribourg, Couvent des Cordeliers, MS 62 stands out among these manuscripts because

---

3 Laura Ackerman Smoller, *The Saint and the Chopped-up Baby: The Cult of Vincent Ferrer in Medieval and Early Modern Europe* (Ithaca: Cornell University Press, 2013), respectively pp. 3 and 13.

4 One of the few articles specifically devoted to the changes between Vicent Ferrer's manuscript and printed sermons is Laurette Godinas, 'Historia de una metamorfosis: del manuscrito al impreso en la tradición de los sermones de San Vicente Ferrer', *Boletín del Instituto de Investigaciones Bibliográficas*, 12 (2007), 13–32.

5 They have been recently summarized by Francisco Gimeno Blay, 'Modelos de transmisión textual de los sermones de San Vicente Ferrer: la tradición manuscrita', *Anuario de Estudios Medievales*, 49 (2019), 137–69. See also Josep Perarnau, 'Els manuscrits d'esquemes i de notes de sermons de sant Vicent Ferrer', *Arxiu de Textos Catalans Antics*, 18 (1999), 158–398. I deal with the most important manuscripts, those that have been edited or on which research has been carried out. The manuscripts and early printed book discussed in this article are listed in Appendix 2.

6 Perugia, Convento di san Domenico, MS 477; Città del Vaticano, Biblioteca Apostolica Vaticana, MS Vat. Lat. 4375; Città del Vaticano, Biblioteca Apostolica Vaticana, MS Vat. Lat. 7730, the only manuscript that splits the sermons between *De tempore* and *De sanctis*.

7 Avignon, Bibliothèque Municipale, MS 610; Fribourg, Couvent des Cordeliers, MS 62; Madrid, Real Academia de la Historia, MS 294; Valencia, Archivo de la Catedral, MS 273.

its whole process of becoming an edition was finished even earlier than other schematic sermons or *reportationes*. In 1406 the author, Friedrich von Amberg, copied sixteen sermons he attended in Fribourg, Murten, Avenches, Stavayer-le-Lac, and Payern (Switzerland) in Lent 1404. As there are no other schematic sermons or *reportationes* from before 1409, this manuscript is actually the oldest among Vicent Ferrer's sermon manuscripts.[8]

Sermon compilations were soon made.[9] They gather sermons from different previous manuscripts that were delivered in different years in order to fill a liturgical year or part thereof. The best known is the Toulouse Compilation begun in 1416, which comprises Bibliothèque Municipale, MS 345 (containing *De tempore* sermons for the whole liturgical year) and Toulouse, Bibliothèque Municipale, MS 346 (containing *De sanctis* sermons).[10] It involves, in addition to the translation of many sermons originally written in Catalan and Spanish into Latin, some changes to the original texts and some discarding of controversial sermons and topics.

The Toulouse Compilation is not the only one to contain certain changes compared to the actual preaching of Vicent Ferrer. For instance, by comparing the versions of the sermon *Attendite a falsis prophetis* in Barcelona, Biblioteca de Catalunya, MS 477, fol. 70v and Avignon, Bibliothèque Municipale, MS 610, fol. 42v, Josep Perarnau showed the omission of controversial content about the Antichrist and flagellation in the latter early compilations. As the preacher himself may have reviewed the sermons, the exclusion of controversial statements can be seen not as censorship, but rather as a decision of the preacher, who might not have wished to let these controversial fragments be copied.

The last group of manuscripts contains scarce sermons, sometimes mixed with other preachers' sermons and works, as in Barcelona, Biblioteca de Catalunya, MS 476, San Lorenzo del Escorial, Biblioteca del monasterio,

---

8 The sermons were partially edited in Segismund Brettle, *San Vicente Ferrer und sein literarischer Nachlass* (Münster in Westfalen: Aschendorffschen Verlagsbuchhandlung, 1924) (sermons 2–5), Josep Perarnau, 'Les primeres "reportationes" de sermons de St Vicent Ferrer: les de Friederich von Amberg, Fribourg, Cordeliers, ms. 62', *Arxiu de Textos Catalans Antics*, 18 (1999), 63–155 (sermons 1 and 6–11), and Bernard Hodel, 'Sermons de s. Vincent', *Mémoire Dominicaine*, 2 (1993), 149–92 (sermons 12–16, with a translation into French). Later, they were edited all together in Vicent Ferrer, *Sermones de cuaresma en Suiza, 1404 (Couvent des Cordeliers, ms. 62)*, ed. by Francisco M. Gimeno Blay and María Luz Mandingorra Llavata (Valencia: Ayuntamiento de Valencia, 2009).

9 In alphabetical order: Ayora, Archivo parroquial, Sermonario de San Vicente Ferrer; Barcelona, Biblioteca de Catalunya MS 477; Clermont-Ferrand, Bibliothèque Municipale, MS 45 (Quadragesimale); Fribourg, Convent des Cordeliers, MS 68; Madrid, Real Academia della Historia, MS 294; Madrid, Real Biblioteca, MS II/413 (Quadragesimale and other sermons); Sevilla, Biblioteca Capitular y Colombina, MS 56–5–31 (Aestivales) and 56–5–32 (Quadragesimale); Toulouse, Bibliothèque Municipale, MSS 345 and 346; Valencia, Colegio del Corpus Christi (or del Patriarca), s.n.; Valencia, Archivo de la Catedral, MSS 168, 274 (*De sanctis*), 276, (277), 278, 279. MS 277 disappeared during the Spanish Civil War.

10 Segismund Brettle, *San Vicente Ferrer und sein literarischer Nachlass* (Münster in Westfalen: Aschendorffschen Verlagsbuchhandlung, 1924), p. 80.

MS M.II.6, Ljubljiana, Drzavna (Licejska) Knjiznica Slovenia, MS 106.23, Madrid, Biblioteca Nacional, MS 4283, Oxford, Bodleian Library, MS Douce 162, or Oviedo, Biblioteca Universitaria, MS 444.

The sermons of Vicent Ferrer were also successful in the printing press, with more than fifty editions between 1475 and 1600. There were two main groups of editions. First, there is a group of almost fifty similar editions between 1475 and 1600, published mainly in Lyon, Köln, and Strasbourg.[11] These are costly Latin editions, usually in three volumes, thought of as model sermons for preachers and as pious reading for clerics. It has traditionally been stated that these editions closely follow the Toulouse Compilation.[12]

A second group of editions was produced in Spain, with more than fifteen different editions between 1550 and 1612, the heyday of religious prophecies and the development of the *Alumbrado* mystical movement, whose earlier development dates back to Vicent Ferrer's preaching campaign in 1411–1412.[13] These editions are much more modest than the Latin ones, and their public is different as well. They contain between four and six sermons about the Apocalypse and the End of Times in Spanish. These editions were thought of as a pious reading for lay people in order to spread mystical and millenarian spirituality. Although these Hispanic editions may have different titles, their content is very similar: an introduction, a short life of Vicent Ferrer, and the sermons. These editions were considered apocryphal for centuries, but that opinion has nowadays changed. While the first sermon is apocryphal (*Ecce positus est hic in ruinam*, Appendix 1, no. 9),[14] sermon 2 is original (*Quaedam mulier de turba dixit*, Appendix 1, no. 27). Other sermons seem to be a mix of

---

11 A list of editions appears at the end of this chapter.

12 Brettle, *San Vicente Ferrer und sein literarischer Nachlass*, pp. 78–80, 106; Josep Perarnau, 'Sermones de sant Vicent Ferrer en los manuscritos de Barcelona, Biblioteca de Catalunya, 477 y Avignon, Musée Calvet, 610', *Escritos del Vedat*, 4 (1974), 611–46 (p. 645); Pedro Cátedra, 'La predicación castellana de San Vicente Ferrer', *Butlletí de la Reial Acadèmia de Bones Lletres de Barcelona*, 39 (1984), 235–309 (p. 264).

13 Marjorie Reeves, *The Influence of Prophecy in the Later Middle Ages: A Study in Joachinism* (Oxford: Clarendon Press, 1969), pp. 446–47, 465–67; María Isabel Toro Pascua, 'Literatura popular religiosa en el siglo XVI: los sermones impresos de Vicente Ferrer', in *Studia aurea: actas del III Congreso de la AISO (Toulouse, 1993)*, ed. by Ignacio Arellano Ayuso, Carmen Pinillos Salvador, Marc Vitse, and Frédéric Serralta, 3 vols (Pamplona: Grupo de Investigación Siglo de Oro, Universidad de Navarra, 1996), III, 521–30. María Isabel Toro Pascua, 'Las versiones castellanas del sermón Ecce positus est hic in ruinam, atribuido a San Vicente Ferrer', in *Actas del VI congreso internacional de la asociación hispánica de literatura medieval (Alcalá de Henares, 12–16 de septiembre de 1995)*, ed. by José Manuel Lucía Megías, 2 vols (Alcalá de Henares: Universidad de Alcalá, 1997), II, 1501–11.

14 It is a very old sermon about the End of Times, perhaps written in the lifetime of Vicent Ferrer that mixes fragments from other sermons, from the letter sent by Vicent to Benedict XIII in 1412 about the Antichrist, and from Joachite writings. It appears in Madrid, Real Academia de la Historia, MS 294, copied in 1448. Apart from these Hispanic editions, the sermon was published separately several times under the title *De fine mundi* in Italy and Germany. See the list of editions at the end of the chapter.

different original sermons. All these sermons are connected with the manuscript Madrid, Real Academia de la Historia, MS 294, instead of with the Toulouse Compilation, and do not appear in the Latin editions.[15]

During the fifteenth century, a series of books about the End of Times were published in the Hispanic Kingdoms, like the Spanish translation of Jean de Roquetaillade's (*c.* 1310–1366/70) *Vade mecum in tribulatione* (1412), the *Libro del cognoscimiento del fin del mundo* (*c.* 1420), the *Libro de los grandes hechos* attributed to Juan Unay (1480–1490?), and Martín Martínez de Ampiés's *Libro del anticristo* (1496), works that bring up to date the prophecies of Gioacchino da Fiore (*c.* 1135–1202), and medieval versions by Hispanic authors like Arnau de Vilanova (1240–1311).[16] Some of this works were printed at the end of the fifteenth and the beginning of the sixteenth century, and the relation with Vicent Ferrer is clear. For instance, the apocryphal sermon *Ecce positus est hic in ruinam* in the Hispanic editions also appears in Martín Martínez de Ampiés's *Libro del anticristo*.[17]

In order to compare manuscript and early printed versions of the same sermons, the most appropriate are those that deal with controversial topics and are preserved in different manuscripts and printed versions. The location of the different sermon versions has been eased by the index of Vicent's sermons prepared by Perarnau.[18] The chosen editions for comparison are those of Köln 1485 and Valencia 1566.[19] The Latin Köln 1485 edition is an early edition in three volumes (*Hiemales, Aestivales, De sanctis*), that can be used as a representative of the very similar editions in Venezia, Lyon, Nürnberg, and Strasbourg.[20]

---

15 Toro Pascua, 'Literatura popular religiosa', p. 523.

16 Other influences date back to Adso de Montier-en-Der's *De ortu et tempore Antichristi*, to Haymon d'Auxerre's *Expositio in apocalypsim* and even to Jerome's *Commentary on Daniel*. María Isabel Toro Pascua, 'Milenarismo y profecía en el siglo xv: la tradición del libro de Unay en la Península Ibérica', *Península: Revista de Estudios Ibéricos* (2003), 29–37 (p. 32); Toro Pascua, 'Imagen y función del anticristo en algunos textos castellanos del siglo xv', *Via Spiritus*, 6 (1999), 27–63 (pp. 43–50); Alain Milhou, 'La chauve-souris, le nouveau David et le roi caché (trois images de l'empereur des derniers temps dans le monde ibérique: xiiiᵉ–xviiᵉ s.', *Mélanges de la Casa de Velázquez*, 18 (1982), 61–78.

17 Martín Martínez de Ampiés's *Libro del anticristo* contains a treatise, *Libro del juicio postrimero*, the sermon *Ecce hic positus est in ruinam* (or *De fine mundi*) and the Epistle of Rabbi Samuel sent to Rabbi Isaac. It was first published in Zaragoza in 1496. Therefore, printed (and exaggerated) prophecies attributed to Vicent Ferrer's existed already before 1500. See Toro Pascua, 'Las versiones castellanas'.

18 Perarnau, 'Aportació a un inventari de sermons'. The selected sermons and their different versions are listed in Appendix 1.

19 Another important edition is that of Valencia 1693–1695 in five volumes, known as the Rocabertí edition, after the name of the archbishop of Valencia who commissioned the edition. It is significant because, unlike previous editions, it takes into account the manuscript from the Colegio del Corpus Christi (or del Patriarca) in Valencia, in order to 'completar sermones o bien para recabar otros que no se encontraban dentro de la redacción tolosana', Cátedra, 'La predicación castellana', p. 288. Nevertheless, as it lies far beyond the chronological scope of this collection of essays, only significant references to this edition will be made.

20 Here, I rely on the opinion of Brettle, *San Vicente Ferrer und sein literarischer Nachlass*,

ORIOL CATALÁN

It is the usually cited early printed edition in Perarnau's index, and the three volumes can be found online.[21] The Valencia edition of 1566, *Sermones de San Vicente Ferrer en los quales trata de la venida del Antichristo y juizio final*, published by Joan Navarro, is a good representative of the sixteenth-century Hispanic editions, and may be found online as well.[22]

A first evident change in the sermons of Vicent Ferrer from manuscript to print is the disappearance of sermons. Thirteen out of thirty-two selected sermons were not published in the fifteenth and sixteenth centuries.[23] However, there are other changes to take into account. For instance, the Latin editions not only depend, as traditionally thought, on the Toulouse Compilation. They sometimes reinstate 'censored' elements in the Toulouse Compilation deriving from other manuscripts, such as Fribourg, Couvent des Cordeliers, MS 68 (an unpublished manuscript that deserves further research). For instance, the sermons *Erunt signa in sole et luna et stellis* (Appendix 1, nos 12 and 13) and *Respicite et levate capita vestra* (Appendix 1, no. 32), for the Second Sunday in Advent, do not appear in the Toulouse Compilation but appear in the edition in Köln 1485. We may therefore say that there was a partial rejection of controversial topics in the sermons published in the fifteenth and sixteenth centuries, a rejection that will be analysed in depth below. We will first analyse some sermons containing social criticism, and then focus on Vicent Ferrer's 'guest topics': the End of Times, the arrival of the Antichrist, and the Last Judgement.

Sermons Containing Social Criticism

Laura Ackerman Smoller suggests that the lives of Vicent Ferrer written in the sixteenth century highlighted some events of his life (miracles and the struggle for the reunification of the Church), while other topics (millenarianism and behaviour) were silenced or at least not promoted.[24] The same seems to have happened with Ferrer's sermons regarding social criticism, as some references about the topic do not appear in the Latin editions.

For example, in the sermon *Hodie est et cras*, about the Apocalypse (Appendix 1, no. 19), Vicent Ferrer does not spare criticism of kings, lords, and friars. The sermon does not appear in the Köln edition:

---

pp. 78–79: 'Alle Drucke der Sermones San Vicentes, die in Deutschland, Frankreich und Italien hergestellt wurden, gehen auf eine einzige handschriftliche Vorlage zurück. Man kann das mit Bestimmtheit sagen, weil sie alle inhaltlich ganz gleich sind und sogar im Incipit und Explicit miteinander übereinstimmen'.

21 http://digital.ub.uni-duesseldorf.de/ink/content/titleinfo/2374444 [accessed 6 January 2021].

22 https://bivaldi.gva.es/es/consulta/registro.cmd?id=4071 [accessed 6 January 2021].

23 Appendix 1, nos 2, 3, 4, 6, 9, 15, 16, 17, 18, 19, 23, 26, and 27.

24 Smoller, *The Saint and the Chopped-up Baby*, pp. 138–43.

CONTROVERSIAL TOPICS IN THE SERMONS OF VICENT FERRER   229

E muchos reyes e enperadores e señores, que reban su ente e sus vasallos, estonçe querrán tener consejo para tornarlo todo a sus dueños. Agora es ora, que estonçe non será ora. E más, algunos clérigos, que no tienen breviario, mas buena lança e buena espada e buena balleta [...] E muchos religiosos, que non tienen la regla ni la saben [...] son locos frayres, que no tienen la regla e religión segúnd son tenudos; e son locos clérigos, que non tienen agora breviario, que non saben dezir oras; e son locos reys e señores, que han muchas rrentas e ponen muchas alcabalas e pechos a las gentes para dar a rufianes e a ladrones. (Madrid, Real Academia de la Historia, MS 294, fol. 164v; *Sermón, sociedad y literatura*, ed. by Cátedra, p. 587)[25]

> [And many kings and emperors and lords, who oppress their subjects and vassals, will then want advice to turn everything over to their owners. Now it is time, later will not be the time. Besides, some clerics, who do not posses a breviary, but a good spear and a good sword and a good crossbow [...] And many clerics, who do not have the rule or even know it [...] they are mad friars, who do not keep the rule and religion as they should, and they are mad clerics, who do not have a breviary, who do not know how to say the Hours; and are mad kings and lords, who have vast incomes and impose many taxes on sales and personal taxes so to give them to thugs and thieves].

Something different happens in the sermon *Latitudo et longitudo* about the Last Judgement (Appendix 1, no. 24), in which Ferrer lashes out against the unjust lords, announcing their eternal damnation. The sermon was not published in the Köln edition, but in the usual way that we will find in many other examples, the controversial fragment appears in another sermon, *In tempore messis* for the *Dominica quarta post octavas Epiphanie* (Appendix 1, no. 22), whose handwritten versions does not contain the accusation:

Sermo Latitudo et longitudo

Grandes reys e duques e condes e grandes señores que non avían justo título en sus señoríos, mas por violençia e por fuerça e por falsas cartas; e non se son governados segúnd justiçia, mas contra justiçia, e de la sangre de sus vasallos, que los desfazen; e ellos van bien vestidos, cargados de piedras preciosas e de aljófar e grandes ornamentos; **destos tales se fará un faz muy grande**, que será maravilla.

Item, de todos malos perlados, papas e cardenales e arçobispos e obispos, que non son entrados en la dignidat por la puerta por pura

---

25 Vicent Ferrer, *Sermón, sociedad y literatura en la Edad Media: San Vicente Ferrer en Castilla (1411–1412). Estudio bibliografico, literario y edicion de los textos ineditos*, ed. by Pedro Cátedra (Salamanca: Junta de Castilla y León de Cultura y Turismo, 1994); references to this edition are given here as *Sermón, sociedad y literatura*, ed. by Cátedra, followed by the relevant page number.

elecçión, mas por ruegos e por presentes; e aún biven en aquello, que lo non quiere dexar

[...] **Item, de frayres e de religiosos** que non tienen la regla, antes son propietarios e son soberbiosos e **luxuriosos.**

[...] **Item los logreros**

[...] **Item los luxuriosos** casados e los otros que fazen luxuria consigo o con otro. (Madrid, Real Academia de la Historia, MS 294, fol. 184r–v; *Sermón, sociedad y literatura*, ed. by Cátedra, pp. 627–28)

> [**Great kings and dukes and counts and great lords** who had no just title to their nobility other than through violence or force or false documents; and they do not govern according to justice, but against justice, and from the blood of their vassals, who defy them; they are well dressed, full of precious stones and pearls and large ornaments; out of these, **a very large sheaf will be made** that will be wonderful [...] **The same of all bad prelates, popes, and cardinals and archbishops and bishops**, who are not entered into the dignity by the door of pure election, but by entreaties and by presents; they still live in that, that they do not want to leave [...] **The same of friars and religious** who do not have the rule, before they are proprietors and they are superb and lustful [...] **The same of the usurers** [...] **The same of the lustful** married and others who commit lust with themselves or with others].

Although the text is not a literal translation, it bears evident similarities in structure as well as vocabulary with the Castilian sermon:

Sermo In tempore messis

Item de omnibus participantibus in eodem crimine, fiet unus fasciculus. Primo de omnibus malis Imperatoribus, regibus et principus, gubernatoribus, et rectoribus fiet unus fasciculus, imo erit magnus fascis et grossus. **Secundo de omnibus malis praelatis,** qui non intraverunt per portam, sed per manum regiam, vel per symoniam, et male vixerunt. Tertio **de omnibus religiosis, qui nihil tenent quod voverunt,** nec de ceremoniis: imo fuerunt inobedientes, proprietarii, **luxuriosi.** Quarto de monialibus fiet alius fascis. Quinto de malis presbiteris, et inhonestis, qui nec dixerunt horas, sed ludunt ad taxilos, tenuerunt concubinas, fecerunt mercancias, etc. Sextus erit de malis iudicibus, advocatis, iuristis, notariis, qui dilatant litigia, devorant viduas, et pauperes, consummunt gentes. Septimus erit de avaris, **usurariis,** latronibus, falsis mercatoribus. Octavus de illis, qui vivunt in bannositatibus. Nonus **de omnibus luxuriosis, lenonibus, meretricibus.** Decimus de omnibus mulieribus vanis, pomposis, quae licet fuerint castae et honestae, ex illis tamen picturis, et vanis ornamentis damnabuntur. (Köln 1485, *Hiemales*, Dominica IV post octavas epiphanie)

[A bundle [*literally* 'a sheaf'] will be made of all who participate in such a crime. First, of all those bad emperors, kings and princes, governors and rulers a bundle will be made, which will be a big fat bundle. Secondly, of all bad clerics that do not enter through the door, but through royal support or simony, and live badly. Thirdly, of all monks that do not obey their vows nor the ceremonies, and what is more, they were disobedient, appropriators, and lustful. Fourth, of the nuns another bundle will be made. Fifth, of bad priests and dishonest ones, who do not say the Hours, but play dice, have concubines, carry out business, etc. Sixth, of bad judges, lawyers, jurists, and notaries who delay litigation, and destroy widows and the poor. Seventh, there will be a bundle of the greedy, usurers, thieves, false merchants. Eighth, of all those who belong to gangs. Ninth, **of all lustful people, procurers, and whoremongers**. Tenth, of all vain women, pompous ones that seem as if they are chaste and honest, but that will be damned on account of their make-up and their jewels].

Sermons about the End of Times, the Antichrist, and the Last Judgement

The End of the World, the Apocalypse, the coming of the Antichrist, and the Final Judgment were some of the most successful, but also the most controversial topics in Vicent Ferrer's preaching, and were treated in a very different way in the Latin and Hispanic editions.

The sermons, *Creatura liberabitur* (in Spanish) and *Ecce positus est hic in ruinam* (in Catalan) (Appendix 1, nos 5 and 10) about the Antichrist and the End of Times, share a similar development. They explain the methods of the Antichrist to seduce Christians: riches, miracles, arguments, and violence. Both sermons have been recently published by Cátedra and by Schib, but they were unpublished for centuries:

Creatura liberabitur

Otrossý, dará otro çevo a los golosos. ¿E qué çevo será? Que tirará la Quaresma del año e de los meses las quatro témporas e de la semana el viernes.

[...] E, otrosí más, **quebrantarán toda la buena ley de matrimonio, que casará cada uno a media carta e dexarán sus mugieres e tomarán quantas quisieren.** E las monjas farán tomar maridos. E a los clérigos dirán los ministros del Antichristo: 'Tomad todos mugieres [...]'. (Madrid, Real Academia de la Historia, MS 294, fol. 145r; *Sermón, sociedad y literatura*, ed. by Cátedra, p. 539)

232 ORIOL CATALÁN

[In addition, he will provide another bait for the greedy. And what will the bait be? That he will remove Lent from the year, and from the months the Ember Days, and from the week, the Friday [...] And, in addition, **they will shatter the good law of marriage so that the whole world will cohabit, and all man will leave their wives and take as many women as they want.** And the nuns will take husbands. And the clerics will say to the ministers of the Antichrist: 'Take all women [...]'].

Ecce positus est hic in ruinam

Soltarà regla de matrimoni, que quiscun hom pugue pendre tantes mulers com li plaurà, a miga carta, e·ls religiosos poran tenir tres o quatre jovenetes en la cel·la. (Valencia, Archivo de la Catedral, MS 277, fol. 263r; *Sermons*, ed. by Sanchis Sivera and Schib, vi (1988), 234)[26]

[**He will break the rule of marriage so that every man can take as many women as he pleases,** and the religious may have three or four young girls in the cell].

However, some of these contents appear in the sermon *Erunt signa in sole et luna et stellis* (Appendix 1, no. 15) in the edition of Köln 1485, although the manuscript versions do not contain this:[27]

Erunt signa in sole et luna et stellis

Item dabit abundantiam ciborum, et escarum, dicens: Comedatis, et bibatis bene, et quare factae sont escae? [...] **Et etiam de anno, amovebit Quadragesimam. De mensibus, quatuor tempora. De hebdomada, diem veneris.** Isto modo habebit omnes gulosos. Item dabit omnes delectationes carnis: **franget totam legem matrimoni, licenciabit clericos, et religiosos ut ducant uxores.** (Köln 1485, *Hiemales*, Dominica secunda adventus, sermo iv)

[He gave plenty of food and nourishment, saying: Let's eat and drink well. What is food made for? [...] **And from the year he removed Lent. From the months, the Ember Days. From the week, the Friday.** In

---

26 Vicent Ferrer, *Sermons*, ed. by Josep Sanchis Sivera and Gret Schib, Els nostres clàssics, col·lecció B, 3, 5, 6–9, 6 vols (Barcelona: Barcino, 1932–1988), here referred to as *Sermons*, ed. by Sanchis Sivera and Schib, followed by the volume and page number. The editors do not provide the pages of the manuscript, so when quoting the volumes edited by Sivera and Schib, I can only refer to the first folio of every sermon.

27 This sermon does not appear in Perarnau's Index, but it is actually a version of the sermon *Creatura liberabitur*. This is a good example of how difficult identifying Vicent Ferrer's sermons can sometimes be. Although having a different *thema* and division, it is actually the same sermon. It almost seems as if the *thema* were changed in order to prevent the identification of the sermon.

this way, everybody would become greedy. He also allowed everybody to enjoy meat; **shattered the whole law of marriage, the clerics were discharged, and the monks (were allowed) to take wives**].

There are other examples of relocation of content in the same sermons, as when the preacher says that during the Apocalypse fire will descend from heaven and images will speak:

Creatura liberabitur

Sant Johán evangelista lo dize en el Apocalipsi en el XIII° capitulo. **Dize que fará descençender fuego del çielo delante todas las personas del mundo [...] E dize sant Juan que fará hablar las ymágenes.** (Madrid, Real Academia de la Historia, MS 294, fol. 146r; *Sermón, sociedad y literatura*, ed. by Cátedra, p. 540)

> [St John the Evangelist says it in the Apocalypse in the thirteenth chapter. **He says that he will make fire descend from heaven in front of all the people of the world [...] And St John says that he will make the images speak**].

Ecce positus est hic in ruinam

Diu sent Johan que davant tota la gent farà cremar les montanyes e farà parlar les ymages de sent Père e de sent Pau. (Valencia, Archivo de la Catedral, MS 277, fol. 263r; *Sermons*, ed. by Sanchis Sivera and Schib, VI (1988), 231)

> [**St John says that in front of all the people he will burn the mountains and will make the images of St Peter and St Paul speak**].

These arguments appear almost literally in the Latin sermon:

Erunt signa in sole

De falsis, et apparentibus miraculis Antichristi, **dicit Beatus Ioannes Apostolus,** Apocalyp. 13, v. 13 **quod faciet descendere ignem de celo, et faciet loqui imagines virtute diabolica.** (Köln 1485, *Hiemales*, Dominica secunda adventus, sermo IV)

> [About the false and apparent miracles of the Anticrist, **John the Apostle said,** Apocalypse 13. 13, **that he caused fire to come down from heaven to earth and made the images speak with diabolical vigour**].

Still in the same sermons there is another relocation of contents when the preacher argues that the followers of the Antichrist will defeat Christian doctors and masters:

Creatura liberabitur

Así serán los del Antichristo, que dirán a los maestros en theología e letrados: 'Venid acá. Pues non queredes creer por riquezas nin por milagros, vayamos a disputaçión' […] **E los siervos del Antichristo començarán a fablar por manera de encantadores e dirán muchas sotilezas con actoridad falsa e farán muy muchos argumentos.** E desque ayan dicho los del Antichristo, querrán fablar los maestros **e non podrán, e dirán: 'Me, me'.** E dirán entonces los del Anticristo a los maestros e letrados: '¿Qué fazedes que non respondedes?'. E ellos non podrán responder e estarán assí como mudos, que non podrán fablar. (Madrid, Real Academia de la Historia, MS 294, fol. 147r; *Sermón, sociedad y literatura*, ed. by Cátedra, p. 542)

> [So will those of the Antichrist, who will say to the masters in theology and lawyers: 'Come here. Because you do not want to believe in riches nor in miracles, let us go to dispute' […] **The servants of the Antichrist will begin to speak in the manner of enchanters and will utter many subtleties with false authority and will make many arguments.** And since those of the Antichrist will have said that they will want to speak to the masters and **they will not be able to, they will say: 'Me, me'.** And then those of the Antichrist will say to the masters and the lawyers: 'What do you do that you do not answer?'. And they will not be able to respond and they will be as mute, who cannot speak].

Ecce positus est hic in ruinam

Los regidors de les ciutats posaran los doctors e mestres en theologia, e los dexebles de Antechrist en cadafals, **e los dexebles argüiran contra aquells suficientmén e aguda per test de bíblia,** e quan hauran dit: 'Responeu vosaltres!', **lo diable los lligarà la lengua, que no poran dir sinó 'Me, me!'** (Valencia, Archivo de la Catedral, MS 277, fol. 263r; *Sermons*, ed. by Sanchis Sivera and Schib, vi (1988), 232)

> [The councillors of the cities will put doctors and masters in theology, and the disciples of Antichrist to the scaffold, **and the disciples will argue against those very sharply and through the texts of the Bible,** and when they will say: 'Respond you!', the devil will tie their tongue so that **they will not be able to say but 'Me, me!'**].

Again, similar expressions appear in the Latin version of the sermon *Erunt signa in sole*:

Erunt signa in sole

Dicent discipuli Antichristi: Veritas non querit angulos, ideo disputemus. Dic practicam disputationis, et quomodo **illi arguent cum argumentis sophisticis, et rationibus palliatis (apparentibus)** quia diabolus loquetur in ore ipsorum, in tantum quod **nec Magistri nostri, nec Doctores poterunt eis respondere; quia diabolus ligabit linguam ipsorum**, permitente Deo propter malam vitam litteratorum. (Köln 1485, *Hiemales*, Dominica secunda adventus, sermo IV)

> [And the disciples of the Antichrist say: the truth seeks no hiding places, therefore let us dispute and talk about the means of discussion and how **they argue with sophistic arguments and apparent reason**, because the devil speaks through their mouths, so that neither **our masters nor our doctors can answer them, because the devil tied their tongues**, God allowing that because of the bad lives of the scholars].

The displacement of controversial contents is a normal phenomenon in early printed editions. Another change of contents from manuscript to print appears is the omission of controversial references, as in the sermons *Frater, sine eiciam festucam* about the Antichrist (Appendix 1, no. 18) and *Respicite et levate capita vestra* for the second week of Advent (Appendix 1, no. 32). These sermons explain why God will allow the coming of the Antichrist with a metaphor of a king betrayed by his subjects. The manuscript versions of *Frater, sine eiciam festucam* and the printed version of *Respicite et levate capita vestra* also blame the faithful's bad behaviour for the coming of the Antichrist. Although all versions contain the *exemplum* of the city and the betrayals, they treat the topic of the Antichrist in different ways:

Frater, sine eiciam festucam

Agora dezid, ¿parésçevos que aquel rey que fizo rrazón? Yo creo que non ay ninguno, que dixiesse que avía fecho mal, pues que tantas trayçiones le avían feho, ca mucho más meresçían.

E aquel capitán traerá muchas gentes, e assí lo dize la actoridad. **Este cavallero es Antichristo, Got e Magot**, 'cuius non est numerus' (Ap. xx° c.) E dize que non averá número en la gente que traerá.

E agora veamos quién es este rey grande tan glorioso e tan esçelente. (Madrid, Real Academia de la Historia, MS 294, fol. 149v; *Sermón, sociedad y literatura*, ed. by Cátedra, p. 550)

> [**Now say, do you think that king was right? I believe that there is no one who says that he had done wrong**, because (his subjects) had made so many betrayals to him, that they deserved much more (punishment).
>
> And that captain will bring many people, and so the authority says. This knight is the Antichrist, Gog and Magog, 'cuius non est numerus' [*see* Apoc. 20. 8]. And he says that there will be no number of the people he will bring.
>
> Now let us see who is this great king so glorious and so excellent].

236 ORIOL CATALÁN

The Köln edition omits the reference to the Antichrist:

Respicite et levate capita vestra

Numquid de hoc debet aliquis admirari aut dicere, quare rex fecit hoc? Et certe non. Imo dicere debet quilibet quod rex fecit optime. (Köln 1485, *Hiemales*, Dominica secunda adventus, sermo v)

> [Should we not wonder at this or say why the king did that? Surely not. Anybody should actually say that the king did the best].

Nevertheless, this silencing is not complete, since other references to the Antichrist appear in different parts of the sermon. The prophetic and millenarian contents were softened, partially eliminated or displaced with respect to the original manuscript versions, but they did not disappear completely from the Latin editions.

Another fundamental topic in Ferrer's sermons is a vision in the Life of St Dominic in the *Legenda aurea*, in which Sts Dominic and Francis could see God carrying three spears (representing the Antichrist, the Destruction of the World, and the Last Judgment), ready to initiate the Apocalypse. Only the intercession of the Virgin Mary grants extra time to humanity to be redeemed before the End of Times.

Together with this vision, sometimes the assertion that the Antichrist was already born appears. Vicent Ferrer had preached about the Antichrist at least since 1403, when he had still not heard about the birth of the Antichrist. Four sermons about the Antichrist appear in Fribourg, Couvent des Cordeliers, MS 62.[28] The topic was already controversial, and Ferrer preferred not to explain to his superiors that he was preaching about these issues.[29] Some years later, around 1408–1410, Vicent Ferrer heard about the birth of the Antichrist, he trusted the witnesses he found in different places, and preached about the topics around 1411–1413, stating that the Antichrist was born in 1403 and providing 'reliable witnesses' to prove such a statement.[30]

The sermon *Reminiscamini quia ego dixi vobis* about the Antichrist (Appendix 1, no. 31) is closely related to the letter that Vicent Ferrer sent to Pope Benedict XIII in 1412 explaining his ideas about the Antichrist.[31] The

---

28 These four sermons are: *Flagellum de funiculis* (fols 51r–53r; Perarnau, no. 351); *Nolite secundum faciem iudicare, sed iustum iudicium iudicate* (fols 53r–55r; Perarnau no. 562); *Nescitis, qua hora filius hominis venturus est* (fols 55v–58r; Perarnau, no. 553); and *Visitavit plebem suam* (fols 61r–63v; Perarnau no. 891).

29 Daileader, *Saint Vincent Ferrer, His World and Life*, pp. 46–48.

30 For a complete analysis of this topic, see José Guadalajara Medina, 'La edad del Anticristo y el año del fin del mundo, según fray Vicente Ferrer', in *Pensamiento medieval hispano: homenaje a Horacio-Santiago Otero*, ed. by José María Soto Rábanos (Madrid: Consejo Superior de Investigaciones Científicas, 1998), pp. 321–42.

31 The letter is published in Francisco Vidal i Micó, *Vida del valenciano apóstol de la Europa San Vicente Ferrer: con reflexiones sobre su doctrina* (Valencia: Juan Mariana, 1857), pp. 579–87,

sermon includes the vision of the three lances and 'eight reliable witnesses' that allowed Vicent Ferrer to assure people that the Antichrist was born in 1403: 'E ha ocho años que es nasçido Antichristo' ['And eight years ago the Antichrist was born'].[32]

The sermon *Quaedam mulier de turba dixit* about the Antichrist (Appendix 1, no. 27),[33] begins by denying the possibility of knowing the date of the end of the world, invoking the biblical sentence *Non est vestrum nosce tempora* (Acts 1. 7). However, Vicent immediately explains the vision of the three lances, the intercession of Mary, and the birth of the Antichrist:

> Duos homines, unus filius militis et alius heremitanus indutus de stupa, qui mihi aparebat homo sancte vite et sanctus in suis gestis, et dixit mihi quod Antichristus erat natus, ut erat revelatum in Toscana quibusdam sanctis heremitanis qui per tredecim annos non comederunt nisi panem et aquam, et tunc jam habebat quinque annos Antichristus quod erat natus et nunc jam vadunt octo annos. (Perarnau, 'Sobre el manuscrit de València', p. 433)
>
> > [Two men, one a son of a soldier, and the other one dressed with a coarse habit, who seemed to me men of saintly life and saints in their gestures, and said to me that the Antichrist was born, as was unveiled in Tuscany to some saint hermits who for thirteen years only consumed bread and water, and by then the Antichrist had been born five years before, and now eight years ago].

A third sermon with similar prophetic content is the already mentioned *Ecce positus est hic in ruinam* on the Antichrist (Appendix 1, no. 10). In this sermon the three spears do not come from the vision of Sts Dominic and Francis, but from 2 Sam. 18. 14: 'Tulit ergo tres lanceas in manu sua et infixit eas in corde Absalom' ['And he took three spears in his hand and thrust them through Absalom's heart']. This sermon focuses on the performance of the Antichrist, but probably also included the intercession of Mary and the birth of the Antichrist, since the sermon ends abruptly: 'Cent anys ha que sà la sentència (ut habetur in legenda Sancti Dominici ordinis predicatorum)' ['The sentence was delivered one hundred years ago (according to the legend of St Dominic of the Order of Preachers)'].[34]

Finally, the sermon *Vos estis sal terrae* (Appendix 1, no. 34), devoted to St Dominic, conveys the same vision, but with no references to the birth of the Antichrist or his age. This sermon (the less controversial of all dealing

---

and Pierre-Henry Fages, *Notes et documents de l'histoire de Saint Vincent Ferrer* (Leuven: Uystpruyst, 1905), pp. 213–24.

32 *Sermón, sociedad y literatura*, ed. by Cátedra, p. 573.

33 This is the only original sermon that appears in the Hispanic editions.

34 *Sermons*, ed. by Sanchis Sivera and Schib, vi (1988), 229–35.

238 ORIOL CATALÁN

with the vision of the three spears) is the only one published in the early printed Latin editions:

> Nam invenio quod iste mundus debuit corrumpi et finiri (bene sunt ducenti anni et ultra elapsi): sed Virgo Maria volens mundum adhuc preservare, posuit salem, scilicet Beatum Dominicum, et salvavit mundum. Nam legitur in Floribus Sanctorum, et in Vita Beati Dominici etiam in duobus locis, visionem quam vidit Beatus Dominicus et Beatus Franciscus, et alii, quando erant Romae laborantes pro confirmatione Ordinum suorum. [...] Cumque una nocte Beatus Dominicus esset in quadam Ecclesia orans, et Beatus Franciscus in alia, visus est eis Christus cum tribus lanceis volens mundum destruere [...]. (Köln 1485, *De sanctis*, In festo sancti Dominici)
>
>> [I think that this world is bound to become corrupt and end (more than two hundred years have passed); but the Virgin Mary, wanting to preserve this world, added some salt, that is, St Dominic, and saved the world. But you can read in Floribus Sanctorum, and in the Life of St Dominic, that in two places St Dominic and St Francis, and others, had a vision when they were in Rome working for the confirmation of their orders [...] Staying one night, St Dominic praying in a church, and St Francis in another one, Christ appeared to them, with three spears, wanting to destroy the world [...]].

Other sermons regarding the Antichrist were not printed until the twentieth century. The sermon *Bonum Facientes* about the burning of the world (Appendix 1, no. 3) recounts the destruction of the world during the reign of the Antichrist and recommends penance to the faithful, while the sermon *In plenitude sanctorum* about the Resurrection (Appendix 1, no. 21) deals with the resurrection of the dead after the coming of the Antichrist and the destruction of the world, and before the Final Judgment.

Two more sermons conveying controversial topics do not appear in early printed editions: the sermon *Benedictus qui venit in nomine Domini* for the First Sunday in Advent (Appendix 1, no. 2) and the sermon *Cum Christo discipuli* (Appendix 1, no. 7), which narrate the development of the Final Judgment and deny the intercession of Mary during the Judgment, a belief that was shared by some people and appears in some gothic paintings in the Hispanic Kingdoms in the early fifteenth century:[35]

Benedictus qui venit in nomine Domini

> Com estarà la verge Maria e los sants?; de la verge Maria dien ialguns, e axí ho pinten los pintors, que estarà agenollada, pregant per nosaltres: no es ver; donchs, com estarà? Ella seurà axí com a conjutge e advocada del

---

35 Albert Toldrà i Vilardell, 'Sant Vicent contra el pintor gòtic: sobre el "triangle" de l'expressió medieval', *Afers*, 41 (2002), 37–55 (p. 47).

seu fill [...]. (Valencia, Archivo de la Catedral, MS 277, fol. 115v; *Sermons*, ed. by Sanchis Sivera and Schib, VI (1988), 273)

> [How will the Virgin Mary and the saints be? About the Virgin Mary, some say, and that is how artists depict the scene, that she will kneel, praying for us: that is not true; so, how will she be? She will sit as a judge and advocate to her son (...)].

Cum Christo discipuli

La Virgen María [...] e sand Juan [...] no osarán abrir la boca para rogar por ninguna creatura, nin estarán las rodillas fincadas, mas la virgen María asentada en una silla al costado de Ihesú Christo. (Madrid, Real Academia de la Historia, MS 294, fol. 178v; *Sermón, sociedad y literatura*, ed. by Cátedra, p. 613)

> [The Virgin Mary [...] and St John [...] will not dare to open their mouths to pray for any creature, nor will they be on their knees, but the Virgin Mary will be sitting on a chair next to Jesus Christ].

Significant changes appear regarding other topics, including the Western Schism. In the sermon *Erunt signa in sole et luna et stellis* (Appendix 1, no. 15), Vicent Ferrer divides Christianity into ten parts, including the three parts in which it was divided during the Schism. By comparing the reference to Benedict XIII in different versions of the sermon, we can identify subtle shifts:

Octava Italicorum, sub Bartholomeo Barensi

Nona Gallicorum, sub Petro de Candia.

Decima vero pars populi Catholici est modo yspaniorum, sub domino **nostro** Papa **vero** vicario Ihesuchristi. (Avignon, Bibliothèque Municipale, MS 610, fol. 206r; *Sermonario de Avignon*, ed. by Gimeno Blay and Mandingorra Llavata, p. 1338)

> [Eighth part, Italy, under Bartholomew of Bari.
>
> Ninth, France, under Peter of Candia.
>
> The tenth part of the Christian people is in Spain, under the **true** vicar of Jesus Christ, **our** Pope].

Octava est Italicorum, sub Bartholomeo Barensi.

Nona est Gallicorum, sub Petro de Candia.

Decima vero pars proprie catholica est | modo Hyspanorum sub Domino Papa **unico** Benedicto **vero** vicario Ihesuchristi. (Toulouse, Bibliothèque Municipale, MS 345, fol. 7va–b)

> [Eighth part, Italy, under Bartholomew of Bari.

Ninth, France, under Peter of Candia.

The tenth part of Christendom is in Spain, under Benedict, **only** Pope, **true** vicar of Jesus Christ].

Octava est Italicorum, sub Bartholomeo Barensi.

Nona eft Gallicorum, sub Petro de Candia.

Decima vero pars populi Catholici est Hispaniorum, sub domino Benedicto **nostro** vicario Iesuchristi. (Köln 1485, *Hiemales*, Dominica secunda adventus, sermo II)

[Eighth part, Italy, under Bartholomew of Bari.

Ninth, France, under Peter of Candia.

The tenth part of the Christian people is Spain, under Benedict, **our** vicar Jesus Christ].

The shift from 'vero' and 'unico' to 'nostro' fits in with the silencing of Ferrer's support for Benedict XIII during the canonization process (1455) and in the lives of Vicent Ferrer written soon after.[36]

To finish with apocalyptic references, it is worth mentioning the *Declaración de Salamanca*, in which Vicent Ferrer identifies himself as a direct envoy of God: 'E agora yo soy embiado espeçialment por este caso, para vos denunçiar e publicar la venida del Antichristo e la fin del mundo' ['Now I am especially sent in this case, to denounce to you and publish the coming of the Antichrist and the end of the world'].[37] Vicent identifies himself with the angel of the Apocalypse, the name by which he has passed into history, and claims to have performed more than three thousand miracles. The sermon does not appear in subsequent collections, and is considered nowadays apocryphal.[38]

Other Controversial Topics

Several arguments against the Jews stated by Vicent Ferrer in his sermons disappeared from the early printed editions. In the sermon *Datus est michi stimulus carnis mee*, for the *Feria tertia post sexagesimam* (Appendix 1, no. 8), the Köln edition omits several negative references to the Jews that appear in the manuscript version: 'E este dolor corporal fue sienpre nesçesario a los jodíos, que jamás nunca quisieron fazer cosa de bien sinon con mal' ['This bodily pain was always necessary to the Jews, who never wanted to do

---

36 Smoller, *The Saint and the Chopped-up Baby*, p. 135.
37 Madrid, Real Academia de la Historia, MS 294, fol. 185v; *Sermón, sociedad y literatura*, ed. by Cátedra, p. 631.
38 *Sermón, sociedad y literatura*, ed. by Cátedra, p. 166.

CONTROVERSIAL TOPICS IN THE SERMONS OF VICENT FERRER   241

anything good without pain'].[39] Something similar happens in the sermon *Redde rationem vilicationis tuae* (Appendix 1, no. 30), for the *Dominica IX post Trinitatem*, in which an argument against the coexistence of Christians and Jews in Valencia, Archivo de la Catedral, MS 279, does not appear in Madrid, Real Academia de la Historia, MS 294 or in later editions:

> Que·ls juheus e moros estiguen en apartat, no entre los christians. Ne sostengats metges infels, ne comprar d'ells vitualles e que estiguen tanquats e murats, car no havem majors enemichs. Christiana no esser dida de aquells, ne menjar ab ells. Si us envien pa, lançau-lo als cans, si us envíen vianda viva prenets-la e no morta, car diu la Scriptura Sancta contra aquest peccats *nescitis quia modicum fermentum totam massam corrumpit?* (Valencia, Archivo de la Catedral, MS 279, fol. 254r; *Sermons,* ed. by Sanchis Sivera and Schib, III (1975), 14)

> [That the Jews and Moors be apart, not among Christians. Do not uphold unfaithful doctors, nor buy food from them, and may they be locked up and enclosed, since we have no major enemies. May Christian women not be their wet nurses, nor eat with them. If they send you some bread, give it to the dogs. If they send you living meat, take it, but not dead meat, because Holy Scripture says against these sins: *Nescitis quia modicum fermentum totam massam corrumpit?*]

Another polemical topic is that of the flagellants. As it is well-known, Vicent Ferrer supported flagellation, which some members of his retinue practised regularly, to the point that Jean Gerson wrote a letter to Vicent Ferrer calling him to stop the processions with penitents promoted by the Dominican friar. Perarnau showed how Vicent Ferrer's defence of flogging, even if within limits that would not endanger the life of the penitent, in the sermon *Attendite a falsis prophetis* (Barcelona, Biblioteca de Catalunya, MS 477, fol. 70v) disappeared, together with other controversial elements, in the Avignon manuscript.[40] Ferrer also defended flogging in the sermon *Quicumque voluerit inter vos maior fieri* (Appendix 1, no. 28).

> Sexto, diu 'Ad flagellandum'. **És una preciosa cosa lo assotar de les disciplines, majorment a homeiers,** que a aquells los és pus propri escampar la sua sang [...] Ítem, és entès en la penitència que dóna lo confessor, que mudets la vida; lo confessor vos dirà: 'Aqueixa vida haveu a mudar!'; dirà: 'Com ho poré fer e què em diran?' No, a fer fa. David: 'Ego in flagellis paratus sum' (Ps. 37. 18); així en disciplines com en assots de la llengua, refrenant aquella.[41]

---

39 Madrid, Real Academia de la Historia, MS 294, fol. 71r; *Sermón, sociedad y literatura,* ed. by Cátedra, p. 383.
40 Perarnau, 'Sermones de Sant Vicent Ferrer', pp. 626–42.
41 Vicent Ferrer, *Sermons de Quaresma,* ed. by Manuel Sanchis Guarner, 2 vols (Valencia: Albatros, 1973), I, 153.

[Sixth, it says 'Ad flagellandum'. **The whipping by lashes, mainly of murderers, is a beautiful thing** because it is proper to them to spill their blood [...] It is equally understood in the penance given by the confessor, to change life; the confessor will tell you: 'That life, you have to change!'; he will say: 'How can I do it and what will they say?' David: 'Ego sum flagellis paratus sum'; Thus in disciplines as in tongue lashes, restraining the tongue].

The Köln 1485 version obviates Vicent Ferrer's favourable opinions of flagellation:

Sextum ad flagelandum. Ecce hic imposicio afflictiva penitentie ieiuniorum, cilicii vel disciplinarum. Unde penitens flagellatur truffis et obprobriis inpenitentium. Ideo sustineat patienter David: 'Ego autem in flagella paratus sum'. (Köln 1485, *Hiemales*, Feria IV post Dominica secunda quadragesima)

[Sixth, about flogging. This is a painful duty of penance, fasting, hair shirts or lashing. So the penitent is whipped because of his swindles and unforgiveable scandals. So, he should bear up patiently like David: 'I am ready for the scourge'].

Vicent Ferrer did not feel comfortable talking about some controversial topics, like predestination. In the sermon *Ambulabunt gentes in lumine tuo* (Appendix 1, no. 1) for the Sunday after the Octave of the Epiphany, the preacher ends the discussion about predestination abruptly:

Aquesta rahó lexa-la, mas fés bones obres e seràs salvat, jatsie sies prescrit, car Déus a quiscú done franch arbitri, e per sa presciència no li és tolt lo franch arbitri, si bé·s sap que tu és de tal natura que no poràs fer bones obres. (Valencia, Archivo de la Catedral, MS 276, fol. 13r; *Sermons*, ed. by Sanchis Sivera and Schib, IV (1977), 296)

[Let this argument go. Just do good deeds and you will be saved, even if you are prescribed, since God gives everyone free will, and because of his prescience nobody is deprived of free will, although he knows that you are of such a nature that you will not be able to do good works].

This digression does not appear in the Avignon manuscript nor in the Köln 1485 edition. Vicent Ferrer preached on the same subject in a more elegant way in the sermon *Ego vobis dico: facite* (Appendix 1, no. 11) about predestination, but this sermon does not appear in the Köln 1485 edition.[42]

---

42 According to Perarnau, 'Cent anys d'estudis dedicats als sermons de Vicent Ferrer', *Arxiu de Textos Catalans Antics*, 18 (1999), 9–62 (p. 30), this sermon was in Vic, Arxiu de la Ciutat, at the end of the nineteenth century, and later in an unknown private collection in Barcelona, so its location is nowadays unknown. It was published by Felipe Mateu i Llopis, 'Sobre la "traditio" de los sermones de San Vicente Ferrer: el de Valencia de 1410 acerca de la predestinación', *Boletín de la Sociedad Castellonense de Cultura*, 35 (1959), 139–53 (pp. 149–50).

CONTROVERSIAL TOPICS IN THE SERMONS OF VICENT FERRER 243

La predestinació divina no tol a nengú lo franch arbitre ni la sciència declar açò. Si un hom és predestinat aquella predestinació no tira lo franch arbitre, car ell pot fer bé o mal. Mas sab Déus que si és predestinat que no farà mal [...] car si predestinació tollia lo franch arbitre que no pogués fer mal, no auria mèrit ni demèrit, axí com les bèsties, e per açò Nostre senyor lexa la creatura en son franch arbitre.[43]

> [Divine predestination does not remove anyone's free will, nor does science declare this. If a man is predestined, that predestination does not remove free will, because he can do well or wrong. But God knows that, if he is predestined, he will not do evil [...] because if predestination removes the free will that could not hurt, there would be no merit or demerit, just like beasts, and therefore Our Lord leaves the creature in free will].

There is also a third sermon about predestination, the sermon *Quos prescivit, et predestinavit* (Appendix 1, no. 29) in which Vicent Ferrer insists that 'divina predestinatio non tollit creature liberum arbitrium' ['divine predestination does not take away man's free will']. This sermon, despite being in the Toulouse Compilation, does not appear in the Köln 1485 edition.

The last controversial topic to be dealt with is that of the Holy Kinship, a reconstruction of the family of Jesus according to which St Anne married three times and had three daughters, all of them named Mary. The stepsisters of Mary would be the mothers of the apostles, with James the Younger, Judas Tadeus, and Simon being the sons of Mary of Alpheus, and James the Elder and John the sons of Mary of Zebedeus. The story of the family of Mary appears in Vicentian sermons for the feasts of Sts Simon and Judas (Appendix 1, no. 4), and in a sermon *De praedestinatione* for the Vigil of the Feast of St Andrew (Appendix 1, no. 23). The legend appears in the sermon of Sts Simon and Judas in the Köln edition, but not in the sermon *Ipse sciebat* for the Vigil of St Andrew. Vicent Ferrer accepted this story because he trusted the visions of Colette de Corbie (1381–1447), a fervent defender of the Holy Kinship, whom he visited in 1417. This kind of story would be forbidden in the Council of Trent, but that did not affect subsequent editions of the sermons.

Conclusion

The 'manipulation' or 'edition' of Vicent Ferrer's sermons had already begun in the first manuscripts, when Vicent Ferrer was still alive and long before the printing press appeared. There seems to be a tendency to hide or soften controversial content since the first compilations. Some of these revisions may have been made or accepted by Vicent Ferrer himself. Another early

---

43 Mateu i Llopis, 'Sobre la "traditio" de los sermones de San Vicente Ferrer', pp. 149–50.

transformation to take into account is the translation of sermons originally delivered and copied in Catalan or Spanish into Latin, which made it difficult to use the sermons as pious reading for laypeople and transformed the liveliness of the oral speech and *reportationes* into a more literary text.

A textual Latin tradition was developed between the canonization of Vicent Ferrer in 1455 and the first sermons' editions in 1472, a selection of sermons that would be faithfully used in later editions. This early selection of contents explains why some contents later considered unorthodox, like the story of the Holy Kinship and other apocryphal stories condemned by the Council of Trent, appear in later editions. The most important changes in late medieval manuscripts and early modern Latin editions include the complete elimination of sermons in some manuscript compilations (Avignon, Bibliothèque Municipale, MS 610; Toulouse, Bibliothèque Municipale, MSS 345 and 346), and in the early printed Latin editions, the softening or partial elimination of contents, content displacement, and the recovering of contents and sermons previously ignored in the Toulouse Compilation. So, contrary to what is often thought, Latin modern editions do not only depend on the Toulouse Compilation, but also on other manuscripts. This point needs further research and a closer comparison between the earliest editions and the manuscripts, but it seems evident that early editions diminished, by using other manuscripts like Fribourg, Couvent des Cordeliers, MS 68, the degree of manipulation or censorship made in the Toulouse and Avignon manuscripts. Finally, the Hispanic editions included apocryphal sermons rejected in the Latin editions, like the sermon *Ecce positus est in hic ruinam*. The changes made in the Latin editions do not appear to have to do with ecclesiastical censorship. Although the appearance of the censorship of printed sermons appears as early as the 1470s and 1480s (the 1487 Bull *Contra impressores librorum reprobatorum* by Innocent VIII (1484–1492)), by then Ferrer's sermons had already been printed in Ulm, Lyon, Köln, and Strasbourg.

The context in which the textual tradition of Vicent Ferrer's printed sermons was formed was different from that of the writing of the Toulouse Compilation (begun in 1416). On the one hand, the Fall of Constantinople in 1453 and the threat of Turkish conquest of Western Christendom promoted the recovery of medieval prophetic traditions (if they had ever disappeared).[44] On the other

---

44 Cornell H. Fleischer, 'A Mediterranean Apocalypse: Prophecies of Empire in the Fifteenth and Sixteenth Centuries', *Journal of the Economic and Social History of the Orient*, 61 (2018), 18–90; Marjorie Reeves, 'Pattern and Purpose in History in the Later Medieval and Renaissance Periods', in Marjorie Reeves, *The Prophetic Sense of History in Medieval and Renaissance Europe*, Variorum Collected Studies, 660 (Aldershot: Ashgate, 1999), pp. 90–111; Marjorie Reeves, *The Influence of Prophecy in the Later Middle Ages*; David Ruderman, 'Hope against Hope: Jewish and Christian Messianic Expectations in the Late Middle Ages', in *Exile and Diaspora: Studies in the History of the Jewish People Presented to Professor Haim Beinart*, ed. by Aharon Mirsky, Avrahám Grossman, and Yosef Kaplan (Jerusalem: Ben-Zvi Institute, 1991), pp. 185–202.

hand, in the same way that Vicent Ferrer had not lost his fame, he had not lost his ability to invoke controversy either. Two issues were controversial in the mid-fifteenth century. The first was the support for Benedict XIII, on which there was a 'carefully controlled testimony elicited at canonization inquests held in Toulouse and, most particularly, in Naples'.[45] The second great topic of controversy was preaching about the imminence of the Apocalypse, including the birth of the Antichrist.[46]

Criticisms of Vicent Ferrer were not minor and even caused the rise of some opinions against the canonization process.[47] In these same years, the Valencian Pope Callixtus III commissioned Pietro Ranzano to write a Life of Vicent Ferrer, in order to appease the opinions of his detractors, quieten the controversy and seek 'to recast Vincent Ferrer primarily as a healer of the Schism and secondarily as a converter of Jews or Muslims',[48] by focusing on other aspects of Vicent's life.[49]

These facts — the rise of millenarianism linked to the Turkish conquest of Constantinople and an ambiguous overcoming of the controversies raised by Vicent Ferrer — explain a certain ambiguity in the changes that occurred in Ferrer's sermons. If there was a growing interest in millenarian themes, orthodoxy (in the incipient censorship of printed books) distrusted the prophetic excesses of Vicent Ferrer. This explains both the disappearance of sermons and the displacement and recovery of controversial content.[50]

---

45 Smoller, *The Saint and the Chopped-up Baby*, p. 135.
46 Smoller, *The Saint and the Chopped-up Baby*, pp. 131–39.
47 Smoller, *The Saint and the Chopped-up Baby*, pp. 131–32.
48 Smoller, *The Saint and the Chopped-up Baby*, p. 139.
49 Smoller, *The Saint and the Chopped-up Baby*, pp. 132–38.
50 This essay is part of the research project 'Writing Religious, Transcultural, Gendered Identities and Alterities in the Medieval and Early Modern Mediterranean' founded by Ministerio de Ciencia, Innovación y Universidades (MICIU), Agencia Estetal de Investigación (AEI), and Fondo Europeo de Desarrollo Regional (FEDER), UE–PGC2018–093472–B–C32.

246   ORIOL CATALÁN

Appendix 1: Selected Sermons

Sermons are listed alphabetically by *thema*. Every sermon includes: the number in Perarnau's index;[51] *thema*; manuscript versions with their opening folios; early editions (Köln 1485 and/or Valencia 1566), with a note where no early editions occur; editions after 1900.

1. 23; *Ambulabunt gentes in lumine tuo*; Avignon, Bibliothèque Municipale, MS 610, fol. 263r; Città del Vaticano, Biblioteca Apostolica Vaticana, MS Vat. Lat. 4375, fol. 25d; Città del Vaticano, Biblioteca Apostolica Vaticana, MS Vat. Lat. 7730, fol. 24r; Perugia, Convento di san Domenico, MS 477, fol. 15v; Valencia, Archivo de la Catedral, MS 276, fol. 13r; Köln 1485, *Hiemales*, In epiphania domini, sermo sextus; *Sermons*, ed. by Sanchis Sivera and Schib, IV (1977), 296; *Sermonario de Avignon*, ed. by Gimeno Blay and Mandingorra Llavata, p. 1626

2. 78; *Benedictus qui venit in nomine Domini*; Città del Vaticano, Biblioteca Apostolica Vaticana, MS Vat. Lat. 7730, fol. 1r; Valencia, Colegio del Corpus Christi (or del Patriarca), s.n., fol. 115v; no early printed editions; *Sermons*, ed. by Sanchis Sivera and Schib, VI (1988), 269–76

3. 86; *Bonum facientes*; Madrid, Real Academia de la Historia, MS 294, fol. 165v; no early printed editions; *Sermón, sociedad y literatura*, ed. by Cátedra, p. 589

4. 114; *Conformes fieri ymaginis filii dei*; Ayora, Archivo parroquial, fol. 234v; Toulouse, Bibliothèque Municipale, MS 346, fol. 159vb; Valencia, Archivo de la Catedral, MS 278, fol. 205r; Köln 1485, *De sanctis*, De sancto Simone et Iuda; *Sermons*, ed. by Sanchis Sivera and Schib, IV (1977), 169–75, *Colección de sermones de Cuaresma y otros según el manuscrito de Ayora*, ed. by Robles, p. 429

5. 122; *Creatura liberabitur a servitute corruptionis*; Madrid, Real Academia de la Historia, MS 294, fol. 143v; no early printed editions; *Sermón, sociedad y literatura*, ed. by Cátedra, p. 535

6. 125; *Crediderunt in eum discipuli eius*; Città del Vaticano, Biblioteca Apostolica Vaticana, MS Vat. Lat. 4375, fol. 27r; Città del Vaticano, Biblioteca Apostolica Vaticana, MS Vat. Lat. 7730, fol. 25v; Perugia, Convento di san Domenico, MS 477, fol. 16v; Valencia, Archivo de la Catedral, MS 276, fol. 19v; Valencia, Colegio del Corpus Christi (or del Patriarca), s.n., fol. 167v; Köln 1485, *Hiemales*, Dominica I post octavas epiphanie, sermo secundo; *Sermons*, ed. by Sanchis Sivera and Schib, V (1984), 7; *Sermonario de Perugia*, ed. by Gimeno Blay and Mandingorra Llavata, p. 140; *Sermonario de San Vicente Ferrer del Real Seminario del Corpus Christi de Valencia*, ed. by Gimeno Blay and Mandingorra Llavata, p. 793

---

51 Josep Perarnau, 'Aportació a un inventari de sermons'.

7. 132; *Cum Christo discipuli eius et turba*; Madrid, Real Academia de la Historia, MS 294, fol. 175r; no early printed editions; *Sermón, sociedad y literatura*, ed. by Cátedra, p. 609

8. 143; *Datus est michi stimulus carnis mee*; Ayora, Archivo parroquial, Sermonario de San Vicente Ferrer, fol. 49v; Città del Vaticano, Biblioteca Apostolica Vaticana, MS Vat. Lat. 4375, fol. 33r; Città del Vaticano, Biblioteca Apostolica Vaticana, MS Vat. Lat. 7730, fol. 29v; Madrid, Real Academia de la Historia, MS 294, fol. 69r; Perugia, Convento di san Domenico, MS 477, fol. 19r; Toulouse, Bibliothèque Municipale, MS 345, fol. 68rb; Köln 1485, *Hiemales*, Dominica in sexagesima, sermo tertius; *Sermón, sociedad y literatura*, ed. by Cátedra, p. 379; *Colección de sermones de Cuaresma y otros según el manuscrito de Ayora*, ed. by Robles, p. 127

9. 226; *Ecce positus est hic in ruinam*; Città del Vaticano, Biblioteca Apostolica Vaticana, MS Vat. Lat. 7071, fol. 32c; Madrid, Real Academia de la Historia, MS 294, fol. 186v; Valencia 1566; *Sermón, sociedad y literatura*, ed. by Cátedra, p. 635

10. 227; *Ecce positus est hic in ruinam*; Valencia, Archivo de la Catedral, MS 277, fol. 263r; no early printed editions; *Sermons*, ed. by Sanchis Sivera and Schib, VI (1988), 229–35

11. 263; *Ego vobis dico: facite*; no manuscript versions known; no early printed editions; Felipe Mateu i Llopis, 'Sobre la "traditio" de los sermones de San Vicente Ferrer: el de Valencia de 1410 acerca de la predestinación', pp. 149–50

12. 282; *Erunt signa in sole et luna et stellis*; Città del Vaticano, Biblioteca Apostolica Vaticana, MS Vat. Lat. 4375, fol. 5r; Città del Vaticano, Biblioteca Apostolica Vaticana, MS Vat. Lat. 7730, fol. 11v; Fribourg, Couvent des Cordeliers, MS 68, fol. 54r; Perugia, Convento di san Domenico, MS 477, fol. 7v; Valencia, Colegio del Corpus Christi (or del Patriarca), s.n., fol. 104r; Köln 1485, *Hiemales*, Dominica secunda adventus, sermo primo; *Sermonario de Perugia*, ed. by Gimeno Gimeno Blay and Mandingorra Llavata, p. 80; *Sermonario de San Vicente Ferrer del Real Seminario del Corpus Christi de Valencia*, ed. by Gimeno Blay and Mandingorra Llavata, p. 501

13. 283; *Erunt signa in sole et luna et stellis*; Fribourg, Couvent des Cordeliers, MS 68, fol. 62r; Köln 1485, *Hiemales*, Dominica secunda adventus, sermo tertius; no twentieth-century editions

14. 285; *Erunt signa in sole et luna et stellis*; Fribourg, Couvent des Cordeliers, MS 68, fol. 67v; Köln 1485, *Hiemales*, Dominica secunda Adventus, sermo quartus; no twentieth-century century editions

15. 286; *Erunt signa in sole et luna et stellis*; Avignon, Bibliothèque Municipale, MS 610, fol. 203r; Fribourg, Couvent des Cordeliers, MS 68, fol. 57r; Toulouse, Bibliothèque Municipale, MS 345, fol. 5va; Köln 1485, *Hiemales*, Dominica secunda adventus, sermo secundo; *Sermonario de Avignon*, ed. by Gimeno Blay and Mandingorra Llavata, p. 1324

16. 351; *Flagellum de funiculis*; Fribourg, Couvent des Cordeliers, MS 62, fol. 51r; no early printed editions; Brettle, *San Vicente Ferrer und sein literarischer Nachlass*, p. 177

17. 355; *Frater, sine eiciam festucam de oculo tuo*; Valencia, Colegio del Corpus Christi (or del Patriarca), s.n., fol. 74r; no early printed editions; *Sermonario de San Vicente Ferrer del Real Seminario del Corpus Christi de Valencia*, ed. by Gimeno Blay and Mandingorra Llavata, p. 368

18. 356; *Frater, sine eiciam festucam de oculo tuo*; Madrid, Real Academia de la Historia, MS 294, fol. 148r; no early printed editions; *Sermón, sociedad y literatura*, ed. by Cátedra, p. 547

19. 405; *Hodie est et cras in clibanum mittitur*; Madrid, Real Academia de la Historia, MS 294, fol. 161r; no early printed editions; *Sermón, sociedad y literatura*, ed. by Cátedra, p. 579

20. 426; *Impletum est tempus pariendi*; Barcelona, Biblioteca de Catalunya, MS 477, fol. 41r; no early printed editions; Perarnau, 'Compilació', p. 253

21. 446; *In plenitude sanctorum*; Madrid, Real Academia de la Historia, MS 294, fol. 170v; no early printed editions; *Sermón, sociedad y literatura*, ed. by Cátedra, p. 599

22. 449; *In tempore messis*; Città del Vaticano, Biblioteca Apostolica Vaticana, MS Vat. Lat. 4375, fol. 29r; Perugia, Convento di san Domenico, MS 477, fol. 67v; Köln 1485, *Hiemales*, Dominica quarta post octavas epiphanie; *Sermonario de Perugia*, ed. by Gimeno Gimeno Blay and Mandingorra Llavata, p. 483

23. 467; *Ipse sciebat quid esse facturus*; Valencia, Archivo de la Catedral, MS 277, fol. 95v; Valencia, Colegio del Corpus Christi (or del Patriarca), s.n., fol. 95v; *Sermonario de San Vicente Ferrer del Real Seminario del Corpus Christi de Valencia*, ed. by Gimeno Blay and Mandingorra Llavata, *Sermons*, ed. by Sanchis Sivera and Schib, VI (1988), 169–75

24. 480; *Latitudo et longitudo*; Madrid, Real Academia de la Historia, MS 294, fol. 180r; no early printed editions; *Sermón, sociedad y literatura*, ed. by Cátedra, p. 621

25. 553; *Nescitis, qua hora filias hominis venturas est*; Fribourg, Couvent des Cordeliers, MS 62, fol. 55v; no early printed editions; Brettle, *San Vicente Ferrer und sein literarischer Nachlass*, p. 184

26. 562; *Nolite secundum faciem iudicare, sed iustum iudicium iudicate*; Fribourg, Couvent des Cordeliers, MS 62, fol. 53r; no early printed editions; Brettle, *San Vicente Ferrer und sein literarischer Nachlass*, pp. 181–82

27. 680; *Quaedam mulier de turba dixit*; Valencia, Colegio del Corpus Christi (or del Patriarca), s.n., fol. 73v; Valencia 1566; Perarnau, 'Sobre el manuscrit de València', p. 433; *Sermonario de San Vicente Ferrer del Real Seminario del Corpus Christi de Valencia*, ed. by Gimeno Blay and Mandingorra Llavata, p. 222

28. 707; *Quicumque voluerit inter vos maior fieri; sit vester minister*; Città del Vaticano, Biblioteca Apostolica Vaticana, MS Vat. Lat. 4375, fol. 96v,

Città del Vaticano, Biblioteca Apostolica Vaticana, MS Vat. Lat. 7609, fols 23r–24v; Valencia, Archivo de la Catedral, MS 273, fols 151–156; Köln 1485, *Hiemales*, Feria quarta post dominicam secundam quadragesimam, sermo primus; Vicent Ferrer, *Sermons de Quaresma*, ed. by Manuel Sanchis Guarner, 2 vols (Valencia: Albatros, 1973), p. 153

29. 726; *Quos praescivit, et praedestinavit*; Barcelona, Biblioteca de Catalunya, MS 477, fol. 45r; Toulouse, Bibliothèque Municipale, MS 346, fol. 209r; no early printed editions; Perarnau, Josep, 'La compilació de sermons', 260–66

30. 730; *Redde rationem vilicationis tuae*; Città del Vaticano, Biblioteca Apostolica Vaticana, MS Vat. Lat. 7730, fol. 77r; Madrid, Real Academia de la Historia, MS 294, fols 126v–130v; Perugia, Convento di san Domenico, MS 477, fol. 49r; Toulouse, Bibliothèque Municipale, MS 345, fol. 192v; Valencia, Archivo de la Catedral, MS 279, fols 254r–256v; Köln 1485, *Aestivales*, Dominica nona post trinitatem, sermo secundus; *Sermón, sociedad y literatura*, ed. by Cátedra, p. 499; *Sermons*, ed. by Sanchis Sivera and Schib, III (1975), 14

31. 739; *Reminiscamini quia ego dixi vobis*; Madrid, Real Academia de la Historia, MS 294, fol. 154r; Valencia, Colegio del Corpus Christi (or del Patriarca), s.n., fol. 74r; no early printed editions; *Sermón, sociedad y literatura*, ed. by Cátedra, p. 561; *Sermonario de San Vicente Ferrer del Real Seminario del Corpus Christi de Valencia*, ed. by Gimeno Gimeno Blay and Mandingorra Llavata, p. 370

32. 749; *Respicite et levate capita vestra*; Città del Vaticano, Biblioteca Apostolica Vaticana, MS Vat. Lat. 1258, fol. 119ra; Città del Vaticano, Biblioteca Apostolica Vaticana, MS Vat. Lat. 4375, fol. 121v; Città del Vaticano, Biblioteca Apostolica Vaticana, MS Vat. Lat. 7730, fol. 14v; Fribourg, Couvent des Cordeliers, MS 68, fol. 72r; Perugia, Convento di san Domenico, MS 477, fol. 64r; Köln 1485, *Hiemales*, Dominica secunda adventus, sermo quintus; *Sermonario de Perugia*, ed. by Gimeno Blay and Mandingorra Llavata, p. 463

33. 891; *Visitavit plebem suam*; Fribourg, Couvent des Cordeliers, MS 62, fol. 61r; no early printed editions; Brettle, *San Vicente Ferrer und sein literarischer Nachlass*, p. 189

34. 907; *Vos estis sal terrae*; Barcelona, Biblioteca de Catalunya, MS 477, fol. 61r; Città del Vaticano, Biblioteca Apostolica Vaticana, MS Vat. Lat. 4375, fol. 99r; Toulouse, Bibliothèque Municipale, MS 346, fol. 129rb; Valencia, Archivo de la Catedral, MS 279, fol. 260r; Valencia, Colegio del Corpus Christi (or del Patriarca), s.n., fol. 91r; Köln 1485, *De sanctis*, In festo sancti Dominici; *Sermons*, ed. by Sanchis Sivera and Schib, III (1975), 21–26; *Sermonario de San Vicente Ferrer del Real Seminario del Corpus Christi de Valencia*, ed. by Gimeno Blay and Mandingorra Llavata, p. 447; Perarnau, 'Compilació', p. 267

35. Not listed by Perarnau; 'Declaración de Salamanca'; Madrid, Real Academia de la Historia, MS 294, fol. 185v; no early printed editions; *Sermón, sociedad y literatura*, ed. by Cátedra, p. 631

Appendix 2: List of Manuscripts and Early Printed Editions

Manuscripts

Avignon, Bibliothèque Municipale, MS 610 (Latin)
Ayora, Archivo parroquial. Sermonario de San Vicente Ferrer (Latin)
Barcelona, Biblioteca de Catalunya, MS 476 (Latin)
Barcelona, Biblioteca de Catalunya, MS 477 (Latin)
Città del Vaticano, Biblioteca Apostolica Vaticana, MS Vat. Lat. 1258 (Latin)
Città del Vaticano, Biblioteca Apostolica Vaticana, MS Vat. Lat. 4375 (Latin)
Città del Vaticano, Biblioteca Apostolica Vaticana, MS Vat. Lat. 7071 (Latin)
Città del Vaticano, Biblioteca Apostolica Vaticana, MS Vat. Lat. 7609 (Latin)
Città del Vaticano, Biblioteca Apostolica Vaticana, MS Vat. Lat. 7730 (Latin)
Clermont-Ferrand, Bibliothèque Municipale, MS 45 (Latin)
Fribourg, Couvent des Cordeliers, MS 62 (Latin)
Fribourg, Couvent des Cordeliers, MS 68 (Latin)
Ljubljiana, Drzavna (Licejska) Knjiznica Slovenia, MS 106.23 (Latin)
Madrid, Biblioteca Nacional, MS 4283 (Spanish)
Madrid, Real Academia de la Historia, MS 294 (Spanish)
Madrid, Real Biblioteca, MS II/413 (Latin)
Oviedo, Biblioteca Universitaria, MS 444 (Spanish)
Oxford, Bodleian Library, MS Douce 162 (Catalan)
Perugia, Convento di san Domenico, MS 477 (Latin)
San Lorenzo del Escorial, Biblioteca del monasterio, MS M.II.6 (Spanish)
Sevilla, Biblioteca Capitular y Colombina, MS 56–5–31 (Latin)
Sevilla, Biblioteca Capitular y Colombina, MS 56–5–32 (Latin)
Toulouse, Bibliothèque Municipale, MS 345 (Latin)
Toulouse, Bibliothèque Municipale, MS 346 (Latin)
Valencia, Archivo de la Catedral, MS 168 (Latin)
Valencia, Archivo de la Catedral, MS 273 (Catalan)
Valencia, Archivo de la Catedral, MS 274 (Latin)
Valencia, Archivo de la Catedral, MS 276 (Catalan)
Valencia, Archivo de la Catedral, MS 277 (Catalan)
Valencia, Archivo de la Catedral, MS 278 (Catalan)
Valencia, Archivo de la Catedral, MS 279 (Catalan)
Valencia, Colegio del Corpus Christi (or del Patriarca), s.n. (Latin)

Early Printed Latin Editions

This list extends the one published by Brettle, *San Vicente Ferrer und sein literarischer Nachlass*, pp. 78–79, with references found in the Universal Short Title Catalogue, the Incunabula Short Title Catalogue and the Gesamtkatalog der Wiegendrucke. Printers included when known.

1475, Ulm: *Sermones de tempore et de sanctis*

1477, Lyon: *Sermones sancti Vincentii*

1482, Köln (Johann Koelhoff): *Sermones Quadragesimales*

1484, Köln: *Sermones per totum annum*

1485, Strasbourg: *Sermones de tempore*

1485, Köln (Heinrich Quentell): *Sermones de tempore et de sanctis*

1487, Köln (Heinrich Quentell): *Sermones de tempore et de sanctis*

1488, Basel (Nicolaus Kesler): *Sermones de tempore*

1488, Milano (Uldericus Scinzenzeler): *Sermones de sanctis*

1488–1489, Strasbourg (Printer of the 1483 Jordanus von Quedlinburg [= Georg Husner]): *Sermones de tempore et de sanctis*

1490, Venezia: *Sermones de tempore et de sanctis*

1490–1491, Lyon (Jean Trechsel): *Sermones de tempore et de sanctis*

1492, Nürnberg (Anton Koberger): *Sermones de tempore et de sanctis*

1493, Lyon (Jean Trechsel): *Sermones de tempore et de sanctis*

1493–1494, Strasbourg (Printer of the 1483 Jordanus von Quedlinburg [= Georg Husner]): *Sermones de tempore et de sanctis*

1496, Venezia (Jacobus Pentius): *Sermones de tempore et de sanctis*

1497, Lyon (Jean de Vingle): *Sermones de tempore et de sanctis*

1497, Lyon (Mathias Huss): *Sermones de tempore et de sanctis*

1498, Strasbourg: *Sermones*

1499, Lyon (Johannes Clein): *Sermones de tempore et de sanctis*

After 1500, Lyon (Simon Berthier): *Sermones de sanctis*

1503, Strasbourg: *Sermones de sanctis*

1505, Lyon: *Sermones de tempore et de sanctis*

1509, Lyon: *Sermones de sanctis*

1513, Lyon (Jean Moylin de Cambrai): *Sermones aestivales*

1516, Lyon: *Sermones hiemales, aestivales, de sanctis*

1518, Lyon: *Sermones de tempore et de sanctis*

1521, Lyon: *Sermones*

1523, Lyon: *Aurei Sermones fructuosissimi et omni tempore praedicabiles*

1525, Lyon: *Sermones aestivales de tempore [...] Sermonum pars tertia, quae de sanctis appeliari solet*

1526, Lyon: *Sermones*

1527–1528, Lyon: *Sermones de tempore*

1529, Lyon: *Sermones*

1530, Lyon: *Sermones*

1539, Lyon: *Sermones hiemales, aestivales, de sanctis*

1550, Lyon: *Sermones de sanctis*

1558, Lyon: *Sermones hiemales*

1570, Antwerpen (Philippus Nutius): *Sermones de tempore et de sanctis*

1572, Venezia (Damianum Diaz): *Sermones aestivales*

1572–1573, Antwerpen (Daniel Vervliet in aed. vid. & haer. Joannes Steelsius): *Sermones de tempore et de sanctis*

1573, Venezia (Bartolomeo Rubini): *Sermones de tempore et de sanctis*

1573, Venezia (Melchiorre Sessa): *Sermones de tempore et de sanctis*

1583, Venezia (Melchiorre Sessa): *Sermones aestivales*

1588, Lyon (Jacques Giunta): *Sermones aestivales*

1615, Mainz: *Sermones de tempore et de sanctis*

1675, Köln: *Sermones de Rosario*

1693–1694, Valencia: *Opera omnia*

1729, Augsburg: *Sermones sancti Vincentii*

Editions of *De fine mundi* (*Ecce est positus hic in ruinam*)

1475, Treviso (Gerardus de Lisa, de Flandria)

1477, Treviso (Hermannus Liechtenstein)

1479, Germany? (Printer of Pseudo-Ferrerius)

1481, Nürnberg (Conrad Zeninger)

1483, Nürnberg (Fratres Ordinis Eremitarum S. Augustini)

c. 1485, Speyer (Johann & Conrad Hist)

1486, Augsburg (Anton Sorg)

1503, Augsburg? (Johann Froschauer)

c. 1505, Augsburg (Johann Froschauer)

Early Modern Hispanic Editions

This list extends the one published by Toro Pascua, 'Las versiones castellanas', 1503, with references found in the Universal Short Title Catalogue.

1550, Valencia (printer unknown)

1561, Toledo (Miguel Ferrer)

1563, Valencia (Juan Mey)

1563, Valencia (Juan Navarro)

1566, Valencia (Juan Navarro)

1567, Valencia (Juan Navarro)

1569, Medina del Campo (printer unknown)

1572, Valladolid (Diego Fernández de Córdoba)

1573, Valencia (Juan Navarro)

1574, Toledo (Francisco de Guzmán)

1576, Toledo (Francisco de Guzmán)

1577, Burgos (Felipe de Junta)

1578, Valencia (Juan Navarro)

1583, Zaragoza (Lorenzo y Diego Robles)

1588, Alcalá de Henares (Sebastián Martínez)

1588, Sevilla (Alonso de la Barrera)

1605, Valencia (Alvaro Franco)

1612, Sevilla (Matías Clavijo)

1621, Sevilla (Matías Clavijo)

Bibliography

Primary Sources

Hodel, Bernard, 'Sermons de s. Vincent', *Mémoire Dominicaine* 2 (1993), 149–92

Mateu i Llopis, Felipe, 'Sobre la "traditio" de los sermones de San Vicente Ferrer: el de Valencia de 1410 acerca de la predestinación', *Boletín de la Sociedad Castellonense de Cultura*, 35 (1959), 139–53

Perarnau, Josep, 'La compilació de sermons de Sant Vicent Ferrer de Barcelona, Biblioteca de Catalunya, Ms. 477', *Arxiu de Textos Catalans Antics*, 4 (1985), 213–402

Vicent Ferrer, *Colección de sermones de Cuaresma y otros según el manuscrito de Ayora*, ed. by Adolfo Robles Sierra (Valencia: Ayuntamiento de Valencia, 1995)

Vicent Ferrer, *Sermón, sociedad y literatura en la Edad Media: San Vicente Ferrer en Castilla (1411–1412). Estudio bibliografico, literario y edicion de los textos ineditos*, ed. by Pedro Cátedra (Salamanca: Junta de Castilla y León de Cultura y Turismo, 1994)

Vicent Ferrer, *Sermonario de Avignon (Avignon, Bibliothèque Municipale ms 610)*, ed. by Francisco M. Gimeno Blay and María Luz Mandingorra Llavata (Valencia: Universitat de València, 2019)

Vicent Ferrer, *Sermonario de Perugia (Convento dei do menicani, ms. 477)*, ed. by Francisco M. Gimeno Blay and María Luz Mandingorra Llavata, and trans. by Daniel Gozalbo Gimeno (Valencia: Ayuntamiento de Valencia, 2006)

Vicent Ferrer, *Sermonario de San Vicente Ferrer del Real Seminario del Corpus Christi de Valencia*, ed. by Francisco M. Gimeno Blay and María Luz Mandingorra Llavata (Valencia: Ayuntamiento de Valencia, 2002)

Vicent Ferrer, *Sermones de cuaresma en Suiza, 1404 (Couvent des Cordeliers, ms. 62)*, ed. by Francisco M. Gimeno Blay and María Luz Mandingorra Llavata (Valencia: Ayuntamiento de Valencia, 2009)

Vicent Ferrer, *Sermones de San Vicente Ferrer, en los cuales trata de la venida del Anticristo y Juicio final* (Valencia: Juan Navarro, 1566)

Vicent Ferrer, *Sermons*, ed. by Josep Sanchis Sivera and Gret Schib, Els nostres clàssics, col·lecció B, 3, 5, 6–9, 6 vols (Barcelona: Barcino, 1932–1988)

Vicent Ferrer, *Sermons de Quaresma*, ed. by Manuel Sanchis Guarner, 2 vols (Valencia: Albatros, 1973)

Secondary Studies

Brettle, Segismund, *San Vicente Ferrer und sein literarischer Nachlass* (Münster in Westfalen: Aschendorffschen Verlagsbuchhandlung, 1924)

Cátedra, Pedro, 'La predicación castellana de San Vicente Ferrer', *Butlletí de la Reial Acadèmia de Bones Lletres de Barcelona*, 39 (1984), 235–309

Daileader, Philip, *Saint Vincent Ferrer, His World and Life: Religion and Society in Late Medieval Europe*, The New Middle Ages (New York: Palgrave Macmillan, 2016)

Fages, Pierre-Henry, *Notes et documents de l'histoire de Saint Vincent Ferrier* (Leuven: Uystpruyst, 1905)

Fleischer, Cornell H., 'A Mediterranean Apocalypse: Prophecies of Empire in the Fifteenth and Sixteenth Centuries', *Journal of the Economic and Social History of the Orient*, 61 (2018), 18–90

Gimeno Blay, Francisco, 'Modelos de transmisión textual de los sermones de San Vicente Ferrer: la tradición manuscrita', *Anuario de Estudios Medievales*, 49 (2019), pp. 137–69

Godinas, Laurette, 'Historia de una metamorfosis: del manuscrito al impreso en la tradición de los sermones de San Vicente Ferrer', *Boletín del Instituto de Investigaciones Bibliográficas*, 12 (2007), 13–32

Guadalajara Medina, José, 'La edad del Anticristo y el año del fin del mundo, según fray Vicente Ferrer', in *Pensamiento medieval hispano: homenaje a Horacio-Santiago Otero*, ed. by José María Soto Rábanos (Madrid: Consejo Superior de Investigaciones Científicas, 1998), 321–42

Milhou, Alain, 'La Chauve-souris, le nouveau David et le roi caché (trois images de l'empereur des derniers temps dans le monde ibérique: XIIIe–XVIIe s.', *Mélanges de la Casa de Velázquez*, 18 (1982), 61–78

Perarnau, Josep, 'Aportació a un inventari de sermons de sant Vicenç Ferrer: temes bíblics, títols i divisions esquemàtiques', *Arxiu de Textos Catalans Antics*, 18 (1999), 479–811

Perarnau, Josep, 'Cent anys d'estudis dedicats als sermons de Vicent Ferrer', *Arxiu de Textos Catalans Antics*, 18 (1999), 9–62

Perarnau, Josep, 'Els manuscrits d'esquemes i de notes de sermons de sant Vicent Ferrer', *Arxiu de Textos Catalans antics*, 18 (1999), 158–398

Perarnau, Josep, 'Les primeres "reportationes" de sermons de St Vicent Ferrer: les de Friederich von Amberg, Fribourg, Cordeliers, ms. 62', *Arxiu de Textos Catalans Antics*, 18 (1999), 63–155

Perarnau, Josep, 'Sermones de sant Vicent Ferrer en los manuscritos de Barcelona, Biblioteca de Catalunya, 477 y Avignon, Musée Calvet, 610', *Escritos del Vedat*, 4 (1974), 611–46

Perarnau, Josep, 'Sobre el manuscrit de València, Col.legi del Patriarca, amb sermons de Sant Vicent Ferrer', *Arxiu de Textos Catalans Antics*, 18 (1999), 399–453

Reeves, Marjorie, *The Influence of Prophecy in the Later Middle Ages: A Study in Joachinism* (Oxford: Clarendon Press, 1969)

Reeves, Marjorie, 'Pattern and Purpose in History in the Later Medieval and Renaissance Periods', in Marjorie Reeves, *The Prophetic Sense of History in Medieval and Renaissance Europe*, Variorum Collected Studies, 660 (Aldershot: Ashgate, 1999), pp. 90–111

Ruderman, David, 'Hope against Hope: Jewish and Christian Messianic Expectations in the Late Middle Ages', in *Exile and Diaspora: Studies in the History of the Jewish People Presented to Professor Haim Beinart, ed. by* Aharon Mirsky, Avrahám Grossman, and Yosef Kaplan (Jerusalem: Ben-Zvi Institute, 1991), pp. 185–202

Smoller, Laura Ackerman, *The Saint and the Chopped-Up Baby: The Cult of Vincent Ferrer in Medieval and Early Modern Europe* (Ithaca: Cornell University Press, 2013)

Toldrà i Vilardell, Albert, 'Sant Vicent contra el pintor gòtic: sobre el "triangle" de l'expressió medieval', *Afers*, 41 (2002), 37–55

Toro Pascua, María Isabel, 'Imagen y función del Anticristo en algunos textos castellanos del siglo xv', *Via Spiritus*, 6 (1999), 27–63

Toro Pascua, María Isabel, 'Literatura popular religiosa en el siglo xvi: los sermones impresos de Vicente Ferrer', in *Studia aurea: actas del iii Congreso de la AISO (Toulouse, 1993)*, ed. by Ignacio Arellano Ayuso, Carmen Pinillos Salvador, Marc Vitse, and Frédéric Serralta, 3 vols (Pamplona: Grupo de Investigación Siglo de Oro, Universidad de Navarra, 1996), iii, 521–30

Toro Pascua, María Isabel, 'Milenarismo y profecía en el siglo xv: la tradición del libro de Unay en la Península Ibérica', *Península: Revista de Estudios Ibéricos* (2003), 29–37

Toro Pascua, María Isabel, 'Las versiones castellanas del sermón Ecce positus est hic in ruinam, atribuido a San Vicente Ferrer', in *Actas del vi congreso internacional de la asociación hispánica de literatura medieval (Alcalá de Henares, 12–16 de septiembre de 1995)*, ed. by José Manuel Lucía Megías, 2 vols (Alcalá de Henares: Universidad de Alcalá, 1997), ii, 1501–11

Vidal i Micó, Francisco, *Vida del valenciano apóstol de la Europa San Vicente Ferrer: con reflexiones sobre su doctrina* (Valencia: Juan Mariana, 1857)

SOPHIE DELMAS

From Nicolas de Biard's *Summa de abstinentia* to the Printed *Dictionarius pauperum*

A Pastoral Compendium for Preachers

The genre of *distinctiones* appeared at the end of the twelfth century. According to Marie-Dominique Chenu such *distinctiones* form 'des espèces de dictionnaires des sens multiples pour chaque mot inscrit dans les récits bibliques'.[1] They correspond to diagrams based on a network of quotations from Scripture and offer basic knowledge concerning the good behaviour of Christians.[2] From the thirteenth century onwards *distinctiones* were enriched by patristic quotations, examples, and *similitudines*. In the fourteenth century the collections of *distinctiones* used by preachers were numerous and widely distributed. The Franciscan Arnaud Royard (d. 1330), *lector* at the convent of Toulouse and later archbishop of Salerno, wrote a prologue for his own collection of *distinctiones*, entitled *Distinctiones super sacram scripturam*, which was dedicated to Robert d'Anjou (1277–1343). Here, he complained that, in his time, there were too many such intellectual tools. The *distinctiones* used in sermons for the people and for the clergy were so numerous as to diminish their value and their quality:

> Quemadmodum, iuxta vulgare proverbium, illud quod est vile facit raritas preciosum, si e contra, iuxta Scripture testimonium, illud qui est preciosum copia facit vile. Temporibus nempe Salomonis tanta fuit argenti

---

1 Marie-Dominique Chenu, 'La Décadence de l'allégorisation; un témoin, Garnier de Rochefort', in *L'Homme devant Dieu: mélanges offert au P. Henri de Lubac*, 3 vols (Paris: Aubier, 1963–1964), II (1964), 129–35 (p. 130), cited by Louis Jacques Bataillon, 'Les Instruments de travail des prédicateurs au XIIIe siècle', in *Culture et travail intellectuel dans l'occident médiéval: bilan des 'Colloques humanisme médiéval' [1960–1980] fondés par le R. P. Hubert, O. P.*, ed. by Geneviève Hasenohr and Jean Longère (Paris: Editions du CNRS, 1981), pp. 197–209 (p. 200).

2 Richard H. Rouse and Mary A. Rouse, 'Biblical Distinctiones in the Thirteenth Century', *Archives d'histoire doctrinale et littéraire du moyen âge*, 41 (1974), 27–37. Gilbert Dahan, *L'Exégèse chrétienne de la Bible en Occident médiéval, XII–XIVe siècle* (Paris: Cerf 1999), pp. 134–38.

Sophie Delmas (delmasophie@gmail.com) is an Associate Member in Medieval History of the Centre National de la Recherche Scientifique.

Circulating the Word of God in Medieval and Early Modern Europe: Catholic Preaching and Preachers across Manuscript and Print (c. 1450 to c. 1550), ed. by Veronica O'Mara and Patricia Stoop, SERMO 17, (Turnhout: Brepols, 2022), pp. 257–277   BREPOLS ❧ PUBLISHERS   10.1484/M.SERMO-EB.5.130458

copia quid nullius precii putabatur. Sed revera, mi domine, tante est hodie distinctionum copia quibus in sermonibus utuntur ad populum et ad clerum quod merito possunt reddi viles in conspectu regie maiestatis maxime pensata vestra vivacitate ingenii et in scriptis sacris experiencia lectionis.[3]

> [So, according to a vernacular proverb, what is vile, scarcity makes it precious; conversely, according to the testimony of Scripture, abundance makes what is precious vile. Indeed, in the time of Solomon, there was such an abundance of silver that it was considered worthless. But in truth, my lord, there is now such an abundance of *distinctiones* being used in the sermons to the people and the clergy that they may rightly be considered worthless in the eyes of your royal majesty, judging by the vivacity of your intelligence and your knowledge of the reading of the sacred texts].

Arnaud Royard was one of the last figures to compose a collection of *distinctiones*. From the fourteenth century onwards, few such collections appeared: rather it was the earlier medieval collections that circulated in manuscript copies and especially in printed editions. Four collections of *distinctiones*, dating from the thirteenth century, were extensively distributed in the later Middle Ages. They were among the most widely read and used Latin texts during this period, with a circulation of well over forty copies.[4] These include the *distinctiones* of the Franciscan Maurice de Provins (between 1248 and 1274), the Dominicans Nicolas de Gorran (between 1272 and 1295), and Nicolas de Biard (between 1272 and 1288).[5]

At the end of the thirteenth century Nicolas de Biard left three works that were diffused by university stationers: a collection of biblical *Distinctiones*, the *Sermones de tempore et de sanctis*, and the *Summa de abstinentia*.[6] This last collection was far more successful than works by any of his contemporaries; this is proven by the fact that at least 184 manuscripts have been preserved.[7]

---

3 Text quoted by Charles-Victor Langlois, 'Arnaud Roiard', in *Histoire littéraire de France* (Paris: A. Colin, 1733–1981), XXXV (1921), 465–66; Brendan Cassidy, 'An Image of King Robert of Naples in a Franco-Italian Manuscript in Dublin', *The Burlington Magazine*, 148 (2006), 31–33.

4 This is the threshold chosen by the coordinators of the FAMA-project of the Institut de Recherche et d'Histoire des Textes, Paris, which aims to catalogue particularly popular medieval works; see http://fama.irht.cnrs.fr/fr/more [accessed 3 May 2021].

5 On the *Distinctiones* of Nicolas de Biard, see Sophie Delmas, 'La Summa de abstinentia attribuée à Nicolas de Biard: circulation et réception', in *Entre stabilité et itinérance: livres et culture des ordres mendiants XIIIe–XVe siècle*, ed. by Nicole Bériou, Martin Morard, and Donatella Nebbiai Dalla Guarda, Bibliologia, 37 (Turnhout: Brepols, 2014), pp. 303–27. On the *Distinctiones* of Nicolas de Gorran, see Silvia Serventi, 'Did Giordano da Pisa Use the *Distinctiones* of Nicolas de Gorran?', in *Constructing the Medieval Sermon*, ed. by Roger Andersson, Sermo: Studies on Patristic, Medieval and Reformation Sermons and Preaching, 6 (Turnhout: Brepols, 2007), pp. 83–116.

6 Antonio Marson Franchini (Oxford University) is pursuing a doctoral degree with the aim of studying and editing the *de festis* collection of Nicolas de Biard.

7 For the manuscripts of the *Summa de absentia*, see Institut de recherche et d'histoire des

FROM *SUMMA DE ABSTINENTIA* TO THE *DICTIONARIUS PAUPERUM*   259

By way of comparison: his *Distinctiones* exist in at least forty-five manuscripts and the *Distinctiones* of Maurice de Provins in at least forty manuscripts, while those of Nicolas de Gorran can be found in sixty-seven manuscripts. The wide distribution of the *Summa de abstinentia* made it a real bestseller in the later Middle Ages. Moreover, the *Summa* was diffused through the well-known pecia-copying system whereby the universities would approve an exemplar, or a main copy text, and the students would order their copies from the scribes who were hired by the universities to make copies. In the current instance there are at least four manuscripts with pecia marks. This is not surprising since the work appears in the Paris pecia-list of 1304 under the title: *83] De abstinentia* (but without an indication of the author).[8] This pastoral bestseller exists in several editions. For instance, we can mention those from Germany (Reutlingen, 1480; Köln, 1501, 1504, and 1505), from Switzerland (Basel, 1481), from the Netherlands (Deventer, 1484), and above all from France (Vienne, 1481; Strasbourg, *c.* 1485, before 1487, 1516, and 1518; Paris, *c.* 1495–1497, 1498, 1512, and finally, 1530). (See Appendix 1 for those printed up to 1501). These editions appear under the title *Dictionarius pauperum*. To the best of my knowledge, Nicolas de Gorran's *Distinctiones* were not published in the sixteenth century. As for those of Maurice de Provins, a partial edition was published in Venice in 1603. The edition by Guido Bartoluccius, *Dictionarium sacrae scripturae Mauricii Hybernici*, published in Venezia in 1603 covers the first letters of the alphabet, from A to E.[9]

The success of the work, however, is not due to its author. Little is known about Nicolas de Biard, except that this Dominican friar composed two collections of *distinctiones*, one entitled *Distinctiones*, the other *Summa de abstinentia*, and one collection of *Sermones de tempore et de sanctis*.[10] The sermons are found in several manuscripts and contain Sunday sermons, sermons for saints, and various other sermons.[11]

The *Summa de abstinentia* will be the main focus of this essay. How can we explain the success, up to early modern times, of this pastoral work written in the thirteenth century, which circulated under the title of *Dictionarius pauperum* in the fifteenth century? In order to answer this question, we will first study the recipients of this intellectual tool (the 'poor' preachers); then

---

textes (IRHT-CNRS), 'Notice de Dictionarius pauperum, Nicolaus de Byardo (12..–12..)', by Pascale Bourgain and Dominique Stutzmann, FAMA: Œuvres latines médiévales à succès, 2018 (http://fama.irht.cnrs.fr/oeuvre/268724; accessed 11 May 2021).

8 Giovanna Murano, *Opere diffuse per exemplar e pecia*, Textes et études du Moyen Âge, 29 (Turnhout: Brepols, 2005), pp. 640–41.

9 *Dictionarium sacrae scripturae Mauricii Hybernici* (Venezia: Guido Bartoluccius, 1603).

10 On the *Distinctiones*, see Louis Jacques Bataillon, 'The Tradition of Nicholas de Biard's Distinctiones', *Viator*, 25 (1994), 245–88.

11 Johannes Baptist Schneyer, *Repertorium der lateinischen Sermones des Mittelalters: für die Zeit von 1150–1350*, 11 vols (Münster: Aschendorffsche Verlagsbuchhandlung, 1969–1989), IV (1972), 248–50.

A Collection for 'Poor' Preachers

The *Summa de abstinentia*, so called in medieval times on account of the term with which it begins (*abstinentia*), circulated from the end of the fifteenth century under the title *Dictionarius pauperum*. It was published in several incunabula (that is, before 1501), but also in editions dating to the sixteenth century, which prove its success.[12] The transition from manuscripts to incunabula was accompanied by new texts. Whereas the manuscripts of the late Middle Ages already contained two different prologues, the incunabula reveal three new introductory or prologue texts.[13] I will take as an example the incunabulum printed in Paris in 1498.[14] On the first page, one can thus read as a subtitle:

> *Dictionarius pauperum* omnibus predicatoribus verbi divini pernecessarius in quo multum succincter continentur materie singulis festivitatibus totius anni tam de tempore quam de sanctis accommodande, ut in tabula huius operis facile et lucide cognoscetur.[15]

> [A *Dictionary of the Poor* is very necessary for all preachers of the Divine Word. It contains in a very concise manner the materials for each feast of the year, both *de tempore* and *de sanctis*, as can be easily and clearly seen in the table of this work].

Then, still in this edition of 1498, before the first heading 'abstinentia', a small paragraph is included which argues along the same lines:

> Incipit Summula omnibus verbi divini seminatoribus pernecessaria que parvum dictionnarium ais de abstinentia intitulatur, in qua diligens indagator materias secundum varietatem temporum applicabiles modumque

---

12 Brigitte Moreau, *Inventaire chronologique des éditions parisiennes du XVI⁰ siècle, d'après les manuscrits de Philippe Renouard*, 5 vols (Paris: Service des travaux historiques de la Ville de Paris, 1972–1992), I (1972), 208 and 379. The term 'incunabulum' is used here in its strict sense to refer to a book printed in Europe in moveable type before 1 January 1501.

13 For the medieval prologues, see Sophie Delmas, 'Les Recueils de distinctiones sont-ils des florilèges?', in *On Good Authority: Tradition, Compilation and the Construction of Authority in Literature from Antiquity to the Renaissance*, ed. by Reinhart Ceulemans and Peter De Leemans, Lectio, 3 (Turnhout: Brepols, 2015), pp. 227–43, especially pp. 232–34.

14 The edition used is from https://gallica.bnf.fr/ark:/12148/bpt6k538912/f.%C2%A0249.item [accessed 11 June 2022].

15 https://gallica.bnf.fr/ark:/12148/bpt6k538912/f. 4.item, folio I.

FROM *SUMMA DE ABSTINENTIA* TO THE *DICTIONARIUS PAUPERUM*   261

accommode adaptandi facile comperiet, si tabulam adapationesque sequentes diligenter consideraverit.[16]

> [This is the beginning of the little Summa, essential for all sowers of the Divine Word, which is entitled 'Little Dictionary' or 'Of Abstinence', in which the diligent one will easily discover useful materials for all circumstances along with [advice] on how to adapt them appropriately, by carefully considering the table and the adaptations that follow it].

These two introductory texts give details of the evolution of the title and the recipients of this intellectual tool. The first text speaks only of a 'dictionary for the poor', while the second mentions a 'little summa', or a 'little dictionary' while recalling its original title 'of abstinence'.

These various titles are found concisely listed in a sixteenth-century annotation on the front page of Paris, Bibliothèque Mazarine, MS 1022: 'Hic liber aliquando dictus est *Flos theologie*, deinde *Summa de abstinentia*, predicatoribus multum necessaria. Nunc autem *Dictionarius pauperum* appelatur' ['This book was sometimes entitled *Flos theologie* or *Summa de abstinentia*, and it is very useful for preachers. Now, however, it is called *Dictionnarius pauperum*']. The succession of these titles is confirmed by the different incunabula editions: we find three different titles, as in the annotation, those of *Flos theologiae*, *Summa de abstinentia*, and then *Dictionarius pauperum* (see Appendix 1).

In this context, we will not consider all the details of the notion of *flores* or *florilèges* that arise here.[17] However, the title *Dictionarius pauperum* should be stressed, as it seems to be the most prominent title in the early modern period. The word *dictionarius* poses no problem as long as the collection is organized alphabetically. We find the same evolution of the title with regard to the collection of Maurice de Provins, entitled *Distinctiones*, from the early Middle Ages; this work is described as a *Dictionnaire* in the Venice edition of 1603.[18] On the other hand, the genitive *pauperum* immediately brings to mind the well-known 'Pauper's Bible' of the later Middle Ages.[19] These *Biblia*

---

16 https://gallica.bnf.fr/ark:/12148/bpt6k538912/f. 4.item, folio II.
17 Delmas, 'Les Recueils de distinctiones sont-ils des florilèges?'.
18 *Dictionarium sacrae scripturae Mauricii Hybernici* (Venezia: Guido Bartoluccius, 1603).
19 Henrik Cornell, *Biblia pauperum* (Stockholm: Thule-Tryck, 1925); Gerhard Schmidt, *Die Armenbibeln des XIV. Jahrhunderts* (Graz: Böhlau, 1959); Karl-August Wirth, 'Biblia pauperum', in *Die deutsche Literatur des Mittelalters: Verfasserlexikon*, ed. by Kurt Ruh, and others, 2nd edn, 14 vols (Berlin: De Gruyter, 1977–2008), I (1977), cols 843–52; Alfred Weckwerth, 'Armenbibeln', in *Theologische Realenzyklopädie*, ed. by Gerhard Krause and Gerhard Müller, 36 vols (Berlin: De Gruyter, 1976–2004), IV (1979), 8–10; Gisela Plotzeck-Wederhake and Günter Bernt, 'Biblia pauperum', in *Lexikon des Mittelalters*, 10 vols (München and other places: Artemis and other publishers, 1980–1999), II (1983), 110; Guy Lobrichon, 'La Bible des Pauvres du Vatican, Palat. Lat. 871: essai sur l'émergence d'une spiritualité laïque dans l'Allemagne de la fin du Moyen Âge', in *La Bible au Moyen Age*, ed. by Guy Lobrichon (Paris: Picard, 2003), pp. 211–38 and finally *Studien zur Biblia pauperum*, ed. by Malena Ratzke, Bruno Reudenbach, and Hanna Wimmer (Bern: Lang, 2016).

pauperum appeared around 1300 and consisted of a series of woodcuts depicting scenes from the Old and New Testaments, which were combined with short explanatory texts printed with metal type. They were characterized by their brevity (a maximum of about fifty pages), their low cost, and their use of typology. They were especially common in Germany, the Netherlands, and France in particular. Interestingly, the early printed texts of the *Dictionarius pauperum* were distributed in the same geographical areas, in France (Paris, Strasbourg, and Vienne), in Germany (Reutlingen and Köln), the Netherlands (Deventer), and Switzerland (Basel).[20]

In seeking to identify these 'poor people', we can refer to what Guy Lobrichon writes about the *Biblia pauperum*:

> Le nom est ambigu en effet. Sans parler des vrais pauvres, les misérables, les déshérités, les bannis de toujours, il y avait au Moyen Âge bien des prétendants au titre de 'pauvres'. Ce pouvait être les moines, qui se disaient volontiers 'pauvres du Christ', les chanoines réguliers du XIIe siècle et d'ensuite aussi bien. C'étaient encore les Frères mendiants, 'pauvres prédicateurs' comme aimaient à se nommer les dominicains, ou frères mineurs, 'les plus pauvres', animés par François d'Assise; ceux-ci étaient nés avec l'aube du XIIIe siècle. C'étaient les membres des constellations hérétiques qui depuis le XIe siècle tentaient de se donner une respectabilité en arborant ce titre, jusqu'à ces 'Pauvres Vaudois', 'Humiliés', 'tout petits frères', qui désiraient d'une ardeur sincère vivre le dépouillement même du Christ dans sa vie d'ici-bas. Autant dire que le nom de 'Bible des pauvres' reste embrumé d'imprécision, dans un nuage que les contemporains n'ont pas cherché à dissiper.[21]

This *Dictionarius pauperum*, like the *Biblia pauperum*, was therefore not addressed to the poor, or the wretched who were not able to buy it.[22] Rather, it was a work for poor preachers who could not afford to buy a large collection. In the same way, the word *summa* in the medieval title of the work should be understood, not as a *sum* or synthesis, but as a 'summary'.[23] The *Summarium* is transmitted in composite manuscripts and miscellanies

---

20 Delmas, 'La Summa de abstinentia attribuée à Nicolas de Biard', p. 310.

21 Lobrichon, 'La Bible des Pauvres du Vatican', p. 297.

22 Finally, it is interesting to note that this title, *Biblia pauperum*, was also commonly used to designate the *Summarium biblicum*, a biblical tool studied by Lucie Doležalová, 'The *Summarium Biblicum*: A Biblical Tool both Popular and Obscure', in *Form and Function in the Late Medieval Bible*, ed. by Eyal Poleg and Laura Light, Library of the Written Word, 27, The Manuscript World, 4 (Leiden: Brill, 2013), pp. 163–84; Lucie Doležalová, 'Mémoriser la Bible au bas Moyen Âge? Le *Summarium Biblicum* aux frontières de l'intelligibilité', in *Le Moyen Âge dans le texte: cinq ans d'histoire textuelle au Laboratoire de médiévistique occidentale de Paris*, ed. by Benoît Grévin and Aude Mairey (Paris: Publications de la Sorbonne, 2016), pp. 135–64.

23 Mariken Teeuwen, *The Vocabulary of Intellectual Life in the Middle Ages*, CIVICIMA: Études sur le vocabulaire intellectuel du Moyen Âge, 10 (Turnhout: Brepols, 2003), pp. 336–38.

FROM *SUMMA DE ABSTINENTIA* TO THE *DICTIONARIUS PAUPERUM* 263

that offer materials used by preachers. The books 'of the poor' — bibles or dictionaries — therefore seem to be summaries of more or less long texts, useful for students and preachers.

An Easy-to-Use Collection: The Adaptations

The writers of the prologues all emphasize the same thing, namely, the presence of very useful tables at the end of the volume. The incunabula, like most manuscripts, contain three tables which, to my knowledge, do not exist for the two other great collections of *distinctiones* of the late Middle Ages, those of Nicolas de Gorran and Maurice de Provins.[24] These tables of contents consist of three elements: 1. adaptations for Saturdays, Sundays, and holy days (*incipiunt adaptationes omnium sermonum in hoc libro contentorum prout competunt sabbatis, dominicis et feriis totius anni*); 2. a list of saints for the whole year (*de sanctis currentibus per totum annum*) with a proposed biblical text, a theme, a reference to one or two chapters; and 3. a list of chapters that are numbered and associated with the corresponding folio. At first glance, this list does not change between the manuscripts and the printed copies, since 133 headings can be listed. However, a comparison of the two lists shows some changes (see Appendix 2). The chapter *De fide* has been divided in the incunabulum into two parts: one part is called *de fide*, the other is the newly entitled *hystoria de fide*. Conversely, the passage devoted in the medieval manuscript to penance proposed two complementary chapters devoted to indiscrete and late penance: the whole has been merged into a single chapter on penance in the printed edition. Another text at the end of the incunabula also discusses at length the usefulness of these tables; it offers in a very concrete way a kind of 'instruction manual', which helps the reader understand how to use them.

This tool first recalls the alphabetical order of the different chapters and the usefulness of the alphabetical table. The future preacher is also instructed where to find pastoral material according to the feast and the proposed theme. For example, for the First Sunday of Advent, about the passage *Abiiciamus opera tenebrarum* (Romans 13. 12), since the 'works of darkness' refer to sins, the preacher is advised to consult the chapter on sin; for 'et induamur arma lucis' ['let us put on weapons of light'], he should refer to the chapter on light; and finally, for 'sicut in die honeste ambulemus' ['let us walk honestly as in the day'], he should consult the chapter on 'walking'.

> Ad habendam contentorum in hac summa elucidationem, duo veniunt consideranda. Primum est pro noticia capitulorum que in numero sunt centum est XXXIII per ordinem alphabeti distincta in quibus de diversis

---

24 See Delmas, 'La Summa de abstinentia attribuée à Nicolas de Biard', pp. 308–09.

materiis tractatur, ratione quorum ponitur tabula ordinem illum exprimens. Secundum est adaptationes sermonum prout dominicis, festis sollennibus et festis totius anni competunt. In quibus adaptionibus debemus notare materiam, considerando capitulum vel capitula ad quod vel que nos remittit. Illicque reperiemus quid pro illo festo simus sermocinaturi. Verbi causa, in dominica prima Adventus est epistola Abiiciamus opera tenebrarum id est peccatta, debemus remittere ad capitulum de peccato. Et induamur arma lucis remittendum est ad capitulum de lumine sicut in die honeste ambulemus, ad capitulum de ambulatione et sic de aliis prout notatur in serie adaptationum in tabula positarum. Hic omnibus bene consideratis et sane digestis quante sit hec summa utilitatis quanteque predicatoribus commoditatis, cunctis qui eam perlegent, facile cognitu erit.[25]

> [To understand the content of this Summa, two elements must be taken into account. The first allows us to know the chapters that are distinguished in alphabetical order and the number of these is 133. There are several subjects, which is why a table is proposed which represents this order. The second one concerns the adaptations of the sermons according to Sundays and holy days anf all the feasts of the year. In these adaptations we have to highlight the subject, taking into consideration the chapter or chapters to which it refers. And here we identify what we should preach for that feast. For example, for the First Sunday of Advent, we find the Epistle 'Let us therefore cast off the works of darkness' (Romans 13. 12), i.e. sins, and we must refer to the chapter on sin. 'And let us put on the armour of light' must refer to the chapter on light, 'Let us walk honestly, as in the day' to the chapter on walking and so on, according to what is noted in the series of adaptations proposed in the table. Once all this has been taken into consideration, as well as the usefulness and convenience of this Summa, to all those who read it, it will be easy to understand].

Following this account of the collection of *Distinctiones*, it is worth looking for some clues as to its dissemination and use in the following centuries.

Summa de abstinentia: 'extracta a magno dictionnario'?

At the end of the incunabulum (Paris, 1498), in the explicit, a final text provides some additional information on:

> Explicit Summula omnibus Verbi divini seminatoribus pernecessaria que est extracta a magno dictionario et potest dici dictionarius pauperum licet de abstinentia intitulatur, in qua diligens indagator materias secundum

---

25 https://gallica.bnf.fr/ark:/12148/bpt6k538912/f. 4.item, tabula (without pagination).

FROM *SUMMA DE ABSTINENTIA* TO THE *DICTIONARIUS PAUPERUM*   265

varietatem temporum applicabiles modumque accommode adaptandi facile comperiet si tabulam adapationesque sequentes diligenter consideraverit.[26]

[End of the 'little Summa' indispensable to the disseminators of the Divine Word which is taken from a large dictionary; and it can be called 'Dictionary of the poor', even if it is entitled 'De abstinentia'. Inside, whoever diligently searches for elements adapted to different circumstances will easily find the way to adapt them if he carefully examines the table and the adaptations that follow].

According to this passage, this *Summula* or *Little Sum* concerning abstinence is 'extracta a magno dictionnario' ['taken from a great dictionary'], and it can be called the 'dictionarius pauperum' ['dictionary of the poor']. This extract causes us to assume that the *Summula* contains only a selection of certain chapters or passages. This explains the use of the title 'flower' (*flos*) id est 'florilège': some of the manuscripts preserved in Munich are entitled 'flowers of theology' or 'flowers of sermons'.[27] Indeed, historians of preaching have wondered which work the *Summa de abstinentia/Dictionarius pauperum* summarizes.[28] As we learn from the prologues of other *Distinctiones* from the early thirteenth century, their authors drew on earlier collections of *distinctiones*; for instance, Tuija Ainonen underlines the 'textual community' formed by the first known collections of *distinctiones*.[29] Thus, in their prologues, at least two authors explicitly allude to their literary debt to their predecessors. The first is Ralph de Longchamp (*c.* 1155–*c.* 1215), who acknowledges borrowings from Alan de Lille (*c.* 1120–1202). He not only shortened the collection of Alan de Lille, but also added new elements, both new subjects and authorities. The second is Durand de Huesca (*c.* 1160–1224) who mentions in his prologue the influence of the collection of Pietro da Capua (d. 1214). He not only shortened it, but also added new entries.

---

26 https://gallica.bnf.fr/ark:/12148/bpt6k538912/f. 4.item, tabula (without pagination).

27 Delmas, 'Les Recueils de distinctiones sont-ils des florilèges?', p. 231.

28 Clément Schmitt, 'Nicolas de Byard', *Dictionnaire de spiritualité, ascétique et mystique, doctrine et histoire*, ed. by Marcel Viller and others, 17 vols (Paris: Beauchesne, 1932–1995), XI (1981), 254–55: 'Un abrégé de ces *Distinctiones*, intitulé *Summa de abstinentia seu Dictionarius pauperum*, a eu plusieurs éditions depuis l'incunable de Paris de 1498', col. 254. Amédée Teetaert explains 'Dans l'édition de 1498, on lit explicitement que ce Dictionarius est un long extrait des Distinctiones qui sont restées inédites', col. 590; see Amédée Teetaert, 'Nicolas Biard', in *Dictionnaire de théologie catholique, contenant l'exposé des doctrines de la théologie catholique, leurs preuves et leur historie*, ed. by Alfred Vacant and others, 15 vols (Paris: Letouzey & Ané, 1902–1950), XI (1930), 589–92.

29 Tuija Ainonen, 'Making New from Old: Distinction Collections and Textual Communities at the Turn of the Thirteenth Century', in *From Learning to Love: Schools, Law, and Pastoral Care in the Middle Ages. Essays in Honour of Joseph W. Goering*, ed. by Tristan Sharp and others, Papers in Mediaeval Studies, 29 (Toronto: Pontifical Institute of Mediaeval Studies, 2017), pp. 48–69.

266   SOPHIE DELMAS

In this case, the simplest hypothesis would be that the *Summa de abstinentia* is an abbreviation of the other, much larger collection of *distinctiones* written by Nicolas de Biard, namely, the *Distinctiones*. As Louis-Jacques Bataillon has rightly observed, this hypothesis does not hold. Even though the chapters in the *Summa de abstinentia* are fewer in number than in the *Distinctiones* (the *Distinctiones* have 254, the *Summa* 133), they are long and often have nothing in common with the *Distinctiones*.[30] The answer to this question probably lies in the reception of the *Summa de abstinentia* in the modern age. In fact, further research shows that the work was printed several times together with *quaestiones* on the Gospels by Johannes de Turrecremata (1388–1468) between 1480 and 1500.[31] I have so far been able to list eight incunabula that associate the work of Nicolas de Biard with that of Johannes de Turrecremata (see Appendix 1). More than eighty incunabula associating the work of Nicolas de Biard and that of Johannes de Turrecremata have been found, which is considerable.

Johannes de Turrecremata was, like Nicolas de Biard, a Dominican (his nephew was the famous Tomás de Turrecremata (1420–1498), the Spanish Dominican friar and the first Grand Inquisitor in Spain). After studies at Paris, he taught in Spain and was successively prior of Valladolid and of Toledo. Professor of theology at the university in Valladolid, he accompanied the Minister General of his order to the Council of Basel in 1431, where he defended the authority of the pope. In 1439 he became cardinal, then bishop of Cadiz, then Orense.[32] He was the author of various works, including the *Tractatus contra madianitas et ismaelitas*. In 1448–1449 he wrote his chief work, *Summa de ecclesia*, defending the Church against both heretics and conciliarists. The work that circulated with that of Nicolas de Biard corresponds to questions on the Gospels (*Quaestiones Evangeliorum de tempore et de sanctis*).

The combined circulation of the texts is no coincidence. They are not merely associated by virtue of publication in one and the same volume. Indeed, Nicolas de Biard's *Summa* and Johannes de Turrecremata's *Quaestiones* were deliberately associated with one another, as can be seen in the prologue that precedes the works of these two Dominicans, in particular, an alphabetical table (*tabula alphabetica*):

---

30 Bataillon, 'The Tradition of Nicholas of Biard's Distinctiones', p. 246.

31 The incunabulum (without pagination) can be found at http://tudigit.ulb.tu-darmstadt.de/show/inc-iii-17 [accessed 5 May 2021].

32 Jules Felix Stockmann, *Joannis de Turrecremata O. P. vitam ejusque doctrinam de corpore Christi mystico* (Bologna: Tipografia 'Studentato missioni', 1951), p. 28; Karl Binder, *Wesen und Eigenschaften der Kirche bei Kardinal Juan de Torquemada, O. P.* (Innsbruck: Verlagsanstalt Tyrolia, 1955); Thomas M. Izbicki, *Protector of the Faith: Cardinal Johannes de Turrecremata and the Defense of the Institutional Church* (Washington, DC: The Catholic University of America Press, 1981).

FROM *SUMMA DE ABSTINENTIA* TO THE *DICTIONARIUS PAUPERUM* 267

Prologus Themata de Tempore

Dum ad pleniorem cognitionem re ordo deducat, necessarium est hic ponere huius solemnissimi ordinem opusculi ut quibus legere placuerit facilius salutiferum reportent fructum. Erit autem ordo operis huius talis quod primo ponentur themata sermonum de tempore tam de epistulis quam de evangeliis ac aliis scriptuis autenticis per totum annum de sanctis et communi sanctorum necnon de quibusdam aliis singularibus et notabilibus materiis cum suis remissionibus pro simplicibus predicare volentibus. Post themata vero ponetur tabula alphabetica in se continens et concludens omnes et singulas materias huius totius operis ut facilior sit recursus volentibus diversas et copiosas habere materias et unuquisque recipere possit quid sibi placitum fuerit. Sequetque tabula secundum ordinem alphabeti ipsius auree materie applicabilis sive floris theologie, demum ipsa enucleata materia sive flos theologie in se. Ultimo ponetur tabula de tempore et de sanctis per circulum anni cum questionibus ex sancto Thoma enucleatis et extratis per illuminatissimum virum dominum Iohannem de Turre cremata, sancte sedis apostolice cardinalem ordinis predicatorum sancti sixti vulgariter nuncupatum. Comportata sunt hec ad laudem dei omnipotentis gloriossissimeque Virginis Marie et omnium sanctorum necnon ad salutem animarum et in salute animarum perficere volentium.

[In order to come to a more complete knowledge of the order of things, it is necessary to present here the order of this very solemn *opusculum* [short or minor work] so that those who will enjoy reading it, can more easily obtain salutary fruit from it. In fact, the order of this work will be as follows: first of all, the biblical themes of the sermons *de tempore*, both from the Epistles and from the Gospels and other authentic writings for the whole year about the saints and the common of saints, and also about other singular and notable materials for those who want to preach to the simple people. After the biblical themes, there is the alphabetical table itself containing and enclosing all the subjects of this work, so that the search is easier for those who want to have varied and rich subjects; in this way, everyone can find what they need. Then follows the table according to the order of the alphabet that applies to this 'golden material' or 'flower of theology', precisely the unadorned material or theology flower in itself. Finally there is the table *de tempore* and *de sanctis* for the whole year with questions taken and extracted from St Thomas by the very illustrious Johannes de Turrecremata, Dominican Cardinal of St Sixtus. They are gathered for the praise of Almighty God, the most glorious Virgin Mary and all the saints, as well as for the salvation of souls and those who want to obtain the salvation of souls].

This prologue presents the different parts of the volume associating the works of Nicolas de Biard and Johannes de Turrecremata. To better understand their contents, I have summarized them in the following list:

1. themata sermonum
   List of biblical themes for the feasts of the time (*themata de tempore*) and of the saints (*themata de sanctis*), of the common of saints and for special occasions (*de commun sanctorum et aliis materiibus singularibus*)
2. tabula alphabetica
   Extensive alphabetical table from 'abstinentia' to 'usura' from Nicolas de Biard's *Summa de abstinentia* and Johannes de Turrecremata's questions
3. tabula secundum ordinem alphabeti ipsius auree materie
   Table of terms in alphabetical order (*abstinentia to vita eterna*) from Nicolas de Biard's *Summa de abstinentia*
4. tabula de tempore et de sanctis per circulum anni cum questionibus ex sancto Thoma enucleatis et extratis
   (in the middle of the book, after the *Summa de abstinentia*) a list of questions by Johannes de Turrecremata, which are based in part on Thomas Aquinas.

The *tabula alphabetica* associates the chapters of Nicolas de Biard's *Distinctiones* with the themes of Johannes de Turrecremata's *Quaestiones*. For example, after the heading *abstinentia* which refers to Nicolas de Biard, one reads the term *abnegare* ('to deny') which does not correspond to a chapter of the *Summa de abstinentia*, but to a discussion of St Katherine of Alexandria ('abscondere thesaurum in agro, id est Christo. Vide Katherine in corpore questionis' ['hiding a treasure in a field, that is, in Christ. See Katherine in the main part of the question']) in the *Quaestiones* of Johannes de Turrecremata.

Finally, according to this table, the *Distinctiones* of Nicolas de Biard and Johannes de Turrecremata's *Quaestiones* are associated with one another, seemingly on the assumption that they formed a large alphabetical dictionary useful for pastoral work. Thus, the statement that the *Summa de abstinentia* 'is taken from a large dictionary' (*extracta a magno dictionnario*) does not correspond to the extraction of certain chapters from an earlier work: in the sixteenth century, the majority of printed material offered Nicolas de Biard's *Summa de abstientia* and Johannes de Turrecremata's *Quaestiones* in a single volume, accompanied by an alphabetical table. For this reason, those who were able to consult the *Summa* separately may have thought that it was taken from a 'great dictionary'.

The *tabula alphabetica* offers not only a list of terms, but also an overview of the plan followed within each distinction. For example, in the first chapter on abstinence, there is a two-fold division, with detestable abstinence, that of hypocrites, the stingy, and the gluttonous on the one hand, and praiseworthy abstinence involving abstinence from sin, food, bad words, bad company on the other.

Conclusion

The *Summa de abstinentia*, entitled at the end of the fifteenth century the *Dictionarius pauperum*, enjoyed an exceptional diffusion, first in manuscripts and then in printed editions, which was far superior to the other collections of *distinctiones* of the Middle Ages. The handy size of the volume, and its numerous tables and adaptations contributed to its success among apprentice preachers, who were no doubt more modest and 'poorer' than their elders. They thus had at their disposal a very practical manual, providing not only alphabetical *distinctiones* (those of Nicolas de Biard), but also ready-to-use *quaestiones* (those of Johannes de Turrecremata), gathered in one and the same volume. Paradoxically for such a work so directed at preachers, (like many other such volumes), the tangible evidence of use tends to be lacking, as noted by Bataillon and Serventi.[33] The former only found a few tenuous examples (with only a few articles copied literally) of Biard using his own *distinctiones* in his own sermons, while the latter's investigation of the potential use of Nicolas de Gorran's *Distinctiones* by Giordano da Pisa (*c.* 1255–1311) is similarly inconclusive; Serventi found no precise literal quotations (something that is always difficult to identify in medieval texts in any case) but emerged with a steady recognition that such works were part of the general arsenal and Latin culture available to preachers. Indeed, at the end of the fifteenth and the beginning of the sixteenth centuries, the work of Nicolas de Biard was one of the most highly recommended books for preachers. Johann Ulrich Surgant (d. 1503), a professor in Basel, published in 1503 the *Regimen studiosorum*, which he wrote for Bruno Amerbach (1484–1519), then a student at the university in Paris. Chapter 19 deals with the use of books. Inspired by Seneca, he advised students to use only a few books instead of getting lost in multiple books. In the *Manuale curatorum* he proposes a list of volumes in which we find the *Flos theologie* by Nicolas de Biard and the *Quaestiones* by Johannes de Turrecremata.[34] Even later, in the eighteenth century, Cardinal Loménie de Brienne (1727–1794), Controller General of the Treasury of King Louis XVI (1754–1793), and great bibliophile, had the 1506 edition in his library.[35]

---

33 See Bataillon, 'The Tradition of Nicholas de Biard's *Distinctiones*' and Serventi, 'Did Giordano da Pisa Use the *Distinctiones* of Nicolas de Gorran?'.

34 Rudolf Hirsch, 'Surgant's List of Recommended Books for Preachers (1502–1503)', *Renaissance Quarterly*, 20 (1967), 199–210.

35 *Catalogue d'une partie des livres de la bibliothèque du cardinal de Lomenie de Brienne, dont la vente se fera Maison de Brienne, rue Saint-Dominique, près la rue de Bourgogne* (Paris: Mauger & Lejeune, 1797), p. 16.

Appendix 1: List of Incunabula including Nicolas de Biard's *Summa de abstinentia*

[Square brackets indicate other known titles for a work].

Author and title of the work	Edition: place, publisher, date
Johannes de Turrecremata, *Quaestiones Evangeliorum de tempore et de sanctis.* Nicolas de Biard, [Dictionarius pauperum] *Flos theologiae sive Summa de abstinentia*	Reutlingen: Michael Greyff, not before 1480
Johannes de Turrecremata, *Quaestiones Evangeliorum de tempore et de sanctis.* Add: Nicolas de Biard, [Dictionarius pauperum] *Flos theologiae sive Summa de abstinentia*	[Vienne]: Eberhard Frommolt, 24 July 1481
Johannes de Turrecremata, *Quaestiones Evangeliorum de tempore et de sanctis.* Add: Nicolas de Biard, [Dictionarius pauperum] *Flos theologiae sive Summa de abstinentia*	Basel: Johann Amerbach, not after 28 September 1481
Johannes de Turrecremata, *Quaestiones Evangeliorum de tempore et de sanctis.* Add: Nicolas de Biard, [Dictionarius pauperum] *Flos theologiae sive Summa de abstinentia*	Deventer: Richardus Pafraet, 20 November 1484
Johannes de Turrecremata, *Quaestiones Evangeliorum de tempore et de sanctis.* Add: Nicolas de Biard, [Dictionarius pauperum] *Flos theologiae sive Summa de abstinentia*	Strasbourg: Printer of the 1483 Jordanus von Quedlinburg (Georg Husner), not after 24 March 1485]
Nicolas de Biard, *Flos theologiae*; Johannes de Turrecremata, *Quaestiones evangeliorum*	Strasbourg: Printer of Jordanus von Quedlinburg, before 1487
Nicolas de Biard, *Dictionarius pauperum* (*Flos theologiae*) *sive Summa de abstinentia*	Paris: Félix Baligault, for Durand Gerlier, [about 1495–1497]
Nicolas de Biard, *Dictionarius pauperum* (*Flos theologiae*) *sive Summa de abstinentia*	Paris: André Bocard, for Durand Gerlier and Jean Petit, 13 November 1498
Nicolas de Biard, *Dictionarius pauperum* (*Summa de abstinentia*)	Köln: Retro Minores, 14 December 1501

Appendix 2: Comparison of the *Capitula* between Manuscripts and Incunabula

Changes are highlighted in bold.

Avignon = Avignon, Bibliothèque Municipale, 308; Reims = Reims Bibliothèque Municipale, 512; Paris = Nicolas de Biard, *Dictionarius pauperum* (Paris: André Bocard, for Durand Gerlier and Jean Petit, 13 November 1498).

Capitula	Avignon	Reims	Paris
1. De abstinentia	269ra	1 bis ra	de abstinentia ca i fol. 2
2. De adulatione	270ra	2va	de adulatione ca ii fol. 3
3. De ambitione [dignitatum]	270rb	3ra	de ambitione ca iii eodem fo.
4. De amicitia	270va	3vb	De amicitia dei ca iiii fo. 4
5. De amore sui ipsius	270va	3vb	de amore proprio ca v fo. 4
6. De amore Dei	270vb	4rb	de amore Dei ca vi fo. 4
7. De amore proximi	272rb	6vb	de amore proximi ca viii fo. 6
8. De amore inimicorum	273ra	7vb	de amore inimicorum ca viii fo. 7
9. De aspectu Dei	273vb	9ra	de aspectu dei ca ix fo. 8
10. Quomodo acquiritur regnum Dei	274rb	10ra	de acquirit. regnum celorum c x f. 9
11. De apertione	274vb	11ra	de apertione aurem ca xi fo. 10
12. Quomodo ambulandum ad Deum	275va	12rb	de ambulare ca xii fo. 11
13. De benedicendo Deo	276va	14ra	de benedicendo Deo ca xiii fo. 12
14. De caritate	277ra	14vb	de caritate ca xiiii fo. 13
15. De custodia sensuum	277vb	15vb	de cogitatione ca xv fo. 14
16. De custodia cordis	278ra	16va	de custodia cordis ca xvi fo. 14
17. De contritione	278va	17va	de contritione ca xvii fo. 15
18. De confessione	279rb	18va	de confessione ca xviii fo. 16
19. De choreis	280rb	20rb	de corcatricibus ca xix fo. 17
20. De cogitatione	280vb	21ra	de cogitatione hominis ca xx fo. 19
21. De consolatione	281va	22va	de consolatione ca xxi fo. 19
22. De compassione [proximi]	282vb	24rb	de compassione ca xxii fo. 20
23. De consuetudine	282vb	24vb	de consuetudine ca xxiii fo. 21
24. De correctione	283rb	25va	de correctione ca xxiiii fo. 21
25. De corpore Christi	284ra	26va	de corpore Christi ca xxv fo. 22
26. De derisoribus [derisionibus]	284vb	28ra	de derisoribus ca xxvi fo. 23
27. De domo	285ra	28va	de domo ca xxvii fo. 24
28. De detractione	285va	29va	de detractione ca xxviii fo. 25
29. De duricia cordis	286rb	30vb	de duritia cordis ca xxix fo. 26
30. De divitiis [temporalibus]	286va	31ra	de divitiis ca xxx fo. 26

Capitula	Avignon	Reims	Paris
31. De dolore	287vb	33ra	de dolore ca xxxi fo. 28
32. De elemosina	288vb	35ra	de elemosina ca xxxii fo. 29
33. De ebrietate	289va	36rb	de ebrietate ca xxxiii fo. 29
34. De erubescentia	289vb	36vb	de erubescentia ca xxxiiii fo. 31
35. De exemplo	290ra	37rb	de exemplo ca xxxv fo. 31
36. De excommunicatione	290vb	38rb	de excommunicatione ca xxxvi fo. 32
37. De exaltatione	291ra	39ra	de exaltatione ca xxxvii fo. 31
38. De fide	291vb	39vb	**de fide ca xxxviii fo. 33** **hystoria de fide ca xxxix fo. 34** **item de eodem ca xl fo. 35**
39. De fidelitate	292va	41rb	de fidelitate ca xli fo. 35
40. De homine	293rb	42va	de fortitudine ca xlii fo. 36
41. De gaudio	293vb	43rb	de gaudio ca xliii fo. 37
42. De gloria	295ra	45ra	de gloria ca xliiii fo. 38
43. De gratia	296ra	46vb	de gratia ca xlv fo. 40
44. De gladio	297rb	48va	de gladio ca xlvi fo. 41
45. De gula	298rb	50ra	de gula ca xlvii fo. 42
46. De humilitate	298va	50vb	de humilitate ca xlviii fo. 43
47. De iactantia	299ra	51va	de iactantia ca xlix fo. 44
48. De innocentia	299rb	51vb	de innocentia ca l fo. 44
49. De instabilitate	299va	52rb	de instabilitate ca li fo. 44
50. De ira	300ra	53ra	de ira ca lii fo. 45
51. De infirmitate spirituali	300rb	53va	de infirmitate ca liii fo. 45
52. De invidia	301ra	54va	de invidia ca liiii fo. 46
53. De inferno	301rb	55ra	de inferno ca lv fo. 47
54. De futuro iudicio	302va	56vb	de iudicio generali ca lvi fo. 48
55. De iudicio [temerario]	303va	58vb	de iudicio temerario clvii f. 50
56. De iudicibus malis	304rb	59vb	de iudicibus ca lviii fo. 51
57. De iusticia	304rb	60ra	de iusticia ca lix fo. 51
58. De iuramento	305vb	62ra	de iuramento ca lx fo. 53
59. De ypocrita	306ra	62vb	de ypocritis ca lxi fo. 53
60. De heretico = de igne purgatorio	306va	63va	de purgatorio ca lxii fo. 54
61. De lumine	307ra	64va	de luce ca lxiii fo. 54
62. De locutione	307vb	65vb	de locutione ca lxiiii fo. 55
63. De luxuria	308rb	66vb	de luxuria ca lxv fo. 56
64. De lacrimis	309ra	68ra	de lachrimis ca lxvi fo. 57
65. De mansuetudine	309va	68vb	de mansuetudine ca lxviii fo. 58

FROM *SUMMA DE ABSTINENTIA* TO THE *DICTIONARIUS PAUPERUM* 273

Capitula	Avignon	Reims	Paris
66. De morte	309vb	69ra	de morte ca lxviii fo. 58
67. De mundicia cordis	311rb	71va	de munditia cordis ca lxic f. 60
68. De mortificatione carnis	312ra	72vb	de mortificatione carnis lxx f. 61
69. De mendacio	312va	73vb	de mendatio ca lxxi fo. 62
70. De murmure	312vb	74ra	de murmuratione ca lxxii fo. 62
71. De mundo fugiendo	313ra	74va	de mundo fugiendo ca lxxiii fo. 62
72. De mirabilibus	313vb	75va	de miribalibus ca lxxiiii fo. 63
73. De misericordia	314rb	76va	de misericordia ca lxxv fo. 64
74. De negligentia	315vb	79ra	de negligentia ca lxxvii fo. 66
75. De obedentia	315vb	79rb	de obedentia ca lxxvii fo. 66
76. De ocioso	317ra	81ra	de otio lxxviii fo. 68
77. De oratione	317rb	81va	de oratione c. lxxix fo. 68
78. De vulgali = De odio vite carnalis	318va	83va	de odio c. lxxx fo. 70
79. **De operatione = De opere bono**	319rb	85ra	
80. De odio proximi	320ra	86va	de odio proximi c. lxxxi fo. 71
81. De ornatu = De ornato corpore	320va	87rb	de ornatu corporis lxxxiii fo. 72
82. De pace	321rb	88rb	de pace lxxxiiii fo. 74
83. De patiencia	322va	90va	de patientia lxxxv fo. 75
84. De inpaciencia	323rb	91vb	de impatientia lxxxvi fo. 76
85. De paupertate	323va	92ra	de paupertate lxxxvii fo. 77
86. De passione Christi	324rb	93vb	de passione Christi lxxxviii fo. 78
87. De peccato [in generali]	324vb	95va	de peccato lxxxix fo. 78
88. **De penitentia**	326ra	96rb	de penitentia ca xc fo. 80
89. **De penitentia indiscreta**	327ra	98rb	
90. **De penitentia tarda**	327rb	98va	
91. De predicatione	328ra	100ra	de predicatione xci fo. 83
92. De perseverantia	328va	100vb	de perseverantia xcii fo. 83
93. De presumptione	328vb	101va	de presumptione xciii fo. 84
94. De prodigalitate	329ra	101vb	de prodigalitate xciiii fo. 84
95. De pigricia	329rb	102rb	de pigritia xcv fo. 84
96. De providentia	329va	102vb	de providentia xcvi fo. 85
97. De preparatione	329vb	103rb	de preparatione xcvii fo. 85
98. **De pecunia (= probatione)**	330va	105ra	
99. Quomodo querendum est Deum	331ra	106ra	Querendum est Deus xcix fo. 88
100. De religiosis	331va	107rb	de religione c fo. 89
101. De repletione	332ra	108rb	de repletione ci fo. 89

Capitula	Avignon	Reims	Paris
102. De resurrectione generali	332va	109va	de resurrectione corporum cii fo. 90
103. De recidivo	332va	109vb	de recidivo ca ciii fo. 91
104. De sapientia	333ra	110va	de sapientia ca ciiii fo. 91
105. De servicio malo	333va	111vb	de servicio dei cv fo. 92
106. De servicio Dei	333vb	112rb	de servicio dyaboli cvi fo. 93
107. De sequendo [Domino]	334rb	113va	de sequela cvii fo. 94
108. De silencio	335rb	115va	de silentio cviii fo. 95
109. De symonia	335va	115vb	de symonia cix fo. 96
110. De societate mala [vitanda]	335va	116ra	de societate mala cx fo. 96
111. De sanctificatione	335vb	116vb	de sanctificatione hominis cxi fo. 96
112. De solitudine	336ra	117rb	de solitudine cxii fo. 97
113. De spe	336rb	117va	de spe cxiii fo. 97
114. De superbia	336vb	118ra	de superbia cxiiii fo. 98
115. De tactu impudico	337ra	119rb	de tactu impudico cxv fo. 98
116. De tepiditate	337rb	120ra	de tepiditate cxvi fo. 99
117. De tempore	337va	120ra	de tempore cxvii fo. 99
118. De temptatione	337va	120vb	de temptatione cxviii fo. 100
119. De thesauro	339rb	124va	de thesauro cxix fo. 102
120. De tribulatione	339vb	125va	de tribulatione cxx fo. 103
121. De timore Domini	341ra	128rb	de timore domini cxxi fo. 105
122. De verbo Dei	341vb	130ra	de verbo dei cxxii fo. 106
123. De velocitate conversionis	342rb	131va	de velocitate cxxiii fo. 108
124. De vita presenti	343rb	134ra	de vita penitenti cxxiiii fo. 109
125. De unitate et concordia	343va	135ra	de unitate spiritus cxxv fo. 110
126. De vocatione Dei	344rb	136vb	de vocatione cxxvi fo. 111
127. De voluntate bona	345ra	138va	de voluntate bona cxxvii fo. 112
128. De voluntate propria	345rb	139va	de voluntate propria cxxviii fo. 113
129. De virginitate	345vb	140va	de virginitate cxxix fo. 113
130. De usurario [usuris]	346va	142va	de usurariis cxxx fo. 115
131. De veritate	346vb	143rb	de veritate cxxxi fo. 115
132. De videndo	347ra	144rb	de videre deum cxxxii fo. 116
133. De vita eterna	347rb	145ra	de vita eterna cxxxiii fo. 117

Bibliography

Manuscripts

Avignon Bibliothèque Municipale, MS 308
Paris, Bibliothèque Mazarine, MS 1022
Reims, Bibliothèque Municipale, MS 512

Early Printed Works

Johannes de Turrecremata, *Quaestiones Evangeliorum de tempore et de sanctis.*
  Nicolas de Biard, [Dictionarius pauperum] *Flos theologiae sive Summa de*
  abstinentia (Reutlingen: Michael Greyff, not before 1480)
Johannes de Turrecremata, *Quaestiones Evangeliorum de tempore et de sanctis.* Add:
  Nicolas de Biard, [Dictionarius pauperum] *Flos theologiae sive Summa de*
  abstinentia ([Vienne]: Eberhard Frommolt, 24 July 1481)
Johannes de Turrecremata, *Quaestiones Evangeliorum de tempore et de sanctis.* Add:
  Nicolas de Biard, [Dictionarius pauperum] *Flos theologiae sive Summa de*
  abstinentia (Basel: Johann Amerbach, not after 28 September 1481)
Johannes de Turrecremata, *Quaestiones Evangeliorum de tempore et de sanctis.* Add:
  Nicolas de Biard, [Dictionarius pauperum] *Flos theologiae sive Summa de*
  abstinentia (Deventer: Richardus Pafraet, 20 November 1484)
Johannes de Turrecremata, *Quaestiones Evangeliorum de tempore et de sanctis.* Add:
  Nicolas de Biard, [Dictionarius pauperum] *Flos theologiae sive Summa de*
  abstinentia (Strasbourg: Printer of the 1483 Jordanus von Quedlinburg (Georg
  Husner), not after 24 March 1485)
Mauritius Hibernicus, *Dictionarium sacrae scripturae Mauricii Hybernici* (Venezia:
  Guido Bartoluccius, 1603)
Nicolas de Biard, *Flos theologiae*; Johannes de Turrecremata, *Quaestiones*
  evangeliorum (Strasbourg: Printer of Jordanus von Quedlinburg, before 1487)
Nicolas de Biard, *Dictionarius pauperum (Flos theologiae) sive Summa de abstinentia*
  (Paris: Félix Baligault for Durand Gerlier, [about 1495–1497])
Nicolas de Biard, *Dictionarius pauperum (Flos theologiae) sive Summa de abstinentia*
  (Paris: André Bocard for Durand Gerlier and Jean Petit, 13 November 1498)
Nicolas de Biard, *Dictionarius pauperum (Summa de abstinentia)* (Köln: Retro
  Minores, 14 December 1501)

Secondary Studies

Ainonen, Tuija, 'Making New from Old: Distinction Collections and Textual
  Communities at the Turn of the Thirteenth Century', in *From Learning to Love:*
  Schools, Law, and Pastoral Care in the Middle Ages. Essays in Honour of Joseph W.
  Goering, ed. by Tristan Sharp and others, Papers in Mediaeval Studies, 29
  (Toronto: Pontifical Institute of Mediaeval Studies, 2017), pp. 48–69

276   SOPHIE DELMAS

Bataillon, Louis Jacques, 'Les Instruments de travail des prédicateurs au XIIIe siècle', in *Culture et travail intellectuel dans l'occident médiéval: bilan des 'Colloques humanisme médiéval' [1960–1980] fondés par le R. P. Hubert, O. P.*, ed. by Geneviève Hasenohr and Jean Longère (Paris: Editions du CNRS, 1981), pp. 197–209

Bataillon, Louis Jacques, 'The Tradition of Nicholas de Biard's Distinctiones', *Viator*, 25 (1994), 245–88

Binder, Karl, *Wesen und Eigenschaften der Kirche bei Kardinal Juan de Torquemada, O. P.* (Innsbruck: Verlagsanstalt Tyrolia, 1955)

Cassidy, Brendan, 'An Image of King Robert of Naples in a Franco-Italian Manuscript in Dublin', *The Burlington Magazine*, 148 (2006), 31–33

Catalogue d'une partie des livres de la bibliothèque du cardinal de Lomenie de Brienne, dont la vente se fera Maison de Brienne, rue Saint-Dominique, près la rue de Bourgogne (Paris: Mauger & Lejeune, 1797)

Chenu, Marie-Dominique, 'La Décadence de l'allégorisation; un témoin, Garnier de Rochefort', in *L'Homme devant Dieu: mélanges offert au P. Henri de Lubac*, 3 vols (Paris: Aubier, 1963–1964), II (1964), 129–35

Cornell, Henrik, *Biblia pauperum* (Stockholm: Thule-Tryck, 1925)

Dahan, Gilbert, *L'Exégèse chrétienne de la Bible en Occident médiéval, XII–XIVe siècle* (Paris: Cerf, 1999)

Delmas, Sophie, 'Les Recueils de distinctiones sont-ils des florilèges?', in *On Good Authority: Tradition, Compilation and the Construction of Authority in Literature from Antiquity to the Renaissance*, ed. by Reinhart Ceulemans and Peter De Leemans, Lectio, 3 (Turnhout: Brepols, 2015), pp. 227–43

Delmas, Sophie, 'La Summa de abstinentia attribuée à Nicolas de Biard: circulation et réception', in *Entre stabilité et itinérance: livres et culture des ordres mendiants XIIIe–XVe siècle*, ed. by Nicole Bériou, Martin Morard, and Donatella Nebbiai Dalla Guarda, Bibliologia, 37 (Turnhout: Brepols, 2014), pp. 303–27

Doležalová, Lucie, 'Mémoriser la Bible au bas Moyen Âge? Le *Summarium Biblicum* aux frontières de l'intelligibilité', in *Le Moyen Âge dans le texte: cinq ans d'histoire textuelle au Laboratoire de médiévistique occidentale de Paris*, ed. by Benoît Grévin and Aude Mairey (Paris: Publications de la Sorbonne, 2016), pp. 135–64

Doležalová, Lucie, 'The *Summarium Biblicum*: A Biblical Tool both Popular and Obscure', in *Form and Function in the Late Medieval Bible*, ed. by Eyal Poleg and Laura Light, Library of the Written Word, 27, The Manuscript World, 4 (Leiden: Brill, 2013), pp. 163–84

Hirsch, Rudolf, 'Surgant's List of Recommended Books for Preachers (1502–1503)', *Renaissance Quarterly*, 20 (1967), 199–210

Izbicki, Thomas M., *Protector of the Faith: Cardinal Johannes de Turrecremata and the Defense of the Institutional Church* (Washington, DC: The Catholic University of America Press, 1981)

Langlois Charles-Victor, 'Arnaud Roiard', in *Histoire littéraire de France* (Paris: A. Colin, 1733–1981), XXXV (1921), 465–66

Lobrichon, Guy, 'La Bible des Pauvres du Vatican, Palat. Lat. 871: essai sur l'émergence d'une spiritualité laïque dans l'Allemagne de la fin du Moyen Âge', in *La Bible au Moyen Age*, ed. by Guy Lobrichon (Paris: Picard, 2003), pp. 211–38

Moreau, Brigitte, *Inventaire chronologique des éditions parisiennes du XVIᵉ siècle, d'après les manuscrits de Philippe Renouard*, 5 vols (Paris: Service des travaux historiques de la Ville de Paris, 1972–1992)

Murano, Giovanna, *Opere diffuse per exemplar e pecia*, Textes et études du Moyen Âge, 29 (Turnhout: Brepols, 2005), pp. 640–41

Plotzeck-Wederhake, Gisela, and Günter Bernt, 'Biblia pauperum', in *Lexikon des Mittelalters*, 10 vols (München and other places: Artemis and other publishers, 1980–1999), II (1983), 110

Ratzke, Malena, Bruno Reudenbach, and Hanna Wimmer, *Studien zur Biblia pauperum* (Bern: Lang, 2016)

Rouse, Richard H., and Mary A. Rouse, 'Biblical Distinctiones in the Thirteenth Century', *Archives d'histoire doctrinale et littéraire du Moyen Âge*, 41 (1974), 27–37

Schmidt, Gerhard, *Die Armenbibeln des XIV. Jahrhunderts* (Graz: Böhlau, 1959)

Schmitt, Clément, 'Nicolas de Byard', *Dictionnaire de spiritualité, ascétique et mystique, doctrine et histoire*, ed. by Marcel Viller and others, 17 vols (Paris: Beauchesne, 1932–1995), XI (1981), 254–55

Schneyer, Johannes Baptist, *Repertorium der lateinischen Sermones des Mittelalters: für die Zeit von 1150–1350*, 11 vols (Münster: Aschendorffsche Verlagsbuchhandlung, 1969–1989)

Serventi, Silvia, 'Did Giordano da Pisa Use the *Distinctiones* of Nicolas de Gorran?', in *Constructing the Medieval Sermon*, ed. by Roger Andersson, Sermo: Studies on Patristic, Medieval and Reformation Sermons and Preaching, 6 (Turnhout: Brepols, 2007), pp. 83–116

Stockmann, Jules Felix, *Joannis de Turrecremata O. P. vitam ejusque doctrinam de corpore Christi mystico* (Bologna: Tipografia 'Studentato missioni', 1951)

Teetaert, Amédée, 'Nicolas Biard', in *Dictionnaire de théologie catholique, contenant l'exposé des doctrines de la théologie catholique, leurs preuves et leur historie*, ed. by Alfred Vacant and others, 15 vols (Paris: Letouzey & Ané, 1902–1950), XI (1930), 589–92

Teeuwen, Mariken, *The Vocabulary of Intellectual Life in the Middle Ages*, CIVICIMA: Études sur le vocabulaire intellectuel du Moyen Âge, 10 (Turnhout: Brepols, 2003)

Weckwerth, Alfred, 'Armenbibeln', in *Theologische Realenzyklopädie*, ed. by Gerhard Krause and Gerhard Müller, 36 vols (Berlin: De Gruyter, 1976–2004), IV (1979), 8–10

Wirth, Karl-August, 'Biblia pauperum', in *Die deutsche Literatur des Mittelalters: Verfasser-lexikon*, ed. by Kurt Ruh, and others, 2nd edn, 14 vols (Berlin: De Gruyter, 1977–2008), I (1977), cols 843–45

PIETRO DELCORNO

A Forgotten Italian Bestseller

Ludovico Pittorio's Omiliario quadragisimale

Food for the soul and precious merchandise: with these two metaphors, Ludovico Pittorio (*c.* 1452–*c.* 1525) depicts his vernacular homilies in the dedicatory letter of his Lenten sermon collection, the *Omiliario quadragisimale*, first printed in Modena in 1506 by Domenico Rococciola (*c.* 1440–1506).[1] At first glance, the humble tone of the dedicatory letter and the location of the edition — definitely not a main hub in the early printing market — would not appear very promising. Yet, over the years, the book became a major bestseller in Italy. It was a gradual process. The second edition was published by Giovanni Angelo Scinzenzeler (d. 1526) in Milan in 1513.[2] This prolific typographer combined the Lenten sermons with Pittorio's *Dominicale e sanctuario*, which significantly had been the first sermon collection *de tempore et de sanctis* printed in Italian, published by Rococciola probably

---

1 Ludovico Pittorio, *Omiliario quadragisimale fondato de verbo ad verbum sule Epistole e Evangelii sì como corrono ogni dì secondo lo ordine dela Romana Giesia* (Modena: Domenico Rococciola, 1506; hereafter Pittorio, *Omiliario 1506*). I was able to consult some digital reproductions of this first edition, kindly provided by Dr Giacomo Mariani. For the reminder of the collection, I rely on Ludovico Pittorio, *Homiliario quadragesimale* (Brescia: Ludovico Brittanico, 1541; hereafter Pittorio, *Omiliario 1541*). The two editions differ only in the spelling of some words. This publication is part of the project 'Lenten Sermon Bestsellers: Shaping Society in Late Medieval Europe (1470–1520)' (project number VI.Veni.191H.018) of the Veni research programme which is financed by the Dutch Research Council (NWO). A first version of this paper was presented at the conference 'Circulating the Word of God in Medieval and Early Modern Europe: Transformative Preaching in Manuscript and Print (*c.* 1450 to *c.* 1550)', University of Hull, 25–27 March 2017. I am grateful to the organizers of the conference as well as the participants for their inputs and suggestions. Moreover, I am particularly indebted to Professor Veronica O'Mara and Dr Patricia Stoop for the invaluable support they gave me in developing this contribution and the patience and accuracy with which they guided the whole process.
2 Ludovico Pittorio, *Dominicale sanctuario e quadragesimale [...] nouamente stampato con molte agionte* (Milano: Giovanni Angelo Scinzenzeler, 1513).

> **Pietro Delcorno** (pietro.delcorno3@unibo.it) is Senior Assistant Professor in Medieval History in the Department of History and Cultures at the University of Bologna.

Circulating the Word of God in Medieval and Early Modern Europe: Catholic Preaching and Preachers across Manuscript and Print (c. 1450 to c. 1550), ed. by Veronica O'Mara and Patricia Stoop, SERMO 17, (Turnhout: Brepols, 2022), pp. 279–309 BREPOLS ❧ PUBLISHERS 10.1484/M.SERMO-EB.5.130459

between 1502 and 1505.[3] By joining the two collections, Scinzenzeler created a set of sermons for the entire liturgical year, a format that became common for the sermons of Pittorio in the 1530s (see Appendix). His Lenten sermon collection was republished in 1518 in Venice by Bernardino Vitali and — again by Scinzenzeler — in 1520 in Milan. No edition was printed in the following decade, during which Pittorio died, probably around 1525. Next, the rhythm of production of the *Omiliario* suddenly soared with four editions between 1530 and 1533, exactly in the period when 'the idea of spreading the Word of God among all Christians reached its peak in Italy'.[4] From that moment onwards, Pittorio's Lenten sermons proved to be unstoppable, reaching the astonishing number of at least thirty-six editions by 1599, when its fortune started to decline, scoring only two other editions in 1607 and 1630.[5] These impressive numbers prove that Pittorio's sermons provided generations of readers (and preachers) with a precious access to materials for meditation (mainly on the Bible) during Lent.

By the fifteenth century, Lent had become a period of intensified religious instruction marked by preaching on a daily basis.[6] Lenten preaching was supposed to lead the faithful in a process of redefinition of their personal and collective identity, culminating in key rites connected with Easter, namely sacramental Confession, participation in the Eucharist, and the commemoration of the Passion. In this regard, Lenten sermon collections were in high demand as crucial tools of pastoral care. As preaching aids that both reflected and produced the religious knowledge of the time, Lenten sermon collections like the one by Pittorio represent fascinating microcosms of late medieval

---

3 Ludovico Pittorio, *Dominicale e santuario* [...] (Modena: Domenico Rococciola, [*c.* 1502–1505]). Previous printed sermon collections in the vernacular were either for Lent, such as those by Roberto Caracciolo (*c.* 1425–1494) and Girolamo Savonarola (1452–1498), or sermon collections organized as treatises, like Antonio da Vercelli, *Consegli della salute del peccatore* [s.n. 1470] or Roberto Caracciolo, *Specchio della fede* (Venezia: Giovanni da Bergamo, 1495).

4 Élise Boillet, 'For Early Modern Printed Biblical Literature in Italian: Lay Authorship and Readership', in *Lay Readings of the Bible in Early Modern Europe*, ed. by Erminia Ardissino and Élise Boillet, Intersections, 68 (Leiden: Brill, 2020), pp. 170–90 (p. 177), which highlights the peak in the 1530s and 1540s.

5 Several of its early editions survive only in one or two copies. *EDIT16: Censimento nazionale delle edizioni italiane del XVI secolo* indicates one copy for Milano 1513; two copies for Venezia 1518. It is plausibe that some editions are entirely lost; see on this topic, Neil Harris, 'La sopravvivenza del libro ossia appunti per una lista della lavandaia', *Ecdotica*, 4 (2007), 24–65; and *Lost Books: Reconstructing the Print World of Pre-Industrial Europe*, ed. by Flavia Bruni and Andrew Pettegree, Library of the Written Word, The Handpress World, 46 (Leiden: Brill, 2016).

6 See *I sermoni quaresimali: digiuno del corpo, banchetto dell'anima / Lenten Sermons: Fasting of the Body, Banquet of the Soul*, ed. by Pietro Delcorno, Eleonora Lombardo, and Lorenza Tromboni, *Memorie Domenicane*, n.s. 48 (Firenze: Edizioni Nerbini, 2017). On the origin of Lenten sermon collections, see Jussi Hanska, '*Sermones quadragesimales*: Birth and Development of a Genre', *Il Santo*, 52 (2012), 107–27.

religious culture.[7] The *Omiliario* stems from this preaching practice, and, at the same time, tries to support and integrate (perhaps even replace) it by envisaging a personal or collective reading of sermons in convents and houses.

Scholars such as Gigliola Fragnito have underlined the relevance of Pittorio's sermons and their extraordinary success in Italy throughout the sixteenth century.[8] Emily Michelson summarizes well some of their main characteristics:

> Pittorio's homilies are direct and conversational. They move from the scriptural reading for the day, presented verse by verse in abbreviated vernacular paraphrases, to a direct and emotional exhortation to penitence and charitable living, as befits the Lenten season. They include no patristic or scholastic references, and they have none of the classical rhetorical flourishes that one might have expected, given Pittorio's classical training.[9]

Still, despite the recognition of the importance and pervasive presence of the *Omiliario* in sixteenth-century Italian society, its sermons have not been subject to any in-depth scrutiny.[10] The *Omiliario* can be considered a forgotten bestseller; or rather, a bestseller that scholars know of, but have forgotten to read. This is even more surprising when one considers that Pittorio is usually listed among the followers of Savonarola (1452–1498) and was active in Ferrara, one of the liveliest Italian cultural centres of the time.[11]

---

7 See Pietro Delcorno, 'Quaresimali "visibili": il serafino, il guerriero, il pellegrino', *Studi medievali*, 60 (2019), 645–88.

8 Gigliola Fragnito, *Proibito capire: la Chiesa e il volgare nella prima età moderna* (Bologna: Il Mulino, 2005), pp. 262–63 (and *ad indecem*).

9 Emily Michelson, *The Pulpit and the Press in Reformation Italy*, I tatti studies in Italian renaissance history(Cambridge, MA: Harvard University Press, 2013), pp. 26–27.

10 Anna Maria Fioravanti Baraldi, 'Testo e immagini: le edizioni cinquecentesche dell'Omiliario quadragesimale di Ludovico Pittorio', in *Girolamo Savonarola da Ferrara all'Europa*, ed. by Gigliola Fragnito and Mario Miegge (Firenze: SISMEL, 2001), pp. 139–53, does not engage with the sermons, offering only a partial description of the editions. Recently, Pittorio's *Psalterio Davidico* (*editio princeps* 1524) received some attention: see Élise Boillet, 'La Fortune du Psalterio Davitico de Lodovico Pittorio en Italie au XVIe siècle', *La bibliofilia*, 115 (2013), 621–28; Élise Boillet, 'Vernacular Biblical Literature in Sixteenth-Century Italy: Universal Reading and Specific Readers', in *Discovering the Riches of the Word: Religious Reading in Late Medieval and Early Modern Europe*, ed. by Sabrina Corbellini, Margriet Hoogvliet, and Bart Ramakers, Intersections, 38 (Leiden: Brill, 2015), pp. 213–33 (pp. 220–23); Élise Boillet, 'Vernacular Sermons on the Psalms Printed in Sixteenth-Century Italy: An Interface between Oral and Written Cultures', in *Voices and Texts in Early Modern Italian Society*, ed. by Brian Richardson, Massimo Rospocher, and Stefano Dall'Aglio (London: Routledge, 2016), pp. 200–11 (pp. 201–03). Pittorio composed this work in 1522, presenting it as his final gift to a group of nuns (probably of Ferrara), saying that he translated each Psalm into the vernacular and commented on it in the form of a homily ('volgarizarli in forma di homelie'); Ludovico Pittorio, *I salmi di David* (Venezia: Al segno della Speranza, 1547), fol. a2 recto.

11 On the religious context of Ferrara, with specific attention paid to its Savonarolan movement, see Tamar Herzig, *Savonarola's Women: Visions and Reform in Renaissance Italy* (Chicago: University of Chicago Press, 2008), which only briefly refers to Pittorio (pp. 67

While a detailed analysis of the entire sermon collection exceeds the limits of an essay, this contribution aims to open up the *Omiliario* and to consider closely some of its sermons, in order to shed light on the cultural and religious relevance of a text that has remained for too long in a sort of hazy limbo. Furthermore, the study of the *Omiliario* calls into question several artificial binary divides, since — as we shall see — it seeks to move beyond divisions such as orality-literacy, popular-learned, laity-clergy. In what follows, I will first introduce Pittorio and the intended audience/readers of his sermons, in particular looking at the dedicatory letter of his *Omiliario*. Next, I will focus on a selected number of his Lenten sermons, so as to gain an insight into how Pittorio put the (moral) interpretation of the Bible at the forefront and was able — at least in some cases — to propose a rich, non-conventional spiritual teaching. Finally, I will discuss a few key elements of the reception history of a book that proved to be appealing for quite a differentiated readership.

Pittorio and his Early Religious Works

Information on the life of Ludovico Pittorio (also known as Luigi Bigi) is in short supply.[12] Born in Ferrara around 1452, he studied in his home town with the renowned humanist Battista Guarini (d. 1503), son of the famous Guarino da Verona. Within the entourage of the court of Ferrara, Pittorio became acquainted with the humanist and philosopher Giovan Francesco Pico della Mirandola (d. 1533), nephew of Giovanni Pico (d. 1494).[13] Probably due to the friendship and influence of Giovan Francesco Pico, in the 1490s Pittorio abandoned his previous poetic compositions, which dealt with secular and erotic themes, and joined the Savonarolan intellectual circle of Ferrara.[14] Three letters of Girolamo Savonarola, written in 1497, attest to

---

and 128). The same is true of the valuable introduction in Gabriella Zarri, *La religione di Lucrezia Borgia: le lettere inedite del confessore* (Roma: Roma nel Rinascimento, 2006), pp. 136 and 139–40. Scholars usually simply refer to Savonarola's letters to Pittorio (see below) and the information provided by Fioravanti Baraldi.

12 See Giancarlo Andenna, 'Pittorio, Ludovico', in *Dizionario biografico degli italiani* (Roma: Istituto della Enciclopedia Italiana, 1960–), 84 (2015), 264–68.

13 See Elisabetta Scapparone, 'Pico, Giovan Francesco', in *Dizionario biografico degli italiani* (Roma: Istituto della Enciclopedia Italiana, 1960–), 83 (2015), pp. 320–22.

14 Already at the end of his secular composition *Candida*, dedicated to Giovan Francesco Pico, there is a *Hymnus ad beatam virginem Dei matrem*; see Ludovico Bigi Pittorio, *Candida* (Modena: Domenico Rococciola, 1491), fols 12 verso–13 verso. The hymn is introduced abruptly so that on the same page there is also the end of the poem *Ad Sextum de eius uxore dormiente*, which praises the beauty of a half-naked sleeping woman ('Una papillarum pars cernitur, altera panno / delitet; haec oculos mulcet, et illa beat'). On Pittorio's Latin poetry, see Silvio Pasquazi, 'La poesia in latino', in *Storia di Ferrara, VII: Il Rinascimento e la letteratura*, ed. by Walter Moretti (Ferrara: Librit, 1994), pp. 100–56 (pp. 121–30).

his personal acquaintance with Pittorio.[15] In 1516 the friar's brother, Alberto Savonarola, left in his will a golden ring to Pittorio, mentioned as 'tantum amico meo' ['my great friend'].[16] Probably in connection with the turbulent events of the rise and fall of Fra Girolamo, Pittorio turned to a more intense spiritual life. According to seventeenth-century local historiographers, at a non-specified time Pittorio became a priest, a piece of information that still requires documentary evidence.[17] Anna Maria Fioravanti Baraldi asserts that Pittorio became a member of the Servite order, yet without any evidence of it and probably by misinterpreting the fact that he was buried in his family tomb, which was in the Servite church in Ferrara.[18] Emily Michelson assumes instead that Pittorio remained a lay man.[19] However, this claim would need to be confirmed as well, as it does not seem fully in line with Pittorio's engagement in the pastoral care of lay people and spiritual guidance of nuns that emerges from his own texts. While only new archival findings may shed light on Pittorio's life, we shall note that the sixteenth-century editions of his works did not feel any need to clarify his social status.[20] This attests to a cultural context where the involvement of lay authors in the production of

---

15 Girolamo Savonarola, *Lettere e scritti apologetici*, ed. by Roberto Ridolfi, Vincenzo Romano, and Armando F. Verde (Roma: Belardetti, 1984), pp. 152–53, 172–74, and 183–84.

16 See Anna Maria Fioravanti Baraldi, 'Ludovico Pittorio e la cultura figurativa a Ferrara nel primo Cinquecento', in *Alla corte degli Estensi: filosofia, arte e cultura a Ferrara nei secoli xv e xvi*, ed. by Marco Bertozzi (Ferrara: Università degli Studi, 1994), pp. 217–46 (p. 221). In a 1514 Latin composition, Pittorio addressed Alberto by recalling Fra Girolamo as a prophet; see Fioravanti Baraldi, 'Testo e immagini', pp. 144–45. In his will, Alberto also left a valuable property to the Ferrarese priest Francesco Caloro, a fervent Savonarolan activist; see Herzig, *Savonarola's Women*, p. 263.

17 Pittorio is defined 'prete divotissimo' ['utmost pious priest'] in Agostino Superbi, *Apparato de gli huomini illustri della città di Ferrara* (Ferrara: Francesco Suzzi, 1620), p. 11. The information is repeated in Antonio Libanori, *Ferrara d'oro imbrunito*, 3 vols (Ferrara: Maresti 1665–1674), iii (1674), p. 189. Superbi (d. 1634) was a Conventual Franciscan theologian, active in Ferrara, where the Cistercian abbot Libanori also lived in the second half of the seventeenth century.

18 See Fioravanti Baraldi, 'Ludovico Pittorio e la cultura figurativa', pp. 222 and 229, and Fioravanti Baraldi, 'Testo e immagini', p. 145 (here, she assumes that Pittorio became a Servite between 1494 and 1496). She refers to Superbi, Libanori, and Marcantonio Guarini (d. 1634), yet they did not affirm that Pittorio was a Servite but only that he was buried in the Servite church. Listing the illustrious people buried there, Marcantonio Guarini, nephew of Battista Guarini, put Pittorio not among the famous Servite friars but among the illustrious 'guests', defining him only as a poet ('poeta latino') and describing the sepulchre; Marcantonio Guarini, *Compendio historico […] delle Chiese […] di Ferrara e delle memorie di que' personaggi di pregio che in esse son sepelliti* (Ferrara: Eredi Vittorio Baldini, 1621), pp. 47–48. The information that Pittorio became a Servite is repeated in Zarri, *La religione di Lucrezia Borgia*, p. 136 and Andenna, 'Pittorio', p. 321. I made the same mistake in Pietro Delcorno, *In the Mirror of the Prodigal Son: The Pastoral Uses of a Biblical Narrative (c. 1200–1550)*, Commentaria, 9 (Leiden: Brill, 2017), p. 444.

19 Michelson, *The Pulpit and the Press*, p. 27.

20 Tellingly the colphon of the first edition of the *Dominicale* uses only the generic and flexible term 'messere' ('Finisse il Dominicale per Messere Ludovico Pictorio da Ferrara'; fol. O6

biblical literature in the vernacular did not encounter resistance (something that increased later on).[21]

The very little that is known about Pittorio's life depends on the information contained in his own religious texts, written in prose and verse, both in Latin and in the vernacular. His first religious texts date to the closing years of the fifteenth century. In 1496 his Latin poetic compositions gathered in the *Opuscolorum christianorum libri tres* were published by Domenico Rococciola.[22] The poems enjoyed a certain success outside Italy, where humanists such as Beatus Rhenanus (1487–1545), Jakob Wimpfeling (1450–1528), and Lefèvre d'Etaples (*c.* 1450–1536) looked at Pittorio as a model of a Christian poet, together with authors such as Battista Mantovano (1447–1516) and Filippo Beroaldo (1481–1550).[23] Particularly in the German regions his poems were printed four times, in different formats.[24] One of them, a meditation on the *Pater noster*, was even translated into German verse and published as an appendix to the sermons on the Lord's Prayer by Johannes Geiler von Kaysersberg (1445–1510), the most celebrated German preacher of the time.[25]

In the same period the *Consolatoria lectione in sul transito della morte* was published (probably in Florence), dedicated to Maria Magdalena Petrata, an Observant Carmelite nun of the monastery of San Gabriele in Ferrara. Pittorio addressed her as his beloved little daughter in Christ, while defining himself as a humble servant of the other nuns.[26] This text is quite interesting, since it exhorts the nun to face her death with full confidence in salvation and as

---

recto), appropriate for any person of high social status such as (learned or noble) lay men or priests. This term seems to exclude Pittorio's belonging to a religious Order.

21 For important general remarks see Élise Boillet, 'For Early Modern Printed Biblical Literature', pp. 170–90. The article builds on ongoing research to create a *Repertorio di letteratura biblica in italiano a stampa (ca 1462–1650)*.

22 Ludovico Pittorio, *Opuscolorum christianorum libri tres* (Modena: Domenico Rococciola, 1496). The three parts are dedicated to prominent political patrons: Giovan Francesco Pico della Mirandola, Alberto Pio da Carpi (1474–1531), and Guidobaldo da Montefeltro (1472–1508).

23 His fame was also due to Giovan Francesco Pico, who praised Pittorio in his *De studio divinae et humanae philosophiae* (1496); see Andrea Severi, *Filippo Beroaldo il Vecchio, un maestro per l'Europa: da commentatore di classici a classico moderno (1481–1550)* (Bologna: Il Mulino, 2015), *ad indicem*.

24 For instance, see the edition published in 1509 in Strasbourg by Matthias Schürer, with two dedicatory letters by Beatus Rhenanus (1485–1547).

25 *Ein betrachtung Ludovici Bigi von Ferraer über das gebett des herren [...]*, in Johannes Geiler von Kaysersberg, *Pater noster: des hochgelerten wurdigen Predicanten [...]* [Strasbourg: Matthias Hupfuff, 1515], fols V3 recto–V4 recto. On this preacher, see the contribution by Rita Voltmer in the present volume.

26 Pittorio's text paraphrased above reads: 'Ludovico Pictorio servo infimo delle Moniale spose di Iesù Christo, infinite spirituali salute dice alla dilectissima e dolce in Christo sua figliuolina suor Maria Magdalena Petrata, professa nello observante e sacro Carmellitan monasterio di sancto Gabriello di Ferrara'; Ludovico Pittorio, *Consolatoria lectione in sul transito della morte* [Firenze: Bartolomeo di Libri, 1490–1500], fol. a1 recto. The monastery was re-founded as a Carmelite nunnery in 1489, under the patronage of the Duchess Eleonora d'Aragona (1450–1493); see

A FORGOTTEN ITALIAN BESTSELLER   285

a joyful encounter with Christ, her groom, and with all the saints — it even exhorts her to imagine the delights of the future talks with her guardian angel in heaven.[27] In the summary especially, this early text forcefully expresses a Christocentric faith, where salvation comes entirely from the sacrifice of Christ and his love. Hence, according to Pittorio, it would be a mistake to desire to live longer to practise more penitence since (as noted by the apostle Paul) no one can be saved on account of his good deeds, but only because of the Passion of Christ:[28]

> Onde se bene voi vivesti li anni di Matusalem e facessi più penitentia voi sola che facessino mai tutti li sancti insieme, a ogni modo la salute vostra consiste nel sangue di Iesù Christo: lui ha pagato per li peccati vostri; nella passione sua habbiate speranza, e sarete salva così hora come da qui a mille anni. (Pittorio, *Consolatoria*, fol. a9 recto–verso)
>
>> [Even if you would live longer than Methuselah and do more penitence than all the other saints together, in any case your salvation would come from the blood of Jesus Christ: he paid for your sins; put your hope in his Passion, and you will be saved now as well as in a thousand years].

Pittorio assumed that the nun would confess her sins and receive the Eucharist before her death. The text is not against sacraments or good deeds; nevertheless, with its firm reassurance of salvation, it significantly gives primacy to God's grace. Even the memory of the sins or faults in her religious life will be transformed into elements to praise the divine mercy.[29]

The *lectione* to Sister Maria Magdalena is part of a small number of texts that attests to Pittorio's commitment (and self-fashioning) as a spiritual mentor of several female communities, not only in Ferrara but also in Milan. Besides the text to the Carmelite nun in Ferrara, there are several letters to the Cistercian nuns of San Michele sul Dosso, in Milan, a brief treatise on sin addressed to Beatrice d'Este, abbess of Sant'Antonio in Polesine, a Benedictine monastery in Ferrara, and a letter to a certain Arcangela, sent immediately after her profession without mentioning her convent. To these texts, one may add the sermon on Holy Communion printed in 1502 and dedicated to Pittorio's own niece, Aurelia Nasella, a nun in the Observant Dominican

---

Thomas Tuohy, *Herculean Ferrara: Ercole d'Este (1471–1505) and the Invention of a Ducal Capital* (Cambridge: Cambridge University Press, 1996), pp. 337 and 486.

27 Pittorio, *Consolatoria*, fol. a4 verso.

28 Pittorio, *Consolatoria*, fol. a9 recto.

29 Pittorio expressed this concept in the following words: 'Niuna cosa ti darà noia, non pure la memoria de peccati, anzi considerandoli non in quanto offesa di Dio, ma in quanto materia delle suoi infinite miserationi farai festa, e iubilosa canterai col propheta: *Misericordias Domini in eternum cantabo*', Pittorio, *Consolatoria*, fol. a3 recto. In early sixteenth-century Italy the mystical and affective language circulated concepts later associated with Lutheran theology; see Michele Camaioni, *Il Vangelo e l'Anticristo: Bernardino Ochino tra francescanesimo ed eresia (1487–1547)* (Bologna: Il Mulino, 2018), pp. 42–56, 82–83, and 215–16.

convent of Santa Caterina Martire, in Ferrara.[30] The letters to the monastery of San Michele depict a lively personal relationship, since they address both the entire community and specific nuns.[31] One of the collective letters hints at the existence of Pittorio's writings in manuscript form. It mentions a sister, named Ludovica, who — it would seem — collected them in a 'quinterno' ['notebook'] either for her personal devotion or the benefit of the community.[32] The original letters and this handwritten booklet has not survived — as far as we know — yet testify to a circulation of some of Pittorio's spiritual texts in manuscript form before getting into print.

This corpus of texts is presented and preserved as an appendix to Pittorio's *Dominicale* published in Modena, once again by Domenico Rococciola, definitely after 1498 and probably after 1502.[33] It continued to be reprinted together with this volume during the sixteenth century, with an additional edition as an appendix to Savonarola's treatises published in Venice in 1547.[34] The *Dominicale* presents some of the letters to the nuns as homilies on key topics for the Christian life, namely: confession, compunction, Holy Communion, and the desire to encounter God (that is, the preparation for death).[35] By defining them as 'sermoni scritti a diverse persone' ['sermons

---

30 See Herzig, *Savonarola's Women*, pp. 128 and 256. I was unable to consult Ludovico Pittorio, *Sermone della comunione* (Firenze: [s.n.], 1502).

31 In a letter to the Abbess Girolama, Pittorio refers with particular affection to Sister Francesca; in a letter to three nuns (Caterina, Paola, Giulia), he mentions several other nuns (besides Girolama and Francesca, the Prioress Maria and Sisters Placita, Chiara, and Ludovica). This letter must date after 1498 (and probably after 1500), since Pittorio presents it as a summary ('cavarne la medolla') and translation into the vernacular of a poetic meditation in Latin included in Pittorio, *Opusculorum christianorum*, fols a7 recto–a8 recto. This text was also printed as an independent pamphlet; see Ludovico Pittorio, *Utile meditatione in sei gradi divisa* (Ferrara: [s.n.], 1502). The Benedictine monastery of San Michele assumed the Cistercian rule in 1498; to my knowledge, there are no studies about this nunnery in that period.

32 'Son contento che D. Ludovica retenga quello nostro quinterno, perché havendovi donato il cuore, sono etiam vostre le facultà, benché siano minime' ['I am glad that lady Ludovica keeps this our notebook, since having given my heart to you, you also possess all my belongings, although they are minimal']; Pittorio, *Dominicale*, fol. y6 verso.

33 See n. 31 for the dating.

34 *Molti devotissimi trattati del reverendo padre frate Hieronimo Savonarola da Ferrara [...] et una espositione del Pater noster et alcuni sermoni devoti di Ludouico Pittorio da Ferrara* (Venezia: Al segno della Speranza, 1547). The publisher conceived the volume as the completition of the edition of Pittorio's Lenten and Sunday sermons, which he printed in the same format in 1546, announcing that he did not include Pittorio's other sermons, which would be published either with his exposition of the Psalms (printed in 1547) or — as happened — with Savonarola's treatises, since their topics were close and the two authors were good friends ('era molto suo familiar amico'); Ludovico Pittorio, *Homiliario* (Venezia: Al segno della Speranza, 1546), fol. 557 verso.

35 The sermon on Holy Communion is addressed 'alli fratelli soi' ['to his brothers']; it addresses a lay audience, probably the members of his confraternity (see below). The relationship of this text with the sermon on the same topic printed in 1502 (see n. 30) remains to be investigated.

written to various people'], Pittorio acknowledges their origin as sermons in the form of letters and implicitly distinguishes them from the sermons of the *Dominicale* that seem to stem from an actual oral performance.[36]

The *Dominicale* clearly suggests Pittorio's commitment as preacher within a confraternal environment.[37] In its dedicatory letter Pittorio depicts himself as a 'minimo e inutile fratello' ['little and unworthy brother'] of the confraternity of San Ludovico in Ferrara and the sermons as originally intended for the religious instruction of the members of this confraternity, as the references to the local context and the uses of the brotherhood show.[38] The letter states that the initiative to publish the book was taken by a certain Ser Ludovico, a devotee probably connected with the confraternity.[39] He considered it extremely useful for 'the illiterate' who have trouble understanding the biblical pericopes during Mass. Pittorio clearly shared this view by envisaging a lay readership and spiritual nourishment resulting from the interplay between personal reading and collective celebration.[40] The fact that Ser Ludovico decided to print these sermons — not that he asked Pittorio to write them[41] — suggests that they already existed in a manuscript format of which we have no trace.

> Circha l'arogantia, me rimetto ala testimonianza de Ser Ludovico, molto huomo de singulare fede. So che'l testificarà como non già io, ma lui e di

---

36 Pittorio, *Dominicale*, fol. X2 recto. On this type of text in the Italian context see Daniela Delcorno Branca, *Le Spirituali sportelle di Agostino di Portico: lettere alle monache di S. Marta di Siena* (Roma: Edizioni di Storia e Letteratura, 2019).

37 On the multifaceted phenomenon of confraternities as organizations of (mainly male) lay members coming from different social backgrounds and engaged in devotional and charitable activities, often developed in connection with and with the participation of friars and priests, and on their role in society, see *Studi confraternali: orientamenti, problemi, testimonianze*, ed. by Marina Gazzini (Firenze: Firenze University Press, 2009) and *A Companion to Medieval and Early Modern Confraternities*, ed. by Konrad Eisenbichler, Brill's Companions to the Christian Tradition, 83 (Leiden: Brill, 2019).

38 This is the address used by Pittorio: 'A tuti li electi de Dio e specialmente huomini devoti de congregatione, Ludovico Pictorio minimo e inutile fratello de la compagnia de Sancto Ludovico da Ferrara, infinite e immortale in Cristo Iesù desidera, salute', Pittorio, *Dominicale*, fol. 1 verso. See particularly the sermons on the patrons of the *congregazione*, St Louis, King of France, and to St Francesco (the brotherhood was founded in 1434 by Gabriele Guastavillani, an Observant Franciscan friar) as well as those to the patrons of Ferrara, St George (Pittorio criticized the *palio* run on that day in the city) and St Maurelio. On this confraternity, see Giuseppe Antenore Scalabrini, *Memorie istoriche delle chiese di Ferrara* (Ferrara: Carlo Coatti, 1773), pp. 338–41.

39 The letter refers to him as 'amico nostro' ['our friend'], suggesting his familiarity (if not his affiliation) with the confraternity. In 1496 Pittorio dedicated a poem to an unspecified Lodovico; Pittorio, *Opuscolorum christianorum*, fols b4 verso–b5 verso.

40 Antonio Pucci (d. 1388) had already presented his versification of the *Diatessaron* and of the Lenten Gospels as a support for a fruitful listening to preaching, probably thinking of a confraternal readership; see Pietro Delcorno, *Lazzaro e il ricco epulone: metamorfosi di una parabola fra Quattro e Cinquecento* (Bologna: Il Mulino, 2014), p. 39.

41 The request for someone to write down the sermon was a commonplace in the introduction to sermon collections.

soa spontanea voluntà ha facto stampare questo nostro libro persuaden-
dosi, sì como lui dice, che'l deba sumamente giovare ai lectori de buona
voluntà, specialmente ali idioti e illiterati, i qualli non intendono così
bene li evangelii e epistole quando se legono a la messa, imperoché non
se contiene qui quasi altro se non la expositione di evangeli et spesso
etiam de le epistole che se recitano ala messa [...]. Veramente ogni fidele
christiano, il qualle non ha il latino ma tutavia se dilecta intendere in
vulgare cose spirituale, doverebbe havere questo libro e legere sempre la
lectione dela festa occurrente 'nanti che'l andassi ala giesa, perché sì nel
legere, sì dipoi nel udire la messa, pigliarà grande consolatione'. (Pittorio,
Dominicale, fol. 1 verso)

> [Concerning [any accusation of] arrogance [for publishing this book],
> I refer to the testimony of Sir Ludovico, a man of great faith. I know
> that he will testify that he and not I, and by his own will caused the
> printing of this book, being persuaded — as he says — that it would
> greatly benefit any reader of good will, especially the rude and illiterate,
> who do not understand the Gospel and the Epistle so well when they
> are read during the Mass; since here there is almost nothing else than
> the explanation of the Gospel pericopes and often of the Epistles that
> are read during the Mass [...]. Truly, every faithful Christian, who
> does not know Latin but loves to understand spiritual things in the
> vernacular, should have this book and always read the pericope of the
> relevant feast from it before going to church, so that first in reading
> and then in hearing the Mass, he will find great consolation].

Furthermore, Pittorio states that those used to mental prayer would also
learn from this book how to develop new interpretations (*sensi*) of the
biblical readings, that is to say, how to engage in a personal meditation and
appropriation of the Scripture. Here, Pittorio uses the technical terms of the
lectio divina by saying that the personal rumination ('in secreto ruminando') of
the meanings of the Bible will give the reader 'tale gusto de Dio' ['so intense a
taste of God'] that one would not have refused to buy this book for all the gold
in the world.[42] Similar affirmations occur also on the title page, which — with
an interesting shift — targets families as possible customers, saying that the
book can be enjoyed not only by readers but also by listeners, hence hinting
at collective reading at home:

> Et è opera così facile, iocunda e salutare che ogni famiglia dove sia chi
> sapa legere la doverebbe havere in casa per conforto e salute dile anime.
> Et chi legerà o odirà cognoscerà ch'io non mento, e remarrà certo più che
> satisfacto e consolato. (Pittorio, *Dominicale*, fol. 1 recto)

---

42 Pittorio, *Dominicale*, fol. 1 verso.

[And it is a work so easy, delightful, and useful that each family with someone who knows how to read should have it at home for the consolation and salvation of the souls. And those who read it or listen to it will know that I do not lie, and will remain for sure more than satisfied and comforted].[43]

The Dedicatory Letter of the *Omiliario*

In 1506 Rococciola published Pittorio's second sermon collection, his *Quadragisimale*.[44] The dedicatory letter is addressed to Beatrice d'Este, the abbess of Sant'Antonio in Polesine (she was still alive in 1513).[45] This important Benedictine convent in Ferrara was firmly connected with the Estense family, as a convent founded by one of its saints, Beatrice II d'Este (1192–1262), who was buried and venerated there: evidently, the abbess's name paid homage to the saintly ancestor.[46] The abbess Beatrice was the sister of Ercole d'Este (d. 1523), not the Duke of Ferrara but the Lord of San Martino in Rio, son of Sigismondo d'Este (1433–1507). Pittorio stated that he composed his work 'sotto l'ombra' ['under the shade'] of Beatrice's illustrious brother and his wife, Angela Sforza (1479–c. 1525), 'mei optimi patroni' ['my excellent patrons'], hence putting himself and his work under the patronage of prominent members of the ruling family of the Duchy of Ferrara, something probably even more urgent after the defeat of his friend and patron Giovan Francesco Pico, who lost control of Mirandola in 1502.[47]

In the letter Pittorio presented the sermons as a spiritual gift to the abbess by saying that — since her duty was 'il pascere le sorelle di cibi sì spirituali sì

---

43 Translated by Boillet, 'For Early Modern Printed Biblical Literature', p. 180. A woodcut occupies two thirds of the title page showing Christ, accompanied by six apostles, who dictates the Gospel to the evangelists represented as *reportatores*, seated at their desks, taking note of their master's lesson.

44 There are internal references to the previous sermon collection; see Pittorio, *Omiliario 1541*, fols 88 recto–153 recto.

45 She was mentioned, still as abbess, in the will of her brother, written in January 1513; see Luigi Napoleone Cittadella, *Notizie amministrative, storiche, artische relative a Ferrara*, 3 vols (Ferrara: Domenico Taddei, 1868), II, 318.

46 The monastery was closely connected with the noble families of Ferrara and had great relevance during the fifteenth century, when it hosted several popes (John XXIII, Eugenius IV during the Council, Pius II); see Chiara Guarnieri, 'Il monastero di S. Antonio in Polesine: un'isola nella città', in *S. Antonio in Polesine: archeologia e storia di un monastero estense*, ed. by Chiara Guarnieri (Borgo San Lorenzo: All'Insegna del Giglio, 2006), pp. 13–15. Archeological evidence shows the affluence of the monastery in the early sixteenth century.

47 Ludovico Pittorio, *Omiliario 1506*, fol. a1 verso. This habit was not new: Roberto Caracciolo put his vernacular sermon collections under the patronage of the Aragonese dynasty of Naples, while Antonio da Bitonto (1385–1465) framed his *Sermones quadragesimales de vitiis* as a dialogue with Guidantonio da Montefeltro, count of Urbino (1377–1443).

corporali' ['to feed her nuns with both spiritual and corporal food'] — these sermons were suitable as table readings during Lent, since the length of each sermon fitted that of a meal, so that the spiritual nourishment would accompany the actual food, even providing them with a more abundant portion on Sunday, which would serve for lunch and dinner.[48] Indeed, the time needed to read one of these sermons is about half an hour, with longer texts for the Sundays that could be split over two meals. However, although Pittorio just introduced the sermons as perfect for the nuns, he confesses that they were not written for them — nor that he was thinking of a female audience. As an excuse, he claims that since women are 'communemente divote' ['usually devout'] they need less spiritual instruction and, by addressing only them, he would run the risk of producing texts too short for the nuns' meals.[49] The apparent conundrum is solved when one realizes that the sermons often address a (male) lay audience, who live a secular life, and not nuns secluded from the world. Furthermore, they never address women directly and generally overlook aspects related to female life.[50] Overall, the tone of the sermons suggests that their original setting was a confraternity, as in the *Dominicale*. The audience is constantly addressed as 'fratelli miei' ['my brothers'] or even 'cari li mei compagni' ['my beloved confrères'], as in the first sermon, where Pittorio also states that, 'fuori de casa' ['in public'], one needs to follow the common customs without any ostentation and should not believe those who foolishly say that one may serve God while trying to have 'dela roba e dele belle donne e dele dignità' ['goods, beautiful women, and honours'].[51] This gender loaded language occurs also when the sermon denounces the hypocrisy of those who do not fast nor perform good deeds, and yet 'fingonsi in publico di essere santi' ['act in public as if they were saints'], by presenting themselves 'le veste inculte e la barba longa e capilli spellacciati' ['with neglected dress, long

---

48 These are the words Pittorio uses: 'Considerando l'ufficio vostro de abbatessa, che è il pascere le Sorelle di cibi sì spirituali sì corporali, pensai che expediente serebbe che de quella povertà la qualle Dio mi ha dato, vi provedesse de lectione da fare legere a la mensa nel tempo della Quaresima. Et così, principalmente per amore vostro e de tutte le altre monache et divote persone ho composto el presente libro intitulato Omiliario quadragisimale, nel quale haveriti ognidì el suo peculiare sermon fondato *de verbo ad verbum* sul epistola e evangelio, sì como correrano secondo l'ordine de la sacrosanta romana Chiesa, dove come vederiti ho advertito di fare questo: che le lectione de le ferie siano sì longe che ciascuna sia bastante per el legere de tutto el desinare, e quelle de le Domeniche per lo desinare e per la ciena insime', Pittorio, *Omiliario 1506*, fol. a1 verso.

49 The exact phrasing of Pittorio is as follows: 'Vero è che in epse non facio il parlare a donne, ma sequo la via di altri, e questo per honesti e rationabili respecti, e specialmente perché essende le donne communemente divote, mi sarebbe spesso accaduto di essere troppo brieve, e così a mezo dil pasto vi seria manchato il cibo spirituale con non picolo scandolo che'l vi sopravanzassono le vivande del corpo e manchassovi quele de l'anima', Pittorio, *Omiliario 1506*, fol. a1 verso.

50 See a clear example in n. 73.

51 Pittorio, *Omiliario 1506*, fol. a3 recto–verso.

beards, and messy hair'], a description that probably hints at the phenomenon of itinerant popular preachers/prophets (*romiti*).[52]

While Pittorio is profuse in humble declarations about himself in the dedicatory letter, he firmly claims that the book is very useful and — thanks to God — 'fructo se ben in si non delicato, almancho per la novità fructo de qualche admiratione' ['a fruit albeit not delicate, yet somehow admirable for its novelty'].[53] Perhaps the latter assertion refers to the interpretation of the Bible in the vernacular, since the author immediately afterwards defends himself from the possible accusation of presumption in 'parlare sopra la sacra scriptura' ['speaking about Holy Writ']. Here Pittorio introduces a second image to present his *Omiliario*, namely that of navigation. Using a commonplace, he acknowledges that Scripture is a vast and deep ocean, where even the sharpest human intellect can be easily submerged.[54] Yet, by trusting in divine mercy and asking God to send his favourable wind in the sails, Pittorio had put his 'navicella' ['little boat'] in such a vast sea hoping to reach the port, thanks also to the prayer of the abbess and other devout people.[55] The widespread nautical imagery is then combined with the semantic field of trade. Once his *navicella* reached the harbour, Pittorio says that he went on the shore and placed there 'le merce' ['his merchandise'] so that the readers could take what they liked from that. Hence, readers are invited to buy beneficial products that come from a dangerous navigation on the sea of Scripture, and that are presented — Pittorio states — without fraud or deceit.[56]

---

52 Pittorio, *Omiliario 1506*, fol. a3 recto. On the *romiti* in early sixteenth-century Italy, see Ottavia Niccoli, *Profeti e popolo nell'Italia del Rinascimento* (Roma: Laterza, 1987), and Camaioni, *Il Vangelo e l'Anticristo*, pp. 79–88.

53 Pittorio, *Omiliario 1506*, fol. a1 verso. The biblical image of the tree that bears fruit and the concept of usefulness as decisive in evaluating preaching were topical and are found in famous passages of Bernardino da Siena; see Delcorno, *Lazzaro e il ricco epulone*, pp. 42–48.

54 'E non si persuada però persona haba totalmente da presomptuoso assompto tanto pexo di parlare sopra la sacra scriptura, perché scio multo ben quello che puono e non puono portare le spalle mie, e che sì profondo pelago affaogano etiam spesso li alti ingigni, nonché un minimo pullice qual sonio io', Pittorio, *Omiliario 1506*, fol. a1 verso. On the image of Scripture as a dangerous ocean, previously used by Iacopo Passavanti (d. 1357), see Carlo Delcorno, 'La trasmissione nella predicazione', in *La Bibbia nel medioevo*, ed. by Giuseppe Cremascoli and Claudio Leonardi (Bologna: EDB, 1996), pp. 65–86 (p. 79).

55 'Confiso io nel'infinita soa bontà, ch'a spirare dovesse nele debile mie velle, misse la navicella al'aqua con speranza de entrare in porto, adiutandome maximamente le oratione dela prefata madre nostra abbatessa e de altre mie devote persone, alle quale spesso racommandava el viagio mio', Pittorio, *Omiliario 1506*, fol. a1 verso. The link between *acque, ingegno, navicella* and *vele* might echo intentionally Dante's incipit of *Purgatorio*.

56 'Et così reducta la nave in porto e su per lo litto distese le merce, in facultà di lectori serà di pigliare se gli serà cosa che gli piaza, e di lassare quello che gli parerà; et veramente quando l'huomo sul mercato non si' sforzato al comprare, non vedo como el puossi iustamente calomniare li mercadanti per fare mostra de le robe soe, maximamente quando sono de sorte che puono più presto giovare che nuocere, e che dentro non vi è nulla de fraude né di inganno', Pittorio, *Omiliario 1506*, fol. a1 verso.

292 PIETRO DELCORNO

Scripture is incontestably at the centre of Pittorio's sermons, whose homiletic style does not indulge in picturesque exempla and is almost without any mention of secular or religious *auctoritates*, with the exception of a very few references to the Church Fathers and classical poets.[57] More relevant seem two mentions of Caterina da Siena (1347–1380), whose revelations are identified as an exegetical authority.[58] Pittorio may be influenced by the 'Biblecentrism' practised and recommended by Savonarola, if not by Giovan Francesco Pico's *De studio divinae et humanae philosophiae* (1496).[59] Probably echoing Fra Girolamo, Pittorio condemns those who look for preachers able to flatter them by preaching 'qualche historia romana, o qualche poesia, o de philosophia, o altro che gli delectasse le orecchie' ['either some Roman story, or some poem, or some philosophy, or anything else that amuses their ears'], as the Apostle had predicted speaking of a time when people would prefer *fabulas* instead of the truth (2 Timothy 4. 3–4).[60]

Nevertheless, in the dedicatory letter, Pittorio was careful in positioning himself by saying that he did not claim to interpret Scripture, but only to deal with its literal sense in developing a moral discourse useful for Christian life; and just to be on the safe side, he added that he submitted all his works, deeds,

---

57 There are two mentions of Augustine (Pittorio, *Omiliario 1541*, fols 31 verso and 65 verso), two of Jerome (fols 72r and 83r), and one of Gregory (fol. 73r, an interesting passage on historical and allegorical reading). Virgil is mentioned three times (fols 19v, 67r, and 121v), with the addition of his verses 'Quid non mortalia pectora cogis, / auri sacra fames?', quoted as proverbial (fol. 56v). Ovid is mentioned, as an adage, on fol. 146r. Pittorio often refers to liturgical prayers, paraphrasing them in the vernacular. More generally, he should be placed within a complex, non-linear transition of style in sixteenth-century Italian preaching; see Carlo Delcorno, 'Dal *sermo modernus* alla retorica borromaica', *Lettere italiane*, 39 (1989), 465–83.

58 'Santa Catherina de Siena, vergine mia divotissima, dice che'l sposo suo Christo Iesù gli disse un giorno [...]' (fol. 87v); 'Et santa Catherina da Siena testifica che la interrogò il suo sposo Christo Iesù di questo ditto, e lui gli rispose secondo la preditta espositione' (fol. 108v). On Caterina's role in Savonarola and the Savoralan movement, see Herzig, *Savonarola's Women*, pp. 27–33.

59 Pittorio dedicated his poem, *Sacrae scripturae non vacasse dolet*, to Pico where he states that he will focus all his attention on the Bible, since he spent too much time seeking an earthly and deceptive glory, while he now refutes the title of poet; Pittorio, *Opuscolorum christianorum*, fol. B4 recto.

60 Interpreting the theophany of the Sinai, where the Jews stood far off, while Moses entered the darkness (see Exodus 20. 20–21), Pittorio allegorically applies it to those who would refuse to hear the Lord's preaching, which means a truthful preacher, and instead would listen to Moses, that is, to hear an adulator who makes them laugh and please them, with the dire consequence that they all 'andarano a trabucchon nela buccha del'inferno' ['will end up tumbling down into the mouth of hell']; Pittorio, *Omiliario 1506*, fol. i2 recto–verso (Wednesday after the Third Sunday of Lent). With the same reference to 2 Timothy 4. 3–4, Savonarola had similar admonitions, particularly against the use of the *Ovidius moralizatus*; see Pietro Delcorno, 'La *parabola* di Piramo e Tisbe: l'allegoria della *fabula* ovidiana in una predica di Johann Meder', *Schede Umanistiche*, 23 (2009), 67–106 (pp. 67–68). Yet, it was a commonplace (*ibid*, p. 69); we cannot be sure that Pittorio took it from Savonarola.

and thoughts to the correction of the Church.[61] We might say that Pittorio expresses here a Catholic *sola Scriptura* principle: the centrality of Scripture but under ecclesiastical authority. This approach probably contributed to his success in the sixteenth century, when the request of a religious discourse founded primarily on the Bible became dominant.[62] Yet, Pittorio cautiously put his book in the area of moral exhortation (and not of theological interpretation), which means at a level that was considered appropriate and commendable for his expected readers, namely lay people and nuns.[63]

Christocentric Piety: 'We are beggars, let us run to the rich man'

The clear address to a lay audience, mainly (if not exclusively) composed of men is evident when Pittorio comments on Jesus entering Jerusalem and going to the temple. The episode allows him to convey very practical rules for the laity by saying, for instance: 'Venuto che fu Christo dentro de la città, credeti voi forsi fratelli che l'andasse incontinente a sbevazare al'hostaria? Nol crediati! Anzi, andò per nostro essempio distesamente a dismontare alla chiesa' ['Once Jesus arrived in town, do you brothers believe perhaps that he went immediately to booze in an inn? Not at all! He went instead directly to visit the church, to give us an example'].[64] Similarly, the expulsion of the merchants from the temple should teach Christians to respect the sanctity of churches, as Pittorio states with a terrifying image of the Lord who checks

---

61 Here are Pittorio's exact words: 'Et per questo testifico ad ogniuno como in ogni parte de questa mia opera [...] non facio professione de commentare né de lucidare la sacra scriptura, ma solamente su la lettera dire cose morale e ala christiana vita consentanee, oltra che etiam in questo e in tutti li atti e ditti e pensieri mei me sottopongo ala correctione de la sancta madre giesa', Pittorio, *Omiliario 1506*, fol. a1 verso. Nevertheless, his sermons also refer to the moral and allegorical meaning of Scripture.

62 The printing success of Pittorio's sermons corresponds to the 1530s, when 'predicare li evangeli' ['preaching the Gospel'] was particularly appreciated in Italy, as demonstrated on a different level by the success of Bernardino Ochino; Camaioni, *Il Vangelo e l'Anticristo*, pp. 159 and 261. See also Gigliola Fragnito, *La Bibbia al rogo: la censura ecclesiastica e i volgarizzamenti della Scrittura, 1471–1605* (Bologna: Il Mulino, 1997) and, in a different context, John Frymire, *The Primacy of the Postils: Catholics, Protestants, and the Dissemination of Ideas in Early Modern Germany* (Leiden: Brill, 2010), pp. 50–74.

63 On the distinction between *praedicatio* and *exhortatio*, see Michel Lauwers, 'Praedicatio — Exhortatio: l'Église, la réforme et les laïcs (XIe–XIIIe siècle)', in *La Parole du prédicateur (ve–xve siècle)*, ed. by Rosa Maria Dessì and Michel Lauwers (Nice: Z'éditions, 1997), pp. 187–232. Pittorio's comment suggests that he wrote these sermons without a degree in theology (hence being labelled just *messere*) — if not even while he was (still) a lay man.

64 Pittorio, *Omiliario 1541*, fol. 23 verso (Tuesday after the First Sunday of Lent). Pittorio probably used to speak to a mixed audience, since he addresses both 'voi gran maestri' ['you, learned men'] and 'voi piccoli e bassi nel popolo' ['you, humble and poor people'] (fol. 23 recto).

from above with a sharp knife in his hand, 'per troncare a sacrileghi il capo' ['ready to cut off the head of the sacrilegious people'].[65] Here and elsewhere, Pittorio sometimes uses a popular, even grotesque language, in line with contemporary preachers such as Bernardino da Feltre (1439–1494) and Valeriano da Soncino (d. 1531).[66]

This type of practical, moral teaching is often combined with a more spiritual interpretation of the Bible, which focuses on the inner life and presents a demanding, non-ritualistic Christian life. The two levels are quite visible in the sermon for Thursday after the Second Sunday of Lent on Lazarus and the Rich Man, where Pittorio uses a well-known preaching commonplace, namely the distinction between the words (*parole*) and their inner meaning, the marrow (*medolla*).[67] First, he comments line by line on the biblical story, echoing well-known preaching topoi on this 'parable' such as the exhortation to the poor to be patient and wait for their eternal reward in the afterlife.[68] Here, Pittorio addresses the poor, with ample use of anaphoric repetitions:

> Tu sei mendico; presto serai summamente richo. Tu sei ulceroso; presto serai impassibile. Tu sei famelico; presto serai per sempre satiato. Tu non puo' caminare; presto serai dali angeli portato. Sta pur constante, e ad imitatione di Lazaro non ti turbare di nulla. Aspecta con patientia l'hora toa, e senza fallo li dolori ti se convertirano in gaudij. (Pittorio, *Omiliario 1506*, fol. i6 verso)

> [You are a beggar; soon you will be incredibly rich. You are covered in sores; soon you will be immortal. You are ravenous; soon you will be sated forever. You cannot walk; soon you will be carried by angels. Keep steady and by imitating Lazarus do not be upset by anything!

---

65 Pittorio, *Omiliario 1541*, fol. 24 recto. It sounds like a miniature version of Savonarola's vision of the sword (1492), often repeated by him and depicted in his *Compendio di rivelazione* (1495).

66 For instance, in the First Sunday of Lent: 'O tignoso vechiazo (così hora ti volgio chiamare, diavolo infernale, perché sono informato che questo nome te dispiace sommamente) [...] Va', sathanasso [...] vatene a scavezzacollo nel inferno' ['O stubborn grumpy old man (I want to address you like that now, infernal devil, since I know that you greatly hate this name) [...] Go, Satan, go daredevil into hell'] (fol. 17 recto). In another sermon Pittorio compares Christ's sacrifice with 'una grassa salvaticina ben arostita' ['a fat game well roasted'] (fol. 61 verso). The tendency to popularize the biblical account, even in grotesque terms, gained momentum with Bernardino da Siena (1380–1444) and reached its peak at the turn of the sixteenth century; see Lucia Lazzerini, *Il testo trasgressivo: testi marginali, provocatori, irregolari dal Medioevo al Cinquecento* (Milano: Franco Angeli, 1988), pp. 79–208.

67 Pittorio, *Omiliario 1506*, fol. i6 recto. On this commonplace, see Oriana Visani and Maria Grazia Bistoni, 'La Bibbia nella predicazione degli agostiniani: il caso di Gregorio di Alessandria', in *Sotto il cielo delle scritture: Bibbia, retorica e letteratura religiosa*, ed. by Carlo Delcorno and Giuseppe Baffetti (Firenze: Olschki, 2009), pp. 115–38 (p. 125).

68 On this enduring preaching theme, see Jussi Hanska, '*And the Rich Man also Died; and He Was Buried in Hell': The Social Ethos in Mendicant Sermons* (Helsinki: Suomen Historiallinen Seura, 1997), pp. 142–74; and Delcorno, *Lazzaro e il ricco epulone*, pp. 187–95.

A FORGOTTEN ITALIAN BESTSELLER   295

Wait patiently for your final hour, and without any doubt your pain will be transformed into joy].

Pittorio exhorts the listeners to convert without hesitation and to meditate continuously on this parable.[69] Yet, he also proposes an unusual and emotionally engaging interpretation, asking his listeners to identify on a spiritual level with the beggar and to knock at the door of the true rich man, Christ, the divine pharmacist, who will open his own 'speciaria' ['pharmacy'] and cure them.

> Charissimi, consideriamo in noi un puocho spiritualmente la condicione di Lazaro. Qual di noi è il quale non sia pieno de ferite de peccati? Qual di noi è il quale non sia povero et egeno di ogni virtù? Qual di noi si può movere per soa sufficientia ad opera veruna di gratia? Perché cagione adonque non ce mettiamo a mendicare dele miche e di superni e celesti doni? Ecco li cani — li rimorsi dela conscientia — ci vano de continuo lecchando e rodendo la marzura dele piaghe. Che stiamo a fare che non gli poniamo su qualche salutare unguento? Ma perché siamo poveri mendicanti, corriamo presto a casa del gran richo! Pichiamo fiducialmente ala porta dela speciaria soa. Costui non è quale fu il richo epulone! Pichiamo, che'l ci aprirà la bottega gratiosamente, immo accumularà beneficio a beneficio. E dapuo la restituita sanità, ce farà per li sancti suoi angeli portare in quella saluberrima patria, dove non serà mai più pericolo di recediva alcuna e dove con Lazaro e con Abraam saremo de continuo e in eterno sani e beati. (Pittorio, *Omiliario 1506*, fol. g1 verso)

>> [My dear [fellows], let us consider briefly the condition of Lazarus on a spiritual level. Who among us is not full of sores caused by sin? Who among us is not poor and destitute of every virtue? Who among us can move by himself to do any work of grace? Why, therefore, don't we start to beg for those crumbs of the superior and divine gifts? Here, the dogs — the remorse of conscience — incessantly lick and gnaw the corruption of our sores. What are we doing? Why do we not put some healing ointment on them? Yet, since we are poor beggars, let us run quickly to the great rich man's house. Let us knock with confidence on the door of his pharmacy. He is not like the Rich Man. Let us knock, since he will open his shop graciously and will even pile upon us benefit after benefit! And after restoring our health, he will command his angels to carry us to that most salvific homeland, where there will be no risk of relapse and where we will be healthy and blessed with Lazarus and Abraham, forever and ever].

Evidently, the sermon goes far beyond a plain explanation of the biblical text with some moral applications. Pittorio outlines a remarkably original

---

69 Pittorio, *Omiliario 1506*, fol. g1 recto. This parable occurs as a powerful *memento mori* in the epigraph of Pittorio's tomb; Guarini, *Compendio historico*, pp. 47–48.

interpretation of the story by inviting his audience to identify with Lazarus and by portraying Christ as the only true and merciful rich man. Such an interpretation does not have clear antecedents, proving the personal touch that Pittorio was able to give to his sermons.[70] Notably, he proposed to the readers an intense and moving Christocentric spirituality, based on the recognition of the primacy of grace (expressed in a tone similar to the letter to Sister Maddalena) and the fact that, in front of God, 'we are all beggars, hoc est verum', to use Martin Luther's words.

Generating Jesus in the Heart and Feeding Him in the Poor

The richness of the spiritual interpretation of the sermon on Lazarus is not present in all the homilies, and yet it is not an isolated case.[71] For instance, on the Third Sunday of Lent Pittorio again combines basic religious advice and an unusual spiritual interpretation of the Gospel. His practical instructions aim at shaping a domestic Christian life supported by writing and memorizing sentences of the Gospel useful for an examination of the conscience.

> Il se voria havere, amantissimi, nel più bello luogo di ogni casa un Christo, el quale col ditto dimostrasse un brieve con queste parole: *Qui non est mecum, contra me est, et qui non colligit mecum, dispergit*. Ma vogliamo almanco noi scriverle, ciascaduno ala lectiera soa, che ben per noi se spesso ce ne racordaremo! [...] Examiniamo fratelli la conscientia nostra e ritrovandola dal nemico obsessa, schaziamolo fuora con la contritione [...] lo quale ci dischatenarà la lingua alla sacramentale confessione e faraci fare opere di admiratione in satisfacione e recompensatione dele passate colpe. (Pittorio, *Omiliario 1506*, fols h1 verso–h2 recto)

> > [My beloved, it would be desirable to have, in the nicest place of every house, an image of Christ pointing with his finger to an inscription with these words: *He who is not with me is against me, and he who does not gather with me scatters* [Luke 11. 23]. We shall at least write them, each of us on the bed's headboard, since it is good for us if we often recall this sentence. [...] Let us brothers examine our conscience and,

---

70 Pittorio may be influenced by a passage from the *Vita Christi* by Ludolf von Sachsen (d. 1378): see Delcorno, *Lazzaro e il ricco epulone*, pp. 32–34. Vicent Ferrer (1350–1419) also identifies Christ as the Rich Man in one of his vernacular sermon; see Pietro Delcorno, '"Faré per manera que vàlgue per molts": i sermoni di Vicent Ferrer sulla parabola di Lazzaro e il ricco epulone', *Erebea*, 1 (2011), 203–30 (pp. 213–15).

71 The following sermon ends with another interesting interpretation. Commenting on the parable of the vineyard, the grape symbolizes the soul planted by God in the soil of the body: it bears different types of fruit and needs to be linked with the tree planted in the middle (the Cross), which holds the grapes upright; Pittorio, *Omiliario 1506*, fol. g3 verso.

when we find it occupied by our enemy, let us send him out by means of contrition [...], which will free our tongues for the sacramental Confession and lead us to perform admirable works such as the satisfaction and reparation of previous sins].

For Pittorio, this inscription (*breve*) also needs to be added virtually as protection for the inner self, so that the interior mirrors the ideal exterior Christian house. When Pittorio states that 'la casa dela conscientia' ['the house of the conscience'] has to be kept clean with 'le schoppe' ['the brooms'] of mental oration, corporal maceration, material and spiritual support of the neighbours, he adds that what keeps the tempter out is that 'vederà che da ogni cantone vi serà el brieve' ['he sees this inscription in every corner'] of the interior house, so that he cannot find an entrance.[72] In keeping an interior purity, the sermon also underlines the power of the Passion to defend believers from any temptation, by saying that the five senses are like doors that need to be locked with the security bars of the five wounds of Christ.

In the last part of the sermon Pittorio comments upon the Gospel episode when a woman from the crowd says to Jesus: 'Blessed is the womb that bore you, and the breasts which nursed you!', to whom Christ replies: 'More than that, blessed are those who hear the word of God and keep it!' (Luke 11. 27–28).[73] The episode allows him to underline the benefits for those who love to read or listen to Scripture: this will give to them not only the necessary strength to follow its teachings, which at first might appear difficult, but will also teach them to carry Christ 'per carità fisso nel core' ['fixed into the hearts with charity']. Remarkably, Pittorio here combines an affective meditation on generating Christ in the hearts with the exhortation of serving him in the poor, as taught by Matthew 25:

> Fratelli miei, noi non potemo portare nel ventre nostro, como fece Maria, el dolce bambino, ben lo possiamo portare nele braze dela speranza, e nel grembio dela fede, e nel cuore dela carità. Praeterea, perché lui ha dicto: '*Quod uni ex istis minimis fecistis, mihi fecistis*. Quello tanto che voi miei christiani harete facto per mio amore ad ogni minimo poverello, vi ni sentirò non mancho grato, quanto l'havesti facto a mi proprio'. Vogliamo portare nel ventre e nele intime viscere del'affecto nostro el poverino amandolo cordialmente, e con le poppe allactiamolo, sustentandolo con le facultà nostre, e così con Maria, benchè diversamente, conciperemo e nutricharemo el figliolo de Dio. (Pittorio, *Omiliario 1506*, fol. h3 recto)[74]

---

72 Pittorio, *Omiliario 1506*, fol. h2 verso.

73 As further evidence that Pittorio mainly thought of a male audience, this reference is not used to propose a model for women but instead to exhort men: 'Non disprecciamo amantissimi le povere donniciolle, perché assai volte hano più del buono che li huomini' ['My beloved, don't despise the poor little women, since they are often better then men']; Pittorio, *Omiliario 1506*, fol. h2 verso.

74 The image of Mary who nurses Christ here overlaps with representations of charity, depicted

[My dear brothers, we could not bear the sweet child [that is, Christ] in our womb as Mary did; yet we can carry him in the arms of hope, in the womb of faith, and in the heart of charity. Moreover, Christ said: '*Quod uni ex istis minimis fecistis, mihi fecistis*; i.e. when you, my Christians, did something to any poor person for my love, I will be grateful for that as if you did it directly to me'. Let us bear the poor person in the womb and in the inner bowels of our affection by loving him heartily, and let us nurse him at our breasts by helping him with our means, and so with Mary, albeit in a different way, we will conceive and feed the little son of God].

This text, in which Christ is generated in the poor through charity, is quite revealing of the way in which Pittorio participated in that evangelical 'religion of charity' that characterized the most fervent religious groups of the time in Italy, and which combined an internalized personal relationship with God with a concrete service to the poor.[75]

The Prodigal Son and Savonarola's Lukewarm Christians

The last sermon that we will consider is devoted to the parable of the prodigal son. On the Saturday after the Second Sunday of Lent, Pittorio advises his audience that the two biblical readings are both quite long, so he has to be concise — and indeed, commenting on the Gospel, he complains twice about the lack of time to deal with many details. Therefore, it is noteworthy, and revealing, that Pittorio diverges from the dominant preaching tradition that focused only on the prodigal son and marginalized the role of the elder brother.[76] Instead, he devotes considerable space to the latter: 'Questo figliolo magior [...] per el presente intendo el tepido christiano, el qualle si persuade che le cerimonie siano quelle che lo mandino in paradiso e non si accorgie che'l è pieno de invidia e di superbia' ['This elder brother [...] currently I interpret him as the lukewarm Christian, who thinks that the religious ceremonies will send him to heaven and does not realize that he is full of envy and pride'].[77] The reference to the lukewarm is repeated four times in the sermon, which closes by attacking 'lo tepido diffuora sancto, ma di dentro

---

as a woman who nurses a child (such as in Piero del Pollaiolo's 1469 painting) or according to the well-known exemplum of Pero breastfeeding her father (the so-called Roman Charity).

75 See Adriano Prosperi, *Tribunali della coscienza: inquisitori, confessori, missionari. Nuova edizione* (Torino: Einaudi, 2009), pp. 16–23 and Michele Camaioni, 'Le opere della "viva fede": i primi cappuccini tra politiche della carità e teologia del cielo aperto', in *Politiche di misericordia tra teorie e prassi: confraternite, ospedali e Monti di Pietà (XIII–XVI secolo)*, ed. by Pietro Delcorno (Bologna: Il Mulino, 2018), pp. 275–309.

76 See Delcorno, *In the Mirror of the Prodigal Son*, pp. 447–49 and *ad indicem*.

77 Pittorio, *Omiliario 1506*, fol. g5 verso.

diavolo incarnato' ['the lukewarm person, who outside looks like a saint but inside is a devil incarnate'].[78]

The polemic against the *tiepidi* was not only one of the most recognizable themes of Savonarola's preaching and one of his buzzwords, but the very interpretation of the elder brother as the symbol of the tepid Christians derives directly from the 1496 Lenten sermon collection of Savonarola (printed in 1497), which also contains explicit critiques of the exterior solemnity of religious ceremonies.[79] Scholars have usually emphasized Pittorio's link with Savonarola, yet always in quite elusive terms. Here, instead, we find a clear textual connection, which proves Pittorio's debt to the spiritual legacy of Fra Girolamo and his knowledge of the predecessor's sermons.[80]

However, in the same homily Pittorio also shows his independence. While in many respects he depends either on a longstanding exegetical tradition or on Savonarola, his interpretation of the shoes the father gives to the returned son is peculiar. The preacher notes that the *calciamenti*, a sort of sandal, are 'disotto asserati e di sopra aperti per dimostrarci che'l se tenga el cuore asserato ale cose terrene e aperto ale celeste' ['closed on the bottom and open on the upper part, so as to show us that one must close one's heart to earthly things and open it to celestial ones'].[81] It is a minor detail, and yet, no antecedent for such an interpretation emerged in my extensive research on the medieval readings of this parable.[82] It suggests that Pittorio was sometimes capable of sending his *navicella* independently into the vast ocean of Scripture.

A Multifaceted Reception of the *Omiliario*

Pittorio's interpretation of the prodigal son's shoes is echoed in a later, quite peculiar text that provides us with a glimpse into the use of the *Omiliario* by late sixteenth-century preachers. The text in question is the sermon on the prodigal son written by Domenico Sala, a secular priest in the small parish of Santa Maria Assunta of Rancio, near Lecco, in the archdiocese of Milan.

---

78 Pittorio, *Omiliario 1506*, fol. g6 recto.

79 See Girolamo Savonarola, *Prediche sopra Amos e Zaccaria*, ed. by Paolo Ghilieri, 3 vols (Roma: Belardetti, 1971–1972), II (1971), 3–26, especially p. 20. On Savonarola's sermons on the prodigal son and his identification of the tepid Christians with the elder brother, see Delcorno, *In the Mirror of the Prodigal Son*, pp. 240–50. On the topic of the *tiepidi* in Savonarola, see Donald Weinstein, *The Rise and Fall of a Renaissance Prophet* (New Haven: Yale University Press, 2011), pp. 87–92.

80 This implicit, yet quite recognizable reference to Savonarola was not obvious in the political context of 1506, that is, after the death of the Duke Ercole (d. 1505) and the (momentary) political ruin of Giovan Francesco Pico, the most prominent political supporters of the Savonarolan movement in the north of Italy; see Herzig, *Savonarola's Women*, pp. 127–53. For another passage where Pittorio possibly depended on Savonarola, see n. 60.

81 Pittorio, *Omiliario 1506*, fol. g5 verso.

82 See Delcorno, *In the Mirror of the Prodigal Son*, p. 443.

Sala composed it in the 1570s for one of the monthly meetings among the clergy of the area. At these gatherings the priests were asked to practise preaching and to submit written copies of their sermons to the ecclesiastical authorities of the diocese.[83] The content and structure of the sermon are rather simple, not surprisingly given the notably modest theological background of Domenico Sala. Yet, Sala writes: 'La scarpa è serrata di soto e aperta di sopra, a significare che il peccator, qual ritorna ala via bona di Cristo, de' lasar le cose terene e risguardar sempre le cose celeste' ['The shoe is closed on the bottom and open on the upper part, so to explain that the sinner, who returns to the good way of Christ, must leave earthly things and always look to celestial things'].[84] Not only are the concepts the same as in Pittorio, but even the terminology. Such a similarity suggests that the priest of Rancio used a copy of the *Omiliario* as his source; something entirely plausible considering the surviving inventories of books of other parishes in the area, which confirm the presence of Pittorio's *Quadragisimale* among the pastoral books available to many diocesan priests.[85] A book originally addressed to nuns and lay people for personal or collective reading also proved to be a useful aid for parish preachers just as a proper model sermon collection should be.

Indeed, the aftermath of the Council of Trent (1545–1563) can be seen as the golden age of the *Omiliario*, which was printed seven times between 1565 and 1571.[86] In the same period, while his clergy mined the sermons of Pittorio for their pastoral duties, the archbishop of Milan, Carlo Borromeo (1538–1584), recommended the works of Pittorio to the lay confraternities of his diocese, where they were still in use for collective reading as late as 1608.[87] Such practice was not limited to Milan, as shown by the statutes of the Compagnia del Nome di Gesù, a lay confraternity in Genoa, where reading the sermons of Pittorio even became an institutionalized practice, as proven by a chapter of the statues, probably added around the mid-sixteenth century:

Della lettione del Pittorio, cap. XXVIIII°.

Ordiniamo che ogni giorno quando si viene a questa devota compagnia del nome di Iesù si debba legere una lettione del libro di detta compagnia,

---

83 See Benjamin Westervelt, 'The Prodigal Son at Santa Justina: The Homily in the Borromean Reform of Pastoral Preaching', *Sixteenth Century Journal*, 32 (2001), 109–26 and Delcorno, *In the Mirror of the Prodigal Son*, pp. 442–44. The sermon is edited in Angelo Turchini, *Parole di Dio, parroci e popolo: prove di predicazione del clero lombardo* (Cesena: Il Ponte Vecchio, 2011), pp. 364–66.

84 Turchini, *Parole di Dio, parroci e popolo*, p. 366.

85 On these lists see Turchini, *Parole di Dio, parroci e popolo*, pp. 90–94. Other priests of the area had a better theological background than Domenico Sala; see Wietse de Boer, 'The Curate of Malgrate or the Problem of Clerical Competence in Counter-Reformation Milan', in *The Power of Imagery: Essays on Rome, Italy and Imagination*, ed. by Peter van Kessel (Roma: Apeiron, 1992), pp. 188–200.

86 It follows a general tendency, see Michelson, *The Pulpit and the Press*, pp. 28–31.

87 See Fragnito, *Proibito capire*, p. 263.

intitolato Ludovico Pittorio, e tale lettione doveranno tutti li fratelli attentamente con gran divotione ascoltare, per esser soggetto molto utile et a noi necessario, contenendovisi il verbo e parola di Dio, Signor nostro, perché come sapete è scritto che *non di solo pane vive l'huomo, ma sì di ogni parola che procede dalla bocca dello omnipotente e benigno Dio*, nostro Signore, e che *beati sono coloro che odono il verbo e parola di Dio e lo custodiscono*. (Burlington, University of Vermont, Silver Special Collections Library, MS 16, fol. 35r)[88]

> [Chapter 29: About the reading of Pittorio.
>
> We order that each day we come to this devout Company of the Name of Jesus, one lesson of the book of this company that is titled Ludovico Pittorio must be read. All the brothers must listen carefully to this reading, with great devotion, because its topic is very useful and necessary for us, since it contains the Word of God, our Lord. Indeed, you know that it is written that *Man shall not live by bread alone, but also by every word that proceeds from the mouth of the omnipotent and benevolent God*, our Lord [Matthew 4. 4], and *blessed are those who hear the Word of God and keep it* [Luke 11. 28]].

For the members of the confraternity, Pittorio's book became a normative text, necessary for their spiritual life, as a sort of avatar of the Bible itself — and of the presence of an actual preacher among them. We may note that the two biblical quotations echoed in this chapter, although quite common for a discourse on the Word of God, are taken from the pericopes of the First and Third Sundays of Lent, where the *Omiliario* comments extensively on this topic, as we have seen.[89]

A further proof of the wide success of Pittorio's sermons, which appealed to both the laity and the clergy, comes from the official approval by another leading figure of the Counter-Reformation movement, the Jesuit Petrus Canisius (1521–1597). In the decades after the Council of Trent, he was deeply involved in the promotion and censorship of sermon collections for both the Duke of Bavaria and the papal *Index librorum prohibitorum*.[90] Hence, the discovery of his approval, dated 1578 and registered on a 1558 copy of the *Omiliario* that was held by the Jesuits of Munich is a precious testimony to the

---

88 The manuscript is described on the webpage of *Textmanuscripts: Les Enluminures* [https://www.textmanuscripts.com/medieval/confraternity-holy-name-jesus-141372; accessed 27 May 2022].

89 For the First Sunday of Lent see Pittorio, *Omiliario 1541*, fols 12 verso–19 recto.

90 See Frymire, *The Primacy of the Postils*, pp. 337–42. Canisius probably knew this type of book from his years in Italy; see Patrizio Foresta, '*Wie ein Apostel Deutschlands': Apostolat, Obrigkeit und jesuitisches Selbstverständnis am Beispiel des Petrus Canisius (1543–1570)* (Göttingen: Vandenhoeck & Ruprecht, 2016), pp. 235–70.

lasting acceptance of this book.[91] Indeed, the support, or at least approval, of prominent spokesmen of the Catholic Counter-Reformation, such as Borromeo and Canisius, who recognized the pastoral value of Pittorio's sermons, is the sign, and partially the reason, for the persistent success of the *Omiliario* in the second part of the century.

Conclusion

Pittorio's *Omiliario* arguably stems from the preaching practice of a Ferrarese confraternity and, in its printed format, while continuing to target a lay readership, it was framed also as a spiritual text for nuns, apt to nourish their souls as table reading during Lent. His sermons, therefore, were from the beginning connected with both oral performance and reading practices and ideally appealed to different forms of Christian life, although their contents were mainly attuned to a male lay audience.

The analysis of the sermons showed how Pittorio offered a simple but not simplistic approach to the Bible and to Christian life. His exegetical sources remain to be fully identified, although we saw that he quoted Caterina da Siena and in one case he clearly depended on Savonarola. His plain exegesis presented first his listeners (if Pittorio really preached these sermons) and then his readers and his emulators as preachers with precious access to the Bible, a practical set of moral exhortations, and at least in some cases quite sophisticated spiritual teaching. The latter focused on an internalized relationship with Christ, with an emphasis on the Cross as the source of salvific grace. In front of him all Christians are like Lazarus the beggar. Yet, the appeal to an inner spiritual life was combined with practical exhortations to engage in charity, particularly to the poor, in line with other spiritual reformers of early sixteenth-century Italy. In his dedicatory letter, Pittorio presented his sermons as food for the soul and precious merchandise, which resulted from a dangerous navigation through the ocean of the Bible. Notwithstanding his humble declaration, he was proudly vocal about the novelty of his achievement. Still, he probably would not have dared to imagine the striking success of his book, which came mainly after his death.

The *Omiliario*, indeed, was able to appeal to a very differentiated readership during a considerable time span. The full story of the reception and the actual use of this bestseller remains to be written.[92] Yet, the few cases considered here

---

91 See the copy by Ludovico Pittorio, *Homiliario [...] per tutta la quadragesima et nele dominiche [...]* (Venezia: Al segno della Speranza, 1558) held by München, Bayerische Staatsbibliothek, Hom. 1217. On its title page, a note of possession reads 'Societatis Jesu Monacj', while on the reverse of the title page, under the letter of the publisher to the readers, the same hand wrote: 'Approbatus a R. P. Caniseo 1578'.

92 Fragnito, *Proibito capire*, pp. 102, 209, 262–63 offers initial remarks on this topic. An invaluable source for this type of research is the RICI database [http://rici.vatlib.it; accessed

show how it responded to the needs of both lay readers and humble parish priests in search of a reliable preaching aid, while at the same time prominent reformers of the sixteenth-century Catholic Church, such as Canisius and Borromeo, supported or approved its use. For almost a century, therefore, this text provided many believers (clerics, nuns, and lay people) with a valuable instrument to have a (mediated) access to the Bible and through which the Word of God circulated within a changing and turbulent society.

---

27 May 2022] that charts the books of the religious orders in Italy on the basis of the enquiry made by the Congregation of the Index between 1596 and 1603.

Appendix: Printed Editions of the *Omiliario quadragisimale* by Ludovico Pittorio

Data are taken from *EDIT16: Censimento nazionale delle edizioni italiane del XVI secolo* [accessed 11 June 2021]. The CNCE is the identification number provided by *EDIT16*. I indicate the editions that also included the *Dominicale*, which were either in one (1v) or two volumes (2v). I also indicate when an editor published the *Dominicale* as a separate book (S), yet in the same year of the *Quadragisimale*.

The last two editions are indicated by the Universal Short Title Catalogue, with the following identification numbers: USTC 4035086 and USTC 4044623 [accessed 30 October 2020].

No.	Place	Publisher	Year	Dom.	CNCE
1	Modena	Domenico Rococciola	1506	—	66679
2	Milano	Giovanni Angelo Scinzenzeler	1513	1v	31326
3	Venezia	[Giovanni Maria Boselli] Bernardino Vitali	1518	—	70161
4	Milano	Giovanni Angelo Scinzenzeler	1520	1v	31369
5	Venezia	[Giovanni Maria Boselli] Bernardino Vitali	1530	—	37988
6	Venezia	[Giovanni Maria Boselli] Bernardino Vitali	1532	—	38024
7	Venezia	Francesco Bindoni and Maffeo Pasini	1532	S	23294
8	Brescia	Ludovico Britannico	1533	—	57672
9	Venezia	Bernardino di Bindoni	1537	S	23129
10	Brescia	Ludovico Britannico	1541	2v	23249
11	Venezia	Francesco Bindoni and Maffeo Pasini	1541	S	23352
12	Venezia	Al segno della Speranza	1546	1v	32982
13	Venezia	Francesco Bindoni and Maffeo Pasini	1548	S	23474
14	Venezia	Giovanni Pavocano	1550	1v	27873
15	Venezia	Comin da Trino	1552	1v	24689
16	Brescia	Ludovico Britannico	1553	2v	58372
17	Venezia	s.n.	1558	1v	49169
18	Venezia	Al segno della Speranza	1558	1v	33224
19	Brescia	Ludovico Britannico	1561	2v	23262
20	Venezia	Francesco Lorenzini da Torino	1565	2v	39748
21	Venezia	Girolamo Scotto	1566	2v	70167
22	Venezia	Girolamo Scotto	1567	2v	32319
23	Venezia	Johann Criegher	1568	1v	25205
24	Venezia	Johann Criegher	1569	1v	25206

No.	Place	Publisher	Year	*Dom.*	CNCE
25	Venezia	Eredi di Marchiò Sessa	1570	1v (?)	30207
26	Venezia	Andrea Muschio	1571	1v	31387
27	Venezia	Francesco Ziletti	1574	2v	40019
28	Venezia	[Varisco Giovanni]	1578	2v	40738
29	Venezia	Altobello Salicato	1578	2v	30532
30	Venezia	[Giovanni Maria Leni]	1579/80	2v	40761
31	Torino	[Eredi Niccolò Bevilacqua] Francesco Lorenzini	1581/82	2v	35706
32	Venezia	Fabio e Agostin Zoppini	1583	2v	40823
33	Venezia	Domenico e Giovanni Battista Guerra	1586	2v	37540
34	Venezia	Giacomo Cornetti	1590	2v	25075
35	Venezia	Eredi di Giovanni Maria Leni	1599	2v	37945
36	Venezia	Sebastian Combi	1599	2v	66636
37	Venezia	Pietro Ricciardi	1607	2v	—
38	Venezia	s.n.	1630	2v	—

Bibliography

Manuscripts

Burlington, University of Vermont, Silver Special Collections Library, MS 16

Early Printed Works

Agostino Superbi, *Apparato de gli huomini illustri della città di Ferrara* (Ferrara: Francesco Suzzi, 1620)

Antonio da Vercelli, *Consegli della salute del peccatore* [s.n. 1470]

Antonio Libanori, *Ferrara d'oro imbrunito*, 3 vols (Ferrara: Maresti 1665–1674)

Girolamo Savonarola, *Molti devotissimi trattati del reverendo padre frate Hieronimo Savonarola da Ferrara [...] et una espositione del Pater noster et alcuni sermoni devoti di Ludouico Pittorio da Ferrara* (Venezia: Al segno della Speranza, 1547)

Johannes Geiler von Kaysersberg, *Pater noster: des hochgelerten wurdigen Predicanten [...]* [Strasbourg: Matthias Hupfuff, 1515]

Ludovico Bigi Pittorio, *Candida* (Modena: Domenico Rococciola, 1491)

Ludovico Pittorio, *Consolatoria lectione in sul transito della morte* [Firenze: Bartolomeo di Libri, 1490–1500]

Ludovico Pittorio, *Dominicale e santuario [...]* (Modena: Domenico Rococciola, [*c.* 1502–1505])

Ludovico Pittorio, *Dominicale sanctuario e quadragesimale [...] nouamente stampato con molte agionte* (Milano: Giovanni Angelo Scinzenzeler, 1513)

Ludovico Pittorio, *Homiliario* (Venezia: Al segno della Speranza, 1546)

Ludovico Pittorio, *Homiliario [...] per tutta la quadragesima et nele dominiche [...]* (Venezia: Al segno della Speranza, 1558)

Ludovico Pittorio, *Homiliario quadragesimale* (Brescia: Ludovico Brittanico, 1541)

Ludovico Pittorio, *Omiliario quadragisimale fondato de verbo ad verbum sule Epistole e Evangelii sì como corrono ogni dì secondo lo ordine dela Romana Giesia* (Modena: Domenico Rococciola, 1506)

Ludovico Pittorio, *Opuscolorum christianorum libri tres* (Modena: Domenico Rococciola, 1496)

Ludovico Pittorio, *I salmi di David* (Venezia: Al segno della Speranza, 1547)

Ludovico Pittorio, *Sermone della comunione* (Firenze: [s.n.], 1502)

Ludovico Pittorio, *Utile meditatione in sei gradi divisa* (Ferrara: [s.n.], 1502)

Marcantonio Guarini, *Compendio historico [...] delle Chiese [...] di Ferrara e delle memorie di que' personaggi di pregio che in esse son sepelliti* (Ferrara: Eredi Vittorio Baldini, 1621)

Roberto Caracciolo, *Specchio della fede* (Venezia: Giovanni da Bergamo, 1495)

Primary Sources

Girolamo Savonarola, *Lettere e scritti apologetici*, ed. by Roberto Ridolfi, Vincenzo Romano, and Armando F. Verde (Roma: Belardetti, 1984)

Girolamo Savonarola, *Prediche sopra Amos e Zaccaria*, ed. by Paolo Ghilieri, 3 vols (Roma: Belardetti, 1971–1972)

Giuseppe Antenore Scalabrini, *Memorie istoriche delle chiese di Ferrara* (Ferrara: Carlo Coatti, 1773)

Secondary Studies

Andenna, Giancarlo, 'Pittorio, Ludovico', in *Dizionario biografico degli italiani* (Roma: Istituto della Enciclopedia Italiana, 1960–), 84 (2015), pp. 264–68

Boer, Wietse de, 'The Curate of Malgrate or the Problem of Clerical Competence in Counter-Reformation Milan', in *The Power of Imagery: Essays on Rome, Italy and Imagination*, ed. by Peter van Kessel (Roma: Apeiron, 1992), pp. 188–200

Boillet, Élise, 'For Early Modern Printed Biblical Literature in Italian: Lay Authorship and Readership', in *Lay Readings of the Bible in Early Modern Europe*, ed. by Erminia Ardissino and Élise Boillet, Intersections, 68 (Leiden: Brill, 2020), pp. 170–90

Boillet, Élise, 'La Fortune du Psalterio Davitico de Lodovico Pittorio en Italie au XVIᵉ siècle', *La bibliofilia*, 115 (2013), 621–28

Boillet, Élise, 'Vernacular Biblical Literature in Sixteenth-Century Italy: Universal Reading and Specific Readers', in *Discovering the Riches of the Word: Religious Reading in Late Medieval and Early Modern Europe*, ed. by Sabrina Corbellini, Margriet Hoogvliet, and Bart Ramakers, Intersections, 38 (Leiden: Brill, 2015), pp. 213–33

Boillet, Élise, 'Vernacular Sermons on the Psalms Printed in Sixteenth-Century Italy: An Interface between Oral and Written Cultures', in *Voices and Texts in Early Modern Italian Society*, ed. by Brian Richardson, Massimo Rospocher, and Stefano Dall'Aglio (London: Routledge, 2016), pp. 200–11

Bruni, Flavia, and Andrew Pettegree, eds, *Lost Books: Reconstructing the Print World of Pre-Industrial Europe*, Library of the Written Word, The Handpress World, 46 (Leiden: Brill, 2016)

Camaioni, Michele, 'Le opere della "viva fede": i primi cappuccini tra politiche della carità e teologia del cielo aperto', in *Politiche di misericordia tra teorie e prassi: confraternite, ospedali e Monti di Pietà (XIII–XVI secolo)*, ed. by Pietro Delcorno (Bologna: Il Mulino, 2018), pp. 275–309

Camaioni, Michele, *Il Vangelo e l'Anticristo: Bernardino Ochino tra francescanesimo ed eresia (1487–1547)* (Bologna: Il Mulino, 2018)

Cittadella, Luigi Napoleone, *Notizie amministrative, storiche, artische relative a Ferrara*, 3 vols (Ferrara: Domenico Taddei, 1868)

Delcorno, Carlo, 'Dal *sermo modernus* alla retorica borromaica', *Lettere italiane*, 39 (1989), 465–83

Delcorno, Carlo, 'La trasmissione nella predicazione', in *La Bibbia nel medioevo*, ed. by Giuseppe Cremascoli and Claudio Leonardi (Bologna: EDB, 1996), pp. 65–86

Delcorno, Pietro, '"Faré per manera que vàlgue per molts": i sermoni di Vicent Ferrer sulla parabola di Lazzaro e il ricco epulone', *Erebea*, 1 (2011), 203–30

Delcorno, Pietro, *In the Mirror of the Prodigal Son: The Pastoral Uses of a Biblical Narrative (c. 1200–1550)*, Commentaria, 9 (Leiden: Brill, 2017)

Delcorno, Pietro, *Lazzaro e il ricco epulone: metamorfosi di una parabola fra Quattro e Cinquecento* (Bologna: Il Mulino, 2014)

Delcorno, Pietro, 'La *parabola* di Piramo e Tisbe: l'allegoria della *fabula* ovidiana in una predica di Johann Meder', *Schede Umanistiche*, 23 (2009), 67–106

Delcorno, Pietro, 'Quaresimali "visibili": il serafino, il guerriero, il pellegrino', *Studi medievali*, 60 (2019), 645–88

Delcorno, Pietro, Eleonora Lombardo, and Lorenza Tromboni, eds, *I sermoni quaresimali: digiuno del corpo, banchetto dell'anima / Lenten Sermons: Fasting of the Body, Banquet of the Soul, Memorie Domenicane*, n.s. 48 (Firenze: Edizioni Nerbini, 2017)

Delcorno Branca, Daniela, *Le Spirituali sportelle di Agostino di Portico: lettere alle monache di S. Marta di Siena* (Roma: Edizioni di Storia e Letteratura, 2019)

Eisenbichler, Konrad, ed., *A Companion to Medieval and Early Modern Confraternities*, Brill's Companions to the Christian Tradition, 83 (Leiden: Brill, 2019)

Fioravanti Baraldi, Anna Maria, 'Ludovico Pittorio e la cultura figurativa a Ferrara nel primo Cinquecento', in *Alla corte degli Estensi: filosofia, arte e cultura a Ferrara nei secoli XV e XVI*, ed. by Marco Bertozzi (Ferrara: Università degli Studi, 1994), pp. 217–46

Fioravanti Baraldi, Anna Maria, 'Testo e immagini: le edizioni cinquecentesche dell'Omiliario quadragesimale di Ludovico Pittorio', in *Girolamo Savonarola da Ferrara all'Europa*, ed. by Gigliola Fragnito and Mario Miegge (Firenze: SISMEL, 2001), pp. 139–53

Foresta, Patrizio, *'Wie ein Apostel Deutschlands': Apostolat, Obrigkeit und jesuitisches Selbstverständnis am Beispiel des Petrus Canisius (1543–1570)* (Göttingen: Vandenhoeck and Ruprecht, 2016)

Fragnito, Gigliola, *La Bibbia al rogo: la censura ecclesiastica e i volgarizzamenti della Scrittura, 1471–1605* (Bologna: Il Mulino, 1997)

Fragnito, Gigliola, *Proibito capire: la Chiesa e il volgare nella prima età moderna* (Bologna: Il Mulino, 2005)

Frymire, John, *The Primacy of the Postils: Catholics, Protestants, and the Dissemination of Ideas in Early Modern Germany*, Studies in Medieval and Reformation Traditions, 147 (Leiden: Brill, 2010)

Gazzini, Marina, ed., *Studi confraternali: orientamenti, problemi, testimonianze* (Firenze: Firenze University Press, 2009)

Guarnieri, Chiara, 'Il monastero di S. Antonio in Polesine: un'isola nella città', in *S. Antonio in Polesine: archeologia e storia di un monastero estense*, ed. by Chiara Guarnieri (Borgo San Lorenzo: All'Insegna del Giglio, 2006), pp. 13–15

Hanska, Jussi, *'And the Rich Man also Died; and He Was Buried in Hell': The Social Ethos in Mendicant Sermons* (Helsinki: Suomen Historiallinen Seura, 1997)

Hanska, Jussi, *'Sermones quadragesimales*: Birth and Development of a Genre', *Il Santo*, 52 (2012), 107–27

Harris, Neil, 'La sopravvivenza del libro ossia appunti per una lista della lavandaia', *Ecdotica*, 4 (2007), 24–65

Herzig, Tamar, *Savonarola's Women: Visions and Reform in Renaissance Italy* (Chicago: University of Chicago Press, 2008)

Lauwers, Michel, *'Praedicatio — Exhortatio*: L'Église, la réforme et les laïcs (XIe–XIIIe siècle)', in *La Parole du prédicateur (v^e-xve siècle)*, ed. by Rosa Maria Dessì and Michel Lauwers (Nice: Z'éditions, 1997), pp. 187–232

Lazzerini, Lucia, *Il testo trasgressivo: testi marginali, provocatori, irregolari dal Medioevo al Cinquecento* (Milano: Franco Angeli, 1988)

Michelson, Emily, *The Pulpit and the Press in Reformation Italy*, I tatti studies in Italian renaissance history (Cambridge, MA: Harvard University Press, 2013)

Niccoli, Ottavia, *Profeti e popolo nell'Italia del Rinascimento* (Roma: Laterza, 1987)

Pasquazi, Silvio, 'La poesia in latino', in *Storia di Ferrara*, VII: *il Rinascimento e la letteratura*, ed. by Walter Moretti (Ferrara: Librit, 1994), pp. 100–56

Prosperi, Adriano, *Tribunali della coscienza: inquisitori, confessori, missionari*, Nuova edizione (Torino: Einaudi, 2009)

Scapparone, Elisabetta, 'Pico, Giovan Francesco', in *Dizionario biografico degli italiani* (Roma: Istituto della Enciclopedia Italiana, 1960–), 83 (2015), pp. 320–22

Severi, Andrea, *Filippo Beroaldo il Vecchio, un maestro per l'Europa: da commentatore di classici a classico moderno (1481–1550)* (Bologna: Il Mulino, 2015)

Tuohy, Thomas, *Herculean Ferrara: Ercole d'Este (1471–1505) and the Invention of a Ducal Capital* (Cambridge: Cambridge University Press, 1996)

Turchini, Angelo, *Parole di Dio, parroci e popolo: prove di predicazione del clero lombardo* (Cesena: Il Ponte Vecchio, 2011)

Visani, Oriana, and Maria Grazia Bistoni, 'La Bibbia nella predicazione degli agostiniani: il caso di Gregorio di Alessandria', in *Sotto il cielo delle scritture: Bibbia, retorica e letteratura religiosa*, ed. by Carlo Delcorno and Giuseppe Baffetti (Firenze: Olschki, 2009), pp. 115–38

Weinstein, Donald, *The Rise and Fall of a Renaissance Prophet* (New Haven: Yale University Press, 2011)

Westervelt, Benjamin, 'The Prodigal Son at Santa Justina: The Homily in the Borromean Reform of Pastoral Preaching', *Sixteenth Century Journal*, 32 (2001), 109–26

Zarri, Gabriella, *La religione di Lucrezia Borgia: le lettere inedite del confessore* (Roma: Roma nel Rinascimento, 2006)

Germanic Lands

RALF LÜTZELSCHWAB

The Neglected Carmelites

Evidence for their Preaching Activities in Late Medieval Germany

Arnold de Liège (d. after 1310), author of one of the most accomplished exempla collections of the Middle Ages, the *Alphabetum Narrationum*, made it very clear: 'Predicator discrete debet predicare secundum conditiones audientium' ['The preacher is supposed to preach in an appropriate manner depending on the circumstances of the audience'].[1] This was certainly also true for preachers belonging to the mendicant orders.[2] The plethora of liturgical sermon collections *per circulum anni* and (to a lesser degree) *ad status* written and/or compiled by mendicant preachers bear witness to this concern.[3] From all the mendicant orders, Dominicans have always had the strongest ties to preaching activities; it is not by chance that in Germany they are called 'Predigerbrüder'. Following the oldest constitutions, they were founded 'to preach and to look after the salvation of the people'.[4] Particularly relevant in this context are the extensive sermon collections by Dominican authors like Hugues de Saint-Cher (*c.* 1200–1263),[5] Jacopo da Varazze

---

1 *Arnoldi Leodiensis Alphabetum Narrationum*, ed. by Elisa Brilli, Corpus Christianorum, Continuatio Mediaevalis, 160 (Turnhout: Brepols, 2015), p. 364, n. 654.
2 The mendicant orders originally comprised only the Franciscans (1209) and the Dominicans (1220); eventually they were joined by the Carmelites (1245), the Hermits of St Augustine (1256), and the Servites (1424), with later orders following.
3 Only five *ad status* collections have come down to us, two of them originating in a mendicant context, see Carolyn Muessig, 'Audience and Preacher: *Ad Status* Sermons and Social Classification', in *Preacher, Sermon, and Audience in the Middle Ages*, ed. by Carolyn Muessig, A New History of the Sermon, 3 (Leiden: Brill, 2003), pp. 255–76.
4 Antoninus H. Thomas, *De oudste Constituties van de Dominicanen: Voorgeschiedenis, tekst, bronnen, ontstaan en ontwikkeling (1215–1237)*, Revue d'histoire ecclésiastique, Bibliothèque, 42 (Leuven: Bureel van de RHE, 1965), p. 311: 'Cum ordo noster specialiter ob predicationem et animarum salutem ab initio noscatur institutus fuisse [...]'.
5 Bernard Hodel, 'Les Sermons reportés de Hugues de Saint-Cher', in *Hugues de Saint-Cher († 1263), bibliste et théologien*, ed. by Louis-Jacques Bataillon, Gilbert Dahan, and

---

Ralf Lützelschwab (luetzel@zedat.fu-berlin.de) is a Research Fellow at the German Study Centre in Venice and a Lecturer in Medieval History at the Freie Universität Berlin.

Circulating the Word of God in Medieval and Early Modern Europe: Catholic Preaching and Preachers across Manuscript and Print (c. 1450 to c. 1550), ed. by Veronica O'Mara and Patricia Stoop, SERMO 17, (Turnhout: Brepols, 2022), pp. 313–338   BREPOLS ✿ PUBLISHERS   10.1484/M.SERMO-EB.5.130460

$(1228/29-1298)^6$ and their Franciscan counterparts[7] — sermons speaking in favour of deeply rooted and visible/audible pastoral concerns. All too often, however, one gets the impression that Carmelite preachers especially took the *discrete* in Arnold de Liège's *dictum* too seriously. Acting *discrete* in the Middle Ages was a prerequisite, even one of the most important traits not only for rulers, but also for academics — and for preachers. One acted in a discreet manner when intellectual qualities, cultural background, and receptivity of the persons dealt with were taken into consideration.[8] And even if the main signification nowadays of 'discreet' has little to do with the medieval signification of the term, *discrete* has always had an alternative secondary meaning (the one we are accustomed to today) referring to somebody being reserved or restrained, somebody speaking between the lines. Reviewing the sermon production of Carmelites, it has to be noted that their discretion seems to be extremely developed.

The sermon production of late medieval Carmelites is still a *terra incognita*. This essay tries to shed light on the importance of Carmelites as preachers and directors in the order's provinces of *Alemania inferior* and *Alemania superior* or Lower and Upper Germany.[9] To this end, the holdings of two important libraries, their genesis, expansion, and fate will be analysed with special attention to pastoral works and sermons therein. To be more precise: the

---

Pierre-Marie Gy, Bibliothèque d'histoire culturelle du Moyen Âge, 1 (Turnhout: Brepols, 2004), pp. 233–52.

6 His four sermon collections are of the utmost importance. Apart from the collections of *Sermones de sanctis* (305 sermons), *Sermones de tempore* (160 sermons) and a *Liber marialis* (160 sermons), one has to mention his collection of *Sermones quadragesimales*, compiled before 1286 (98 sermons); see Jacopo da Varazze, *Sermones quadragesimales*, ed. by Giovanni Paolo Maggioni, Edizione nazionale dei testi mediolatini, 13 (Firenze: SISMEL, 2005); Giovanni Paolo Maggioni, 'Chastity Models in the Legenda Aurea and in the Sermones de Sanctis of Jacobus de Voragine', *Medieval Sermon Studies*, 52 (2008), 19–30; Suzanne Hevelone, 'Preaching the Saints: The *Legenda Aurea* and *Sermones de sanctis* of Jacobus de Voragine' (unpublished doctoral dissertation, Boston College, 2010).

7 Of particular relevance is Bertrand de la Tour, see Patrick Nold, 'Bertrand de la Tour O. Min.: Manuscript List and Sermon Supplement', *Archivum Franciscanum Historicum*, 95 (2002), 3–51, and Patrick Nold, *Pope John XXII and his Franciscan Cardinal: Bertrand de la Tour and the Apostolic Poverty Controversy* (Oxford: Oxford University Press, 2003).

8 The relationship between 'discrete' and 'integer' has not been researched so far. Arnold de Liège's dictum is very close to Nicolas de Biard's remark about the ideal preacher: 'Predicatorem oportet lucere vita et doctrina' ['The preacher is supposed to shine by his life and doctrine']; see Nicolas de Biard, *Dictionarius pauperum omnibus praedicatoribus verbi divini pernecessarius de tempore et de sanctis* (Strasbourg: Johann Knoblouch, 1516), fol. CXLV.

9 *Monasticon Carmelitanum: die Klöster des Karmelitenordens (O. Carm.) in Deutschland von den Anfängen bis zur Gegenwart*, ed. by Edeltraud Klueting, Stephan Panzer, and Andreas H. Scholten, Monastica Carmelitana, 2 (Münster: Aschendorff, 2012), pp. 24–49 (*Alemania inferior*), and pp. 50–60 (*Alemania superior*). The province of Lower Germany roughly comprised all convents in the Netherlands and the western part of the Holy Roman Empire whereas the province of Upper Germany covered the south-east, especially Bavaria and Hungary.

THE NEGLECTED CARMELITES   315

essay's focus will be on the Carmelite convents of Straubing and Mainz, the former belonging to the order's province of Upper Germany, the latter being part of the province of Lower Germany. Its aim is to contribute to a better understanding of the richness of both convents' libraries and of the special role sermons played therein. These libraries not only collected and conserved books related to the order, but followed practical purposes supporting pastoral activities both in the confessional and in the pulpit.

The Carmelites in New Surroundings

The Carmelites were, due to their strong veneration of the Virgin Mary, also called 'brethren of Our Lady'. However, this order has never attracted the scholarly attention that the Franciscans and the Dominicans managed to attract. The reason for this neglect may lie within its history and the difficulties it encountered organizing and structuring itself at its very beginnings. Carmelites, initially a group of hermits dwelling on the hills of Mount Carmel, are a phenomenon of the Holy Land. In the thirteenth century, as the Kingdom of Jerusalem began to disintegrate, many Western Christians in the East chose exile instead of submission to Muslim rule or even death: among them, the Carmelites. They had to move to Europe in order to secure their own life and the order's *propositum*.[10] If they had not opted for exile, they would not have survived. This displacement entailed serious problems. In Europe eremitical existence was, at least theoretically, highly valued, but in practice hardly lived.[11] In the cities, the privileged new dwelling places of the Carmelites, an eremitical existence could not be maintained. Pope Innocent IV (1243–1254) took the initiative in bringing the order à jour.[12] In 1247 a new rule

---

10 Markus Schürer, 'Das "propositum" in religiös-asketischen Diskursen: historisch-semantische Erkundungen zu einem zentralen Begriff der mittelalterlichen "vita religiosa"', in *Oboedientia: zu Formen und Grenzen von Macht und Unterordnung im mittelalterlichen Religiosentum*, ed. by Sébastien Barret and Gert Melville, Vita regularis, 27 (Münster: LIT, 2005), pp. 99–128.

11 Andrew Jotischky, 'The Image of the Greek: Western Pilgrims' Views of Eastern Monks and Monasteries in the Holy Land, *c.* 1200–1500', *Speculum*, 94 (2019), 674–703; *Eremitismo e habitat rupestre: atti del VI Convegno internazionale sulla civiltà rupestre in ricordo di Giuseppe Giacovazzo*, ed. by Enrico Menestò, Atti dei Convegni della Fondazione San Domenico, 6 (Spoleto: Fondazione Centro Italiano di Studi sull'alto Medioevo, 2015); still worth reading: Herbert Grundmann, 'Deutsche Eremiten, Einsiedler und Klausner im Hochmittelalter', *Archiv für Kulturgeschichte*, 45 (1963), 60–90.

12 *Bullarium Carmelitanum a fratre Eliseo Monsignani*, Pars Prima (Roma: Plachi, 1715), pp. 8–11; Innocent IV, *Les Registres d'Innocent IV*, ed. by Élie Berger (Paris: Thorin, 1884), I, no. 3287 (*Paganorum incursus*; 1247.10.04); no. 3288 (*Quae honorem conditoris*; 1247.10.01); Marie-Hyacinthe Laurent, 'La Lettre "Quae Honorem Conditoris" (1er octobre 1247)', *Ephemerides Carmeliticae*, 2 (1948), 5–16. The opening to society via *cura animarum* entailed an adaptation of material and financial resources; see Hans-Joachim Schmidt, 'L'Économie contrôlée des couvents des Carmes: le témoignage des rapports de visites dans la province de Germania

316 RALF LÜTZELSCHWAB

was imposed; Carmelites lost their eremitical character becoming a mendicant order instead. Its new focus was pastoral care. A more radical change is hardly conceivable. A *vita eremitica* was replaced by a *vita communis*. One could go even further: searching for God in solitude was henceforth considered inappropriate. Preaching, hearing confession, dispensing sacraments were the new challenges. The Carmelites did everything in their power to catch up with the other mendicant orders taking their study systems as a model.[13] And they succeeded. They became involved in a ministry of preaching and teaching whose distinctiveness was rooted in individual prayer, in a strong Marian spirituality, but especially in a special founding myth.[14] Choosing (or better: 'inventing') the Old Testament prophet Elias as founder of the Order, Carmelites became by far the oldest order in Christendom.[15] In the late thirteenth century the order was divided by the general chapter into twelve provinces, with the province of the 'Holy Land' or *Terra Sancta* first in order

---

inferior', in *Économie et religion: L'Expérience des ordres mendiants (XIIIᵉ–XVᵉ siècle)*, ed. by Nicole Bériou and Jacques Chiffoleau, Collection d'histoire et d'archéologie médiévales, 21 (Lyon: Presses Universitaires de Lyon, 2009), pp. 247–69.

13 Emanuele Boaga, 'L'organizzazione dello studio e degli *studia* presso i carmelitani tra il XIIIᵉ il XIV secolo', in *Studio e studia: le scuole degli ordini mendicanti tra XIII e XIV secolo. Atti del XXX Convegno internazionale (Assisi, 11–13 ottobre 2001)*, Atti dei Convegni della Società internazionale di studi francescani e del Centro interuniversitario di studi francescani, 12 (Spoleto: Fondazione CISAM, 2002), pp. 175–95.

14 Valerie Edden, 'Marian Devotion in a Carmelite Sermon Collection of the Late Middle Ages', *Mediaeval Studies*, 57 (1995), 101–29; Richard Copsey, 'Simon Stock and the Scapular Vision', *The Journal of Ecclesiastical History*, 50 (1999), 652–83.

15 Joachim Smet, *The Carmelites: A History of the Brothers of Our Lady of Mount Carmel* (Roma: Institutum Carmelitanum, 1975); Kaspar Elm, 'Elias, Paulus von Theben und Augustinus als Ordensgründer: ein Beitrag zur Geschichtsschreibung und Geschichtsdeutung der Eremiten- und Bettelorden des 13. Jahrhunderts', in *Geschichtsschreibung und Geschichtsbewusstsein im Spätmittelalter*, ed. by Hans Patze (Sigmaringen: Thorbecke, 1987), pp. 371–97 (p. 383); Kaspar Elm, 'Die Bedeutung historischer Legitimation für Entstehung, Funktion und Bestand mittelalterlichen Ordenswesens', in *Herkunft und Ursprung: historische und mythische Formen der Legitimation*, ed. by Peter Wunderli (Sigmaringen: Thorbecke, 1994), pp. 71–90; Andrew Jotischky, *The Carmelites and Antiquity: Mendicants and their Past in the Middle Ages* (Oxford: Oxford University Press, 2002); Richard Copsey, *Carmel in Britain: Studies on the Early History of the Carmelite Order, III: The Hermits from Mount Carmel* (Roma: Institutum Carmelitanum, 2004); Frances Andrews, *The Other Friars: The Carmelite, Augustinian, Sack, and Pied Friars in the Middle Ages*, Monastic Orders, 2 (New York: Boydell, 2006); Edeltraud Klueting, '"historiam provinciae et conventuum tenere": zur Geschichtsschreibung des Karmelitenordens (O. Carm.)', in *Bettelorden in Mitteleuropa: Geschichte, Kunst, Spiritualität. Referate der gleichnamigen Tagung vom 19. bis 22. März 2007 in St. Pölten*, ed. by Heidemarie Specht and Ralf Andraschek-Holzer, Geschichtliche Beilagen zum St. Pöltner Diözesanblatt, 32, Beiträge zur Kirchengeschichte Niederösterreichs, 15 (St. Pölten: Diözesanarchiv St. Pölten, 2008), pp. 87–105; Jean-Marie Carbasse, 'Les Deux Lois: le prophète Élie et le feu du Ciel', in *La Religiosité du droit*, ed. by Jacqueline Hoareau-Dodinau and Guillaume Métairie, Cahiers de l'Institut d'Anthropologie juridique, 35 (Limoges: Presses Universitaires de Limoges, 2013), pp. 173–84; and Davide Ferraris, 'Il culto del profeta Elia tra Oriente e Occidente', *Rivista di storia e letteratura religiosa*, 52 (2016), 47–64.

THE NEGLECTED CARMELITES 317

to keep alive the memory of its own beginnings. The complete list (in order of seniority is: 1. *Terra Sancta*; 2. Sicily; 3. England; 4. Provence; 5. Tuscany; 6. France; 7. Lower Germany; 8. Lombardy; 9. Aquitaine; 10. Spain; 11. Upper Germany; 12. Scotland-Ireland.

Carmelites paved their way into the big universities, especially Paris, where in the fourteenth century brethren like John Baconthorpe (d. 1348),[16] Michele Aiguiani (d. 1400),[17] and Guido Terreni (d. 1342)[18] exercised considerable influence on theological studies.[19] One has to say, however, that the Carmelites never succeeded in forming an own 'school' based on eminent teachers coming from within the Order. Sermons, 'die bedeutendste Form religiöser Kommunikation', were part of the regular pastoral routine.[20] As a consequence, there should be hundreds, even thousands of Carmelite sermons. Carmelite preaching, however, seems a particularly underdeveloped research field.[21] The number of Carmelite sermons Johann Baptist Schneyer cited in his *Repertorium* is frustratingly low; only one sermon is mentioned.[22] This is also true for the

---

16 Richard Copsey, *Biographical Register of Carmelites in England and Wales 1240–1540* (Faversham: Saint Albert's Press, 2020), pp. 85–93; still useful is Bartolomé Xiberta, 'De magistro Johanne Baconthorp, O. Carm.', *Analecta Ordinis Carmelitarum*, 6 (1927), 3–128.

17 Copsey, *Biographical Register of Carmelites in England and Wales 1240–1540*, pp. 251–54. His Holy Saturday sermon on the Lamentation of the Virgin Mary is edited by Paul Chandler, 'The Lamentation of the Virgin: A Planctus Mariae Sermon by Michael Aiguani of Bologna, O. Carm.', in *The Land of Carmel: Essays in Honor of Joachim Smet, O. Carm.*, ed. by Paul Chandler and Keith Egan (Roma: Institutum Carmelitanum, 1991), pp. 209–29 (text pp. 220–29).

18 *Guido Terreni, O. Carm. († 1342): Studies and Texts*, ed. by Alexander Fidora, Textes et Études du Moyen Age, 78 (Brepols: Turnhout, 2015), pp. vii–xiii.

19 Chris Schabel, 'Carmelite Quodlibeta', in *Theological Quodlibeta in the Middle Ages: The Fourteenth Century*, ed. by Chris Schabel, Brill's Companions to the Christian Tradition, 7 (Leiden: Brill, 2007), pp. 493–543; Stephen F. Brown, 'The Early Carmelite Parisian Masters', in *Philosophy and Theology in the Studia of the Religious Orders and at Papal and Royal Courts: Acts of the xv^{th} Annual Colloquium of the Société Internationale pour l'Étude de la Philosophie Médiévale (University of Notre Dame, 8–10 octobre 2008)*, ed. by Kent Emery, William J. Courtenay, and Stephen M. Metzger (Turnhout: Brepols, 2012), pp. 479–91.

20 Bernhard Lang, 'Predigt als intellektuelles Ritual: eine Grundform religiöser Kommunikation kulturwissenschaftlich betrachtet', in *Literarische und religiöse Kommunikation in Mittelalter und Früher Neuzeit*, ed. by Peter Strohschneider (Berlin: De Gruyter, 2009), pp. 292–323 (p. 293).

21 Emanuele Boaga, 'Predicazione. Carmelitani', *Dizionario degli Istituti di perfezione*, 7 (1983), 524–27; Eef Overgaauw, 'Das Predigtwesen im Karmeliterorden: Predigten in Handschriften aus dem Karmeliterkloster Boppard', in *Predigt im Kontext*, ed. by Volker Mertens, Hans-Jochen Schiewer, Regina D. Schiewer, and Wolfram Schneider-Lastin (Berlin: De Gruyter, 2013), pp. 473–90.

22 Johann Baptist Schneyer, *Repertorium der lateinischen Sermones des Mittelalters für die Zeit von 1150–1350*, 11 vols (Münster: Aschendorff, 1969–1980), III (1971), 432. This sermon, preached by the bishop of Terralba at the pontifical court in Avignon, belongs to the plethora of writings that arose in connection with the *visio beatifica* controversy of the 1330s and has been edited; see Marc Dykmans, 'Jean XXII et les Carmes: la controverse de la vision', *Carmelus*, 17 (1970), 151–92 (Latin edition on pp. 163–92).

318 RALF LÜTZELSCHWAB

digital follow-up to Schneyer in which one more Carmelite preacher is cited, Franciscus de Senis with fifty-three sermons.[23] Schneyer, however, might be wrong in this case: three of the existing four manuscripts ascribe these sermons to the Dominican Aldobrandinus de Toscanella (*fl.* 1314). My own research has shown how much material still exists, more or less hidden in manuscripts or early printed books, all too often quite easily traceable via new and/or digitized manuscript catalogues. In fact, there are about 200 sermons of Carmelite provenance — a number constantly growing owing to my current research. The lion's share of these sermons belongs, however, to the end of the fourteenth and the fifteenth centuries. So far, we do not know of any Carmelite sermon before 1300, which could reflect the Carmelites' difficult starting conditions in the West on the one hand, the lack of corresponding library catalogues of the thirteenth century on the other hand.

The Florence Catalogue (1391)

What do we know about the sermon material hidden in the order's libraries? Early catalogues of Carmelite libraries are a rare species. The first one we have goes back to 1391 and describes the situation in Florence.[24] It is the only extant catalogue of a Carmelite library before 1400. This case is mentioned because in many ways it should set the standard for catalogues to come, both in content and composition as will become clear with regard to the Straubing catalogue. In Florence one large portion of the convent's holdings, in total about 700 manuscripts, were sermons or, more generally speaking, preaching material. The index of authors compiled by the catalogue's editor, Kenneth Humphreys, reveals a wealth of diverse but unfortunately unidentified sermon literature in the library.[25] Quite often only incipits and explicits are given, which are too often insufficient to identify sermons. In the case of Florence we know for sure that sermon collections by Jacopo da Varazze OP (1228/29–1298), Bertrand de la Tour OFM (1262–1332), Jean d'Abbeville (*c.* 1180–1237) and Bernard de Clairvaux O. Cist. (*c.* 1090–1153) filled up the shelves, but we find

---

23 Ludwig Hödl and Wendelin Knoch, *Repertorium der lateinischen Sermones des Mittelalters für die Zeit von 1350 bis 1500 (CD-ROM)* (Münster: Aschendorff, 2001).

24 Kenneth W. Humphreys, *The Library of the Carmelites of Florence at the End of the Fourteenth Century*, Studies in the History of Libraries and Librarianship, 2 (Amsterdam: Erasmus Booksellers, 1964).

25 Humphreys, *The Library of the Carmelites of Florence at the End of the Fourteenth Century*, pp. 90–100. See also *The Friars' Libraries*, ed. by Kenneth W. Humphreys, Corpus of British Medieval Library Catalogues, 1 (London: British Library, 1999). Humphreys edits the catalogues of the Carmelite convents at Aylesford, Boston, Hulne, Lincoln, London, Norwich, and Oxford. An analysis of the books mentioned does not show any sermon or sermon collections by Carmelite authors. A volume by John Beston O. Carm. on vices and virtues may at least be considered a preaching tool; *The Friars' Libraries*, ed. by Humphries, p. 184, n. 39: 'Beston Carmelita de virtutibus et vitiis oppositis'.

THE NEGLECTED CARMELITES   319

only two Carmelite sermon authors: Michaele Aiguani (*c.* 1320–1400) (with the entry numbers 154 and 432),[26] and Guido Terreni (*c.* 1270–1342) (with the entry number 565).[27] This number should be kept in mind: in the library of an order in which preaching constitutes a *raison d'être*, we can only identify the sermons by two Carmelite authors. Given the total of 700 manuscripts this is a meagre 0.3%. An astonishing fact indeed. With this figure in mind, let us turn towards the situation of late medieval Germany.

The Straubing Catalogue (1414)

In 1500 the order had sixty monasteries in German-speaking lands with four *studia generalia* in Vienna, Cologne, Mainz, and Trier.[28] Carmelites had first settled in Cologne (*c.* 1256) and Würzburg (1260) and expanded rather rapidly. When, in 1348 after a few futile attempts (at the end of the thirteenth century and in 1318), the province 'Alemania' was divided into the provinces of Upper and Lower Germany, it included thirty-five monasteries.[29] Reliable calculations of the number of brethren do not exist, although we do find indications of the size of some monasteries in the *Chronicon universale* by Jakob Milendunck (d. 1682). Here, the chronicler records the acts of the provincial chapters held in the province of Lower Germany.[30] Just one example: in 1348, the province of Lower Germany comprised 563 brethren, ninety-eight of them belonging to the convent in Cologne.[31] Not all monasteries were a success

---

26 Humphreys, *The Library of the Carmelites of Florence at the End of the Fourteenth Century,*
   p. 50, n. 154: 'Sermones, incipiunt: Induimini. Finit. Ergo et cetera. Q. 7'; ibid, p. 72, n. 432:
   'Sermones quadragesimales qua sta ferri in papiro cum postibus incipit. Faciem. Et finit.
   Domini', and so on. His *sermones quadragesimales* are only known in one manuscript,
   Ravenna, Biblioteca Classense, MS 400; see Copsey, *Biographical Register of Carmelites in
   England and Wales 1240–1540,* p. 254.
27 Humpheys, *The Library of the Carmelites of Florence at the End of the Fourteenth Century,* p. 85,
   n. 565: '1. In primis sermones dominicales ghuidonis in perghameno cum postibus. Incipit.
   Nondum. Finit. Liber'.
28 Nicole Priesching, 'Die Karmeliten (Ordo Fratrum B.M.V. de Monte Carmelo)', in
   Orden und Klöster im Zeitalter von Reformation und katholischer Reform 1500–1700, ed. by
   Friedhelm Jürgensmeier and Regina Elisabeth Schwerdtfeger, 2 vols (Münster: Aschendorff,
   2005–2006), II (2006), 89–110; *Monasticon Carmelitanum,* ed. by Klueting, Panzer, and
   Scholten, pp. 17–64.
29 In 1440, a third province, Saxonia, came into being; see *Monasticon Carmelitanum,* ed. by
   Klueting, Panzer, and Scholten, pp. 61–64. It existed until the 1520s. Deckert is still the
   authority on the history of the province of Upper Germany; see Adalbert Deckert, *Die
   Oberdeutsche Provinz der Karmeliten nach den Akten ihrer Kapitel von 1421 bis 1529,* Archivum
   Historicum Carmelitanum, 1 (Roma: Institutum Carmelitanum, 1961).
30 The 'Karmeliterbücher' in the Institut für Stadtgeschichte (ISG), Frankfurt am Main contain
   the acts of the provincial chapters as written down by Milendunck. In order to acquire reliable
   figures, one has to count successively from year to year; see Jakob Milendunck, *Chronicon
   universale (Historia provinciae),* II (1200–1500), III (1500–1599), ISG Frankfurt/M. KB 43/44.
31 *Monasticon Carmelitanum,* ed. by Klueting, Panzer, and Scholten, p. 25.

story. In particular, the province of Upper Germany, which had its difficulties in implementing serious reforms propagated by the order's generals John Soreth (1451–1471) and Nicolas Audet (1524–1562), recorded tremendous losses during the Reformation of the first half of the sixteenth century: only eleven out of twenty-six convents survived.[32]

Founded in 1368, the Carmelite convent in the Bavarian city of Straubing is exceptional in so far as it is the only convent in Germany that has an uninterrupted history from its foundation to the present.[33] Until recently, its library has always been highly praised for its abundant content.[34] Straubing is all the more exceptional, given the existence of a library catalogue going back to the year 1414. This catalogue owes its existence to a visitation in 1414 by Heinrich Graefenberger (provincial from 1393–1421), and it lists 176 manuscripts with a substantial amount of preaching material and other pastoral works.[35] In 1414 the library's holdings were divided into several monastic spaces: sacristy, choir, priory, and the library itself. The books were assigned to eleven thematic sections and had signatures. According to the catalogue's

---

32 Adrianus Staring, *Der Karmelitergeneral Nikolaus Audet (1481–1562) und die katholische Reform des 16. Jahrhunderts*, Textus et studia historica Carmelitana, 3 (Roma: Institutum Carmelitanum, 1959); Edeltraud Klueting, *Monasteria semper reformanda: Kloster- und Ordensreformen im Mittelalter*, Historia profana et ecclesiastica, 12 (Münster: Aschendorff, 2005), pp. 101–18 (pp. 113–15); John Soreth, *Expositio Paraenetica in Regulam Carmelitarum*, ed. by Bryan Deschamp, Corpus Christianorum, Continuatio Mediaevalis, 259 (Turnhout: Brepols, 2016), pp. xxxv–lxxi.

33 Adalbert Deckert, *Karmel in Straubing* (Roma: Institutum Carmelitanum, 1962); Christine Riedl-Valder, 'Straubing', in *Monasticon Carmelitanum: die Klöster des Karmelitenordens (O. Carm.) in Deutschland von den Anfängen bis zur Gegenwart*, ed. by Edeltraud Klueting, Stephan Panzer and Andreas H. Scholten (Münster: Aschendorff, 2012), pp. 693–710. The oldest inventory of the monastery's archive goes back to 1545. The archive's holdings were dispersed in 1802 due to secularization. At this time, Straubing became a so-called 'Aussterbekloster' or 'Central Convent' where all brethren of the province unwilling to leave the order were concentrated.

34 Alfons Huber, 'Geschichte der Karmelitenbibliothek Straubing', in *Handschriften und alte Drucke aus der Karmelitenbibliothek Straubing: Ausstellung Gäubodenmuseum Straubing* (Straubing: Gäubodenmuseum, 1986), pp. 5–14; Matthäus Hösler, 'Straubing Karmelitenbibliothek', in *Handbuch der historischen Buchbestände in Deutschland*, ed. by Eberhard Dünninger and Irmela Holtmeier, 27 vols (Hildesheim: Olms, 1992–2000), XIII (1997) (Bayern S–Z), 58–60; Alfons Huber, *Bibliothek des Karmeliterklosters Straubing*, Schnell Kunstführer, 2807 (Regensburg: Schnell and Steiner, 2013).

35 Adalbert Deckert, 'Bibliotheks-Katalog des Straubinger Karmelitenklosters von 1414', *Jahresbericht des historischen Vereins für Straubing und Umgebung*, 68 (1965), 84–93; Alfons Huber, 'Die Bibliothek des Straubinger Karmelitenklosters im Mittelalter', in *Ratisbona Sacra: das Bistum Regensburg im Mittelalter. Ausstellung anlässlich des 1250 jährigen Jubiläums der kanonischen Errichtung des Bistums Regensburg durch Bonifatius 739–1989* (München: Schnell & Steiner, 1989), pp. 287–89. Deckert's edition has been replaced by Christine Elisabeth Ineichen-Eder, 'Straubing: Karmeliterkloster St Maria', *Mittelalterliche Bibliothekskataloge Deutschlands und der Schweiz*, IV/1: *Bistümer Passau und Regensburg*, ed. by Christine Elisabeth Ineichen-Eder (München: Beck, 1977), pp. 504–13; Hösler, 'Straubing Karmelitenbibliothek'.

THE NEGLECTED CARMELITES   321

description, the codices were located in a *pulpitum*, a presumably large frame with an inclined surface.

In the second half of the fifteenth century the purchase or bequest of many incunabula led to a considerable increase in the number of volumes. A library catalogue from 1768 (with some *additamenta* up to 1776) lists 200 incunabula and 276 early printed books. Thirty-eight of them consist of sermons, and 276 are early printed books with thirty-seven sermon volumes.[36] Whereas all the sermon incunabula belonged to the section 'concionatores latini' or Latin preachers, the early printed books appeared in both sections, the 'concionatores latini' (thirty-one) and the 'concionatores germanici' or German preachers (six).[37] The predominance of Latin preaching material is striking. The 1768 catalogue with a total of 13,421 volumes, however, does not represent the total of the convent's books when it was threatened by closure in 1802. At the beginning of the nineteenth century, the current book holdings must have been a little fewer than 16,000 volumes.[38] Unfortunately, however, the medieval library is lost. Today only single volumes survive scattered in different libraries.[39] Numbers speak for themselves: seventy-six out of the 176 manuscripts mentioned in the 1414 catalogue contain sermons, almost 44% of the whole. Even by mendicant standards this is an extremely high number.

In general, decoding the sometimes enigmatic references in medieval catalogues is not an easy task. Straubing's catalogue of 1414 is no exception to the rule. Three examples will suffice to illustrate this point:

1. Titles like 'Omelie per dominicas et sermones' are of absolutely no use beyond the fact that they show the existence of sermon literature on the library's shelves. There is clearly no hope in identifying author or particular work.

2. Indications like 'Burchardus ad Carthusienses. Item pericula viciorum. Sermones de sancta Maria Magdalena. Item sermones de beata virgine' are misleading, because we never know if the manuscript cited is a miscellaneous codex. This would make it difficult to identify the sermons about Mary Magdalene or the Virgin as genuine works of a certain Burchard. Or does the scribe refer to Bernard de Clairvaux?

---

36 The oldest incunabulum contained sermons by Leonardo da Udine, printed in 1475 (Ulm) (ISTC nn. L*155, L*158); see Paul Ruf, *Säkularisation und Bayerische Staatsbibliothek*, 1: *die Bibliotheken der Mendikanten und Theatiner (1799–1802)* (Wiesbaden: Harrassowitz, 1962), pp. 520–31. In 1802 the monastery was chosen as 'Aussterbekloster' for the province. It was only in 1842 when King Ludwig I of Bavaria officially re-opened the convent.

37 The total number of books belonging to these two sections is 689 volumes for the 'conciniatores latini' and 1080 volumes for the 'conciniatores germanici'.

38 Ruf, *Säkularisation und Bayerische Staatsbibliothek*, p. 522.

39 The 1768 catalogue only mentions one manuscript belonging to the section *concionatores latini*. It is Meffreth's [Pseudo-Petrus Meffordis of Leipzig?] *Hortulus reginae cum manuscriptis*.

3. Some titles may be ambiguous. The sermon collection entitled 'Viridarius' might be the work of Nikolaus Magni de Jauer (1355–1435),[40] the famous rector of the university of Heidelberg, as well as of the Carmelite prior general Johannes Grossi (1360–1435).

However, not everything is difficult or ambiguous. The 1414 catalogue shows other examples of sermon literature ascribed to specific authors. In these cases the identification usually does not pose major problems. We find sermons by authors like Berthold von Regensburg OFM (d. 1272) or Conradus de Brundelsheim O. Cist. (d. 1321),[41] by Antonio Azaro Parmense OP (d. *c.* 1310),[42] Johannes Contractus OFM (fourteenth century),[43] Peregrinus de Oppeln OP (d. after 1333),[44] and others. The majority of the identifiable material belongs to the Dominican Jacopo da Varazze (d. 1298) with eleven manuscripts of his various sermon collections.[45] Most of these authors belong to the regular clergy with Dominicans and Franciscans in foremost position. But: where are the Carmelites? Where are Carmelite authors in a well-equipped library bursting with sermons? The answer is simple: they are not totally absent, but their presence is very 'discrete'. Just one volume bears a Carmelite author's name: in a miscellaneous manuscript we find sermons *de tempore* by the Carmelite Johannes Grossi.[46] He is quite prominent because he acted as prior general of the order from 1411. His most famous work is the *Viridarium*, written between 1411–1417, from which two examples could also be found on the shelves of the Carmelites at Straubing.[47] His sermons, however, appear to have circulated only minimally. If we trust the indication

---

40 Deckert, 'Bibliotheks-Katalog des Straubinger Karmelitenklosters von 1414', p. 88: *Viridarius de sanctis*; see Krzysztof Bracha, *Des Teufels Lug und Trug: Nikolaus Magni von Jauer, Ein Reform-theologe des Spätmittelalters gegen Aberglaube und Götzendienst* (Dettelbach: Röll, 2013).

41 Deckert, 'Bibliotheks-Katalog des Straubinger Karmelitenklosters von 1414', 'Primo sermones Rusticani de tempore et sermones Socci per adventum' (p. 87).

42 Deckert, 'Bibliotheks-Katalog des Straubinger Karmelitenklosters von 1414', 'Anthonius Parmensis dominicis diebus et speculum humane salvacionis' (p. 87).

43 Deckert, 'Bibliotheks-Katalog des Straubinger Karmelitenklosters von 1414', 'Contractus de sanctis' (p. 88).

44 Deckert, 'Bibliotheks-Katalog des Straubinger Karmelitenklosters von 1414', 'Peregrinus de sanctis'(p. 88).

45 Deckert, 'Bibliotheks-Katalog des Straubinger Karmelitenklosters von 1414', nos 45, 56, 70, 71, 113–17, 140, and 174. For his most famous work, see Jacopo da Varazze, *Legenda aurea*, ed. by Giovanni Paolo Maggioni, Millenio medievale, 6 (Firenze: SISMEL, 1998). His four sermon collections had an enormous impact, the large number of preserved manuscripts being the ultimate proof of their importance.

46 Deckert, 'Bibliotheks-Katalog des Straubinger Karmelitenklosters von 1414', p. 89 n. 73: 'Flores de tempore. Bartholomeus de tempore et exempla. Sermones de tempore fratris Johannis Gossi [*sic*] ordinis fratrum Carmelitarum'; see Copsey, *Biographical Register of Carmelites in England and Wales 1240–1540*, pp. 71–73; Gabriel Wessels, 'Aliquid de Statu Ordinis durante schismate occidentali (1378–1417)', *Analecta Ordinis Carmelitarum*, 3 (1914), 140–52.

47 Deckert, 'Bibliotheks-Katalog des Straubinger Karmelitenklosters von 1414', 'Viridarius de sanctis' (n. 60); *ibid*, 'Viridarius per quadragesimam' (n. 124).

THE NEGLECTED CARMELITES   323

in the *Bibliotheca Carmelitana Nova*, recently confirmed by Richard Copsey's *Biographical Register of Carmelites in England and Wales*, only one manuscript with sermons by Grossi has survived the ages. Nowadays it is kept at the Staatsbibliothek München.[48] These sermons have never been edited. There is, however, more sermon material of Carmelite provenance. Three volumes of Lenten sermons appear as *Carmelita per quadragesimam*.[49] Unfortunately, as of now, scholars are unable to identify this 'Carmelita'.

It is notable that in 1414 most of the sermon manuscripts was protected by a special security feature: they were chained ('in hac parte pulpiti appensa sunt hec volumina'). This speaks in favour of the special importance these sermon manuscripts held for the brethren. Apparently they represented the core of the reference library with no chance whatsoever of being lent. Those *volumina catenata* were considered precious items, not necessarily for their inherent value, but for the significance in light of the order's main *propositum*: pastoral work.

Twenty-six of the 200 incunabula cited in the 1768 catalogue ended up in the Staatsbibliothek München. One can be found in Oslo. The monastery itself is still in possession of 160 of them.[50] But a situation which is good in itself (original holdings still in place) may become awkward; the case of Straubing is particularly revealing in this respect.[51] Having no access to the monastery library at the moment, the only thing one could do was to check the twenty-four incunabula preserved in Munich. The result is discouraging: only one volume contains sermons, to be more precise: the *Quadragesimale* by the Franciscan Johannes Gritsch (1405–1475), printed in Lyon in 1492.[52] But this finding is completely logical: when at the beginning of the nineteenth century the personnel of the Königliche Bibliothek in Munich got access to the library, its choice did not fall upon *praedicabilia* or sermons. For them, this was the least interesting material imaginable. Chances are therefore high that relevant sermon incunabula may be found at Straubing.

---

48 München, Staatsbibliothek, Clm 23855, fols 132v–228r.
49 Deckert, 'Bibliotheks-Katalog des Straubinger Karmelitenklosters von 1414', nn. 110–12.
50 Ruf, *Säkularisation und Bayerische Staatsbibliothek*, pp. 520–31. Only fifteen manuscripts remained in 1768. In 2018 the convent in Straubing comprised 185 incunabula in total; thirty-four contained sermon material.
51 For several years Straubing has been threatened with closure. The monastery's ordinary research library has recently been sold and only the literature from 1500 to 1800 is still on place. There is no reliable catalogue of the monastery's incunabula section, neither online nor in print.
52 Ludwig Hain, *Repertorium bibliographicum in quo libri omnes ab arte typographica inventa usque ad annum MD typis expressi ordine alphabetico vel simpliciter enumerantur vel adcuratius recensentur*, 2 vols in 2 parts (Stuttgart: Cotta, 1827), I, part 2, n. 8076: *Quadragesimale Johannes Gritsch OFM* (Lyon, 1492). The Carmelite Monastery was acquired by the Free State of Bavaria in October 2018. In the future, the rooms of the former monastery will become part of the 'Straubing Campus' of the Technical University of Munich. One area is to be sectioned off for the three remaining Indian monks.

324   RALF LÜTZELSCHWAB

The Carmelite Library at Mainz

In the fifteenth century Mainz belonged to the order's province of Lower Germany. Carmelites had lived in this important imperial city since at least 1271. The earliest evidence for the existence of a library goes back to a visitation protocol, written by Petrus de Nieukerk, provincial from 1430–1444 and 1456–1462, in 1434. At that time the convent was supposed to own 173 manuscripts.[53] Only a small part of the convent's medieval manuscript holdings survives, to be more precise: thirty-nine of them, copied and/or written from the second half to the end of the fifteenth century. Three remaining sermon manuscripts are no exception to this rule.[54]

A doctoral dissertation in which the Carmelite library is reconstructed and analysed from its very beginnings up to the dissolution of the brethren in 1802 successfully sheds light on the genesis, development, and transformation of this important book collection.[55] After the convent's suppression, the majority of the library holdings ended up in the municipal library, the Stadtbibliothek of Mainz. The author of this 1200-page *opus magnum*, Annelen Ottermann, has worked in the Stadtbibliothek for decades and is considered one of the best specialists of its internal structure. What she has achieved is really remarkable. Assessing what remains in the library was a very complex process, because incunabula and printed books were not integrated into the Stadtbibliothek in discrete sections, but distributed into the appropriate, already existing thematic sections. The main task consisted in physically investigating every single print in the library's book storage rooms. Numbers speak for themselves: the relevant holdings in the Stadtbibliothek comprise no fewer than 130,000 volumes. At the end of the day, Ottermann was able to identify 1589 manuscripts and prints from the thirteenth to the beginning of the nineteenth century as the former property of the Carmelites. Let us have a closer look at the volumes we are particularly interested in: among the thirty-nine manuscripts we find the *Sermones de tempore* of the Augustinian Jordanus von Quedlinburg (*c.* 1300–1370/80, OESA) with very little traces of use.[56] But the codex shows an entry which is a testimony to the manuscript's

---

53   This number had increased up to 186 manuscripts in 1486. In 1441 the province's biggest convent in Brussels owned 317 manuscripts; see Henricus Gabriel Johannes Lansink, 'Bücher und Bibliotheken bei den Karmeliten der niederdeutschen Provinz im Mittelalter', in *Contributions à l'histoire des bibliothèques et à la lecture aux Pays-Bas avant 1600 / Studies over het boekenbezit en boekengebruik in de Nederlanden voor 1600*, Archief- en bibliotheekwezen in België, Extranummer, 11 / Archives et bibliothèques de Belgique, Numero spécial, 11 (Bruxelles: Association des archives et bibliothecaires, 1974), pp. 225–45.

54   Mainz, Stadtbibliothek, MS II 26 (Gerson); Mainz, Stadtbibliothek, MS II 27 (after 1427); Mainz, Stadtbibliothek, MS II 34; see Annelen Ottermann, *Die Mainzer Karmelitenbibliothek: Spurensuche — Spurensicherung — Spurendeutung*, Berliner Arbeiten zur Bibliotheks- und Informationswissenschaft, 27, 2 vols (Berlin: Logos, 2016), II, 357, 561.

55   Ottermann, *Die Mainzer Karmelitenbibliothek.*

56   Mainz, Stadtbibliothek, MS II 41 (mid-fifteenth century).

THE NEGLECTED CARMELITES   325

use in pastoral care: 'Hunc sermonem predicavit fr[ater] adam de Duren Anno 1489 lector istius conventus et est satis [...] illum' ['This sermon was preached by Brother Adam de Düren in 1489, lector of this convent, and that is quite [...]'] (where the text is not legible).[57] Adam de Düren, who in 1489 also acted as *lector sententiarum* in the Carmelite convent at Trier, apparently refrained from composing his own sermon, using Jordanus von Quedlinburg instead. We should not underestimate the importance of this statement for it finally refers to a real preaching act *hic et nunc*.

In Mainz we also find Alan de Lille's (*c.* 1120–1202) *Summa de arte praedicandi*, sermons by the Cistercian Conradus de Brundelsheim (d. 1321),[58] and the Dominican Johannes Herolt (*c.* 1380–1468),[59] all in manuscripts. Herolt's *Sermones discipuli super epistolas Pauli* even bear an owner's mark: 'Sermones Discipuli super ep[istu]las Pauli ex p[a]rte fratris Johannis Budingen filius huius scilicet Maguntini factus professus in die s[anc]ti tho[me] ap[osto]li a[nn]o etx. Lxii' ['Sermons by Discipulus on Paul's letters that belonged to Johannes Budingen, a son of this convent in Mainz, who made his profession on St Thomas's Day in 1462'].[60] The owner, Johannes de Budingen (d. 1496), belonged to a group of six Carmelites who in 1467 were given the right to preach by the archbishop of Mainz, Adolf von Nassau. The marginalia within the text show clearly that Johannes de Budingen worked with these sermons. His hand can also be identified in a manuscript containing Jean Gobi's (*c.* 1300–1350, OP) *Scala coeli*.[61] Let us speculate a little: it may be reasonable

---

57 Mainz, Stadtbibliothek, MS II 41, fol. 241r; see Ottermann, *Die Mainzer Karmelitenbibliothek*, p. 594.

58 Romuald Bauerreiß, 'Wer ist der mittelalterliche Prediger "Soccus"?', *Studien und Mitteilungen zur Geschichte des Benediktiner-Ordens und seiner Zweige*, 65 (1953–1954), 75–80; F.J. Worstbrock, 'Konrad von Brundelsheim', in *Die deutsche Literatur des Mittelalters: Verfasserlexikon*, ed. by Kurt Ruh and others, 14 vols, 2nd edn (Berlin: De Gruyter, 1978–2008), v (1985), cols 147–53; Kathrin Janz-Wenig, 'Mittelalterphilologie am Beispiel einer Predigtsammlung: die Sammlung der "Sermones Socci"', in *Mittelalterphilologien heute: eine Standortbestimmung. 1: die germanischen Philologien*, ed. by Alessandra Molinari (Würzburg: Königshausen & Neumann, 2016), pp. 79–98.

59 John W. Dahmus, 'Late Medieval Preachers and Lay Perfection: The Case of Johannes Herolt, O. P.', *Medieval Perspectives*, 1 (1986), 122–34; Richard G. Newhauser, 'From Treatise to Sermon: Johannes Herolt on the *novem peccata aliena*', in *De ore Domini: Preacher and Word in the Middle Ages*, ed. by Thomas Leslie Amos, Eugene A. Green, and Beverly Mayne Kienzle, Studies in Medieval Culture, 27 (Kalamazoo: Western Michigan University, 1989), pp. 185–209. The *Sermones discipuli de tempore et de sanctis cum promptuario exemplorum et miraculis Beatae Mariae Virginis* was the most widely reprinted sermon collection of the fifteenth century; see Anne T. Thayer, 'Learning to Worship in the Late Middle Ages: Enacting Symbolism, Fighting the Devil, and Receiving Grace', *Archiv für Reformationsgeschichte*, 99 (2008), 36–65 (p. 39).

60 Mainz, Stadtbibliothek, MS II 28, fol. 175r.

61 *La Scala coeli de Jean Gobi*, ed. by Marie-Anne Polo de Beaulieu (Paris: Centre National de la Recherche Scientifique, 1991); Marie-Anne Polo de Beaulieu, 'Des histoires et des images au service de la prédication: la Scala coeli de Jean Gobi Junior (+ 1350)', in *De l'homélie au sermon: histoire de la prédication médiévale*, ed. by Jacqueline Hamesse and Xavier Hermand,

326   RALF LÜTZELSCHWAB

to assume that Johannes von Budingen not only plundered Herolt in order to construct his own sermons (from which nothing remains, alas), but might have used the Dominican's sermons in their entirety.

At Mainz the number of incunabula and post-incunabula (that is, before the 1550s) is high: 289 volumes that formerly belonged to the Carmelites are preserved either in the Stadtbibliothek Mainz or in the Gutenberg-Museum. Sermons and sermon literature represent the strongest segment within the reconstructed holdings of the library.[62] Four incunabula contain sermons by Johannes Herolt,[63] eight incunabula substantial portions of Roberto Carracciolo's OFM (c. 1425–1495) sermons.[64] One can add sermons by Vicent Ferrer OP (1350–1419),[65] and Johannes de Werdena OFM (d. c. 1437),[66] Johannes Nider's OP (1380–1438) *Formicarius* and four incunabula with Lenten sermons by Conrad Grütsch OFM (c. 1409–1475).[67] The Franciscan Pelbartus de Temeswar (c. 1435–1504) is particularly well represented by seven incunabula.[68] A *Vocabularius praedicantium* (*sive variloquus*) compiled by Johannes Melber (active c. 1453) shows a decidedly practical approach to preaching realities.[69]

The situation at Straubing reminds us of that in Mainz with its reconstructed Carmelite library, despite all the problems and shortcomings such a

---

Publications de l'institut d'études médiévales: textes, études, congrès, 14 (Louvain-la-Neuve: Collège Erasme, 1993), pp. 279–312.

62 Ottermann, *Die Mainzer Karmelitenbibliothek*: 'Predigten, als einzelne oder in Sammlungen, stellen das stärkste Segment innerhalb des Rekonstruktionsbestands dar' (p. 583).

63 Johannes Herolt, *Sermones discipuli de tempore et de sanctis cum promptuario exemplorum et miraculis Beatae Mariae Virginis* (Basel: Johann Amerbach, 1482; Nürnberg: Anton Koberger, 1483; Reutlingen: Michael Greyff, 1482) and Johannes Herolt, *Liber Discipuli de eruditione Christifidelium* (Strasbourg: Johann Prüss, 1490).

64 *Sermones quadragesimales de peccatis* (Venedig: Andreas Asulanus, 1488); *Sermones quadragesimales de poenitentia* (Köln: Johann Koelhoff, the Elder, 1473); *Sermones de timore divinorum iudiciorum* (Köln: Johann Manthen, 1475); *Sermones de laudibus sanctorum* (four copies; Antwerpen: Gerard Leeu, 1490; Speyer: Peter Drach, 1490; Basel: Nicolaus Kessler, 1490; Reutlingen: Michael Greyff, before 1492).

65 *Sermones de tempore et de sanctis* (Strasbourg, 1493/94).

66 Sermon collection *Dormi secure*.

67 Christine Stöllinger, 'Grütsch, Conrad', in *Die deutsche Literatur des Mittelalters: Verfasserlexikon*, ed. by Kurt Ruh and others, 14 vols, 2nd edn (Berlin: De Gruyter, 1978–2008), III (1981), cols 291–94.

68 Ildikó Bárczi, 'La Diversité thématique dans les prédications de Pelbart de Temesvár', *Archivum franciscanum historicum*, 100 (2007), 251–310; Balász Kertész, 'Two Hungarian Friars Minor (Franciscan Observants) in the Late Middle Ages: Pelbart de Temesvár and Oswald de Lasko', in *Infima aetas Pannonica: Studies in Late Medieval Hungarian History*, ed. by Péter E. Kovácz and Kornél Szovák (Budapest: Corvina, 2009), pp. 60–78.

69 Susanne Brüggemann, 'Vocabularius praedicantium: ein lateinisch-deutsches Wörterbuch für die Prediger von Johannes Melber, Dokumentation zur Restaurierung der Inkunabel 4 Inc.s.a. 1248a aus den Beständen der Bayerischen Staatsbibliothek', in *Habent sua fata libelli: Integration von Wissenschaft und Praxis in der Buchrestaurierung*, ed. by Helmut Bansa (München: Saur, 2000), pp. 103–19.

THE NEGLECTED CARMELITES   327

methodological approach entails. In both libraries we find the same authors. In both cases the library was a library for users providing plenty of material in the fields of *praedicatura* and *docentura*. With regard to Mainz, however, we know even more: 75% of the surviving reconstructed holdings are the result of a non-contingent increase. Especially in view of pastoral practice, the library shows signs of a systematic building process. But in the end one fact cries out for explanation.

Sermons by Carmelite Authors?

The question of the whereabouts of sermons by Carmelites authors may also be formulated the other way round: were Carmelites second-hand preachers but first-hand directors — directors in the sense of the German 'Seelenführer' or spiritual guide? For the decades immediately following the Reformation the answer is obvious. The province of Upper Germany faced a total collapse. There was restricted manpower; preachers were difficult to find. Fortunately, we have the *acta* of Andreas Stoß, who from 1534–1538 acted as provincial.[70] Andreas belonged to an illustrious family: his father was the highly gifted carver Veit Stoß, famous as the creator of the breath-taking high altar in Kraków's St Mary's Church. Andreas Stoß left a collection mainly of copies of letters (or drafts of them) sent to various ecclesiastical and secular dignitaries. The reality that shines through is sad, even dramatic. Apparently, the province's existence was at stake. Andreas Stoß's complaint that 'So aber vnserem orden, auch andern, mangel ist an personen vnd in sunderhait an predicanten' ['That in our Order, as well as in others, there is a shortage of manpower and especially in preachers'] is omnipresent.[71] In some cases, the *ultima ratio* was to supply preachers belonging to other orders or to the secular clergy. After a visitation of the Carmelite convent in Straubing, Stoß wrote:

> Ea de re conventus caret predicante, quin deficio in predicantibus in provincia. Conclusimus ego, vicedominus et conventus, ex quo conventum cum fratre, qui predicare novit, providere non possum, sol man alterius religionis vel secularem sacerdotem catholicum annemen, donec possum habere nostre professionis unum.[72]
>
> [For this reason, the convent lacks a preacher because I do not have preachers in the province. I, the prior, and the convent have decided,

---

70 *Acta des Karmelitenprovinzials Andreas Stoß (1534–1538)*, ed. by Adalbert Deckert and Matthäus Hösler, Archivum Historicum Carmelitanum, 5 (Roma: Institutum Carmelitanum, 1995).

71 *Acta des Karmelitenprovinzials Andreas Stoß (1534–1538)*, ed. by Deckert and Hösler, p. 349 (Würzburg, 1537.05.16); p. 350 (Bamberg 1537.08.01).

72 *Acta des Karmelitenprovinzials Andreas Stoß (1534–1538)*, ed. by Deckert and Hösler, p. 393 (draft, 1538); see *ibid*, p. 406 (1538.06.04) where a Franciscan is nominated as the new preacher of the Carmelite convent in Rottenburg.

328 RALF LÜTZELSCHWAB

that one should accept a monk of another order or a Catholic secular priest as long as I can have someone belonging to our order].

In arduis, Andreas Stoß was alone. He could not expect any help from the order's general Nicolas Audet who in 1534 wrote to Stoß:

[…] litere vestre testantur magnam admodum provincie nostre Alemanie Superioris desolacionem et calamitatem. Compatimur illi ex intimis animi precordys […]. Multa et varia sunt consilia, auxilia vero perpauca et rara.[73]

[[…] Your letters bear witness to the great desolation and distress of your province of Upper Germany. We suffer with you in our inner heart […]. There are many and various counsels, but little and rare help].

Under these circumstances, the order had other, more urgent problems, than providing convents with competent preachers. Times of disaster do not operate in favour of sermon production.

But what about the pre-Reformation period of the fifteenth century? Without any doubt, the high points of Carmelite sermon production were the late fourteenth and especially the fifteenth centuries — periods in which hundreds of sermons were transmitted. The reason for this is evident: efficient institutional structures existed. The order had at its disposal eminent *magistri* acting as renowned preachers. Even two missing *Artes praedicandi* can be assigned to this period.[74] We also encounter two fourteenth–century sermons written in the Middle German vernacular. One sermon is part of an elaborate commentary on John 1. 1–14 (*Das Buch von der himmlischen Gottheit*) that found its way into a plenary for Sundays and feast days, where the remarks of Frederic the Carmelite (Friedrich der Karmelit), acting in 1386 as provincial of the province of Upper Germany, on the prologue of John's Gospel appear in the form of a vernacular sermon.[75] The other sermon goes back to John the Carmelite (Hane der Karmelit), who in all probability can be identified with Johannes Vogele, the prior of Cologne's Carmelite convent in the 1340s.[76] He

---

73 *Acta des Karmelitenprovinzials Andreas Stoß (1534–1538)*, ed. by Deckert and Hösler, p. 187 (1534.06.01); see Staring, *Der Karmelitergeneral Nikolaus Audet*, pp. 269–92.

74 The authors of these *Artes praedicandi* were John Folsham (d. 1348), provincial prior in England (*De arte predicandi*) and Goswinus Hex (d. 1475), suffragan bishop of Utrecht (*De modo predicandi Liber unus*); see Harry Caplan, *Mediaeval Artes Praedicandi: A Hand-List* (Ithaca: Cornell, 1934), pp. 19–20, and 32; Thomas-Marie Charland, *Artes Praedicandi: contribution à l'histoire de la rhétorique au Moyen Age*, Publications de l'institut d'etudes médiévales d'Ottawa, 7 (Paris: Publications de l'institut d'etudes médiévales, 1936), pp. 38 and 54; Copsey, *Biographical Register of Carmelites in England and Wales 1240–1540*, pp. 147–48.

75 Gisela Kornrumpf, 'Friedrich der Karmelit', in *Die deutsche Literatur des Mittelalters: Verfasserlexikon*, ed. by Kurt Ruh and others, 14 vols, 2nd edn (Berlin: De Gruyter, 1978–2008), II (1979), cols 948–50.

76 Lauri Seppänen, 'Hane der Karmelit', in *Die deutsche Literatur des Mittelalters: Verfasserlexikon*, ed. by Kurt Ruh and others, 14 vols, 2 edn (Berlin: De Gruyter, 1978–2008), III (1981), cols 429–31.

left a vernacular sermon on Matthew 14. 36 (*Omnes querebant eum tangere*) which is very close spiritually to the kind of speculative mysticism practised by Meister Eckhart.[77] Neither one, however, influenced the order's sermon production in a substantial way.

Conclusion

Carmelites succeeded in working their way into the inner circles of power. Their roles as counsellors or confessors contributed to the preservation of what they uttered.[78] The more prominent the preachers were, the greater the chances of their sermons being transmitted for posterity. But at a simple parish level, sermons were seldom considered worth being kept, written down, or integrated into the libraries. However, the sheer quantity of non-Carmelite preaching material in those libraries shows that they had everything they wanted at their disposal in order to construct appropriate, 'discrete' sermons. But on the whole, these sermons were mass-produced goods, sufficient to respond to the needs of a rather undemanding population, and not bravura pieces representing the cutting edge of late medieval rhetoric. Only a few Carmelite preachers reached the dizzying heights of their Dominican or Franciscan counterparts. The Carmelites Grossi, Aiguiani, or Terreni were towering preaching figures. Their works were usually present in the libraries — amidst a huge array of sermon collections written by preachers of the other mendicant orders.[79] It would therefore not be accurate to say that there were no genuine Carmelite sermons. What surprises, however, is the scarcity of well-made examples of the *sermo modernus*. Future library discoveries might change this picture.

---

77 Antje Willing, 'Die Predigt *Omnes querebant eum tangere* Hanes des Karmeliten', in *Paradisus anime intelligentis. Studien zu einer dominikanischen Predigtsammlung aus dem Umkreis Meister Eckharts*, ed. by Burkhard Hasebrink, Nigel F. Palmer, and Hans-Jochen Schiewer (Tübingen: Niemeyer, 2009), pp. 201–26.

78 Stephen Patrington and Robert Mascall acted as the confessors of Henry IV (d. 1413), while Thomas Netter from Saffron Walden in Essex, who was the provincial of the English Carmelites from 1414 until his death in 1430, assumed the same position under Henry V (d. 1422); see David Knowles, *The Religious Orders in England*, 3 vols (Cambridge: Cambridge University Press, 1950–1959), II (1955), 144–48; Richard Copsey, *Biographical Register of Carmelites in England and Wales 1240–1540*, pp. 414–25. As Copsey points out, only a short extract of one of Netter's sermons has stood the test of time. All other sermons are lost, even the one preached at Henry V's funeral.

79 It is no surprise that neither Straubing nor Mainz had printed (medieval) Carmelite sermons on their library shelves. Anne Thayer in her ground-breaking work on model sermon collections in incunabula does not even mention the Carmelites; see Anne T. Thayer, *Penitence, Preaching and the Coming of the Reformation*, St Andrews Studies in Reformation History (Aldershot: Ashgate, 2002).

Straubing and Mainz are no exception to the rule.[80] They represent normal libraries of middle-sized convents with a huge amount of preaching material and large numbers of sermon collections written and/or compiled by non-Carmelite authors. The little information we have about other Carmelite libraries in Europe point in the same direction. And this situation continued well into the times of incunabula and early printed books, something that Szymon Sułecki convincingly showed with regard to the Carmelite library in Kraków in which printed *praedicabilia* dominated the shelves.[81] It comes as no surprise that the bulk of this printed preaching material did not originate in Carmelite surroundings. This, however, changed quickly with the arrival of the Carmelites' reform movement of the sixteenth-century towering figures, Teresa de Ávila (1515–1582) and John of the Cross (1542–1591). Their works were printed in huge numbers and heavily influenced subsequent Carmelite authors and their sermons.[82] To sum it up: there was no pressing need for Carmelites to activate their own inventive skills. Preaching material was available in sufficient quantity — and apparently the Brethren of Our Lady made the best of this wealth.

---

80 One could add the Carmelite convent in Esslingen, where only fifteen books survived (among them Brundelsheims *Sermones de sanctis*); see Iris Holzwart-Schäfer, *Das Karmeliter-kloster in Esslingen (1271–1557): ein südwestdeutscher Mendikantenkonvent zwischen Ordensideal und Alltagswirklichkeit*, Esslinger Studien, Schriftenreihe, 22 (Ostfildern: Thorbecke, 2011), pp. 272–75.

81 Szymon Sułecki, *The Library of the Carmelite Monastery in Piasek in Cracow*, Textus et Studia Historica Carmelitana, 45 (Roma: Institutum Carmelitanum, 2018).

82 Jane E. Ackermann, 'The Carmelite Ancestry of Teresa of Avila and John of the Cross', *Carmelus*, 46 (1999), 8–33; Elena Carrera, *Teresa of Avila's Autobiography: Authority, Power and the Self in Mid-Sixteenth-Century Spain* (Oxford: Oxford University Press, 2005); Peter Tyler, *St John of the Cross* (London: Continuum, 2010); Colin Thompson, 'Dangerous Visions: The Experience of Teresa of Avila and the Teaching of John of the Cross', in *Angels of Light? Sanctity and Discernment of Spirits in the Early Modern Period*, ed. by Claire Copeland and Jan Machielsen (Leiden: Brill, 2013), pp. 53–74; Paul Murray, 'St John of the Cross: The Thinker, the Poet, the Mystic', *Angelicum*, 96 (2019), 255–74.

Bibliography

Manuscripts and Archives

Frankfurt am Main, Institut für Stadtgeschichte, Jakob Milendunck, *Chronicon universale (Historia provinciae)*, II (1200–1500), III (1500–1599), KB 43/44
Mainz, Stadtbibliothek, MS II 26
Mainz, Stadtbibliothek, MS II 27
Mainz, Stadtbibliothek, MS II 28
Mainz, Stadtbibliothek, MS II 34
Mainz, Stadtbibliothek, MS II 41
München, Staatsbibliothek, Clm 23855
Ravenna, Biblioteca Classense, MS 400

Early Printed Works
[with ISTC references]

Johannes Herolt, *Liber Discipuli de eruditione Christifidelium* (Strasbourg: Johann Prüss, 1490, ISTC ih00095000)
Johannes Herolt, *Sermones discipuli de tempore et de sanctis cum promptuario exemplorum et miraculis Beatae Mariae Virginis* (Basel: Johann Amerbach, 1482, ISTC ih00106000; Nürnberg: Anton Koberger, 1483, ISTC ih00109000; Reutlingen: Michael Greyff, 1482, ISTC ih00102000)
Nicolas de Biard, *Dictionarius pauperum omnibus praedicatoribus verbi divini pernecessarius de tempore et de sanctis* (Strasbourg: Johann Knoblouch, 1516)
Roberto Carracciolo, *Sermones de laudibus sanctorum* (Antwerpen: Gerard Leeu, 1490, ISTC ic00149000; Speyer: Peter Drach, 1490, ISTC ic00146000; Basel: Nicolaus Kessler, 1490, ISTC ic00148000; Reutlingen: Michael Greyff, before 1492, ISTC ic00151000)
Roberto Carracciolo, *Sermones de timore divinorum iudiciorum* (Köln: Johann Manthen, 1475, ISTC ic00184000)
Roberto Carracciolo, *Sermones quadragesimales de peccatis* (Venezia: Andreas Asulanus, 1488, ISTC ic00160000)
Roberto Carracciolo, *Sermones quadragesimales de poenitentia* (Köln: Johann Koelhoff, the Elder, 1473, ISTC ic00173000)
Vicent Ferrer, *Sermones de tempore et de sanctis* (Strasbourg: Georg Husner, 1493/94, ISTC if00136000)

Primary Sources

Andreas Stoß, *Acta des Karmelitenprovinzials Andreas Stoß (1534–1538)*, ed. by Adalbert Deckert and Matthäus Hösler, Archivum Historicum Carmelitanum, 5 (Roma: Institutum Carmelitanum, 1995)

Arnold de Liège, *Arnoldi Leodiensis Alphabetum Narrationum*, ed. by Elisa Brilli, Corpus Christianorum, Continuatio Mediaevalis, 160 (Turnhout: Brepols, 2015)

Bullarium Carmelitanum a fratre Eliseo Monsignani, Pars Prima (Roma: Plachi, 1715)

The Friars' Libraries, ed. by Kenneth W. Humphreys, Corpus of British Medieval Library Catalogues, 1 (London: British Library, 1999)

Guido Terreni, *Guido Terreni, O. Carm. († 1342): Studies and Texts*, ed. by Alexander Fidora, Textes et Études du Moyen Age, 78 (Brepols: Turnhout, 2015)

Innocent IV, *Les Registres d'Innocent IV*, ed. by Élie Berger (Paris: Thorin, 1884)

Jacopo da Varazze, *Legenda aurea*, ed. by Giovanni Paolo Maggioni, Millenio medievale, 6 (Firenze: SISMEL, 1998)

Jacopo da Varazze, *Sermones quadragesimales*, ed. by Giovanni Paolo Maggioni, Edizione nazionale dei testi mediolatini, 13 (Firenze: SISMEL, 2005)

Jean Gobi, *La Scala coeli de Jean Gobi*, ed. by Marie-Anne Polo de Beaulieu (Paris: Centre National de la Recherche Scientifique, 1991)

John Soreth, *Expositio Paraenetica in Regulam Carmelitarum*, ed. by Bryan Deschamp, Corpus Christianorum, Continuatio Mediaevalis, 259 (Turnhout: Brepols, 2016)

Thomas, Antoninus H., *De oudste Constituties van de Dominicanen: Voorgeschiedenis, tekst, bronnen, ontstaan en ontwikkeling (1215–1237)*, Revue d'histoire ecclésiastique, Bibliothèque, 42 (Leuven: Bureel van de RHE, 1965)

Secondary Studies

Ackermann, Jane E., 'The Carmelite Ancestry of Teresa of Avila and John of the Cross', *Carmelus*, 46 (1999), 8–33

Andrews, Frances, *The Other Friars: The Carmelite, Augustinian, Sack, and Pied Friars in the Middle Ages*, Monastic Orders, 2 (New York: Boydell, 2006)

Bárczi, Ildikó, 'La Diversité thématique dans les prédications de Pelbart de Temesvár', *Archivum franciscanum historicum*, 100 (2007), 251–310

Bauerreiß, Romuald, 'Wer ist der mittelalterliche Prediger "Soccus"?', *Studien und Mitteilungen zur Geschichte des Benediktiner-Ordens und seiner Zweige*, 65 (1953–1954), 75–80

Boaga, Emanuele, 'L'organizzazione dello studio e degli studia presso i carmelitani tra il XIII e il XIV secolo', in *Studio e studia: Le scuole degli ordini mendicanti tra XIII e XIV secolo. Atti del XXX Convegno internazionale (Assisi, 11–13 ottobre 2001)*, Atti dei Convegni della Società internazionale di studi francescani e del Centro interuniversitario di studi francescani, 12 (Spoleto: Fondazione CISAM, 2002), pp. 175–95

THE NEGLECTED CARMELITES 333

Boaga, Emanuele, 'Predicazione. Carmelitani', *Dizionario degli Istituti di perfezione*, 7 (1983), 524–27

Bracha, Krzysztof, *Des Teufels Lug und Trug: Nikolaus Magni von Jauer, ein Reformtheologe des Spätmittelalters gegen Aberglaube und Götzendienst* (Dettelbach: Röll, 2013)

Brown, Stephen F., 'The Early Carmelite Parisian Masters', in *Philosophy and Theology in the Studia of the Religious Orders and at Papal and Royal Courts: Acts of the xvth Annual Colloquium of the Société Internationale pour l'Étude de la Philosophie Médiévale (University of Notre Dame, 8–10 octobre 2008)*, ed. by Kent Emery, William J. Courtenay, and Stephen M. Metzger (Turnhout: Brepols, 2012), pp. 479–91

Brüggemann, Susanne, 'Vocabularius praedicantium: ein lateinisch-deutsches Wörterbuch für die Prediger von Johannes Melber, Dokumentation zur Restaurierung der Inkunabel 4 Inc.s.a. 1248a aus den Beständen der Bayerischen Staatsbibliothek', in *Habent sua fata libelli: Integration von Wissenschaft und Praxis in der Buchrestaurierung*, ed. by Helmut Bansa (München: Saur, 2000), pp. 103–19

Caplan, Harry, *Mediaeval Artes Praedicandi: A Hand-List* (Ithaca: Cornell, 1934)

Carbasse, Jean-Marie, 'Les Deux Lois: le prophète Élie et le feu du Ciel', in *La Religiosité du droit*, ed. by Jacqueline Hoareau-Dodinau and Guillaume Métairie, Cahiers de l'Institut d'Anthropologie juridique, 35 (Limoges: Presses Universitaires de Limoges, 2013), pp. 173–84

Carrera, Elena, *Teresa of Avila's Autobiography: Authority, Power and the Self in Mid-Sixteenth-Century Spain* (Oxford: Oxford University Press, 2005)

Chandler, Paul, 'The Lamentation of the Virgin: A Planctus Mariae Sermon by Michael Aiguani of Bologna, O. Carm.', in *The Land of Carmel: Essays in Honor of Joachim Smet, O. Carm.*, ed. by Paul Chandler and Keith Egan (Roma: Institutum Carmelitanum, 1991), pp. 209–29

Charland, Thomas-Marie, *Artes Praedicandi: contribution à l'histoire de la rhétorique au Moyen Age*, Publications de l'institut d'etudes médiévales d'Ottawa, 7 (Paris: Publications de l'institut d'etudes médievales, 1936)

Copsey, Richard, *Biographical Register of Carmelites in England and Wales 1240–1540* (Faversham: Saint Albert's Press, 2020)

Copsey, Richard, *Carmel in Britain: Studies on the Early History of the Carmelite Order*, III: *The Hermits from Mount Carmel* (Roma: Institutum Carmelitanum, 2004)

Copsey, Richard, 'Simon Stock and the Scapular Vision', *The Journal of Ecclesiastical History*, 50 (1999), 652–83

Dahmus, John W., 'Late Medieval Preachers and Lay Perfection: The Case of Johannes Herolt, O. P.', *Medieval Perspectives*, 1 (1986), 122–34

Deckert, Adalbert, 'Bibliotheks-Katalog des Straubinger Karmelitenklosters von 1414', *Jahresbericht des historischen Vereins für Straubing und Umgebung*, 68 (1965), 84–93

Deckert, Adalbert, *Karmel in Straubing* (Roma: Institutum Carmelitanum, 1962)

Deckert, Adalbert, *Die Oberdeutsche Provinz der Karmeliten nach den Akten ihrer Kapitel von 1421 bis 1529*, Archivum Historicum Carmelitanum, 1 (Roma: Institutum Carmelitanum, 1961)

Dykmans, Marc, 'Jean XXII et les Carmes: la controverse de la vision', *Carmelus*, 17 (1970), 151–92

Edden, Valerie, 'Marian Devotion in a Carmelite Sermon Collection of the Late Middle Ages', *Mediaeval Studies*, 57 (1995), 101–29

Elm, Kaspar, 'Die Bedeutung historischer Legitimation für Entstehung, Funktion und Bestand mittelalterlichen Ordenswesens', in *Herkunft und Ursprung: historische und mythische Formen der Legitimation*, ed. by Peter Wunderli (Sigmaringen: Thorbecke, 1994), pp. 71–90

Elm, Kaspar, 'Elias, Paulus von Theben und Augustinus als Ordensgründer: ein Beitrag zur Geschichtsschreibung und Geschichtsdeutung der Eremiten- und Bettelorden des 13. Jahrhunderts', in *Geschichtsschreibung und Geschichtsbewusstsein im Spätmittelalter*, ed. by Hans Patze (Sigmaringen: Thorbecke, 1987), pp. 371–97

Ferraris, Davide, 'Il culto del profeta Elia tra Oriente e Occidente', *Rivista di storia e letteratura religiosa*, 52 (2016), 47–64

Grundmann, Herbert, 'Deutsche Eremiten, Einsiedler und Klausner im Hochmittelalter', *Archiv für Kulturgeschichte*, 45 (1963), 60–90

Hain, Ludwig, *Repertorium bibliographicum in quo libri omnes ab arte typographica inventa usque ad annum MD typis expressi ordine alphabetico vel simpliciter enumerantur vel adcuratius recensentur*, 2 vols in 2 parts (Stuttgart: Cotta, 1827)

Hevelone, Suzanne, 'Preaching the Saints: *The Legenda Aurea* and *Sermones de sanctis* of Jacobus de Voragine' (unpublished doctoral dissertation, Boston College, 2010)

Hodel, Bernard, 'Les Sermons reportés de Hugues de Saint-Cher', in *Hugues de Saint-Cher († 1263), bibliste et théologien*, ed. by Louis-Jacques Bataillon, Gilbert Dahan, and Pierre-Marie Gy, Bibliothèque d'histoire culturelle du Moyen Âge, 1 (Turnhout: Brepols, 2004), pp. 233–52

Hödl, Ludwig, and Wendelin Knoch, *Repertorium der lateinischen Sermones des Mittelalters für die Zeit von 1350 bis 1500 (CD-ROM)* (Münster: Aschendorff, 2001)

Holzwart-Schäfer, Iris, *Das Karmeliterkloster in Esslingen (1271–1557): ein südwestdeutscher Mendikantenkonvent zwischen Ordensideal und Alltagswirklichkeit*, Esslinger Studien, Schriftenreihe, 22 (Ostfildern: Thorbecke, 2011)

Hösler, Matthäus, 'Straubing Karmelitenbibliothek', in *Handbuch der historischen Buchbestände in Deutschland*, ed. by Eberhard Dünninger and Irmela Holtmeier, 27 vols (Hildesheim: Olms, 1992–2000), XIII (1997) (Bayern S–Z), 58–60

Huber, Alfons, *Bibliothek des Karmeliterklosters Straubing*, Schnell Kunstführer, 2807 (Regensburg: Schnell & Steiner, 2013)

Huber, Alfons, 'Die Bibliothek des Straubinger Karmelitenklosters im Mittelalter', in *Ratisbona Sacra: das Bistum Regensburg im Mittelalter. Ausstellung anlässlich des 1250 jährigen Jubiläums der kanonischen Errichtung des Bistums Regensburg durch Bonifatius 739–1989* (München: Schnell & Steiner, 1989), pp. 287–89

Huber, Alfons, 'Geschichte der Karmelitenbibliothek Straubing', in *Handschriften und alte Drucke aus der Karmelitenbibliothek Straubing: Ausstellung Gäubodenmuseum Straubing* (Straubing: Gäubodenmuseum, 1986), pp. 5–14

Humphreys, Kenneth W., *The Library of the Carmelites of Florence at the End of the Fourteenth Century*, Studies in the History of Libraries and Librarianship, 2 (Amsterdam: Erasmus Booksellers, 1964)

Ineichen-Eder, Christine Elisabeth, 'Straubing: Karmeliterkloster St Maria', *Mittelalterliche Bibliothekskataloge Deutschlands und der Schweiz*, IV/1: *Bistümer Passau und Regensburg*, ed. by Christine Elisabeth Ineichen-Eder (München: Beck, 1977), pp. 504–13

Janz-Wenig, Kathrin, 'Mittelalterphilologie am Beispiel einer Predigtsammlung: die Sammlung der "Sermones Socci"', in *Mittelalterphilologien heute: eine Standortbestimmung*, 1: *die germanischen Philologien*, ed. by Alessandra Molinari (Würzburg: Königshausen & Neumann, 2016), pp. 79–98

Jotischky, Andrew, *The Carmelites and Antiquity: Mendicants and their Past in the Middle Ages* (Oxford: Oxford University Press, 2002)

Jotischky, Andrew, 'The Image of the Greek: Western Pilgrims' Views of Eastern Monks and Monasteries in the Holy Land, *c.* 1200–1500', *Speculum*, 94 (2019), 674–703

Kertész, Balász, 'Two Hungarian Friars Minor (Franciscan Observants) in the Late Middle Ages: Pelbart de Temesvár and Oswald de Lasko', in *Infima aetas Pannonica: Studies in Late Medieval Hungarian History*, ed. by Péter E. Kovácz and Kornél Szovák (Budapest: Corvina, 2009), pp. 60–78

Klueting, Edeltraud, '"historiam provinciae et conventuum tenere": zur Geschichtsschreibung des Karmelitenordens (O. Carm.)', in *Bettelorden in Mitteleuropa: Geschichte, Kunst, Spiritualität. Referate der gleichnamigen Tagung vom 19. bis 22. März 2007 in St. Pölten*, ed. by Heidemarie Specht and Ralf Andraschek-Holzer, Geschichtliche Beilagen zum St. Pöltner Diözesanblatt, 32, Beiträge zur Kirchengeschichte Niederösterreichs, 15 (St. Pölten: Diözesanarchiv St. Pölten, 2008)

Klueting, Edeltraud, *Monasteria semper reformanda: Kloster- und Ordensreformen im Mittelalter*, Historia profana et ecclesiastica, 12 (Münster: Aschendorff, 2005)

Klueting, Edeltraud, Stephan Panzer, and Andreas H. Scholten, eds, *Monasticon Carmelitanum: die Klöster des Karmelitenordens (O. Carm.) in Deutschland von den Anfängen bis zur Gegenwart*, Monastica Carmelitana, 2 (Münster: Aschendorff, 2012)

Knowles, David, *The Religious Orders in England*, 3 vols (Cambridge: Cambridge University Press, 1950–1959)

Kornrumpf, Gisela, 'Friedrich der Karmelit', *Die deutsche Literatur des Mittelalters: Verfasserlexikon*, ed. by Kurt Ruh and others, 14 vols, 2nd edn (Berlin: De Gruyter, 1978–2008), II (1979), cols 948–50

Lang, Bernhard, 'Predigt als intellektuelles Ritual: eine Grundform religiöser Kommunikation kulturwissenschaftlich betrachtet', in *Literarische und religiöse*

Kommunikation in Mittelalter und Früher Neuzeit, ed. by Peter Strohschneider (Berlin: De Gruyter, 2009), pp. 292–323

Lansink, Henricus Gabriel Johannes, 'Bücher und Bibliotheken bei den Karmeliten der niederdeutschen Provinz im Mittelalter', in *Contributions à l'histoire des bibliothèques et à la lecture aux Pays-Bas avant 1600 / Studies over het boekenbezit en boekengebruik in de Nederlanden voor 1600*, Archief- en bibliotheekwezen in België, Extranummer, 11 / Archives et bibliothèques de Belgique, Numero spécial, 11 (Bruxelles: Association des archives et bibliothecaires, 1974), pp. 225–45

Laurent, Marie-Hyacinthe, 'La Lettre "Quae Honorem Conditoris" (1ᵉʳ octobre 1247)', *Ephemerides Carmeliticae*, 2 (1948), 5–16

Maggioni, Giovanni Paolo, 'Chastity Models in the Legenda Aurea and in the Sermones de Sanctis of Jacobus de Voragine', *Medieval Sermon Studies*, 52 (2008), 19–30

Menestò, Enrico, ed., *Eremitismo e habitat rupestre: atti del VI Convegno internazionale sulla civiltà rupestre in ricordo di Giuseppe Giacovazzo*, Atti dei Convegni della Fondazione San Domenico, 6 (Spoleto: Fondazione Centro Italiano di Studi sull'alto Medioevo, 2015)

Muessig, Carolyn, 'Audience and Preacher: *Ad Status* Sermons and Social Classification', in *Preacher, Sermon, and Audience in the Middle Ages*, ed. by Carolyn Muessig, A New History of the Sermon, 3 (Leiden: Brill, 2003), pp. 255–76

Murray, Paul, 'St John of the Cross: The Thinker, the Poet, the Mystic', *Angelicum*, 96 (2019), 255–74

Newhauser, Richard G., 'From Treatise to Sermon: Johannes Herolt on the *novem peccata aliena*', in *De ore Domini: Preacher and Word in the Middle Ages*, ed. by Thomas Leslie Amos, Eugene A. Green, and Beverly Mayne Kienzle, Studies in Medieval Culture, 27 (Kalamazoo: Western Michigan University, 1989), pp. 185–209

Nold, Patrick, 'Bertrand de la Tour O. Min.: Manuscript List and Sermon Supplement', *Archivum Franciscanum Historicum*, 95 (2002), 3–51

Nold, Patrick, *Pope John XXII and his Franciscan Cardinal: Bertrand de la Tour and the Apostolic Poverty Controversy* (Oxford: Oxford University Press, 2003)

Ottermann, Annelen, *Die Mainzer Karmelitenbibliothek: Spurensuche — Spurensicherung — Spurendeutung*, Berliner Arbeiten zur Bibliotheks- und Informationswissenschaft, 27, 2 vols (Berlin: Logos, 2016)

Overgaauw, Eef, 'Das Predigtwesen im Karmeliterorden: Predigten in Handschriften aus dem Karmeliterkloster Boppard', in *Predigt im Kontext*, ed. by Volker Mertens, Hans-Jochen Schiewer, Regina D. Schiewer, and Wolfram Schneider-Lastin (Berlin: De Gruyter, 2013), pp. 473–90

Polo de Beaulieu, Marie-Anne, 'Des histoires et des images au service de la prédication: la Scala coeli de Jean Gobi Junior († 1350)', in *De l'homélie au sermon: histoire de la prédication médiévale*, ed. by Jacqueline Hamesse and Xavier Hermand, Publications de l'institut d'études médiévales: textes, études, congrès, 14 (Louvain-la-Neuve: Collège Erasme, 1993), pp. 279–312

Priesching, Nicole, 'Die Karmeliten (Ordo Fratrum B.M.V. de Monte Carmelo)', in *Orden und Klöster im Zeitalter von Reformation und katholischer Reform 1500–1700*, ed. by Friedhelm Jürgensmeier and Regina Elisabeth Schwerdtfeger, 2 vols (Münster: Aschendorff, 2005–2006), II (2006), 89–110

Riedl-Valder, Christine, 'Straubing', in *Monasticon Carmelitanum: die Klöster des Karmelitenordens (O. Carm.) in Deutschland von den Anfängen bis zur Gegenwart*, ed. by Edeltraud Klueting, Stephan Panzer and Andreas H. Scholten (Münster: Aschendorff, 2012), pp. 693–710 Ruf, Paul, *Säkularisation und Bayerische Staatsbibliothek*, I: *die Bibliotheken der Mendikanten und Theatiner (1799–1802)* (Wiesbaden: Harrassowitz, 1962)

Schabel, Chris, 'Carmelite Quodlibeta', in *Theological Quodlibeta in the Middle Ages: The Fourteenth Century*, ed. by Chris Schabel, Brill's Companions to the Christian Tradition, 7 (Leiden: Brill, 2007), pp. 493–543

Schmidt, Hans-Joachim, 'L'Économie contrôlée des couvents des Carmes: le témoignage des rapports de visites dans la province de Germania inferior', in *Économie et religion: L'Expérience des ordres mendiants (XIIIᵉ–XVᵉ siècle)*, ed. by Nicole Bériou and Jacques Chiffoleau, Collection d'histoire et d'archéologie médiévales, 21 (Lyon: Presses Universitaires de Lyon, 2009), pp. 247–69

Schneyer, Johann Baptist, *Repertorium der lateinischen Sermones des Mittelalters für die Zeit von 1150–1350*, 11 vols (Münster: Aschendorff, 1969–1980)

Schürer, Markus, 'Das "propositum" in religiös-asketischen Diskursen: historisch-semantische Erkundungen zu einem zentralen Begriff der mittelalterlichen "vita religiosa"', in *Oboedientia: zu Formen und Grenzen von Macht und Unterordnung im mittelalterlichen Religiosentum*, ed. by Sébastien Barret and Gert Melville, Vita regularis, 27 (Münster: LIT, 2005), pp. 99–128

Seppänen, Lauri, 'Hane der Karmelit', in *Die deutsche Literatur des Mittelalters: Verfasserlexikon*, ed. by Kurt Ruh and others, 14 vols, 2nd edn (Berlin: De Gruyter, 1978–2008), III (1981), cols 429–31

Smet, Joachim, *The Carmelites: A History of the Brothers of Our Lady of Mount Carmel* (Roma: Institutum Carmelitanum, 1975)

Staring, Adrianus, *Der Karmelitergeneral Nikolaus Audet (1481–1562) und die katholische Reform des 16. Jahrhunderts*, Textus et studia historica Carmelitana, 3 (Roma: Institutum Carmelitanum, 1959)

Stöllinger, Christine, 'Grütsch, Conrad', in *Die deutsche Literatur des Mittelalters: Verfasserlexikon*, ed. by Kurt Ruh and others, 14 vols, 2nd edn (Berlin: De Gruyter, 1978–2008), III (1981), cols 291–94

Sułecki, Szymon, *The Library of the Carmelite Monastery in Piasek in Cracow*, Textus et Studia Historica Carmelitana, 45 (Roma: Institutum Carmelitanum, 2018)

Thayer, Anne T., 'Learning to Worship in the Late Middle Ages: Enacting Symbolism, Fighting the Devil, and Receiving Grace', *Archiv für Reformationsgeschichte*, 99 (2008), 36–65

Thayer, Anne T., *Penitence, Preaching and the Coming of the Reformation*, St Andrews Studies in Reformation History (Aldershot: Ashgate, 2002)

Thompson, Colin, 'Dangerous Visions: The Experience of Teresa of Avila and the Teaching of John of the Cross', in *Angels of Light? Sanctity and Discernment of*

Spirits in the Early Modern Period, ed. by Claire Copeland and Jan Machielsen (Leiden: Brill, 2013), pp. 53–74

Tyler, Peter, *St John of the Cross* (London: Continuum, 2010)

Wessels, Gabriel, 'Aliquid de Statu Ordinis durante schismate occidentali (1378–1417)', *Analecta Ordinis Carmelitarum*, 3 (1914), 140–52

Willing, Antje, 'Die Predigt *Omnes querebant eum tangere* Hanes des Karmeliten', in *Paradisus anime intelligentis: Studien zu einer dominikanischen Predigtsammlung aus dem Umkreis Meister Eckharts*, ed. by Burkhard Hasebrink, Nigel F. Palmer, and Hans-Jochen Schiewer (Tübingen: Max Niemeyer, 2009), pp. 201–26

Worstbrock, F.J., 'Konrad von Brundelsheim', in *Die deutsche Literatur des Mittelalters: Verfasserlexikon*, ed. by Kurt Ruh and others, 14 vols, 2nd edn (Berlin: De Gruyter, 1978–2008), v (1985), cols 147–53

Xiberta, Bartolomé, 'De magistro Johanne Baconthorp, O. Carm.', *Analecta Ordinis Carmelitarum*, 6 (1927), 3–128

NATALIJA GANINA

Johannes Kreutzer

A Preacher in Strasbourg and Basel and his Work in Manuscript and Early Print

The Alsatian preacher Johannes Kreutzer was famous during his lifetime in the fifteenth century,[1] but later — as will be shown in this essay — he came to be one of the 'great unknowns' apart from one appearance in early print.[2] He was popular as a preacher in Strasbourg, but for complicated reasons was banished from the city in the mid-fifteenth century, later becoming one of the founders of the university in Basel. As a well-educated theologian and a gifted preacher, he also gained respect among the Dominican Observant reformers. In fact, Johannes Meyer (1422–1485), whose *Buch der Reformacio Predigerordens* did so much to tell the story of the reform movement, dedicated his *Liber de viris illustribus ordinis praedicatorum* to Kreutzer.[3] It would seem, according to later commentators, that Kreutzer's sermons possessed some power, and that his exhortations led to the growth of piety.[4] And, indeed, exploration of Kreutzer's manuscript tradition in the twentieth century demonstrates that

---

*   This essay is dedicated to the memory of Nigel F. Palmer (1946–2022).

1   I owe sincere gratitude to Nigel F. Palmer for having drawn my attention to this early print and for his valuable advice as well as to the co-editors of this volume Veronica O'Mara and Patricia Stoop from whose attentive reading and improving proposals this essay has benefited greatly.

2   See Médard Barth, 'Dr Johannes Kreutzer (gest. 1468) und die Wiederaufrichtung des Dominikanerinnenklosters Engelporten in Gebweiler', *Archiv für elsässische Kirchengeschichte*, 8 (1933), 181–208, 'ein großer Verkannter' (p. 184); *'Bräute Christi': Legenden und Traktate aus dem Straßburger Magdalenenkloster. Edition und Untersuchungen*, ed. by Natalija Ganina, Kulturtopographie des alemannischen Raums, 7 (Berlin: De Gruyter, 2016), pp. 113–26.

3   Johannes Meyer, *Liber de viris ordinis praedicatorum*, ed. by Paulus von Löe, Quellen und Forschungen zur Geschichte des Dominikanerordens in Deutschland, 12 (Leipzig: Harrassowitz, 1918), ch. 16; see the discussion in Barth, 'Dr Johannes Kreutzer', p. 196; Anne Huijbers, *Zealots for Souls: Dominican Narratives of Self-Understanding during Observant Reforms, c. 1388–1517* (Berlin: De Gruyter, 2018), p. 25.

4   Barth, 'Dr Johannes Kreutzer', pp. 192 and 206 with further references.

Natalija Ganina (fulminata@mail.ru) is Professor of the Department of Germanic and Celtic Philology in the Philological Faculty of the Lomonosov Moscow State University.

Circulating the Word of God in Medieval and Early Modern Europe: Catholic Preaching and Preachers across Manuscript and Print (c. 1450 to c. 1550), ed. by Veronica O'Mara and Patricia Stoop, SERMO 17, (Turnhout: Brepols, 2022), pp. 339–363   BREPOLS ❧ PUBLISHERS   10.1484/M.SERMO-EB.5.130461

340   NATALIJA GANINA

Kreutzer was a significant spiritual author in his day. Nevertheless, all his works have remained unpublished until now and, even more importantly, there is a complex relationship between what is known about him as a preacher and the (relatively scant) evidence from the manuscript tradition.[5] Indeed, if it were not for an early printed treatise (*c.* 1509) from Basel by Nikolaus Lamparter (d. 1529?) that makes use of some of Kreutzer's material, even less would be known about the work of this preacher. The aim of this study is therefore to outline something of Kreutzer's history and reputation, discuss the complexities of Kreutzer's manuscript tradition, and examine the textual transmission across manuscript and print, while also paying attention to the fluidity between treatise and sermon in the Germanic tradition before moving on to the early print.

The Clerical Career of Johannes Kreutzer

Johannes Kreutzer was born between 1424 and 1428 in Guebwiller (Gebweiler) in Alsace and, according to a report by the sixteenth-century Strasbourg chronicler Maternus Berler (who died after 1555), came from a wealthy family.[6] He studied at the university in Erfurt: his name is mentioned in the university's matriculation book on 4 November 1442.[7] After finishing his studies in Erfurt, Kreutzer became a 'lútpriester' or parish priest at the St. Lorenzaltar of Strasbourg Cathedral in 1454. Having been appointed to the position of the cathedral parish priest and the 'Großpoenitentiar' in the oldest town parish,[8] Kreutzer must have been preaching in accordance with his duties at the 'Pfarrgottesdienst' or parish service. At this time, Kreutzer's qualification of *Magister artium* was insufficient for a 'Domprädikatur' or

---

5   Four spiritual treatises by Kreutzer, *Geistlicher Mai, Geistliche Ernte*, and *Herbstmost I* and *II* are published in an edition of a manuscript miscellany from St. Magdalena in Strasbourg, dated from the fifteenth century (Moscow, Russian State Library, F. 68, № 446); see *'Bräute Christi'*, ed. by Ganina, pp. 217–350. An edition of his Commentary on the Song of Songs is in progress.

6   *Code historique et diplomatique de la ville de Strasbourg*, ed. by Georges Frédéric Schutzenberger and others, 1 vol. in 2 parts (Strasbourg: Silbermann, 1843–1848), I (1848), part 2, 70, 73.

7   *Acten zur Geschichte der Universität Erfurt (1392–1636)*, ed. by Johann Christian Hermann Weißenborn, Geschichtsquellen der Provinz Sachsen und angrenzender Gebiete, 8/1–3, 3 vols (Halle: Hendel, 1881–1899), I (1881), 191b; Wieland Schmidt, 'Johannes Kreutzer: ein elsässischer Prediger des 15. Jahrhunderts', in *Festschrift Helmut de Boor zum 75. Geburtstag am 24. März 1966*, ed. by the Direktoren des Germanischen Seminars der Freien Universität Berlin (Tübingen: Niemeyer, 1966), pp. 150–92 (p. 155).

8   Strasbourg Cathedral was the first and oldest parish in the city. The cult of St. Lorenz in Strasbourg had ancient roots, while the St. Lorenzaltar served as the parish altar until 1494; see Médard Barth, *Handbuch der elsässischen Kirchen im Mittelalter*, Archives de l'Église d'Alsace, 27–29 (= new series, 11–13), 3 vols (Strasbourg: Société d'histoire de l'Église d'Alsace, 1960–1963), II (1962), col. 1440.

cathedral preacher's position, so he only became a cathedral preacher in Basel in 1459 after the resumption of his theological studies at the university in Heidelberg from 1457.

From 1454 onward Kreutzer was involved in a conflict between the secular clergy and the four mendicant orders in Strasbourg.[9] In the regular-secular debate over the 'ultimum vale' (an arbitrary determined tax collected by the Strasbourg parish clergy from the relatives of citizens who chose to be buried at a cloister cemetery) Kreutzer fought on the side of the secular clergy against the four mendicant orders.[10] The mendicant party won by supporting the Strasbourg magistrate, and submitted allegations against the secular clergy to the pope in Rome. In this connection, the Carmelite prior Heinrich von Köln excommunicated Kreutzer on 6 November 1455. As Kreutzer had been very popular in the town, the magistrate decided to banish him from Strasbourg under the influence of the mendicant party and for fear of unrest in Strasbourg: 'dasz ir nit mer in unser Stadt kommen sollent, weder nun noch hienach, dann wir uch nit me in unser Stadt wissen noch haben wollent' ['that you should not come to our city neither now nor later because we do not want to have you in our city'].[11] Kreutzer was thus forced to leave Strasbourg on 9 June 1456. However, his name did not sink into oblivion in Strasbourg. The renowned preacher Johannes Geiler von Kaysersberg (1445–1510), who was also associated with Basel and Strasbourg, mentions him in his sermon on the First Sunday of Lent in 1508. Geiler believes that God punished Kreutzer's enemies, namely by avenging them in the manner of the Old Testament:

> Nym zům ersten doctor Creutzer, der was ein frum bidermann. Euwer seind vil da, die in kentt haben, vnd ich seine erste predigt hort, die er in dem orden thet, da er ein predigermünch ward zů Basel. Der ist hie zů Straßburg zů Sant Laurentzen ein leutpriester geweßt vnd ein Vicarivss vnserm chor. Als der durchechtet ist worden von vnnützen schlechten leuten, daz weiß man auch wol. Sie sein auch schier als ellendglich vmbkummen: der ein ertranck, der <ander> fiel zů tod, der drit erstach sich selbs.[12]

> [First of all, let us take Doctor Kreutzer, who was a pious honest man. There are many of you who knew him, and I heard his first sermon which he delivered to the order as he became a Friar Preacher at Basel.

---

9 Barth, 'Dr Johannes Kreutzer', pp. 184–91; Schmidt, 'Johannes Kreutzer', pp. 156–58; Elisabeth Vogelpohl, *Lassen, Tun und Leiden als Grundmuster zur Einübung geistlichen Lebens: Studien zu Johannes Kreutzer*, Münsteraner Theologische Abhandlungen, 50 (Altenberge: Oros, 1997), pp. 50–53.
10 Barth, 'Dr Johannes Kreutzer', p. 186.
11 Schmidt, 'Johannes Kreutzer', p. 158. Hereinafter the translations are my own.
12 Johannes Geiler von Kaysersberg, *Die Emeis* (Strasbourg: Johannes Grüninger, 1517), fol. XXr; on Geiler's relationship to Kreutzer see Rita Voltmer, *Wie der Wächter auf dem Turm, ein Prediger und seine Stadt: Johannes Geiler von Kaysersberg und Straßburg*, Beiträge zur Landes- und Kulturgeschichte, 4 (Trier: Porta Alba, 2005), pp. 157–61.

The same had been a parish priest here at St. Lorenz in Strasbourg as well as a vicar of our choir. It is well-known how he was persecuted by worthless wicked people. Soon, they perished miserably too: one drowned, the other fell to his death, the third stabbed himself].

This passage was almost literally repeated by the German humanist Jakob Wimpfeling (1450–1528) as well as by the Strasbourg chronicler Maternus Berler and the Strasbourg Lutheran pastor and historian Oseas Schadaeus (1586–1626) in the sixteenth and the seventeenth centuries.[13] These statements bear witness to the fact that Kreutzer enjoyed a good reputation among devout Strasbourg citizens and commentators long after his death.

After his banishment in 1456, Kreutzer headed to Rome to justify himself. A commission was established at the papal court under the leadership of Arnold von Rotberg (c. 1394–1396/7 May 1458), bishop of Basel (the first mention of Basel in Kreutzer's biography). But the matter could not be solved immediately. Kreutzer visited Rome again in 1457, where Arnold von Rotberg defended him most decisively, and the Church ban was lifted.[14] Nevertheless, Kreutzer never returned to Strasbourg. He came to Heidelberg to complete his university education from the winter term of 1457. Here he obtained a degree in theology as 'baccalaureus biblicus, sententiarius, formatus', which was a necessary requirement for a doctorate in the theological faculty.[15]

An impetus for Kreutzer's doctoral study might have been provided by his contacts with the Basel spiritual elite. The cathedral preacher's position was founded in Basel in 1456 and remained vacant for more than a year, until Kreutzer proved himself to be a suitable candidate.[16] Kreutzer got elected as a 'Domherr' or canon and cathedral preacher in Basel in 1459. Not only was this position very important for the town, it was also crucial for Kreutzer's career, marking his social advancement.[17] He preached his first sermon at

---

13 Jakob Wimpfeling, *Catalogus episcoporum Argentinensium* (Strasbourg: Johannes Grüninger, 1508), p. 110; Schutzenberger, *Code historique et diplomatique de la ville de Strasbourg*, 1 (1848), part 2, p. 71; Oseas Schadaeus, *Summum argentoratensivm templum, das ist Außführliche vnd Eigendtliche Beschreibung deß viel Künstlichen, sehr Kostbaren, vnd in aller Welt berühmten Münsters zu Strassburg* (Strasbourg: Zeßners Erben, 1617), p. 82; see Barth, 'Dr Johannes Kreutzer', p. 190.

14 Julius Mann, *Die Kirchenpolitik der Stadt Straßburg am Ausgang des Mittelalters* (Strasbourg: Herder, 1914), p. 42; Vogelpohl, *Lassen, Tun und Leiden*, p. 53.

15 Wilhelm Vischer, *Geschichte der Universität Basel von der Gründung 1460 bis zur Reformation 1529* (Basel: Georg, 1860), p. 211; Schmidt, 'Johannes Kreutzer', pp. 158–59.

16 Rudolf Wackernagel, *Geschichte der Stadt Basel*, 3 vols in 4 parts (Basel: Heilbing & Lichtenhahn, 1907–1924), II, 2 (1916), 855; Bernhard Neidiger, 'Basel BS — Dominikaner', in *Helvetia Sacra*, IV/5: *Die Dominikaner und Dominikanerinnen in der Schweiz*, ed. by Urs Amacher and others (Basel: Schwabe, 1999), part 1, p. 178.

17 With regard to the term 'Prädikatur' in Basel see Eduard Lengwiler, *Die vorreformatorischen Prädikaturen in der deutschen Schweiz: von ihrer Entstehung bis 1530* (Fribourg: Kanisiusdruckerei, 1955), pp. 1–79.

FIGURE 4. Foundation Ceremony of the Universität Basel, 4 April 1460. First row, from left to right: Rector Georg von Andlau, an unknown cleric, Bishop Johann von Venningen, presumably Johannes Kreutzer, and Hans von Flachslanden. Register of the rector of the Universität Basel, I (1460–1567). Basel, Universitätsbibliothek, Cod. AN II 3, fol. 2v. Reproduced with permission.

344   NATALIJA GANINA

Basel Cathedral on the day of St. Heinrich (13 July) of the same year.[18] And Wieland Schmidt supposes that the election of Kreutzer as a canon was closely connected with the foundation of the university of Basel.[19]

On the 12 November 1459 Pope Pius II (1405–1464) promulgated a papal bull approving the university of Basel foundation. The inauguration ceremony took place on 4 April 1460 and a well-known miniature from the matriculation book shows a portrait of Johannes Kreutzer among other participants in the celebration (see Figure 4).[20]

Thus, Kreutzer became one of the founding fathers of the university. From the opening of the university in Basel in 1460, he was appointed as professor there, and he was also the first Dean of the Faculty of Arts (from 1 May to 18 October 1460).[21] From the beginning, he gave lectures in the Theological Faculty, albeit not in the position of a full professor.[22] Once Kreutzer earned a doctorate in theology at the university of Heidelberg in 1461, he was appointed to the *Magister regens* in theology. In 1462 he was elected as the fourth rector of the university in Basel and held this position in 1462/63.

In cooperation with the Basel Dominicans, Kreutzer actively promoted the reform of the Upper Rhine nunneries and the implementation of strict observance. He inspired the reform of the Dominican convent in his home town of Guebwiller in 1461, owing, *inter alia*, to the support of his friend Petrus Mör, the prior of the Guebwiller Dominican convent.[23] Kreutzer then marked

---

18 St. Heinrich II (6 May 972–13 July 1024) was especially venerated in Basel. See Wackernagel, *Geschichte der Stadt Basel*, II, 2 (1916), 771–72; Schmidt, 'Johannes Kreutzer', p. 161.

19 Schmidt, 'Johannes Kreutzer', pp. 161–62.

20 '*Bräute Christi*', ed. by Ganina, p. 121.

21 Vischer, *Geschichte der Universität Basel*, p. 286.

22 Schmidt, 'Johannes Kreutzer', pp. 162–63.

23 On the history of the Dominicans and the Dominican Sisters in Alsace, especially in Guebwiller, see Jean-Luc Eichenlaub, 'L'Ordre dominicain en Alsace', in *Dominicains et dominicaines en Alsace, XIIIe–XXe siècles: actes du colloque de Guebwiller 8–9 avril 1994*, ed. by Jean-Luc Eichenlaub (Colmar: Conseil Général du Haut-Rhin, 1996), pp. 9–12; Sonia Pelletier-Gautier, 'Floraison dominicaine dans la deuxième moitié du XVe siècle à Guebwiller', in *Dominicains et dominicaines en Alsace*, ed. by Eichenlaub, pp. 53–60. On the Observant Reform from the point of view of Johannes Meyer see Thomas Lentes, 'Bild, Reform und Cura Monialium: Bildverständnis und Bildgebrauch im Buch der Reformacio Predigerordens des Johannes Meyer (✝ 1485)', in *Dominicains et Dominicaines en Alsace*, ed. by Eichenlaub, pp. 177–95; Anne Winston-Allen, 'Rewriting Women's History: Medieval Nuns' Vitae by Johannes Meyer', in *Medieval German Voices in the 21st Century: The Paradigmatic Function of Medieval German Studies for German Studies*, ed. by Albrecht Classen, Internationale Forschungen zur vergleichenden Literaturwissenschaft, 46 (Amsterdam: Rodopi, 2000), pp. 145–54; Carl Pfaff, 'Bild und Exempel: die observante Dominikanerin in der Sicht des Johannes Meyer O. P.', in *Personen der Geschichte — Geschichte der Personen: Studien zur Kreuzzugs-, Sozial- und Bildungsgeschichte. Festschrift für Rainer Christoph Schwinges zum 60. Geburtstag*, ed. by Christian Hesse and others (Basel: Schwabe, 2003), pp. 221–35; Heike Uffmann, *Wie in einem Rosengarten: monastische Reformen des späten Mittelalters in den Vorstellungen von Klosterfrauen*, Religion in der Geschichte, 14 (Bielefeld: Verlag für Regionalgeschichte, 2008), pp. 72–76. See also Madlen Doerr,

JOHANNES KREUTZER   345

a change of career by taking monastic vows in Guebwiller on 4 August 1465, on the feast of St Dominic, the founder of the order.[24] On the occasion of joining the Dominican order, Kreutzer bequeathed his entire property to the Dominican nunnery of Engelporten in Guebwiller. This reformed nunnery, which had been ruined, was rebuilt due to Kreutzer's efforts. The re-establishment of Engelporten took place on 20 August 1466. Kreutzer, having just finished his noviciate on 5 August 1466, preached a sermon before the nuns and many other people from Guebwiller and various towns and villages came to hear the famous preacher.[25] On 11 September 1467 Kreutzer was instructed by the Provincial Minister Peter Wellen to take on lector duties at the Nürnberg Dominican convent. Six months later he had to go back to Alsace where he was elected as the prior of the Guebwiller convent on 24 March 1468.[26] There he had to provide assistance to his combatants as the situation of the Observants worsened because of confrontation within the Dominican order in Germany and other countries. Kreutzer committed himself to fighting for the Observant party, developing wide-ranging activities within the order. He journeyed to Rome in 1468 to defend the cause of the Observant reform and was urged to travel to Rome for a second time. Exhausted from the journey, he died in Rome on 16 June 1468.

The Manuscripts of Kreutzer's Works

The vernacular tradition of Kreutzer's works known at present comprises five manuscripts containing completely preserved texts (they are fully described in the Appendix). These are Berlin, Staatsbibliothek zu Berlin, Preußischer Kulturbesitz, MS germ. qu. 158, from the Strasbourg Dominican nunnery of St. Nikolaus in undis; Berlin, Staatsbibliothek zu Berlin, Preußischer Kulturbesitz, MS germ. qu. 202, probably also from St. Nikolaus in undis; Moscow, Russian State Library, F. 68, N° 446 and New York, Columbia University Library, Rare Book and Manuscript Library, MS X242.1.S, from the Strasbourg 'Reuerinnenkloster' St. Magdalena (a convent of *sorores poenitentes*); and Stuttgart, Württembergische Landesbibliothek, MS theol. et phil. 4° 190, from the Clarissan convent of Pfullingen (Baden-Württemberg).[27] Two others

---

'Klarissen und Dominikanerinnen in Freiburg im 15. Jahrhundert: Sozialstruktur und Reform' (unpublished doctoral dissertation, Albert-Ludwigs-Universität, Freiburg, 2011/12; https://freidok.uni-freiburg.de/data/10034 [accessed 10 February 2021]), pp. 231–33.

24 Barth, 'Dr Johannes Kreutzer', p. 197; Schmidt, 'Johannes Kreutzer', p. 166.

25 Barth, 'Dr Johannes Kreutzer', p. 204; the same day Johannes Meyer dates the dedication of his *Liber de viris illustribus* to Kreutzer, having welcomed him into the Dominican order, especially to the priory in Guebwiller, see Huijbers, *Zealots for Souls*, p. 25.

26 Barth, 'Dr Johannes Kreutzer', p. 197.

27 On the reasons for this provenance (attribution of the binding), see *'Bräute Christi'*, ed. by Ganina, pp. 128–41.

containing extracts from his work are found in Berlin, Staatsbibliothek zu Berlin, Preußischer Kulturbesitz, MS germ. oct. 31, and Berlin, Staatsbibliothek zu Berlin, Preußischer Kulturbesitz, MS germ. qu. 344. Finally, the early printed book, *Disz ist ein schöne und fast nutzbar betrachtung des lidens Jesu Christi mit einer erkantnusz ob es dem menschen verdienstlich sig und got dem herren angenem* (*Betrachtung des Leidens Christi*) published in Basel by Nikolaus Lamparter in *c.* 1509 contains Kreutzer's treatise *Herbstmost I* (sig. B3v–B5v).[28] The title, which may be translated as 'This is a good and useful contemplation of the Passion of Jesus Christ with an insight that it would be advantageous for a person and pleasant to God the Lord', provides an indication of its purpose.

Kreutzer: His Sermons and Treatises

Kreutzer's contemporaries, particularly Johannes Meyer, Petrus Mör, and Johannes Geiler von Kaysersberg, praised Kreutzer as an outstanding preacher.[29] Due to Kreutzer's reputation, his manuscripts have usually been interpreted as 'sermons'. For instance, the aforementioned Strasbourg Lutheran pastor and historian Oseas Schadaeus notes in the sixteenth century: 'Dieses Johannis Crützers Predigten sind noch vorhanden, aber, so viel mir bewußt, nie getruckt worden' ['The sermons of this Johannes Kreutzer still exist but, as far as I know, they have never been printed'].[30] Nevertheless, only a small number of the known works by Kreutzer can be regarded as sermons according to their formal attributes. In other words, we have here a man who was regarded as a famous preacher in his day but, without those contemporary comments, we should not be able to gain access to this reputation if we were only to judge from the surviving manuscripts. And it should be noted that all of these have strong links to female convents, with two each ascribed to the Dominican convent of St. Nikolaus in undis and to the Reuerinnenkloster St. Magdalena

---

28   Verzeichnis der Druck des 16. Jahrhunderts online (hereafter VD), no. ZV 4516. The only extant full copy is Basel, Universitätsbibliothek, FP VI 19:2; a fragment of the treatise is kept in Freiburg, Universitätsbibliothek, O 8284; on the Basel copy, see Emil Weller, *Repertorium typographicum: die deutsche Literatur im ersten Viertel des sechzehnten Jahrhunderts* (Nördlingen: Beck, 1864–1885), I (1864), 133, no. 1095; Volker Honemann, *Deutsche Literatur in der Laienbibliothek der Basler Kartause 1480–1520*, Studien und Texte zum Mittelalter und zur frühen Neuzeit, 22 (unpublished Habilitationsschrift, Freie Universität Berlin, 1982; revised print Münster: Waxmann, 2020); Volker Honemann, 'Kreutzer, Johannes', in *Die deutsche Literatur des Mittelalters: Verfasserlexikon*, ed. by Kurt Ruh and others, 14 vols, 2nd edn (Berlin: De Gruyter, 1978–2008), V (1985), cols 358–63 (col. 361); 'Bräute Christi', ed. by Ganina, pp. 133–34.

29   Johannes Meyer, *Liber de viris illustribus*, p. 76 (the letter of Petrus Mör to Johannes Kreutzer from 28 January 1465 cited by Meyer), p. 82 ('Appendix'); Geiler von Kaysersberg, *Die Emeis*, fol. XXr. For a discussion of Geiler von Kaysersberg, see the essay by Rita Voltmer in the current collection.

30   Schadaeus, *Summum argentoratensivm templum*, p. 82.

in Strasbourg, and one to the Clarissan convent in Pfullingen. As far as we can tell, no effort was made to print any of Kreutzer's sermons and, as we shall see, contemporary attempts to preserve his sermons seem also to have been fairly limited. Leaving aside the problems of the vicissitudes of time and the often haphazard ways of manuscript survival, it is a salutary reminder of how little we know about the circumstances of sermon production and preservation in the Middle Ages and most particularly the attitudes of the sermonists themselves towards what was essentially an oral phenomenon. Kreutzer's case also demonstrates that we perhaps pay insufficient attention to the links between the sermon as a preached event and its preservation as a written memorialization or spur to contemplation.

Indeed, what is most typical of Kreutzer's surviving œuvre are spiritual allegorical treatises. Many of these texts are connected with significant moments of the Church year, as is obvious from their titles as much in German as in English, such as *Geistliches Fastnachtsküchlein* [*Spiritual Shrovetide's Cake*], *Osterjubel* [*Easter Jubilation*] *I* and *II*, *Geistlicher Osterfladen* [*Spiritual Easter Flatbread*], *Geistliche Martinsnacht* [*Spiritual Martin's Night*] *I* and *II*, and *Geistliche Weihnachten* [*Spiritual Christmas*]. A whole group of treatises, such as the *Geistlicher Mai* [*Spiritual May*], the *Geistliche Ernte* [*Spiritual Harvest*], and the *Herbstmost* [*Autumn Wine*] *I* and *II*, however, belong to the Church year sequence only formally and offer a far broader devotional and literary perspective. We may assume that these works, addressed to women, were created to instruct and inspire Dominican nuns, because Kreutzer's spiritual guidance of Dominican nuns is also evidenced by his treatise *Unterweisung einer Klosterfrau* or *Instruction for a Monastic Woman* in Berlin, Staatsbibliothek zu Berlin, Preußischer Kulturbesitz, MS germ. qu. 158, fols 168v–221r, which develops the theme of the bridal mystic on the basis of the exegesis of Psalm 104. 4. The most comprehensive of Kreutzer's work is the *Hoheliedauslegung*, a *Commentary on the Song of Songs* (Berlin, Staatsbibliothek zu Berlin, Preußischer Kulturbesitz, MS germ. qu. 158, fols 2r–167v) which remained uncompleted because of his death.

All of the extant sermons are recorded in Berlin, Staatsbibliothek zu Berlin, Preußischer Kulturbesitz, MS germ. qu. 158 (fols 241v–282r). This paper manuscript, with a provenance in St. Nikolaus in undis in Strasbourg, was written after 1469.[31] Like the other Kreutzer manuscript linked to this convent, Berlin, Staatsbibliothek zu Berlin, Preußischer Kulturbesitz, MS germ. qu. 202, it was written by multiple scribes. But unlike the two Kreutzer manuscripts associated with the convent of St. Magdalena in Strasbourg (Moscow, Russian State Library, F. 68, Nº 446 and New York, Columbia University Library, Rare Book and Manuscript Library, MS X242.1.S.) where the nun Katharina Ingoldt

---

31 See, *Das lyrische Œuvre von Heinrich Laufenberg in der Überlieferung des 15. Jahrhunderts: Untersuchungen und Editionen*, ed. by Balázs J. Nemes, *Zeitschrift für deutsches Altertum*, Beiheft 22 (Stuttgart: Hirzel, 2015), pp. 28–30.

played a major part in the scribal production of the first and a minor part in the second, we cannot link either of the Berlin manuscripts to any particular nun or nuns, though we may assume that the female religious in St. Nikolaus in undis may well have been responsible for them, given its prestigious reputation in this regard in German-speaking lands. The inclusion of sermons seems to be rather secondary compared to the main aim of this manuscript to offer a record of Kreutzer's most significant work, the *Hoheliedauslegung*. This also applies to their place in the manuscript after a text series dealing with spiritual guidance, namely, the *Unterweisung einer Klosterfrau* (fols 168v–221r) and two letters on James 4. 8 (*Nohent úch zů got*), the first to a monk (fols 221v–233r), the second to nuns (fols 233r–241v).

The sermon group in Berlin, Staatsbibliothek zu Berlin, Preußischer Kulturbesitz, MS germ. qu. 158 consists of eleven texts: the sermon *Vom nutz zitlichen lidens* (fols 241v–246r) and a series of ten sermons on Communion and its reception in a worthy manner (fols 246r–282r). The first and the second texts do not contain the term 'sermon' in their headings: 'Dis sint vil gúter púnctelin vom nutz zitlichen lidens vnd wie sich der mönsche dor inn halten sol' ['These are many good brief points on the benefits of temporal suffering'] (fol. 241v), 'Von dem heiligen sacrament, wer do sölle zú gon oder nit vnd wenn daz triben vß got sy vnd ob es heilsam syge, allein geistlichen enpfohen daz heilige sacrament vnd waz der mönsche an im haben sölle, der daz sacrament enpfohen wil' ['On Holy Communion: who may partake or should not partake of it, and when this desire is from God, and if it might have been salutary to receive Holy Communion only in a spiritual way, and what a person should have who wants to receive Communion'] (fol. 246r). The reference 'bredig' or 'sermon' only occurs in the third text heading: 'Ein ander bredig von dem heiligen sacrament' ['Another sermon on Holy Communion'] (fol. 249r). In fact, some sermons within this group, especially the text with the heading 'Disse bredige seit von ix meinungen, welliche der mönsche het, so mag er wol zůgon' ['This sermon tells about nine meanings that allow a person to partake of the Sacrament properly'] (fols 270v–278v), can be defined as 'treatises' as well, both by the lack of main reference to a Gospel verse and because of their treatise-like structure with many detailed points dedicated to spiritual guidance.

It is not clear at what time these surviving sermons or treatise-like sermons by Kreutzer were created. It can only be concluded that these texts represent a very small part of his suggested sermon œuvre. A well-developed system of rhetorical strategies and devices in Kreutzer's treatises may indicate his experience in the pulpit. At the beginning of modern research on Kreutzer's works, Médard Barth suggested that the treatises and letters by this dedicated preacher might have been adaptations of his sermons.[32] Indeed, Hans-Jochen Schiewer points out the real or fictive 'sermon prehistory' of many spiritual

---

32 Barth, 'Dr Johannes Kreutzer', p. 182.

treatises.[33] Textual analysis of Kreutzer's *Hoheliedauslegung* and the *Unterweisung einer Klosterfrau* shows that adaptation of his own writings was one of his working principles: in these treatises the author uses large passages from the *Geistlicher Mai*. As we know that the *Hoheliedauslegung* was his last work (owing to a notice on Kreutzer's death in Berlin, Staatsbibliothek zu Berlin, Preußischer Kulturbesitz, MS germ. qu. 158, fols 167v–168r), it can be stated that the *Geistlicher Mai* provided some basic material for a more comprehensive later work. Likewise, some earlier sermons by Kreutzer could be transformed into treatises; the seventeenth-century evidence of 'many sermons by Kreutzer' may reflect the popular notion of the preacher's written heritage, although at that time, of course, many further manuscripts containing his sermons may have existed. In any case, one of the things that is most obvious about Kreutzer's œuvre is the narrow dividing-line between what might be called a sermon and what might be called a treatise, and, as we shall see below, when he made it into print, it was not with a sermon but with a treatise.

Particularly important in this regard are the conclusions drawn by Volker Honemann on preaching methods in the late fifteenth century. First, the old sermon genres did not appear in their pure form, so that the borders between the sermon and the homily became indistinct. Second, famous preachers such as Johannes Geiler von Kaysersberg widely used Latin and German treatises as templates for their sermons instead of Latin sermon corpora like that by Meffreth or the *Dormi secure*,[34] while treatises were easily transformed into sermons. For example, Geiler made such use of the *Paradisus animae* by Pseudo-Albert for his own *Seelenparadies* and transformed the treatise *De oratione dominica* by Johannes Nider (*c.* 1380–1438) into sermons on the *Pater noster*, and Nider's *Formicarius* was used by Geiler for his *Emeis*.[35] Third, it should be noted that catalogue records of the Basel Charterhouse library, for instance, tend to list under 'Sermones' theological treatise literature owing to the fact that the genres are to some extent related.[36] Furthermore, Honemann's observations throw light on the external circumstances of sermon dissemination at the time. A large number of written evidence shows that the sermon had a great revival in Basel

---

33 Hans-Jochen Schiewer, 'Texttypologie: Typ und Polyfunktionalität (Predigt)', in *Jahrbuch für internationale Germanistik*, 24 (1992), pp. 44–47 (pp. 45–46). I owe thanks to Regina Schiewer for her friendly help with access to this publication.

34 On Meffreth and the *Dormi Secure* see Anne T. Thayer, *Penitence, Preaching and the Coming of the Reformation*, St Andrews Studies in Reformation History (Aldershot: Ashgate, 2002); John W. Dahmus, 'Dormi Secure: The Lazy Preacher's Model of Holiness for His Flock', in *Models of Holiness in Medieval Sermons: Proceedings of the International Symposium (Kalamazoo, May 4–7, 1995)*, ed. by Beverley Mayne Kienzle (Louvain-la-Neuve: Fédération internationale des Instituts d'études médiévales, 1996), pp. 301–16.

35 Honemann, 'Deutsche Literatur in der Laienbibliothek der Basler Kartause', p. 160; see also Honemann, *Deutsche Literatur in der Laienbibliothek der Basler Kartause 1480–1520*. On Geiler's use of Latin and German treatises to model his sermons see in general Voltmer, *Wächter auf dem Turm*, pp. 66–81, and particularly pp. 945–47 (*Emeis*) and pp. 1001–02 (*Seelenparadies*).

36 Honemann, 'Deutsche Literatur in der Laienbibliothek der Basler Kartause', p. 157.

around 1500, while the 'Prädikatur' was crucial for the main churches and such churches competed to get talented preachers. Hearing sermons became very popular and was even preferred to 'plain' spiritual lectures.[37]

However, the textual transmission of sermons mainly depended on people who could record and disseminate those texts. For example, Geiler's sermons were recorded by the nuns of St. Magdalena in Strasbourg in 1503–1505 as noted in the print of his *Seelenparadies*.[38] We can hardly expect that anybody regularly recorded Kreutzer's sermons in his early tumultuous years in Strasbourg because he had not yet earned the respect that Geiler did later. However, it is also true that it only takes one person to decide to take notes or transcribe a sermon, whatever the fame of the preacher. Whether or not this was ever done for Kreutzer's sermons in Strasbourg, we cannot say. The question about Kreutzer's Basel years also remains open considering that no manuscripts of his works from Basel have been preserved. There is no known evidence of his manuscripts after the 1470s either. The latter can be explained by the fact that the manuscript tradition of his works obviously belongs to the Observant Reform text transmission within a limited period in the late fifteenth century (for which we can see the manuscripts from Strasbourg and Pfullingen in the Appendix).[39]

Kreutzer and Early Print

Most important is the evidence of the early Basel print *Betrachtung des Leidens Christi* by Nikolaus Lamparter where Kreutzer's treatise *Herbstmost I* is transmitted at the beginning of the sixteenth century. It is the *Herbstmost I* that effectively acts as the bridge between the medieval and the early modern Kreutzer. Without its appearance in print, Johannes Kreutzer might have been forgotten as simply a preacher from Alsace who had gained some fame and indeed notoriety in Strasbourg and Basel in the 1450s and 1460s. The

---

37 Honemann, 'Deutsche Literatur in der Laienbibliothek der Basler Kartause', p. 157.

38 Honemann, 'Deutsche Literatur in der Laienbibliothek der Basler Kartause', p. 159.

39 For a brief account of the widespread argument in German scholarship that the production of literature was linked to monastic reform see, for example, Werner Williams-Krapp, 'Ordensreform und Literatur im 15. Jahrhundert', *Jahrbuch der Oswald von Wolkenstein Gesellschaft*, 4 (1986–1987), pp. 41–51. For the importance played by nuns in the production of such literature, particularly sermons, see, for instance, Cynthia J. Cyrus, *The Scribes for Women's Convents in Late Medieval Germany* (Toronto: University of Toronto Press, 2009); Anne Winston-Allen, *Convent Chronicles: Women Writing about Women and Reform in the Late Middle Ages* (University Park, PA: Penn State University Press, 2005); and Regina Dorothea Schiewer, 'Books in Texts — Texts in Books: The *St. Georgener Predigten* as an Example of Nuns' Literacy in Late Medieval Germany', in *Nuns' Literacies in Medieval Europe: The Hull Dialogue*, ed. by Virginia Blanton, Veronica O'Mara, and Patricia Stoop, Medieval Women: Texts and Contexts, 26 (Turnhout: Brepols, 2013), pp. 223–37. See also Werner Williams-Krapp, *Die Literatur des 15. und 16. Jahrhunderts: Modelle literarischer Interessenbildung*, II:1 (Berlin: De Gruyter, 2020).

remainder of this essay will focus on an analysis of this text in an attempt to demonstrate the sort of text that Kreutzer readers would have encountered in the first decade of the sixteenth century.

This text belongs to the 'May-Autumn Group' of Kreutzer's devotional treatises close to the tradition of German mysticism. Like longer treatises of this group, it was created for nuns who were Kreutzer's spiritual daughters. It offers an allegorical instruction on how to make a young autumn wine ('herbstmost'). The text opens with an introduction in terms of the 'Dingallegorie':

> Wylt du <denn, du edle gottesliephaberin,> einen andechtigen süßen most lesen vnd adellich vnd süsseclich getrencket vnd ersüsset werden in dem edelen liden Cristy, so erheb din gemüt vnd rüst dich vff mit der zarten liephaberin vnd herbsterin der herren, die vß höher begird sich vff disen lieplichen herbst frouwete, do sie sprach in irem gesangen büchelin: 'Ach, min geminter ist mir der cypertrybel in dem wingarten Engady'. Vnd daz du denn mit ir gar wißlich den herbst inlesest vnd zů foß tragest, so loß dir daz edele geblümete jungfrowelich hertz Marien den edelen rebstock sin. Loß dir den schönen lüstlichen cypertrybel den süssen lieplichen vnd mynneklichen gespontzen Cristum sin. Loß daz messer, do mit man in abschnidet vnd lißet, din schärppffe klore vnd erlúchtete vernunfft sin. Loß dir daz leßezúberlin, dar in man den trybel lißet, din gedechtnisse sin. Loß daz heymfúren vnd intragen din versamelt gemüt sin. Loß daz trotten, werffen vnd kmysten alle bitter verserunge des güttigen frintlichen heren sin.[40]

> > [If you, O noble female lover of God, want to collect a grape harvest to make a devout sweet young wine, and to drink your fill and to be delighted in the noble Passion of Christ, lift up your spirit and make yourself ready with that tender lover and harvester of the Lord who rejoiced over this lovely harvest as she said in her little book of the Song of Songs: 'Oh, my beloved is to me as a bunch of Cyprus grapes in the vineyards of Engedi'. Then, in order to collect this harvest with her very wisely and to bring it to a vat, let the noble floral virgin heart of Mary be your noble vine. Let the sweet lovely and loving spouse Christ be your fair pleasing bunch of Cyprus grapes. Let your sharp, clear and enlightened reason be the knife with which they cut it off and collect it. Let your memory be the basket in which they collect the grapes. Let your disciplined mind be the taking home and the carrying in. Let all bitter pains of the kind friendly Lord be the treading, the throwing, and the squeezing].

The focus of the two *Herbtsmost* treatises is the comparison of the blood of Christ to young autumn wine, a metaphor with a local Alsatian colour that is common to Kreutzer's allegorical treatises, for instance, the *Geistlicher*

---

40 'Bräute Christi', ed. by Ganina, pp. 299, ll. 10–20 to 300, ll. 1–2.

NATALIJA GANINA

Mai has a list of wines that are used in a description of spiritual joy. After an extended allegory of the grape harvest depicting a reflection on the Passion, the *Herbstmost I* offers five prayers to the Wounds of Christ in the following order: his left foot, his right foot, his left hand, his right hand, and his heart, while the degree of emotionality keeps increasing from one point to another. In contrast to this, the *Herbsmost II* is an epistle based on themes of bridal mysticism without a meditation of the Passion of Christ as well as without any highlighting of the Heart of Jesus. The *Herbstmost I* was included in its entirety in the compilation of *c.* 1509 by Lamparter, to which we shall now turn, first outlining its overall context before moving to the *Herbsmost I* proper.

The early Basel print *Betrachtung des Leidens Christi* consists of three sections, each of which is marked by an initial. The headings and incipits of these sections read as follows:

> 1. Wie vnd in wie mangerley wyse man das hochwirdig liden Ihesu Christi, vnsers herren, betrachten mag vnd soll, das es dem menschen verdienlich vnd gott dem herren angenem sy.
>
> Es ist zů wissen, das man daz wirdig lyden vnd leben vnsers lieben herren Ihesu Christi in mangerley wyse vnd ordnung betrachten mag. Da von doch etlichen menschen gar wenig nutz vnd frucht entspringt oder kumpt, wie wol das sie vndertwilen grossen ernst vnd innigkeit dar innen hand vnd entpfindent, wan sie hand die selben andacht dick me von natur dann von gnaden. Vnd darumb so gewinnent sie nit die gewaren frucht vnd den nutz des lidens Ihesu Christi. Vnd diß ist die sach, wann sie dem herren nit redlich nochvolgendt vnd sich imm mit irem leben nit gelichen nach irem vermögen. Vnd also werden sie dann mit irem natúrlichen gestifften andacht dick betrogen vnd verwyset. Aber welcher mensch da will durch das liden Ihesu Christi gereiniget werden vnd von imm gelert vnd erleichtert werden, der sol nachuolgen der lere, die da der andåchtig inbrunstig vnd heylig lerer Bonauentura gelert hat in sechs wåg vnd wyse [...]. (Sig. A2rv)

> > [How and in how many ways one might and should contemplate the most venerable Passion of Jesus Christ, our Lord, so that it would be advantageous for a person and pleasant to God the Lord.
> >
> > It is good to know that one can contemplate the venerable Passion and life of our beloved Lord Jesus Christ in various ways and order. Nevertheless, for many, little fruit comes from it, although they meanwhile both have and feel there great fervour and ardency, because they have this same devoutness rather by nature than by grace. That is why they do not win true fruit and the benefit of the Passion of Jesus Christ. And that is the matter, because they do not follow the Lord properly and do not imitate him with their life to the best of their ability. And thus they are after that greatly deceived and expelled by their naturally based devoutness. However, if one wants to be purified

through the Passion of Jesus Christ and to be taught and relieved from it, this person should follow the doctrine that the pious fervent and holy teacher Bonaventura taught in six ways and manners [...]].

2. Ein kurtze vnderichtung, da by der mensch mercken mag, ob er das liden Christi recht vnd wol betrachtet hab nach nutz vnd nachuolgung.[41]

Wiltu wissen, ob du da liden Christi rǎcht vnd wol betrachtet habest, des nym do by war. So du komest von einem liden vnsers herren, ob du dann mit dir bringest die frucht, bezeichnet in dinem leben. Daz sint die frúcht, so wir das liden vnsers herren recht vnd wol betrachtet hand: ob wir dann diemǔtiger, gedultiger vnd senffmǔtiger vnd gelǎßner sind dann vor, vnd was vns lidens vnd widerwertigkeit zǔvellet, das wir das bas geliden kǒnnent dann vor. Und ob dir din gebrǎsten me abgewúrckt sint dann vor. Vnd also von allen tugenden das da iemer sein soll von recht. Das sind die zeichen, das du das liden vnsers herren Ihesu Christi recht betrachtet hast vnd das liden vnsers herren Ihesu Christi recht gewurckt hat in dir [...]. (Sig. A8r)

> [2. A brief instruction, whereby one may notice whether he contemplated the Passion of Christ well and truly according to advantage and following.
>
> If you would like to know whether you contemplated the Passion of Christ well and truly, consider this thereby. If you have returned from the Passion service of our Lord, whether you are bringing with you the fruits that are indicated by your life. These are the fruits indicating that we contemplated the Passion of our Lord well and truly: if we became more humble, more patient, and gentler, and calmer than before, and when any suffering and adversity befall us, we are able to endure it better than before. And if your flaws are overcome to a higher degree than before. The same about all virtues which should ever be there in truth. These are the signs that you truly contemplated the Passion of our Lord Jesus Christ and that the Passion of our Lord Jesus Christ has truly acted in you [...]].

3. Ein sǔsser andǎchtiger herbstmost in vermanens wyse in das hochwirdigen <liden>[42] vnsers herren Ihesu Christi.

Wiltu einen andǎchtigen sǔssen herbstmost[43] lesen vnd adelich vnd sǔssiglich getrenckt vnd ersǔsset werden in dem edlen liden Christi, so erheb din gemǔt vnd rǔste dich vff mit der zarten liebhaberin vnd

---

41 'nach nutz vnd nachuolgung' is a handwritten record after the printed heading.
42 '<liden>' is lacking in the heading.
43 'herbstmost': 'herstbmost'.

allerliebsten herbsterin des herren, die da vß hoher begirde sich vff disen lustgebenden herbst fröwte, do sie sprach in irem gesangbůchlin: — Min geminter ist mir ein zippertrúbel in den wingarten Engadi'. Vnd daz du denn mit ir gar wyßlich den herbst inlåsest vnd zů vasß tragest, so laß dir daz edel geblůmt jungfrôlich hertz Marie den edlen råbstock sein. Laß dir den schonen lustlichen zippertrúbel den sůssen lieplichen vnd minnenglichen gesponsen Jesum Christum sin. Las dir das måsser, da mit man in abzwick tvnn liset, din scharpffe clare erlůhte vernunfft sin. Laß dir daz låßzúberli, dar in man den trúbel liset, din gedåchnúß sin. Laß dir daz heimfůren vnd intragen din versamet gemůte sin. Laß dir das tråtten, trotten, múrßen vnd knútzen alle bittere verserung des gůtigen fründtlichen herren sein [...]. (sig. B3v)

> [3. A sweet devout young autumn wine in a recollecting manner on the most venerable Passion of our Lord Jesus Christ.
>
> If you want to collect a grape harvest to make a devout sweet young wine, and to drink your fill in a noble and sweet manner and to be delighted in the noble Passion of Christ, lift up your spirit and make yourself ready with that tender lover and harvester of the Lord who rejoiced over this pleasant harvest as she said in her little book of the Song of Songs: 'My beloved is to me as a bunch of Cyprus grapes in the vineyards of Engedi'. Then, in order to collect this harvest with her very wisely and to bring it to a vat, let the noble floral virgin heart of Mary be your noble vine. Let the sweet lovely and loving spouse Jesus Christ be your fair pleasing bunch of Cyprus grapes. Let your sharp, clear and enlightened reason be the knife, with which they cut off branches. Let your memory be the basket, in which they collect the grapes. Let your disciplined mind be the taking home and the carrying in. Let all bitter pains of the kind friendly Lord be the treading, the trampling, the crushing, and the squeezing].

The first and second sections were identified by Honemann as a vernacular translation of the *Stimulus amoris* by Pseudo-Bonaventura, part I, chap. IV, *Circa passionem sex consideranda*, followed by an adaptation of part I, chap. IX.[44] Thus, the book consists in fact of two parts, the translation of the *Stimulus amoris* and the *Herbstmost I* respectively, but the compiler presents the Pseudo-Bonaventuran adaptation as two sections by means of two brief edifying introductions. It should be noted that Kreutzer's text appears without such introductions in the manuscript tradition of the *Herbstmost I*.

The title page of the Basel early print is highlighted by a woodcut of the Crucifixion. The first part is opened by the woodcut of Christ in the Garden of Gethsemane, between the second and the third part (the *Stimulus amoris* and the *Herbstmost I*); the woodcut of the Man of Sorrows is used; and the

---

44 Honemann, 'Deutsche Literatur in der Laienbibliothek der Basler Kartause', pp. 88–89.

third part, the *Herbstmost I*, is followed by a woodcut of the Coronation of the Virgin. This design fully complies with the idea of reflection on the Passion ('Passionsbetrachtung'). The whole layout of this early print is closely allied to manuscript culture due to hand-painted initials, red strikethroughs, and handwritten marginalia.

The conceptual programme of the Basel early print can be described as follows:

1. Spiritual guidance towards reflection on the Passion based on the *Stimulus amoris*
2. Practical implementation of the 'six ways' for the imitation of Christ
3. Devotion and prayer

The *Herbstmost* has a particular role in this programme as the conclusion of the book, offering a performative text that provides elevated and moving prayers to express and affirm a reader's devotion. The whole book could undoubtedly have been used for devotional reflections at any time, especially if it belonged to a monastery, but the introduction to the second section (starting at fol. A8r?) may reveal its special functions within the Church year. The sentence 'So du komest von einem liden vnsers herren' ['If you have returned from the Passion service of our Lord'] indicates that the book was intended to be read in Holy Week.

Conclusion

As pointed out in a comprehensive work by Romy Günthart, Basel was a significant centre for printing.[45] The author notes that such a reputation was based mainly on print production from the early sixteenth century.[46] There were twenty printers in Basel around 1500 who published both vernacular and Latin texts. Nikolaus Lamparter started his work at that time and printed relatively few German books, for example, the *Narrenschiff* by Sebastian Brant.[47] There were two main sources of vernacular print production in Basel, namely, manuscripts and reprints of books from the South German region, in particular from Augsburg and Kirchheim. As there is no evidence of other books containing any texts by Kreutzer, we can suggest that the Basel early print was based on manuscript tradition. This could have been a manuscript miscellany because the structure of this early print reminds us of such a miscellany. However, it remains unknown whether the manuscripts of Kreutzer's works kept being copied much longer than the 1470s or if the print may have come from an earlier manuscript.

---

45 On Lamparter see Romy Günthart, *Deutschsprachige Literatur im frühen Basler Buchdruck (ca. 1470–1510)* (Münster: Waxmann, 2007), pp. 5, 13, 24.
46 Günthart, *Deutschsprachige Literatur*, p. 13.
47 Günthart, *Deutschsprachige Literatur*, pp. 5, 24 (without reference to *Betrachtung des Leidens Christi*).

The catalogues of the Basel Charterhouse library do not give any indications of Kreutzer's texts, excepting the treatise *Herbstmost I* in the framework of the compilation *Betrachtung des Leidens Christi* discussed here. On the other hand, this compilation is listed there several times (D 64/3+4, D 70/2+3, D/73 8+9).[48] Meanwhile, the works of Kreutzer's literary successors Johannes Geiler von Kaysersberg and Stephan Fridolin are widely represented in those late medieval catalogues.[49] This seems to imply that the Basel Charterhouse library did not possess a notable written heritage by Kreutzer. This lack, documented by the Basel Charterhouse library catalogues, may be explained in part by the fact that Kreutzer's works and his popularity as preacher were mainly the preserve of the Observant Reform Dominicans of the late fifteenth century. We recall that Geiler only referred to his own hearing of a Kreutzer's sermon and not to written or indeed printed sources.[50] Unlike Kreutzer's oral sermons in Alsace and Basel, his written œuvre, with the exception of the *Herbstmost I*, did not overcome the gap between the intimate circles of Observant supporters and the wider audience; in other words, his work in manuscript would seem to have remained within the confines of the Observant convents.

Ultimately we may never know why *Herbstmost I* rather than any of the other texts by Johannes Kreutzer (either sermons or treatises surviving in manuscript) was printed in Basel in *c.* 1509. It may have been simply owing to its focus on the meditation of the Passion of Christ and the Heart of Jesus, which would have fitted in well with contemporary European meditational traditions. Yet at any rate, the appearance of the *Herbstmost I* in a devotional early print provides evidence of Kreutzer's reception in Basel, demonstrating the polyfunctional usage of his text in the local devotional tradition. On a more general level, it also demonstrates the ways in which there are gaps in transmission history between the Middle Ages and the Reformation period. These gaps, which can either be deliberate or accidental depending on circumstances, may also show up alterations and distortions in interpretations of preachers and their works over time. In this particular case we have in Johannes Kreutzer a reforming mid-fifteenth-century preacher who was not afraid to engage in conflict with authority, who was sufficiently esteemed to help found a university, who acted as a guiding light for female religious and yet is 'known' today — if he is 'known' at all — only as an (anonymous) contributor to a little meditational printed book from the early sixteenth century.

---

48 Honemann, 'Deutsche Literatur in der Laienbibliothek der Basler Kartause', pp. 114–15, 116, 118, 120, 128.
49 See Almut Breitenbach and Stefan Matter, 'Image, Text, and Mind: Franciscan Tertiaries Rewriting Stephan Fridolin's *Schatzbehalter* in the Pütrichkloster in Munich', in *Nuns' Literacies in Medieval Europe: The Antwerp Dialogue*, ed. by Virginia Blanton, Veronica O'Mara and Patricia Stoop, Medieval Women: Texts and Contexts, 28 (Turnhout: Brepols, 2017), pp. 297–316.
50 Johannes Geiler von Kaysersberg, *Die Emeis*, fol. XXr.

JOHANNES KREUTZER **357**

Appendix: Johannes Kreutzer's Works

The vernacular tradition of Kreutzer's works known at present comprises five manuscripts containing completely preserved texts, two extracts, and an early print:[51]

Complete Works

1. Berlin, Staatsbibliothek zu Berlin, Preußischer Kulturbesitz, MS germ. qu. 158.[52] Paper; 322 fols; 214 × 143 (160 × 90) mm; Low Alemannic; 1469; many scribes; from Strasbourg, St. Nikolaus in undis.

   The miscellany opens with Kreutzer's *Hoheliedauslegung* (fols 5r–167v). The manuscript also contains treatises, such as the *Unterweisung einer Klosterfrau* on fols 168v–221r, and letters by Kreutzer, including two letters on James 4. 8 (*Nohent úch zů got*), the first to a monk (fols 221v–233r), the second to nuns (fols 233r–241v). Kreutzer's only extant sermons are preserved in this codex on fols 241v–282r, namely, *Vom nutz zitlichen lidens* (fols 241v–246r) and a series of ten sermons on Communion and its reception in a worthy manner (fols 246r–282r). The treatise *Herbstmost I* occurs here on fols 313v–315v. The table of contents offers an explicit reference to Kreutzer's authorship: 'Die Tofel dis búches, daz do ist die vßlegunge úber Cantica canticorum des ersten cappittel, also daz der erwúrdige meister Johannes Krútzer mit sin selbes henden geschriben het etlichen sinen geistlichen kinden zú trost, wellicher siner geschrift dis búch abgeschriben ist vnd waz in dissem búch stot ist alles des vorgenannten meister Johannes Crútzers lere' ['The table of contents of this book, that is the commentary on the first chapter of the Song of Songs, as the venerable master Johannes Kreutzer wrote them with his own hands for consolation of some of his spiritual children, from which manuscript by him this book is copied, and all contents of this book are teachings by the above mentioned master Johannes Kreutzer'] (fol. 2r).

---

51 Kreutzer's Latin oeuvre still remains unexplored. There is a university document 'Acta in vesperiis [...] magistri J. Cruczer de Basilea canonici et predicatores in theologia licenciati per R. de Bruxella', dated 3 August 1461 (Città del Vaticano, Biblioteca Apostolica Vaticana, Fondo Palatino, MS 370, fols 357–370), and two further Latin works by Kreutzer, namely, his theses on the 'ultimum vale' debate and praise of true believers, are recapitulated in a Latin memoir note (Città del Vaticano, Biblioteca Apostolica Vaticana, Fondo Palatino, MS 368, fol. 45rv); see Francis Rapp, *Réformes et réformation à Strasbourg: église et société dans le diocèse de Strasbourg (1450–1525)*, Collection de l'Institut des Hautes Études Alsaciennes, 23 (Paris: Ophrys, 1974), pp. 151–52, nn. 72, 79, 85.
52 *'Bräute Christi'*, ed. by Ganina, pp. 128–29, 134–35.

2. Berlin, Staatsbibliothek zu Berlin, Preußischer Kulturbesitz MS germ. qu. 202.[53] Paper; 427 fols; 209 × 144 (*c.* 145 × 90) mm; Low Alemannic; late fifteenth century; nine scribes; probably from Strasbourg, St. Nikolaus in undis.

A miscellany containing treatises by various authors (mostly by Kreutzer, but also by anonymous authors) according to the order of the Church year from Christmas to the Eve of St Martin. The treatise *Herbstmost I* is recorded in this manuscript on fols 347v–350r. The texts are mostly handed down anonymously.

3. Moscow, Russian State Library, F. 68, N° 446.[54] Parchment (fols 2–73); and paper (fols 75–154); 154 fols (the parchment fascicle consists of 74 fols); 195/200 × 135/40 mm (text space varies from 130 × 90 mm (*Life of St Katherine of Alexandria*) to 132/33 × 85/87 mm (*Life of St Barbara*); Low Alemannic; scribe's date 17 October 1477 (the parchment fascicle); scribe: the nun Katharina Ingolt (*Life of St Katherine of Alexandria* and a *Life of St Barbara*) in the parchment fascicle; some marginal glosses by Katharina Ingolt can also be found in the paper fascicle. Strasbourg, Reuerinnenkloster St. Magdalena.

The paper fascicle contains Kreutzer's treatises *Geistlicher Mai, Geistliche Ernte, Herbstmost I* and *II*, dating to 1472–1475 (fols 75r–154r). *Herbstmost I* is recorded on fols 149v–152r. There is no mention of Kreutzer's authorship in this manuscript.

4. New York, Columbia University Library, Rare Book and Manuscript Library, MS X242.1.S.[55] Paper; 213 fols; leaf size 204 × 139 (140 × 85) mm; Low Alemannic; 14 April 1485; scribe: nun Katharina Ingolt; from Strasbourg, Reuerinnenkloster St. Magdalena.

The miscellany contains a German translation of Thomas a Kempis's *Imitatio Christi* by the Dominican monk Johannes Zierer. There are only two treatises by Kreutzer in this manuscript, namely, the *Geistliche Martinsnacht II* and *I* (in reverse order on fols 137r–139r and 168r–169r) which are handed down anonymously.

5. Stuttgart, Württembergische Landesbibliothek, MS theol. et phil. 4° 190, also called the *Pfullinger Liederhandschrift* because of its song supplement (fols 169r–179r).[56] Paper; 179 fols; 210 × 140–42 mm; text space 135–45 × 95–100 to 120 mm; 1478–1480, one scribe. East Alemannic (Swabian). It can be shown that the manuscript originates from the Clarissan nunnery of Pfullingen.[57]

---

53 '*Bräute Christi*', ed. by Ganina, pp. 129–31, 134–35.
54 '*Bräute Christi*', ed. by Ganina, pp. 1–10, 131.
55 '*Bräute Christi*', ed. by Ganina, pp. 30, 131.
56 '*Bräute Christi*', ed. by Ganina, pp. 132–33, 136–41.
57 See n. 27.

This is a manuscript miscellany that consists of two parts: (1) Kreutzer's treatises, mostly in parallel tradition to Berlin, Staatsbibliothek zu Berlin, Preußischer Kulturbesitz, MS germ. qu. 202, albeit in a different order; (2) a song supplement (the *Pfullinger Liedersammlung*, fols 169r–179r). The treatise *Herbstmost I* occurs on fols 111v–114v, which is introduced by a repetition of initial sentences from the previous treatise *Geistliche Ernte*. There is no mention of Kreutzer's authorship in this manuscript.

Extracts

1. Berlin, Staatsbibliothek zu Berlin, Preußischer Kulturbesitz, MS germ. oct. 31.[58] Paper; 268 fols; *c.* 146 × 102 mm; language: Upper Rhenish; third quarter of the fifteenth century, most probably from the 1470s; from Strasbourg, St. Nikolaus in undis.

   This miscellany contains prayers and some mystical texts such as the *Hohenflüge der Seele*, likely written by Ulrich the Johanniter, among them an extract from the *Herbstmost I* on fols 182v–185r.[59] Thomas Lentes defines it as 'Betrachtungsanleitung zu den fünf Wunden Christi'; he connects it to a discussion on religious gestures.[60] This extract shows the actual reception of Kreutzer's works in the religious practice of Strasbourg Dominican nuns.

2. Berlin, Staatsbibliothek zu Berlin, Preußischer Kulturbesitz, MS germ. qu. 344. Paper; 232 fols; leaf size 215 × 147 mm; text space *c.* 150 × 100 mm; a manuscript miscellany dating from the fifteenth to the seventeenth century; from the manuscript collection of the teacher and poet Daniel Sudermann (1550–1631), who was interested in the medieval German mystic. The manuscript contains an early modern extract from the *Hoheliedauslegung* and the *Unterweisung an eine Klosterfrau* apparently made by Kreutzer. These treatises were copied by Sudermann from the codex Berlin, Staatsbibliothek zu Berlin, Preußischer Kulturbesitz, MS germ. qu. 158, fols 185r–188v, 152r–155r, and 173r–174v respectively.[61]

---

58 *Bräute Christi'*, ed. by Ganina, pp. 133–34.
59 An edition of the *Hohenflüge der Seele* is published by Stephen Mossman and Nigel F. Palmer, 'Ulrich der Johanniter vom Grünen Wörth and his Adaptation of the "Liber amoris": A Critical Edition of the "Hoheliedpredigt" and of its German Precursor the "Höhenflüge der Seele"', in *Schreiben und Lesen in der Stadt: Literaturbetrieb im spätmittelalterlichen Straßburg*, ed. by Stephen Mossman, Nigel F. Palmer, and Felix Heinzer, Kulturtopographie des alemannischen Raums, 4 (Berlin: De Gruyter, 2012), pp. 469–520.
60 Thomas Lentes, 'Gebetbuch und Gebärde: religiöses Ausdrucksverhalten in den Gebetbüchern aus dem Dominikanerinnen-Kloster St. Nikolaus in undis zu Straßburg (1350–1550)' (unpublished doctoral dissertation, Westfälische Wilhelms-Universität Münster, 1996), pp. 1046–47.
61 The latter manuscript contains numerous handwritten notes and comments by Sudermann.

Early Print

1. *Disz ist ein schöne und fast nutzbar betrachtung des lidens Jesu Christi mit einer erkantnusz ob es dem menschen verdienstlich sig und got dem herren angenem* ([Basel]: Nikolaus Lamparter, *c.* 1509); 14 fols; woodcuts; 8°: *Herbstmost I* (sig. B3v–B5v). The only extant full copy is Basel, Universitätsbibliothek, FP VI 19:2; a fragment of the treatise is kept in Freiburg, Universitätsbibliothek, O 8284

Bibliography

Manuscripts

Berlin, Staatsbibliothek zu Berlin, Preußischer Kulturbesitz, MS germ. oct. 31
Berlin, Staatsbibliothek zu Berlin, Preußischer Kulturbesitz, MS germ. qu. 158
Berlin, Staatsbibliothek zu Berlin, Preußischer Kulturbesitz, MS germ. qu. 202
Berlin, Staatsbibliothek zu Berlin, Preußischer Kulturbesitz, MS germ. qu. 344
Città del Vaticano, Biblioteca Apostolica Vaticana, Fondo Palatino, MS 368
Città del Vaticano, Biblioteca Apostolica Vaticana, Fondo Palatino, MS 370
Moscow, Russian State Library, F. 68, N° 446
New York, Columbia University Library, Rare Book and Manuscript Library, MS X242.1.S
Stuttgart, Württembergische Landesbibliothek, MS theol. et phil. 4° 190

Early Printed Works

Betrachtung des Leidens Christi ([Basel]: Nikolaus Lamparter, *c.* 1509)
Jakob Wimpfeling, *Catalogus episcoporum Argentinensium* (Strasbourg: Johannes Grüninger, 1508)
Johannes Geiler von Kaysersberg, *Die Emeis* (Strasbourg: Johannes Grüninger, 1517)
Oseas Schadaeus, *Summum argentoratensivm templum, das ist Außführliche vnd Eigendtliche Beschreibung deß viel Künstlichen, sehr Kostbaren, vnd in aller Welt berühmten Münsters zu Strassburg* (Strasbourg: Zeßners Erben, 1617)

Primary Sources

Acten zur Geschichte der Universität Erfurt (1392–1636), ed. by Johann Christian Hermann Weißenborn, Geschichtsquellen der Provinz Sachsen und angrenzender Gebiete, 8/1–3, 3 vols (Halle: Hendel, 1881–1899)
'Bräute Christi': Legenden und Traktate aus dem Straßburger Magdalenenkloster, Edition und Untersuchungen, ed. by Natalija Ganina, Kulturtopographie des alemannischen Raums, 7 (Berlin: De Gruyter, 2016)
Code historique et diplomatique de la ville de Strasbourg, ed. by Georges Frédéric Schutzenberger and others, 1 vol. in 2 parts (Strasbourg: Silbermann, 1843–1848)

Johannes Meyer, *Liber de viris illustribus ordinis praedicatorum*, ed. by Paulus von
Löe, Quellen und Forschungen zur Geschichte des Dominikanerordens in
Deutschland, 12 (Leipzig: Harrassowitz, 1918)
*Das lyrische Œuvre von Heinrich Laufenberg in der Überlieferung des 15. Jahrhunderts:
Untersuchungen und Editionen*, ed. by Balázs J. Nemes, *Zeitschrift für deutsches
Altertum*, Beiheft 22 (Stuttgart: Hirzel, 2015)
'Ulrich der Johanniter vom Grünen Wörth and his Adaptation of the "Liber
amoris": A Critical Edition of the "Hoheliedpredigt" and of its German
Precursor the "Höhenflüge der Seele"', ed. by Stephen Mossman and
Nigel F. Palmer, in *Schreiben und Lesen in der Stadt: Literaturbetrieb im
spätmittelalterlichen Straßburg*, ed. by Stephen Mossman, Nigel F. Palmer, and
Felix Heinzer, Kulturtopographie des alemannischen Raums, 4 (Berlin: De
Gruyter, 2012), pp. 469–520

Secondary Studies

Barth, Médard, 'Dr Johannes Kreutzer (gest. 1468) und die Wiederaufrichtung des
Dominikanerinnenklosters Engelporten in Gebweiler', *Archiv für elsässische
Kirchengeschichte*, 8 (1933), 181–208
Barth, Médard, *Handbuch der elsässischen Kirchen im Mittelalter*, Archives de
l'Église d'Alsace, 27–29 (= new series, 11–13), 3 vols (Strasbourg: Société
d'histoire de l'Église d'Alsace, 1960–1963)
Breitenbach, Almut, and Stefan Matter, 'Image, Text, and Mind: Franciscan
Tertiaries Rewriting Stephan Fridolin's *Schatzbehalter* in the Pütrichkloster in
Munich', in *Nuns' Literacies in Medieval Europe: The Antwerp Dialogue*, ed. by
Virginia Blanton, Veronica O'Mara, and Patricia Stoop, Medieval Women:
Texts and Contexts, 28 (Turnhout: Brepols, 2017), pp. 297–316
Cyrus, Cynthia J., *The Scribes for Women's Convents in Late Medieval Germany*
(Toronto: University of Toronto Press, 2009)
Dahmus, John W., 'Dormi Secure: The Lazy Preacher's Model of Holiness for
His Flock', in *Models of Holiness in Medieval Sermons: Proceedings of the
International Symposium (Kalamazoo, May 4–7, 1995)*, ed. by Beverley Mayne
Kienzle (Louvain-la-Neuve: Fédération internationale des Instituts d'études
médiévales, 1996), pp. 301–16
Doerr, Madlen, 'Klarissen und Dominikanerinnen in Freiburg im 15. Jahrhundert:
Sozialstruktur und Reform' (unpublished doctoral dissertation, Albert-
Ludwigs-Universität, Freiburg im Breisgau, 2011/12)
Eichenlaub, Jean-Luc, 'L'Ordre dominicain en Alsace', in *Dominicains et domini-
caines en Alsace, XIIIᵉ–XXᵉ siècles: actes du colloque de Guebwiller 8–9 avril 1994*,
ed. by Jean-Luc Eichenlaub (Colmar: Conseil Général du Haut-Rhin, 1996),
pp. 9–12
Günthart, Romy, *Deutschsprachige Literatur im frühen Basler Buchdruck
(ca. 1470–1510)* (Münster: Waxmann, 2007)
Honemann, Volker, *Deutsche Literatur in der Laienbibliothek der Basler Kartause
1480–1520*, Studien und Texte zum Mittelalter und zur frühen Neuzeit, 22

(unpublished Habilitationsschrift, Freie Universität Berlin, 1982; revised print Münster: Waxmann, 2020)

Honemann, Volker, 'Kreutzer, Johannes', in *Die deutsche Literatur des Mittelalters: Verfasserlexikon*, ed. by Kurt Ruh and others, 14 vols, 2nd edition (Berlin: De Gruyter, 1978–2008), V (1985), cols 358–63

Huijbers, Anne, *Zealots for Souls: Dominican Narratives of Self-Understanding during Observant Reforms, c. 1388–1517* (Berlin: De Gruyter, 2018)

Lengwiler, Eduard, *Die vorreformatorischen Prädikaturen in der deutschen Schweiz: von ihrer Entstehung bis 1530* (Fribourg: Kanisiusdruckerei, 1955)

Lentes, Thomas, 'Bild, Reform und Cura Monialium: Bildverständnis und Bildgebrauch im Buch der Reformacio Predigerordens des Johannes Meyer († 1485)', in *Dominicains et dominicaines en Alsace, XIIIe–XXe siècles: actes du colloque de Guebwiller 8–9 avril 1994*, ed. by Jean-Luc Eichenlaub (Colmar: Conseil Général du Haut-Rhin, 1996), pp. 177–95

Lentes, Thomas, 'Gebetbuch und Gebärde: religiöses Ausdrucksverhalten in den Gebetbüchern aus dem Dominikanerinnen-Kloster St. Nikolaus in undis zu Straßburg (1350–1550)' (unpublished doctoral dissertation, Westfälische Wilhelms-Universität Münster, 1996)

Mann, Julius, *Die Kirchenpolitik der Stadt Straßburg am Ausgang des Mittelalters* (Strasbourg: Herder, 1914)

Neidiger, Bernhard, 'Basel BS — Dominikaner', in *Helvetia Sacra*, IV/5: *Die Dominikaner und Dominikanerinnen in der Schweiz*, ed. by Urs Amacher and others (Basel: Schwabe, 1999)

Pelletier-Gautier, Sonia, 'Floraison dominicaine dans la deuxième moitié du XVe siècle à Guebwiller', in *Dominicains et dominicaines en Alsace, XIIIe–XXe siècles: actes du colloque de Guebwiller 8–9 avril 1994*, ed. by Jean-Luc Eichenlaub (Colmar: Conseil Général du Haut-Rhin, 1996), pp. 53–60

Pfaff, Carl, 'Bild und Exempel: die observante Dominikanerin in der Sicht des Johannes Meyer O. P.', in *Personen der Geschichte — Geschichte der Personen: Studien zur Kreuzzugs-, Sozial- und Bildungsgeschichte. Festschrift für Rainer Christoph Schwinges zum 60. Geburtstag*, ed. by Christian Hesse and others (Basel: Schwabe, 2003), pp. 221–35

Rapp, Francis, *Réformes et réformation à Strasbourg: église et société dans le diocèse de Strasbourg (1450–1525)*, Collection de l'Institut des Hautes Études Alsaciennes, 23 (Paris: Ophrys, 1974)

Schiewer, Hans-Jochen, 'Texttypologie: Typ und Polyfunktionalitat (Predigt)', *Jahrbuch für Internationale Germanistik*, 24 (1992), pp. 44–47

Schiewer, Regina Dorothea, 'Books in Texts — Texts in Books: The *St. Georgener Predigten* as an Example of Nuns' Literacy in Late Medieval Germany', in *Nuns' Literacies in Medieval Europe: The Hull Dialogue*, ed. by Virginia Blanton, Veronica O'Mara, and Patricia Stoop, Medieval Women: Texts and Contexts, 26 (Turnhout: Brepols, 2013), pp. 223–37

Schmidt, Wieland, 'Johannes Kreutzer: ein elsässischer Prediger des 15. Jahrhunderts', in *Festschrift Helmut de Boor zum 75. Geburtstag am 24. März 1966*,

ed. by the Direktoren des Germanischen Seminars der Freien Universität
Berlin (Tübingen: Niemeyer, 1966), pp. 150–92

Thayer, Anne T., *Penitence, Preaching and the Coming of the Reformation*, St Andrews
Studies in Reformation History (Aldershot: Ashgate, 2002)

Uffmann, Heike, *Wie in einem Rosengarten: monastische Reformen des späten Mittelalters in den Vorstellungen von Klosterfrauen*, Religion in der Geschichte, 14
(Bielefeld: Verlag für Regionalgeschichte, 2008)

Vischer, Wilhelm, *Geschichte der Universität Basel von der Gründung 1460 bis zur
Reformation 1529* (Basel: Georg, 1860)

Vogelpohl, Elisabeth, *Lassen, Tun und Leiden als Grundmuster zur Einübung
geistlichen Lebens: Studien zu Johannes Kreutzer*, Münsteraner Theologische
Abhandlungen, 50 (Altenberge: Oros, 1997)

Voltmer, Rita, *Wie der Wächter auf dem Turm, ein Prediger und seine Stadt:
Johannes Geiler von Kaysersberg und Straßburg*, Beiträge zur Landes- und
Kulturgeschichte, 4 (Trier: Porta Alba, 2005)

Wackernagel, Rudolf, *Geschichte der Stadt Basel*, 3 vols in 4 parts (Basel: Heilbing
& Lichtenhahn, 1907–1924)

Weller, Emil, *Repertorium typographicum: die deutsche Literatur im ersten Viertel des
sechzehnten Jahrhunderts*, 3 vols (Nördlingen: Beck, 1864–1885)

Williams-Krapp, Werner, *Die Literatur des 15. und 16. Jahrhunderts: Modelle
literarischer Interessenbildung*, II:1 (Berlin: De Gruyter, 2020)

Williams-Krapp, Werner, 'Ordensreform und Literatur im 15. Jahrhundert',
Jahrbuch der Oswald von Wolkenstein Gesellschaft, 4 (1986–1987), pp. 41–51

Winston-Allen, Anne, *Convent Chronicles: Women Writing about Women and
Reform in the Late Middle Ages* (University Park, PA: Penn State University
Press, 2005)

Winston-Allen, Anne, 'Rewriting Women's History: Medieval Nuns' Vitae
by Johannes Meyer', in *Medieval German Voices in the 21st Century: The
Paradigmatic Function of Medieval German Studies for German Studies*,
ed. by Albrecht Classen, Internationale Forschungen zur vergleichenden
Literaturwissenschaft, 46 (Amsterdam: Rodopi, 2000), pp. 145–54

RITA VOLTMER

Instructio, correctio, and *reformatio*

Johannes Geiler von Kaysersberg and the Transmission of his Sermons

The secular priest and learned theologian Johannes Geiler von Kaysersberg (1445–1510; see Figure 5) is considered as one of the most important preachers of the late Middle Ages and the early modern period. He has to be regarded as an exceptional figure because of his preaching style, his Catholic reform agenda, the use of the printing press as its tool, the transmission of hundreds of his sermons in early print, and — last but not least — his afterlife of 'Protestantisation'. In Strasbourg, he aimed at no less than a religious and political reform of urban society. At the upper level, the magistrates should preside over a godly city, where ecclesiastical privileges and the primacy of a reformed clergy were protected, where urban policy followed the Ten Commandments and severe prosecution had outrooted any vices. At the lower level, all citizens, segregated rigorously into laity and clergy as well as along gender lines, should conduct a life of penitence and preparation for a blessed death. Religious houses should adopt the harsh rules of observance. Strasbourg was to transform itself into a New Jerusalem, a monastery under the abbot Jesus Christ. Using the pulpit as a platform for agitation, Geiler summoned both the religious authorities and the Strasbourg magistrates to fulfil their duties in bringing to life his great plan of Christian *reformatio in partibus*.[1] His reputation as a strict reformer became notorious, since his

---

1 Rita Voltmer, *Wie der Wächter auf dem Turm, ein Prediger und seine Stadt: Johannes Geiler von Kaysersberg und Straßburg*, Beiträge zur Landes- und Kulturgeschichte, 4 (Trier: Porta Alba, 2005), pp. 433–734; Rita Voltmer, 'Political Preaching and a Design of Urban Reform: Johannes Geiler of Kaysersberg and Strasbourg', *Franciscan Studies*, 71 (2013), 71–88; Rita Voltmer, 'Klerikaler Antiklerikalismus? Die Kritik am geistlichen Stand bei Johannes Geiler von Kaysersberg (1445–1510)', in *Kirchlicher und religiöser Alltag im Spätmittelalter*, ed. by Andreas Meyer, Schriften zur südwestdeutschen Landeskunde, 69 (Stuttgart: Thorbeke, 2010), pp. 48–76. On Geiler's attempts to reform the system of welfare and poor relief in Strasbourg, see in detail, Rita Voltmer, '*Die fueß an dem leichnam der christenhait / seind die hantwercks leüt. arbaiter / baüleüt / und das gemayn volck ...* Die Straßburger

Rita Voltmer (voltmer@uni-trier.de) is a Senior Lecturer in Medieval and Early Modern History at the University of Trier.

Circulating the Word of God in Medieval and Early Modern Europe: Catholic Preaching and Preachers across Manuscript and Print (c. 1450 to c. 1550), ed. by Veronica O'Mara and Patricia Stoop, SERMO 17, (Turnhout: Brepols, 2022), pp. 365–408 BREPOLS ❦ PUBLISHERS 10.1484/M.SERMO-EB.5.130462

FIGURE 5. Johannes Geiler von Kaysersberg, painted by Hans Burgkmair the Elder, in 1490. München, Bayerische Staatsgemäldesammlungen, Inv.-Nr. 3568.

INSTRUCTIO, CORRECTIO, AND REFORMATIO 367

performance in Augsburg during the autumn and winter of 1488/89 initially prevented the establishment of a preaching chair there.[2]

Roughly estimated, in Strasbourg, Geiler delivered 4500 sermons both as Cathedral preacher and as pastoral guide to nunneries and monasteries. Around 1300 sermons survive in various textual formats. Among them are texts in the vernacular and in Latin, edited or authenticated by himself, as well as printed and unprinted transcripts or *reportationes*,[3] made *inter alia* by women religious. In disregarding Geiler's great urban reform agenda, sermon studies have followed for too long the mere hagiographical myth that he never wanted his sermons to be printed. The fact that the preacher used the print medium to spread his reform agenda was mostly overlooked or downplayed. However, as a member of an elite network in Strasbourg, Geiler began with the circulation of his work from the start. Tracts, based on sermons, or sermons for reading were published either by himself or — with his consent — by friends and familiars, including his preaching programme, held during the last quarter of 1488 in Augsburg.

Shortly after his death, a flood of partly pictorial enriched prints commenced, based either on Geiler's sermon journals or on *reportationes*. In transmitting and re-constructing his sermons, different actual as well as virtual areas of work (meaning the place and subject of work) were interrelated, including the areas of the preacher, his secretary, the different note takers of his orally preached sermons, and, finally, the editors, printers, and visual artists. While the editions containing Latinised sermons, which originally were given in the vernacular, were directed at a clerical readership, the vernacular served the interests of a lay clientele seeking not only pious uplifting but also entertainment. In both versions, woodcuts decorated the prints, with the images opening up another

---

Unterschichten im polit-theologischen System des Johannes Geiler von Kaysersberg', in *Städtische Gesellschaft und Kirche im Spätmittelalter*, ed. by Sigrid Schmitt and Sabine Klapp, Geschichtliche Landeskunde, 62 (Stuttgart: Steiner, 2008), pp. 189–232; Rita Voltmer, 'Zwischen polit-theologischen Konzepten, obrigkeitlichen Normsetzungen und städtischem Alltag: Johannes Geiler von Kaysersberg und das Straßburger Fürsorgewesen', in *Norm und Praxis der Armenfürsorge in Spätmittelalter und Früher Neuzeit*, ed. by Jens Aspelmeier and Sebastian Schmidt, Vierteljahrschrift für Sozial- und Wirtschaftsgeschichte, 189 (Stuttgart: Steiner, 2006), pp. 91–135. In order not to overburden the text, Geiler's sermons, printed up to 1522, are cited with short titles, which are provided in full in the annexed list of sources. An annotated bibliography of Geiler's work is to be found in Voltmer, *Wie der Wächter auf dem Turm*, pp. 942–1014.

2   See Werner Williams-Krapp, '"Durch ihn werde widerwillen vnd erneuwerungen gesät vnd vffpracht": zu den Reforminitiativen Friederichs von Zollern und Johann Geilers von Kaysersberg in Augsburg', in *Reformen vor der Reformation: Sankt Ulrich und Afra und der monastisch-urbane Umkreis im 15. Jahrhundert*, ed. by Klaus Wolf and Gisela Drossbach, Studia Augustana, 18 (Berlin: De Gruyter, 2018), pp. 205–16.

3   On the techniques of making *reportationes* see in general Nicole Bériou, *L'Avènement des maîtres de parole: la prédication à Paris au XIIIe siècle*, Collection des études augustiniennes: Série Moyen Âge et Temps modernes, 31–32, 2 vols (Turnhout: Brepols, 1998), I, 89–102, 216–38; Voltmer, *Wie der Wächter auf dem Turm*, pp. 75–77.

level of interpretation. The volatile word of the preacher, stabilized first in writing and then in print, was placed in a pictorial and thus a third context, distancing itself further from its lost orality.

With the Lutheran Reformation in Strasbourg, the production of Geiler's sermons in print first came to a standstill. However, the Protestantisation of the preacher's word, labelled as Luther's forerunner, started in parallel. His printed sermons were listed on the papal *Index librorum prohibitorum* of forbidden books until the year 1900. Whereas the extensive corpus of Geiler's sermons together with his pastoral lectures for reading can now be regarded as professionally researched, both by Germanists[4] and by historians, the many attempts to edit his œuvre *in toto* have so far failed entirely.

In this essay I study Geiler's attempts to circulate spiritual care and his reform programme with the help of manuscripts and the printing shops. In categorizing his oral as well as his written sermons, I examine the workshops of those who were occupied with their transmission. I concentrate on Geiler's sermons leaving out the vast range of notes, letters, opinions, and *gravamina* left by his own hand, backing his reform agenda. Finally, the essay discusses why since the sixteenth century most projects to edit Geiler's sermons have failed, and why sermon studies still have to rely on those manuscripts and prints that were meant to stabilize the volatile preacher's word, and thus make it — in its best pedagogic and didactic sense — repeatable.

Undoing the Myth: Geiler's Written and Printed Sermons as Tools of *reformatio*

The argument that Geiler had never wished his sermons to be published is simply a hagiographical myth, created after the life and work of the late preacher became the subject of two *vitae*.[5] They provided, concurrently, researchers in future with the two most influential, but one-dimensional images of Geiler's personality and aim in life. The historiographer and schoolmaster Jakob Wimpfeling (1450–1528), a contemporary friend and comrade-in-arms, labelled Geiler as the incarnated Church reform programme, neglecting the latter's general approach towards urban reform. Young Beatus Rhenanus (1485–1547) transfigured Geiler into an ideal humanistic paragon, gaining

---

4 Johannes Geiler von Kaysersberg, *Johannes Geiler von Kaysersberg: die Augsburger Predigten*, ed. by Kristina Freienhagen-Baumgardt and Werner Williams-Krapp, Deutsche Texte des Mittelalters, 92 (Berlin: De Gruyter, 2015); Johannes Geiler von Kaysersberg, *Johannes Geiler von Kaysersberg: sämtliche Werke, 1. Teil: Die deutschen Schriften, Abt. 1: Die zu Geilers Lebzeiten erschienenen Schriften*, ed. by Gerhard Bauer, Ausgaben deutscher Literatur des 15. bis 18. Jahrhunderts, 3 vols (Berlin: De Gruyter, 1989–1995).

5 Voltmer, *Wie der Wächter auf dem Turm*, pp. 50–51; Jakob Wimpfeling and Beatus Rhenanus, *Jakob Wimpfeling und Beatus Rhenanus: Das Leben des Johannes Geiler von Kaysersberg*, ed. by Otto Herding (München: Fink, 1970).

INSTRUCTIO, CORRECTIO, AND REFORMATIO   369

most of his information from the priest Gangolf Steinmetz, who had served the preacher as secretary and in 1505 as witness to the latter's will, but who had probably been sacked because of his shortcomings.[6]

Both *vitae* tried to outdo each other in the hagiographical super elevation of Geiler. In using humanistic ascriptions they praised his scholarship, preaching art, true faith, ascetic life, modesty, freedom from fear, and — certainly — his stability against all kinds of hostility. Both *vitae*, but mainly Wimpfeling's, were written to prove the saintly life of the Cathedral preacher and to prepare the way for his canonization. In the light of critical observation, these *vitae* served less the memory of Geiler. In looking for fame as humanistic men of letters, Wimpfeling and Rhenanus linked their names with that of the famous preacher. The character, person, and the work of Geiler became the playthings of others and their respective interests. Even the more than thirty lamentations, which were published very soon after Geiler's death, had in mind not only mourning, but the battling over the most polished necrology in humanistic style.[7]

The humanistic clichés, which entwined the life of Geiler, are not yet abandoned. Based on the assertion of Beatus Rhenanus, it has been assumed that the preacher had nothing to do with the multiplication of his sermons through manuscripts and printing, and that he only tacitly tolerated it.[8] This argument overlooked the fact that the contentious preacher, who with watchful eyes observed Strasbourg and its bookmarket, would never have left printing against his interest without any comment. Moreover, it downplayed the further fact that by strictly following both, his role model Jean Gerson (1363–1429) and his official duties of *instructio, correctio, reformatio*, and *purgatio*,[9] Geiler had already started in 1480 or 1481 to publish tracts, based on his sermons.[10]

---

6   See Laurent Naas, 'L'Influence de Geiler de Kaysersberg (1446 [*sic*]–1510) ou l'émergence de l'idée de réforme de l'Eglise chez Beatus Rhenanus', in *Beatus Rhenanus (1485–1547) et une réforme de l'Eglise: engagement et changement*, ed. by James Hirstein, Studia humanitatis Rhenana, 4 (Turnhout: Brepols, 2018), pp. 91–112.

7   Uwe Israel, *Johannes Geiler von Kaysersberg (1445–1510): der Straßburger Münsterprediger als Rechtsreformer*, Berliner historische Studien, 27 (Berlin: Duncker & Humblodt, 1997), pp. 390–93.

8   See Volker Mertens, 'Authentisierungsstrategien in vorreformatorischer Predigt: Erscheinungsform und Edition einer oralen Gattung am Beispiel Johannes Geilers von Kaysersberg', *Editio*, 16 (2002), 70–85 (pp. 71, 77). My views about Geiler, making use of the print, have been accepted; see Volker Mertens, '*figuren und gemelt*: reale und evozierte Bilder in Geilers Narrenschiff-Predigten', in *Die Predigt zwischen Mündlichkeit, Bildlichkeit und Schriftlichkeit*, ed. by René Wetzel and Fabrice Flückiger, Medienwandel — Medienwechsel — Medienwissen, 13 (Zürich: Chronos, 2010), pp. 241–59 (p. 242).

9   In 1478 the preaching office had been established in Strasbourg. The foundation charter, ranking the preacher at the top of urban society, literally obliged Geiler to carry out the assignments above; Voltmer, *Wie der Wächter auf dem Turm*, pp. 139–40.

10 These are: *Totenbüchlein* (1480/81), *Oratio in Synodo* (1482), *Heilsame Lehre* (1489), *Pilger* (1494, 1499), *Beichtgedicht* (1497, following a text of Hans Folz), *Sterbe-ABC* (1497), *Romfahrt* (1500); see Geiler von Kaysersberg, *Johannes Geiler von Kaysersberg*, ed. by

370 RITA VOLTMER

For the most part, these were concise *artes moriendi* or brief confessional mirrors in the vernacular. Printing shops in Strasbourg, Augsburg, Basel, or Speyer took part in distributing the doctor's words. For example, under the strong impression of the latter's sermons, given in Augsburg during the autumn and winter of 1488, Johannes Schobser and Johannes Schönsperger (1455–1521), both printers there, published *Heilsame Lehre*, which claimed to be a condensed sermon by Geiler himself and handed down to a familiar person.[11] Probably Peter Attendorn in Strasbourg (in 1490) found the tract worthy of a reprint.[12] It was republished in 1502 in Frankfurt an der Oder in the vernacular and then translated into Latin (*Arbor salutis anime*).[13] In 1497 the Basel printer Michael Furter brought together in a collection three tracts, based on Geiler's sermons, which served as *ars moriendi* and mirror of confessions. From the pulpit, the preacher himself often advertised these cheap booklets, which were especially intended for the urban readership.[14] In addition to the prints, the same and other manuscripts of Geiler's sermons circulated both in Strasbourg convents and in female religious houses in Colmar or Freiburg. It is precisely this parallel transmission of Geiler's lectures that cannot have happened without his approval, because he had recycled the Augsburg preaching programme, printed in 1508 in Augsburg under the title *Predigten teütsch*, in Strasbourg.[15]

Geiler was not only occupied in delivering printed spiritual care to the urban lay audience, as well as women and men religious. As early as 1482 his opening speech at the Strasbourg Synod (*Oratio in Synodo*), given in the same year, was published, in which he had already outlined his far-reaching political-theological reform programme for both bishop and magistrate in Strasbourg.[16] After 1500, Geiler continued giving sermons for reading into

---

Bauer, I (1989); Voltmer, *Wie der Wächter auf dem Turm*, pp. 952, 976, 987, 998, 1007, and 1009; Oliver Duntze, *Ein Verleger sucht sein Publikum: die Straßburger Offizin des Matthias Hupfuf (1497/98–1520)*, Archiv für Geschichte des Buchwesens, 4 (München: Saur, 2007), pp. 145–46, 368.

11 See Christoph Reske, *Die Buchdrucker des 16. und 17. Jahrhunderts im deutschen Sprachgebiet: auf der Grundlage des gleichnamigen Werkes von Josef Benzing*, Beiträge zum Buch- und Bibliothekswesen, 51, 2nd edn (Wiesbaden: Harrassowitz, 2015), pp. 33 and 677.

12 Geiler von Kaysersberg, *Johannes Geiler von Kaysersberg*, ed. by Freienhagen-Baumgardt and Williams-Krapp, p. xi. Geiler von Kaysersberg, *Johannes Geiler von Kaysersberg*, ed. by Bauer, I (1989), 481–82, identifies the print from 1490 as having been made in Ulm.

13 Geiler von Kaysersberg, *Johannes Geiler von Kaysersberg*, ed. by Bauer, I (1989), 477–93; Voltmer, *Wie der Wächter auf dem Turm*, p. 976.

14 These are *Totenbüchlein* (1480/81), *Beichtgedicht* (1497), and *Sterbe-ABC* (1497); Herbert Kraume, *Die Gerson-Übersetzungen Geilers von Kaysersberg: Studien zur deutschsprachigen Gerson-Rezeption*, Münchener Texte und Untersuchungen zur deutschen Literatur des Mittelalters, 71 (München: Artemis, 1980), pp. 99–105.

15 See Geiler von Kaysersberg, *Johannes Geiler von Kaysersberg*, ed. by Freienhagen-Baumgardt and Williams-Krapp, pp. xi–xii; Voltmer, *Wie der Wächter auf dem Turm*, pp. 943–45, 952–53, 960–61, 968–69, 971–72, 975–76, 983–84, 986, 990–91, 1002, 1005–06, 1011, and 1013.

16 Voltmer, *Wie der Wächter auf dem Turm*, pp. 433–35. The Synodal sermon was reprinted

INSTRUCTIO, CORRECTIO, AND REFORMATIO 371

print.[17] Some of them became bestsellers, both in print and in manuscript; some were later inserted in larger collections of Geiler's sermons.[18]

Time was pressing after 1500, for the preacher had already fallen seriously ill and made his will in 1505. With the help of his secretary Jakob Otter (1485–1547), who worked out Geiler's Latin sermon journals, the latter wanted to bring his œuvre to press, urged by his friend Wimpfeling and other members of the urban elite. Whereas the Latin sermon collections served as handbooks and manuals for clerics and colleagues in preaching,[19] some *reportationes* of his cloister sermons, noted by the women religious from Strasbourg convents, were printed in Augsburg.[20] Wimpfeling's correspondence shows that Geiler's sermon journals as well as the convent manuscripts were put into print with almost hectic activity. This never happened without Geiler's will and input, and neither are the corresponding references in the dedication letters of the prints purely authentication strategies.

In disregard of both, the general context of Geiler's politico-religious agenda and his printing policy, sermon studies still emphasize the ideal that preaching meant strict orality, where every word, every emphasis, every facial expression, and every gesture of the preacher was of eminent relevance, communicating with the church room, the sacred space of preaching, and the audience.[21] The preaching event was considered a unique, unrepeatable action of spiritual enlightenment, which could and should be brought neither to the written format nor to print. However, for exactly this very reason, the audience was concerned to capture the preacher's word, to stabilize it in memory and

---

in 1489 (in Jakob Wimpfeling, *Directorium statuum seu verius tribulatio seculi*) and 1518 (*Sermones et varii tractatus*).

17 These are: *Trostspiegel* (1503), *Passion* (1506 in Latin and in the vernacular), *Zacheus* (1508); see Geiler von Kaysersberg, *Johannes Geiler von Kaysersberg*, ed. by Bauer, I (1989) and II (1991); Voltmer, *Wie der Wächter auf dem Turm*, pp. 987–88, 1010, 1013; Duntze, *Ein Verleger sucht sein Publikum*, pp. 148–49, 164–65, 381, 439; Moritz Wedell, 'Zachäus auf dem Palmbaum: enumerativ-ikonische Schemata zwischen Predigtkunst und Verlegergeschick (Geilers von Kaysersberg *Predigen Teütsch*, 1508, 1510)', in *Die Predigt zwischen Mündlichkeit, Bildlichkeit und Schriftlichkeit*, ed. by René Wetzel and Fabrice Flückiger, Medienwandel — Medienwechsel — Medienwissen, 13 (Zürich: Chronos, 2010), pp. 261–304.

18 The *Trostspiegel*, for example, was reprinted until 1598 (Hamburg); see Geiler von Kaysersberg, *Johannes Geiler von Kaysersberg*, ed. by Bauer, I (1989), 523–36.

19 In 1508 in a Latin version Otter brought to print the Lenten sermons of the year 1507, originally held in the vernacular (*Fragmenta passionis*); in 1509 he published the Lenten cycle of 1508 on the Lord's Prayer in a Latin version (*De oratione dominica*). Geiler's vernacular sermons on Sebastian Brant's *Narrenschiff*, held in 1498 and 1499, likewise, were ready to be printed in February 1510 while Geiler was still alive (*Navicula fatuorum*); Voltmer, *Wie der Wächter auf dem Turm*, pp. 966, 957, 984–85.

20 *Predigten teütsch* in 1508; see Geiler von Kaysersberg, *Johannes Geiler von Kaysersberg*, ed. by Bauer, II (1991); Voltmer, *Wie der Wächter auf dem Turm*, p. 998.

21 See Beverly Mayne Kienzle, 'Medieval Sermons and their Performance: Theory and Record', in *Preachers, Sermon and Audience in the Middle Ages*, ed. by Carolyn Muessig, A New History of the Sermon, 3 (Leiden: Brill, 2002), pp. 89–124.

on paper. And precisely for this reason, Geiler used short reading sermons by his own hand, manuscripts, and prints as tools to instruct and consolidate simple Christians, to bring forward the *correctio* of the ecclesiastical and secular authorities, and, thus, the *reformatio* and *purgatio* of the entire urban society.

Geiler's Position in Strasbourg: Duties, Networks, Contacts with Printers

In comparing the secular priest Johannes Geiler with his itinerant preaching colleagues from the mendicant orders, three basic differences have to be emphasized, whose impact on the transmission of his sermons is significant.[22] First of all, Johannes Geiler was a learned theologian with a doctorate, who had previously worked as a professor at the universities of Freiburg and Basel. Together with his priestly fellows Peter Schott the Younger (1460–1490) and Wimpfeling, Geiler openly battled against both the non-observant branches of the mendicant orders as well as the noble and worldly canons in Strasbourg. Fiercely, he opposed the mendicant way of preaching, especially during the Lenten time. Geiler labelled it devilish, whilst defining his own art as the true traditional means of the catechetical education of the audience. In fact, Geiler found new ways of preaching, particularly in shortening and controlling his speaking time in the pulpit (see Figure 6) and in using the literary work of secular scholars or writers like Sebastian Brant as guiding frameworks.

Secondly, in particular for Geiler an urban preaching office (*Prädikatur*) was established at the Cathedral in Strasbourg in 1478. Its charter burdened him with a wide range of duties: he had to preach in the Cathedral every Sunday, every saint's day, including the saint's eve, and every day during Lent. He had to mentor the most prominent nunneries and monasteries in Strasbourg with regular preaching. Moreover, he had to give sermons on special occasions like synods, the funerals of bishops and canons, or the election and installation of a new bishop. To his duties belonged the announcing of new indulgences and church parades, organized by the magistrate. In addressing these different audiences in different religious and social milieux, Geiler used different languages in preaching, and this produced variations in the preservation of the preacher's word in manuscripts and prints.

Thirdly, for thirty-two years, Johannes Geiler held the preaching office in Strasbourg. His non-itinerant, stable position provided him with the opportunity to perceive the urban space from a critical perspective of long continuity. He adjusted the framing topics of his annual sermon cycles in line with recent events, and thus, year by year refreshed the attention of the audiences. However, we need to avoid the impression that every sermon

---

22 For the following paragraphs see (with full references), Voltmer, *Wie der Wächter auf dem Turm*, pp. 132–228.

was a high-levelled sacred act of shared spiritual experience. In fact, people attended Geiler's preaching for pure entertainment, since he was, indeed, a celebrity, famous for his jokes and farcical comparisons. On the other hand, many a listener felt annoyed by his invectives. There were regular disruptive actions on the part of those who repeatedly became the target of his fierce attacks; these included the *jeunesse doré*, belonging to the urban patricians, as well as overly worldly-minded canons and mendicants. Besides, during his sermons, other holy as well as worldly services were going on in the Cathedral. Nevertheless, Johannes Geiler has to be labelled as the best-documented and well-known preacher of medieval and early modern times. Printers from Augsburg and Strasbourg were therefore eager to lay their busy hands on his work and to publish it in print.

Geiler, endorsed by the Emperor Maximilian I (1459–1519) himself, who appointed him as his court chaplain, was by no means a lone warrior. In Strasbourg he belonged to the network of powerful families that dominated the ruling magistrate there. It had been Peter Schott the Elder (1427/34–1504), 'the most distinguished public figure of his days in Strasbourg'[23] and the latter's wife Susanna (d. 1498), who had brought the preacher to Strasbourg. Schott became his lifelong patron. He supported *inter alia* the reformation of the Strasbourgian convents according to the rules of observance. His daughter Anna became highly praised as a learned nun in the house of St. Margareta and St. Agnes. Throughout his lifetime, Geiler maintained a deep friendship with Schott's only son Peter the Younger, who — under the influence of the preacher — became a cleric in the collegiate church of Jung St. Peter in Strasbourg. The family network of the Schotts included not only ties with the ruling elite, but also with the women's convents and the collegiates as well as the printing houses, since the printer Martin Schott (d. 1499) was called a cousin of Peter Schott the Younger.[24] Geiler's pedagogic and politico-religious zeal was backed by companions such as Peter Schott the Younger, Sebastian Brant, and Jakob Wimpfeling or by women religious from enclosed houses, whom he trusted the most like Susanne Hörwart or Ursula Stingel from St. Magdalena (*Reuerinnen*). Patrons, friends, and appreciated nuns, as well as — after 1500 — a secretary supported the preacher, either to produce manuscripts or to deliver sermons to print.

Johannes Geiler maintained close contact with printing shops, as he had taken a deep interest in the new technology. It was part of Geiler's almost

---

23 Peter Schott, *The Works of Peter Schott (1460–1490)*, I: *Introduction and Text*; II: *Commentary*, ed. by Murray A. Cowie and Marian L. Cowie (Chapel Hill: University of North Carolina Press, 1963–1971), II (1971), 756.

24 For information on the Schott family, see Schott, *The Works of Peter Schott*, ed. by Cowie and Cowie, II (1971), 753–57; Voltmer, *Wie der Wächter auf dem Turm*, pp. 29, 73, 142, 164–65; Charles Schmidt, *Zur Geschichte der ältesten Bibliotheken und der ersten Buchdrucker zu Strassburg* (Strasbourg: C.F. Schmidt's Universitäts-Buchhandlung Friedrich Bull, 1882), pp. 111, 121–26. In 1522 Johannes Schott, Martin's son, printed Geiler's gospel book *Postille*.

daily routine to order and to buy new books.[25] Already in Basel, he engaged *inter alia* in editing manuscripts from other authors, whom he thought as important.[26] According to Wimpfeling's correspondence with the printing office of Amerbach in Basel, the preacher continued his relationship with print shops in Strasbourg. His most elaborate effort had been — together with Peter Schott the Younger — the editing of Jean Gerson's *Opera omnia*, which appeared in 1488 in three volumes published by Johann Prüss (1447–1510) in Strasbourg. It was supplemented in 1502 with a fourth volume, edited by Wimpfeling.[27] Most noteworthy, this volume contained French sermons *ad populum* by Gerson, based on *reportationes* by lay people, which had not taken in the preaching *ad verbum*, but *ad sententiam*.[28] Together with Sebastian Brant and Wimpfeling, Johannes Geiler's impact on the flourishing book markets in Basel, Augsburg, and Strasbourg cannot be over estimated, especially concerning prints in the vernacular. The library stocks of monasteries and female religious houses as well as private book collections show that the prints of Geiler's sermons were widely distributed and esteemed.[29]

Against this background, it seems more than unlikely that Johannes Geiler would have been fundamentally opposed to the notation and printing of his sermons. The preacher's handling of the writings of third authors points to the fact that he used the circulation of manuscripts and printing as most welcome media for reproducing his agenda, be it the lectures for laity, lay brothers, and nuns, or be it his call for politico-religious reform. Pastoral lectures in particular could be repeated as often as desired through reading, thus deepening their beneficial influence on heart and soul, bringing forth more spiritual fruit. In this respect, Geiler resolutely followed the approaches of Jean Gerson and other reform theologians of the fifteenth century. Generally, he showed the habitus of a scholar, trained in the milieu of imperial cities and their universities. As a man of letters, his professional interests naturally included the finding and producing of manuscripts to put them into print.

---

25 Jakob Wimpfeling, *Jakob Wimpfeling: Briefwechsel*, ed. by Otto Herding and Dieter Mertens (München: Fink, 1909), pp. 229, 332, 373–76, 482, 493, 505, 550, 570, 612.

26 Romy Günthart, *Deutschsprachige Literatur im frühen Basler Buchdruck (ca. 1470–1510)*, Studien und Texte zum Mittelalter und zur frühen Neuzeit, 11 (Münster: Waxmann, 2007), 145–48.

27 Kraume, *Die Gerson-Übersetzungen*, pp. 79–90.

28 Wimpfeling, *Jakob Wimpheling*, ed. by Herding and Mertens, pp. 364–66.

29 See Günthart, *Deutschsprachige Literatur*, pp. 255–60; Volker Honemann, *Deutsche Literatur in der Laienbibliothek der Basler Kartause 1480–1520*, Studien und Texte zum Mittelalter und zur frühen Neuzeit, 22 (unpublished Habilitationsschrift Freie Universität Berlin, 1982; revised print Münster: Waxmann, 2020). The library for the lay brothers in the Charterhouse of Basel possessed almost the entire printed sermon œuvre of Geiler, with some books in several copies.

Geiler's Orally Produced Sermons: Categories

Roughly, we can classify Geiler's sermons in the vernacular and in Latin in three types.[30]

The first are Lenten cycles, other minor cycles, and single sermons, delivered in the Cathedral in the vernacular during the liturgical year.[31] I assume that his audience included all social milieux, the patriciate and the poor, magistrates and higher clergy, canons and vicars. Even the non-observant mendicants listened to his preaching, since they showed themselves to be very well informed about Geiler's attacks against their order.[32] Likewise, we know that visitors to the city paid tribute to the famous doctor in the Cathedral.[33] Only eleven of the thirty Lenten cycles were preserved, some only fragmentarily. Apart from these, Geiler delivered sermon cycles, which covered, for example, the Sundays after Trinity or Advent, Christmas time, and Epiphanies.

The second category consists of minor cycles or single sermons preached in the Strasbourg convents: St. Magdalena (*Reuerinnen*), St. Clara im grünen Wörd (Clarissans, observant), St. Katharina (Dominicans, reformed, non-observant), St. Margareta and St. Agnes (Dominicans, observant), St. Nikolaus in undis (Dominicans, observant),[34] St. Johann im grünen Wörd (knights of St John)

---

30 The categories are based on Voltmer, *Wie der Wächter auf dem Turm*, pp. 197–228, 757–923, 942–1023.

31 See in general Rita Voltmer, '"Preaching during the Holy Week is like being Killed on the Wheel": The Design, Performance, and Recording of Johannes Geiler of Kaysersberg's Lenten Sermons', in *I sermoni quaresimali: digiuno del corpo, banchetto dell'anima / Lenten Sermons: Fast of the Body, Banquet of the Soul*, ed. by Pietro Delcorno, Eleonora Lombardo, and Lorenza Tromboni, Memorie domenicane, n. s., 48 (Firenze: Edizioni Nerbini, 2017), pp. 277–92.

32 On Geiler's fierce and open battle against the Strasbourgian Dominicans that took place in the Cathedral and on the latter's pulpits, see Voltmer, *Wie der Wächter auf dem Turm*, pp. 185–92.

33 For example François Bonivard from Geneva; in 1509, Hans Baldung Grien might well have listened to Geiler's sermons concerning witchcraft and sorcery; see Rita Voltmer, 'Preaching on Witchcraft? The Sermons of Johannes Geiler of Kaysersberg (1445–1510)', in *Contesting Orthodoxy in Medieval and Early Modern Europe: Heresy, Magic and Witchcraft*, ed. by Louise Nyholm Kallestrup and Raisa Maria Toivo, Palgrave Historical Studies in Witchcraft and Magic (Basingstoke: Palgrave Macmillan, 2017), pp. 193–215; Rita Voltmer, 'Du discours à l'allegorie: représentations de la superstition, de la magie et de la sorcellerie dans les sermons de Johannes Geiler de Kaysersberg', in *Sorcellerie savante et mentalités populaires*, ed. by Antoine Follain and Maryse Simon, Sciences de l'histoire (Strasbourg: Presses universitaire de Strasbourg, 2013), pp. 45–88.

34 A list of female religious houses in Strasbourg may be consulted in Sigrid Hirbodian, 'Pastors and Seducers: The Practice of the *Cura monialium* in Mendicant Convents in Strasbourg', in *Partners in Spirit: Women, Men, and Religious Life in Germany, 1100–1500*, ed. by Fiona J. Griffiths and Julie Hotchin, Medieval Women: Texts and Contexts, 24 (Turnhout: Brepols, 2014), pp. 303–37 (pp. 329–33); see also Anna Sauerbrey, *Die Straßburger Klöster im 16. Jahrhundert: eine Untersuchung unter besonderer Berücksichtigung der Geschlechtergeschichte*, Spätmittelalter, Humanismus, Reformation, 69 (Tübingen: Mohr Siebeck, 2012), pp. 38–51.

FIGURE 6. Johannes Geiler von Kayersberg in the pulpit in Strasbourg Cathedral. Engraving in *Heilsame Predigt* (Strasbourg: Johannes Grüninger, 1513), fol. III verso (VD16 G 782; copy München, Bayerische Staatsbibliothek, Rar. 2241#Beibd.2).

and the Wilhelmites (Augustinian Hermits).[35] Some of these sermons were part of the greater cycles, which Geiler held in the Cathedral. His audience could follow him literally from pulpit to pulpit. Some of the convent sermons that took place in female religious houses were compiled and printed in the vernacular. However, the manuscripts of Geiler's convent sermons, which circulated in many observant nunneries in the Upper Rhineland, are neither fully catalogued nor explored. It remains a most remarkable fact that with his sermons, Geiler built a bridge between the enclosed women religious, who were forced to very strict observance, and the surrounding urban space of Strasbourg.

Thirdly, there are a few Latin sermons addressing the higher clergy at certain events, for instance, at the opening of the synod in 1482, the election of a new bishop in 1506, or the orations at the funerals of bishops and canons. Overall, not more than six or seven occasions are known, in which

---

35 Geiler had strong relationships with the Strasbourgian Carthusians, but there is no information about sermons delivered there.

INSTRUCTIO, CORRECTIO, AND REFORMATIO

Geiler had to preach in Latin. Since the higher clergy being thus addressed did not want to hear his fierce calls for reform, the canons very often cut short the preacher's speaking time or postponed his sermon.[36] This was precisely the reason why Geiler — in facing a hesitant, careless, and hostile clergy — redoubled his efforts to persuade the temporal authorities, the housefathers, and the members of the ruling elite to implement his reform agenda in Strasbourg.

The Transmission of Geiler's Sermons: Interrelated Areas of Work

Studies in medieval German sermons, initiated by Volker Mertens, Hans-Jochen Schiewer, and their collaborateurs, have provided helpful tools to categorize the transmission of medieval sermons in their different scriptual formats.[37] In adapting their model, a homologous tradition refers to those texts that Geiler either wrote down himself, or in whose composition he was redactionally involved, or which he had authorized or which were based on his own notes and preaching journals. Likewise, translations of those manuscripts and prints have to be defined as a homologous tradition. A heterologous tradition refers to those texts that were based on *reportationes*, transcripts, notations, and postscripts that had not been revised by Geiler.

Different people engaged in notation and *reportationes*: women religious in the nunneries; clerics listening to Geiler in the Cathedral such as Jakob Otter or Johannes Pauli (1455–1530/33); learned laymen such as Johannes Adolphus Muling (d. 1523) or the enthusiastic weaver Jörg Preining (around 1440–1526/27) in Augsburg; many anonymous persons, whose names are lost in manuscripts and prints.[38] The canon and famous Swiss historiographer from Geneva, François Bonivard (1493–1570), visited Strasbourg in his youth

---

36 See in general Voltmer, 'Klerikaler Antiklerikalismus?'.

37 All detailed information with reference to the work of Mertens and Schiewer is found in Voltmer, *Wie der Wächter auf dem Turm*, pp. 81–90, 942–1014. In addition see Beverly Mayne Kienzle, 'Conclusion', in *The Sermon*, ed. by Beverly Mayne Kienzle, Typologie des sources du Moyen Âge occidental, 81–83 (Turnhout: Brepols, 2000), pp. 963–83 (pp. 974–78).

38 Jörg Preining was a well-educated, self-appointed lay priest who may have been close to the Waldensians and whose critical statements about the Church ultimately led to his banishment from Augsburg in 1504. Highly impressed by the already famous Strasbourg Cathedral preacher, Preining produced fascicles of each series of sermons in order to compile and distribute them as text samples. It remains a mystery how Preining managed to produce such a quantity and quality of transcripts. The thesis that Johannes Geiler himself could have handed over his notes (always written in Latin) to the religious enthusiast Preining (not knowledgeable in Latin), is not at all convincing. Geiler stayed extremely hostile to self-proclaimed lay preachers, especially when they smacked of heresy as Preining did; Voltmer, *Wie der Wächter auf dem Turm*, pp. 75–77; Mertens, 'Authentisierungsstrategien', p. 80.

after 1500. He heard Geiler in the Cathedral. We owe to him the latter's only transmitted sermon in the French language.[39]

The transmission of Geiler's Augsburg sermons illustrate how *reportationes* in the vernacular could easily be carried out: a group of reporters can be assumed, which supplied Jörg Preining with several corresponding transcripts, written down during or shortly after Geiler's preaching sessions and compiled collectively.[40] Some scholars in German sermon studies bring forward the argument that in the German vernacular no shorthand, comparable to the Latin one, was known, and thus, the notation of sermons in the vernacular was far more difficult, if not impossible.[41] According to this argument, postscripts of sermons had to rely on sparse points of outlining and a strong memory. However, this verdict has to be discussed, since German scribes in different text formats — *inter alia* sermons — used abbreviations, both in Latin or in the vernacular.[42] The reporting collective in Augsburg may have used abbreviations, formed by individual ways in abbreviating writing, to capture the volatile words of Geiler.[43] It seems obvious that likewise women religious used the same techniques in taking down notes on sermons collectively, compiling the parts to a coherent text and discussing it with the preacher.[44] Mertens and Schiewer have since conceded that sermons in the German vernacular could also be recorded by notation and as *reportatio*.[45] Whereas Geiler revised the *reportationes* carried out by women religious in Strasbourg, others were made without his participation. However, close reading of the preacher's complete œuvre, including his letters, opinions, and *gravamina* together with corresponding material, provides the conclusion that the various forms of writing that helped to circulate the doctor's word have to be considered as authentic. They coherently convey his preaching programme and reform agenda. In general, different areas of work connected in transmitting sermons from orality to script to print and to visual illustration, using various methods and techniques. The interwoven paths of transmission in manuscripts and

---

39 Voltmer, *Wie der Wächter auf dem Turm*, pp. 89, 378–83, 972.

40 See Kienzle, 'Conclusion', pp. 975–76.

41 Again in Mertens, 'Authentisierungsstrategien', p. 81; Mertens, '*figuren und gemelt*', p. 244.

42 Karin Schneider, *Paläographie und Handschriftenkunde für Germanisten: eine Einführung*, Sammlung kurzer Grammatiken germanischer Dialekte. B: Ergänzungsreihe, 8, 3rd edn (Berlin: De Gruyter, 2014), pp. 86–91.

43 Geiler von Kaysersberg, *Johannes Geiler von Kaysersberg*, ed. by Freienhagen-Baumgardt and Williams-Krapp, pp. xxvii–xxxiii.

44 See Nigel F. Palmer, 'Die Münchner Perikopenhandschrift Cgm 157 und die Handschriftenproduktion des Straßburger Reuerinnenklosters im späten 15. Jahrhundert', *Kulturtopographie des deutschsprachigen Südwestens im späteren Mittelalter*, ed. by Barbara Fleith and René Wetzel, Kulturtopographie des alemannischen Raums, 1 (Berlin: De Gruyter, 2009), pp. 263–300 (p. 283).

45 Mertens, 'Authentisierungsstrategien', p. 77; Hans-Jochen Schiewer, 'German Sermons in the Middle Ages', in *The Sermon*, ed. by Beverly Mayne Kienzle, Typologie des sources du Moyen Âge occidental, 81–83 (Turnhout: Brepols, 2000), pp. 861–961 (pp. 923–24).

INSTRUCTIO, CORRECTIO, AND REFORMATIO   379

prints as well as in the vernacular or in Latinised versions often ran in parallel. It is therefore not adequate to look only at the manuscripts or only at the Latin prints; rather, a close reading of all forms of transmission is necessary. Likewise, the editors, their access to Geiler's notes as well as *reportationes* and their motives have to be taken into account. A look in the workshop of Johannes Geiler, his secretary Jakob Otter, his nephew Peter Wickram (d. 1540), and finally, his reporter, the Franciscan Johannes Pauli, provides better insight into the process of transmitting volatile orality into the libraries of the preacher's audience.

In his workshop composing his sermons, Geiler made notes in advance, mostly very early in the morning, but he went to the pulpit without any written guidance.[46] During the preaching, he changed his plans by speaking at length on one point, and not mentioning the others. He altered his notes after returning to his study, adding more material as references. Although Geiler's sermons were overwhelmingly given in the vernacular, the notes were made in Latin. However, the preacher added a term, a sentence, or a figure of speech in the vernacular to specify the meaning. Thus, he shifted from the vernacular to Latin, back and forth. He sampled the notes in specific journals. In the Lenten period or during other liturgical based cycles, each sermon had to be adjusted to the daily Gospel and the feast of the daily saint. Therefore, a sermon might be composed of at least three parts: first, a short interpretation of the daily Gospel or lesson, secondly, a passage on the daily saint's life, and finally, the respective part of a sequel.

Already in 1480/81 Geiler had started publishing tracts, which were based on his sermons. Women religious noted down his convent sermons, which were later discussed and revised by himself. Up to 1500, the preacher had not forced the printing of his famous Lenten cycles and sermon sequels. However, after the turn of the century, he announced to friends that he did not want to choose any new topics for preaching. Instead, he wanted to re-order his sermon journals.[47] The workshop of the preacher thus included the workshop of his revising secretary. After 1501, at first to help him with his notes, Geiler employed the priest Gangolf Steinmetz, a former *familiarus* of the late Peter Schott the Younger. Probably Steinmetz was sacked after 1505 because of his inadequacy; perhaps he left the preacher's service for other reasons.[48]

In 1507 the preacher got better support from the priest Jakob Otter, who was recommended to him by Wimpfeling. Otter at the same time served as chaplain and confessor in the convent of St. Magdalena. He therefore had

---

46 See with full references Voltmer, '"Preaching during the Holy Week"', pp. 282–87.
47 Voltmer, *Wie der Wächter auf dem Turm*, pp. 71–73.
48 In 1505 Steinmetz signed Geiler's will as a witness. If he had to leave the latter's service, it would explain why he, bearing a grudge against Otter and his success in getting Geiler's sermons printed, fed Beatus Rhenanus with the information that the preacher had not wanted to publish his sermons.

easy access to the convent's *reportationes*, mostly written down by Susanna Hörwart and Ursula Stingel and revised by Geiler.

Otter started with editing both the convent sermons and the Lenten cycles, which had been preached in the Cathedral.[49] In 1508 the so-called *Predigten teütsch*, which contained Strasbourg convent sermons, were printed in Augsburg, where the audience still had a vivid memory of Geiler, who had first preached some of the now printed topics there.[50] Allegedly, the printing was done without Geiler's knowledge or involvement, as the printer Hans Otmar (d. 1514/17) assures us in the colophon. However, this remark can only refer to the print alone, because some of the sermons presented there explicitly refer to the collaboration of the preacher. Their manuscripts were already circulating for years in female convents of the Upper Rhineland.[51] This sermon collection was followed in 1510 by the so-called *Granatapfel*, first printed in Augsburg with Hans Otmar, reprinted in 1511 and 1516 in Strasbourg by Johann Knoblouch (d. 1528).[52] Also in 1510, seven treatises by Jean Gerson appeared in Strasbourg. The collection was called *Irrig Schaf*, published by Matthias Schürer (d. 1519). Geiler had been responsible for their translation into the vernacular and very probably had prepared their printing before death stopped him.[53] He had used the respective topics in the sermons both for the audience in the Cathedral and in the convents. It is safe to assume that it had been Otter, who had accompanied this printing to its finalization. Finally, the *Seelenparadies*, based on *reportationes* made in St. Magdalena, was printed in 1510 in Strasbourg by Schürer.[54] The three editions of *Granatapfel*, *Irrig Schaf*, and *Seelenparadies* likewise aimed at instructing lay people as well as female and male religious in offering material for catechetical and spiritual care, mostly stemming from convent sermons in Strasbourg. In the process of editing, both the preacher's and his secretary's areas of work were interrelated with that of the sermon's female reporters.

Based on Geiler's journals, Otter brought to print the two vernacular Lenten cycles on the so-called 'Gingerbread' (*Fragmenta passionis*, given in 1507, printed in 1508) and on the Lord's Prayer (*De oratione dominica*,

---

49 Voltmer, *Wie der Wächter auf dem Turm*, pp. 91–94.

50 Voltmer, *Wie der Wächter auf dem Turm*, p. 998 together with the entries to the respective sermons and sermon cycles; see the edition of *Predigten teütsch* in Geiler von Kaysersberg, *Johannes Geiler von Kaysersberg*, ed. by Bauer, II (1991).

51 Geiler von Kaysersberg, *Johannes Geiler von Kaysersberg*, ed. by Freienhagen-Baumgardt and Williams-Krapp, p. xi.

52 Voltmer, *Wie der Wächter auf dem Turm*, pp. 972–73, together with the entries to the respective sermons and sermon cycles. It has been suggested that Otmar published the fascicles separately as a sequel; Honemann, *Deutsche Literatur*, pp. 44–45.

53 Kraume, *Die Gerson-Übersetzungen*, pp. 121–26. *Irrig schaf* was reprinted 1514 by Johannes Grüninger in Strasbourg.

54 Otter had definitely prepared the printing of *Seelenparadies*; Voltmer, *Wie der Wächter auf dem Turm*, pp. 92–93; see the edition of *Seelenparadies* in Geiler von Kaysersberg, *Johannes Geiler von Kaysersberg*, ed. by Bauer, III (1995).

preached in 1508, printed in 1509), both edited in a Latinised version. Both were translated into the vernacular by Muling, a former corrector in some printing houses of Strasbourg, who had been an eyewitness of Geiler's preaching in Strasbourg.[55] These translations were printed some years later: *Lebkuchen* in 1514, *Pater Noster* in 1515. In swift sequence, Otter published in Strasbourg, again based on Geiler's sermon journals, the Latinised versions of three of Geiler's vernacular Lenten sermons: *Navicula fatuorum* (printed in 1510; see Figure 7), *Navicula penitentie* (printed in 1511),[56] and *Peregrinus* (printed in 1513), which topics Geiler had interwoven in a sequel between 1498 and 1502.[57] The *Navicula fatuorum* was certainly prepared for printing by Otter under the supervision of Geiler, who was still alive then. For the other two Lenten cycles, Geiler must at least have had a desire to have them printed. The Latin versions sought readers amongst clerics, learned lay people, students, or theologians. Likewise, they may have served as preaching handbooks.[58] However, the respective vernacular versions of *Navicula penitentie* (*Schiff der Penitenz*, printed in 1514 in Augsburg) and *Peregrinus* (*Pilgerschaft*, printed in 1512 in Basel) aimed at different audiences.

Around 1513 the dispute about Geiler's spiritual heritage escalated, since his nephew Peter Wickram, as his less than congenial successor in the preaching office, wanted a piece of the profitable business of his uncle's printed sermons. Jakob Otter was forced to pass Geiler's journals over to him.[59] Wickram ordered his secretary, Jakob Biethen, to publish a Latinised version of the so-called *Sermones prestantissimi*, a great cycle of sermons, stretching from 1495 to 1497, which contained Geiler's most elaborated *ars moriendi*, given

---

55 See Voltmer, *Wie der Wächter auf dem Turm*, pp. 98–99; Duntze, *Ein Verleger sucht sein Publikum*, pp. 165–67, 300, 453–54. Muling kept a deep interest in Geiler's sermon, which is shown in his annotations to an exemplar of *Granatapfel*; see Armin Schlechter, 'Lesespuren von Johann Adelphus Muling in einer Ausgabe des Granatapfel von Johannes Geiler von Kaysersberg', in *Grundlagen: Forschungen, Editionen und Materialien zur deutschen Literatur und Sprache des Mittelalters und der Frühen Neuzeit*, ed. by Rudolf Bentzinger, Ulrich-Dieter Oppitz, and Jürgen Wolf, Zeitschrift für deutsches Altertum und deutsche Literatur, Beiheft 18 (Stuttgart: Hirzel, 2013), pp. 247–55.

56 Already in 1512 the Catholic theologian Johannes Eck (not to be confused with the Lutheran theologian Johann Eck), admirer of Geiler and fierce opponent of Luther, had published (by Johannes Grüninger) with *Schiff des Heils* a short version of *Schiff der Penitenz*, lavishly decorated with woodcuts. Geiler's vernacular *Schiff der Penitenz*, printed in 1513, includes a text on Christ's Passion, which has been wrongly attributed to Geiler, but, indeed, was written by Eck; see Jonathan Reinert, *Passionspredigt im 16. Jahrhundert: das Leiden und Sterben Jesu Christi in den Postillen Martin Luthers, der Wittenberger Tradition und altgläubiger Prediger*, Spätmittelalter, Humanismus, Reformation, 119 (Tübingen: Mohr Siebeck, 2020), pp. 125–26.

57 See Voltmer, *Wie der Wächter auf dem Turm*, pp. 984–85, 991–95, 999–1000; Rita Voltmer, '"Preaching during the Holy Week"'.

58 With reference to the *Navicula fatuorum* Mertens, '*figuren und gemelt*', p. 244, agrees with my interpretation.

59 On Peter Wickram, see Voltmer, *Wie der Wächter auf dem Turm*, pp. 94–98.

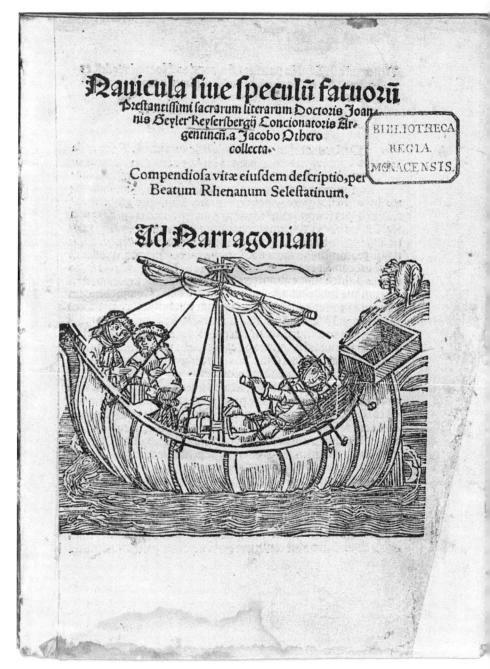

FIGURE 7. Title page of *Navicula fatuorum*, published by Jakob Otter (Strasbourg: Matthias Schürer, 1510) (VD16 ZV 6437; copy München, Bayerische Staatsbibliothek, 4 P.lat. 728).

INSTRUCTIO, CORRECTIO, AND REFORMATIO 383

partly in the Cathedral and in Strasbourg convents.[60] Biethen announced in the dedication that the preacher himself had wished very dearly that these sermons be published. Printed in 1514 by Johannes Grüninger (*c.* 1455–*c.* 1532), the book was lavishly decorated with several woodcuts, showing Death in terrible action. In 1521 a vernacular version from an unknown editor appeared which was not a simple translation, but relied on additional material. Obviously, the anonymous editor had used *reportationes*, made by anonymous nuns and lay people, which offered not only more sermons, but also a better inner coherence than the Latinised version of Biethen.[61]

Two sermons from a sub-cycle of the great *ars moriendi* cycle, both delivered in the St. Magdalena convent in Strasbourg in 1495, are available in several versions: first, in a vernacular version, written down by nuns, revised and extended by Geiler. This version circulated in at least four manuscripts in convents of the Upper Rhineland. It was printed in the collection *Predigten teütsch* (1508).[62] A Latinised version of the same sermon, based on Geiler's sermon notes, is to be found in *Sermones prestantissimi* (1514), whereas a second vernacular version, based on both the Latin print and additional *reportationes*, was printed in *De arbore humana* (1521).[63]

There are further examples of transmitting Geiler's sermons in parallel: in 1520 Grüninger had published sermons by Geiler, noted and compiled by 'an honourable virgin', under the title *Drei Marien*.[64] The collection contained several sermons, preached during the *ars moriendi* cycle between April and July 1496. In comparison with their parallel edition in *Sermones prestantissimi* and *De arbore humana*, these *reportationes* are characterized by a more detailed presentation of the *facetia*, but a more deficient rendering of the theological content. One of these sermons can also be found in *Postille* (1522), most likely not a *reportatio* of the Franciscan Johannes Pauli. Eleven of the sermons in *Drei Marien* have no parallel tradition in another vernacular or Latinised edition of Geiler's sermons.

In 1518 Wickram himself used Geiler's notes for editing some sermons in Latin (*Sermones et varii tractatus*), which for the most part had been given in the vernacular and which had been published in print. In the foreword, he openly insulted the preceding editions in the vernacular, which had been prepared by Muling (*Lebkuchen*, printed in 1514) and Johannes Pauli (*Evangelienbuch*, 1515 and 1517; *Brösamlin*, 1517).[65] The latter was denounced wrongly as being a converted Jew and of having blended his own fantasies

---

60 Voltmer, *Wie der Wächter auf dem Turm*, pp. 759–81, 1009; Voltmer, '"Preaching during the Holy Week"', p. 280. The *Ars moriendi* cycle contained at least ten sub-cycles.

61 Voltmer, *Wie der Wächter auf dem Turm*, pp. 947–50.

62 *Geiler von Kaysersberg, Johannes Geiler von Kaysersberg*, ed. by Bauer, II (1991), 186–96.

63 Voltmer, *Wie der Wächter auf dem Turm*, pp. 943–45.

64 Voltmer, *Wie der Wächter auf dem Turm*, pp. 958–59.

65 See Luzian Pfleger, 'Der Franziskaner Johannes Pauli und seine Ausgaben Geilerscher Predigten', *Archiv für Elsässische Kirchengeschichte*, 3 (1928), 47–96 (pp. 54–60).

into the quasi-holy words of Geiler. Wickram's polemics spared Jakob Otter for good reason, since both used the sermon journals of Geiler; obviously, they were born from a grudge. In particular, Wickram intended to ridicule the prints in the vernacular and to praise his own Latinised editions, which had the air of learned educational humanism. Wickram wanted to immortalize his own reputation as a man of letters in linking his name with his famous uncle and the latter's circle of comrades like Sebastian Brant or Wimpfeling.

The comparison of Wickram's Latinised reconstructions of Geiler's vernacular sermons shows clearly how much the actual lecture could differ from the sparse notes, which the preacher had afterwards taken down. This is exemplified by Geiler's New Year's sermons (1497–1508), edited by Wickram in *Sermones et varii tractatus*, some of which are available in parallel in a vernacular record by Johannes Pauli. Geiler used the custom of presenting a small gift to friends and acquaintances on New Year's Day as the topic for these sermons, in which he figuratively gave his listeners a precious stone at the beginning of each year. Emblematically, he interpreted twelve gemstones, each symbolizing a Christian virtue.[66] Nevertheless, by no means, did Geiler limit the exposition of the topic to one day, as the Latinised version implies, but stretched the subject's treatment over several dates.[67]

To the Franciscan mendicant Johannes Pauli we owe congenial *reportationes* of most of Geiler's sermons, given between 1504 and 1509.[68] Pauli possessed the necessary talent for recording the doctor's sermons as they were preached. He may have done so in a Latin shorthand.[69] As a learned preacher himself, the Franciscan was trained in the *ars memorativa* and well informed about the handbooks, *ars praedicandi*, manuals, and samples of legends or collections of examples. Pauli, likewise, used journals to take down his notes on Geiler's sermons, which he carefully annotated with the date and location of their presentation. However, his recording techniques show significant differences in comparison with the *reportationes* already mentioned, since the Franciscan tried to purge a specific sermon from those elements, which might disrupt the line of argument in its main part, the topic of the running cycle. For example, Geiler's references to the daily saint or to the Gospel were recorded and edited separately in the *Evangelienbuch*. This is the reason why two or three parts of the same sermon, given in the Cathedral, can be found in three

---

66 During the Lenten cycle in 1501/02, Geiler interpreted the same gemstones as symbols of the twelve virtues of convent women; Voltmer, *Wie der Wächter auf dem Turm*, p. 957.

67 Whereas Wickram edited only one sermon for New Year's Day in 1505, Pauli, who had missed the first one, recorded the following six sermons. Geiler therefore stretched the topic to seven sermons from 1 January to 1 February 1505; Voltmer, *Wie der Wächter auf dem Turm*, pp. 877, 880–81, 886, 956–57.

68 Voltmer, *Wie der Wächter auf dem Turm*, pp. 99–107, 289–90.

69 Mertens, 'figuren und gemelt', p. 244.

differing printed collections of sermons, prepared by Pauli. In some cases, Pauli provided reference to his editing technique.[70]

At least since 1512 Johannes Pauli had maintained a close relationship with the Strasbourg printer Johannes Grüninger, who planned to publish Geiler's *Opera omnia*. The Franciscan started working on the edition of Lenten cycles and a book, assembling Geiler's lectures on the Gospels during an ideal ecclesiastical year (*sermones ad tempore*). The *Evangelienbuch* contained sermons, beginning with the First Sunday of Advent and ending with the Twenty-Fifth Sunday after Trinity, including eight Sundays after Epiphany, a Lenten period, the Sundays after Easter Sunday and the twenty-five Sundays after Trinity, followed by several sermons for Marian feasts, saints' days, and other religious festivals. Thanks to Pauli's explicit and implicit references, some of the sermons can be dated precisely. In 1515, the first edition of Geiler's *Evangelienbuch* contained 136 sermons. The second and third editions in 1517 and in 1522 contained 142 sermons.[71] In parallel, the Franciscan put together material for two Lenten cycles, the so-called *Ameise*, definitely given in 1509 and printed in 1516 as well as 1517, and *Sünden des Munds* given in 1505 and printed in 1518.[72] He then gathered all the remaining extracts and scraps, which could still be found in his journals on Geiler's sermons. They were edited in the so-called *Brösamlin* in 1517, containing in two parts fragments of sermon cycles and single sermons, given during the years of 1506 until 1509. As numerous references by Pauli prove, the second part of the *Brösamlin* collection is closely linked with his edition of Geiler's Gospel book: in his journals, Pauli had overlooked some of Geiler's sermons when compiling the latter's *Evangelienbuch*, which were now printed in *Brösamlin*. Other sermons Pauli had withheld, so that the *Evangelienbuch* would not become too extensive. Moreover, Pauli translated the Latinised *Navicula fatuorum* in the manner of Geiler's preaching style in the vernacular, perhaps because in 1498 and 1499, the Franciscan might had heard some of the sermons in the Cathedral.[73] As close reading reveals, Pauli's

---

70 Voltmer, *Wie der Wächter auf dem Turm*, pp. 876–82.

71 Voltmer, *Wie der Wächter auf dem Turm*, pp. 851–69.

72 Voltmer, *Wie der Wächter auf dem Turm*, pp. 945–47, 1008–09. *Sünden des Munds* was printed together with the reading sermon *Baum der Seligkeit* (or *Alphabet in 23 Sermons*), which had first been published in 1512 in Strasbourg (printer unknown). Geiler had preached these sermons in 1490 in the convent of St. Margareta and St. Agnes; a manuscript circulated in Strasbourg convents, for example, in St. Nikolaus in undis. Wickram delivered a Latinised version (*Sermones alphabeticis*) in *Sermones et varii tractatus* (1518); Voltmer, *Wie der Wächter auf dem Turm*, pp. 951–52.

73 On Pauli and his techniques of editing see Voltmer, *Wie der Wächter auf dem Turm*, pp. 99–107, 828–32, 841–69, 876–82; Mertens, '*figuren und gemelt*', pp. 242–45; without any reference to Voltmer's book and thus outdated is Gerald Kapfhammer, 'Inszenierung von Authentizität: Johannes Pauli und die Veröffentlichung der Predigten Geilers von Kaysersberg', in *Autorbilder: zur Medialität literarischer Kommunikation in Mittelalter und Früher Neuzeit*, ed. by Gerald Kapfhammer and others, Tholos, 2 (Münster: Rhema, 2007), pp. 270–84.

version, printed in 1520, gives a far better impression of Geiler's famous cycle than the Latinised edition of Otter.[74] Probably Pauli had used handwritten *reportationes*, stemming from a third party.[75]

In 1522 the so-called *Postille* appeared, edited by an unknown scribe.[76] Like the previous three Gospel books by Johannes Pauli, it started on the First Sunday of Advent and ended on the Twenty-Fifth Sunday after Trinity, followed by several *sermones ad sanctis*. It contained 115 sermons. My close reading has brought to light an astonishing fact: at times, the *Postille* contains sermons with the most uncorrupted text passages, whereas the several editions of the *Evangelienbuch* only present an abstract or the outlines of a sermon, which is given fully in the *Postille* or *Brösamlin*.[77] This finding leads to the conclusion that both the *Evangelienbuch* and the *Postille* together with the *Brösamlin* go back to the original sermon journals, compiled by Johannes Pauli, who probably had sold the journals containing his notes of the doctor's sermons to Grüninger. When at some point after 1521 Grüninger gave up the plans to edit Geiler's complete œuvre, he probably sold Pauli's original journal to the printer Johannes Schott (1477–around 1550), who published it under a pseudonym and the title *Postille* in 1522.[78] The *Evangelienbuch* (printed in 1515) published by Pauli also contains a sermon from Geiler's Lenten cycle in 1508, which the Franciscan had noted in detail, but which had only been briefly reproduced in the Latin edition commissioned by Otter on the basis of Geiler's sermon notes (*De oratione dominica*) and their translation by Muling (*Pater Noster*).[79]

---

74 Gerhard Bauer, 'Die Predigten Johannes Geilers von Kaysersberg über Sebastian Brants Narrenschiff und ihre Überlieferung durch Jakob Otters *Navicula Fatuorum* (1510) und Johannes Paulis *Narrenschiff* (1520)', in *Sébastian Brant, son époque et 'La Lef des fols'*, ed. by Gonthier-Louis Fink, Collection Recherches germaniques, 5 (Strasbourg: Presses universitaire de Strasbourg, 1995), pp. 96–113.

75 See Ralf-Henning Steinmetz, 'Über Quellenverwendung und Sinnbildungsverfahren in den "Narrenschiff"-Predigten Geilers von Kaisersberg: am Beispiel und mit dem lateinischen und dem deutschen Text der Predigten über die *Bulnarren*', in *Predigt im Kontext*, ed. by Volker Mertens and others (Berlin: De Gruyter, 2013), pp. 89–124 (p. 92), without any reference to Voltmer's book.

76 On the still unknown Heinrich Wesszmer see Voltmer, *Wie der Wächter auf dem Turm*, pp. 107–10. Bauer, 'Die Predigten', pp. 105–06, agrees with my thoughts about Pauli being the editor of *Postille*, a thesis that I had firstly promoted in 1991 in my Master's thesis.

77 Voltmer, *Wie der Wächter auf dem Turm*, pp. 887–923 (concordance of the four editions with comparative remarks); the similarities and interconnections between *Evangelienbuch* (1515, 1517, 1522), *Brösamlin* (1517) and *Postille* (1522) have been recognized by Charles Schmidt, *Histoire littéraire de l'Alsace à la fin du XVᵉ et au commencement du XVIᵉ siècle*, 2 vols (Paris: Librairie Sandoz et Fischbacher, 1879), II, 390.

78 Voltmer, *Wie der Wächter auf dem Turm*, pp. 108–10.

79 Voltmer, *Wie der Wächter auf dem Turm*, p. 989.

An Example: Transmitting Geiler's Sermons on the Christian Pilgrim

To outline the very complex process of transmitting Geiler's preaching, we have to take a very close look at the different, sometimes closely interrelated formats in which these sermons were stabilized in script and in print. The transmitting process concerning Geiler's sermons on the Christian pilgrimage gives a remarkable example, because he had preached at least three times on this topic, based on a tract of Jean Gerson, first in 1488 in Augsburg, again in 1489 in the Strasbourg convent of St. Magdalena, and finally in 1500 in the Cathedral during the Lenten period.[80]

The Augsburg sermons, including Geiler's preaching on the Christian pilgrim, had been recorded in four manuscripts by a collective of scribes, initiated by Jörg Preining. This version (*Pilger I*) presented the exegesis of twenty characteristics of the pilgrim in at least twenty sermons, dealing at the end with the pilgrim's return home. These versions never made it into print.[81] In 1494 a short tract on the same topic was published in Augsburg, probably with Geiler's consent, with eighteen simple woodcuts (*Pilger II*).[82] Who the scribe of this version was remains unknown. In 1499 the tract was reprinted. Not divided into sermons, it presented the pilgrim's nineteen characteristics, but sequenced them differently than *Pilger I*; it ended with the pilgrim's return to his fatherland.[83] Together with other sermon cycles and single sermons, which the preacher had given in Strasbourg convents, a tract concerning the Christian pilgrim was published in the collection *Predigten teütsch* in Augsburg in 1508 by Hans Otmar, reprinting a shorter version of 1494 (*Pilger III*). Several manuscripts containing parts of the later printed *Predigten teütsch* and authenticated as Geiler's word, were transmitted around 1500 in female convents in Strasbourg, Colmar, and Freiburg.[84]

In 1489 Johannes Geiler chose again the figure of the Christian pilgrim as a topic for a cycle of sermons, this time held at St. Magdalena in Strasbourg. These were noted down by a group of nuns in a manuscript, which recorded twenty-three sermons, laying out the nineteen characteristics of the pilgrim, but leaving the cycle unfinished without him returning home. This fourth version (*Pilger IV*) seems to have circulated in other convents in the Upper

---

80 See the synopsis in Voltmer, *Wie der Wächter auf dem Turm*, pp. 1019–23.
81 Geiler von Kaysersberg, *Johannes Geiler von Kaysersberg*, ed. by Freienhagen-Baumgardt and Williams-Krapp, pp. xxvii–xxxiii.
82 Richard Muther, *Die deutsche Bücherillustration der Gothik und Frührenaissance (1460–1530)* (München: Hirth, 1922), p. 36.
83 See Geiler von Kaysersberg, *Johannes Geiler von Kaysersberg*, ed. by Bauer, I (1989), 494–503. Bauer counts only eighteen characteristics, leaving out his return home.
84 Geiler von Kaysersberg, *Johannes Geiler von Kaysersberg*, ed. by Bauer, II (1991), 757–70; Geiler von Kaysersberg, *Johannes Geiler von Kaysersberg*, ed. by Freienhagen-Baumgardt and Williams-Krapp, p. xi; Kraume, *Die Gerson-Übersetzungen*, pp. 107–21.

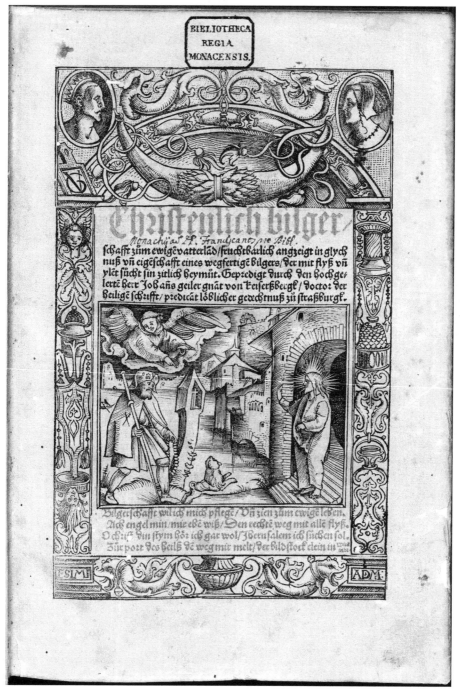

FIGURE 8. Title page of *Pilgerschaft*, published by Jakob Otter (Basel: Adam Petri, 1512) (VD16 G 727; copy München, Bayerische Staatsbibliothek, Res/2 P.lat. 874).

INSTRUCTIO, CORRECTIO, AND REFORMATIO   389

Rhineland, as at least two copies have survived, one most probably stemming from St. Nikolaus in undis, whereas the other was sent to St. Ursula in Augsburg.[85]

During the Lenten cycle of the year 1500 Geiler again took up the topic of the Christian pilgrimage, after he had exegeted Brant's *Narrenschiff* during the fasting times of 1498 and 1499. He extended the topic, so that its fifty-one sermons were able to fill the whole Lent, even stretching beyond. This time, the pilgrim was described in twenty-five characteristics, closing with an additional sermon on Sunday *Cantate*. Some characteristics were divided into sub-categories. Johannes Geiler took down Latin notes about the sermons in his journals, as he was accustomed to do.

Around 1512 Jakob Otter started to publish the Lenten cycle of 1500 in the vernacular (*Pilgerschaft*; see Figure 8). He had at hand only Geiler's sermon journals with the latter's Latin notes, together with a manuscript concerning those sermons, which the preacher had held at St. Magdalena in 1489 (*Pilger IV*) and which must have been the template for the version, preserved at St. Nikolaus in undis. Otter's edition was thought of as reading sermons for members of the laity, lacking too many learned references that would have been useful only for preachers and clerics. However, the print needed signs of orality to strengthen the air of a sermon given by Geiler. In creating a certain 'predication fiction', Otter organized the cycle into twenty-five chapters on the respective qualities of the pilgrim, leaving out the structure of the daily-preached sermons.[86] Close reading has revealed that to complete the material he had used the manuscript from St. Magdalena, which, indeed, contained many traces of orality. The result was a mere virtual construction, wherein Otter had transferred the preaching situation from St. Magdalena to the Cathedral, simulating Geiler in communication with the audience there.

In 1513 Otter published a Latinised version of this very Lenten cycle (*Peregrinus*). This time, the version was directed at learned men, clerics, and preachers. It followed the daily routine of the fasting period and included references for further reading from other preaching manuals. It is not yet clear whether and to what extent the preaching situation from the St. Magdalena convent, preserved in *reportationes* had been used in this Latinised version. Incidentally, Otter used the same techniques in re-constructing Geiler's Lenten cycle on the so-called *Schiff der Penitenz*, published in a Latinised (*Navicula penitentie*, printed in 1511) and a vernacular version (printed in 1514).[87] The Latin print was subdivided into 118 sermons, which served as model sermons,

---

85 See Berlin, Staatsbibliothek zu Berlin, Preußischer Kulturbesitz, MS germ. qu. 163, and Karlsruhe, Badische Landesbibliothek Donaueschingen, MS 294; Voltmer, *Wie der Wächter auf dem Turm*, p. 991.

86 Voltmer, *Wie der Wächter auf dem Turm*, pp. 991–95. On 'predication fiction', see Thom Mertens, 'De Middelnederlandse preek: een voorbarige synthese', in *De Middelnederlandse preek*, ed. by Thom Mertens, Patricia Stoop, and Christoph Burger, Middeleeuwse Studies en Bronnen, 116 (Hilversum: Verloren, 2009), pp. 9–66 (pp. 10, 17, 63).

87 Voltmer, *Wie der Wächter auf dem Turm*, pp. 985, 999–1000.

whereas the vernacular text of 1514 was made for lay people and religious for reading, structured along the lines of the thirty-three qualities of the *Schiff der Penitenz*. Otter re-used text passages from the vernacular *Pilgerschaft* (1512) to fill in the gaps in Geiler's notes. In here, he strictly followed the preaching agenda of Geiler, who had recycled parts of the Lenten cycle on the Christian pilgrimage to bolster his exegesis of the *Schiff der Penitenz*.

The Printer's and the Artist's Workshop

Not less than a third of the book market in Strasbourg was occupied in publishing texts from Geiler, Wimpfeling, or Brant. Much of their printed work was illustrated by woodcuts, which were added for different reasons.[88] Sometimes the images served only to structure the text and for pure decoration. Sometimes the images added a new dimension of meaning by stimulating the reader's imagination; at other times, they enabled the illiterate to participate. Some woodcuts showed complicated allegories that needed further knowledge to be interpreted. Others had purely explanatory, didactic functions. The connection between text and image thus varied between pure decoration and a symbiosis with a new level of meaning. Moreover, frontispieces were intended to stimulate purchases.[89] Geiler knew about the emotion-triggering effect of the image. In the pulpit and in instructing the simple lay people as well as women religious he stimulated their imaginary and their memory with lively allegories and ecphrasis. As a master in the *ars memorativa* and imagery, he pointed to visible, explicable pictures, for instance, by including in his interpretation the wall paintings and statues in the Cathedral.[90] In doing so, he explained the woodcuts and paintings as figurative examples.[91] He may even have brought books like Brant's *Narrenschiff* into the pulpit.[92] Additionally, the doctor evoked powerful images to explain the invisible, for example, in describing the horrors of death or the torments of Christ's Passion.[93] Geiler held the position that a simple Christian did indeed need images to contemplate. However, the further a person ascended in contemplation, the less he or she needed visual

---

88 Günthart, *Deutschsprachige Literatur*, pp. 59–61.

89 Honemann, *Deutsche Literatur*, pp. 274–77.

90 Voltmer, *Wie der Wächter auf dem Turm*, pp. 205–17, 261, 405; Helga Schüppert, 'Geiler von Kaysersberg: ein Beitrag zur Imagologie der Predigt', in *Albertus Magnus und der Albertismus: deutsche philosophische Kultur des Mittelalters*, ed. by Maarten J. F. M. Hoenen and Alain de Libera, Studien und Texte zur Geistesgeschichte des Mittelalters, 48 (Leiden: Brill, 1995), pp. 333–52.

91 Mertens, '*figuren und gemelt*', pp. 248–56.

92 Geiler used different versions of Brant's *Narrenschiff* in his sermons; see Mertens, '*figuren und gemelt*', pp. 246–47.

93 Volker Honemann, 'Der Tod bei Geiler von Kaysersberg', in *Zeit, Tod und Ewigkeit in der Renaissance-Literatur*, ed. by James Hogg, Analecta Cartusiana, 117, 3 vols (Salzburg: Institut für Anglistik und Amerikanistik, 1987), I, 90–107 (pp. 96–97).

support. On the contrary, one had to avoid too strong figurative imaginings, because spiritual delving into a naked Christ hanging on the cross or into the beauty of the Virgin Mary could provoke the opposite: sinful thinking. More than once Geiler harshly criticized the new visual art in painting female saints in revealing contemporary clothing, which could have sparked the fantasy of young priests.[94] Johannes Geiler therefore adopted a thoroughly ambivalent attitude towards the painted or printed image. Depending on the case, it could support the written word or contradict it and nullify its effect. Unfortunately, however, we know nothing about whether he influenced the visual decoration of his printed sermons in any way. Yet, the publication of his works employed a remarkable number of artists, such as Hans Burgkmair the Elder (1473–1531), Urs Graf the Elder (1485–1528), Hans Baldung Grien (1484/85–1545), and Hans Schäuffelin (1480/85–1538/40).[95] For example, *Granatapfel*, published first in 1510 in Augsburg by Hans Otmar, contained six frontispieces, introducing the respective fascicles, which most probably had been sold as single pieces.[96] The woodcuts had been orginally designed by Hans Burgkmair.[97] In 1511 (and 1516) the sermon collection was reprinted in Strasbourg by Johann Knoblouch. Hans Baldung Grien, since 1509 a citizen there, reproduced the woodcuts from Augsburg in his characteristic style.[98]

Apart from case studies, a thorough analysis of the relationship between image and text in the printings of Geiler's sermons is lacking so far.[99] A migration of images can be observed.[100] It has already been established that

---

94 See Annette Volfing, 'Geiler von Kaysersberg and Late Medieval Contemplative Practice: Gerson, Bridal Mysticism and the Force of the Imagination', *Oxford German Studies*, 43 (2014), 229–45; Voltmer, *Wie der Wächter auf dem Turm*, pp. 207–08, 261.

95 On the artists and pictorial decoration of Geiler's prints, see in general Maria Consuelo Oldenbourg, *Die Buchholzschnitte des Hans Baldung Grien: ein bibliographisches Verzeichnis ihrer Verwendung*, Studien zur deutschen Kunstgeschichte, 335 (Baden-Baden: Valentin Koerner, 1985); Maria Consuelo Oldenbourg, *Die Buchholzschnitte des Hans Schäufelein: ein bibliographisches Verzeichnis ihrer Verwendung, mit einem Anhang über Buchholzschnitte des Monogrammisten IS mit der Schaufel*, Text- und Bildband, Studien zur deutschen Kunstgeschichte, 340–41, 2 vols (Baden-Baden: Heitz, 1964); Muther, *Die deutsche Bücherillustration*; Paul Kristeller, *Die Strassburger Bücher-Illustration im xv. und im Anfange des xvi. Jahrhunderts*, Beiträge zur Kunstgeschichte, n.s. 7 (Leipzig: Bär & Hermann, 1888).

96 Apart from several cycles and a single sermon by Geiler, *Granatapfel* contains two texts from different authors; Voltmer, *Wie der Wächter auf dem Turm*, pp. 972–73.

97 See Muther, *Die deutsche Bücherillustration*, p. 133, who counts only five woodcuts, missing the frontispieces of *Sieben Schwerter*.

98 Muther, *Die deutsche Bücherillustration*, pp. 212 and 219, assumes a reprint of *Granatapfel* by Johannes Grüninger in 1510, followed by a third edition by Knoblouch. This assumption is wrong; Muther's Grüninger version never existed.

99 For the illustrations of Geiler's so-called sermons on witchcraft, see Voltmer, 'Preaching on Witchcraft?'; Voltmer, 'Du discours à l'allegorie'. For the illustrations in Geiler's *Narrenschiff* and in the second print of *Navicula fatuorum* (1511), see Schüppert, 'Geiler von Kaysersberg', and Mertens, '*figuren und gemelt*'.

100 See in general Rita Voltmer, 'Wissen, Medien und die Wahrheit: Überlegungen zu Transfer-prozessen von Hexenwissen', in *Hexenwissen: zum Transfer von Magie- und Zauberei-*

in some prints there is only a very loose link between text and image, while other prints seem to contain carefully coordinated illustration programmes.[101] The policy of the printers remains to be observed here. Whether and to what extent a text was decorated with images that explained, commented on or reproduced the written word depended on many conditions, for instance, whether suitable woodcuts were already available or whether the budget allowed for the production of new ones. A print could thus be decorated with woodcuts by different artists. Printers used images several times in different contexts. Printing blocks were borrowed from each other, sold or copied.[102] A common rule — the vernacular prints were illustrated, the Latin ones were not — cannot be established, because the extent and quality of the visual decoration depended on the particular printer.

Since 1508 Matthias Schürer had brought a significant number of Geiler's sermons, edited by Jakob Otter, to print. He was contested by his Strasbourg colleague Johannes Grüninger, who with the help of Muling in 1508 had already published a highly disputed collection of Geiler's so-called *scommata*.[103] Grüninger announced that he would start publishing the preacher's *Opera omnia*, starting in 1512 with the so-called collection *Himmelfahrt Mariens*, containing one sermon on the Virgin Mary's Assumption and three on her Immaculate Conception. Johannes Pauli had written the sermons down; they were reprinted in a shortened version in the *Evangelienbuch* of 1515. In 1513 the print of *Heilsame Predigt* followed, the German version of Geiler's synodal sermon (1482), translated by Wimpfeling. In there the preacher had announced his reform agenda.[104] Grüninger may also have taken over the main business from Matthias Schürer in 1514 in reprinting one of the latter's respective editions (*Irrig Schaf*).[105] In the following years until 1521, Grüninger employed Pauli, Muling, and other unnamed contributors to provide him either with reconstructed Geiler sermons, based on *reportationes*, or translations of

---

Imaginationen in interdisziplinärer Perspektive, ed. by Heinz Sieburg, Rita Voltmer, and Britta Weimann, Trierer Hexenprozesse, 9 (Trier: Paulinus, 2017), pp. 3–46 (pp. 28–32).

101 Kristeller, *Die Strassburger Bücher-Illustration*, pp. 35–36.

102 Oldenbourg, *Die Buchholzschnitte des Hans Baldung Grien*, pp. 152–55.

103 The print was stopped by the magistrate and — after its revision — reprinted in 1509; Voltmer, *Wie der Wächter auf dem Turm*, pp. 98–99.

104 See Charles Schmidt, *Répertoire bibliographique Strasbourgeois jusque vers 1530*, I: *Jean Grüninger 1483–1531* (Strasbourg: Heitz & Mündel, 1894); Schmidt, *Histoire littéraire de l'Alsace*, II, 373. Grüninger made this announcement in the colophon of *Schiff des Heils*, a short version of *Navicula penitentie*, produced by Johann Eck. On Grüninger's printing office, see Schmidt, *Zur Geschichte*, pp. 112–18; Reske, *Die Buchdrucker*, pp. 948–49; Catarina Zimmermann-Homeyer, *Illustrierte Frühdrucke lateinischer Klassiker um 1500: innovative Illustrationskonzepte aus der Straßburger Offizin Johannes Grüningers und ihrer Wirkung*, Wolfenbütteler Abhandlungen zur Renaissanceforschung, 36 (Wiesbaden: Harrasowitz, 2018).

105 See Reske, *Die Buchdrucker*, pp. 953–54.

INSTRUCTIO, CORRECTIO, AND REFORMATIO   393

already published material.[106] Obviously, Grüninger tried to dominate the book market and thus preferred to publish the sermons in the vernacular, decorated lavishly with images of high quality.[107] His general impact on the art of book illustrations has to be emphasized. In particular, the illustrations in Geiler's great cycle on Death and the *ars moriendi*, printed in 1514 (Latinised) and 1521 (vernacular), influenced the visual presentations of the *Dance of Death* in general.[108] To complete his collection of Geiler's sermons, Grüninger even printed Latin or Latinised samples of sermons, given to him by Jakob Biethen and the latter's client Peter Wickram. Why Johannes Grüninger had given his permission to print Wickram's polemics against Pauli and Muling remains an enigma, since the defamed works had been printed in his own workshop.

Up to 1522 many print shops in the Upper Rhineland looked out for Geiler's sermons in the vernacular as well as in Latin. The prints fed the increasing hunger of the urban citizens not only for catechetical texts, but also likewise for entertainment. We may assume that the prints promoted further religious discussions. Yet, the printers' business with Geiler's sermons did not last for long, because in 1522 Lutheran preaching started in the Cathedral of Strasbourg. Between 1523 and 1547, the Reformation process, adopted by the magistrate, changed the printers' business as well as the desires and needs of the readers. Henceforth, the transmission of new ideas became the focus of the printers' policy. Even the Catholic Johannes Grüninger gave up his plans of editing Geiler's collected works any further. Instead, he took a stand against the Protestant Reformation and focussed on the works of anti-Lutheran polemics.

Geiler's sermons were not entirely forgotten. Slowly, but consistently, a 'Protestantisation' of the preacher's words and deeds started, a remarkable process of rewriting history, which construction has yet to be traced in detail. As part of this Protestant invention of tradition, texts stemming

---

106 In 1514: *Lebkuchen* (translation made by Muling of the Latinised version *Fragmenta passionis*), *Sermones prestantissimi* (based on Geiler's journals, made by Jakob Biethen); *Irrig Schaf* (a reprint of 1510, made by Schürer); in 1515: *Evangelienbuch* (*reportationes* by Johannes Pauli, reprinted in revised versions in 1517 and 1522); in 1516 *Ameise* (*reportationes* by Pauli, reprinted in 1517); in 1517: *Brösamlin* (*reportationes* by Johannes Pauli); in 1518: *Sünden des Munds* (*reportationes* by Johannes Pauli); *Baum der Seligkeit* (a reprint from 1512, by an unknown printer); *Sermones et varii tractatus* (based on Geiler's journals, made by Peter Wickram); in 1520: *Narrenschiff* (translation by Pauli); *Drei Marien* (*reportationes* by an unknown woman); 1521: *De arbore humana* (translation and *reportationes* by an unknown editor).

107 The artist, who signed with HF, illustrated *Brösamlin* (with sixteen woodcuts) and *Sünden des Munds* (with ten woodcuts); his images were, indeed, illustrations and interpretations of the text, not mere decoration; see Muther, *Die deutsche Bücherillustration*, p. 263. Muther very often misreads the year of printing.

108 The Lutheran Niklaus Manuel, poet, artist, and magistrate in Bern, in 1516/17 painted the famous Dance of Death, which was highly influenced by the illustrations from *Sermones prestantissimi*; see Wilfried Kettler, *Der Berner Totentanz des Niklaus Manuel: Philologische, epigraphische sowie historische Überlegungen zu einem Sprach- und Kunstdenkmal der frühen Neuzeit* (Frankfurt am Main: Lang, 2009), p. 67.

from Geiler were settled and printed in a Reformation context. In 1543, for example, a satirical anti-Catholic dialogue was reprinted. The text had been written in 1526 by Niklaus Manuel (1484–1530) from Bern, who was well acquainted with Geiler's sermons. The dialogue, which could be performed as a Shrovetide play, took place among a young maiden, her mother, and several clerical seducers, who wanted to lure her into a nunnery.[109] Most significantly, in the 1543 print, the satire went along with Geiler's so-called *Sendtbrief*, a reading sermon of introduction, which he had sent to the Magdalens in Freiburg in 1499. Léon Dacheux (1835–1903) assumed that the *Sendtbrieff* had been printed by Bartholomeus Grüninger, son of Johannes, in Colmar.[110] Neither Dacheux nor Bauer has contested its originality, but it remains entirely unknown how it found its way to be printed together with Manuel's dialogue. However, published in the context of an anti-Catholic attack, Geiler's instructions for maintaining a strict observant conduct in female houses religious supported Manuel's harsh critics. In 1574 the Lutheran pastor Nicolaus Höniger (1548–1598) published in Basel Brant's and Geiler's versions of the *Narrenschiff* as a kind of synopsis. Neither text kept its original wording; instead, they were coloured by Lutheranism.[111]

The 'Protestantisation' of Johannes Geiler went on. Daniel Specklin (1536–1589), the famous Strasbourgian fortification builder, announced Geiler in his chronicle, written in 1587, to be one of the forerunners of Martin Luther (1483–1546). Specklin was an adamant Protestant chronographer, born twenty-six years after Geiler's death. He falsified facts, dates, and the conditions of the preacher's life, and invented sermons. His aim was to turn Geiler into a Church Father of Protestantism, a figure most desired by Lutherans in their search for tradition and legitimation. The project of redesigning Geiler bore fruit because in 1597 and 1598 the Lutheran pastor David Wolder (d. 1604) published a version of the preacher's famous *Trostspiegel*, now in the Low German vernacular.[112] Ironically, the Protestant inventors of tradition were backed by the Roman Catholic Church: in 1520, Jakob Otter had converted to Lutheranism, and thus Geiler's sermons, which had been edited by his secretary, were listed in 1559 amongst the forbidden books on the papal *Index librorum prohibitorum*. A revision in 1564 took Geiler's sermon collections

---

109 Jakob Bächtold, *Bibliothek älterer Schriftwerke der deutschen Schweiz und ihres Grenzgebietes*, II: *Niklaus Manuel* (Frauenfeld: J. Huber, 1878), pp. clviii–clxvi.

110 See Geiler von Kaysersberg, *Johannes Geiler von Kaysersberg*, ed. by Bauer, I (1989), xxxv; Johannes Geiler von Kayserberg, *Die ältesten Schriften Geilers von Kaysersberg*, ed. by Léon Dacheux (Freiburg im Breisgau: Herder'sche Verlagshandlung, 1882), pp. cxxix, 209–24.

111 See Mertens, 'figuren und gemelt', p. 247; Joachim Hamm, 'Narren mit *Außlegung*: zum *Welt Spiegel oder Narren Schiffe* (Basel 1574) des Nikolaus Höniger von Königshofen', in *Traditionelles und Innovatives in der geistlichen Literatur des Mittelalters*, ed. by Jens Haustein and others, *Meister-Eckhart-Jahrbuch*, Beiheft 7 (Stuttgart: Kohlhammer, 2019), pp. 407–26.

112 See Geiler von Kaysersberg, *Johannes Geiler von Kaysersberg*, ed. by Bauer, I (1989), 530–32. These prints seem to be lost.

INSTRUCTIO, CORRECTIO, AND REFORMATIO   395

under his own name from the *Index*. Again in 1590 the work of the famous preacher, who had defended the privileges and doctrines of the Catholic Church so very bitterly, returned to the *Index* and remained there until the year 1900.[113] Up to the nineteenth century, Catholic editors such as Johann Caspar Bencard (1649–1720), Abbé Léon Dacheux or the canon Philipp de Lorenzi (1818–1898) had to ask permission to edit the preacher's sermons.

The Aftermath

Johann Caspar Bencard, who maintained print shops in Dillingen and Augsburg, tried again in 1708 to publish a significant set of Geiler's sermons, who was still seen to be a famous preacher at that time.[114] Two volumes appeared on the book market, which contained the supplemented and revised vernacular versions of the *Narrenschiff* and the *Schiff der Penitenz*.[115] During the twentieth century, besides Johann Scheible's (1809–1866) reprint of Höniger's Protestant version of Brant's and Geiler's *Narrenschiff*,[116] some French and German Catholics, mostly clerics, attempted to publish selections of Geiler's sermons.[117] The reasons for this renewed interest in the Cathedral preacher must probably be seen as an attempt to rehabilitate him as an arch-Catholic man of letters. Only Abbé Léon Dacheux, however, remained faithful to the original early modern prints, while others, especially Philipp de Lorenzi, canon of the Trier Cathedral, purged them of allegedly religious and morally obnoxious content.[118]

In 1912 the newly founded Society of Alsatian Literature (*Gesellschaft für Elsässische Literatur*) instructed the great expert in Alsatian Church history, Luzian Pfleger (1876–1944), to edit the complete work of Johannes Geiler, including prints and manuscripts.[119] Pfleger quickly had to realize that no notes

---

113 On Specklin and Geiler's 'Protestantisation', see Voltmer, *Wie der Wächter auf dem Turm*, pp. 51–52, 128–31; and Israel, *Johannes Geiler von Kaysersberg*, pp. 18–36.

114 On Bencard see Reske, *Die Buchdrucker*, pp. 170–71.

115 Johannes Geiler, *Fatuo-Sophia Caesare-Montana. Das ist: Die Kaysersbergische Narragonische Schiffahrt oder der so geannte Sittliche Narren-Spiegel [...]* (Augsburg & Dillingen: Johann Caspar Bencard, 1708); Johannes Geiler, *Geistliche Schiffahrt/ aus Schlaraffen und Welt-Affen-Land oder aus Narragonien zu dem geliebten und gelobten Land nacher Jerusalem/ Das ist Geistlich-Sittliches Buß-Schifflein zu dem Himmlischen Jerusalem [...]* (Augsburg & Dillingen: Johann Caspar Bencard, 1708).

116 Sebastian Brant and Johannes Geiler, 'Weltspiegel, oder Narrenschiff [...]', in *Das Kloster. Weltlich und geistlich. Meist aus der älteren deutschen Volks-, Wunder-, Curiositäten- und vorzugsweise komischen Literatur. Zur Kultur- und Sittengeschichte in Wort und Bild*, ed. by Johann Scheible, 12 vols (Stuttgart: Eigenverlag, 1845–1849), I (1845), 215–813.

117 See Voltmer, *Wie der Wächter auf dem Turm*, pp. 118–21, 1024–26.

118 Geiler von Kaysersberg, *Die ältesten Schriften*, ed. by Dacheux; Johannes Geiler von Kaysersberg, *Geiler von Kaisersberg: ausgewählte Schriften nebst einer Abhandlung über Geilers Leben und echte Schriften*, ed. by Philipp De Lorenzi, 4 vols (Trier: Ed. Groppe, 1881–1883).

119 The society pursued the highly ambitious plan to edit the *opera omnia* not only of Geiler

396   RITA VOLTMER

or transcripts from the hand of Geiler himself had survived. Moreover, some manuscripts containing sermon series from Strasbourg nunneries had been destroyed by the great fire in Strasbourg during the war of 1870/71.[120] As a stroke of luck during the seventeenth century, the collector Daniel Sudermann (1550–1631) had bought some volumes. *Inter alia* they contained sermons by Johannes Geiler.[121] From this stock, Pfleger published three previously unknown sermon series.[122] However, the First World War had put an end to all further efforts to produce a complete edition of the preacher's work. Pfleger nevertheless tried to continue in preparing the *Opera omnia*, but was finally convinced to abandon the project both because of the diversity of the textual tradition and the unresolved question of authenticity.[123]

In 1968 the linguist Gerhard Bauer signed a contract to edit Geiler's *Opera omnia* in approximately eight volumes.[124] However, he had underestimated both the quantity and the complicated textual tradition of Geiler's works. His editorial work was constrained by narrow text-critical requirements. Some reviewers harshly criticized Bauer for attempting to cling to the anachronistic textual concept of originality that necessitated elaborate variant apparatuses.[125] Bauer expanded his schedule to at least thirteen volumes including several sub volumes. The first volume appeared in 1989, but for lack of funding the editing finished in 1995 with only three volumes published. Already in 1990 Volker Mertens and Hans-Jochen Schiewer had initiated a project to edit in four volumes a repertory of medieval unprinted sermons in the vernacular.[126]

---

but also of Sebastian Brant, Thomas Murner, and Johann Fischart; Ernst von Borries, *Erster Jahresbericht der Gesellschaft für Elsässische Literatur* (Strasbourg: n.p., 1912), pp. 2, 4.

120 See Luzian Pfleger, 'Zur handschriftlichen Überlieferung Geilerscher Predigttexte', *Archiv für Elsässische Kirchengeschichte*, 6 (1931), 195–205; Gustav Friedrich Haenel, *Catalogi librorum manuscriptorum, qui in bibliothecis Galliae, Helvetiae, Belgii, Britaniae M., Hispaniae, Lusitaniae asservantur* (Leipzig: Sumtibus I. C. Hinrichs, 1830), pp. 466–67. Pfleger (and in following him, Voltmer) deciphered Geiler's sermons on the 7 *Peinen der geistlichen Höllen* erroneously to 'Von Sieben Steinen der geistlichen Höllen'; Pfleger, 'Zur handschriftlichen Überlieferung', p. 195; Voltmer, *Wie der Wächter auf dem Turm*, p. 111.

121 Hans Hornung, *Daniel Sudermann als Handschriftensammler: ein Beitrag zur Strassburger Bibliotheksgeschichte* (unpublished doctoral dissertation, Universität Tübingen, 1956).

122 Luzian Pfleger, '"Von den zwölf schefflin": eine unbekannte Predigt Geilers von Kaysersberg', *Archiv für Elsässische Kirchengeschichte*, 6 (1931), 206–16; Luzian Pfleger, '"Von den xv aest": eine unbekannte Predigt Geilers von Kaysersberg', *Archiv für Elsässische Kirchengeschichte*, 10 (1935), 139–51; Luzian Pfleger, '"Von der artt der kind": eine unedierte Predigt Geilers von Kaysersberg', *Archiv für Elsässische Kirchengeschichte*, 15 (1941/42), 129–48.

123 Pfleger, 'Der Franziskaner Johannes Pauli', p. 50.

124 See Gerhard Bauer, 'Johannes Geiler von Kaysersberg, ein Problemfall für Drucker, Herausgeber, Verleger, Wissenschaft und Wissenschaftsförderung', *Daphnis*, 23 (1994), 559–89.

125 Mertens, 'Authentisierungsstrategien', pp. 83–84.

126 The sermon collection in the Staatsbibliothek in Berlin houses around 3000 sermons, of which 2100 are not published yet; Schiewer, 'German Sermons in the Middle Ages', pp. 885–91; Volker Mertens and Hans-Jochen Schiewer, 'Erschließung einer Gattung: Edition, Katalogisierung und Abbildung der deutschsprachigen Predigt des Mittelalters', *Editio*, 4 (1990), 93–111. The first volume has been announced as *Repertorium der*

INSTRUCTIO, CORRECTIO, AND REFORMATIO

This most important and well-designed project was partly based on the famous collection of Daniel Sudermann, now in Berlin, Staatsbibliothek zu Berlin, Preußischer Kulturbesitz, which contained sermon manuscripts from the Strasbourg observant Dominican nunnery St. Nikolaus in undis. Geiler had regularly served as spiritual adviser and preacher there.[127] Unfortunately, none of the planned volumes made it into print, but parts of the project's outcome are available in an online database, while other parts are accessible on demand and are circulating in the community of medieval sermon researchers.[128] At least in 2015, the critical edition appeared of those sermons delivered by Johannes Geiler during his stay in Augsburg in 1488/89.[129] In light of this still open-ended history of Geiler's *Opera omnia edited*, anybody who wants to study his sermons has to use the early modern prints and manuscripts. Admittedly, with a few exceptions and apart from the edited sermons by Bauer, Geiler's sermons both in manuscripts and early modern prints can easily be downloaded in digitized form. However, these formats do not make up for the lack of a critical edition that is indispensible for interdisciplinary sermon studies.

Conclusion

During more than thirty years of preaching, instruction, and battling for reform, Johannes Geiler produced various forms of texts, translations, tracts, sermons, or *gravamina*. He definitely used the printing press to spread his ideas of politico-religious reform and of spiritual education. The transmission of his sermons had been a very complex operation in different interrelated areas of work, undertaken with different interests and following different aims. Finally, a few points need to be stressed again.

A clear distinction between the use of either Latin or the vernacular cannot be drawn: Geiler's duties obliged him to preach in the Cathedral as well as in convents, mostly in the vernacular, but very seldom in Latin. He wrote down the notes of these sermons in his journals, mostly in Latin, but sometimes in the vernacular. Women religious, secular priests such as the cleric Peter

---

ungedruckten deutschsprachigen Predigten des Mittelalters: der Berliner Bestand, Band I: *Die Handschriften aus dem Straßburger Dominikanerinnenkloster St. Nikolaus in undis und benachbarte Provenienzen,* , ed. by Volker Mertens and Hans-Jochen Schiewer.

127 See Andreas Rüther and Hans-Jochen Schiewer, 'Die Predigthandschriften des Straßburger Dominikanerinnenklosters St. Nikolaus in undis: historischer Bestand, Geschichte, Vergleich in *Die deutsche Predigt im Mittelalter,* ed. by Volker Mertens (Tübingen: Niemeyer, 1992), pp. 169–93.

128 PiK (Predigt im Kontext): pik.ku-eichstaett.de [accessed 21 June 2022]. Thanks to Volker Mertens, who allowed me access to those parts of the repertory that referred to Geiler's sermons, I was able to include this vital information in my dissertation.

129 Geiler von Kaysersberg, *Johannes Geiler von Kaysersberg,* ed. by Freienhagen-Baumgardt and Williams-Krapp.

Wickram, or the Franciscan mendicant Pauli, and many unknown reporters either worked with these journals or wrote down the preacher's words directly from his lips, noting them either in the vernacular or in Latin. Geiler himself supervised many editions, based on the vernacular notes of women religious or on his own Latin journals. Printers and artists wanted to share the profit in publishing the word of the famous doctor. Whilst the Latin texts were mainly aiming at the learned men of the clergy, like students, theologians, or preachers, the vernacular prints looked for buyers amongst the laity with their need for catechetical uplifting and entertainment. Alongside the prints, manuscripts of Geiler's sermons were still circulating in the religious houses in the Upper Rhineland. Some sermons were thus transmitted in parallel versions, based on *reportationes*, translations, and his own journals. Other sermons were split up with their parts printed in different collections. The inserted signs of orality sometimes stemmed from the original, sometimes from another preaching situation. Sermons from convents were mixed with those from the Cathedral.

The fluid orality of Geiler's sermons is lost. The once spoken word was stabilized in written texts and in images. On many levels, the word shifted from orality to textuality, combined with the visuality of the woodcuts. A blend between different levels of interpretation and re-interpretation opened up, which affected the different social and religious milieux, in which this blend was consumed. We do not know how far the impact of editors and printers went in re-constructing the doctor's word, but we have seen how Otter simulated lively preaching situations between Geiler and his respective audience. The re-interpretation of the preacher's word reached a new level of hype during his Protestantisation.

Sermon studies should not mourn about the preacher's lost spoken words, seeking them in signs of orality, which might be faked simply as tools of authentification. The history of how, why and in what context Geiler's sermons have been recorded, written down, illustrated, and printed is in itself a most important aspect in the history of creating and transmitting knowledge.

INSTRUCTIO, CORRECTIO, AND REFORMATIO

Appendix: The Non-Edited Printed Sermons of Johannes Geiler von Kaysersberg

The printed sermons, discussed above, here set out in chronological order, are cited with short titles in the text and its footnotes, with the short titles given below in square brackets.

Oratio habita in sinodo Argen. in presentia Episcopi et cleri [...] (Strasbourg: Heinrich Knoblochtzer, 1482) [*Oratio in Synodo*]

Arbor salutis anime. Ex vernacula lingua in latinum traducta foeliciter incipit (Frankfurt an der Oder: Martin Tretter, 1502) [*Arbor salutis anime*]

Passionis Christi unum ex quattuor evangelistis textum (Strasbourg: Johann Knoblouch, 1506, reprint in 1507) [*Passion*]

Fragmenta passionis domini nostri Jesu Christi. A celeberrimo (divini eloquii oratore) domino Joanne Geiler ex Keisersberg Theologo / sub typo placente mellee predicate. Per Jacobum Ottherum familiarem eius in hunc modum collecta (Strasbourg: Matthias Schürer, 1508) [*Fragmenta passionis*]

Margarita facetiarum [...] Scommata Joannis Keisersberg concionatoris Argentinensis [...] (Strasbourg: Johannes Grüninger, 1508; revised reprint under the title *Tropi D. Joannis Keisersbergii concionatoris ecclesie Argentinensis viri illuminatissimi foelicirer incipiunt*, 1509) [*Scommata*]

Celeberrimi sacrarum litterarum Doctoris Joannis Geiler Keisersbergii Argentinensium concionatoris bene meriti. De oratione dominica Sermones. Per Jacobum Ottherum nemetensem hac forma (Strasbourg: Matthias Schürer, 1509) [*De oratione dominica*]

Das buch Granatapfel. im latin genant Malogranatus. helt in ym gar vil und manig haylsam und süsser underweysung und leer / den anhebenden / auffnemenden und volkommen mennschen / mittsampt gaystlicher bedeütung des außganngs der kinder Israhel von Egipto. Item ain merkliche underrichtung der gaistlichen spinnerin / Item etlich predigen von dem hasen im pfeffer. Und von den siben schwertern / und schayden / nach gaistlicher außlegung. Meerers tails gepredigt durch den hochgeleerten doctor Johannem Gayler von Kaysersperg, etc. (Augsburg: Hans Otmar, 1510; reprint Strasbourg, Johann Knoblouch, 1511 and 1516) [*Granatapfel*]

Das Irrig Schafe. Das irrig Schafe Sagt von cleinmütigkeit und böser anfechtung. Der hellisch Lew Sagt uns von böser anfechtung. Christliche Künigin Von underscheid tödtlicher und teglicher sünden. Der dreyeckechte Spiegel der gebot / der beicht und wol sterben. Der Eschengrüdel Anfang der menschen in dem dienst gottes. Dz Clappermaul Sagt von der hinderred. Der Trostspiegel Des unvernünfftigen traurens. Gebredigt / und geteutschet / durch den wirdigen und hochgelerten Doctorem Johannes Geiler von Keisersberg / mitsampt den obbestimpten Tractäten (Strasbourg: Matthias Schürer, 1510; reprint Johannes Grüninger, 1514) [*Irrig Schaf*]

Navicula sive speculum fatuorum prestantissimi sacrarum literarum Doctoris Joannis Geyler Keysersbergii Concionatoris Argentinensis a Jacobo Othero collecta.

Comprendio vitae eiusdem descriptio per Beatum Rhenanum Selestantinum
(Strasbourg: Matthias Schürer, 1510; reprint Johannes Knoblouch, 1511)
[*Navicula fatuorum*]

Navicula Penitentie per excellentissimum sacre pagine doctorem Joannem Keyserspergium Argentinensium Concionatorem predicata A Jacobo Otthero Collecta
(Strasbourg: Matthias Schürer, 1511; reprinted several times) [*Navicula Penitentie*]

Christenlich bilgerschafft zuom ewigen vatterland / fruchtbarlich angzeigt in glychnuß und eigenschafft eines wegfertigen bilgers / der mit flyß und ylent suocht sin zitlich heymuot [...] (Basel: Adam Petri, 1512) [*Pilgerschaft*]

Des hochgelerten doctor Keiserspergs Alphabet in .xxiii. Predigen so er gethon und die geordnet hat an einen baum .xxiii. est ufzesteigen zuo ewigem leben gut zelesen und davon man wol gebessert mag werden (Strasbourg: Anonymous, 1512; reprint Johannes Grüninger, 1518) [*Baum der Seligkeit*]

Predig der himelfahrt Mariens. Dis seind vier predig von unser lieben Frawen. Eine seit von irer himmelfart / wie sie gott der herr geeret hatt / mit sibenerlei Eeren / Und in der aller letsten eeren / da würt ußgelegt ein frag an welchem ort im himelreich / gott mit allen seinen ußerwelten sein wonung hatt / Und uff welchem stuol / oder tron Maria sitz. Aber die andern dry predigen / sagen von dryerlei empfengnis Marie. Auch welche empfengnis under den dryen die christenlich kirch begat uff den tag irer empfengnis [...] (Strasbourg: Johannes Grüninger, 1512) [*Himmelfahrt Mariens*]

Ein heilsam kostliche Predig Doctor iohans geiler von Keisersperg predicanten der loblichen stat Straßburg Die er zuo bischoff Albrechten von Straßburg und andern erwirdigen prelaten / und seiner gantzen Ersamen priesterschafft vor zeiten gethon hat / ir und ires gesinds regiment und reformation antreffenuß wolgeziertem latein durch iacobum wimpfelingen darzuo durch grosse bit bwegt [sic] in tütsche sprach verwandt und trausferiert [sic] (Strasbourg: Johannes Grüninger, 1513) [*Heilsame Predigt*]

Peregrinus. Doctissimi sacre doctoris Joannis Geiler Keyserspergii Concionatoris Argentinensis celebratissimi a Jacobo Otthero discipulo sui congestus (Strasbourg: Matthias Schürer, 1513) [*Peregrinus*]

Doctor keiserspegrs [sic] passion Des Herren Jesu. Fürgeben und geprediget gar betrachtiglich (particuliert) und geteilt in stückes weiß eins süßen Lebkuochen ußzuogeben (per quadragesimam) als durch die gantze fasten allen tag wol ein Predig daruß zuonemen ist. Neulich uß dem latyn in tütsche sprach tranßveriert / durch Johannem Adelphum Physicum von Straßburg (Strasbourg: Johannes Grüninger, 1514) [*Lebkuchen*]

Das schiff der penitentz und buoßwürckung / gepredigt in dem hohen stifft / in unser lieben frauwen münster zuo Stroßburg [...] in teütsch gewendt vom latin / auß seiner aygnen handtgeschrifft (Augsburg: Hans Otmar, 1514) [*Schiff der Penitenz*]

Sermones prestantissimi sacrarum literarum Doctoris Joannis Geilerii Keiserspergii Concionatoris Argentinensis fructuosissimi de tempore et de sanctis accomodandi. De arbore humana. De xii excelentiis arboris crucifixi. De xii fructibus spiritus sancti. De xiii conditionibus mortis sub typo maioris villani arborum cesaris

dorfmeier. holtzmeier. De morte virtuali sive gratie De Dispositione ad felicem
mortem. De xxiii obsequiis mortuis impendendis que sermonibus de morte virtuali
annectuntur. (Strasbourg: Johannes Grüninger, 1514; reprint 1515) [*Sermones*
prestantissimi]

Das Evangelibuoch: Das buoch der Ewangelien durch das gantz iar / Mitt Predig
und Ußlegungen durch den wirdigen hochgelerten Doctor Johannes geiler von
Keisersperg [...] die er in seinen fier letsten Jare gepredigt hat. Und daz uß seinnem
mund von wort zuo wort geschriben (Strasbourg: Johannes Grüninger, 1515;
revised reprints in 1517 and 1522) [*Evangelienbuch*]

Doctor Keiserspergs pater noster. Des hochgelerten wurdigen predicanten der loblichen
statt Straßburg. Ußlegung / über das gebette des herren / so wir täglich sprechen.
Vatter unser der du bist in den hymeln, etc. (Strasbourg: Matthias Hupfuf, 1515)
[*Pater Noster*]

Die Emeis. Dis ist das buoch von der Omeissen [...] Und sagt von Eigenschafft der
Omeissen. Und gibt underweisung von den Unholden und Hexen / und von
gespenst der geist / und von dem Wütenden heer wunderbarlich und nützlich
zewissen / was man darvon glauben oder halten soll (Strasbourg: Johannes
Grüninger, 1516, reprinted in 1517) [*Ameise*]

Die Brösamlin doct. Keiserspergs uffgelesen von Frater Johann Paulin barfüser ordens.
Und sagt von den funfftzehen Hymelschen staffelen die Maria uff gestigen ist / und
gantz von den vier Leuwengeschrei. Auch von dem Wannenkromer / der Kauflüt
sunderlich hüpsche matery bei .lxii. predigen / nutzlich und guot den menschen die
dz lesen / on zweifel wol dardurch gebesseret werden. Hienach so folget ein gemeine
taffel uber den tractat genant Keiserspergs Brösamlin / puncten etlicher predigen /
die frater Johannes Pauli zuosamen gesamlet hat die in keinem tractat begriffen
seind [...] (Strasbourg: Johannes Grüninger, 1517) [*Brösamlin*]

Das buch der sünden des munds. Von dem hochgelerten Doctor Keysersperg / die er
nent die blatren am mund davon er xxix predigen und leeren gethon hat [...]
(Strasbourg: Johannes Grüninger, 1518) [*Sünden des Munds*]

Sermones et varii tractatus Keiserspergii iam recens excusi [...] (Strasbourg: Johannes
Grüninger, 1518) [*Sermones et varii tractatus*]

An dem Ostertag hat der hochgelert Doctor keisersperg geprediget von den dry marien
wie sie unsern heren iesum cristum wolten salben. Und von den mucken die unß
die salben verderben. Von den senffkörnlin. Und von den früchten des wolsterbens.
Angeschriben von einer ersamen iunckfrawen und die erbeten das sie sollchs in
den druck gelasen hat / in hoffnung zuo guot allen menschen [...] (Strasbourg:
Johannes Grüninger, 1520) [*Drei Marien*]

Des hochwirdigen doctor Keiserspergs narenschiff so er geprediget hat zuo straßburg
in der hohen stifft daselbst predicant der zeit .1498. dis gebrediget. Und uß latin
in tütsch bracht / darin vil weißheit ist zuo lernen und leert auch die narrenschel
hinweck werffen. ist nütz und guot alen menschen (Strasbourg: Johannes
Grüninger, 1520) [*Narrenschiff*]

Das buoch arbore humana. Von dem menschlichen Baum / Geprediget von dem hoch-
gelerten Doctor Johannes Keysersperg / darin geschicklich und in gottes lob zuo

lernen ist / des holtzmeyers des dotz / frölich zu warten / Einem yeden menschen nütz und guot (Strasbourg: Johannes Grüninger, 1521) [*De arbore humana*]

Doctor keiserspergs Postill: Uber die fyer Evangelia durchs jor / sampt dem Quadragesimal / und von ettlichen heyligen / newlich ußgangen (Strasbourg: Johannes Schott, 1522) [*Postille*]

Fatuo-Sophia Caesare-Montana. Das ist: Die Kaysersbergische Narragonische Schiffahrt oder der so genannte Sittliche Narren-Spiegel [...] (Augsburg & Dillingen: Johann Caspar Bencard, 1708)

Geistliche Schiffahrt/ aus Schlaraffen und Welt-Affen-Land oder aus Narragonien zu dem geliebten und gelobten Land nacher Jerusalem/ Das ist Geistlich-Sittliches Buß-Schifflein zu dem Himmlischen Jerusalem [...] (Augsburg & Dillingen: Johann Caspar Bencard, 1708)

Johannes Eck and Johannes Geiler, *Das Schiff des Heils auff das aller kürtzest hie uß geleget nach der Figur, die Doctor Johannes von Eck gemacht hat zu Ingolstat auß den predigten des wirdigen Herren doctor Johannes geiler on Keisersperg etwan Predicant zu Straßburg in dem Elsas* (Strasbourg: Johannes Grüninger, 1512) [*Schiff des Heils*]

Bibliography

Manuscripts

Berlin, Staatsbibliothek zu Berlin, Preußischer Kulturbesitz, MS germ. qu. 163
Karlsruhe, Badische Landesbibliothek Donaueschingen, MS 294

Primary Sources

The edited sermons of Geiler, discussed above, are cited with short titles in the text and its footnotes; the short titles are given in square brackets below.

Jakob Wimpfeling, *Jakob Wimpfeling: Briefwechsel*, ed. by Otto Herding and Dieter Mertens (München: Fink, 1990)

Jakob Wimpfeling, *Jakob Wimpfeling und Beatus Rhenanus: das Leben des Johannes Geiler von Kaysersberg*, ed. by Otto Herding (München: Fink, 1970)

Johannes Geiler von Kaysersberg, *Die ältesten Schriften Geilers von Kaysersberg*, ed. by Léon Dacheux (Freiburg im Breisgau: Herder'sche Verlagshandlung, 1882) [*Sendtbrief*]

Johannes Geiler von Kaysersberg, *Geiler von Kaisersberg: ausgewählte Schriften nebst einer Abhandlung über Geilers Leben und echte Schriften*, ed. by Philipp De Lorenzi, 4 vols (Trier: Ed. Groppe, 1881–1883)

Johannes Geiler von Kaysersberg, *Johannes Geiler von Kaysersberg: die Augsburger Predigten*, ed. by Kristina Freienhagen-Baumgardt and Werner Williams-Krapp, Deutsche Texte des Mittelalters, 92 (Berlin: De Gruyter, 2015) [*Pilger I*]

Johannes Geiler von Kaysersberg, *Johannes Geiler von Kaysersberg: sämtliche Werke,
1. Teil: die deutschen Schriften, Abt. 1: Die zu Geilers Lebzeiten erschienenen
Schriften*, ed. by Gerhard Bauer, Ausgaben deutscher Literatur des 15. bis 18.
Jahrhunderts, 3 vols (Berlin: De Gruyter, 1989–1995) [*Beichtgedicht, Heilsame
Lehre, Passion, Pilger II, Romfahrt, Sterbe-Abc, Totenbüchlein, Trostspiegel;
Predigten teütsch, Berg des Schauens, Pilger III, Zacheus; Seelenparadies*]

Peter Schott, *The Works of Peter Schott (1460–1490)*, I: *Introduction and Text*, II:
Commentary, ed. by Murray A. Cowie and Marian L. Cowie, 2 vols (Chapel
Hill: University of North Carolina Press, 1963–1971)

Pfleger, Luzian, '"Von den XV aest": eine unbekannte Predigt Geilers von Kaysersberg', *Archiv für Elsässische Kirchengeschichte*, 10 (1935), 139–51

Pfleger, Luzian, '"Von den zwölf schefflin": eine unbekannte Predigt Geilers von
Kaysersberg', *Archiv für Elsässische Kirchengeschichte*, 6 (1931), 206–16

Pfleger, Luzian, '"Von der artt der kind": eine unedierte Predigt Geilers von
Kaysersberg', *Archiv für Elsässische Kirchengeschichte*, 15 (1941/42), 129–48

Sebastian Brant and Johannes Geiler, 'Weltspiegel, oder Narrenschiff [...]',
in *Das Kloster. Weltlich und geistlich. Meist aus der älteren deutschen Volks-,
Wunder-, Curiositäten- und vorzugsweise komischen Literatur. Zur Kultur- und
Sittengeschichte in Wort und Bild*, ed. by Johann Scheible, 12 vols (Stuttgart:
Selbstverlag, 1845–1849), I (1845), 215–813

Secondary Studies

Bächtold, Jakob, *Bibliothek älterer Schriftwerke der deutschen Schweiz und ihres
Grenzgebietes*, II: *Niklaus Manuel* (Frauenfeld: J. Huber, 1878)

Bauer, Gerhard, 'Johannes Geiler von Kaysersberg, ein Problemfall für Drucker,
Herausgeber, Verleger, Wissenschaft und Wissenschaftsförderung', *Daphnis*, 23
(1994), 559–89

Bauer, Gerhard, 'Die Predigten Johannes Geilers von Kaysersberg über Sebastian
Brants *Narrenschiff* und ihre Überlieferung durch Jakob Otthers *Navicula
Fatuorum* (1510) und Johannes Paulis *Narrenschiff* (1520)', in *Sébastian
Brant, son époque et 'La Lef des fols'*, ed. by Gonthier-Louis Fink, Collection
Recherches germaniques, 5 (Strasbourg: Presses universitaire de Strasbourg,
1995), pp. 96–113

Bériou, Nicole, *L'Avènement des maîtres de parole: la prédication à Paris au XIIIe siècle*,
Collection des études augustiniennes: Série Moyen Âge et Temps modernes,
31–32, 2 vols (Turnhout: Brepols, 1998)

Borries, Ernst von, *Erster Jahresbericht der Gesellschaft für Elsässische Literatur*
(Strasbourg: n. p., 1912)

Duntze, Oliver, *Ein Verleger sucht sein Publikum: die Straßburger Offizin des Matthias
Hupfuff (1497/98–1520)*, Archiv für Geschichte des Buchwesens, 4 (München:
Saur, 2007)

Günthart, Romy, *Deutschsprachige Literatur im frühen Basler Buchdruck
(ca. 1470–1510)*, Studien und Texte zum Mittelalter und zur frühen Neuzeit, 11
(Münster: Waxmann, 2007)

Haenel, Gustav Friedrich, *Catalogi librorum manuscriptorum, qui in bibliothecis Galliae, Helvetiae, Belgii, Britaniae M., Hispaniae, Lusitaniae asservantur* (Leipzig: Sumtibus I. C. Hinrichs, 1830)

Hamm, Joachim, 'Narren mit *Außlegung*: zum *Welt Spiegel oder Narren Schiffe* (Basel 1574) des Nikolaus Höniger von Königshofen', in *Traditionelles und Innovatives in der geistlichen Literatur des Mittelalters*, ed. by Jens Haustein and others, *Meister-Eckhart-Jahrbuch*, Beiheft 7 (Stuttgart: Kohlhammer, 2019), pp. 407–26

Hirbodian, Sigrid, 'Pastors and Seducers: The Practice of the *Cura monialium* in Mendicant Convents in Strasbourg', in *Partners in Spirit: Women, Men, and Religious Life in Germany, 1100–1500*, ed. by Fiona J. Griffiths and Julie Hotchin, Medieval Women: Texts and Contexts, 24 (Turnhout: Brepols, 2014), pp. 303–37

Honemann, Volker, *Deutsche Literatur in der Laienbibliothek der Basler Kartause 1480–1520*, Studien und Texte zum Mittelalter und zur frühen Neuzeit, 22 (unpublished Habilitationsschrift Freie Universität Berlin, 1982; revised print Münster: Waxmann, 2020)

Honemann, Volker, 'Der Tod bei Geiler von Kaysersberg', in *Zeit, Tod und Ewigkeit in der Renaissance-Literatur*, ed. by James Hogg, Analecta Cartusiana, 117, 3 vols (Salzburg: Institut für Anglistik und Amerikanistik, 1987), pp. 90–107

Hornung, Hans, *Daniel Sudermann als Handschriftensammler: ein Beitrag zur Strassburger Bibliotheksgeschichte* (unpublished doctoral dissertation, Universität Tübingen, 1956)

Israel, Uwe, *Johannes Geiler von Kaysersberg (1445–1510): der Straßburger Münsterprediger als Rechtsreformer*, Berliner historische Studien, 27 (Berlin: Duncker & Humblodt, 1997)

Kapfhammer, Gerhard, 'Inszenierung von Authentizität: Johannes Pauli und die Veröffentlichung der Predigten Geilers von Kaysersberg', in *Autorbilder: zur Medialität literarischer Kommunikation in Mittelalter und Früher Neuzeit*, ed. by Gerald Kapfhammer and others, Tholos, 2 (Münster: Rhema, 2007), pp. 270–84

Kettler, Wilfried, *Der Berner Totentanz des Niklaus Manuel: philologische, epigraphische sowie historische Überlegungen zu einem Sprach- und Kunstdenkmal der frühen Neuzeit* (Frankfurt am Main: Lang, 2009)

Kienzle, Beverly Mayne, 'Conclusion', in *The Sermon*, ed. by Beverly Mayne Kienzle, Typologie des sources du Moyen Âge occidental, 81–83 (Turnhout: Brepols, 2000), pp. 963–83

Kienzle, Beverly Mayne, 'Medieval Sermons and their Performance: Theory and Record', in *Preachers, Sermon and Audience in the Middle Ages*, ed. by Carolyn Muessig, A New History of the Sermon, 3 (Leiden: Brill, 2002), pp. 89–124

Kraume, Herbert, *Die Gerson-Übersetzungen Geilers von Kaysersberg: Studien zur deutschsprachigen Gerson-Rezeption*, Münchener Texte und Untersuchungen zur deutschen Literatur des Mittelalters, 71 (München: Artemis, 1980)

INSTRUCTIO, CORRECTIO, AND REFORMATIO 405

Kristeller, Paul, *Die Strassburger Bücher-Illustration im XV. und im Anfange des XVI. Jahrhunderts*, Beiträge zur Kunstgeschichte, n.s. 7 (Leipzig: Bär & Hermann, 1888)

Mertens, Thom, 'De Middelnederlandse preek: een voorbarige synthese', in *De Middelnederlandse preek*, ed. by Thom Mertens, Patricia Stoop, and Christoph Burger, Middeleeuwse Studies en Bronnen, 116 (Hilversum: Verloren, 2009), pp. 9–66

Mertens, Volker, 'Authentisierungsstrategien in vorreformatorischer Predigt: Erscheinungsform und Edition einer oralen Gattung am Beispiel Johannes Geilers von Kaysersberg', *Editio*, 16 (2002), 70–85

Mertens, Volker, '*figuren und gemelt*: reale und evozierte Bilder in Geilers Narrenschiff-Predigten', in *Die Predigt zwischen Mündlichkeit, Bildlichkeit und Schriftlichkeit*, ed. by René Wetzel and Fabrice Flückiger, Medienwandel — Medienwechsel — Medienwissen, 13 (Zürich: Chronos, 2010), pp. 241–59

Mertens, Volker, and Hans-Jochen Schiewer, 'Erschließung einer Gattung: Edition, Katalogisierung und Abbildung der deutschsprachigen Predigt des Mittelalters', *Editio*, 4 (1990), 93–111

Muther, Richard, *Die deutsche Bücherillustration der Gothik und Frührenaissance (1460–1530)* (München: Hirth, 1922)

Naas, Laurent, 'L'Influence de Geiler de Kaysersberg (1446 [*sic*]–1510) ou l'émergence de l'idée de réforme de l'Eglise chez Beatus Rhenanus', in *Beatus Rhenanus (1485–1547) et une réforme de l'Eglise: engagement et changement*, ed. by James Hirstein, Studia humanitatis Rhenana, 4 (Turnhout: Brepols, 2018), pp. 91–112

Oldenbourg, Maria Consuelo, *Die Buchholzschnitte des Hans Baldung Grien: ein bibliographisches Verzeichnis ihrer Verwendung*, Studien zur deutschen Kunstgeschichte, 335 (Baden-Baden: Valentin Koerner, 1985)

Oldenbourg, Maria Consuelo, *Die Buchholzschnitte des Hans Schäufelein: ein bibliographisches Verzeichnis ihrer Verwendung, mit einem Anhang über Buchholzschnitte des Monogrammisten IS mit der Schaufel*, Text- und Bildband, Studien zur deutschen Kunstgeschichte, 340–41, 2 vols (Baden-Baden: Heitz, 1964)

Palmer, Nigel F., 'Die Münchner Perikopenhandschrift Cgm 157 und die Handschriftenproduktion des Straßburger Reuerinnenklosters im späten 15. Jahrhundert', in *Kulturtopographie des deutschsprachigen Südwestens im späteren Mittelalter*, ed. by Barbara Fleith and René Wetzel, Kulturtopographie des alemannischen Raums, 1 (Berlin: De Gruyter, 2009), pp. 263–300

Pfleger, Luzian, 'Der Franziskaner Johannes Pauli und seine Ausgaben Geilerscher Predigten', *Archiv für Elsässische Kirchengeschichte*, 3 (1928), 47–96

Pfleger, Luzian, 'Zur handschriftlichen Überlieferung Geilerscher Predigttexte', *Archiv für Elsässische Kirchengeschichte*, 6 (1931), 195–205

Reinert, Jonathan, *Passionspredigt im 16. Jahrhundert: das Leiden und Sterben Jesu Christi in den Postillen Martin Luthers, der Wittenberger Tradition und altgläubiger Prediger*, Spätmittelalter, Humanismus, Reformation, 119 (Tübingen: Mohr Siebeck, 2020)

Reske, Christoph, *Die Buchdrucker des 16. und 17. Jahrhunderts im deutschen Sprachgebiet: auf der Grundlage des gleichnamigen Werkes von Josef Benzing*, Beiträge zum Buch- und Bibliothekswesen, 51, 2nd edn (Wiesbaden: Harrassowitz, 2015)

Rüther, Andreas, and Hans-Jochen Schiewer, 'Die Predigthandschriften des Straßburger Dominikanerinnenklosters St. Nikolaus in undis: historischer Bestand, Geschichte, Vergleich', in *Die deutsche Predigt im Mittelalter*, ed. by Volker Mertens (Tübingen: Niemeyer, 1992), pp. 169–93

Sauerbrey, Anna, *Die Straßburger Klöster im 16. Jahrhundert: eine Untersuchung unter besonderer Berücksichtigung der Geschlechtergeschichte*, Spätmittelalter, Humanismus, Reformation, 69 (Tübingen: Mohr Siebeck, 2012)

Schiewer, Hans-Jochen, 'German Sermons in the Middle Ages', in *The Sermon*, ed. by Beverly Mayne Kienzle, Typologie des sources du Moyen Âge occidental, 81–83 (Turnhout: Brepols, 2000), pp. 861–961

Schlechter, Armin, 'Lesespuren von Johann Adelphus Muling in einer Ausgabe des Granatapfel von Johannes Geiler von Kaysersberg', in *Grundlagen: Forschungen, Editionen und Materialien zur deutschen Literatur und Sprache des Mittelalters und der Frühen Neuzeit*, ed. by Rudolf Bentzinger, Ulrich-Dieter Oppitz, and Jürgen Wolf, Zeitschrift für deutsches Altertum und deutsche Literatur, Beiheft 18 (Stuttgart: Hirzel, 2013), pp. 247–55

Schmidt, Charles, *Histoire littéraire de l'Alsace à la fin du XVe et au commencement du XVIe siècle*, 2 vols (Paris: Librairie Sandoz & Fischbacher, 1879)

Schmidt, Charles, *Répertoire bibliographique Strasbourgeois jusque vers 1530, I: Jean Grüninger 1483–1531* (Strasbourg: Heitz & Mündel, 1894)

Schmidt, Charles, *Zur Geschichte der ältesten Bibliotheken und der ersten Buchdrucker zu Strassburg* (Strasbourg: C. F. Schmidt's Universitäts-Buchhandlung Friedrich Bull, 1882)

Schneider, Karin, *Paläographie und Handschriftenkunde für Germanisten: eine Einführung*, Sammlung kurzer Grammatiken germanischer Dialekte. B: Ergänzungsreihe, 8, 3rd edn (Berlin: De Gruyter, 2014)

Schüppert, Helga, 'Geiler von Kaysersberg: ein Beitrag zur Imagologie der Predigt', in *Albertus Magnus und der Albertismus: deutsche philosophische Kultur des Mittelalters*, ed. by Maarten J. F. M. Hoenen and Alain de Libera, Studien und Texte zur Geistesgeschichte des Mittelalters, 48 (Leiden: Brill, 1995), pp. 333–52

Steinmetz, Ralf-Henning, 'Über Quellenverwendung und Sinnbildungsverfahren in den "Narrenschiff"-Predigten Geilers von Kaisersberg: am Beispiel und mit dem lateinischen und dem deutschen Text der Predigten über die *Bulnarren*', in *Predigt im Kontext*, ed. by Volker Mertens and others (Berlin: De Gruyter, 2013), pp. 89–124

Volfing, Annette, 'Geiler von Kaysersberg and Late Medieval Contemplative Practice: Gerson, Bridal Mysticism and the Force of the Imagination', *Oxford German Studies*, 43 (2014), 229–45

Voltmer, Rita, 'Du discours à l'allegorie: représentations de la superstition, de la magie et de la sorcellerie dans les sermons de Johannes Geiler de Kaysersberg', in *Sorcellerie savante et mentalités populaires*, ed. by Antoine Follain and Maryse Simon, Sciences de l'histoire (Strasbourg: Presses universitaire de Strasbourg, 2013), pp. 45–88

Voltmer, Rita, '*Die fueß an dem leichnam der christenhait / seind die hantwercks leüt. arbaiter / bauleüt / und das gemayn volck …* Die Straßburger Unterschichten im polit-theologischen System des Johannes Geiler von Kaysersberg', in *Städtische Gesellschaft und Kirche im Spätmittelalter*, ed. by Sigrid Schmitt and Sabine Klapp, Geschichtliche Landeskunde, 62 (Stuttgart: Steiner, 2008), pp. 189–232

Voltmer, Rita, 'Klerikaler Antiklerikalismus? Die Kritik am geistlichen Stand bei Johannes Geiler von Kaysersberg (1445–1510)', in *Kirchlicher und religiöser Alltag im Spätmittelalter*, ed. by Andreas Meyer, Schriften zur südwestdeutschen Landeskunde, 69 (Stuttgart: Thorbeke, 2010), pp. 48–76

Voltmer, Rita, 'Political Preaching and a Design of Urban Reform: Johannes Geiler of Kaysersberg and Strasbourg', *Franciscan Studies*, 71 (2013), 71–88

Voltmer, Rita, '"Preaching during the Holy Week is like being Killed on the Wheel": The Design, Performance, and Recording of Johannes Geiler of Kaysersberg's Lenten Sermons', in *I sermoni quaresimali: digiuno del corpo, banchetto dell'anima / Lenten Sermons: Fast of the Body, Banquet of the Soul*, ed. by Pietro Delcorno, Eleonora Lombardo, and Lorenza Tromboni, *Memorie domenicane*, n.s., 48 (Firenze: Edizioni Nerbini, 2017), pp. 277–92

Voltmer, Rita, 'Preaching on Witchcraft? The Sermons of Johannes Geiler of Kaysersberg (1445–1510)', in *Contesting Orthodoxy in Medieval and Early Modern Europe: Heresy, Magic and Witchcraft*, ed. by Louise Nyholm Kallestrup and Raisa Maria Toivo, Palgrave Historical Studies in Witchcraft and Magic (Basingstoke: Palgrave Macmillan, 2017), pp. 193–215

Voltmer, Rita, *Wie der Wächter auf dem Turm, ein Prediger und seine Stadt: Johannes Geiler von Kaysersberg und Straßburg*, Beiträge zur Landes- und Kulturgeschichte, 4 (Trier: Porta Alba, 2005)

Voltmer, Rita, 'Wissen, Medien und die Wahrheit: Überlegungen zu Transferprozessen von Hexenwissen', in *Hexenwissen. zum Transfer von Magie- und Zauberei-Imaginationen in interdisziplinärer Perspektive*, ed. by Heinz Sieburg, Rita Voltmer, and Britta Weimann, Trierer Hexenprozesse, 9 (Trier: Paulinus, 2017), pp. 3–46

Voltmer, Rita, 'Zwischen polit-theologischen Konzepten, obrigkeitlichen Normsetzungen und städtischem Alltag: Johannes Geiler von Kaysersberg und das Straßburger Fürsorgewesen', in *Norm und Praxis der Armenfürsorge in Spätmittelalter und Früher Neuzeit*, ed. by Jens Aspelmeier and Sebastian Schmidt, Vierteljahrschrift für Sozial- und Wirtschaftsgeschichte, 189 (Stuttgart: Steiner, 2006), pp. 91–135

Wedell, Moritz, 'Zachäus auf dem Palmbaum: enumerativ-ikonische Schemata zwischen Predigtkunst und Verlegergeschick (Geilers von Kaysersberg *Predigen Teütsch*, 1508, 1510)', in *Die Predigt zwischen Mündlichkeit, Bildlichkeit und Schriftlichkeit*, ed. by René Wetzel and Fabrice Flückiger, Medienwandel — Medienwechsel — Medienwissen, 13 (Zürich: Chronos, 2010), pp. 261–304

Williams-Krapp, Werner, '"Durch ihn werde widerwillen vnd erneuwerungen gesät vnd vffpracht": zu den Reforminitiativen Friederichs von Zollern und Johann Geilers von Kaysersberg in Augsburg', in *Reformen vor der Reformation: Sankt Ulrich und Afra und der monastisch–urbane Umkreis im 15. Jahrhundert*, ed. by Klaus Wolf and Gisela Drossbach, Studia Augustana, 18 (Berlin: De Gruyter, 2018), pp. 205–16

Zimmermann-Homeyer, Catarina, *Illustrierte Frühdrucke lateinischer Klassiker um 1500: innovative Illustrationskonzepte aus der Straßburger Offizin Johannes Grüningers und ihrer Wirkung*, Wolfenbütteler Abhandlungen zur Renaissanceforschung, 36 (Wiesbaden: Harrasowitz, 2018)

The Low Countries

THOM MERTENS

The Gouda Gospel Sermons

The Glosses of a Successful Middle Dutch Pericope Collection (1477–1553)

In Middle Dutch, around 3,700 different sermons have been handed down — 11,000 sermons, if we include the duplicates — in more than 550 manuscripts.[1] In this vast numer of texts we can discern three major genres: sermons based on the *divisio* of a theme, sermons commenting on a pericope, and the informal, admonishing collation, which were popular in the *Devotio moderna*.[2] In this essay I want to discuss a representative of the second genre, the pericope sermon.

The genre of pericope sermons wanders between Bible translation, Bible commentary and the sermon. It is related to the sermon because it is the written form of the sermon that was delivered orally on Sundays and Holy Days. It is related to Bible translation because it often contains a translation or paraphrase of the Bible pericope that was read in Latin as the Epistle or the Gospel in the Mass. It is related to the Bible commentary because it comments on this pericope, usually giving a moral interpretation, sometimes based on a literal or spiritual interpretation of the pericope. Because of this affinity to Bible commentary, in some Middle Dutch manuscripts and prints these pericope sermons are called *exposicien, verclaringe, glose*, that is, *explanations* or *glosses*.

There are ten cycles of Middle Dutch pericope sermons, ranging from the thirteenth until the late fifteenth century: seven virtually complete cycles, and

---

1 *Repertorium van Middelnederlandse preken in handschriften tot en met 1550 / Repertorium of Middle Dutch Sermons Preserved in Manuscripts from before 1550*, ed. by Maria Sherwood-Smith and Patricia Stoop (I–III), Daniël Ermens and Willemien van Dijk (IV–VII), Miscellanea Neerlandica, 29, 7 vols (Leuven: Peeters, 2003–2008), VII (2008), 1 (hereafter *Repertorium van Middelnederlandse preken*). For abbreviations used in this essay, see the Abbreviations and Selected Online Resources at the beginning of this volume.

2 For the collation, see Thom Mertens, 'Collatio und Codex im Bereich der Devotio moderna', in *Der Codex im Gebrauch: Akten des Internationalen Kolloquiums 11.–13. Juni 1992*, ed. by Christel Meier, Dagmar Hüpper, and Hagen Keller, Münstersche Mittelalter-Schriften, 70 (München: Fink, 1996), pp. 163–82; Lydeke van Beek, *Leken trekken tot Gods Woord: Dirc van Herxen (1381–1457) en zijn Eerste Collatieboek*, Middeleeuwse Studies en Bronnen, 120 (Hilversum: Verloren, 2009), pp. 61–77.

Thom Mertens (thom.mertens@uantwerpen.be) is an Emeritus Professor of the Ruusbroec Institute at the University of Antwerp.

Circulating the Word of God in Medieval and Early Modern Europe: Catholic Preaching and Preachers across Manuscript and Print (c. 1450 to c. 1550), ed. by Veronica O'Mara and Patricia Stoop, SERMO 17, (Turnhout: Brepols, 2022), pp. 411–444 BREPOLS ❧ PUBLISHERS 10.1484/M.SERMO-EB.5.130463

412   THOM MERTENS

three cycles for Lent.[3] None of these cycles is available in a modern edition. These sermons may be laid out as follows:

Thirteenth Century

1 Berlin Cycle

Thirteenth century; 125 sermons; 3 (+3) manuscripts[4]

Fourteenth Century

2 The Hague Cycle: Gregory the Great, *Homiliae* XL *in evangelia*

(Middle Dutch translation of the Latin text, rearranged in liturgical order) 1380–1381; 40 sermons; 19 (+19) manuscripts; 1 printed edition (1479)[5]

3 Zwolle Cycle

c. 1380–*c*. 1425; 3 versions (adaptations of a lost version from *c*. 1323–1347?); 59 sermons; 9 (+5) manuscripts[6]

---

3 Mainly based on *Repertorium van Middelnederlandse preken*, and Gerrit Cornelis Zieleman, *Middelnederlandse epistel- en evangeliepreken*, Kerkhistorische bijdragen, 8 (Leiden: Brill, 1978). The cycles were named by Gerrit Cornelis Zieleman after the city where the most important manuscript is kept (or the text was printed first, in the case of the Gouda Cycle). See also Gerrit Cornelis Zieleman, 'Das Studium der deutschen und niederländischen Predigten des Mittelalters', in *Sô predigent eteliche: Beiträge zur deutschen und niederländischen Predigt im Mittelalter*, ed. by Kurt Otto Seidel, Göppinger Arbeiten zur Germanistik, 378 (Göppingen: Kümmerle, 1982), pp. 5–48 (pp. 40–44). It is not clear to what extent the assembled collection in Brussel, Koninklijke Bibliotheek, MS 1268–1269 should be distinguished as an independent cycle (see Zieleman, *Middelnederlandse epistel- en evangeliepreken*, pp. 78–81).

4 3 (+3) = 3 corpus manuscripts (+3 manuscripts with incidental transmission) ['corpus manuscript' is understood here as: more than one third of the sermons in the form of a coherent sermon collection]. It should be noted that the numbers are stated with reservation. Most cycles do not constitute a homogeneous body of texts and so the separate cycles are sometimes difficult to define. Therefore the number of sermons and the number of manuscripts involved is difficult to determine precisely, and subject to discussion. On the Berlin Cycle, see also Esther Jonker, *Het Amsterdams Perikopenboek: volkstalige vroomheid in veertiende-eeuws Vlaanderen* (Leiden: Leiden University Press, 2010); with a Summary in English on pp. 147–49. Jonker demonstrates that each pericope and each sermon has its own transmission (pp. 42–49, 148).

5 *Repertorium van Middelnederlandse preken*, VII (2008), 101–02; Maria Sherwood-Smith, 'The Last Judgement in Middle Dutch Sermons and its Role in the Dutch Translation of the Homilies of Gregory the Great', in *The Last Judgement in Medieval Preaching*, ed. by Thom Mertens, Hans-Jochen Schiewer, and Maria Sherwood-Smith, Sermo: Studies on Patristic, Medieval, and Reformation Sermons and Preaching, 3 (Turnhout: Brepols, 2013), pp. 79–97.

6 See Zieleman, *Middelnederlandse epistel- en evangeliepreken*, pp. 75–77, 90–159; *Repertorium van Middelnederlandse preken*, VII (2008), 100; Daniël Ermens, 'Een onbekend handschrift met evangeliepreken uit de tekstgroep Zwolle: Heverlee, Abdij van Park, 5', *Ons Geestelijk Erf*, 81 (2010), 194–242. Zieleman attributes one version to Geert Grote (1340–1384) and another to Johannes Scutken (d. 1423), both prominent members of the *Devotio moderna*. See respectively Gerrit C. Zieleman, 'Der Verfasser der sog. Zwoller Predigten des späten 14. Jahrhunderts', in *Die deutsche Predigt im Mittelalter: Internationales Symposium am Fachbereich Germanistik der Freien Universität Berlin vom 3.–6. Oktober 1989*, ed. by Volker Mertens and Hans-Jochen Schiewer (Tübingen: Niemeyer, 1992), pp. 223–55; G. C. Zieleman, 'Evangeliën

THE GOUDA GOSPEL SERMONS   413

4 **Copenhagen Cycle**: *Een nuttelijc boec den kerstenen menschen*
   c. 1395; 61 sermons (free adaptation of sermons by Jacobus de Voragine)[7] + 5
   non-sermon texts; 17 (+11) manuscripts, 3 printed editions (1482, 1489, 1501)[8]

5 **Paris Cycle**
   before 1400 (or after 1477);[9] 67 sermons (Sundays 57; *festa duplica* 10); 1
   (+2) manuscripts

Fifteenth Century

6 **Nijmegen Cycle**
   1421 or earlier; 54 sermons (summer part); 1 manuscript (1421)

7 **Gouda Cycle**: *Alle die epistelen ende ewangelien mitten sermonen*
   1477; 51 sermons; at least 41 printed editions (1477–1553); 3 (+1) manuscripts[10]

Lent Cycles

1 **Hamburg (Staats- und Universitätsbibliothek, Cod. Theol. 1099)**
   before 1450?; 40 sermons for the 40 weekdays of Lent; 1 manuscript
   (*c.* 1425–1450)

2 **Leiden (Universiteitsbibliotheek, BPL 61)**
   1477 or earlier; 43 sermons; 2 manuscripts

---

door het jaar met hun glossen: een onderzoek naar de bijdrage van Johan Scutken (+ 1423)
aan een laatmiddeleeuws religieus genre in de volkstaal', in *De Middelnederlandse preek*, ed. by
Thom Mertens, Patricia Stoop, and Christoph Burger, Middeleeuwse Studies en Bronnen,
116 (Hilversum, Verloren, 2009), pp. 102–31.

7 See Rüdiger Schnell, 'Konstanz und Metapmorphosen eines Textes: eine Überlieferungs- und
   geschlechtergeschichtliche Studie zur volkssprachlichen Rezeption von Jacobus de Voragine
   Ehepredigten', *Frühmittelalterliche Studien*, 33 (1999), 319–95 (pp. 377–90), and Zieleman's
   remarks on Schnell's observations: Zieleman, 'Evangeliën door het jaar', p. 111 n. 47.

8 See Daniël Ermens, '"Een nuttelijc boec den kerstenen menschen" (ca. 1400):
   heilsgeschiedenis voor beginners', in *De letter levend maken: opstellen aangeboden aan
   Guido de Baere bij zijn zeventigste verjaardag*, ed. by Kees Schepers and Frans Hendrickx,
   Miscellanea Neerlandica, 39 (Leuven: Peeters, 2010), pp. 265–84 (pp. 267–68).

9 The last sermon has 1477 as its *terminus post quem*, but is possibly added afterwards
   (Zieleman, *Middelnederlandse epistel- en evangeliepreken*, p. 73).

10 See below, Appendix 2. The manuscripts seem to have been copied from printed editions:
   none of these manuscripts contains all fifty-one sermons. Zieleman, *Middelnederlandse
   epistel- en evangeliepreken*, pp. 55–57, mentions two manuscripts. A third manuscript
   (Heverlee, Abdij van Park, MS 5) is mentioned in *Repertorium van Middelnederlandse
   preken*, V (2008), 454–78, especially p. 477 (no. HV.5/064), and thoroughly discussed by
   Daniël Ermens in his 'Een onbekend handschrift'. The fourth 'manuscript' is a print of
   Gheraert Leeu's *Alle die epistelen ende ewangelien vanden gheheelen iaere* (Gouda, 24 May
   1477 [CA 686]): in the margins of one of the copies (London, British Library, IB 47301)
   the sermons are added in a late fifteenth-century hand; see Suzan Folkerts, 'Reading
   the Scriptures during the Early Reformation: Continuities in the Production and Use
   of Printed Dutch Bibles', in *Renaissance und Bibelhumanismus*, ed. by J. Marius, J. Lange
   van Ravenswaay, and Herman J. Selderhuis, Refo500 Academic Studies, 65 (Göttingen:
   Vandenhoeck & Ruprecht, 2020), pp. 159–77 (p. 163).

3 Berlin, Staatsbibliothek zu Berlin, Preußischer Kulturbesitz, MS germ. qu. 1580)

1492 or earlier; 112 sermons (Lent and the week after Easter), including 7 sermons of Gregory the Great, *Homiliae XL in evangelia*; 1 manuscript (1492)

In this essay I will discuss the most successful cycle: number 7 of the list, *Alle die epistelen ende ewangelien mitten sermonen*, a Middle Dutch lectionary with a series of Sunday Gospel sermons (see Appendix 1). It is also called the 'Gouda Cycle' for it was printed in the city of Gouda in Holland for the first time. I refer to the sermons contained in this cycle as the 'Gouda Gospel Sermons'. *Alle die epistelen ende ewangelien mitten sermonen* surpassed all other cycles in dissemination and it survived unto the middle of the sixteenth century. I will describe the origin, the development and the form of the collection, and the form of the sermons contained in it. I will search for the author(s) of the different text elements and I will try to explain the success of this collection.

The Gouda Gospel Sermons

The Gouda Gospel Sermons were published in 1477, the year that in the Low Countries the first books in the vernacular were printed in movable type. In January in Delft a Dutch 'Bible' was finished (only the Old Testament, without the Book of Psalms).[11] In Gouda on 24 May of the same year Gheraert Leeu (*c.* 1445/50–93) printed his first book: *Alle die epistelen ende ewangelien vanden gheheelen iaere*, a Middle Dutch pericope collection without sermons.[12] This first book of Gheraert Leeu is technically not perfect. Its font has its imperfections and Leeu did not yet manage to get his right margins justified.[13] About six months later Gheraert Leeu printed a collection of Gospel pericopes with

---

11 CA 290. A facsimile edition was published in 1977: *De Delftse bijbel van 1477: facsimile van de oorspronkelijke druk*, with an introduction by C. C. de Bruin, 3 vols (Amsterdam: Buijten & Schipperheijn, 1977); for a digital edition of the text see www.bijbelsdigitaal.nl [accessed 21 June 2022]. On the Delft Bible of 1477, see Mart van Duijn, 'Printing, Public, and Power: Shaping the First Printed Bible in Dutch (1477)', *Church History and Religious Culture*, 93 (2013), 275–99; Mart van Duijn, 'Defining the Delft Bible (1477): From Printer–Public Dynamics to Extant Copies', in *Cultures of Religious Reading in the Late Middle Ages: Instructing the Soul, Feeding the Spirit, and Awakening the Passion*, ed. by Sabrina Corbellini, Utrecht Studies in Medieval Literacy, 25 (Turnhout: Brepols, 2013), pp. 117–40; Mart van Duijn, *De Delftse Bijbel: een sociale geschiedenis, 1477–circa 1550*, Bijdragen tot de geschiedenis van de Nederlandse boekhandel, n.s. 19 (Zutphen: Walburg Pers, 2017), pp. 193–255: descriptions of the sixty-one extant copies.

12 CA 686; 1477.EpEv.dut.GL.a in the *Biblia Sacra* database. Nine copies are preserved. For corrections to the list in *Biblia Sacra*, see Folkerts, 'Reading the Scriptures', p. 162 n. 4. See 'Het Goudse fonds van Gheraert Leeu (volgens ISTC)', in *Een drukker zoekt publiek: Gheraert Leeu te Gouda 1477–1484*, ed. by Koen Goudriaan and others, Bijdragen Oudheidkundige Kring 'Die Goude', 23 (Delft: Eburon, 1993), pp. 224–45 (p. 224, no. 1).

13 *De vijfhonderdste verjaring van de boekdrukkunst in de Nederlanden: catalogus tentoonstelling*

THE GOUDA GOSPEL SERMONS 415

a collection of sermons on the Sunday Gospels: *Alle die ewangelien vanden gheheelen iaer ende vanden sonnendaghen mitter glosen*.[14] The next year the Utrecht printer Johan Veldener (d. after 1486) combined those three elements in a collection which proved to be very successful, a bestseller: *Alle die epistelen ende ewangelien mitten sermonen*.[15] It was printed more than forty times in the next seventy-five years (see Appendix 2). Between 4 November 1478 and 30 July 1479, Veldener published a variant setting (*Doppeldrück*) of this work, also dated 4 November 1478.[16] The fourth edition of Veldener, 1481, was the first illustrated edition of *Alle die epistelen ende ewangelien mitten sermonen*. It was profusely illustrated with fifty-one woodcuts, forty-six of which were different; thirty-nine were new. The woodcuts were not printed at the beginning of the relevant Epistle or Gospel, as was customary, but in the middle of the text, in the vicinity of the passages they were meant to illustrate.[17] Most editions after 1481 are illustrated.

The Middle Dutch Bible manuscripts usually offered complete books of the New Testament, with a liturgical reading scheme facilitating para-liturgical use. In print, however, the lectionary-form became the dominant form of Middle Dutch Bible translation. Lay people preferred to read the New Testament in conformity with the ecclesiastical year, as is also clear from handwritten notes in the prints which assure a correct accordance with the liturgical reading

---

in de Koninklijke Bibliotheek Albert I (Brussel: Koninklijke Bibliotheek Albert I, 1973), pp. 291–93 (no. 125).

14 CA 685; *Biblia Sacra*: 1477.EpEv.dut.GL.b. Three copies of this edition are extant. For corrections to the list in *Biblia Sacra*, see Folkerts, 'Reading the Scriptures', p. 162 n. 5. The counting of the number of copies may be less reliable because Veldener published a variant setting of this print (see below, n. 16). For my research I used a PDF-facsimile of the Stuttgart copy (Stuttgart, Württembergische Landesbibliothek, Inc. 4° 6647b: Digitale Sammlungen der Württembergischen Landesbibliothek / Alte und wertvolle Drucke: https://digital. wlb-stuttgart.de/purl/bsz348361432 [accessed 22 July 2020]). In this PDF fol. 31v is lacking and from this point, each verso side precedes its corresponding recto side; also lacking are the fols 130v, 131v, and 189v.

15 CA 687; *Biblia Sacra*: 1478.EpEv.dut.JVe.a. At least ten copies are preserved. For corrections to the list in *Biblia Sacra*, see Folkerts, 'Reading the Scriptures', p. 162, n. 6.

16 CA 687a; *Biblia Sacra* 1478.EpEv.dut.JVe.b. Gerard van Thienen shows that CA 687a was later than CA 687; see Gerard van Thienen, 'Papieronderzoek van de in de Nederlanden gedrukte incunabelen', in *For Bob de Graaf, Antiquarian Bookseller, Publisher, Bibliographer: Festschrift on the Occasion of his 65th Birthday*, ed. by Anton Gerits (Amsterdam: Gerits & Sons, 1992), pp. 160–73. I thank Dr Goran Proot for his clear discussion of this case. A variant setting (*Doppeldrück*) tries to imitate another print down to the last detail, including the impressum and date of publication. See Martin Boghardt, *Analytische Druckforschung: ein methodischer Beitrag zu Buchkunde und Textkritik* (Hamburg: Hauswedell, 1977), pp. 110–11; Marita Mathijsen, *Naar de letter: handboek editiewetenschap*, 2nd edn (Den Haag: Constantijn Huygens Instituut, 1997), pp. 138 and 229.

17 CA 690. See Ina Kok, *Woodcuts in Incunabula Printed in the Low Countries*, Bibliotheca bibliographica neerlandica: series major, 2, 4 vols (Houten: HES & De Graaf, 2013), I, 47–48 (no. 22), III, 170–74 (nos 22.1–39); the third edition (30 July 1479 [CA 688]) featured only a closing woodcut.

THOM MERTENS

order, such as 'dese ewangelie behoert up den vridach' ['This Gospel belongs to Friday'].[18] The lectionary-form was cheaper to print than complete New Testaments.[19] Moreover, this form gave the opportunity of adding sermons to the biblical text.

The Form of the Collection

I will discuss here the collection in its definitive form, the edition by Johan Veldener in Utrecht from 4 November 1478.[20] This edition also has no title page, but an incipit:

> Hier beghinnen alle die epistelen ende ewangelien mitten sermonen vanden ghehelen jaere die een na den anderen volghende: ende oec mede die prophecien ghenomen wt der bibelen volmatelijc [*read:* volmaectelijc] ende gherechtelijck ouer gheset wt den latine in goeden duytsche. ghelikerwijs alsmen houdende is inder heyligher kerken.

> [Here begin all the Epistles and Gospels with the sermons of the entire year, one following after the other, and also the prophecies[21] taken from the Bible, completely [*read:* perfectly] and correctly translated from Latin into good Dutch, as they are observed in the Holy Church].

The collection consists of a temporale, and a sanctorale, both in the order of the liturgical year, completed with the pericopes and the sermon for the Feast of Dedication of the Church:[22]

---

18 On traces of users in Middle Dutch pericope books, see Suzan A. Folkerts, 'Middle Dutch *Epistles and Gospels*: The Transfer of a Medieval Bestseller into Printed Editions during the Early Reformation', in *Vernacular Bible and Religious Reform in the Middle Ages and Early Modern Era*, ed. by Wim François and August den Hollander, Bibliotheca Ephemeridum Theologicarum Lovaniensium, 287 (Leuven: Peeters, 2017), pp. 53–73 (pp. 59–61; example cited on p. 61).

19 See Suzan Folkerts, 'Reading the Bible Lessons at Home: Holy Writ and Lay Readers in the Low Countries', *Church History and Religious Culture*, 93 (2013), 215–35 (p. 234); Folkerts, 'Middle Dutch *Epistles and Gospels*', pp. 53–59, 61, 70–71; Folkerts, 'Reading the Scriptures', pp. 162–65; Suzan Folkerts, 'Appropriating the Passion: On the Uses of Middle Dutch Gospels in Manuscript and Print', in *The Same and Different: Strategies of Retelling the Bible within the 'New Communities of Interpretation' (1350–1570)*, ed. by Lucie Doležalová and Géraldine Veysseyre, New Communities of Interpretation (Turnhout: Brepols, forthcoming), in the section 'The Passion Harmony in Printed Lectionaries'.

20 I cite the first edition, printed by Johan Veldener in Utrecht, 4 November 1478 (CA 687), the full-colour electronic facsimile of the copy Utrecht, Universiteitsbibliotheek, MAG 130 D 23 (Rariora), available on https://objects.library.uu.nl/reader/ [accessed on 20 March 2020].

21 With regard to 'prophecies' the Epistle pericopes taken from the Prophets and other Old Testament books are meant. See *Novum Testamentum Devotionis Modernae / Het Nieuwe Testament van de Moderne Devotie*, ed. by C. C. de Bruin, Corpus Sacrae Scripturae Medii Aevi, series major, 2:2 (Leiden: Brill, 1979), p. ix.

22 In German research this type of text collection is called a (glossed) *Plenar*. It consists

THE GOUDA GOSPEL SERMONS 417

Temporale (197 occasions): openings 1a–271b[23]

    Sundays: Epistle, Gospel, sermon

    Wednesdays: Epistle, Gospel

    Fridays: Gospel

    [272a: blank]

Sanctorale (98 occasions): openings 272b–324a

    Epistle, Gospel

Dedication of the Church: openings 324a–326a

    Epistle, Gospel, sermon

Colophon: opening 326a

The temporale spans the period from the First Sunday in Advent to the Twenty-Sixth Sunday after Pentecost.[24] It contains 197 liturgical occasions: Sundays, Wednesdays, and Fridays.[25] On Sundays there is an Epistle, a Gospel, and a sermon. On Wednesdays the Epistle and Gospel pericopes are given; on Fridays just the Gospel pericope. There are some exceptions to this set-up: the Epistle and Gospel for all weekdays in Lent are given, just as the lessons, Epistle and Gospel for the four series of Ember Days (*quatuor tempora*); and there are some individual exceptions or irregularities, for example: there are four

---

of translations of the Epistle and Gospel pericopes of the Sundays and holy days of the ecclesiastical year, of which only the Gospels texts are glossed. See Regina D. Schiewer and Hans-Jochen Schiewer, 'Predigt im Spätmittelalter', in *Literarische und religiöse Textsorten und Textallianzen um 1500*, ed. by Alexander Schwarz, Franz Simmler, and Claudia Wich-Reif, Textsorten und Textallianzen um 1500, 1 (Berlin: Weidler, 2009), pp. 727–71 (pp. 752–53), and the literature cited there. Fundamental for the German tradition is Nigel F. Palmer, 'Deutsche Perikopenhandschriften mit der Glosse: zu den Predigten der spätmittelalterlichen deutschen Plenarien und Evangelistare', in *Deutsche Bibelübersetzungen des Mittelalters*, ed. by Heimo Reinitzer, Vestigia Bibliae, 9–10 (Bern: Peter Lang, 1991), pp. 273–96.

23 In the edition the openings (or: spreads) are numbered. These numbers are used for cross references in the book. This is why I use them too, with addition of 'a' for the left page and 'b' for the right page (for example, opening 12a = fol. 11v; opening 12b = fol. 12r). Editions from 1479 onwards usually have a table of contents at the end (which also refer to the openings).

24 The text counts the Sundays 'after the Octave of Pentecost', which wording further down has been shortened to 'the third Sunday' and so on.

25 Traditionally, Wednesdays and Fridays, that is, the liturgical 'station days' have been penitential days and therefore they could have their own Mass lessons. See *Liturgisch Woordenboek*, ed. by L. Brinkhoff and others, 3 vols (Roermond: Romen, 1958–1970), II (1968), 2582–84 (i.v. *Statio*), 2931–32 (i.v. *Woensdag, I*), and 2888–89 (i.v. *Vrijdag, II*); Joseph Andreas Jungmann, *Missarum sollemnia: eine genetische Erklärung der Römischen Messe*, 5th edn, 2 vols (Bonn: Nova et Vetera, 2003; repr. from Freiburg im Breisgau.: Herder, 1962), I, 511–16; John Harper, *The Forms and Orders of Western Liturgy from the Tenth to the Eighteenth Century: A Historical Introduction and Guide for Students and Musicians* (Oxford: Clarendon Press, 1991), p. 136.

Sundays without a sermon;[26] the Epistle and Gospel is given for the Mondays after the Fourth and Fifth Sunday after Easter instead of the Wednesdays.

The sanctorale contains ninety-eight feasts. For all of them the Epistle and Gospel texts are given, but no sermon. The only exception is the ninety-ninth occasion at the end of the sanctorale: the Feast of the Dedication of the Church, which has an Epistle and a Gospel and a sermon. There are fifty sermons for the Sunday Gospels in the temporale, and one for the Feast of the Dedication of the Church at the end of the sanctorale, in sum fifty-one.

The Form of the Sermons

Each sermon begins with the theme in Latin and an indication of the biblical place where this theme may be found. The theme is always taken from the Gospel reading. Mostly it is the first sentence of the pericope, but sometimes it is taken from a sentence further on.

SERMO

CVm audisset Iohannes in vincula opera cristi Mathei xi § In desen heiligen ewangelio worden ons bewijst twee puncten tot onse lere Dat eerste is dat herodes iohannem dede vangen ende inden kerker leggen [...] Dat ander punt is dat iohannes vten karker daer hi lach gheuanghen twee van sinen iongheren sende tot ihesum, als ghi ghehoert hebt int ewangelium [...] (Sermon 3, openings 11a–12a)

[Sermon

Cum audisset Iohannes in vincula opera Cristi (Matthew 11). In this hòly Gospel we are taught two points. The first is that Herod had John captured and placed in the dungeon. [...] The other point is that John, from the dungeon in which he was imprisoned, sent two of his disciples to Jesus, as you have heard in the Gospel. [...]].

Obviously, the theme serves to identify the pericope that is discussed in the sermon. In a number of cases the references to the Bible placed at the beginning of the pericope and at the beginning of the sermon differ, one of the two being wrong. There are remarkably many mistakes of this kind, mostly a wrong chapter number, sometimes a wrong evangelist. This suggests that the sermons were written as a separate collection, and only afterwards were

---

26 The Sunday in the Octave of Epiphany; Palm Sunday (which has a Passion Harmony instead of the Gospel); Trinity Sunday (has the same Gospel as the Sixth Sunday after Easter, with Sermon 25); Twenty-Fourth Sunday after Pentecost (the Gospel pericope coincides for the larger part with the pericope of the Fourth Sunday in Lent, with its corresponding Sermon 17). On the Passion Harmony see Folkerts, 'Appropriating the Passion', especially the section 'The Passion Harmony in Printed Lectionaries'.

integrated into the pericope collection. The Latin theme at the beginning of a sermon is not taken from the complete Bible text but from a Latin pericope: anaphora have been made explicit, for example: *Et ut appropinquavit, videns civitatem flevit super illam* ['And when He drew near, seeing the city, He wept over it', Luke 19. 41] is rephrased as *Cum appropinquasset Jhesus Jherusalem, flevit super eam* ['When Jhesus had drawn nearer to Jerusalem, He wept over it', Sermo 36, opening 222b].

There is no division of the theme, that is, no *divisio intra*, by which the theme is divided to structure the sermon, but almost all sermons are subdivided in two or more points (a maximum of five points). The majority of the sermons discuss two points: thirty-two out of fifty-one.[27] The division is done with a rather conventional expression: 'In desen heiligen ewangelio worden ons bewijst twee puncten tot onse lere Dat eerste is [...]' ['In this Gospel two points are taught to us. The first one is [...]', Sermon 3, opening 11a]; 'In desen heiligen ewangelio worden ons bescreuen drie punten tot onser lere Dat eerste is [...]' ['In this Gospel three points are written to instruct us. The first one is [...]', Sermon 14, opening 65b]; 'Nv vinde ic drie punten der vroetheit in desen rentemeiste<r> die ons oec noet sijn Die eerste vroetheit was [...]' ['Now I find three points of wisdom in this steward, which we need. The first (kind of) wisdom is [...]', Sermon 35, opening 219b]. Sometimes these points take the form of a simple *divisio extra*: 'god den vader die goet saet heeft gesaeiet ende dat in drien ackeren Die eerste acker is [...]' ['God the Father, who sows His good seed and He did so into three fields. The first field is [...]', Sermon 10, opening 47a], or the Gospel on the miraculous multiplication of the five loaves of bread and two fishes: 'Dat eerste broet is [...]' ['The first loaf is [...]', Sermon 17, opening 100b]. Often a point is subdivided in yet another number of points.

The explanation almost always provides a moral, emblematic (as in the German *Dingallegorische*) interpretation of an object, a person, an act, or an event.

> Ende doe hi quam anden berghe van olyueten doe sende hi petrum ende phillippum. [...] Bi desen twe jongeren soe verstaen wi alle predicaren die dat woert gods prediken ende leren den volcke Dese sullen mit predicacien beesteliken menschen dat sijn alle sondaren tot gode brengen Want die sondare is ghelijc eenre beesten. want dat beest heeft altoes die oghen in die eerde. Hier bi verstaen wi die ghierighe menschen. die altoes hoer oghen hoere begheerten slaen op verganclike dinghen [...] (Sermon 1, opening 2b–3a)

> > [The pericope tells about Jesus's triumphal entry into Jerusalem, on Palm Sunday, Matthew 21. 1–9]. When He came to Mount Olivet, He sent Peter and Philip out [to fetch an ass in a nearby village on which Jesus would be seated to make his entry]. [...] We interpret these

---

27 Another two sermons announce two points, but in fact discuss three points (Sermons 22 and 42).

two disciples as all preachers who preach the Word of God and teach it to the people. These [preachers] will bring bestial people — that is, all sinners — to God. For the sinner is like an animal, because an animal always directs its eyes to the earth. We interpret them [that is, the sinners] as desirous people, who have the eyes of their desire always on transitory things [...]].

Sometimes the explanation is confirmed by a quotation from the Bible or an authority like St Augustine or St Gregory,[28] or by a very short, rudimentary exemplum.[29] Usually, a sermon ends with a one-sentence exhortation.

A few sermons have a concluding formulation (Sermons 11, 35, 50, 51). The last sermon of the temporale has one, and the sermon on the Dedication of the Church at the end of the sanctorale: '[...] tot welcken ewighe leuen ons moet brengen die vader die soen ende die heilighe gheest. Amen'. ['[...] to which eternal life must bring us the Father, the Son and the Holy Spirit. Amen', Sermon 50, opening 221b], and 'Dat moet ons gonnen die vader die soen ende die heilighe gheest. Amen'. ['May the Father, the Son and the Holy Spirit give this to us. Amen', Sermon 51, opening 336a].

The sermons are usually short: about one and half pages in print, about forty-five to fifty lines, on average about 380 words.[30] They have a factual-moral slant and are intellectually not very demanding. Sometimes the public is addressed as 'lieve broeders' ['dear brothers', Sermons 1 and 3] and 'lieve menschen' ['dear people', Sermon 4].[31] Usually, addresses serve more as a means to mark the structure of the text: 'Nv lieue broders' ['Now, dear brothers [...]', Sermon 3, opening 11b], or 'Nu lieuen menschen' ['Now, dear people [...]', Sermon 4, opening 19b].

The author addresses his audience as plural *ghi* ('you'): 'soe leestmen dit ewangelium als ghi ghehoert hebt dat [...]' ['So, as you have heard, (in) this Gospel is read that [...]', Sermon 18, opening 114a]. The author refers to himself in the first person singular, but not very often: 'dat proue ic v bi .iiij. redenen' ['I will show this to you by three arguments', Sermon 4, opening 19a], 'Hier om rade ic v [...]' ['Therefore I advise you to [...]', Sermon 5, opening 30a],

---

28 Quoted authorities: St Augustine (12 times: Sermons 1 (2 ×), 5, 9, 11, 17, 21, 23, 33, 35, 39, 42), St Gregory (6 times: Sermons 14 (2 ×), 27, 29, 38, 41), St Bernard de Clairvaux (3 times: Sermons 6, 9, 44), St Jerome (2 times: Sermons 2, 31), 'Tulius' (that is, Marcus Tullius Cicero) (Sermon 22), St Ambrose (Sermon 14), St John Chrysostom (Sermon 47).

29 In Sermon 6 (of a thief), 8 (an ill lady), 9 (a king's child), 12 (a holy father), 16 (a holy father), 43 (Makarios), and 51 (Paul the Hermit) (openings 36a, 40b, 45b–46a, 55a–b, 87b, 246a, 325b–326a).

30 Sermon 1 is exceptionally long (*c.* 928 words); the second longest is Sermon 2 (*c.* 535 words), the shortest Sermon 39 (*c.* 205 words). The sermons tend to become shorter as the temporale progresses.

31 Zieleman ('Evangeliën door het jaar', p. 118 n. 82) asserts that the address 'lieve broeders' ['dear brothers'] suggests a provenance from a male convent, but in my view this is a too exclusive interpretation of a masculinist wording, comparable with the fact that most Epistle pericopes open with the address 'Broeders'.

THE GOUDA GOSPEL SERMONS   421

or 'Dit heilighe ewangelium exponeert hem seluen als ghi ghehoert hebt hier om wil ic een cort sermoen maken. mer twee dinghen wil ic ontbinden' ['This holy Gospel explicates itself, as you have heard. Therefore I want to make a short sermon. But two things I want to explain', Sermon 12, openings 54b–55a].

Sin, confession and penitence are frequent subjects. The words 'biechten' ('to confess') or 'biechte' ('confession') appear in twelve sermons.[32] Some subjects are fit for a lay audience, like Sunday observance (Sermon 6), marriage and raising children (Sermon 7), and the prohibition against talking in the church (Sermons 51).

Authorship

The pericopes seem to have a different author than the sermons. The pericopes are taken from the northern Netherlandish translation of the New Testament.[33] This translation was made in the early years of the *Devotio moderna* in the last decade of the fourteenth century, between 1387 and 1399 to be precise.[34] Referring to a passage in *De viris illustribus* by the Windesheim historiographer Johannes Busch (d. 1479 or later), most scholars attribute it to Johannes Scutken (d. 1423), who lived as a *clericus* in the monastery of Windesheim.[35] He was a well educated, gifted person with sufficient capacities to be ordained a priest and to become a choir monk. Nevertheless he preferred to keep the — usually transitory — state of *clericus* all his life and did not want to be professed as a regular canon.[36]

So the pericopes stem from an existing translation of the New Testament, which was about eighty years old at that time.[37] One would assume that Leeu

---

32 Sermons 3, 4, 5, 9, 15, 16, 19, 32, 33, 35, 38, 40.

33 Edition: *Novum Testamentum Devotionis Modernae*.

34 Suzan Folkerts, 'De Noord-Nederlandse vertaling van het Nieuwe Testament (eind veertiende eeuw)', in *De Bijbel in de Lage Landen: elf eeuwen van vertalen*, ed. by Paul Gilliaerts and others (Heerenveen: Royal Jongbloed, 2015), pp. 164–76 (pp. 170–72); Folkerts, 'Middle Dutch *Epistles and Gospels*', pp. 54, 56, 57.

35 See Johannes Busch, *De viris illustribus*, ch. 64, *Des Augustinerpropstes Iohannes Busch Chronicon Windeshemense und Liber de reformatione monasteriorum*, ed. by Karl Grube, Geschichtsquellen der Provinz Sachsen und angrenzender Gebiete, 19 (Halle: Hendel, 1886; reprint: Farnborough: Gregg International Publishers, 1968), p. 192; Folkerts, 'De Noord-Nederlandse vertaling', pp. 166–68. According to Zieleman, Busch does not refer to a translation of the New Testament by Scutken, but to one of the versions of the Zwolle Cycle of pericope sermons (Zieleman, 'Evangeliën door het jaar').

36 In the early *Devotio moderna* there was more room to choose one's own way of living on the margins of official standard possibilities; see John Van Engen, 'The Work of Gerlach Peters (d. 1411): Spiritual Diarist and Letter-Writer, a Mystic among the Devout', *Ons Geestelijk Erf*, 73 (1999), 150–77 (pp. 164–71).

37 Jan Deschamps, 'De verspreiding van Johan Scutkens vertaling van het Nieuwe Testament en de oudtestamentische perikopen', *Nederlands Archief voor Kerkgeschiedenis*, 56 (1975), 159–79 (pp. 164–67); this is also published under the same title in *In navolging: een bundel studies*

took his Gospel pericopes from his *Alle die epistelen ende ewangelien vanden gheheelen iaere*, which he had printed in May 1477. But we have to be careful. For example, *Alle die epistelen ende ewangelien* lacks the pericope for Sermon 50: Matthew 9. 18–26 for the Twenty-Sixth Sunday after Pentecost.[38] A thorough investigation may establish the relations and dependencies of both texts. At any rate, we do not know who compiled this pericope collection from the northern Netherlandish translation of the New Testament, but we may have to look for him in the same circles as the author of the sermons.

Unfortunately, it is not known who wrote the sermons. A Latin or other source can not be identified.[39] Gheraert Leeu was the first to print these sermons[40] and we assume that they were written for the occasion. We do not know whether the author lived in the same town as Leeu, but if so, two religious convents come to mind as the home base of the author of the sermons: the convent of Observant Friars Minor and the so-called Collatiehuis.

In Gouda the first convent of Observant Friars Minor in the Cologne province of the order was established, in 1418. After decades of problems, it flourished around the middle of the fifteenth century.[41] The Friars Minor furthered the liturgical participation of the laity.[42]

---

aangeboden aan C. C. de Bruin bij zijn afscheid als hoogleraar te Leiden, ed. by M. J. M. de Haan and others (Leiden: Brill, 1975), pp. 159–79 (pp. 164–67); Suzan Folkerts, 'The Cloister or the City? The Appropriation of the New Testament by Lay Readers in an Urban Setting', in *Cultures of Religious Reading in the Late Middle Ages: Instructing the Soul, Feeding the Spirit, and Awakening the Passion*, ed. by Sabrina Corbellini, Utrecht Studies in Medieval Literacy, 25 (Turnhout: Brepols, 2013), pp. 175–99; Folkerts, 'De Noord-Nederlandse vertaling van het Nieuwe Testament', pp. 172–75; Folkerts, 'Appropriating the Passion', the section on 'The Passion Harmony in Printed Lectionaries'; Thom Mertens, 'Pragmatic Forms of Middle Dutch Bible Translation', in *Every(wo)man's Books of Salvation: The Most Popular Medieval Religious Texts in Europe, Their Circulation and Reception*, ed. by Florence Bourgne and Géraldine Veysseyre (Turnhout: Brepols, forthcoming), pragmatic form no. 3.7.

38 *Alle die epistelen ende ewangelien vanden gheheelen iaere* (CA 686) has the Epistle for the Twenty-Sixth Sunday after Pentecost (opening 112b), but the Gospel pericope is wanting.

39 A possible clue is the fact that at least two sermons are related to sermons in Low German plenaries of the time (see below, nn. 69 and 70). This clue needs further research.

40 For the four manuscripts, each of them supposedly copied from a print, see n. 10 and Appendix 2. None of these four manuscripts contains all fifty-one sermons.

41 Johannes Taal, *De Goudse kloosters in de Middeleeuwen* (Hilversum: Brand, 1960), pp. 28–34; Koen Goudriaan, 'De verdwenen kloosters', in *Gouda*, ed. by Wim Denslagen, De Nederlandse monumenten van geschiedenis en kunst (Zeist: Rijksdienst voor Monumentenzorg / Zwolle: Waanders, 2001), pp. 171–211 (pp. 187–88); *Kloosterlijst: beknopt overzicht van de Nederlandse kloosters tot 1800*, 'G16: Gouda, Franciscanen II'.

42 Bert Roest, *Franciscan Literature of Religious Instruction before the Council of Trent*, Studies in the History of Christian Traditions, 117 (Leiden: Brill, 2004), pp. 366, 368, 369; Koen Goudriaan, 'The Church and the Market: Vernacular Religious Works and the Early Printing Press in the Low Countries, 1477–1540', in Koen Goudriaan, *Piety in Practice and Print: Essays on the Late Medieval Religious Landscape*, ed. by Anna Dlabačová and Ad Tervoort (Hilversum: Verloren, 2016), pp. 240–56 (p. 240); Koen Goudriaan, 'The Franciscans, the Laity and the Printing Press', in Goudriaan, *Piety in Practice and Print*, pp. 279–308; Koen Goudriaan, 'Een kerkelijk catechese-offensief?: misverklaringen op de drukpers rond 1500',

THE GOUDA GOSPEL SERMONS   423

The Brethren of the Common Life lived in the Collatiehuis or St Paul's convent on condition that they delivered a collation (that is, an admonitory sermon) every Sunday afternoon to interested lay people.[43] Presumably these sermons were related to the Gospel pericope of the day and a collection of pericope sermons may well be a derivation of this activity.[44] After 1483, probably *circa* 1494, the Gouda Collatiebroeders started a printing press, primarily with commercial motives. They were not a competitor of Leeu because Leeu had moved his printing press from Gouda to Antwerp in 1484. Furthering Christian belief was of course the basis of their activities, but as publishers the Collatiebroeders lacked a coherent strategy. The idea that they used the printing press deliberately as a tool for their apostolate cannot sufficiently be substantiated.[45]

In 1506 the Friars and the Collatiebroeders worked together, publishing a very successful explanation of the Mass for the laity, of which adapted translations were made in Latin, English, and French. The Collatiebroeders asked the Observant Franciscan Friar Gerrit van der Goude (*fl.* 1500–1513?) to 'arrange some material in order to hear Mass devoutly',[46] which he did by composing his *Boexken vander missen*.[47] This is a clear example of a Gouda Friar

---

in *Terug naar Gouda: religieus leven in de maalstroom van de tijd*, ed. by Paul H. A. M. Abels, Jan Jacobs, and Mirjam van Veen (Zoetermeer: Meinema, 2014), pp. 73–95. All the texts discussed in these publications are explanations of the Mass, or aids for attending Mass (Passion meditations; how to prepare for Communion, and so forth); there are no pericope books or pericope sermons.

43 A. H. L. Hensen, 'Henric van Arnhem's Kronyk van het fraterhuis te Gouda', *Bijdragen en Mededeelingen van het Historisch Genootschap*, 20 (1899), 1–46; Taal, *De Goudse kloosters*, pp. 34–38; Thom Mertens, 'Collatio und Codex', pp. 164–69 (esp. p. 168 n. 24); A. G. Weiler, *Volgens de norm van de vroege Kerk: de geschiedenis van de huizen van de broeders van het Gemene leven in Nederland*, Middeleeuwse studies, 13 (Nijmegen: Katholieke Universiteit, Centrum voor Middeleeuwse Studies, 1997), pp. 138–49; *Monasticon Fratrum Vitae Communis*, ed. by Wolfgang Leesch, Ernest Persoons, and Anton G. Weiler, Archief- en Bibliotheekwezen van België, Special Issues 18–20, 3 vols (Brussel: Archief- en Bibliotheekwezen van België, 1977–2004), III (2004), 195–220; Goudriaan, 'De verdwenen kloosters', pp. 189–95; *Kloosterlijst*, 'G 18: Gouda, Broeders des gemenen levens: Collatiebroeders'.

44 Weiler mentions no writing activity from the Collatiebroeders, except the house chronicle of Hendrik van Arnhem (see n. 43). See *Monasticon Fratrum*, III (2004), 208, § 3.3 ('Authors and Editors').

45 Koen Goudriaan, 'Apostolate and Printing: The *Collaciebroeders* of Gouda and their Press', in *Between Lay Piety and Academic Theology: Studies Presented to Christoph Burger on the Occasion of his 65ᵗʰ Birthday*, ed. by Ulrike Hascher-Burger, August den Hollander, and Wim Janse, Brill's Series in Church History, 46 (Leiden: Brill, 2010), pp. 433–52.

46 Cf. '[…] dat ick doch wat soude willen ordineren om devoteliken misse te horen', cited by Goudriaan, 'The Church and the Market', p. 240.

47 Gouda: Collatiebroeders, 1506 (NK 982); see Benjamin De Troeyer, *Bio-bibliographia Franciscana Neerlandica, saeculi XVI*, 2 vols (Nieuwkoop: De Graaf, 1969–1970), I (1969), 7–13, II (1970), 105–14 (nos 173–92); Andrew Pettegree and Malcolm Walsby, *Netherlandish Books: Books Published in the Low Countries and Dutch Books Printed Abroad before 1601* (Leiden: Brill, 2011), I, 594–95 (nos 13596–631); Goudriaan, 'Een kerkelijk catechese-offensief?', pp. 84–95; Anna Dlabačová, 'Seeing beyond Signs: Allegorical Explanations

Minor composing a text for the local printing press, but the evidential value is low because it stems from almost thirty years after the publication of Leeu's *Alle die ewangelien vanden gheheelen iaer ende vanden sonnendaghen mitter glosen*.

If we look for evidence in the Gouda Gospel Sermons themselves: they seem to show a certain sympathy for religious orders. Marriage is presented as an order, analogous to religious orders:

> Dat eerste punt is dat ihesus cristus god ende mensche huwelic heuet ghemaect Ander oerdene hebben ghesticht santen. als sinte benedictus die swerte oerdene. sincte bernaert die graeuwe. sinte franciscus die minre broeders. mer huwelike staet heeft allene ghemaect god. mer huwelike staet heeft allene ghemaect god Och hoe salich sijn si die aldus groten abt ende prelaet hebben (Sermon 7, opening 23b).

> [The first point is that Jesus Christ, God and man, created marriage. Other orders have been founded by saints, such as St Benedict the Black Order, St Bernard the Grey Order, St Francis the Friars Minor. But the marital state was made solely by God. How blessed are those who have such a great abbot and prelate!].

Sermon 46 also holds religious orders in high esteem. God has sent messengers three times to invite people to the wedding: the Old Testament prophets, the New Testament apostles, and the preachers today: 'dat sijn predikers minre broeders augustinen ende onse vrouwen broeders' ['that is, preachers [*or:* Dominicans?*], Friars Minor, Augustinians [*or:* regular canons of St Augustine?*], and Carmelites'].[48] These two passages suggest an appreciation for religious orders, but in both cases the Friar Minors are not mentioned first. This seems to weaken their position as candidate authors of the cycle.

So, when we search in Gouda for the author, there were at least two institutions whose members could have written the sermons on the Sunday Gospels, published by Gheraert Leeu in 1477: the Observant Friars Minor and the Collatiebroeders. For the time being, these are just possibilities, not certainties.

The text of *Die epistelen ende ewangelien mitten sermonen* was revised at least twice. The 1493 print by Jacob van Breda in Deventer is the first edition to report in its incipit that the text is 'anderwerf verbetert ende ghecorrigeert' ['for the second time emended and corrected']. This wording implies a first revision, but when this took place is not clear from the incipits of earlier prints. Maybe *anderwerf* has to be interpreted more neutrally as 'again', the 1493 print presenting a first revision. The 1528 print by Willem Vorsterman reports that it offers a third revision: 'derdewerf verbetert ende ghecorrigeert' ['for the third

---

of the Mass in Medieval Dutch Literature', in *Quid est sacramentum? Visual Representation of Sacred Mysteries in Early Modern Europe, 1400–1700*, ed. by Walter S. Melion, Elizabeth Carson Pastan, and Lee Palmer Wandel (Leiden: Brill, 2020), pp. 199–226 (pp. 212–19).

48 Sermon 46, opening 140b.

THE GOUDA GOSPEL SERMONS   425

time emended and corrected'], clearly understanding the *anderwerf* of earlier prints as 'for the second time'. Further research has to show what the scope of these revisions was. It is possible that they only affected the sermons or just the pericopes. An analysis of the variants for the (randomly chosen) Fourth Sunday of Lent in a number of editions shows no major differences between the revisions.[49] In the four editions of Peter van Os van Breda (1487–1493), the Epistle pericope has been revised to some extent. In the print by Symon Cock from 1553, the text of the Epistle is partly adapted to the authoritative Leuven Bible of 1548, but the text of the Gospel is not.[50]

Success

Leeu's Gospels with glosses (CA 685), especially in Veldener's format of *Die epistelen ende ewangelien mitten sermonen* were very successful between 1477 and 1553, in particular in the first decades. Between 1477 and 1522 no separate edition of all four Gospels together or the New Testament was printed in Dutch, or at least no edition from this period has come down to us.[51] There are two editions of complete Bibles in Köln in 1478 in Low German dialects, which are near to the Eastern Dutch dialects.[52] And in 1516–1518 there are three editions of a virtually complete Bible.[53] In 1522 there is a sudden change

---

49 The texts for the Fourth Sunday in Lent include Galatians 4. 22–31 (Epistle), John 6. 1–14 (Gospel), and Sermon 17. The sample was taken from the editions at my disposal (in PDF, photographs, or checked in the original manuscripts): the manuscripts from Brussels and London, and the printed editions nos 1–4, 6–10, 12–22, 25, 26, 28, 29, 31, 33, 35, 36, 38–40 from Appendix 2.

50 See Wim François, 'De Leuvense Bijbel (1548) en de katholieke bijbelvertalingen van de tweede helft van de zestiende eeuw', in *De Bijbel in de Lage Landen: elf eeuwen van vertalen*, ed. by Paul Gilliaerts and others (Heerenveen: Royal Jongbloed, 2015), pp. 266–303; Wim François, 'Bible Production and Bible Readers in the Age of Confessionalisation: The Case of the Low Countries', in *Lay Readers of the Bible in Early Modern Europe*, ed. by Erminia Ardissino and Élise Boilett, Intersections, 68 (Leiden: Brill, 2020), pp. 190–216 (pp. 196–202).

51 See *Biblia sacra*, 1477–1522; Suzan Folkerts and Arend Elias Oostindiër, 'New Bibles and Old Reading Habits Around 1522: The Position of the New Testament Translation of the Devotio Moderna among Dutch Printed Bibles', *Quaerendo*, 47 (2017), 175–98 (pp. 179–81).

52 *Biblia Sacra* 1478.B.dut.HQ.a and 1478.B.dut.HQ.b; C. C. de Bruin, *De Statenbijbel en zijn voorgangers: Nederlandse bijbelvertalingen vanaf de Reformatie*, revised by F. G. M. Broeyer (Haarlem: Nederlands Bijbelgenootschap / Brussel: Belgisch Bijbelgenootschap, 1993), p. 36. According to *Biblia Sacra*, the language of these editions is Dutch; Sonderegger designates them as *niederdeutsch* (Low German); see Stefan Sonderegger, 'Geschichte deutschsprachiger Bibelübersetzungen in Grundzügen', in *Sprachgeschichte: ein Handbuch zur Geschichte der deutschen Sprache und ihre Erforschung*, ed. by Werner Besch and others, 2 vols, 2nd edn (Berlin: De Gruyter, 1998–2004), I (1998), 229–84 (p. 257); Folkerts, 'Reading the Scriptures', pp. 165–73, discerns a Low Saxon (*unde-*)version and a Low Renish (*ende-*)version (p. 166).

53 *Den bible int corte* (NK 366–68; *Biblia Sacra* 1516.OTpart.dut.CdG.a, 1518.Bpart.dut.CdG.a, 1518.Bpart.dut.CdG.b); see Isaac Le Long, *Boek-zaal der Nederduytsche Bybels* (Amsterdam: Vieroot, 1732), pp. 466–70; De Bruin, *De Statenbijbel en zijn voorgangers*, pp. 37–38.

under the influence of the Reformation: Luther's German translation of the New Testament is translated and from this moment on the canon of the Holy Scripture plays an important role in Bible editions.[54] But in the years 1477–1522 the pericope collections with the sermons are absolutely the dominant form of editions of texts from the New Testament.[55]

Obviously, there was a strong preference for Bible reading in the form of pericopes with sermons. How is this to be explained? It is known that already before the beginning of the Reformation there was an increasing interest in Bible reading.[56] Did this increasing interest in Bible reading promote the demand for collections of pericopes with sermons, or do we have to assume that lay people sought an increasing involvement in the liturgy of the Church? Vernacular Mass and Office books did exist, but we do not see an increase in numbers there.[57] And texts explaining the Holy Mass to the laity do not advise lay people to take a pericope collection with them to Mass, but to meditate during Mass on the Passion of Jesus Christ, presenting the Mass as a re-enactment of the Passion.[58] The vernacular texts used during Mass were prayers, especially prayers for Holy Communion. So without doubt, 'Epistles and Gospels with Sermons' are a para-liturgical genre, but it is not likely that they were intended to be used (or were actually used) in church during Mass. It is more likely that they were used at home to prepare — or rather to digest — the Sunday Mass, possibly in reading sessions on Sunday afternoons.[59]

This is one side of the story: the needs of the laity. On the other side we have the concerns of the Church regarding lay people reading the Bible. There was no official ban on reading the Bible, but authors had a more or less severe view on this. From the different views we may deduce a double hierarchy of

---

54 August A. den Hollander, *De Nederlandse bijbelvertalingen, 1522–1545*, Bibliotheca bibliographica Neerlandica, 37 (Nieuwkoop: De Graaf, 1997), pp. 13–21; Wim François, 'Naar een "confessionalisering" van bijbelvertalingen in de zestiende eeuw: inleiding', in *De Bijbel in de Lage Landen: elf eeuwen van vertalen*, ed. by Paul Gilliaerts and others (Heerenveen: Royal Jongbloed, 2015), pp. 204–19; François, 'Bible Production and Bible Readers'; Folkerts, 'Middle Dutch *Epistles and Gospels*', especially p. 56.

55 Folkerts, 'Middle Dutch *Epistles and Gospels*', pp. 61, 73–74.

56 Goudriaan, 'The Church and the Market', pp. 243–44.

57 On the vernacular Mass and Office Books in manuscripts: Youri Desplenter, *Al aertrijc segt lofsanc: Middelnederlandse vertalingen van Latijnse hymnen en sequensen*, Studies op het gebied van de oudere Nederlandse letterkunde, 3, 2 vols (Gent: Koninklijke Academie voor Nederlandse Taal- en Letterkunde, 2008), I, 327–28, 403–33; Youri Desplenter, 'The Latin Liturgical Song Subtitled: Middle Dutch Translations of Hymns and Sequences', *Church History and Religious Culture*, 88 (2008), 395–413 (pp. 402–03); Thom Mertens, 'Praying in the Vernacular: Middle Dutch Imitative Forms of the Divine Office from the 1370s to 1520s', in *Nuns' Literacies in Medieval Europe: The Hull Dialogue*, ed. by Virginia Blanton, Veronica O'Mara, and Patricia Stoop, Medieval Women: Texts and Contexts, 26 (Turnhout: Brepols, 2013), pp. 133–46 (pp. 142–44).

58 See n. 42.

59 See Mertens, 'Collatio und Codex', p. 174.

appropriateness of Bible reading for the laity:[60] the New Testament was deemed to be more appropriate than the Old Testament; and in both testaments: the narrative books more appropriate than the discursive books (that is, Wisdom Books, Epistles), and these books in their turn were considered more appropriate than prophetic books. According to this twofold hierarchy, the Old Testament prophets were most inappropriate and the New Testament's Gospels and Acts of the Apostles the most appropriate. But all authors agree that the pericopes read and explained during Mass were the safest form of Bible reading. The main instruments for guiding the devotion of the laity were the liturgy with sermons, and the sacrament of Confession. From this we may deduce that the initiative to compose 'Epistles and Gospels with Sermons' was taken by ecclesiastical authorities. But, as Koen Goudriaan has shown, it is not likely that there was a deliberate publication strategy on the part of the Church in the Low Countries.[61] Nevertheless, we may assume that the Church looked at this form of Bible reading with a benevolent eye.

In a pericope collection with sermons lay people possessed a guided and measured form of Bible reading. And the aspect of the cost also played a role in this.[62] A complete New Testament was more expensive; and even more so, if the text were provided with a running commentary (something like that was not even published in the late medieval Low Countries).

The printers are the third party involved. Their publication list was not based primarily on ideological or missionary interests. Their activities were not subject to some kind of direction or supervision by the Church.[63] The main interest of the printers was to sell books.[64] They had to find a reading public and they sought to print what the public wanted to buy. So we return to the public. The interest of book buying lay readers seems to be the most important explanation.

In my view, the success of *Die epistelen ende evangelien metten sermoenen* has to be explained by a fortunate combination of interests — in order of

---

60 *Was dürfen Laien lesen? Gerhard Zerbolt von Zutphen, De libris teutonicalibus / Een verclaringhe vanden deutschen boeken, lateinisch und mittelniederländisch*, ed. by Nikolaus Staubach and Rudolf Suntrup (Münster: Aschendorff, 2019), pp. 29–33, 78–80, 166–70 (§ 3.3); Nikolaus Staubach, 'Gerhard Zerbolt von Zutphen und die Apologie der Laienlektüre in der Devotio moderna', in *Laienlektüre und Buchmarkt im späten Mittelalter*, ed. by Thomas Kock and Rita Schlusemann, Gesellschaft, Kultur und Schrift: Mediävistische Beiträge, 5 (Frankfurt am Main: Peter Lang, 1997), pp. 221–89; Mikel Kors, 'Die Bibel für Laien: Neuansatz oder Sackgasse? Der Bibelübersetzer von 1360 und Gerhard Zerbolt von Zutphen', in *Kirchenreform von unten: Gerhard Zerbolt von Zutphen und die Brüder vom gemeinsamen Leben*, ed. by Nikolaus Staubach, Tradition — Reform — Innovation, 6 (Frankfurt am Main: Peter Lang, 2004), pp. 243–46; Folkerts, 'Middle Dutch *Epistles and Gospels*', pp. 72–73.
61 Goudriaan, 'The Church and the Market', pp. 253–55.
62 Already mentioned in 1937 by C. C. de Bruin, *De Statenbijbel en zijn voorgangers* (Leiden: Sijthoff, 1937), pp. 79–80; Folkerts, 'Middle Dutch *Epistles and Gospels*', p. 61; see also n. 19.
63 Koen Goudriaan, 'Boekdistributie langs kerkelijke kanalen in de Late Middeleeuwen', *Jaarboek voor Nederlandse Boekgeschiedenis*, 8 (2001), 43–58; Goudriaan, 'Apostolate and Printing', p. 434.
64 Folkerts, 'Middle Dutch *Epistles and Gospels*', p. 67.

importance: the interest of the readers-buyers, the interest of the printers, and the interest of the Church.

This success lasted unto the middle of the sixteenth century. When the Protestant Bible translations were published — in Dutch from 1522 on — the Catholic Church and Emperor Charles V (1500–1558) increasingly mistrusted reading the Bible in the vernacular and they condemned the accompanying texts, which interpret the Bible text. The Council of Trent (1545–1563) did not take a stand in this matter and left the problem to the regional ecclesiastical and secular authorities. Charles V wanted to promote correct, Catholic translations in his attempt to stamp out heterodox translations. The Leuven theologians, who played a prominent part in the discussions in the Low Countries, at first tolerated the reading of the Bible text in an orthodox translation and without paratextual elements. This view developed into a decidedly negative attitude towards reading the Bible in the vernacular. In 1552–1553 they advocated an imperial prohibition of all vernacular Bibles. In Rome too, the opposition against reading the Bible in the vernacular grew. The Catholic Church wished to emphasize the link between the Bible and the liturgy and the exclusive mediating role of the Church in the interpretation of the Bible, through the spoken sermon.[65] The last known edition of *Alle die epistelen ende ewangelien mitten sermonen* was published in 1553. Pericope books continued to be a popular genre, but without any glosses and sermons. In the years from 1547 to the 1580s eight editions were published, under the title *Evangelien ende Epistelen alsoo men die doort gantsche Jaer op alle Sondaghen, ende ander heylighe daghen inder heyligher Kercken houdt*.[66] In the next (almost) two decades no Dutch Roman Catholic Bibles or pericope books were printed.[67] The production resumed in 1599 with the so called 'Moerentorf Bible' and in 1607 with pericopes that where translated from the Tridentine Roman missal, published in 1570. About 180 editions appeared in the subsequent two centuries.[68]

---

65 See Den Hollander, *De Nederlandse bijbelvertalingen*; Wim François, 'The Catholic Church and the Vernacular Bible in the Low Countries: A Paradigm Shift in the 1550s?', in *Discovering the Riches of the Word: Religious Reading in Late Medieval and Early Modern Europe*, ed. by Sabrina Corbellini, Margriet Hoogvliet, and Bart Ramakers, Intersections, 38 (Leiden: Brill, 2015), pp. 234–81; François, 'Bible Production and Bible Readers'; the essays of August den Hollander and Wim François in *De Bijbel in de Lage Landen*, pp. 203–303.

66 Numbers according to *Biblia Sacra*.

67 François, 'Catholic Church and the Vernacular Bible', pp. 265–68; François, 'De Leuvense Bijbel', pp. 298–99, 301. *Belgica typographica* mentions an edition of *Evangelien ende epistelen […] op alle de sondaghen ende heylighe daghen* (Antwerpen: H. Swingen (printer), J. van Keerbergen (bookseller), 1600); because of the shortened title it is not clear which text exactly is concerned. See *Belgica typographica: 1541–1600*, ed. by Elly Cockx-Indestege, Geneviève Glorieux, and Bart Op De Beeck, Collection du Centre national de l'archéologie et de l'histoire du livre, 2, 4 vols (Nieuwkoop: De Graaf, 1968–1994), I (1968), 81 (no. 1092).

68 Number according to *Biblia Sacra*. See also Bern. Alfrink, 'Over Nederlandsche pericopenvertalingen', *Studia Catholica*, 12 (1936), 200–18, 306–27.

THE GOUDA GOSPEL SERMONS 429

Appendix 1: List of the Gouda Gospel Sermons

This list is based on the *Alle die epistelen ende ewangelien mitten sermonen vanden ghehelen jaere* (Utrecht: Johan Veldener, 1478 [CA 687]) after the copy in Utrecht, Universiteitsbibliotheek, MAG: 130 D 23 (Rariora). The textual differences between the sermons in this edition and those in *Alle die ewangelien vanden gheheelen iaer ende vanden sonnendaghen mitter glosen* (Gouda: Gheraert Leeu, 1477 [CA 685]) are negligible.

The sermon number (provided by me), the occasion, the theme, and the number of words are given, followed by a very short summary of the content, indicating the main points of the sermon. The number of words is approximate. It can vary, partly because the word separation in Middle Dutch has some variation. The Middle Dutch text makes little distinction between Jesus, Christ, the Lord, and God. In the summary, this is not done either.

Sermon 1: First Sunday of Advent; no theme (Gospel of the day: Matthew 21. 1–9); approx. 928 words. Four kinds of tribute and service to Christ: (1) of his disciples, (2) of the donkey and her young, (3) of the people at the triumphal entry into Jerusalem, (4) of the children who shouted 'Hosanna in excelsis'.[69]

Sermon 2: Second Sunday of Advent; theme: Luke 21. 25; approx. 535 words. Two points: (1) the signs of the Last Judgment, (2) Christ's coming to judge.

Sermon 3: Third Sunday of Advent; theme: Matthew 11. 2; approx. 515 words. Two points: (1) Herod had John captured, (2) John sent two of his disciples out of the dungeon to Jesus.

Sermon 4: Fourth Sunday of Advent; theme: John 1. 19; approx. 498 words. Two points: (1) John called himself a voice in the wilderness, (2) John exhorts us to prepare the way for the Lord.

Sermon 5: First Sunday after Christmas; theme: Luke 2. 33; approx. 491 words. Two points: (1) Simeon blessed Jesus, (2) Simeon prophesied that Jesus would become a sign that will be contradicted.

Sermon 6: First Sunday after [the Octave of] the Epiphany; theme: Luke 2. 42; approx. 440 words. Three points: (1) we must observe Sunday duty, (2) we must educate the children well (exemplum of a thief reproaching his father for an insufficient education), (3) if we have lost Christ in the joy of sin, we must find Him in sorrow of penance.

---

69 This sermon is related to a sermon for Saturday before Palm Sunday in Middle Low German glossed plenaries; see the synoptic edition of the three versions in København, Det Kongelige Bibliotek, MS 94 fol., the so-called 'Lübeck plenary' (*Evangelia durch das ganze Jahr mit der Glosse*, Lübeck: Lukas Brandis, c. 1475 [GW M34205]), and *Eyn Spegel der mynschliken Behaltenisse* (Lübeck: Lukas Brandis, c. 1476 [GW M43046]), in Winfried Kämpfer, *Studien zu den gedruckten mittelniederdeutschen Plenarien: ein Beitrag zur Entstehungsgeschichte spätmittelalterlicher Erbauungsliteratur*, Niederdeutsche Studien, 2 (Münster: Böhlau, 1954), pp. 221–24: the four points are (almost) the same as in the Middle Dutch version but the interpretations differ.

Sermon 7: Second Sunday after the Octave of the Epiphany; theme: John 2. 1; approx. 425 words. Marital status should be honoured because of four points: (1) Jesus Christ instituted marriage, (2) marriage was instituted before Adam and Eve sinned, (3) marriage was instituted in Paradise, (4) Jesus Christ honoured marriage.

Sermon 8: Third Sunday after the Octave of the Epiphany; theme: Matthew 8. 1; approx. 434 words. Two points: (1) the mercy of the Lord Jesus Christ to heal a leper (exemplum of a leprous lady who had to be bathed in the blood of a king to recover), (2) what is to be understood by this leper.

Sermon 9: Fourth Sunday after the Octave of the Epiphany; theme: Matthew 8. 23; approx. 521 words. Two points: (1) we must always be afraid (exemplum of a king's child who is damned),[70] (2) when we are in distress, we must ask God for help.

Sermon 10: Fifth Sunday after the Octave of the Epiphany; theme: Matthew 13. 24; approx. 386 words. God has sowed his seed in three fields: (1) the Kingdom of Heaven, (2) the earthly Paradise, (3) the heart of the people.

Sermon 11: Sunday Septuagesima; theme: Matthew 20. 1; approx. 466 words. Three points: (1) by the father of the family we understand God the Father, (2) this father has planted a vineyard, (3) the father went out to find workmen.

Sermon 12: Sunday Sexagesima; theme: Luke 8. 5; approx. 375 words. Two points: (1) who sows good seed will harvest good fruit, (2) who sows his seed before him (exemplum of a holy father who sees a soul sitting at two tables, a richly laid table and an empty table).

Sermon 13: Sunday Quinquagesima; theme: Luke 18. 31; approx. 386 words. Two points: (1) Christ predicted His passion to His apostles, (2) Jesus cured a blind man.

Sermon 14: First Sunday of Lent; theme: Matthew 4. 1; approx. 469 words. Three points: (1) Jesus was led by the Holy Spirit in the desert, (2) He fasted there for forty days, (3) He was tempted by the devil.

Sermon 15: Second Sunday of Lent; theme: Matthew 15. 22; approx. 412 words. Two points: (1) the woman and her daughter, who was

---

70 This exemplum is also found in a Middle Low German sermon on the same theme (Matthew 8. 23) for the Third Sunday after the Epiphany; see *Mittelniederdeutsche Predigtfragmente aus einer Handschrift der Universitätsbibliothek zu Helsingfors*, ed. by Pekka Katara, Annales Academiae Scientiarum Fennicae, series B, 20,3 (Helsinki: Suomalainen Tiedeakatemia, 1926), pp. 69–73. The Low German sermon is not the same as the Middle Dutch sermon. Katara (p. 92, no. 11,62) corrects Wolfgang Stammler's attribution of this exemplum to Caesarius von Heisterbach's *Dialogus miraculorum*; the source of the exemplum is still unknown. See also Pekka Katara, 'Das Predigtmärlein von der unvollkommenen Beichte eines Königssohnes', *Neuphilologische Mitteilungen*, 29 (1928), 74–77 (p. 74).

THE GOUDA GOSPEL SERMONS   431

tormented by the devil, (2) how the woman succeeded in that the Lord answered her.

Sermon 16: Third Sunday in Lent; theme: Luke 11. 14; approx. 396 words. Two points: (1) the mute (exemplum of a holy father who asked the devil what he hates most in man), (2) the great grace of the Lord.

Sermon 17: Fourth Sunday in Lent; theme: John 6. 9; approx. 425 words. [Two points:] (1) five loaves of bread, (2) two fishes.

Sermon 18: Fifth Sunday in Lent (Passion Sunday); theme: John 8. 59; approx. 453 words. Two points: (1) the wrongness of the Jews, (2) the grace of Jesus Christ.

Sermon 19: Easter; theme: Mark 16. 1; approx. 413 words. 'Many points': (1) the reason why the three women wanted to anoint the dead body of Jesus, (2) they all three were called Mary, (3) Christ wanted to be buried in a stone tomb, (4) the guardians of the tomb were afraid of the angel whereas the three Marys were not, (5) the angel specifically named Peter when he said: 'Go and tell his disciples and Peter that He has risen'.

Sermon 20: First Sunday after Easter (Low Sunday); theme: John 20. 19; approx. 353 words. Three points: (1) Jesus visited His disciples with closed doors, (2) He stood among them, (3) He greeted them with 'Peace be to you'.

Sermon 21: Second Sunday after Easter; theme: John 10. 11; approx. 437 words. Two points: (1) Jesus compares Himself to a good shepherd, (2) the evil of the devil.

Sermon 22: Third Sunday after Easter; theme: John 16. 16; approx. 444 words. Two [*read*: three] points: (1) the shortness of life, (2) the sadness of the good people on earth, (3) the joy of eternal life.

Sermon 23: Fourth Sunday after Easter; theme: John 16. 5; approx. 384 words. Two points: (1) the comfort of the Holy Spirit, (2) the Holy Spirit will rebuke the world.

Sermon 24: Fifth Sunday after Easter; theme: John 16. 23; approx. 471 words. Two points: (1a) the comfort of the Holy Spirit,[71] (1b) the gentleness of the Lord, (2) what we will pray for.

Sermon 25: Sixth Sunday after Easter; theme: John 15. 26; approx. 304 words. Four things to prepare for the coming of the Holy Spirit: (1) purification of sins, (2) prayer, (3) abstinence and fasting, (4) listening to the Word of God and remembering it.

Sermon 26: Pentecost; theme: John 14. 23; approx. 251 words. Two things are needed: (1) perfect love for God, (2) peace.

---

71   The first lines of the body of Sermon 24 are almost identical to those of Sermon 23.

Sermon 27: Second Sunday after Pentecost; theme: Luke 16. 19; approx. 309 words. Two points: (1) the state of the rich man on earth, (2) his state after his life.

Sermon 28: Third Sunday after Pentecost; theme: Luke 14. 16; approx. 342 words. Two points: (1) the man prepared a supper, (2) the excuses of the invited guests who did not want to attend.

Sermon 29: Fourth Sunday after Pentecost; theme: Luke 15. 1; approx. 316 words. Two points: (1) the grace that the Lord sought for the lost sheep, (2) the joy of the angels when one repents.

Sermon 30: Fifth Sunday after Pentecost; theme: Luke 6. 36; approx. 361 words. Mercy consists of three things: (1) condemn nobody, (2) give to the poor, (3) forgive neighbours.

Sermon 31: Sixth Sunday after Pentecost; theme: Luke 5. 1; approx. 336 words. Two points: (1) the great devotion of the people, (2) the ship that Christ boarded.

Sermon 32: Seventh Sunday after Pentecost; theme: Matthew 5. 20; approx. 340 words. Three brothers with whom we will make peace: (1) Christ, (2) our guardian angel, (3) our fellow Christians.

Sermon 33: Eighth Sunday after Pentecost; theme: Mark 8. 1; approx. 300 words. Two points: (1) the mercy of the Lord, (2) Christ took care of those who followed Him.

Sermon 34: Ninth Sunday after Pentecost; theme: Matthew 7. 17; approx. 323 words. Two points: (1) the good man is like a good tree, (2) the evil man is like a bad tree.

Sermon 35: Tenth Sunday after Pentecost; theme: Luke 16. 1; approx. 381 words. Three points of wisdom from the steward: (1) he considered that his task could be taken from him, (2) his concern to render account, (3) he made friends who could receive him.

Sermon 36: Eleventh Sunday after Pentecost; theme: Luke 19. 41; approx. 301 words. Two points: (1) the mercy of the Lord, (2) the blindness of sinners.

Sermon 37: Twelfth Sunday after Pentecost; theme: Luke 18. 10; approx. 262 words. (1) The pride of the Pharisee, (2) the humility of the publican.

Sermon 38: Thirteenth Sunday after Pentecost; theme: Mark 7. 32; approx. 294 words. Two points: (1) the deaf person, (2) the people who brought this person to Christ.

Sermon 39: Fourteenth Sunday after Pentecost; theme: Luke 10. 30; approx. 205 words. Brief moral interpretations of man, Jerusalem, Jericho, murderers, priests and Levites, the Samaritan, and mercy.

THE GOUDA GOSPEL SERMONS · 433

Sermon 40: Fifteenth Sunday after Pentecost; theme: Luke 17. 12–13; approx. 333 words. Two points: (1) the lepers, (2) how they got well.

Sermon 41: Sixteenth Sunday after Pentecost; theme: Matthew 6. 24; approx. 281 words. [Three points:] (1) people who serve the world, (2) the devil, (3) God.

Sermon 42: Seventeenth Sunday after Pentecost; theme: Luke 7. 11; approx. 300 words. Two [*read:* three] points: (1) the dead young man, (2) the people who buried the dead young man, (3) how this young man rose from the dead.

Sermon 43: Eighteenth Sunday after Pentecost; theme: Luke 14. 11; approx. 253 words. Two points: (1) we shall not exalt ourselves, (2) Christ directs us to humility (exemplum of Makarios surpassing the devil in humility).

Sermon 44: Nineteenth Sunday after Pentecost; theme: Matthew 22. 37; approx. 315 words. Four things that lead us to love for God: (1) natural love, (2) the love that God showed us by His Passion, (3) the forgiveness of our sins, (4) the joy of love for God.

Sermon 45: Twentieth Sunday after Pentecost; theme: Matthew 9. 2; approx. 338 words. Two points: (1) the lame, (2) the grace of healing.

Sermon 46: Twenty-First Sunday after Pentecost; theme: Matthew 22. 2; approx. 282 words. Two points: (1) the gentleness of the Lord to celebrate a wedding, (2) the invited guests.

Sermon 47: Twenty-Second Sunday after Pentecost; theme: John 4. 46; approx. 281 words. Two points: (1) the little king whose son was sick, (2) the little king as an example.

Sermon 48: Twenty-Third Sunday after Pentecost; theme: Matthew 18. 28; approx. 265 words. Two points: (1) the Lord's mercy towards all sinners, (2) His justice on the Day of Judgment.

Sermon 49: Twenty-Fifth Sunday after Pentecost; theme: Matthew 22. 19; approx. 307 words. Three things that we have to give proof of: (1) truth in our words, (2) good works, (3) a pure soul when we die.

Sermon 50: Twenty-Sixth Sunday after Pentecost; theme: Matthew 9. 18; approx. 270 words. Two points: (1) the dead girl, (2) how she was raised from the dead.

Sermon 51: Dedication of the Church; theme: Luke 19. 9; approx. 389 words. The blessings of a church: (1) God prefers to hear prayer in a church, (2) preaching takes place in the church and the body of Christ is consecrated there, (3) sins are forgiven in the church (exemplum: Paul the Hermit sees a soul come out of the church purified).

Appendix 2: Preliminary List of Manuscripts and Printed Editions

This list is preliminary because it is mostly based on second-hand data. The assignment of printed editions to the second or third revision is based on the incipits of these editions (a first revision is not mentioned). I have given a number of editions the label 'uncertain' because their bibliographic data were incomplete.

Most editions are identified with their number in the bibliographies of Campbell, *Annales de la typographie néerlandaise au 15e siècle* (CA) or Nijhoff and Kronenberg, *Nederlandsche bibliographie van 1500 tot 1540* (NK);[72] for the other editions the source in which they are found is mentioned. Descriptions of each incunable can be found on-line in the Incunabula Short Title Catalogue (ISTC), and the Gesamtkatalog der Wiegendrucke (GW).[73]

Manuscripts

The text in each manuscript is presumably based on one of the printed editions.

1 Brussel, Koninklijke Bibliotheek, MS II 5445
Third quarter of the sixteenth century. Fols 1ra–172vb: Epistles and Gospels of the temporale, with Sermons 1–47 and 49–50.

2 Den Haag, Koninklijke Bibliotheek, MS 133 B 19
1508. Fols 286r–398r: Epistles and the incipits of the Gospels, with Sermons 1–47 and 49–51.

3 Heverlee, Abdij van Park, MS 5
Date uncertain. Fol. 177r–v: Sermon 47.

4 London, British Library, IB 47301
Sermons 1–9 and 11–51 handwritten in the margins of the incunable *Alle die epistelen ende ewangelien vanden gheheelen iaere* (Gouda: Gheraert Leeu, 4 May 1477; CA 686).

---

72 M. F. A. G. Campbell, *Annales de la typographie néerlandaise au 15e siècle: 1°–4° Supplement*, 4 vols ('s-Gravenhage: Nijhoff, 1878–1890; repr.'s-Gravenhage: Nijhoff, 1962); Wouter Nijhoff and M. E. Kronenberg, *Nederlandsche bibliographie van 1500 tot 1540*, 3 vols in 6 parts ('s-Gravenhage: Nijhoff, 1923–1971).

73 See Incunabula Short Title Catalogue and Gesamtkatalog der Wiegendrucke [both accessed on 25 February 2021]. I would like to thank Dr Suzan Folkerts (Athenaeumbibliotheek, Deventer) for generously sharing her photographs and research data on prints of pericope books with me, and Dr Anna Dlabačová (University Leiden) and Jean Vilbas (Bibliothèque Municipale, Douai) for photographing some relevant pages.

THE GOUDA GOSPEL SERMONS   435

Printed Editions

Combined with the Gospels

1   Gouda: Gheraert Leeu, 1477 [after 7 October] (CA 685, ISTC ie00064800, GW M34243)

Combined with the Epistles and the Gospels

2   Utrecht: Johan Veldener, 4 November 1478 (CA 687, ISTC ie00064900, GW M34250)

3   Utrecht: Johan Veldener, 1478, [after] 4 November (CA 687a, ISTC ie00065000, GW M34251)

4   Utrecht: Johan Veldener, 30 July 1479 (CA 688, ISTC ie00066000, GW M34253)

5   Hasselt: Peregrinus Barmentlo, 1480 (CA 689, ISTC ie00066300, GW M34246)

6   Utrecht: Johan Veldener, 9 October 1481 (CA 690, ISTC ie00066500, GW M34255)

7   Delft: Jacob Jacobszoon van der Meer, 1481 (CA 691, ISTC ie00067000, GW M34226)

8   Delft: Jacob Jacobszoon van der Meer, 1481 (CA 691a, ISTC ie00067100, GW M34228)

9   Leiden: Heynricus Heynrici, 1483 (CA 692, ISTC ie00067500, GW M34248)

10 Gouda: printer of 'Teghen die strael der minnen', 23 June 1484 (CA 693, ISTC ie00068000, GW M34240)

11 Delft: Jacob Jacobszoon van der Meer, 1484 (CA 694, ISTC ie00068300, GW M34230)

12 Haarlem: Jacob Bellaert, 8 April 1486 (CA 695, ISTC ie00068500, GW M34244)

13 Delft: Jacob Jacobszoon van der Meer, 29 November 1486 (CA 696, ISTC ie00069000, GW M34231)

14 Zwolle: Peter van Os van Breda, 5 January 1487 (CA 697, ISTC ie00069500, GW M34258)

15 Delft: Jacob Jacobszoon van der Meer or Christiaen Snellaert, 3 September 1487 (CA 698, ISTC ie00070000, GW M34233)

16 Zwolle: Peter van Os van Breda, 10 November 1488 (CA 699, ISTC ie00070500, GW M34260)

17 Delft: Christiaen Snellaert, 1488 (CA 700, ISTC ie00071000, GW M34234)

18 Zwolle: Peter van Os van Breda, 14 February 1491 (CA 702, ISTC ie00071500, GW M34263)

19 Zwolle: Peter van Os van Breda, 26 March 1493 (CA 704, ISTC ie00071800, GW M34264)

Second Revision

20 Deventer: Jacob van Breda, 1 March 1493 (CA 703, ISTC ie00071750, GW M34236)

21 Deventer: Jacob van Breda, 4 March 1496 (CA 705, ISTC ie00071850, GW M34238)

22 Antwerpen: Govaert Back, 3 July 1496 (CA 706, ISTC ie00071900, GW M34224)

23 Delft: Henrick Eckert van Homberch, *c.* 1498 (GW M3422450)

24 Antwerpen: Henrick Eckert van Homberch, *c.* 1502? (NK 3005)[74]

25 Leiden: Jan Seversz., 9 August 1503 (NK 899)

26 Antwerpen: Henrick Eckert van Homberch, 9 June 1506 (NK 900)

27 Antwerpen: Adriaen van Berghen, 1507 (NK 901)

28 Antwerpen: Michiel Hillen van Hoochstraten, 1508 (NK 902)

29 Antwerpen: Michiel Hillen van Hoochstraten, 1514 (*Biblia Sacra* 1514. EpEv.dut.MHvH.a)

30 Antwerpen: Henrick Eckert van Homberch, 1517 (NK 904)

31 Antwerpen: Willem Vorsterman, 1518 (NK 905)

32 Antwerpen: Henrick Eckert van Homberch, 1520 (NK 3006)

33 Amsterdam: Doen Pietersoen, 1521 (NK 906)

34 Antwerpen: Willem Vorsterman, 29 May 1523 (NK 907)

35 Antwerpen: Willem Vorsterman, no date (NK 903 (= NK 0484?), *Biblia Sacra* 15XX.EpEv.dut.WV.a)

36 Antwerpen: Willem Vorsterman, no date (*Biblia Sacra* 15XX.EpEv.dut. WV.b, NK 0484?)

---

74 Folkerts, 'Middle Dutch *Epistles and Gospels*', p. 55 n. 4, assumes that the 1502 version (NK 3005) 'in all probability' is the same as the 1520 version (NK 3006), but differences in the spelling of the incipits (according to the bibliographical descriptions in NK) suggest that these are two different prints. NK 3005 dates 'c. 1502?', but *Biblia Sacra* 1502.EpEv.dut.HEvH.a is sure about the year 1502.

Third Revision

37 Antwerpen: Willem Vorsterman, 12 February 1528 (*Biblia Sacra* 1528.EpEv. dut.WV.a)
38 Antwerpen: Symon Cock, January 1533 (NK 908)
39 Antwerpen: Willem Vorsterman, between 1523 and 1538? (NK 4340)
40 Antwerpen: Willem Vorsterman, 8 November 1538 (NK 909)
41 Antwerpen: Symon Cock, 6 November 1553 (STCV 12923559)

Uncertain

1 Utrecht: Johan Veldener, 30 July 1479 (*Biblia Sacra* 1479.EpEv.dut.JVe.b)
2 Zwolle: Peter van Os van Breda, 1490 (CA 701, GW M34262)
3 Antwerpen: Willem Vorsterman, 1514 (NK 0485)
4 Antwerpen: Willem Vorsterman, 18 June 1521 (NK 0486)
5 Antwerpen: Symon Cock, 4 November 1531 (NK 0487)
6 Antwerpen: Willem Vorsterman, 18 June 1541 (Le Long, *Boek-zaal*, 588)

Bibliography

Manuscripts

Brussel, Koninklijke Bibliotheek, MS 1268–1269
Brussel, Koninklijke Bibliotheek, MS II 5445
Den Haag, Koninklijke Bibliotheek, MS 133 B 19
Heverlee, Abdij van Park, MS 5
København, Det Kongelige Bibliotek, MS 94 fol.
London, British Library, IB 47301 (extensive, written marginal notes)

Early Printed Works

Alle die epistelen ende ewangelien mitten sermonen vanden ghehelen jaere (Utrecht:
Johan Veldener, 4 November 1478) [CA 687]
Alle die epistelen ende ewangelien mitten sermonen vanden ghehelen jaere (Utrecht:
Johan Veldener, between 4 Nov. 1478 and 30 July 1479) [CA 687a]
Alle die epistelen ende ewangelien vanden gheheelen iaere (Gouda: Gheraert Leeu, 24
May 1477) [CA 686]
Alle die ewangelien vanden gheheelen iaer ende vanden sonnendaghen mitter glosen
(Gouda: Gheraert Leeu, After 7 October 1477) [CA 685]
Boexken vander missen (Gouda: Collatiebroeders, 1506) [NK 982]
Delft Bible (Jacob Jacobszoon van der Meer and Mauricius Yemantszoon, 10
January 1477) [CA 290]
Den Bible int corte (Antwerpen, Claes de Grave, 1516; 2nd edn 1519, 3rd edn 1519)
[NK 366–68]
Evangelia durch das ganze Jahr mit der Glosse (Lübeck: Lukas Brandis, *c.* 1475)
[GW M34205]
Eyn Spegel der mynschliken Behaltenisse (Lübeck: Lukas Brandis, *c.* 1476)
[GW M43046]

Primary Sources

De Delftse bijbel van 1477: facsimile van de oorspronkelijke druk, with an introduction
by C. C. de Bruin, 3 vols (Amsterdam: Buijten & Schipperheijn, 1977)
Gerard Zerbolt, *De libris teutonicalibus: was dürfen Laien lesen? Gerhard Zerbolt
von Zutphen, De libris teutonicalibus / Een verclaringhe vanden deutschen boeken,
lateinisch und mittelniederländisch*, ed. by Nikolaus Staubach and Rudolf
Suntrup (Münster: Aschendorff, 2019)
Johannes Busch, *De viris illustribus: des Augustinerpropstes Iohannes Busch Chroni-
con Windeshemense und Liber de reformatione monasteriorum*, ed. by Karl Grube,
Geschichtsquellen der Provinz Sachsen und angrenzender Gebiete, 19 (Halle:
Hendel, 1886; reprint: Farnborough: Gregg International Publishers, 1968)

Mittelniederdeutsche Predigtfragmente aus einer Handschrift der Universitätsbibliothek zu Helsingfors, ed. by Pekka Katara, Annales Academiae Scientiarum Fennicae, series B, 20,3 (Helsinki: Suomalainen Tiedeakatemia, 1926)

Novum Testamentum Devotionis Modernae / Het Nieuwe Testament van de Moderne Devotie, ed. by C. C. de Bruin, Corpus Sacrae Scripturae Medii Aevi, series major, 2:2 (Leiden: Brill, 1979)

Secondary Studies

Alfrink, Bern., 'Over Nederlandsche pericopenvertalingen', *Studia Catholica*, 12 (1936), 200–18, 306–27

Boghardt, Martin, *Analytische Druckforschung: ein methodischer Beitrag zu Buchkunde und Textkritik* (Hamburg: Hauswedell, 1977)

Brinkhoff, L., and others, eds, *Liturgisch Woordenboek*, 3 vols (Roermond: Romen, 1958–1970)

Campbell, M. F. A. G., *Annales de la typographie néerlandaise au 15e siècle: 1°–4° Supplement*, 4 vols ('s-Gravenhage: Nijhoff, 1878–1890; repr. 's-Gravenhage: Nijhoff, 1962)

Cockx-Indestege, Elly, Geneviève Glorieux, and Bart Op De Beeck, eds, *Belgica typographica: 1541–1600*, Collection du Centre national de l'archéologie et de l'histoire du livre, 2, 4 vols (Nieuwkoop: De Graaf, 1968–1994)

de Bruin, C. C., *De Statenbijbel en zijn voorgangers* (Leiden: Sijthoff, 1937)

de Bruin, C. C., *De Statenbijbel en zijn voorgangers: Nederlandse bijbelvertalingen vanaf de Reformatie*, revised by F. G. M. Broeyer (Haarlem: Nederlands Bijbelgenootschap / Brussel: Belgisch Bijbelgenootschap, 1993)

De Troeyer, Benjamin, *Bio-bibliographia Franciscana Neerlandica, saeculi XVI*, 2 vols (Nieuwkoop: De Graaf, 1969–1970)

De vijfhonderdste verjaring van de boekdrukkunst in de Nederlanden: catalogus tentoonstelling in de Koninklijke Bibliotheek Albert I (Brussel: Koninklijke Bibliotheek Albert I, 1973)

den Hollander, August A., *De Nederlandse bijbelvertalingen, 1522–1545*, Bibliotheca bibliographica Neerlandica, 37 (Nieuwkoop: De Graaf, 1997)

Deschamps, Jan, 'De verspreiding van Johan Scutkens vertaling van het Nieuwe Testament en de oudtestamentische perikopen', *Nederlands Archief voor Kerkgeschiedenis*, 56 (1975), 159–79 [also published in *In navolging: een bundel studies aangeboden aan C. C. de Bruin bij zijn afscheid als hoogleraar te Leiden*, ed. by M. J. M. de Haan and others (Leiden: Brill, 1975), pp. 159–79]

Desplenter, Youri, *Al aertrijc segt lofsanc: Middelnederlandse vertalingen van Latijnse hymnen en sequensen*, Studies op het gebied van de oudere Nederlandse letterkunde, 3, 2 vols (Gent: Koninklijke Academie voor Nederlandse Taal- en Letterkunde, 2008)

Desplenter, Youri, 'The Latin Liturgical Song Subtitled: Middle Dutch Translations of Hymns and Sequences', *Church History and Religious Culture*, 88 (2008), 395–413

Dlabačová, Anna, 'Seeing beyond Signs: Allegorical Explanations of the Mass in Medieval Dutch Literature', in *Quid est sacramentum? Visual Representation of Sacred Mysteries in Early Modern Europe, 1400–1700*, ed. by Walter S. Melion, Elizabeth Carson Pastan, and Lee Palmer Wandel (Leiden: Brill, 2020), pp. 199–226

Ermens, Daniël, '"Een nuttelijc boec den kerstenen menschen" (ca. 1400): heilsgeschiedenis voor beginners', in *De letter levend maken: opstellen aangeboden aan Guido de Baere bij zijn zeventigste verjaardag*, ed. by Kees Schepers and Frans Hendrickx, Miscellanea Neerlandica, 39 (Leuven: Peeters, 2010), pp. 265–84

Ermens, Daniël, 'Een onbekend handschrift met evangeliepreken uit de tekstgroep Zwolle: Heverlee, Abdij van Park, 5', *Ons Geestelijk Erf*, 81 (2010), 194–242

Folkerts, Suzan, 'Appropriating the Passion: On the Uses of Middle Dutch Gospels in Manuscript and Print', in *The Same and Different: Strategies of Retelling the Bible within the 'New Communities of Interpretation' (1350–1570)*, ed. by Lucie Doležalová and Géraldine Veysseyre, New Communities of Interpretation (Turnhout: Brepols, forthcoming)

Folkerts, Suzan, 'The Cloister or the City? The Appropriation of the New Testament by Lay Readers in an Urban Setting', in *Cultures of Religious Reading in the Late Middle Ages: Instructing the Soul, Feeding the Spirit, and Awakening the Passion*, ed. by Sabrina Corbellini, Utrecht Studies in Medieval Literacy, 25 (Turnhout: Brepols, 2013), pp. 175–99

Folkerts, Suzan A., 'Middle Dutch *Epistles and Gospels*: The Transfer of a Medieval Bestseller into Printed Editions during the Early Reformation', in *Vernacular Bible and Religious Reform in the Middle Ages and Early Modern Era*, ed. by Wim François and August den Hollander, Bibliotheca Ephemeridum Theologicarum Lovaniensium, 287 (Leuven: Peeters, 2017), pp. 53–73

Folkerts, Suzan, 'De Noord-Nederlandse vertaling van het Nieuwe Testament (eind veertiende eeuw)', in *De Bijbel in de Lage Landen: elf eeuwen van vertalen*, ed. by Paul Gilliaerts and others (Heerenveen: Royal Jongbloed, 2015), pp. 165–76

Folkerts, Suzan, 'Reading the Bible Lessons at Home: Holy Writ and Lay Readers in the Low Countries', *Church History and Religious Culture*, 93 (2013), 215–35

Folkerts, Suzan, 'Reading the Scriptures during the Early Reformation: Continuities in the Production and Use of Printed Dutch Bibles', in *Renaissance und Bibelhumanismus*, ed. by J. Marius, J. Lange van Ravenswaay, and Herman J. Selderhuis, Refo500 Academic Studies, 65 (Göttingen: Vandenhoeck & Ruprecht, 2020), pp. 159–77

Folkerts, Suzan, and Arend Elias Oostindiër, 'New Bibles and Old Reading Habits Around 1522: The Position of the New Testament Translation of the Devotio Moderna among Dutch Printed Bibles', *Quaerendo*, 47 (2017), 175–98

François, Wim, 'Bible Production and Bible Readers in the Age of Confessionalisation: The Case of the Low Countries', in *Lay Readers of the Bible in Early Modern Europe*, ed. by Erminia Ardissino and Élise Boilett, Intersections, 68 (Leiden: Brill, 2020), pp. 190–216

François, Wim, 'The Catholic Church and the Vernacular Bible in the Low Countries: A Paradigm Shift in the 1550s?', in *Discovering the Riches of the Word: Religious Reading in Late Medieval and Early Modern Europe*, ed. by Sabrina Corbellini, Margriet Hoogvliet, and Bart Ramakers, Intersections, 38 (Leiden: Brill, 2015), pp. 234–81

François, Wim, 'De Leuvense Bijbel (1548) en de katholieke bijbelvertalingen van de tweede helft van de zestiende eeuw', in *De Bijbel in de Lage Landen: elf eeuwen van vertalen*, ed. by Paul Gilliaerts and others (Heerenveen: Royal Jongbloed, 2015), pp. 266–303

François, Wim, 'Naar een "confessionalisering" van bijbelvertalingen in de zestiende eeuw: inleiding', in *De Bijbel in de Lage Landen: elf eeuwen van vertalen*, ed. by Paul Gilliaerts and others (Heerenveen: Royal Jongbloed, 2015), pp. 204–19

Goudriaan, Koen, 'Apostolate and Printing: The *Collaciebroeders* of Gouda and their Press', in *Between Lay Piety and Academic Theology: Studies Presented to Christoph Burger on the Occasion of his 65th Birthday*, ed. by Ulrike Hascher-Burger, August den Hollander, and Wim Janse, Brill's Series in Church History, 46 (Leiden: Brill, 2010), pp. 433–52

Goudriaan, Koen, 'Boekdistributie langs kerkelijke kanalen in de Late Middeleeuwen', *Jaarboek voor Nederlandse Boekgeschiedenis*, 8 (2001), 43–58

Goudriaan, Koen, 'The Church and the Market: Vernacular Religious Works and the Early Printing Press in the Low Countries, 1477–1540', in Koen Goudriaan, *Piety in Practice and Print: Essays on the Late Medieval Religious Landscape*, ed. by Anna Dlabačová and Ad Tervoort (Hilversum: Verloren, 2016), pp. 240–56

Goudriaan, Koen, 'The Franciscans, the Laity and the Printing Press', in Koen Goudriaan, *Piety in Practice and Print: Essays on the Late Medieval Religious Landscape*, ed. by Anna Dlabačová and Ad Tervoort (Hilversum: Verloren, 2016), pp. 279–308

Goudriaan, Koen, 'Een kerkelijk catechese-offensief?: misverklaringen op de drukpers rond 1500', in *Terug naar Gouda: religieus leven in de maalstroom van de tijd*, ed. by Paul H. A. M. Abels, Jan Jacobs, and Mirjam van Veen (Zoetermeer: Meinema, 2014), pp. 73–95

Goudriaan, Koen, 'De verdwenen kloosters', in *Gouda*, ed. by Wim Denslagen, De Nederlandse monumenten van geschiedenis en kunst (Zeist: Rijksdienst voor Monumentenzorg / Zwolle: Waanders, 2001), pp. 171–211

Harper, John, *The Forms and Orders of Western Liturgy from the Tenth to the Eighteenth Century: A Historical Introduction and Guide for Students and Musicians* (Oxford: Clarendon Press, 1991)

Hensen, A. H. L., 'Henric van Arnhem's Kronyk van het fraterhuis te Gouda', *Bijdragen en Mededeelingen van het Historisch Genootschap*, 20 (1899), 1–46

'Het Goudse fonds van Gheraert Leeu (volgens ISTC)', in *Een drukker zoekt publiek: Gheraert Leeu te Gouda 1477–1484*, ed. by Koen Goudriaan and others, Bijdragen Oudheidkundige Kring 'Die Goude', 23 (Delft: Eburon, 1993), pp. 224–45

Jonker, Esther, *Het Amsterdams Perikopenboek: volkstalige vroomheid in veertiende-eeuws Vlaanderen* (Leiden: Leiden University Press, 2010)

Jungmann, Joseph Andreas, *Missarum sollemnia: eine genetische Erklärung der Römischen Messe*, 2 vols, 5th edn (Bonn, Nova et Vetera: 2003; repr. from Freiburg im Breisgau: Herder, 1962)

Kämpfer, Winfried, *Studien zu den gedruckten mittelniederdeutschen Plenarien: ein Beitrag zur Entstehungsgeschichte spätmittelalterlicher Erbauungsliteratur*, Niederdeutsche Studien, 2 (Münster: Böhlau, 1954)

Katara, Pekka, 'Das Predigtmärlein von der unvollkommenen Beichte eines Königssohnes', *Neuphilologische Mitteilungen*, 29 (1928), 74–77

Kok, Ina, *Woodcuts in Incunabula Printed in the Low Countries*, Bibliotheca bibliographica neerlandica: series major, 2, 4 vols (Houten: HES & De Graaf, 2013)

Kors, Mikel, 'Die Bibel für Laien: Neuansatz oder Sackgasse? der Bibelübersetzer von 1360 und Gerhard Zerbolt von Zutphen', in *Kirchenreform von unten: Gerhard Zerbolt von Zutphen und die Brüder vom gemeinsamen Leben*, ed. by Nikolaus Staubach, Tradition — Reform — Innovation, 6 (Frankfurt am Main: Peter Lang, 2004), pp. 243–46

Le Long, Isaac, *Boek-zaal der Nederduytsche Bybels* (Amsterdam: Vieroot, 1732)

Leesch, Wolfgang, Ernest Persoons, and Anton G. Weiler, eds, *Monasticon Fratrum Vitae Communis*, Archief- en Bibliotheekwezen van België, Special Issues 18–20, 3 vols (Brussel: Archief- en Bibliotheekwezen van België, 1977–2004)

Mathijsen, Marita, *Naar de letter: handboek editiewetenschap*, 2nd edn (Den Haag: Constantijn Huygens Instituut, 1997)

Mertens, Thom, 'Collatio und Codex im Bereich der Devotio moderna', in *Der Codex im Gebrauch: Akten des Internationalen Kolloquiums 11.–13. Juni 1992*, ed. by Christel Meier, Dagmar Hüpper, and Hagen Keller, Münstersche Mittelalter-Schriften, 70 (München: Fink, 1996), pp. 163–82

Mertens, Thom, 'Pragmatic Forms of Middle Dutch Bible Translation', in *Every(wo)man's Books of Salvation: The Most Popular Medieval Religious Texts in Europe, Their Circulation and Reception*, ed. by Florence Bourgne and Géraldine Veysseyre (Turnhout: Brepols, forthcoming)

Mertens, Thom, 'Praying in the Vernacular: Middle Dutch Imitative Forms of the Divine Office from the 1370s to 1520s', in *Nuns' Literacies in Medieval Europe: The Hull Dialogue*, ed. by Virginia Blanton, Veronica O'Mara, and Patricia Stoop, Medieval Women: Texts and Contexts, 26 (Turnhout: Brepols, 2013), pp. 133–46

Nijhoff, Wouter, and M. E. Kronenberg, *Nederlandsche bibliographie van 1500 tot 1540*, 3 vols in 6 parts ('s-Gravenhage: Nijhoff, 1923–1971)

Palmer, Nigel F., 'Deutsche Perikopenhandschriften mit der Glosse: zu den Predigten der spätmittelalterlichen deutschen Plenarien und Evangelistare', in *Deutsche Bibelübersetzungen des Mittelalters*, ed. by Heimo Reinitzer, Vestigia Bibliae, 9–10 (Bern: Peter Lang, 1991), pp. 273–96

Pettegree, Andrew, and Malcolm Walsby, *Netherlandish Books: Books Published in the Low Countries and Dutch Books Printed Abroad before 1601* (Leiden: Brill, 2011)

Roest, Bert, *Franciscan Literature of Religious Instruction before the Council of Trent*, Studies in the History of Christian Traditions, 117 (Leiden: Brill, 2004)

Schiewer, Regina D., and Hans-Jochen Schiewer, 'Predigt im Spätmittelalter', in *Literarische und religiöse Textsorten und Textallianzen um 1500*, ed. by Alexander Schwarz, Franz Simmler, and Claudia Wich-Reif, Textsorten und Textallianzen um 1500, 1 (Berlin: Weidler, 2009), pp. 727–71

Schnell, Rüdiger, 'Konstanz und Metapmorphosen eines Textes: eine Überlieferungs- und geschlechtergeschichtliche Studie zur volkssprachlichen Rezeption von Jacobus de Voragine Ehepredigten', *Frühmittelalterliche Studien*, 33 (1999), 319–95

Sherwood-Smith, Maria, 'The Last Judgement in Middle Dutch Sermons and its Role in the Dutch Translation of the Homilies of Gregory the Great', in *The Last Judgement in Medieval Preaching*, ed. by Thom Mertens, Hans-Jochen Schiewer, and Maria Sherwood-Smith, Sermo: Studies on Patristic, Medieval, and Reformation Sermons and Preaching, 3 (Turnhout: Brepols, 2013), pp. 79–97

Sherwood-Smith, Maria, and Patricia Stoop (I–III), Daniël Ermens and Willemien van Dijk (IV–VII), *Repertorium van Middelnederlandse preken in handschriften tot en met 1550 / Repertorium of Middle Dutch Sermons Preserved in Manuscripts from before 1550*, Miscellanea Neerlandica, 29, 7 vols (Leuven: Peeters, 2003–2008)

Sonderegger, Stefan, 'Geschichte deutschsprachiger Bibelübersetzungen in Grundzügen', in *Sprachgeschichte: ein Handbuch zur Geschichte der deutschen Sprache und ihre Erforschung*, ed. by Werner Besch and others, 2 vols, 2nd edn (Berlin: De Gruyter, 1998–2004), I (1998), 229–84

Staubach, Nikolaus, 'Gerhard Zerbolt von Zutphen und die Apologie der Laienlektüre in der Devotio moderna', in *Laienlektüre und Buchmarkt im späten Mittelalter*, ed. by Thomas Kock and Rita Schlusemann, Gesellschaft, Kultur und Schrift: Mediävistische Beiträge, 5 (Frankfurt am Main: Peter Lang, 1997), pp. 221–89

Taal, Johannes, *De Goudse kloosters in de Middeleeuwen* (Hilversum: Brand, 1960)

van Beek, Lydeke, *Leken trekken tot Gods Woord: Dirc van Herxen (1381–1457) en zijn Eerste Collatieboek*, Middeleeuwse Studies en Bronnen, 120 (Hilversum: Verloren, 2009)

van Duijn, Mart, 'Defining the Delft Bible (1477): From Printer–Public Dynamics to Extant Copies', in *Cultures of Religious Reading in the Late Middle Ages: Instructing the Soul, Feeding the Spirit, and Awakening the Passion*, ed. by Sabrina Corbellini, Utrecht Studies in Medieval Literacy, 25 (Turnhout: Brepols, 2013), pp. 117–40

van Duijn, Mart, *De Delftse Bijbel: een sociale geschiedenis, 1477–circa 1550*, Bijdragen tot de geschiedenis van de Nederlandse boekhandel, n.s., 19 (Zutphen: Walburg Pers, 2017)

van Duijn, Mart, 'Printing, Public, and Power: Shaping the First Printed Bible in Dutch (1477)', *Church History and Religious Culture*, 93 (2013), 275–99

Van Engen, John, 'The Work of Gerlach Peters (d. 1411): Spiritual Diarist and Letter-Writer, a Mystic among the Devout', *Ons Geestelijk Erf*, 73 (1999), 150–77

van Thienen, Gerard, 'Papieronderzoek van de in de Nederlanden gedrukte incunabelen', in *For Bob de Graaf, Antiquarian Bookseller, Publisher, Bibliographer: Festschrift on the Occasion of his 65th Birthday*, ed. by Anton Gerits (Amsterdam: Gerits & Sons, 1992), pp. 160–73

Weiler, A. G., *Volgens de norm van de vroege Kerk: de geschiedenis van de huizen van de broeders van het Gemene leven in Nederland*, Middeleeuwse studies, 13 (Nijmegen: Katholieke Universiteit, Centrum voor Middeleeuwse Studies, 1997)

Zieleman, G. C., 'Evangeliën door het jaar met hun glossen: een onderzoek naar de bijdrage van Johan Scutken (+ 1423) aan een laatmiddeleeuws religieus genre in de volkstaal', in *De Middelnederlandse preek*, ed. by Thom Mertens, Patricia Stoop, and Christoph Burger, Middeleeuwse Studies en Bronnen, 116 (Hilversum, Verloren, 2009), pp. 102–31

Zieleman, Gerrit Cornelis, *Middelnederlandse epistel- en evangeliepreken*, Kerkhistorische bijdragen, 8 (Leiden: Brill, 1978)

Zieleman, Gerrit Cornelis, 'Das Studium der deutschen und niederländischen Predigten des Mittelalters', in *Sô predigent etelîche: Beiträge zur deutschen und niederländischen Predigt im Mittelalter*, ed. by Kurt Otto Seidel, Göppinger Arbeiten zur Germanistik, 378 (Göppingen: Kümmerle, 1982), pp. 5–48

Zieleman, Gerrit C., 'Der Verfasser der sog. Zwoller Predigten des späten 14. Jahrhunderts', in *Die deutsche Predigt im Mittelalter: Internationales Symposium am Fachbereich Germanistik der Freien Universität Berlin vom 3.–6. Oktober 1989*, ed. by Volker Mertens and Hans-Jochen Schiewer (Tübingen: Niemeyer, 1992), pp. 223–55

KEES SCHEPERS

Diverging Perceptions

Johannes Tauler in Sixteenth-Century Printed Editions

In the second and third quarter of the fourteenth century the Dominican Johannes Tauler (1300–1361) became famous as an inspirational preacher. He likely delivered his sermons to female monastic communities in Strasbourg, Basel, Cologne, and possibly some other, unidentified places. Tauler was known for his ability to galvanize his audiences and readers with his sublime message expressed in a down-to-earth manner, using language every listener in his non-academic audience could understand and relate to. In his sermons, Tauler would take any given biblical theme and interpret it in surprising and exciting ways to instill into his audience the conviction that each person has the potential to develop and experience the connection with the Divine in the innermost part of his or her soul. Some eighty-three sermons by Tauler are believed to exist. They survive in eleven manuscript collections, mostly containing different selections of sermons.[1]

Tauler retained this reputation as a preacher and author of mystical sermons after his death, and as a consequence his works were widely disseminated in countless manuscripts all through the fifteenth century.[2] His fame and stature grew further once his sermons began to appear in print from the late fifteenth century onward. In the sixteenth century, after Martin Luther had come onto the stage, Tauler was appropriated by both Protestants and Catholics alike. In this contribution I will consider this earliest phase of appropriation by Catholics and Protestants of the works of Tauler in print, in particular by

---

1 No definitive critical edition of Tauler's sermons exists. Scholars have to make do with two editions, each with a series of sermons different from the other edition: Johannes Tauler, *Sermons de J. Tauler et autres écrits mystiques*, ed. by A. L. Corin, Bibliothèque de la Faculté de Philosophie et Lettres de l'Université de Liège, 33 and 42, 2 vols (Paris: Champion, 1924–1929), and Johannes Tauler, *Die Predigten Taulers: aus der Engelberger und der Freiburger Handschrift, sowie aus Schmidts Abschriften der ehemaligen Strassburger Handschriften*, ed. by Ferdinand Vetter, Deutsche Texte des Mittelalters, 11 (Berlin: Weidmann, 1910).
2 A comprehensive survey of the manuscripts containing Tauler sermons can be found in the database PiK (Predigt im Kontext).

Kees Schepers (kees.schepers@uantwerpen.be) is an Associate Professor in the Ruusbroec Institute at the University of Antwerp.

Circulating the Word of God in Medieval and Early Modern Europe: Catholic Preaching and Preachers across Manuscript and Print (c. 1450 to c. 1550), ed. by Veronica O'Mara and Patricia Stoop, SERMO 17, (Turnhout: Brepols, 2022), pp. 445–471   BREPOLS ❧ PUBLISHERS   10.1484/M.SERMO-EB.5.130464

pointing out the differences in the redacted versions that can be linked to the different creeds.

The diverging trajectories of the two types of appropriation start with two sixteenth-century printed editions of Johannes Tauler's works. They determined the course of their reception and success in the Catholic and Protestant traditions for centuries to come. The 1543 Tauler edition, printed in Cologne, ensured Tauler's enduring fame in the Catholic world all across Western Europe.[3] It engendered numerous translations in several languages. The remarkable 1565 edition, printed in Emden, did the same for Tauler's stature among Protestants.[4] Even though the 1565 edition does not explicitly say so, it is clearly a translation and reworking of the 1543 edition (with the same works, in the same order). This circumstance provides the opportunity for a methodologically valid comparison between both editions. In this contribution only a brief comparison of these huge editions can be made as a full comparison would require a separate study. I will describe the differences, sometimes surprisingly subtle, between these two editions, both with regard to the texts themselves and to their para-textual framing.

It is important to stress from the outset that the reputation of Tauler from the sixteenth century onward was based on the vastly expanded oeuvre attributed to him in the 1543 edition. Tauler was no longer seen as merely a preacher of mystical sermons. All of a sudden he was considered the author of treatises, letters, songs, and prophecies. Because of the attribution of numerous texts in different genres, Tauler had become an author of great literary scope and depth, with a literary persona that was markedly different from his persona during his lifetime, when he had only been known as a preacher.

Tauler the Catholic: The 1543 Köln Edition

The 1543 edition, which was printed by Jaspar von Gennep in Köln in 1543, has had the biggest influence on the shaping of Tauler's reputation. The exact title is a mouthful: 'Des erleuchten D. Johannis Tauleri von eym waren Euangelischen leben. Gôtliche Predig, Leren, Epistolen, Cantilenen, Prophetien. Alles eyn

---

3   *Des erleuchten D. Johannis Tauleri von eym waren Euangelischen leben. Gôtliche Predig, Leren, Epistolen, Cantilenen, Prophetien. Alles eyn kostpar Seelen schatz, in alten geschryben Büchern fůnden, vnd nů erstmals ins liecht kommen* (Köln: Jaspar von Gennep, 1543) The translations of quotations from this edition are mine. The edition may be consulted at: https://dspace.library.uu.nl/handle/1874/21182 [accessed 30 December 2020].

4   *Des Hoochverlichten D. Johannis Tauleri van eenen volcomen Euangelisschen leuen Christelijcke Predicatien oft Sermonen op allen Sondaghen ende Feestdagen vanden gantsen Jaer. Wt den Hoochduytsche in Nederlantsche sprake ghetrouwelijck ouergheset* (Franckfort: Peter van Dueren, 1565 [Emden: Willem Gailliart]). The translations of quotations from this edition are mine. The edition may be consulted here: https://digitale.bibliothek.uni-halle.de/vd16/content/pageview/2592494 [accessed 30 December 2020].

kostpar Seelen schatz, in alten geschryben Büchern fûnden, vnd nû erstmals ins liecht kommen' ['From the enlightened master Johannes Tauler, about a true evangelical life. Divine sermons, treatises, letters, songs, prophecies. Everything being a precious treasure for the soul, found in ancient written books, and now published for the first time]'. The importance of this edition cannot be overstated. It is crucial in understanding the transition from the late medieval to early modern Tauler.[5] Even though several earlier editions of Tauler's sermons had been printed since 1498, the 1543 edition presents a whole 'new' Tauler as a consequence of the alleged 'discovery' and attribution of numerous, previously unknown texts (some of which were certainly not written by him). At the same time the edition constitutes the final phase in the construction of the corpus of sermons attributed to Tauler. Earlier editions had contained different, overlapping sermon collections. This 1543 edition contains the largest collection of sermons, into which the earlier collections had been integrated. The collection was even expanded with sermons that had been unknown before. Its editor calls it the first *Opera omnia* of Tauler's works.

The timing of the edition is no accident. During the second quarter of the sixteenth century, when the bridges between the Catholic and Reformation-minded worlds were starting to collapse, there were still many Catholics who hoped to stifle the Protestant reform movement simply by showing that sincere spirituality was still alive and well within the Catholic tradition. After 1517 and before 1545 (the start of the 'official' Counter or Catholic Reformation) there were numerous bottom-up attempts to roll back the tide of Protestantism through Catholic Reform. This entailed an invigoration of authentic 'Catholic' spirituality. Such attempts form the backdrop for the development of a particular type of mysticism during this era in the Low Countries and the neighbouring Rhineland. An important centre was the St. Barbara Charterhouse in Cologne. Mystical culture was promoted by the Cologne Carthusians through their numerous editions. An important part of their publication offensive was the printing of classic fourteenth-century mystical authors. The Carthusians were part of what has been labelled a sixteenth-century mystical renaissance.[6]

---

5 A remarkable fact is that the 1543 edition was translated and copied in Middle Dutch in (at least) two manuscripts, both most likely from the Sint-Agnes convent in Arnhem; see Tobias Benzinger, 'Von der Handschrift zum Druck und zurück: Ursachen und Auswirkungen eines markanten Medienwechsels', *Meister-Eckhart-Jahrbuch*, 14 (2021), 167–90.

6 Another important exponent of this sixteenth-century mystical renaissance is the convent of Sint-Agnes in Arnhem that had close ties to the Charterhouse in Cologne. See Kees Schepers, 'A Web of Texts: Sixteenth-Century Mystical Culture and the Arnhem Sint-Agnes Convent', in *Nuns' Literacies in Medieval Europe: The Kansas City Dialogue*, ed. by Virginia Blanton, Veronica O'Mara, and Patricia Stoop, Medieval Women: Texts and Contexts, 27 (Turnhout, Brepols, 2015), pp. 168–77; Kees Schepers, 'The Arnhem Mystical Sermons and the Sixteenth-Century Mystical Renaissance in Arnhem and Cologne', in *Mysticism and Reform, 1400–1750*, ed. by Sara S. Poor and Nigel Smith, ReFormations: Medieval and Early Modern (Notre Dame, IN: University of Notre Dame Press, 2015), pp. 84–123; Ineke Cornet, *The Arnhem Mystical Sermons: Preaching Liturgical Mysticism in the Context of Catholic*

And even though they are not strictly connected to the 1543 Tauler edition, it fits perfectly within their anti-Lutheran publication offensive. It should be noted, as well, that the printer was apparently in close contact with the Carthusians, since he had printed several books at their commission. At the very least, they must have known that Von Gennep was going to print the Tauler edition. It is quite possible that he did so at their request.[7]

The 1543 edition brought about three major changes with regard to the perception of Tauler (see Figure 9). First, as mentioned above, numerous works were attributed to Tauler that had never been attributed to him. His oeuvre was thus considerably expanded. Second, the edition presented Tauler not merely as a preacher but also as an author versed in a wide array of literary genres. In doing so, it transformed Tauler into a highly regarded author of great literary span. Third, Tauler, as a person, was presented in a whole new light. This was done in the introductory letter and especially in his alleged biography that provided him with a completely new persona.

We are fortunate that the editor, who calls himself Petrus Noviomagus, is very explicit about his editorial work in a dedicatory letter (fols Aijra–Aiijrb).[8] He informs the reader about his objectives and about his knowledge of Tauler and his works. This Petrus Noviomagus has since the late nineteenth century been identified with the saint and doctor of the Church Petrus Canisius (1521–1597), although this identification has always been disputed, and, in recent years, even more so.[9]

Reform, Brill's Series in Church History, 77 (Leiden: Brill, 2019). See also Markus Polzer, 'Arnhem and the Tauler Revival: New Evidence Concerning a Second Manuscript from the St Agnes Convent in Arnhem Containing Johannes Tauler's *Von eym waren Euangelischen leben*', *Ons Geestelijk Erf*, 84 (2013), 55–73.

7 Gérald Chaix, *Réforme et contre-réforme catholiques: recherches sur la chartreuse de Cologne du xvie siècle*, Analecta Cartusiana, 80, 3 vols (Salzburg: Institut für Anglistik und Amerikanistik, Universität Salzburg, 1981). On Von Gennep, see https://www.deutsche-biographie.de/sfz20345.html [accessed 1 October 2020].

8 The prologue or dedicatory letter (it is called *Vorred* in the heading) by Petrus Noviomagus is edited in Petrus Canisius, *Beati Petri Canisii Epistolae et Acta*, ed. by O. Braunsberger, 8 vols (Freiburg: Herder, 1896), I, 79–93.

9 Even though it is (for now) impossible to prove, I personally consider it to be inconceivable that Petrus Canisius would have edited these mystical texts. The main reason is that nowhere in his oeuvre and his extensive correspondence (other than in this dedicatory letter) does he mention Tauler, nor does he mention the closely related mystical authors Ruusbroec and Eckhart. Some scholars have argued that Canisius later avoided mentioning Tauler out of prudence. This argument I find to be unconvincing. It is not just that the mystical authors Johannes Tauler and Meister Eckhart, and even Jan van Ruusbroec, are completely absent in Canisius's correspondence, Canisius, moreover, apparently lacks affinity with mysticism altogether. See Aug[ust] Jundt, *Histoire du panthéisme populaire au Moyen-Age et au xvie siècle* (Paris: Sandoz & Fischbacher, 1875), pp. 63–65. See also A. De Pelsemaeker, 'Canisius éditeur de Tauler', *Revue d'ascétique et de mystique*, 36 (1960), 102–08; J. Brodrick, *Saint Peter Canisius, S. J. 1521–1597* (London: Sheed and Ward, 1935), pp. 38–40. A recent argument against the attribution to Petrus Canisius is offered by R. J. M. van de Schoor, 'Canisius als Herausgeber: die Ausgaben von Tauler (1543), Kyrill (1546) und Leo dem Großen (1546)', *Ons Geestelijk Erf*, 82 (2011), 161–86.

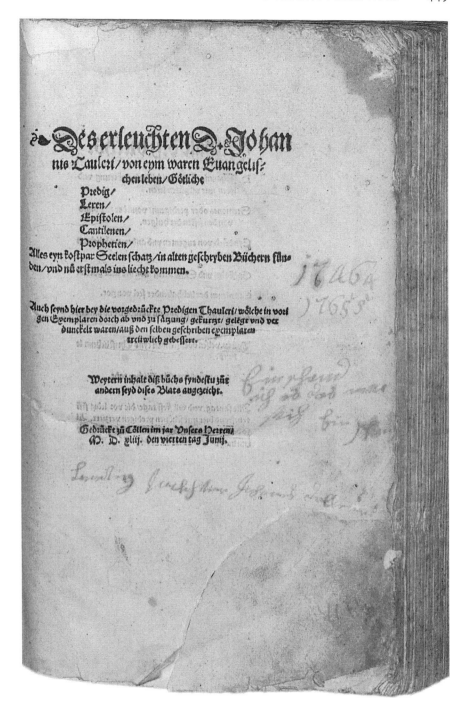

FIGURE 9. Title page of the 1543 Köln edition of Tauler's Works. Universiteit Antwerpen, Ruusbroecgenootschap, 3112 A 3. Reproduced with permission.

450   KEES SCHEPERS

Noviomagus first explains his reasons for editing Tauler's works once more. This had, after all, already been done five times before.[10] In the first paragraph, which he addresses to Georgius Skodberg whom he calls 'hochwirdiger here', he says that he himself had already for a long time enjoyed 'die sermones oder predig' of Tauler:

> Hochwirdiger here unter ander gůten büchern die vns dat wort gots, vmb vnse sele inn disem jamerthall zů speisen, reichlig mit theylen, haben mir allezeitt fürderlich wol angestanden die Sermones oder predig des erleuchten D. Johannis Tauleri als eyn kostpar bůch das vns den rechten kurtzsten weg zů vnsen vrsprung, das Got ist, mitt klaren worten treüwelig entdeckt und weiset. (fol. Aijra)

> [Venerable Lord, among other good books that generously inform us about the Word of God, to nourish our soul in this vale of tears, I have always liked the sermons or homilies of the enlightened master Johannes Tauler for being useful as a precious book that faithfully reveals and shows us, in plain words, the proper, shortest way to our origin, that is, God].

He then proceeds by saying that he has been frustrated to find many mistakes in the earlier printed editions. Confronted with this fact, he decided to try to find what he calls the 'original' manuscript versions.[11] Noviomagus asked around and finally, in 1542, he found them, so he says, in the monastery of St. Gertrud in Cologne and in some other unmentioned places.[12] Noviomagus asserts that these manuscripts contained some of the best works of Tauler. What is striking, however, is that he identifies an oeuvre that, all of a sudden, has been vastly expanded, containing not just *predige* ['sermons'] but also *lerunge, epistolen und cantilenen* ['treatises, letters, and songs']. These are genres Tauler had never been connected to (except for some songs). Noviomagus also identifies the ultimate objective of a perfect, Christian life as union with God:

> In welchen vil gute, ja die beste Taulerus predige, lerunge, epistolen vnd cantilenen alls von eynem volkomen christlichen leben, wie wir vns mit got vereynigen vnd eyn geyst mit im werden sollen gar klarlich geschreyben steen, die biss her nye getruckt noch offenbar gewesen. (fol. Aijra)

---

10   The editions are: Leipzig: Konrad Kacheloven, 1498: *Sermon des großgelarten in gnade[n] erlauchte[n] doctoris Johannis Thauleri predigerr ordens [...]*; Augsburg: Hans Otmar, 1508; Basel: Adam Petri, 1521 and 1522; and Halberstadt: Lorenz Stuchs, 1523. See Henrik Otto, *Vor- und frühreformatorische Tauler-Rezeption: Annotationen in Drucken des späten 15. und frühen 16. Jahrhunderts*, Quellen und Forschungen zur Reformationsgeschichte, 75 (Heidelberg: Gütersloh, 2003). The titles of the editions are listed on p. 341.

11   'Darumb hab ich mich mit fleiss nach den ware geschreyben exemplaren zů überkommen vmbgefragt' ['Therefore I have zealously asked around to find the original written exemplars'].

12   Jutta Prieur, *Das Kölner Dominikanerinnenkloster St. Gertrud am Neumarkt*, Kölner Schriften zur Geschichte und Kultur, 3 (Köln: DME-Verlag, 1983).

DIVERGING PERCEPTIONS   451

[In which [that is, the manuscripts] many good, yes, the best sermons, teachings, letters and songs of Tauler — all dealing with a perfect Christian life, that is to say, how we should unite with God and become one spirit with him — are written, which have never been printed or published before].

Noviomagus quickly arrives at the conclusion: the new and better versions must be put into print, on the one hand to provide better versions of the sermons already known; on the other to make the unknown texts available for the first time.

What makes the 1543 Tauler edition a Catholic edition? We need to realize that the editor obviously did not need to do much to make it Catholic. Simply the fact that Tauler was a Dominican priest who wrote sermons for an often monastic community already makes his work 'Catholic', one could say. Tauler furthermore referred to liturgical acts and ecclesiastical traditions that came to be seen as specifically 'Catholic' after 'Lutherans' had rejected many of them as their doctrinal and ecclesiastical views evolved. Tauler's work, therefore, when left unchanged, automatically ends up on the Catholic side of the confessional divide. The only instances where the 1543 edition becomes explicitly Catholic occur when opposition against Lutheranism is expressed. This is only done in the dedicatory letter. In the following I will point out those instances where Noviomagus manifests his confessional adherence.

The first very obvious testimony to Noviomagus's Catholic credentials is the fact that he addresses the dedicatory letter to Georgius Skodberg (d. 1551), the exiled archbishop of Lund in Sweden. Skodberg was archbishop from 1520 to 1521, but fled to Denmark due to conflict with King Christian II (1481–1559). Skodberg finally went to live in Cologne, where he was in close contact with the milieu of the earliest Jesuits and the Cologne Carthusians. He befriended Petrus Canisius, who had considered becoming a Carthusian before becoming the first Dutch Jesuit. At the opening of his dedicatory letter Noviomagus writes: 'Dem hochwerdigen in Got vatter vnd heren, heren Georgio von Schotborch, ertzbuschoff zů Londen, Primat von Sweden, Geboren legat, etc., wunsch ich, Petrus Nouiomagus, Gnad von got mit erbietung meins willigen gehorsamen diensts' ['To the venerable father and master in God, master Georgius Skodberg, archbishop of Lund, Primate of Sweden, born legate, etc., I, Peter Noviomagus, wish grace from God, and I offer my willing, obedient service'] (fol. Aijra).

In his letter Noviomagus is generally not very explicit about the historical context, but there are two further instances where historical reality creeps into his argument for publishing Tauler's works. The first instance is when Noviomagus observes that Tauler was extremely good at identifying and even foreseeing the plague of doctrinal error that he, Noviomagus, deems to be pervasive in his time. This important observation deserves to be mentioned in full:

Da by ist er [Tauler] von dem heilgen geyst so reichlig erleuchtet vnd überformet inn got das er durch den geyst der prophetien die grosse plagen

vn*d* irru*ng* im heilgen glauben (die nu über uns, got erbarms, gefalle*n*)
furgesehen un*d* mit klaren worte*n* beschreibe*n* hat. (fol. Aijrb)

> [On top of that he [Tauler], was so enlightened by the Holy Spirit and
> transformed in God, that he foresaw, through the spirit of prophecy,
> the great plagues and deviations from the holy faith — that now,
> God have mercy, have befallen us — and he described them in the
> clearest of terms].

The letter provides another glimpse into the ongoing debate with Lutheran doctrine, when Noviomagus tells his readers that Tauler at no time rejects the merits of good works. This, of course, was one of the main points of controversy between Lutherans and the Catholic Church, with Lutherans arguing for 'sola gratia'. In sum, the dedicatory letter frames Tauler as an established authority whose works may help to develop a mystical spirituality, and in doing so, will help to ward off the onslaught of contemporaneous heresies. The letter makes the edition emphatically Catholic and presents it as a tool in the defence against Lutheranism.

The editor does not stop at this, and he proceeds to describe the qualities of Tauler. Foremost, according to Noviomagus, is indeed his ability to express divine wisdom using plain language, characterized by clear words and comprehensible images and comparisons (*gleichnissen*). This sets him apart from a writer like Dionysius the Areopagite, whose language is called nebulous, although he expounds on the same connection between man and the Divine.

Nevertheless, there can sometimes be a problem with the comprehensibility of his sermons, but that is due, Noviomagus argues, to the fact that the sermons were written down by people who listened to his sermons being delivered. This problem, on the other hand, often gets solved when Tauler expresses himself more clearly on the same subject in other sermons. In conclusion, with regard to the comprehensibility of Tauler's texts, it is necessary for any reader to read and reread the entire corpus of texts.

Towards the end of the long dedicatory letter Noviomagus notes that during Tauler's lifetime there were numerous other authors whom he calls 'Freunde Gottes' ['friends of God']. He mentions Meister Eckhart (*c.* 1260–1328), Heinrich Seuse (1295–1366), Jan van Ruusbroec (1293–1381), and Geert Grote (1340–1384). Noviomagus suddenly reveals that it might well be that some of the texts attributed to Tauler are not actually his, but he immediately adds that that should not bother anyone, since all of these writers were inspired by the Holy Spirit.[13] It is important to note that this last mention of this crucial text-historical information might not have got through to every reader, especially since the outlook of the book, its title-page, and

---

13 I refer to my earlier comment (n. 9) that the complete absence of all of these writers in Petrus Canisius's correspondence suggests that Petrus Noviomagus is not Canisius.

the texts themselves, do not take up this issue; hence the reader might never suspect that not all texts are by Tauler.

To appreciate the rather light-hearted and careless way in which Noviomagus deals with the grave uncertainties regarding the attribution of texts, it is interesting to see how his predecessors handled the same issue. It is especially interesting to consider the editorial information in the 1522 Basel edition.[14] Here the introduction notes that the edited texts — only sermons, no other genres — are subdivided into three categories. The first section contains the sermons that are considered authentic Tauler sermons. The second has the sermons that were probably written by Tauler, although some might have been written by others. They were, however, surely written in the same period and in the same spirit. This section ends with the note: 'Hier enden sich die sermo und predigen die man gemeinlich dem hochgelerten andechtigen vatter doctor Johanni Tauler zuschreibt' ['Here end the sermons and homilies that are commonly attributed to the learned and devout doctor, father Johannes Tauler'] (fol. 242rb). The third category is that of sermons by teachers from whom Tauler drew his inspiration.

Since Noviomagus tells us that he knew and used the earlier editions, we may safely assume that he had seen and evaluated this subdivision. Therefore, it is all the more surprising that he applies a less rigid philological approach than his predecessor had done. The doubtful sermons had all been neatly collected in the second section in the Basel edition. Noviomagus, however, extends the doubt regarding authorship over the entire collection of sermons. He disregards the order of the Basel edition and no longer applies the subdivision between authentic and doubtful sermons; they are all lumped together under the heading of Tauler. Whereas the Basel edition provided a whole section of sermons that were considered authentic, the 1543 version no longer presents the reader with such relative certainty. It, moreover, includes some twenty-nine sermons that had never been published before. They are entirely unstudied, and thus constitute one of the many aspects of this edition that deserve an in-depth study.[15]

On the other hand, Noviomagus does not include the sermons from the third section. He thus leaves out sermons that were certainly not Tauler's. If this could be regarded a manifestation of text-critical awareness, such awareness is again conspicuously absent in his decision uncritically to include the whole host of genres not formerly attributed to Tauler.

---

14 *Joannis Tauleri des seligen lerers Predig, fast fruchtbar zů eim recht christlichen leben: Deren Predigen garnah hie in disem bůch des halbteyls meer seind den[n] in andern vorgetruckten büchere[n] [...]* (Basel: Adam Petri, 1522). The edition may be consulted here: https://reader.digitale-sammlungen.de/resolve/display/bsb10149257.html [accessed 30 December 2020].

15 There is no practical, concise way to refer to these twenty-nine sermons that show up when comparing the 1543 edition with the earlier editions and with the Vetter and Corin editions.

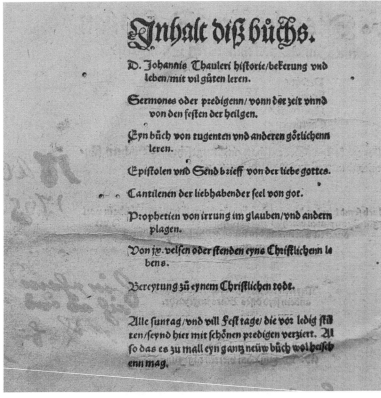

FIGURE 10. Table of Contents of the 1543 Köln edition of Tauler's Works. Universiteit Antwerpen, Ruusbroecgenootschap, 3112 A 3, fol. Aiv. Reproduced with permission.

After the dedicatory letter follows a text entitled *Historia und Leben des Erwurdigen Doctors Johannis Tauleri*. It has long been established that this alleged biography is in fact an adapted version of the so-called *Meisterbuch* that has nothing to do with Tauler.[16] The *Meisterbuch* contains a dialogue between a master and a lay person. In the *Historia* the master is identified with Johannes Tauler. This identification was already made in the first printed version of Tauler's sermons in 1498 in Leipzig.[17] The 1543 edition of the *Historia* is a further enhancement, as it were, of the reputation of Tauler that had already been fundamentally changed by the attribution of genres that he had not been connected with before. It is therefore important to mention the new

---

16 See Georg Steer, 'Merswin, Rulman', in *Die deutsche Literatur des Mittelalters: Verfasserlexikon*, ed. by Kurt Ruh and others (Berlin: De Gruyter, 1978–2008), VI (1987), cols 420–42 (col. 435), XI (2004), col. 993; Heinrich Denifle, *Taulers Bekehrung, kritisch untersucht*, Quellen und Forschungen zur Sprach- und Kulturgeschichte der Germanischen Völker, 36 (Strasbourg: Trübner, 1879).

17 See Steer, 'Merswin, Rulman', col. 435.

DIVERGING PERCEPTIONS   **455**

characteristics that were added. The most important innovation is certainly the fact that Tauler is presented as a knowledgeable preacher who initially lacked the grace of divine inspiration. The critical lay person confronts him with this grave shortcoming. This sends the preacher into near depression, and it takes him a while to acknowledge this fact and submit himself to God, leaving his pride behind. When, eventually, as a consequence of this conversion, he does receive divine inspiration, he becomes the imposing authority that this edition suggests him to be. There can be no doubt that this conversion story heightened Tauler's standing immensely. No longer was he merely well educated; he was divinely inspired.

After the *Historia* and the *Sermons*, edited with little philological zeal, follows a long series of newly attributed works. By far the longest of those additional works, and the most influential (as we will see) is *Eyn bůch von tugenten und anderen gótlichenn leren*, as it is called in the very brief Table of Contents on fol. Aiv (a detailed description of the content follows in the *Register* on fols Aiiira–Avivb; see Figure 10).[18]

In the edition itself, on fol. 279ra the text is introduced in the following manner: 'Des erleüchten D. Johannis Tauleri gótliche leren. Wie mann durch geystliche übungen und tugenden zu lieblicher vereinung gots kommen sol neüw gefunden' ['Divine teachings from the enlightened master Johannes Tauler; how one may arrive at a loving union with God through spiritual exercises and virtues; newly found']. This is the treatise that later became rather well-known as the *Institutiones*.[19] The *Leren* were for a large part responsible for the fame of Tauler. Scholarship has established that the text is a clever compilation, using, among others, texts of Eckhart, Ruusbroec, and the treatise *Vanden twaelf dogeden*.[20]

The other highlights from the additional works are also identified in the abbreviated table of contents on the verso of the title page. They are letters, songs, and prophecies. Only the songs have received scholarly attention

---

18   The additional works as listed in the Register are (the chapter numbers and the folio numbers where the texts can be found in the edition are indicated): *Tractat vonn tugenden*, cap. 1, fol. 279ra; *gaven*, cap. 39, fol. 318va; *Epistolen und Sendbrieff*, cap. 40, fol. 321vb; *Cantilene*, cap. 67, fol. 331vb; *Prophetie*, cap. 67 [*sic*], fol. 332vb; *Von ix. velsen odder stenden*, cap. 73, fol. 333va; *Klar spiegel*, cap. 74, fol. 336vb; *Meyster Eckarts wirtschaft*, cap. 75, fol. 337va; *Eyn bild reiche form eyns volcomnen menschen*, no chapter number, fol. 338ra.

19   The *Institutiones* (the title is found in the Latin translation by Surius) is often referred to as the *Institutiones Taulerianae*, which is a confusing title as it suggests that this is the original title, whereas it is only a given title. The actual title is: *D. Ioannis Thauleri, sublimis et illuminati theologi, saluberrimae ac plane divinae institutiones aut doctrinae, recens inventae, quibus, instruimur, uti per spirituales exercitationes virtutesque, ad amabilem Dei unionem pertingatur*.

20   See Ine Kiekens, '"Want wi van doechden scriven willen": een literair- en cultuurhistorische studie van het ontstaan en de doorwerking van *Vanden twaelf dogheden*' (unpublished doctoral dissertation, Universiteit Antwerpen, 2018).

456   KEES SCHEPERS

in recent years, particularly from Almut Suerbaum.[21] It is obvious that this sudden expansion did much to alter the image of Tauler. It means that he became an author who was able to convey his message of the possible union with the Divine, using different literary genres. This extension of his literary competence added to his stature.

The Influence of the 1543 Edition

The 1543 edition is ultimately the source for the later Europe-wide fame of Tauler, both in the Catholic and Protestant worlds. Only one step was still needed to make this possible: the production of a Latin translation. The prolific Carthusian translator Laurentius Surius (1523–1578) took on this task. His Latin translation of the 1543 edition was published in 1548.[22] Not surprisingly, Surius saw fit to translate the entire *Opera omnia*, which clearly suited his objective to bring trustworthy masters of fourteenth-century mysticism to the fore (a few years later he also completed the translation of Jan van Ruusbroec's works, for example).[23] With his translation he ensured the entry of Tauler, who had become an imposing figure in spiritual literature, into the broader European realm.

How did Surius deal with the 1543 edition? What did he do with the sermons, many of which are of uncertain authorship, with the *Historia*, which had suddenly been connected to Tauler, and with the added works? The general answer is that he largely does not question the attributions made by Noviomagus. In particular, Surius does not question that the *Historia* is about Tauler, and the large font in which the title *Historia* and the name *Ioannis Thauleri* are printed certainly gives the readership the impression that what they have before their eyes is indeed a biography of Tauler. The *Leren*, equally important with regard to the literary profile of Tauler, are also considered to be Tauler's. The Surius translation — surprisingly — even has some minor, additional texts that were not in the 1543 edition. In this case, however, Surius does provide an explanation for their inclusion in the edition, and here he reflects on their authorship.[24] All in all, Surius does not alter the literary profile

---

21 Almut Suerbaum, 'Tauler Reception in Religious Lyric: (The pseudo-)Tauler Cantilenae', *Ons Geestelijk Erf*, 84 (2013), 41–54. See also K. Ruh, 'Tauler-Cantilenen', in *Die deutsche Literatur des Mittelalters: Verfasserlexikon*, ed. by Kurt Ruh and others (Berlin: De Gruyter, 1978–2008), IX (1995), cols 657–62, XI (2004), col. 1489.

22 D. Joannis Thauleri [...] *Tam de tempore quam de sanctis conciones plane piissimae, caeteraque [...] opera omnia [...]/ nunc primum ex Germanico idiomate in Latinum transfusa sermonem [...] interprete Laurentio Surio Lubecensi* ... (Köln: Joannis Quentel, 1548).

23 D. Ioannis Rusbrochii summi atque sanctissimi viri, quem insignis quidam theologus alterum Dionysium Areopagitam appellat, opera omnia. Nunc demum post annos ferme ducentos e Brabantiae Germanico idiomate reddita Latine per F. Laurentium Surium. Carthusiae Coloniensis alumnum (Köln: Joannis Quentel, 1552).

24 Albert Ampe, 'Een kritisch onderzoek van de *Institutiones Taulerianae*', *Ons Geestelijk Erf*, 40 (1966), 167–240 (pp. 167–69).

of Tauler that emerged from the 1543 edition. What he did do, however, is raise his status even further by making the texts available in Latin, the language of the higher echelons of religious life and of scholarly literature.

A peculiar example of the influence of the Noviomagus edition in the Catholic tradition is the 1557 printed edition in Middle Dutch of some of Tauler's works. This edition represents a further phase in the development of Tauler's literary profile as an author:

> Van volcomentheyt alre deuchden. Een seer innich boecxken des seer verlichten Doctoers Johannis Tauleri. Predicant tot Colen dwelcke met rechte wel ghenoemt mach worden Dat merch der sielen [...] overgheset wt die overlantsche tale in onse nederlandtsche duytsche tale.
>
> [On the perfection of all virtues. A very devout book by the very enlightened doctor Johannes Tauler, preacher in Cologne, that could justifiably be called The Marrow of the Soul [...] translated from German into our Netherlandish Dutch language].

The latter part of the title 'Dat merch der sielen' is commonly used to refer to the book that was later published in numerous editions. The translator is Antony van Hemert (active *c.* 1550), a canon regular from Eindhoven. He informs us that he translated the work from German. The book was printed in 1557 in Antwerp by Symon Cock (1481–1562). It is a highly peculiar edition because it contains a translation of Tauler's *Opera* in the 1543 edition *without* the sermons. The edition thus exclusively contains works that were *not* written by Tauler. Of course, this is knowledge in hindsight; Van Hemert saw it differently. For him it was precisely the works other than the sermons that contain the core of Tauler's teaching. The Van Hemert edition had become possible ever since the reputation of Tauler as an author versed in a wide range of genres had been firmly established. As a consequence it seemed quite acceptable to omit the sermons. These sermons were most suited to those who lived as monastics; by omitting them Van Hemert's edition focused on Tauler's more generally instructive oeuvre instead.

Tauler the Protestant: The 1565 Emden Edition

As we have seen, any sixteenth-century edition of Tauler that seeks to present his works largely unchanged quite naturally becomes Catholic as the Catholic Church sought to remain true to its traditions. Therefore, turning an edition of Tauler's works into a Protestant book requires quite a bit more effort. And indeed, such effort was made in the 1565 edition (see Figure 11). This earliest Protestant Tauler-edition in Dutch has the following title:

> Des Hoochverlichten D. Johannis Tauleri van eenen volcomen Euangelisschen leuen Christelijcke Predicatien oft Sermonen op allen

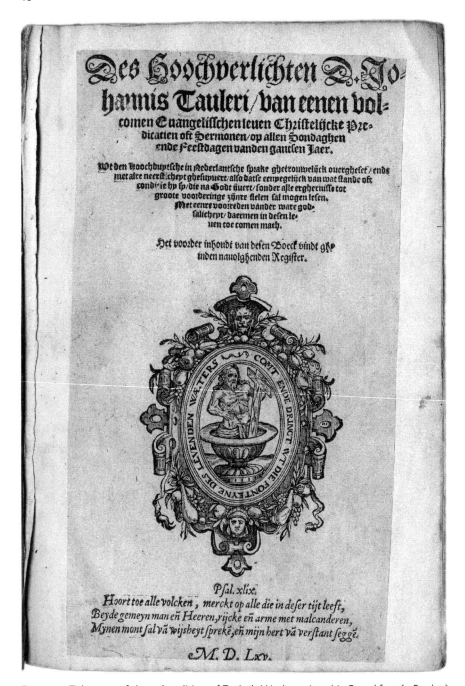

FIGURE 11. Title page of the 1565 edition of Tauler's Works, printed in Franckfort (= Emden). Universiteit Antwerpen, Ruusbroecgenootschap, 3116 B 10. Reproduced with permission.

DIVERGING PERCEPTIONS   459

Sondaghen ende Feestdagen vanden gantsen Jaer. Wt den Hoochduytsche in Nederlantsche sprake ghetrouwelijck ouergheset.

> [From the highly enlightened Johannes Tauler, about a perfect evangelical life; Christian homilies or sermons for all Sundays and Holy Days of the entire year. Faithfully translated from High German into the Dutch language].

The edition is remarkable both for its content and for its place in the history of printing. I will briefly address the latter aspect first. The colophon on the last page reads: 'Tot Franckfort, by Peter van Dueren, M D Lxv'. However, no printer of such name is known.[25] In fact, Peter van Dueren did not exist, and the name is a pseudonym for Willem Gailliart (*c.* 1507–1574), a printer from Emden in the most northern part of Germany, close to the border of the modern-day Netherlands. Both Emden and Frankfurt harboured large communities of Dutch Protestant refugees and exiles at the time. The reason for Gailliart using a fake identity and address was most likely purely opportunistic: apparently he had legal problems over the use of the typographical material of another printer.[26]

The introductory text of the 1565 edition is unusual and long (fols Aira–Aiijvb). It does not say a word about the reasons for this edition, nor does it identify its intended readership or give information about the origin of the text. Needless to say, it remains unclear what kind of revisions were carried out. The reader has to return to the title page, more specifically to the subtitle, to gain a little bit of insight into the genesis of the edition. Here it is stated that the text was translated from German. The fact, however, that it was translated from the 1543 edition — a Catholic edition — is left unmentioned, quite possibly to let sleeping dogs lie as by 1543 a Tauler edition from Noviomagus in Cologne would certainly be perceived as Catholic. The entire subtitle reads:

> Wt den Hoochduytsche in Nederlandsche sprake getrouwelijck overgheset ende met alre neersticheyt ghesuyvert also datse eenyegelijck van wat stande of condicie hy sy die na God ijvert sonder alle erghernisse tot groote voorderinge zijnre sielen sal moghen lesen.

> [Faithfully translated from High German into Dutch, and carefully purged, so that everybody, from whatever walk of life he may be who longs for God, may read it for the benefit of his soul without any annoyance].

---

25 See *Dutch Typography in the Sixteenth Century: The Collected Works of Paul Valkema Blouw*, ed. by Ton Croiset van Uchelen and Paul Dijstelberge, Library of the Written Word, The Handpress World, 18 (Leiden: Brill, 2013), pp. 196–98.

26 *Dutch Typography in the Sixteenth Century*, ed. by Croiset van Uchelen and Dijstelberghe, pp. 196–98.

The motive for this edition is also hinted at in a phrase in the subtitle. The crucial phrase is 'sonder alle erghernisse' ['without any annoyance']. Only after a cursory analysis of the edition, comparing it with the 1543 edition, it becomes clear that this likely means without having to take offence at any traces of Catholicism.

The edition opens with an introductory text. It has a title/heading in which its purpose is explained: 'Vander ware godsalicheyt daer toe een mensche in desen leven comen mach. Ghestelt alhier in de plaetse van Prologe oft Voorreden, tot een inleydinghe int navolghende Boeck' ['On true blessedness in God to which a person may arrive in this life. It is placed here in lieu of a prologue or preface, as an introduction to the following book'] (fol. Air). Even though the introductory text is far more extensive than the dedicatory letter of Noviomagus, its author does not address the works of Tauler in any way. The introductory text contains an exposition on a subject that is apparently dear to his heart. It deals entirely with the subject of *Godtsalicheyt*, a concept that is hard to translate, but the phrase 'blessedness in God' renders its meaning adequately. The introduction gives a more extensive definition of *Godtsalicheyt*: 'Inden eersten en*de* voor al moet men weten dat de godtsalicheyt niet anders en is dan een ruste die de Gheest Godts door Christum inden mensche werckt' ['In the first place and before anything one should know that "blessedness in God" is nothing but a stillness or serenity the Holy Spirit instils through Christ into a human person']. The concept of *Godtsalicheyt* seems to be specifically Lutheran.[27] Apparently, it is the conceptual framework within which the work of Tauler is read and understood.

Godtsalicheit is omnipresent in the introduction to the edition. Tauler, on the other hand, is oddly absent. As noted, there is no explicit mention of Tauler's oeuvre in the title/heading that precedes the introduction. His work is simply referred to as '[dat] navolghende boeck' ['the following book']. Only in the final paragraph, which connects the introductory text with the edited works, is Tauler's name finally mentioned: 'ende dat is de ware godsalicheyt daer van ghy breeder verclaringe vint inde navolgende Domini Taulerus boecken' ['And that is the true blessedness in God about which you will find a more extensive explanation in the following books of Master Tauler'] (fol. Aiijvb). Only by comparing both editions does it become clear that what might be termed undesirable elements were carefully and competently purged from the 1565 edition. The editor makes some careful choices in this regard. He allows many elements of Catholic doctrine to pass that Lutheran doctrine did not vehemently oppose. In fact, the elements that seem to have been purged

---

27 *Deutsches Wörterbuch von Jacob und Wilhelm Grimm*, 16 vols, Leipzig 1854–1961, online version: http://dwb.uni-trier.de/de/ [accessed 1 October 2020]: '*gottseligkeit, f.,* frömmigkeit (...) die abstraktbildung zu gottselig wird von Luther, besonders in der bibelübersetzung, in bedeutung und gebrauch und bis in einzelne sprachliche wendungen hinein weitgehend festgelegt. die verbreitung in der protestantischen literatur des 16. jhs. vollzieht sich wie bei dem zugrunde liegenden adj. überaus schnell'.

from the edition are those that explicitly refer to the Catholic Church as an institution, and to the sacramental role of its priests.

The mere fact that the 1565 edition was published by Gailliart in Emden suggests that this was an edition aimed at a Protestant readership. Both the printer and the place of print are firmly Protestant.[28] But that is obviously not enough to make a Catholic text acceptable for Protestant readers. Therefore the 1565 translation of the 1543 edition certainly required meaningful changes with regard to the content of the texts. In order to detect those meaningful changes, I have made a comparison of some of the sermons (especially sermons 40, 46, 54, 55, and 69 in the edition by Vetter). I did not study possible adaptations in the other attributed genres. However, I can mention one very conspicuous case of texts that were deleted in the 1565 edition. The final two chapters of the *Institutiones* in the 1543 edition are entitled 'Von bereytung das heilige sacrament wirdigklich zu entfangen / vnd vonden übergrossen gnaden vnd fruchten da in verborgen Cap. xxxviij' ['On preparing to receive the Holy Sacrament in a worthy manner, and on the immense grace and fruit that is hidden in it. Chapter 38'] and 'Von xij. vnsprechlichen grossen gaben vnd gnaden / die got gibt allen die in werdigklich entfangen in dem heilgen sacrament Das xxxix Cap' ['On twelve unspeakably great gifts and mercies that God gives to those who worthily receive him in the Holy Sacrament. Chapter 39']. Both chapters were omitted on the 1565 edition for the very obvious reason that they deal with the sacrament of Holy Communion in a way that would be unacceptable for any Protestant denomination.

I am neither the first nor the last to look at the 1565 edition. In 1994 the edition was one element discussed in an article by Maarten Hoenen.[29] However, he did not compare the 1565 edition with the 1543 edition — the connection to which he seems to have overlooked — but directly with the Tauler sermons in the Vetter edition. Very recently, Ine Kiekens made a fairly extensive comparison between the 1543 and 1565 editions.[30] Her comparison differs from my own, however, in that she looked at adaptations in the *Leren*, a text that I did not consider as I only examined the sermons. Nevertheless, the results of her comparison are very comparable to mine. Kiekens devised useful categories for comparison — also comparable to the ones I myself have used. Her categories are partly based on a study by Von Habsburg on

---

28 See Martin Tielke, 'Johan Gailliart (Galliart, Gaillart, Geillyaert, Gheylliaert, Guaillart)', in *Biographisches Lexikon für Ostfriesland*, ed. by Martin Tielke, 4 vols (Aurich: Ostfriesische Landschaftliche Verlags- und Vertriebsgesellschaft, 1993–2007), I (1993), 156–57. Online available at: www.ostfriesischelandschaft.de/fileadmin/user_upload/bibliothek/blo/Gailliart.pdf [accessed 1 October 2020].

29 Maarten J. F. M. Hoenen, 'Johannes Tauler (+ 1361) in den Niederlanden: Grundzüge eines philosophie- uns rezeptionsgeschichtlichen Forschungsprogramm', *Freiburger Zeitschrift für Philosophie und Theologie*, 41 (1994), 389–444.

30 Kiekens, '"Want wi van doechden scriven willen"'.

the Protestant appropriation of Thomas a Kempis.[31] Kiekens noted that the 1565 edition left out or changed textual elements having to do with different aspects of Catholic doctrine. She found that 'Catholic' elements were omitted. These omissions fall into the following categories: purgatory, the veneration of saints, the Church as an institution, the role of priests, the value of good works, and the interpretation of *Gelassenheit* or 'detachment'.

In my comparison I identify two main categories of adaption. The first adaptation was to use a Protestant version of the Bible; the second, and more fundamental adaptation process involved the excision of specific references to the sacramental Church and to priesthood. The adaptation process was carried out remarkably discreetly and skilfully: the adaptations consist mainly of deletions and, if one read only this 1565 version, one would not suspect that passages had been omitted. The deleted content mainly has to do with aspects of the sacramental Church that were unacceptable from a Protestant perspective. And in this regard the excisions are in fact quite radical, as we will see. With regard to theological doctrine, it is important to note that early Lutheranism did not object to the veneration of Mary and the saints. It respected them as examples for one's own life and faith.[32] What Lutheranism did oppose was the belief that Mary or the saints could be mediators to achieve redemption, therefore it prohibited praying *to* the saint.

As noted, one of the textual aspects that clearly make the 1565 edition Protestant is the fact that it uses Protestant Bible translations. The translator does not consistently use the same version it seems; but whatever version he chooses, it is always Protestant. Sometimes his biblical quotes are closest to the so-called Biestkens Bible of 1560, sometimes to the Liesvelt Bible of 1526. The Biestkens Bible was based on Luther's German translation. No place of printing is mentioned, but in recent research it has been established that it was most likely printed in Groessen, a small village near Arnhem in the eastern part of the Netherlands. The printing shop existed only a few years, from 1558 to 1562, and exclusively published Protestant books. In 1562 its printing types were taken over by a printer in Emden.[33] The Biestkens Bible was intended to replace the Liesvelt Bible, the first complete Bible in Dutch translation that was first published in Antwerp in 1526 and was largely based

---

31 Maximilian von Habsburg, *Catholic and Protestant Translations of the Imitatio Christi, 1425–1650: From Late Medieval Classic to Early Modern Bestseller*, St Andrews Studies in Reformation History (Farnham: Ashgate, 2011).

32 See Carol Piper Heming, *Protestants and the Cult of the Saints in German-Speaking Europe, 1517–1531*, Sixteenth Century Essays and Studies, 65 (Kirksville, MO: Truman State University, 2003).

33 Anne Jaap van den Berg and Boukje Thijs, 'Biestkensbijbel', *Met andere woorden*, 25 (2006), 23–28.

on the translation of Luther.[34] Both Bibles were particularly in use among Lutherans and Mennonites.[35]

The closeness to these two Bibles seems to connect the Tauler translation to a specific niche of the Protestant world. Given the fact that some doctrinal differences between Lutherans and Mennonites did exist, it might be possible through more extensive research eventually to determine whether the Tauler edition was geared toward one of these two Protestant groups in particular.

In earlier scholarship, particularly in an article from 1994 by Maarten Hoenen, the 1565 edition was connected to a third Protestant Bible, the so-called Deux-Aes Bible, that was printed by Gilles van Erven in Emden in 1562.[36] This Bible was in use mainly in reformed (Calvinist) churches. However, the biblical quotes in the Tauler edition seem to be somewhat less close to the Deux-Aes. This becomes clear from the following examples.[37] In this first quote (Song of Songs 2. 7) the Tauler text is closest to Biestkens.

1565 Edition

Ick beswere u *ghy* dochteren Jerusalem byden rheen ende by den herten, dat ghy myn vriendinne niet op en wect *noch en roert* tot dattet haer selver behaecht (fol. 180vb).

[I adjure you, O ye daughters of Jerusalem, by the roes, and the harts of the fields, that you stir not up, nor make the beloved to awake, till she please].[38]

Biestkens 1560	Deux-Aes 1562	Liesvelt 1526
Ick beswere v *ghy* dochteren Ierusalems by den Rehen, oft by den Hinden opten velde, dat ghy mijne vriendinne niet op en wect, *noch en roert,* tot dattet haer seluen behaecht.	Ick besweere v, *ghy* dochteren Ierusalems, by den Rheen ofte by den Hinden op den velde, dat ghy mijn vriendinne niet op en weckt, *noch op en stuert,* tot dat het haer selue behaecht.	Ic beswere v dochteren Hierusalem, biden reehen oft byden hijnden opten velde, dat ghi mijne vriendinne niet op en wect, *noch en roert,* tot dattet haer selue behaecht.

In the following example, Wisdom 18. 14–15, Biestkens and Deux-Aes diverge in an identical manner from the version of Liesvelt, which is closest to the Tauler edition. There can be no doubt that in this case the Liesvelt Bible is the (distant) source.

---

34 Marginal notes that betrayed Liesvelt's Protestant leanings got him in trouble with the authorities. Liesvelt was convicted at a trial in Antwerp and beheaded in 1545.

35 Van den Berg and Thijs, 'Biestkensbijbel'.

36 Anne Jaap van den Berg and Boukje Thijs, 'Deux-Aesbijbel', *Met andere woorden,* 26 (2007), 23–29.

37 I refer to the digital editions of these Bibles that may be consulted at: https://www.bijbelsdigitaal.nl/ [accessed 21 June 2022].

38 Translation from the Douay-Rheims Bible [www.drbo.org; accessed 21 June 2022].

1565 Edition

Als alle dinghen in een stilswijghen waren *ende de nacht int midden zijns loops was here soo spranck u almachtich woort uut den hemel ende quam van uwen coninclijcken sale* (fol. 180va).

[For while all things were in quiet silence, and the night was in the midst of her course, Thy almighty word leapt down from heaven from thy royal throne].

Biestkens 1560	Deux-Aes 1562	Liesvelt 1526
Want doen alle dinck stille was ende rustede, ende euen recht middernacht was Voer dijn Almachtighe woort af vanden Hemel, wt Coninclijcken Throne.	Want doe alle dinck stille was ende rustede, ende euen recht middernacht was Voer dijn Almachtighe Woordt, af van den Hemel, wt Konincklicken Throone.	Want als alle dingen gerust geswijch hielden, *ende den nacht int middel zijns loops was HERE so spranc v almachtige woort wt den hemel ende quam van uwen coninclicken* throon.

Psalms 49. 1–3 in the 1565 edition (which is Psalm 48. 2–4 in the Douay-Rheims Bible) has the same version as Biestkens and Deux-Aes, and differs from Liesvelt.

1565 Edition

Hoort toe alle volcken, merckt op alle die in deser tijt leeft, beyde gemeyn man ende Heeren, rijcke ende arme *met **malcanderen***. Mynen mont sal van wijsheyt spreken, ende mijn hert van verstant seggen. (title page).

[Hear these things, all ye nations: give ear, all ye inhabitants of the world. All you that are earthborn, and you sons of men: both rich and poor together. My mouth shall speak wisdom: and the meditation of my heart understanding].

Biestkens 1560	Deux-Aes 1562	Liesvelt 1526
Hoort toe alle Volcken, mercket op, alle die in deser tijt leeft. Beyde ghemeyn man ende Heeren, beyde rijcke ende arme ***met malcanderen***. Mijnen mont sal van wijsheyt spreken, ende mijn hert van verstant segghen.	Hoort toe alle volcken: merckt op, alle die in deser tijt leeft. Beyde ghemeyne man ende heeren, beyde rijck ende arm ***met malcanderen***. Mynen mont sal van wijsheyt spreken, ende mijn herte van verstande segghen.	Hoort toe alle volcken. aenmerct alle die in deser tijt leuen. beyde gemeyne mannen ende heeren, beyde rijcke ende arme ***te samen***. Mijnen mont sal van wijsheyt spreken, ende mijn herte van verstant seggen.

It would be important to determine exactly what Bible version the Tauler edition is closest to, given the fact that the Biestkens and Liesvelt Bible were mainly used by Lutherans and Mennonites, whereas the Deux-Aes Bible found its users mostly among in Reformed Churches.

For this contribution I have made a limited comparison of the contents in the 1543 and 1565 editions, particularly by comparing some sermons; a full comparison would require a larger research project. However, even a limited comparison allows me to present clear examples of adaptations in the Protestant edition. As noted earlier, these adaptations are in fact mostly deletions.

In the first example both the authority of the Holy Church and of its priests is underscored in the version of the 1543 edition. The translation in the 1565 edition radically omits the entire paragraph.

Diligis dominum deum tuum[39]

Köln 1543, fol. 198r	Emden 1565, fol. 154v
Als nu diser mensch diss alles durchlitten hatt, so steet er *recht als der priester thut ob dem altar der ist von gots ordnung in der heilgen kirchen heilig geweycht, unde alles dat er umb und an hat ist alles heilig und hat den warden leichnam unsers herren in seinem gewalt zu heben und zu legen wo er wil, hyn under her, auff under nider* unde getar doch nit sprechen pater noster.	Als nu dese mensche dit al doorgheleden heeft, so staet hi, en derre doch niet Onse Vader spreken.

[When this person has suffered through everything, then he stands [*just like a priest on the altar that has been consecrated by God's ordinance of the Holy Church, and everything that he has around and on him is sacred, and he has the authority to raise the venerable body of Christ and to place it wherever he wants, here or there, up or down*], and still he does not dare to speak the Pater noster].

From the following paragraph, dealing with guilt, remorse and forgiveness, a reference to the sacrament of Confession was deleted.

Iohannes est nomen eius[40]

Köln 1543, fol. 229rb	Emden 1565, fol. 180ra
In disem nidersehen inn seyn gebrechen sol sich der mensch demütigen unnd sich legen für die fuss gottes das er sich erbarm über in **und sich biechtenn vor gottes stathelter** unnd soll hoffen das got alle schulde farenn last.	In dezen neder sien in zijn ghebreken sal hem de mensche verootmoedighen ende hem legghen voor de voeten Gods dat hy hem ontferme over hem ende sal dan hopen dat Godt alle schult quijtscheldt

[In this looking down upon one's shortcomings a person shall humble himself and lie down before the feet of God, so that he may have mercy on him *and he* [this person] *shall confess before God's representative* [i.e. a priest], and he must hope that God will absolve all guilt].

In the same sermon a remarkably long paragraph on the function and qualities of a priest is omitted.

---

39 *Die Predigten Taulers*, ed. by Vetter, no. 54, pp. 253–55.
40 *Die Predigten Taulers*, ed. by Vetter, no. 40, pp. 162–69.

466   KEES SCHEPERS

Köln 1543, fol. 229va	Emden 1565, fol. 180ra
Diser gotgedechtiger mensch dat ist ein inwendiger mensch der sol eyn prister sein und soll yngeen in sancta sanctorum und das volck alles darusz bleiben. [*followed by a paragraph of 27 lines*]	Dese Godtgedachtige man dat is een inwendich mensche die sal een priester zijn ende sal ingaen in dat heylich der heylighen ende dat volc sal altesamen daer buyten blijven [*a paragraph of 27 lines is omitted*].

[This God-devoted person, that is a contemplative person, must be (like) a priest and he shall enter the *Sancta sanctorum*, and the people shall remain outside].

In this long paragraph Tauler describes the many liturgical acts a priest performs. Remarkably, he adds that even though the actual priesthood is reserved for men, the spiritual priesthood can also be adopted by women.

The following paragraph is also completely deleted. It again contains a reference to Confession as well as a mention of the pope.

In omnibus requiem quesivi[41]

Köln 1543, fol. 242vb	Emden 1565, fol. 190v
Kinder ich môiss vch sagen von liebe ich bin vnrecht begriffen als ob ich gesprochen haben. Ich wolt nyemants *beycht* hôren er wôlt mir dan geloben das er thûn wôlt was ich wôlle das ist gar vnrecht gesprochen was ich wôlle Ich will von nyemants nichts dan wie geschriben steet und das selb bit ich mir nyemants zû gelobenn. Ich mag nyemants *absolvieren* in einem synn im seien dan seyn sünd leyd. Noch auch der *babst* er hab dan einen willen zû bessern seyn leben und sich vor sünden zu hüten und auch vor den ursachen der sünden nach seinem vermügen.	*Omitted*

[Children, I must tell you out of love that I have been misunderstood; as if I had said that I did not want to hear anyone's confession unless he promises that he would do what I want him to do. That is a completely false statement of what I want. I do not want anything from anyone other than what is prescribed and even that I do not ask anyone to promise me. I am unable to absolve anyone in any way, unless he is sorry for his sins. Not even the pope can do that, unless he [the penitent] is willing to improve his life and stay away from sin and also from the causes of sin, as much as he can].

The following paragraph is again missing in the 1565 edition, most likely because of the fact that even though the dedication of a church building is also known

---

41   *Die Predigten Taulers*, ed. by Vetter, no. 46, pp. 201–07.

in the Lutheran tradition, there is far less attention paid to the actual building, and much less to the yearly service to commemorate the dedication.[42]

In domo tua oportet me manere[43]

Köln 1543, fol. 259vb	Emden 1565, fol. 213ra
Liebe kinder es ist hüt kirch weyhe in disem gegenwertigenn gots hauss. Unnd alle die weiss vnd übung der heyligen christlichen kirchenn weyset vns alle geystlich auff den inwendigen menschen da selbst in der warheyt kirchweyhe vnd ein war gótlich verneüwung seyn soll on vnderlass.	*Omitted*

[Dear children, today is the Feast of the Dedication of the Church in this present house of God. And every mode and practice in the holy Christian Church steer us all spiritually toward the inner person where the true dedication of the church and a true divine renewal should continuously take place].

With the deletion of the following paragraph a list of just about every aspect of Catholic life was left out.

Sequere me[44]

Köln 1543, fol. 252rab	Emden 1565, fol. 213ra
Ich hab entfangen von gots gnaden vnd von der heilgn Christen-heit meinen orden, mein kappen, vnd dise kleider vnd meyn priesterschafft zu sein eyn lerer vnd beicht zu hóren. Nun keem es also das mir disz der Bapst wolt nemen vnd die heilge kirch (von der ich es hab) ich solt inn es lassen und nit fragen warumb sie es theten (were ich anders eyn gelassen mensch) vnd solt eyn grauwen rock anthún (mócht ich in haben) vnd solt ich nit mer in dem closter seyn bei den brúdern noch nit mer priesterlich mesz thún noch beicht hóren vnd predigen, So sprach ich In gots namen so sey es mit mir.	*Omitted*

[I have received from God's grace and from holy Christendom my religious order, my cope, and these clothes and my priesthood, to be a teacher and to hear confession. If it were to happen that the pope wanted to take this away from me, as well as the holy Church (from whom I have received it), I should leave it to them and not ask why they did it (if I were to be a spiritually detached person) and I should put on a grey cloak (if I had one); and if I were not to be in the monastery anymore with my brethren, nor were allowed to say Mass and hear confession and preach, then I should say: for God's sake, this is how it has to be].

---

42 See Allmut Polmer-Schmidt and Bernward Schmidt, 'Ritual and its Negation: "Dedicatio Ecclesiae" and the Reformed first Sermon', in *Foundation, Dedication and Consecration in Early Modern Europe*, ed. by Maarten Debelke and Minou Schraven, Intersections, 22 (Leiden: Brill, 2012), pp. 315–32.

43 *Die Predigten Taulers*, ed. by Vetter, no. 69, pp. 377–80.

44 *Die Predigten Taulers*, ed. by Vetter, no. 55, pp. 253–58.

Conclusion

These preliminary comparisons — and examples can be multiplied *ad libitum* — indeed make clear that everything that has to do with the authority of the Church and its priests, and consequently with the sacraments they administer, has been deleted. A more extended comparison might bring to light more subtle changes, such as the changing of terminology or the insertion of terms. One of the terms that was definitely inserted, is precisely the term *Godtsalicheyt*, referring to the concept so dear to the heart of the editor, since he expounded on it in the introduction.

Having focused on what is left out of the 1565 edition, we should not forget what was retained: everything that has to do with the introverted mystical life. Tauler's principal point in all of his sermons — also in the 1565 edition — is that every person who turns away from every (sinful) worldly distraction and sinks into his or her innermost being, may find God's presence there. And with everything sacramental having been omitted, this focus on the mystical life within a Protestant tradition is even stronger in the 1565 edition than in the 1543 edition. Even though the 1565 edition surely was a major feat — the adapted version attests to a very skilful editor — it seems to have had surprisingly limited success. It was reprinted only once, in 1588 by Barent Adriaensz in Amsterdam.[45]

From the mid-sixteenth century onward, and after Tauler's oeuvre had been enlarged by the 1543 edition, a Catholic and a Protestant Tauler go their separate ways. The Catholic Tauler stays on the traditional course, and is employed as a tool to combat Lutheranism. The Protestant Tauler sets off on a distinctly different route, with the substance of his mystical teachings cut loose from its ecclesiastical embedding. A limited comparison between both editions makes clear that the 1565 edition rigorously applies a series of adaptions intended to make the Catholic edition acceptable for a new, Protestant audience. The 1565 edition uses Protestant versions of the Bible and excises every mention of the authority of the Church and the sacramental role of its priests. It seems that the new Protestant Tauler was appreciated most among Lutherans and Mennonites. The details of his authorial persona and mystical teachings, as they emerge from the 1565 edition, will need to be determined in further research.

---

45 *Des hoochverlichten D. Iohannis Tauleri, van eenen volcomen euangelischen leuen Christelijcke predicatien oft sermonen, op allen sondaghen ende feestdaghen vanden ghantsen iaer.* Interestingly, Adriaensz also published the works of Menno Simons (after whom the Mennonites are named).

Bibliography

Early Printed Works Attributed to Johannes Tauler

D. Ioannis Rusbrochii summi atque sanctissimi viri, quem insignis quidam theologus alterum Dionysium Areopagitam appellat, opera omnia. Nunc demum post annos ferme ducentos e Brabantiae Germanico idiomate reddita Latine per F. Laurentium Surium. Carthusiae Coloniensis alumnum (Köln: Joannis Quentel, 1552)

D. Joannis Thauleri [...] Tam de tempore quam de sanctis conciones plane piissimae, caeteraque [...] opera omnia [...] / nunc primum ex Germanico idiomate in Latinum transfusa sermonem [...] interprete Laurentio Surio Lubecensi [...] (Köln: Joannis Quentel, 1548)

Des erleuchten D. Johannis Tauleri von eym waren Euangelischen leben. Götliche Predig, Leren, Epistolen, Cantilenen, Prophetien. Alles eyn kostpar Seelen schatz, in alten geschryben Büchern fünden, vnd nů erstmals ins liecht kommen (Köln: Jaspar von Gennep, 1543)

Des Hoochverlichten D. Johannis Tauleri van eenen volcomen Euangelisschen leuen Christelijcke Predicatien oft Sermonen op allen Sondaghen ende Feestdagen vanden gantsen Jaer. Wt den Hoochduytsche in Nederlantsche sprake ghetrouwelijck ouergheset (Franckfort: Peter van Dueren, 1565 [Emden: Willem Gailliart])

Des hoochverlichten D. Iohannis Tauleri, van eenen volcomen euangelischen leuen Christelijcke predicatien oft sermonen, op allen sondaghen ende feestdaghen vanden ghantsen iaer (Amsterdam: Barent Adriaensz, 1588)

Joannis Tauleri des heilige[n] lerers Predig, fast fruchtbar zů eim recht christlichen leben: Deren Predigen gar nah hie in disem bůch des halbteyls meer seind dan[n] in andern vorgetruckten büchere[n] [...] (Basel: Adam Petri, 1521)

Joannis Tauleri des hillige[n] lerers Predige faste fruchtbar vn[de] nutlick to eine[n] Christlyken leuende. Welkorer Predige gar na hyr yn düssem boke des halue[n] deels mehr synt wan yn andere[n] vorgedruckten bokere[n] [...] (Halberstadt: Lorenz Stuchs, 1523)

Joannis Tauleri des seligen lerers Predig, fast fruchtbar zů eim recht christlichen leben: Deren Predigen garnah hie in disem bůch des halbteyls meer seind den[n] in andern vorgetruckten büchere[n] [...] (Basel: Adam Petri, 1522)

Sermon des großgelarten in gnade[n] erlauchte[n] doctoris Johannis Thauleri predigerr ordens [...] (Leipzig: Konrad Kacheloven, 1498)

Sermones des hochgeleerten in gnaden erleüchten doctoris Johannis Thaulerii sannt dominici ordens die da weißend auff den nächesten waren weg im gaist zu wanderen durch überswebendenn syn, von latein in teutsch gewendt manchem menschen zu säliger fruchtbarkaitt (Augsburg: Hans Otmar, 1508)

Van volcomentheyt alre deuchden. Een seer innich boecxken des seer verlichten Doctoers Johannis Tauleri. Predicant tot Colen dwelcke met rechte wel ghenoemt mach worden Dat merch der sielen [...] overgheset wt die overlantsche tale in onse nederlandtsche duytsche tale (Antwerpen: Symon Cock, 1557)

Primary Sources

Johannes Tauler, *Die Predigten Taulers: aus der Engelberger und der Freiburger Handschrift, sowie aus Schmidts Abschriften der ehemaligen Strassburger Handschriften*, ed. by Ferdinand Vetter, Deutsche Texte des Mittelalters, 11 (Berlin: Weidmann, 1910)

Johannes Tauler, *Sermons de J. Tauler et autres écrits mystiques*, ed. by A. L. Corin, Bibliothèque de la Faculté de Philosophie et Lettres de l'Université de Liège, 33 and 42, 2 vols (Paris: Champion, 1924–1929)

Petrus Canisius, *Beati Petri Canisii Epistolae et Acta*, ed. by O. Braunsberger, 8 vols (Freiburg: Herder, 1896)

Secondary Studies

Ampe, Albert, 'Een kritisch onderzoek van de *Institutiones Taulerianae*', *Ons Geestelijk Erf*, 40 (1966), 167–240

Benzinger, Tobias, 'Von der Handschrift zum Druck und zurück: Ursachen und Auswirkungen eines markanten Medienwechsels', *Meister-Eckhart-Jahrbuch* 14 (2021), 167–90

Berg, Anne Jaap van den, and Boukje Thijs, 'Biestkensbijbel', *Met andere woorden*, 25 (2006), 23–28

Berg, Anne Jaap van den, and Boukje Thijs, 'Deux-Aesbijbel', *Met andere woorden*, 26 (2007), 23–29

Brodrick, J., *Saint Peter Canisius, S.J. 1521–1597* (London: Sheed and Ward, 1935)

Chaix, Gérald, *Réforme et contre-réforme catholiques: recherches sur la chartreuse de Cologne du XVIe siècle*, Analecta Cartusiana, 80, 3 vols (Salzburg: Institut für Anglistik und Amerikanistik, Universität Salzburg, 1981)

Cornet, Ineke, *The Arnhem Mystical Sermons: Preaching Liturgical Mysticism in the Context of Catholic Reform*, Brill's Series in Church History, 77 (Leiden: Brill, 2019)

Croiset van Uchelen, Ton, and Paul Dijstelberge, eds, *Dutch Typography in the Sixteenth Century: The Collected Works of Paul Valkema Blouw*, Library of the Written Word, The Handpress World, 18 (Leiden: Brill, 2013)

De Pelsemaeker, A., 'Canisius éditeur de Tauler', *Revue d'ascétique et de mystique*, 36 (1960), 102–08

Denifle, Heinrich, *Taulers Bekehrung, kritisch untersucht*, Quellen und Forschungen zur Sprach- und Kulturgeschichte der Germanischen Völker, 36 (Strasbourg: Trübner, 1879)

Habsburg, Maximilian von, *Catholic and Protestant Translations of the Imitatio Christi, 1425–1650: From Late Medieval Classic to Early Modern Bestseller*, St Andrews Studies in Reformation History (Farnham: Ashgate, 2011)

Heming, Carol Piper, *Protestants and the Cult of the Saints in German-Speaking Europe, 1517–1531*, Sixteenth Century Essays and Studies, 65 (Kirksville, MO: Truman State University, 2003)

Hoenen, Maarten J. F. M., 'Johannes Tauler († 1361) in den Niederlanden: Grund-züge eines philosophie- uns rezeptionsgeschichtlichen Forschungsprogramm', *Freiburger Zeitschrift für Philosophie und Theologie*, 41 (1994), 389–444

Jundt, Aug[ust]., *Histoire du panthéisme populaire au Moyen-Age et au XVIᵉ siècle* (Paris: Sandoz & Fischbacher, 1875)

Kiekens, Ine, '"Want wi van doechden scriven willen": een literair- en cultuurhistorische studie van het ontstaan en de doorwerking van *Vanden twaelf dogheden*' (unpublished doctoral dissertation, Universiteit Antwerpen, 2018)

Otto, Henrik, *Vor- und frühreformatorische Tauler-Rezeption: Annotationen in Drucken des späten 15. und frühen 16. Jahrhunderts*, Quellen und Forschungen zur Reformationsgeschichte, 75 (Heidelberg: Gütersloh, 2003)

Polmer-Schmidt, Allmut, and Bernward Schmidt, 'Ritual and its Negation: "Dedicatio Ecclesiae" and the Reformed First Sermon', in *Foundation, Dedication and Consecration in Early Modern Europe*, ed. by Maarten Debelke and Minou Schraven, Intersections, 22 (Leiden: Brill, 2012), pp. 315–32

Polzer, Markus, 'Arnhem and the Tauler Revival: New Evidence Concerning a Second Manuscript from the St Agnes Convent in Arnhem Containing Johannes Tauler's *Von eym waren Euangelischen leben*', *Ons Geestelijk Erf*, 84 (2013), 55–73

Prieur, Jutta, *Das Kölner Dominikanerinnenkloster St. Gertrud am Neumarkt*, Kölner Schriften zur Geschichte und Kultur, 3 (Köln: DME-Verlag, 1983)

Ruh, K., 'Tauler-Cantilenen', in *Die deutsche Literatur des Mittelalters: Verfasserlexikon*, ed. by Kurt Ruh and others, 14 vols, 2nd edn (Berlin: De Gruyter, 1978–2008), IX (1995), cols 657–62, XI (2004), col. 1489

Schepers, Kees, 'The Arnhem Mystical Sermons and the Sixteenth-Century Mystical Renaissance in Arnhem and Cologne', in *Mysticism and Reform, 1400–1750*, ed. by Sara S. Poor and Nigel Smith, ReFormations: Medieval and Early Modern (Notre Dame, IN: University of Notre Dame Press, 2015), pp. 84–123

Schepers, Kees, 'A Web of Texts: Sixteenth-Century Mystical Culture and the Arnhem Sint-Agnes Convent', in *Nuns' Literacies in Medieval Europe: The Kansas City Dialogue*, ed. by Virginia Blanton, Veronica O'Mara, and Patricia Stoop, Medieval Women: Texts and Contexts, 27 (Turnhout, Brepols, 2015), pp. 168–77

Schoor, R. J. M. van de, 'Canisius als Herausgeber: die Ausgaben von Tauler (1543), Kyrill (1546) und Leo dem Großen (1546)', *Ons Geestelijk Erf*, 82 (2011), 161–86

Steer, Georg, 'Merswin, Rulman', in *Die deutsche Literatur des Mittelalters: Verfasserlexikon*, ed. by Kurt Ruh and others, 14 vols, 2nd edn (Berlin: De Gruyter, 1978–2008), VI (1987), cols 420–43, XI (2004), col. 993

Suerbaum, Almut, 'Tauler Reception in Religious Lyric: (The pseudo-)Tauler Cantilenae', *Ons Geestelijk Erf*, 84 (2013), 41–54

Tielke, Martin, 'Johan Gailliart (Galliart, Gaillart, Geillyaert, Gheylliaert, Guaillart)', in *Biographisches Lexikon für Ostfriesland*, ed. by Martin Tielke, 4 vols (Aurich: Ostfriesische Landschaftliche Verlags- und Vertriebsgesellschaft, 1993–2007), I (1993), 156–57

PATRICIA STOOP

Strategies of Publishing

The Case of Franciscus Costerus

The Jesuit Franciscus Costerus (1532–1619) was an important pioneer of the Catholic Reformation and a strongly polemical figure. In the last twenty-five years of his life he was a passionate preacher. His attacks against Lutheran and Calvinist theologians as well as against more pagan forms of Humanism, in both his sermons and his widely-dispersed treatises, gave him the nickname *Ketterhamer* or the *Heretics' Hammer*. The fact that Costerus's sermons circulated in both manuscript and print raises issues about their authorship and dissemination as well as their readership. It also brings up questions of what effect these different kinds of publishing had on the extant sermons. In order to shed light on these topics I will focus within the context of this essay on the oldest printed sermon collection, the *Catholijcke sermoonen op de evangelien van de sondaghen* that was initially printed in Antwerp between 1598 and 1604, and the oldest text, Brussel, Koninklijke Bibliotheek, MS 614, which contains sermons from the period between 11 June 1592 and the end of 1594. The paratexts in both the manuscript and the early printed cycle offer interesting clues about the genesis of the sermons and the collections in which they are preserved. Whereas the dedications and the prologue to the printed collection show how Costerus wrote and published his Gospel sermons to support the Catholic cause in the Low Countries, the manuscript shows clear signs of Costerus's support of monastic life as well as the collaborative effort of women to save his sermons for the benefit of their devotion in a tradition extending back to the Middle Ages.

Franciscus Costerus

Franciscus Costerus — or Frans de Coster in Dutch — was born on 16 (or 13?) June 1532 in Mechelen (see Figure 12). In 1548 he enrolled at the university of Leuven where he studied philosophy. He obtained his diploma

> **Patricia Stoop** (patricia.stoop@uantwerpen.be) is a Researcher in the Department of Literature and an Associate Member of the Ruusbroec Institute at the University of Antwerp.

Circulating the Word of God in Medieval and Early Modern Europe: Catholic Preaching and Preachers across Manuscript and Print (c. 1450 to c. 1550), ed. by Veronica O'Mara and Patricia Stoop, SERMO 17, (Turnhout: Brepols, 2022), pp. 473–496 BREPOLS ❧ PUBLISHERS 10.1484/M.SERMO-EB.5.130465

474 PATRICIA STOOP

as *magister artium* on 19 March 1551.[1] Hereafter he studied theology until he joined the Jesuits in Cologne on 8 November 1552. From 5 April 1553 onwards he continued his noviciate and studies in Rome, where he lived in the house of Ignacio de Loyola (1491–1556), the founder of the Jesuit order. He was ordained priest on 9 April 1556.

Jos Andriessen and, in his footsteps, Els Agten, divide Costerus's life into three periods.[2] From 1556 until 1565 Costerus was a teacher at the Gymnasium Tricoronatum in Cologne, which was the model institute of Jesuit training in Germany and the most important institute of the Jesuits after the Collegium Romanum in Rome.[3] In 1557 he became novice master, and one year later, he was chosen prefect of studies, which he remained until 1564. During his time at the Gymnasium in Cologne, he also achieved his doctorate in theology.

In the second period, from 1565 until 1589, Costerus held several important administrative functions. In 1565, at the second general congregation of the Jesuits, he was appointed vice-provincial of the *Provincia Germania Inferior*, which included the Low Countries, the bishopric of Liège, and the Rhineland. He guided the Jesuit order in one of the most turbulent periods in the history of the Low Countries: the Iconoclastic Fury (1566), the upsurge of Calvinism in the Southern Low Countries, and the subsequent arrival of Fernando Álvarez de Toledo y Pimentel (1507–1582), the Duke of Alva, who was not positively disposed towards the Jesuits, offered huge challenges. Twelve years later, in May 1567, Costerus was appointed provincial of the Dutch province. In this function, which he occupied until November 1571, he founded colleges in Douai and Saint-Omer (nowadays located in France, just south of the Belgian border), led the opposition in Limburg against the rising Protestantism, and thus consolidated the position of the Jesuits in the Southern Low Countries. From 1571 onwards Costerus worked as rector of the Jesuit colleges of Douai and Bruges, until he was ordered to return to

---

1 Costerus has received a good deal of attention in (Jesuit) scholarship in the twentieth century. This biography is based on: J. Jageneau, 'De jonge Franciscus Costerus S.J.: Student aan de Leuvensche Alma Mater (1548–1552)', *Ons Geestelijk Erf*, 9 (1935), 198–204 and 302–11; J. Andriessen, 'Costerus (Coster, De Coster, De Custer, De Costere), Franciscus', in *Nationaal Biografisch Woordenboek*, 23 vols (Brussel: Paleis der Academiën, 1964–), I (1964), cols 333–41 (available online at https://www.kvab.be/nl/nationaal-biografisch-woordenboek; accessed 21 June 2022); Els Agten, 'Costerus en Van den Leemputte: twee katholieke bijbelvertalingen uit de eerste helft van de zeventiende eeuw', in *De Bijbel in de Lage Landen: elf eeuwen van vertalen* ed. by Paul Gillaerts and others, pp. 395–405 (Heerenveen: Royal Jongbloed, 2015). For a short biography in English, see Els Agten, *The Catholic Church and the Dutch Bible: From the Council of Trent to the Jansenist Controversy (1564–1733)*, Brill's Series in Church History, 80 (Leiden: Brill, 2020), pp. 135–41.

2 Andriessen, 'Costerus (Coster, De Coster, De Custer, De Costere), Franciscus', cols 334–35; Agten, *The Catholic Church and the Dutch Bible*, pp. 136–37.

3 For the history of the Gymnasium Tricoronatum, see Josef Kuckhoff, *Die Geschichte des Gymnasium Tricoronatum: ein Querschnitt durch die Geschichte der Jugenderziehung in Köln vom 15. bis zum 18. Jahrhundert* (Köln: Bachem, 1931).

FIGURE 12. Portrait of Franciscus Costerus, designed by Lucas Vorsterman I (1595–1675) in Antwerp in 1619. Engraving, *c.* 120 × 85 mm. Rijksmuseum Amsterdam, RP–P–OB–33.098. Reproduced with permission.

the Gymnasium in Cologne. There he showed himself to be a polemicist and a writer of controversial treatises. In 1577 he was chosen as provincial of the Rhine Province. In this period he founded a number of sodalities, and frequently preached against the heretics.[4] In 1585 Costerus was asked to return to the Low Countries, where he was appointed provincial for the second time.

---

4 For Costerus's role in the founding of Jesuit sodalities, see Judith Pollmann, *Catholic Identity and the Revolt of the Netherlands 1520–1635*, The Past & Present Book Series (Oxford: Oxford University Press, 2011), pp. 137–42.

476 PATRICIA STOOP

There he continued to found new sodalities and Jesuit colleges and to preach against new religious movements.

In the last thirty years of his long life Costerus lived and worked in Brussels as a preacher, confessor, and writer. He wrote over forty works, ordinarily in Latin and Dutch, that were strongly opposed to the Reformation and intended to support his fellow Catholics in both the Northern and Southern Low Countries.[5] He published various meditation books such as *De cantico salve regina septem mediationes* and *De vita et lavdibvs deiparae Mariae virginis, meditationes qvinqvaginta*, both printed by Christoffel Plantin (1520–1589) in 1587.[6] His *Libellus sodalitatis*, which in 1586 was also printed in the printing house of Plantin (*ex officina Christophori Plantini*), was immensely widespread. No fewer than eight reprints, in Latin, Dutch, and French were published.[7] Equally important are his influential book *Enchiridion controversiarum praecipuarum nostri temporis de religione*, printed in 1585 in Cologne by Arnold

---

5 A (not entirely complete) overview of Costerus's extensive oeuvre may be found in: Ferdinand Van der Haeghen and others, *Bibliotheca Belgica: bibliographie générale des Pays-Bas*, 6 vols (Brussel: Editions culture et civilisation, 1964–1970; repr. 1979), I (1964), 847–954; 'Coster, François', in Carlos Sommervogel and others, *Bibliothèque de la compagnie de Jesus*, 12 vols (Brussel: Schepens, 1890–1932), II (1891), cols 1510–34; and Andrew Pettegree and Malcolm Walsby, *Netherlandish Books: Books Published in the Low Countries and Dutch Books Printed Abroad before 1601*, 2 vols (Leiden: Brill, 2011), I, 396–98 (nos 8992–9046).

6 See Sommervogel and others, 'Coster, François', cols 1517–18. Middle Dutch versions of both texts were printed by Plantin's widow, Jeanne Rivière (*c.* 1521–1596), in 1590: *Seven meditatien op den lof-sanck Salve Regina* and *Vijftich meditatien van het leuen ende lof der Moeder Godts ende Maeghet Maria*. Both Plantin and Trognesius had strong connections with the Jesuits in Antwerp, and printed, among many other texts, school books for them. See Stijn Van Rossem, 'Het gevecht met de boeken: de uitgeversstrategieën van de familie Verdussen' (unpublished doctoral dissertation, Universiteit Antwerpen, 2014), p. 144.

7 See Sommervogel and others, 'Coster, François', cols 1511–14. The Latin versions of the *Libellus sodalitatis, hoc est Christianarum institutionum libri quinque* editions were published in 1587, 1593, 1597, 1601, and 1607. The Dutch versions, entitled *Het boecksen der broederschap, dat is vijf boecken der christelijcker leeringhen, voor de broederschap der H. maghet Maria* were printed in 1596 and 1604, and the French (*Le livre de la confrerie, c'est à dire les cinq livres des institutions chrestiennes*) in 1590. See Dirk Imhof, *Jan Moretus and the Continuation of the Plantin Press: A Bibliography of the Works Published and Printed by Jan Moretus I in Antwerp (1589–1610)*, Bibliotheca Bibliographica Neerlandica, Series major, III (Leiden: Brill, 2014), pp. 211–17 (the dates in Sommervogel differ slightly from the ones Imhof mentions). See also J. Andriessen, 'Uit de voorgeschiedenis van Franciscus Costerus's "Libellus sodalitatis"', *Ons Geestelijk Erf*, 35 (1961), 422–26. Agten, *The Catholic Church and the Dutch Bible*, p. 137 refers to reprints in 1603, 1604, and 1607; where she found this information is not clear to me; in n. 247 she refers to J. Jagenau, 'Twee catechismusuitgaven van P. Fr. Costerus S. J. in 1566 en 1568', *Ons Geestelijk Erf*, 8 (1934), 341–46, but he discusses a different, much earlier, catechism (*De Christelijcke leeringhe*) by Costerus that was first published in 1566 (but has not been preserved) and reprinted in 1568 by Emmanuel Philippe Trognesius (d. 1614) in Antwerp, who was active as a printer between 1564 and 1570. In 1934 this edition was present in the Grootseminarie in Bruges. See also Andriessen, 'Costerus (Coster, De Coster, De Custer, De Costere), Franciscus', col. 336. Thus far I have not been able to find this 1568 edition.

Mylius (1540–1604) in the printing office of Arnold Birckmann (d. 1541);[8] his translation of the New Testament in 1614 with accompanying brief explanations, *Nieu Testament onses Heeren Iesu Christi met korte uytlegghingen*, which was published by Joachim Trognesius in Antwerp; and, most essentially in this context, the series of *Catholijcke sermoonen*, which were printed between 1598 and 1616.[9]

Costerus's Sermon Collections

Costerus's sermons have been preserved in two manuscript collections and in six voluminous printed sermon cycles.[10] The oldest manuscript, Brussel, Koninklijke Bibliotheek, MS 614, contains fifty-one sermons preached at several places in Brussels in the period between 11 June 1592 and the end of 1594. The texts are collected by the canonesses regular of the Augustinian convent of Jericho, but Costerus did not preach all of them in that convent. The later manuscript is Wien, Österreichische Nationalbibliotheek, MS 13696. It contains forty-four sermons on the seven penitential psalms (*Sermones 44 super septem psalmos poenitentialis*), preached in 1595.[11]

The six printed sermon cycles, all in folio size, were all published in Antwerp and survive in numerous copies.[12] The first cycle was printed by

---

8 See Sommervogel and others, 'Coster, François', cols 1514–17. The *Enchiridion* also had several reprints, in Latin (1586, 1587, 1589, 1593, 1596, 1599, 1608, 1612, and 1621), in Dutch (1591), and in German (1595 and 1602). The thirteen Latin and German prints are mentioned in the Universal Short Title Catalogue. The Dutch version, entitled *Schildt der catholijcken, teghen de ketterijen, inhoudende de principaelste gheschillen die in onsen tijden opgeresen zijn in t'gelooue* (Antwerpen: ex officina Plantiniana, Jeanne Rivière and Jan I Moretus, 1591) is mentioned in STCV: de bibliografie van het handgedrukte boek (www.stcv.be; accessed 14 July 2020). On the impact of the *Enchiridion*, see Pollmann, *Catholic Identity*, pp. 147–50.

9 Costerus's Bible Translation has been preserved in two editions. Els Agten hypothesizes that the A-edition was printed by Trognesius, whereas the B-edition 'was probably a pirated edition that was printed in the Northern Low Countries and circulated in that area' (Agten, *The Catholic Church and the Dutch Bible*, pp. 138–39; citation on p. 139). See also Agten, 'Costerus en Van den Leemputte', pp. 397–400.

10 Costerus's printed collections of sermons received attention in K. Porteman, 'Na 350 jaar: de "sermoonen" van Franciscus Costerus', *Ons Geestelijk Erf*, 43 (1969), 209–69.

11 Sommervogel and others, 'Coster, François', cols 1533–34; Ernest Persoons, 'Handschriften uit kloosters in de Nederlanden in Wenen', *Archief- en Bibliotheekwezen in België*, 38 (1967), 59–107 (p. 89, no. 206).

12 The transmission of Costerus's sermon collections is very complex, as the different cycles were printed in several forms and/or bound together in different orders, and not necessarily in the order that Costerus wrote them. For example, the copy that is now preserved at Antwerpen, Ruusbroecgenootschap, 3048 A 1, preserves all three cycles of the *Catholijcke sermoonen op de evangelien van de sondaghen* in the order of the ecclesiastical year. First it contains the fourteen sermons for the period between Advent and Quinquagesima (part 2), followed by the fifteen sermons for Lent until the Feast of the Holy Trinity (part 3), and finally by the twenty-four sermons after Pentecost (part 1). The copy that is now Antwerpen,

FIGURE 13. Title page of *Catholiicke sermoonen op de evangelien van de sondaghen naer Sinxen tot den Advent* (Antwerpen: Joachim Trognesius, 1598). Universiteit Antwerpen, Ruusbroecgenootschap, 3048 A 1. Reproduced with permission.

Joachim Trognesius (1556/59–1624), who was active as a printer from 1583 until *c.* 1620, and contains fifty-three *Catholijcke sermoonen op de evangelien van de sondaghen.*[13] Costerus wrote the cycle, which covers the full ecclesiastical year, in three stages. He started with the twenty-four sermons for the Sundays after Pentecost: *Catholiicke sermoonen op de evangelien van de sondaghen naer Sinxen tot den Advent* (see Figure 13). They were dedicated — like the two other volumes — to Matthias Hovius (1542–1620), archbishop of Mechelen, on 20 March 1597 (and printed in 1598) and preceded by an extensive prologue (*Voor-rede*).[14] The *Vierthien catholiicke sermoonen op de evangelien der sondaghen van den Advent tot den Vasten* are dated to 4 December 1600 (and printed in 1601), and the third part — *Viifthien catholiicke sermoonen op de evangelien der sondaghen van den Vasten tot de H. Driivvldicheyt* — to 8 August 1603 (printed in 1604).

Shortly after Costerus finished his sermons on the Gospels, he wrote a collection on the Epistles, in two volumes: *Catholiicke sermoonen op d'epistelen van de sondaghen van den Advent tot den Vasten* and *Catholiicke sermoonen op d'epistelen van den sondaghen na Sinxen tot den Advent.* These sermons

---

Ruusbroecgenootschap, 3048 A 10 follows the same order. However, whereas the cycles for Advent–Quinquagesima and the Sundays after Pentecost only contain sermons on the Gospels, the cycle for the period between Lent and Holy Trinity combines the sermons on the Gospels with the sermons on the Epistles, which are considered a different cycle that was printed by Joachim Trognesius in 1606 (see below) and which indeed was published separately elsewhere, for example, in Antwerpen, Ruusbroecgenootschap, 3048 A 1 (only the Gospels) and 3048 A 6 (only the Epistles). To complicate matters considerably, the half-page title with the correct indication of the content (*Viiftien catholiicke sermoonen op d'epistelen ende evangelien der sondaghen van het beghinsel des Vastens tot de heylighe Driivuldicheit* is preceded by a beautifully decorated full title page that wrongly indicates that this part of the book should contain the fifteen sermons to the Gospels only: *Viifthien catholiicke sermoonen op de evangelien der sondaghen van den Vasten tot de H. Driivvldicheyt.* It bears 1604 as its date, although in that year the sermons on the Epistles supposedly had not been printed yet (see below). Another example of the fact that information on the title pages is to be handled with great care is to be found in Antwerpen, Ruusbroecgenootschap, 3047 A 2. The title page claims that the volume contains the *Vijftien catholiicke sermoonen op d'Epistelen ende Evangelien der sondaghen van den Vasten tot de H. Driivuldichheydt* printed by Trognesius in 1617, but actually contains the fourteen Sermons on the Sunday Gospels for the period between Advent and Lent (*Vierthien Catholiicke sermoonen op de evangelien der sondaghen van den Advent tot den Vasten*), which was written in 1600 and appeared in print much earlier (but was reprinted several times). At which point this copy was printed cannot be determined. In any case, it is clear that the title pages of Costerus's early printed volumes should not be taken at face value and that mapping the full dispersal of his printed sermon collections (and by extension, his other works) could teach us more about the reception of Costerus's comprehensive oeuvre and the history of printing in general.

13 Anne Rouzet, 'Trognesius, Joachim' in *Dictionnaire des imprimeurs, libraires et éditeurs des XV*[e] *et XVI*[e] *siècles dans les limites géographiques de la Belge actuelle* (Nieuwkoop: De Graaf, 1975), pp. 224–25.

14 See Gerrit Vanden Bosch, 'Frans de Coster S. J., *Vierthien catholiicke sermoonen* (1618)', in *Jesuit Books in the Low Countries 1540–1773: A Selection from the Maurits Sabbe Library*, ed. by Paul Begheyn, Bernard Deprez, Rob Faesen, and others (Leuven: Peeters, 2009), pp. 40–43.

initially were also printed by Joachim Trognesius, most likely in 1606, but ten years later they were reprinted by his colleague Hieronymus Verdussen (1552–1632) under the title *Sermoonen op alle de epistelen van de sondaghen van der gheheelen jaer*.[15] In the following two years, 1617–1618, Trognesius also published a reprint of these sermons, which he combined with the sermons on the Gospels mentioned before.[16]

The third and the fourth cycle were printed by Hieronymus Verdussen in 1616, the same year in which he (re)printed the aforementioned *Sermoonen op alle de epistelen van de sondaghen van der gheheelen jaer*.[17] The two cycles, *Acht sermoonen ter eeren der H. moeder Godts op de acht capitelen van Salomons III. boeck ghenoempt Canticvm canticorvm* and the *Catholiicke sermoonen op de octave van't H. Sacrament des avtaers* were bound together. According to the prologue of Verdussen's *Sermoonen op alle de epistelen van de sondaghen van der gheheelen jaer*, these three collections were meant to be published together:

> Ende gemerct ic tot noch toe mijn beste gedaen hebbe, om V.L. met Godts VVoordt te vertroosten; soo seynde ick V.L. nu voor d'leste de Sermoonen op de Epistelen vande Sondagen van den geheelen Iaere, met tvvee Sermoon-octauen, dat is, sesthien Sermoonen; acht van't H. Sacrament des Autaers, ende d'andere acht vande H. Moeder Godts Maria; om uvve deuotie daer mede te verstercken (RG 3048 A 6, part 1, fols *2v–*3r).

> [And, considering that I have done my best thus far to comfort you with God's Word, I send you now finally the sermons on the Epistles for the complete year, with two sermon octaves, that is sixteen sermons, eight on the Holy Sacrament of the Altar, and eight on God's Holy Mother Mary, to strengthen your devotion to them].

Also in 1616, his colleague Joachim Trognesius printed the *Catholiicke sermoonen op alle de heylichdaghen des jaers*.[18]

The sixth and final cycle of sermons by Costerus was published posthumously. In 1643 Caesar Joachim Trognesius (born in 1590), son and successor of Joachim Trognesius, published a collection of sermons on Lent: *Schat der sermoonen op elcken dach des gheheelen Vastens*.[19]

---

15 Sommervogel and others, 'Coster, François', col. 1525. For a biography of Hieronymus Verdussen, see Van Rossem, 'Het gevecht met de boeken', pp. 25–28.

16 Franciscus Costerus, *Viiftien catholiicke sermoonen op d'epistelen ende evangelien der sondaghen van het beghinsel des Vastens tot de heylighe Driivvldicheydt* (Antwerpen: Joachim Trognesius, 1617; reprinted in 1618); *Vierthien catholiicke sermoonen op de epistelen ende evangelien der sondaghen van den Advent tot den Vasten* (Antwerpen: Joachim Trognesius, 1618); and *Catholiicke sermoonen op de epistelen ende evangelien van de sondagen naer Sinxen tot den Aduent* (Antwerpen: Joachim Trognesius, 1618).

17 Sommervogel and others, 'Coster, François', cols 1525–26.

18 Sommervogel and others, 'Coster, François', col. 1525.

19 Sommervogel and others, 'Coster, François', col. 1526.

Printed Gospel Sermons

It is clear from the dedications to Matthias Hovius that Costerus started writing his *Catholiicke sermoonen op de evangelien der sondaghen*, his oldest collection of sermons, at the request of his superiors: 'Eervveerdichsten Heere, het is my van mijnen Ouersten beuolen, dat ick in onse Neder-landtsche spraecke sommighe Sermoonen soude schrijuen, tot behoef der Catholijcken, die door eenich belet Godts vvoordt niet en connen hooren' ['Most venerable Father, I have been ordered by my superiors that I should write some sermons in our Dutch language, in favour of the Catholics, who for some hindrance are not able to hear God's Word'] (Antwerpen, Ruusbroecgenootschap, 3048 A 1 [hereafter 3048 A 1], part 1, fol. *2r).

From the dedication that precedes the second part, the *Vierthien catholiicke sermoonen op de evangelien der sondaghen van den Advent tot den Vasten*, we learn that his sermons were aimed foremost at the Catholics 'die in de vvederspannighe oft rebelle landen onder de ketters vvoonen' ['who live in the rebellious regions among the heretics'] (3048 A 1, part 2, fol. *2r), in the northern part of the Low Countries, even though all his books were 'seer straffelijck verboden' ['very strictly forbidden'] in Holland, 'als oft ick hunnen archsten vijandt waer' ['as if I were their worst enemy'] (3048 A 1, part 2, fol. *2v).[20]

In all three dedications to Hovius, Costerus is very clear about his motivation to write this cycle of Gospel sermons. He repeatedly expressed his wish to comfort and to teach the Catholic believers, to strengthen their sincere faith, to foster virtuous life, and to bring the lost sheep onto the right path.[21] Moreover, he exerted himself to offer a counter-weight — in line with the ancient, unambiguous Catholic doctrine (on the 'voet-padt onser Vaderen' ['footpath of our Father's]) — to the heretics who, each at their sole discretion, try to pull away people from the Catholic truth and bring them to eternal damnation by

> [...] sermoonen ende Predicatien voor alle plaetsen en tijden; Huys-postillen diemen inde huysen leest, ende in de herberghen den gasten ende reysenden mannen voor-stelt; Schips-prediken, om in de schepen

---

20 In the dedication to part 3, Costerus states that 'sommige van onse vvederpartijen' ['some of the opponents'] also read his sermons, either for their spiritual learning, or to misuse it and to fight against the Holy Church. See 3048 A 1, part 3, fol. *2r.

21 See 3048 A 1, part 2, fol. *2v. Very similar wordings can be found in the dedication preceding the *Catholiicke sermoonen op alle de heylichdaghen des jaers*: 'Hier toe hebbe ick desen Sermoon-boeck gheschreven, ende late die nu uytgaen, om de Catholijcken in dese Godlicke vvaerheydt t'ondervvijsen, ende de tvvijfelachtighe te verstercken, ende de verdoolde schapen in den rechten wech te brenghen' ['For this reason I have written this sermon book, and I publish it now in order to teach the Catholics in the Godly truth, to strengthen those in doubt, and to bring the lost sheep onto the right path'] (Antwerpen, Ruusbroecgenootschap, 3048 A 8, part 1, fols a3v–a4r).

482 PATRICIA STOOP

ende vveghen te lesen; Lijck-prediken voor de doode; Disch-redenen, om ouer tafel | te vermaecken; Sermoonen op S. Pauvvels brieuen, ende op de vier Euangelisten, ende dierghelijcke andere (3048 A 1, part 2, fol. *2r–v).

> [[...] sermons and preachings for all places and times; house postils which are read in the houses, and introduced to guests and travelling men in the taverns; ship sermons to read on the ships and the roads; funeral sermons for the dead; table sermons to entertain at the table; sermons on St Paul's Letters and the four evangelists, et cetera].

Here Costerus fulminated against the Protestants who 'd'een op sijn Luthers, d'ander op sijn Calvijns' ['the one in the Lutheran way, the other in the Calvinist way'] explain Scripture according to their own ideas, because they lack divine inspiration (3048 A 1, part 2, fol. *2v). In the dedication that precedes part 3, he also lashes out against the Protestants, complaining that

> Ons nieu volcksken komt na 1500. iaren, sonder Godlicke mirakelen, sonder Godlicke ghetuyghenisse, sonder uytnemende gheleertheydt, ende versmaden al het oudt, willende na hun goedtduncken alle leeringhen, ghebruycken ende Sacramenten deformeren, alle cerimonien te niet doen, ende eenen-ieghelicken vvijs-maken dat onse H. Catholijcke Kercke tot noch toe maer eenen modder-plasch gevveest en is, vol van alle vuylicheyt, superstitien, ende afgoderije' (3048 A 1, part 3, fol. *2v).

> [Our new people appear after 1500 years, without divine miracles, without testimony of God, without excellent erudition, and condemn all the old, while they wish to deform all teachings, uses, and sacraments according to their discretion, and destroy all ceremonies, and make everyone believe that our Holy Catholic Church thus far only has been a muddy puddle, filled with filth, superstition, and idolatry].

In order to teach his Catholic audience, Costerus used a methodology that he called new:

> Ick ghebruycke hier een nieuvve maniere, die in andere Sermoon-schrijuers niet en is: te vveten, dat ick niet een sententie sonder haer vvt-legginghe ende leeringhe achter en laete, op dat de materien dies te ouervloedigher zijn, ende den Leser daer vvt neme vvat hem aenstaet (3048 A 1, part 1, fol. *2r).

> [I use a new manner here, which cannot be found in other sermon writers, namely: I do not leave any sentence behind without its explanation and lesson, so that the materials are all the more profuse and the reader can take from it what suits him].

However, this method of verse by verse discussion of the pericope of the day is not as new as Costerius suggests; perhaps it was a way of getting people interested in his sermons. In the Low Countries, for example, the so-called

STRATEGIES OF PUBLISHING   483

pericope sermons were structured this way.[22] The reason that Costerus opted for this kind of sermon seems quite obvious: he aimed at biblical exegesis — 'uytlegghen' is the word that he uses repeatedly. This is what he considers to be the main task of a priest: he should explain what the Epistles and the Gospels selected by the Holy Church mean, so that the people can store the information in their memories and conform their lives to divine teachings. The ultimate goal is to win souls and to bring those to heaven.[23]

For the use of his sermon collections, Costerus had five methods in mind, which he mentioned in the dedication to Hovius that preceded part 1 of his sermon collection and explained at length in the *Voor-rede* that followed this dedication.[24] First he explained how teachers should expound Scripture in schools; second how preachers should preach it (in the *Voor-rede* itself this is the third manner); third, how listeners should hear God's Word; and finally how others should read it and meditate upon it. The second aspect received most attention in the dedications to Hovius: Costerus clearly considered his sermon collections as a rich source of material for other preachers: 'Zijnder eenighe Catholijcke Predicanten, die hen hier mede begheeren te behelpen, die sullen stoffe vinden om veel iaren te prediken' ['If there are any Catholic preachers who wish to make do with this, they will find preaching material for many years'] (3048 A 1, part 1, fol. *2r). They could, he stated, 'in eenighe sententie blijuen' ['stay with one sentence'] or 'tvvee oft dry puncten vvt nemen, die sy verbreyden' ['or take out two or three points, on which they elaborate'] (3048 A 1, part 1, fol. *2r). In order to be able to serve as model sermons for other priests who needed assistance in their own preaching activities, Costerus added 'veel exempelen ende vvaerachtige historien' ['many exempla and truthful stories'] (3048 A 1, part 1, fol. *2r) in the tradition of the holy Church Fathers as well as the medieval custom.[25] At the request of some of the readers who thought that the twenty-four sermons for the

---

22   The pericope sermons, which were one of the three main genres of the Middle Dutch sermon, were first explored in Gerrit Cornelis Zieleman, *Middelnederlandse epistel- en evangeliepreken*, Kerkhistorische bijdragen, 8 (Leiden: Brill, 1978). An example of a pericope sermon in Middle Dutch may be found in Thom Mertens, 'De Middelnederlandse preek: een voorbarige synthese', in *De Middelnederlandse preek*, ed. by Thom Mertens, Patricia Stoop, and Christoph Burger, Middeleeuwse Studies en Bronnen, 116 (Hilversum: Verloren, 2009), pp. 9–66 (pp. 44–53). For an English translation of this article, see Thom Mertens, 'The Middle Dutch Sermon: A Preliminary Synthesis', in Thom Mertens, *Spiritual Literature in the Late Medieval Low Countries*, ed., trans. and intro. by John Arblaster and others (Turnhout: Brepols, forthcoming). For the ten cycles that may be distinguished, and especially for the 'Gouda cycle' (*Alle die epistelen ende ewangelien mitten sermonen*) that was printed by Gerard Leeu in 1477, see the essay by Thom Mertens in this volume.

23   3048 A 1, part 1, fol. **3r.

24   The *Voor-rede* can be found in 3048 A 1, part 1 on fols *3r–***5v. The role and attitude of the preacher, the ways to construct sermons as well as to perform them, is extensively discussed on fols **2v–***2v.

25   In order to make the materials accessible, all the sermon collections are preceded by extensive lists of subjects, of exempla, and of moralizing stories (all in two columns). The

period after Pentecost were too short, Costerus made his sermons of the winter cycle longer, so that they could find materials for many years on each Gospel. Because, he added, 'alle iaer het selue te lesen, brengt een vernoeyen den genen die gheerne iet nieuvvs hebben' ['reading the same every year generates aversion in the ones who like to have something new'] (3048 A 1, part 2, fol. *2r).[26] Thus he created, as Gerrit Vanden Bosch puts it, 'some kind of popular theological and pastoral encyclopedia for the use of preachers'.[27]

We may conclude that Costerus's printed sermons are the result of his individual writing process, which is executed on demand and in support of those people who have no access to true Christian faith, which — in Costerus's view — had been transmitted from hand to hand since the time of the apostles, without interruption. Whether and to what extent they are actually based on the sermons preached for his fellow believers in the last twenty-five years of his life, as is often stated in the scholarly literature, is subject to discussion.[28] It is clear from the extant manuscripts that Costerus was a dedicated preacher. Moreover, Caesar Joachim Trognesius wrote in his prologue to the 1643 posthumous edition of the *Schat der sermoonen op elcken dach des gheheelen Vastens*, 'Terstond met sijne leersen aen ghingh hij op den predickstoel' ['Immediately, with his boots on, he entered the pulpit'].[29] Neither the dedications and the prologue to the *Catholijcke sermoonen op de evangelien van de sondaghen* nor the sermons themselves, however, show any indications that Costerus wrote down what he had preached before or what he was going to preach later on. In this respect we have the same problem as in many sermon incunabula: to figure out what is the relationship between God's Word as preached and God's Word as printed. In his dedication to the oldest cycle for the period between Pentecost and Advent he claims that his sermons are a compilation of old and new materials from the Bible:

> Ick bekenne dat dese Sermoonen vvt mijn hoofdt niet en comen, noch van mijn verstandt gedicht en zijn. Ick hebbe vvt veel Leeraers vergadert, soe oude Vaders, soo nieuvve schrijuers, vvat ick hier voordt-brenghe, op dat

---

'Tafelen der dinghen' ['Tables of items'] of Part 1 takes up twenty-three pages; the table of Part 2 consists of thirty-eight pages; and the table of Part 3 of no fewer than forty-eight pages.

26 The winter cycle, which in this case started with Advent and ended with Pentecost, was split into two parts. In that way, according to Costerus, the second part could be published more quickly, and if the complete sermon cycle were to be reprinted, it could be printed in smaller volumes by turning it into three booklets, which could be carried around more easily, either to church or somewhere else (3048 A 1, part 2, fol. *2v). Whether people actually did carry around Costerus's sermon volumes is questionable, because even when the three parts were bound separately, they remained hefty folio-size books.

27 Vanden Bosch, 'Frans de Coster S. J., *Vierthien catholiicke sermoonen* (1618)', p. 42.

28 Andriessen, 'Costerus (Coster, De Coster, De Custer, De Costere), Franciscus', col. 338; Porteman, 'Na 350 jaar', 213; and Agten, *The Catholic Church and the Dutch Bible*.

29 See Porteman, 'Na 350 jaar', 213.

den Catholijcken Leser, naer Christi vermaeninghe, oude ende nieuvve dinghen vvt den scat der Schrifture ontfanghen (3048 A 1, part 1, fol. *2v).[30]

> [I confess that these sermons do not stem from my head nor are versed by my mind. What I produce here I have collected from many teachers, both old Fathers and new writers, so that the Catholic reader, according to Christ's admonition, may receive old and new things from the treasure of Scripture].

This statement should probably in part be read as a humility trope and a *captatio benevolentiae*, as the extant sermons show a well-thought-out design and contain much more elaborate digressions than is suggested here. They start with the Gospel pericope of the Sunday — in the case of the First Sunday of Advent that is Luke 21. 25–33 — followed by a 'Corte vvtlegghinghe van d'Euangelie' ['Short explanation of the Gospel'] in which the Gospel text is briefly interpreted, and lengthy moralizing 'leeringhen' ['lessons'] that verse by verse discuss the Gospel text (in the typical *divisio*-structure).[31] Each section is interspersed with many citations from the Bible and the Church Fathers, and exempla to make the sermon more colourful and intelligible (which is in line with his admonitions to other preachers in the *Voor-rede*). Each sermon is finally concluded with a prayer. The whole set-up of the project seems to imply that Costerus's (Gospel) sermon collections that made it to the printing press are the product of the writing table, rather than of the pulpit.

Sermons in Manuscript

Whereas the printed sermons most likely were never preached by Costerus, the sermons in Brussel, Koninklijke Bibliotheek, MS 614 that were copied in the Brussels convent of Jericho clearly indicate that they go back to actual preached sermons (see Figure 14).[32] This sizeable manuscript (369 folios; 309 × 204 mm) was written at some point between the end of 1594 — the last sermon that carries a date (Sermon 39) is preached on 5 September of that year, but it is followed by eleven sermons without a date that were probably

---

30 In the dedication to the second part he phrases it slightly differently: 'Ende daerom, vvat ik hier by brenghe, en is niet nieuvv, maer oudt ende ghemeyn: het vvelck nochtans somtijdts met nieuvve redenen ende gelijckenissen verclaert vvordt, ende naer de leeringhe der heyligher Kercke vvt gheleyt' ['And therefore, what I bring forth here is not new, but old and universal. However, it is sometimes explained with new reasonings and parables, and explained according to the doctrine of the Holy Church'] (3048 A 1, part 2, fol. *2v).

31 The 'leeringhen' of the first sermon, for example, comprise over nine pages with two columns of sixty-eight lines. The second sermon is no fewer than twenty and a half pages long.

32 For a description of the manuscript, see Patricia Stoop, *Schrijven in commissie: de zusters uit het Brusselse klooster Jericho en de preken van hun biechtvaders (ca. 1456–1510)*, Middeleeuwse Studies en Bronnen, 127 (Hilversum: Verloren, 2013), pp. 419–20.

preached later that autumn — and 1621, the year of the death of Sister Katharina Moleman, who likely wrote the manuscript.[33] The captions of the sermons refer repeatedly to the occasions and the places where Costerus preached: 'Dit sermoen is ghepredickt int iaer ons heeren M Vᶜ XCIII des woensdaechs na sincxenen in sinter Goelen kerke van den eerweerdighen pater der societeyt Jhesu ghenaemt Costerus' ['This sermon has been preached in the year of our Lord 1593, on Wednesday after Pentecost in the church of Sint-Goedele by the honourable father of the Society of Jesus named Costerus'] (Sermon 1, fol. 1r);[34] and 'Hier na volghen zeer schoon sermonen die ghepredict syn binnen onsen clooster van Jherico int jaer ons heeren M Vᶜ XCII van [...]' ['Hereafter follow the very beautiful sermons which have been preached in our convent in the year of our Lord 1592 by [...]' (the name of the preacher has not been written in; Sermon 4, fol. 25r).[35]

Interestingly, the collection contains sermons that were preached in several locations.[36] Sermons 1–3 (fols 1r–24v) were preached in the collegiate church of Sint-Goedele on the Wednesday, Thursday, and Friday after Pentecost in 1593; Sermon 6 (fols 39r–42r) in the convent of the canonesses regular of Sint-Elisabeth op de berg Sion on the Sunday after Ascension Day 1592; and the rest in the convent of Jericho itself. Sermon 4 (fols 25r–30v) was preached on 11 June 1592, the Feast of St Barnabas, and Sermon 5 (fols 30v–39r) on 15 July (of the same year?), on the Feast of the Dispersion of the Apostles (*Divisio apostolorum*), that is, the Great Commission when the apostles were sent out to preach the gospel to all nations in Matthew 28. 19. The other forty-four sermons (Sermon 7–51, fols 42v–369v) form one cycle on the eight chapters of *Cantica canticorum*, which Costerus considered 'een tractacie es vol troost ende consolatie' ['a treatise filled with comfort and consolation'] (Sermon 7, fol. 42v).[37] In the period between Pentecost Monday 1593 and the

---

33 I am assuming that Katharina Moleman is the scribe of the manuscript, because on fol. 30v she mentions that she copied Sermon 5 from the text a secular woman wrote down (see below, p. 489), and the whole codex is written by one person.

34 The page has a modern folio number 10. As the first nine folios are empty and the rest of the manuscript has not been foliated, I consider this first page with text folio 1 and continue the numbering from there.

35 Occasionally, the date and place of the sermon are given at the end. Sermon 25 (fol. 192v), for example, has the following explicit: 'Ghepredickt op den kermisse dach den 22 mey 1594 pater Costerius' ['Preached at the Day of the Dedication of the Church, 22 May 1594 by Father Costerus'].

36 Usually, this type of (convent) sermons is recorded and kept by the (female) inhabitants of the institution where they were preached. Like Sister Books, these sermon collections, which in the late Middle Ages came into being in the context of the *Devotio moderna*, were a form of *Hausüberlieferung*. See Thom Mertens, 'Ein Prediger in zweifacher Ausführung: die Kollationen des Claus von Euskirchen', in *Predigt im Kontext*, ed. by Volker Mertens and others (Berlin: De Gruyter, 2013), pp. 421–32 (p. 422).

37 To this biblical book he would later devote a whole sermon collection: *Acht sermoonen ter eeren der H. moeder Godts op de acht capitelen van Salomons III. boeck ghenoempt Canticvm canticorvm* (Antwerpen: Verdussen, 1616). He considered the Song of Songs 'het

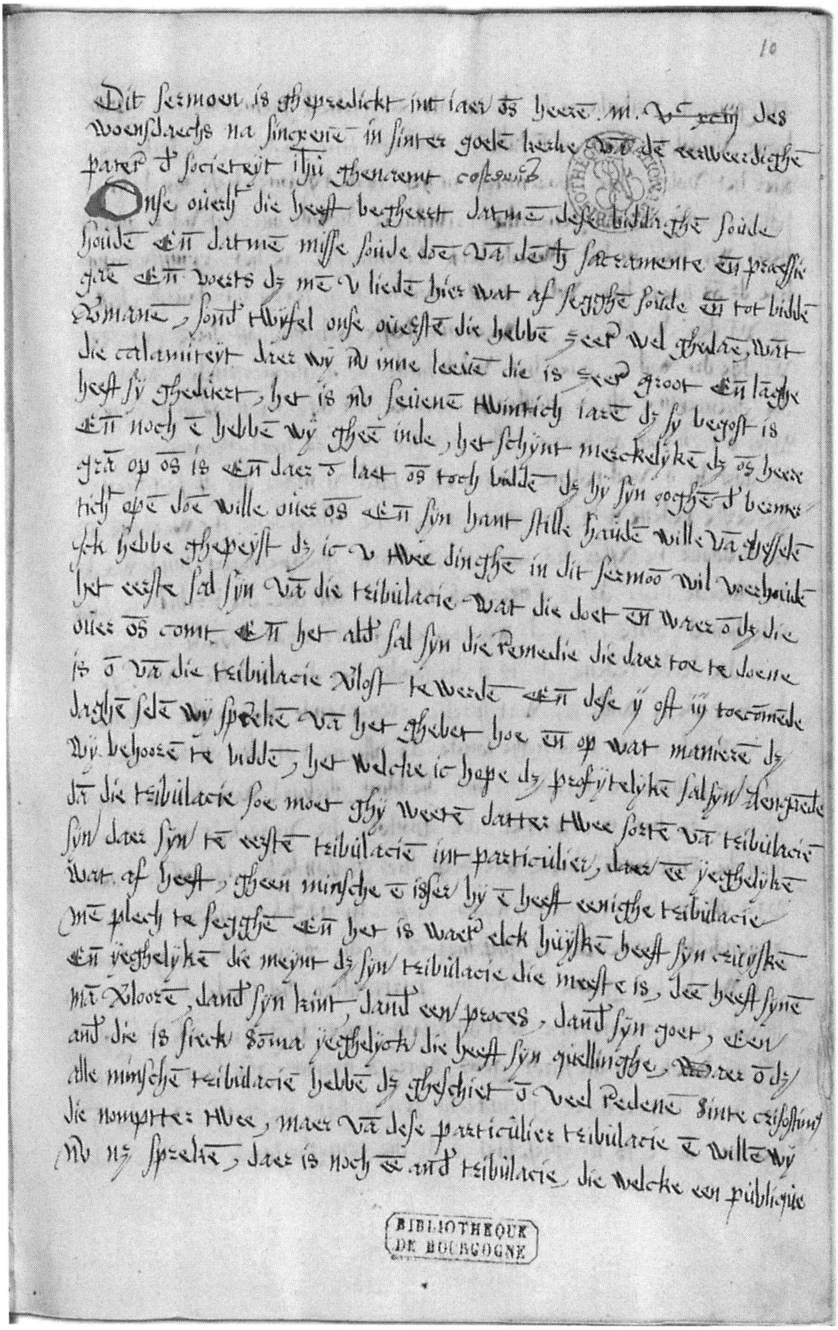

FIGURE 14. Beginning of the sermon preached by Costerus in the church of Sint-Goedele in Brussels on the Wednesday after Pentecost 1593. Brussel, Koninklijke Bibliotheek, MS 614, fol. 10r. Reproduced with permission.

end of July 1593 he delivered ten sermons on the first chapter, and between the end of March (the Feast of the Annunciation of Mary on 25 March?) and the autumn (?) of 1594, he discussed the other seven chapters in thirty-four sermons. In the intermediary period, Costerus went to Rome, as we can read in the heading of Sermon 17 in the collection: 'Seer cort hier naer is hy naer Roome ghereyst ende is weder commen in die vastenen int jaer ons heeren M Vᶜ XCIIII op onser liever vrouwen. Ende deerste weke daer na is hy tot ons commen vervolghende syn materie beginnende het tweede capittel van cantica' ['Shortly after this, he travelled to Rome, and he returned at Lent in the year of our Lord 1594 on the day of Our Lady. And in the first week thereafter he came to us in order to continue his subject, beginning with the second chapter of Cantica'] (fol. 134r).

The fact that four of the sermons in this collection have been preached outside the convent walls of Jericho raises questions about who initially wrote down these sermons. As Jericho is an enclosed convent, the sisters in principle were not allowed to attend Costerus's sermons in another church. However, according to its incipit, Sermon 1 (fols 1r–10v) was related to a Mass and procession of the Holy Sacrament: 'Onse overheit die heeft begheert datmen dese biddaghe soude houden ende datmens misse souden doen van den heiligen sacramente ende processie gaen ende voerts dat men u lieden hier af wat segghen soude ende tot bidden vermanen' ['Our authorities have desired that this day of prayer would be observed, and that Mass of the Holy Sacrament would be celebrated and a procession held, and furthermore that we would tell you something about it and exhort you to prayer'] (Sermon 1, fol. 1r). Would the canonesses of Jericho be allowed — or supposed — to participate in this procession and thus to leave the convent by way of exception?[38]

---

excellenste der ganscher Schrifturen' ['the most excellent part of Scripture'], as he mentions in the prologue to his printed sermon collection on *Cantica canticorum* (Antwerpen, Ruusbroecgenootschap, 3048 A 6, part 3, fol. + 2v). A quick exploration of the manuscript and the early print shows that the sermons are different texts. In the manuscript, the bride from *Cantica* is compared to the human soul, whereas the bride in the early printed book is compared to Mary, the mother of God to whom the book is dedicated. The next interesting question is to what extent the texts differ in structure as well as content, as this may shed more light on the authorship of female religious.

38 According to Gisela Muschiol, 'Women's procession routes were generally restricted to the internal space of the monastery, and very few processions led women beyond their cloister walls and into the surrounding villages'. See Gisela Muschiol, 'Gender and Monastic Liturgy in the Latin West (High and Late Middle Ages)', in *The Cambridge History of Medieval Monasticism in the Latin West*, ed. by Alison I. Beach and Isabelle Cochelin, 2 vols (Cambridge: Cambridge University Press, 2020), II, 803–15 (p. 808). However, the *Barking Ordinale* (Oxford, University College, MS 169) shows that the nuns of Barking Abbey in Essex did leave their abbey on the Rogation days to process publicly to other churches, unless the weather was really bad; see Anne Bagnall Yardley, *Performing Piety: Musical Culture in Medieval Nunneries*, The New Middle Ages (New York: Palgrave Macmillan, 2006), pp. 156–58. Ch. 5, 'Pomp and Piety: Processional Practices in Nunneries' (pp. 113–58) extensively describes the rituals that were related to processions. A comparable small trace

Or had they heard that Costerus had preached in those other Brussels' (convent) churches and did they request reports from these sermons? This was the case with the sermon that was initially written down from Costerus's lips ('uut synen mont') in Jericho by a 'werlyke joffrouwe' ['worldly lady'] — was she allowed access to the (enclosed areas?) of the convent or did the convent church have a screen that allowed the nuns to sit apart from the laity while service was conducted?[39] — and subsequently copied into Brussels, Koninklijke Bibliotheek, MS 614 by Sister Katharina Moleman:

> Dit was ghepredict op die scheedinghe | der apostolen in ons clooster van Jherico van een gheleert man ende priste uut die societyt Jhesu ende van een werlyke joffrouwe uut synen mont ghecomponeert ende ghescreven diet doer myn versueck my heeft gheleent ende hebt uut den haren ghescreven, ic suster Katherina Moleman, hopende een beter (Sermon 5, fols 30v–31r).
>
>> [This has been preached at the Dispersion of the Apostles in our convent of Jericho by a learned man and priest of the *Societas Jesu* and was composed and written by a worldly lady from his lips. She lent it out to me at my request. I, Katharina Moleman, have copied it from hers, hoping for a better life].

Sermon 19 (fols 144r–149r) demonstrates that other sermons — in all probability the majority of them — were redacted within the convent walls of Jericho, albeit not necessarily by Katharina Moleman.[40] According to its rubric, this particular sermon was written from Costerus's lips by Sister Hester Malcoet (d. 18 April 1624), who was canoness in Jericho for thirty-eight years and served nine years as its sub-prioress:[41]

> Dit sermoen is ghepredict den 30 dach meerte int jaer ons heeren 1594 van den eerwerdeghen pater Costerius ende uut synen mont ghescreven van suster Hester Malcoet, religiose in ons closter van Jherico (Sermon 19, fol. 144r).

---

of processions by nuns through town can be found in Mercedes Pérez Vidal, 'The Corpus Christi Devotion: Gender, Liturgy, and Authority among Dominican Nuns in Castile in the Middle Ages', *Historical Reflections / Réflexions Historiques*, 42 (2016), 35–47 (p. 40). In this case the prioress of the Dominican nuns of Toledo led processions outside enclosure. It is also known that a small delegation of canonesses from Jericho left the convent to celebrate the anniversary of Maria van Pee (d. 1511), their former prioress, in her new convent of Vredenberg in Breda in 1500. See Stoop, *Schrijven in commissie*, p. 89. So for very special reasons some of the nuns were allowed to leave enclosure. It seems conceivable that a procession to celebrate the Holy Sacrament was one of those.

39 This is the only indication in the (archival) sources from Jericho that shows that the convent was open to people other than the sisters or their supervising priests.

40 Eleven sermons refer to Jericho explicitly; as the forty-four sermons on *Cantica canticorum* all form part of the same cycle, I assume that all these sermons were preached within that monastery.

41 See Stoop, *Schrijven in commissie*, pp. 24–25 n. 13.

[This sermon was preached on 30 March in the year of our Lord 1594 by the venerable Father Costerus and written from his lips by Sister Hester Malcoet, sister in our convent of Jericho].

Hester, however, most probably was not the sister who copied this sermon into the preserved manuscript, as that is written in one hand. Most likely she — like the worldly lady — produced the exemplar, which subsequently was copied by Sister Katharina into the manuscript that is preserved in the Koninklijke Bibliotheek in Brussels today.

Although it is explicitly stated that the sermons were written from Costerus's lips by several people and in diverse contexts, the texts show little difference in style and execution. All sermons in the codex are fully elaborated texts, with a narrative and lively character and fewer citations from the Bible and other *auctoritates* than the printed sermons have. They have been written from a first-person singular or plural perspective, often in the form of a dialogue and with many references to the context in which the sermons were preached.[42] Thus the impression is created for the recipients

---

42 Sermon 1 discusses how to deal with tribulations. This choice is motivated by 'die calamiteyt daer wij nu inne leeven' ['the calamity in which we live now'] (fol. 1r). At fol. 6v, the second point of the sermon gives advice on how to escape from these tribulations: 'Dat is het tweede poent dat ic u in dit sermoen segghen wille, wat raet datter is om dese tribulacie te ontgane. Dat is dat wy tot onsen here gaen ghelyc sy hier voermaels deden ende roepen: heere, wilt ons toch bermertich sijn. Maer sult ghy segghen: hier syn soe veel heylighe lieden int stadt, die welcke gheduerichlyc bidden; daer syn die heylighe capusienen die soe grooten penitencie doen dat sy eens deels naeckt gaen; daer syn die clarissen die allen daghe vasten ende nemmermeer vlees en eeten, sy eeten stockvis als sy dien hebben ende eenen stinckenden herinck als syen hebben; daer syn die heijlighe minnebruers die welcke aerm syn ende en hebben gheen renten, sy gaen bedelen achter straten ende nochtans soe syn daer veel eel mans kinderen inne ghegaen. Ende dese lieden, selt ghy segghen, die en doen niet dan bidden voer het volck ende hulpt dat niet? Jaet, het helpt veele, want soe Sint-Jacob seet, het ghebedt van eenen rechtverdighen minsche, dat is zeer crachtich' ['That is the second point that I want to explain in this sermon: what advice there is to escape from this tribulation. That is that we go to our Lord like they did before and pray: Lord, have mercy upon us. You will say, however: there are so many holy people in town, who pray continuously; there are the holy Capuchins who perform such great penance that they walk around partly naked; there are the Clarisses that fast every day and never eat meat. They eat hake if they have it and a smelly herring if they have it; there are the holy Friars Minor who are poor and do not have income. They beg on the streets and still many noblemen's children join them. And, you will say, those people do nothing other than pray for the folk and does that not help? Yes, it helps greatly, because as St James says, the prayer of a righteous person is very powerful']. Interestingly, Sermons 1–3 contain far more references to events in the secular world, and specifically events and groups of people in Brussels, than the other sermons in the volume that focus on the duties and virtues of monastic women. Perhaps the sermons reflect the fact that Costerus preached these sermons in a collegiate church, on the occasion of a procession, and therefore for a larger audience. On fol. 13v it is suggested that the audience consisted of women: the audience is addressed as 'myn dochter' ['my daughter']. However, this address may be the result of the redactional process that is apparent in this manuscript (see below).

that when they heard the written texts read to them, for example, during the refectory readings, or when they were reading the written sermons, that they were listening to Costerus himself.[43] Although this does not mean that the preserved sermons are a literal representation of what Costerus preached in the churches and convents in Brussels, the way in which the written sermons are phrased creates a sense of authenticity that would encourage belief.[44] The fact that the sermons in the manuscript show smaller differences in style than one would expect if they were direct copies of what different women in different places had written down, seems to imply that the redactional process of the book was controlled by one single person. This person — Sister Katharina Moleman? — made editorial adaptations and thus continued the medieval tradition of sermon writing within Jericho which showed a complex, collective effort to produce sermon collections that would support the spiritual life of the members of the community.

Conclusion

The early printed volumes with Costerus's Gospel sermons and the manuscript from the Brussels convent of Jericho show some interesting contrasts when it comes to authorship, readership, and strategies of publishing. The first one relates to the relationship between the oral act of preaching and the manual act of transcription. In the case of the printed sermon collections there are no indications that the sermons have any relationship to the act of preaching at all. In my view, these sermons are the result of hard labour at a writing table, the product of the individual writing process of Franciscus Costerus

---

43 For the use of sermon collections as refectory reading, see Mertens, 'De Middelnederlandse preek', p. 17 and Stoop, *Schrijven in commissie*, pp. 325–26.

44 Since Gerrit Zieleman published his pioneering research on Middle Dutch sermons, the liturgical act of preaching (*predicatie*) and the written sermon (*preek*) as a literary genre, which could be based on an actual spoken sermon, are considered two separate genres in Middle Dutch sermon studies, which is not necessarily a one-to-one relationship; see Zieleman, *Middelnederlandse epistel- en evangeliepreken*, p. 9. See also Mertens, 'De Middelnederlandse preek', pp. 10 and 63. In 'The Middle Dutch Sermon' Mertens explains the relevance of the predication fiction as follows: 'De versterking van de predicatiefictie heeft vermoedelijk tot doel de teksten levendiger te maken, zodat het publiek de inhoud zich gemakkelijker eigen kon maken. Ook straalde het gezag van de predicatiesituatie af op de geschreven preek' ['The augmentation of this predication fiction was presumably intended to make the texts livelier so that the audience would be able to master the content more easily. The written sermon would thus also be imbued with the authority of the predication context'] (p. 17). The relationship between the oral sermon as a (para)liturgical act and the written sermon, and the presence or absence of predicatory features is extensively discussed in Thom Mertens, 'Relic or Strategy: The Middle Dutch Sermon as a Literary Phenomenon', in *Speculum Sermonis: Interdisciplinary Reflections on the Medieval Sermon*, ed. by Georgiana Donavin, Gary J. Nederman, and Richard Utz, Disputatio, 1 (Turnhout: Brepols, 2004), pp. 293–314 (pp. 293–94).

himself. As a result, the preaching fiction that is so present in the handwritten sermons is absent in the printed volumes. Is this because Costerus wanted his printed collections to be able to serve a broad range of purposes? After all, he considered his work a treasure trove that should make the true faith available to a Catholic audience. Additionally, he had a multiple use for his sermons in mind: not only should they be read, listened to, or meditated upon, they also should be used for expounding in schools and as a preaching aid. Texts that have less prominent preaching features could perhaps more easily meet these multiple goals.

The sermons in the manuscript from Jericho, on the other hand, contain many references to sermons preached in three religious institutions in Brussels over a short period of about two and a half years. In this case, the authorship is shared by several persons. Although it is impossible to know to what extent the preserved sermons represent what Costerus preached in the collegiate church of Sint-Goedele or in the convent churches of Sint-Elisabeth op de berg Sion and Jericho, we must consider Costerus the *auctor intellectualis* of the spoken sermons. Subsequently, the sermons were redacted by several women. The sermons tell us that this authorial role was executed by Sister Hester Malcoet and the anonymous worldly lady, but possibly also a canoness from Sint-Elisabeth op de berg Sion, an anonymous member in the audience in Sint-Goedele, and Katharina Moleman or other sisters in Jericho acted as redactors. Afterwards, all these first versions were collected and most likely substantially edited as to make the manuscript volume a coherent collection. At a final stage the texts were copied into Brussels, Koninklijke Bibliotheek, MS 614, most likely by Katharina Moleman. Thus, the manuscript shows, like the medieval sermon manuscripts from Jericho, a collective, layered authorship that involved a dynamic merging of the work of a priest and several women.[45]

Another contrast is that the sermons in the manuscript were written down on the initiative of the women who wanted to use Costerus's texts in support of their own religious life and that of their community members, whereas the initiative for the printed sermons initially was taken by Costerus's superiors, in support of the Catholic believers, especially those who were oppressed by the Calvinists and the Lutherans in the Dutch Republic in the troubled period of the late sixteenth and early seventeenth centuries. Thus, his sermons served as an important tool in the missionary offensive, for which the Jesuits are renowned.

Furthermore, the ways of publishing had an impact on the dissemination of the sermons. The sermons in the manuscript — and this will apply to the

---

45 On the authorial roles in the process of sermon writing in the medieval collections from Jericho, see Stoop, *Schrijven in commissie*, ch. 4 and 5 and Patricia Stoop, 'Female Authorship in the Augustinian Convent of Jericho and the Translation of Conrad of Saxony's *Speculum beatae Mariae virginis* in Sermons by Maria van Pee and Janne Colijns', *Journal of Medieval Religious Cultures*, 42 (2016), 248–68 (especially pp. 248–49).

Vienna manuscript as well — had a very limited audience. They circulated among (groups of) women — both religious and lay — in the Brussels region, and after they found their way into the fair copy, they stayed within the convent walls of Jericho. There they were used in support of the spiritual life of female religious, even though the first three sermons in the collection have clear signs that Costerus had preached for a broader audience. The printed sermons, on the other hand, were disseminated widely. Except for the Sermons for Lent, which were printed posthumously by Caesar Joachim Trognesius in 1643, all collections are preserved in several copies.

Interestingly, the varied modes of transmission reflect the multiple audiences and multiple purposes of Costerus's preaching. On the one hand, the printed sermons display his awareness of his missionary task as well as the role of the clerical hierarchy in printed book production (in the form of the encouragement by Costerus's superiors and the support of the archbishop Matthias Hovius). The books were aimed at a broad audience of men and women, lay and religious alike. The Brussels manuscript, on the other hand, demonstrates how women's agency and literary strategies played a role in the publishing and preservation of a preacher's religious ideas, even if the sermons were available to a more limited audience. Thus, the case of Franciscus Costerus demonstrates how sermon production and transmission were balanced on a fascinating divide between a public and a private enterprise.

The *Catholijcke sermoonen op de evangelien van de sondaghen* and the *Catholiicke sermoonen op d'epistelen van de sondaghen* especially were published a number of times, and therefore can be considered real bestsellers. Costerus's sermons show that early modern sermons in the Dutch vernacular, both in manuscript and print, built on a long existing, medieval tradition. Moreover, they show that sermons published in both media could easily exist and function well next to one another, even a century and a half after the development of the printing press.

Bibliography

Manuscripts

Brussel, Koninklijke Bibliotheek, MS 614
Oxford, University College, MS 169
Wien, Österreichische Nationalbibliothek, MS 13696

Early Printed Works by Franciscus Costerus

Acht sermoonen ter eeren der H. moeder Godts op de acht capitelen van Salomons III. boeck
  ghenoempt Canticvm canticorvm (Antwerpen: Hieronymus Verdussen, 1616)
Het boecksken der broederschap, dat is vijf boecken der christelijcker leeringhen, voor
  de broederschap der H. maghet Maria (Antwerpen: ex officina Plantiniana and
  Jan I Moretus, 1596)
Catholiicke sermoonen op alle de heylichdaghen des jaers (Antwerpen: Joachim
  Trognesius, 1616)
Catholiicke sermoonen op d'epistelen van den sondaghen na Sinxen tot den Advent
  (Antwerpen: Joachim Trognesius, 1606?)
Catholiicke sermoonen op d'epistelen van de sondaghen van den Advent tot den Vasten
  (Antwerpen: Joachim Trognesius, 1606?)
Catholiicke sermoonen op de epistelen ende evangelien van de sondagen naer Sinxen tot
  den Aduent (Antwerpen: Joachim Trognesius, 1618)
Catholiicke sermoonen op de evangelien van de sondaghen naer Sinxen tot den Advent
  (Antwerpen: Joachim Trognesius, 1598)
Catholiicke sermoonen op de octave van't H. Sacrament des avtaers (Antwerpen:
  Hieronymus Verdussen, 1616)
De cantico salve regina septem meditationes (Antwerpen: Christoffel Plantin, 1587)
De vita et lavdibvs deiparae Mariae virginis, meditationes qvinqvaginta (Antwerpen:
  Christoffel Plantin, 1587)
Enchiridion controversiarum praecipuarum nostri temporis de religione (Köln: Arnold
  Mylius, in officina Birckmannica, 1585)
Libellus sodalitatis, hoc est Christianarum institutionum libri quinque (Antwerpen: ex
  officina Plantiniana, 1586)
Le livre de la confrerie, c'est à dire les cinq livres des institutions chrestiennes
  (Antwerpen: ex officina Plantiniana and Jan I Moretus, 1590)
Nieu Testament onses Heeren Iesu Christi met korte uytlegghingen (Antwerpen:
  Joachim Trognesius, 1614)
Schat der sermoonen op elcken dach des gheheelen Vastens (Antwerpen: Caesar
  Joachim Trognesius, 1643)
Schildt der catholijcken, teghen de ketterijen, inhoudende de principaelste gheschillen die
  in onsen tijden opgeresen zijn in t'gelooue (Antwerpen: ex officina Plantiniana,
  Jeanne Rivière and Jan I Moretus, 1591)
Sermoonen op alle de epistelen van de sondaghen van der gheheelen jaer (Antwerpen:
  Hieronymus Verdussen, 1616)

Seven meditatien op den lof-sanck Salve Regina (Antwerpen: ex officina Plantiniana, Jeanne Rivière, 1590)

Vierthien catholiicke sermoonen op de epistelen ende evangelien der sondaghen van den Advent tot den Vasten (Antwerpen: Joachim Trognesius, 1618)

Vierthien catholiicke sermoonen op de evangelien der sondaghen van den Advent tot den Vasten (Antwerpen: Joachim Trognesius, 1601)

Viifthien catholiicke sermoonen op de evangelien der sondaghen van den Vasten tot de H. Driivvldicheyt (Antwerpen: Joachim Trognesius, 1604)

Viiftien catholiicke sermoonen op d'epistelen ende evangelien der sondaghen van het beghinsel des Vastens tot de heylighe Driivvldicheydt (Antwerpen: Joachim Trognesius, 1617; reprinted in 1618)

Vijftich meditatien van het leuen ende lof der Moeder Godts ende Maeghet Maria (Antwerpen: ex officina Plantiniana, Jeanne Rivière, 1590)

Secondary Studies

Agten, Els, *The Catholic Church and the Dutch Bible: From the Council of Trent to the Jansenist Controversy (1564–1733)*, Brill's Series in Church History, 80 (Leiden: Brill, 2020)

Agten, Els, 'Costerus en Van den Leemputte: twee katholieke bijbelvertalingen uit de eerste helft van de zeventiende eeuw', in *De Bijbel in de Lage Landen: elf eeuwen van vertalen*, ed. by Paul Gillaerts and others (Heerenveen: Royal Jongbloed, 2015), pp. 395–405

Andriessen, J., 'Costerus (Coster, De Coster, De Custer, De Costere), Franciscus', in *Nationaal Biografisch Woordenboek*, 23 vols (Brussel: Paleis der Academiën, 1964–), I (1964), cols 333–41

Andriessen, J., 'Uit de voorgeschiedenis van Franciscus Costerus's "Libellus sodalitatis", *Ons Geestelijk Erf*, 35 (1961), 422–26

Imhof, Dirk, *Jan Moretus and the Continuation of the Plantin Press: A Bibliography of the Works Published and Printed by Jan Moretus I in Antwerp (1589–1610)*, Bibliotheca Bibliographica Neerlandica, Series major, III (Leiden: Brill, 2014)

Jageneau, J., 'De jonge Franciscus Costerus S. J.: Student aan de Leuvensche Alma Mater (1548–1552)', *Ons Geestelijk Erf*, 9 (1935), 198–204 and 302–11

Jagenau, J., 'Twee catechismusuitgaven van P. Fr. Costerus S. J. in 1566 en 1568', *Ons Geestelijk Erf*, 8 (1934), 341–46

Kuckhoff, Josef, *Die Geschichte des Gymnasium Tricoronatum: ein Querschnitt durch die Geschichte der Jugenderziehung in Köln vom 15. bis zum 18. Jahrhundert* (Köln: Bachem, 1931)

Mertens, Thom, 'De Middelnederlandse preek: een voorbarige synthese', in *De Middelnederlandse preek*, ed. by Thom Mertens, Patricia Stoop, and Christoph Burger, Middeleeuwse Studies en Bronnen, 116 (Hilversum: Verloren, 2009), pp. 9–66

Mertens, Thom, 'The Middle Dutch Sermon: A Preliminary Synthesis', in Thom Mertens, *Spiritual Literature in the Late Medieval Low Countries*, ed., trans. and intro. by John Arblaster and others (Turnhout: Brepols, forthcoming)

Mertens, Thom, 'Ein Prediger in zweifacher Ausführung: die Kollationen des Claus von Euskirchen', in *Predigt im Kontext*, ed. by Volker Mertens and others (Berlin: De Gruyter, 2013), pp. 421–32

Mertens, Thom, 'Relic or Strategy: The Middle Dutch Sermon as a Literary Phenomenon', in *Speculum Sermonis: Interdisciplinary Reflections on the Medieval Sermon*, ed. by Georgiana Donavin, Gary J. Nederman, and Richard Utz, Disputatio, 1 (Turnhout: Brepols, 2004), pp. 293–314

Muschiol, Gisela, 'Gender and Monastic Liturgy in the Latin West (High and Late Middle Ages)', in *The Cambridge History of Medieval Monasticism in the Latin West*, ed. by Alison I. Beach and Isabelle Cochelin, 2 vols (Cambridge: Cambridge University Press, 2020), II, 803–15

Pérez Vidal, Mercedes, 'The Corpus Christi Devotion: Gender, Liturgy, and Authority among Dominican Nuns in Castile in the Middle Ages', *Historical Reflections / Réflexions Historiques*, 42 (2016), 35–47

Persoons, Ernest, 'Handschriften uit kloosters in de Nederlanden in Wenen', *Archief- en Bibliotheekwezen in België*, 38 (1967), 59–107

Pettegree, Andrew, and Malcolm Walsby, *Netherlandish Books: Books Published in the Low Countries and Dutch Books Printed Abroad before 1601*, 2 vols (Leiden: Brill, 2011)

Pollmann, Judith, *Catholic Identity and the Revolt of the Netherlands 1520–1635*, The Past & Present Book Series (Oxford: Oxford University Press, 2011)

Porteman, K., 'Na 350 jaar: de "sermoonen" van Franciscus Costerus', *Ons Geestelijk Erf*, 43 (1969), 209–69

Rouzet, Anne, 'Trognesius, Joachim', in *Dictionnaire des imprimeurs, libraires et éditeurs des xve et xvie siècles dans les limites géographiques de la Belge actuelle* (Nieuwkoop: De Graaf, 1975), pp. 224–25

Sommervogel, Carlos, and others, 'Coster, François', *Bibliothèque de la compagnie de Jesus*, 12 vols (Brussel: Schepens, 1890–1932), II (1891), cols 1510–34

Stoop, Patricia, 'Female Authorship in the Augustinian Convent of Jericho and the Translation of Conrad of Saxony's *Speculum beatae Mariae virginis* in Sermons by Maria van Pee and Janne Colijns', *Journal of Medieval Religious Cultures*, 42 (2016), 248–68

Stoop, Patricia, *Schrijven in commissie: de zusters uit het Brusselse klooster Jericho en de preken van hun biechtvaders (ca. 1456–1510)*, Middeleeuwse Studies en Bronnen, 127 (Hilversum: Verloren, 2013)

Van der Haeghen, Ferdinand, and others, *Bibliotheca Belgica: bibliographie générale des Pays-Bas*, 6 vols (Brussel: Editions culture et civilisation, 1964–1970; repr. 1979)

Van Rossem, Stijn, 'Het gevecht met de boeken: de uitgeversstrategieën van de familie Verdussen' (unpublished doctoral dissertation, Universiteit Antwerpen, 2014)

Vanden Bosch, Gerrit, 'Frans de Coster S. J., *Vierthien catholiicke sermoonen* (1618)', in *Jesuit Books in the Low Countries 1540–1773: A Selection from the Maurits Sabbe Library*, ed. by Paul Begheyn, Bernard Deprez, Rob Faesen, and others (Leuven: Peeters, 2009), pp. 40–43

Yardley, Anne Bagnall, *Performing Piety: Musical Culture in Medieval Nunneries*, The New Middle Ages (New York: Palgrave Macmillan, 2006)

Zieleman, Gerrit Cornelis, *Middelnederlandse epistel- en evangeliepreken*, Kerkhistorische bijdragen, 8 (Leiden: Brill, 1978)

Indices

In the essays above complete contextual information is given in the main volume, notes, bibliographies, and/or appendices for the texts in manuscript and early print discussed by each contributor. Full bibliographical detail for all archival, manuscript, and early printed works is recorded in the individual bibliographies. The inclusion of this extensive material here is therefore unwarranted as such duplication would merely result in inflated indices. The indices below, People; Places; and Religious Institutions, Movements, and Orders, exclude the detailed appendices, biblical citations, bibliographical material, and quotations; they concentrate on matter that cannot otherwise be easily located in the volume.

Index of People

The People index includes the names of biblical, classical, hagiographical, medieval, and early modern people (plus a few people up to the nineteenth century) that occur in the body of the volume and are discussed in the notes. Biblical figures are exclusive of Christ and the Virgin Mary and the names of printers are only listed if they are found in the course of the discussion rather than as bibliographical entries. People are listed under their first names, with both the native and/or Latin forms given as relevant, for instance, 'Jacobus de Voragine/Jacopo da Varazze' or 'Christiern Pedersen'. Saints, popes, and royal personages are distinguished. Where no second name occurs, an indentifier is added, such as 'Archangela, nun', apart from those people that are well known such as 'Virgil'.

Abraham Andreae Angermannus: 161 n. 1
Adam de Düren: 325
Adolf von Nassau: 325
Adso de Montier-en-Der: 227 n. 16
Aesop: 140
Agostino Superbi: 283 n. 17–18
Alan de Lille: 265, 325
Alberto Pio da Carpi: 284 n. 22
Alberto Savonarola: 283, 283 n. 16
Albertus de Padua: 196
Albertus Magnus: 148, 207
Aldobrandinus de Toscanella: 318
Alexander of Hales: 60

Ambrose, saint: 125, 420 n. 28
Andreas Stoß: 327–28
Angela Sforza: 289
Anna, daughter of Christiern Pedersen: 139
Anna Schott: 373
Anne, saint: 243
Anthonius, cleric from Mediaş: 196
Antonio Azaro Parmense: 117, 117 n. 31, 322
Antonio da Bitonto: 289 n. 47
Antonio Libanori: 283 nn. 17–18
Antonio Possevino: 126
Antonio Pucci: 287 n. 40

498 INDICES

Antony van Hemert: 457
Arcangela, nun: 285
Arnau de Vilanova: 227
Arnaud Royard: 257–58
Árni Magnússon: 135 n. 4
Arnold Birckmann: 477
Arnold de Liège: 313–14, 314 n. 8
Arnold Mylius: 476–77
Arnold von Rotberg: 342
Arthur Tudor, son of Henry VII,
    king of England: 76
Augustine of Hippo, saint: 51,
    51 n. 7, 51 n. 9, 54, 125, 148,
    292 n. 57, 420, 420 n. 28
Aurelia Nasella: 285

Barent Adriaensz: 468, 468 n. 45
Bartholomeus Gallus: 92
Bartholomeus Ghotan: 119 n. 40
Bartholomeus Grüninger: 394
Battista Guarini: 282, 283 n. 18
Battista Mantovano: 284
Beatrice d'Este: 35, 41, 285, 289
Beatrice II d'Este, saint: 289
Beatus Rhenanus: 284, 284 n. 24,
    368–69, 379 n. 48
Benedict XIII, pope: 223, 226 n. 14,
    236, 239–40, 245
Bernard André: 88 n. 40
Bernard de Clairvaux, saint:
    55, 55 n. 20, 148, 202, 318, 321,
    420 n. 28
Bernardino da Busti: 30, 52, 54,
    57–61
Bernardino da Feltre: 294
Bernardino Ochino: 293 n. 62
Bernardino Vitali: 280
Bernardinus de Senis *alias*
    Bernardino da Siena: 28, 204,
    207, 291 n. 53, 294 n. 66
Berthold von Regensburg: 322
Bertrand de la Tour: 314 n. 7, 318

Birgitta of Sweden, saint: 110,
    121 n. 43
Bonaventura, saint: 58, 135 n. 6,
    201 n. 56
Bruno Amerbach: 269
Burchard, anonymous: 321

Caesar Joachim Trognesius: 480,
    484, 493
Caesarius von Heisterbach:
    430 n. 17
Callixtus III, pope: 223, 245
Carlo Borromeo, saint: 300, 302–03
Caterina, a nun in San Michele sul
    Dosso: 286 n. 31
Caterina da Siena: 292, 302
Charles V, emperor: 428
Chiara, a nun in San Michele sul
    Dosso: 286 n. 31
Christian II, king of Denmark:
    138–40, 451
Christian III, king of Denmark:
    133, 156
Christiern Pedersen: 29, 32, 40,
    133–57 *passim*, 168
Christina Horn: 116
Christina Vasa, queen of Sweden:
    116 n. 28
Christoffel Plantin: 476, 476 n. 6
Christopher, saint: 134 n. 2, 138
Clemens Petri: 111, 111 n. 15, 127
Clement VII, pope: 80
Colette de Corbie, saint: 243
Conrad Grütsch: 326
Conradus de Brundelsheim:
    206 n. 77, 207, 322, 325
Cuthbert, saint: 61

Daniel Specklin: 394, 395 n. 113
Daniel Sudermann: 359, 359 n. 61,
    396–97
Dante Alighieri: 291 n. 55

David Wolder: 394
Denis the Carthusian: 61
Desiderius Erasmus: 88 n. 38, 93
Dionysius the Areopagite: 452
Domenico Rococciola: 41, 279,
 284, 286, 289
Domenico Sala: 299–300, 300 n. 85
Dominic, saint: 236–38
Durand de Huesca: 265

Eckhart, Meister: 329, 448 n. 9,
 452, 455
Edward VI, king of England: 80
Eiler Hagerup: 143
Eleonora d'Aragona, duchess:
 284 n. 26
Elisha, biblical figure: 65
Elizabeth of York, consort of
 Henry VII, king of England: 89
Else Jacobsdatter: 139
Emmanuel Philippe Trognesius:
 476 n. 7
Ercole d'Este, duke of Ferrara: 289
Ercole d'Este, lord of San Martino
 in Rio: 289, 299 n. 80
Ericus Erici Sorolainen: 124
Erik, saint: 111 n. 10
Eugenius IV, pope: 289 n. 46

Felix, member of the parish clergy
 in Jelna [?]: 194
Fernando Álvarez de Toledo y
 Pimentel: 474
Filippo Beroaldo: 284
Francesca, a nun in San Michele
 sul Dosso: 286 n. 31
Francesco Caloro: 283 n. 16
Francesco d'Assisi *alias* Francis,
 saint: 60, 236–38, 287 n. 38
Francesco d'Asti: 118
Franciscus Costerus *alias* Frans de
 Coster: 30, 39, 41, 473–93 *passim*

Franciscus de Senis: 318
François Bonivard: 375 n. 33, 377
Frederik Knudsen: 153 n. 43
Frederik I, king of Denmark: 139
Friedrich der Karmelit: 328
Friedrich von Amberg: 255

Gabriele Guastavillani: 287 n. 38
Gangolf Steinmetz: 369, 379
Geert Grote: 412 n. 6, 452
Georg Norman: 127
Georg von Andlau: 343 Figure 4
George, saint: 29, 196–97 n. 37,
 209, 287 n. 38
Georgius, priest in Daia: 205
Georgius, priest in Ulieş: 205
Georgius Skodberg: 450–51
Gerrit van der Goude: 423
Gheraert Leeu: 413 n. 10, 414, 422,
 424
Gilles van Erven: 463
Gioacchino da Fiore: 227
Giovan Francesco Pico della
 Mirandola: 282, 282 n. 14, 284
 nn. 22–23, 289, 292, 292 n. 59, 299
Giovanni Angelo Scinzenzeler:
 279–80
Giovanni Pico della Mirandola: 282
Girolama, abbess in San Michele
 sul Dosso: 286 n. 31
Girolamo Savonarola: 28, 73,
 280 n. 3, 282–83, 283 n. 16,
 292, 299
Giulia, a nun in San Michele sul
 Dosso: 286 n. 31
Goswinus Hex: 328 n. 74
Gregory I (the Great), pope:
 121 n. 43, 125, 135 n. 6, 204 n. 66,
 292 n. 57, 412, 414, 420, 420 n. 28
Gregory XIII, pope: 126
Guarino da Verona: 282
Guibert de Tournai: 52, 52 n. 11, 54

500 INDICES

Guidantonio da Montefeltro,
  count of Urbino: 289 n. 47
Guido Bartoluccius: 259
Guido Terreni: 317, 319
Guidobaldo da Montefeltro, duke
  of Urbino: 284 n. 22
Guillermus, anonymous: 55 n. 21, 56
Guillermus Parisiensis: 142,
  168 n. 28, 205, 205 nn. 72–73, 207
Gustav I Vasa, king of Sweden: 120,
  123, 127, 142, 165, 165 n. 18

Hane der Karmelit: 328
Hans Baldung Grien: 375 n. 33, 391
Hans Brask: 143, 162 n. 3
Hans Burgkmair the Elder: 366
  Figure 5, 391
Hans Folz: 369 n. 10
Hans Holbein the Younger: 89
Hans Mikkelsen: 143
Hans Otmar: 380, 380 n. 52, 387, 391
Hans Pauli Montanus: 125,
  125–26 n. 56
Hans Schäuffelin: 391
Hans Tausen: 175
Hans von Flachslanden: 343
  Figure 4
Haymon d'Auxerre: 227 n. 16
Heinrich Graefenberger: 320
Heinrich II, saint: 344, 344 n. 18
Heinrich Quentell: 138 n. 17
Heinrich Seuse: 135 n. 6, 452
Heinrich von Köln: 341
Heinrich Wesszmer: 386 n. 76
Hendrik van Arnhem: 423 n. 44
Henricus de Langenstein: 196
Henricus Lelle alias Henricus
  Lolle: 113–14
Henrik Gabriel Porthan: 108,
  121 n. 43
Henrik Smith: 138 nn. 17–19,
  138 n. 21

Henry, saint: 111, 111 n. 10, 112
Henry IV, king of England:
  329 n. 78
Henry V, king of England: 83,
  329 n. 78
Henry VII, king of England:
  76–77, 88–89
Henry VIII, king of England: 23,
  76–77, 80, 94
Hester Malcoet: 489–90, 492
Hieronymus Verdussen: 480,
  480 n. 15
Honorius III, pope: 60
Horace: 178
Hugues de Saint-Cher: 30, 62–63,
  65, 313

Iacopo Passavanti: 291 n. 54
Ignacio de Loyola, saint: 39, 474
Innocent IV, pope: 315
Innocent VIII, pope: 244
Isaac, rabbi: 227 n. 17

Jacob van Breda: 424
Jacobus de Clusa: 208
Jacobus de Voragine alias Jacopo
  da Varazze: 18, 21 n. 12, 52, 116,
  118–19, 122, 194, 196, 313, 318, 322,
  413
Jacques de Lausanne: 118
Jacques Lefevre d'Etaples: 62
Jakob Biethen: 381, 383, 393,
  393 n. 106
Jakob Milendunck: 319, 319 n. 30
Jakob Otter: 37, 371, 377–94 passim
Jakob Wimpfeling: 49, 284, 342,
  342 n. 13, 368–69, 371–74 passim,
  379, 384, 390, 392
James IV, king of Scotland: 89
James Ravynell: 75
James the Elder, saint/apostle: 243
James the Younger, saint/apostle: 243

Jan van Ruusbroec: 448 n. 9, 452, 456

Jaspar von Gennep: 446, 448, 448 n. 7

Jean Barbier: 138

Jean Calvin: 24

Jean d'Abbeville: 318

Jean de Roquetaillade: 227

Jean Gerson: 37, 202, 204, 241, 369, 374, 380, 387

Jean Gobi: 325

Jeanne Rivière: 476 n. 6

Jerome, saint: 199 n. 43, 227 n. 16, 292 n. 57, 420 n. 28

Joachim Trognesius: 476 n. 6, 477, 477 n. 9, 479, 479 n. 12, 480, 484

Joan Navarro: 228

Jodocus Badius Ascensius *alias* Josse Bade: 138

Johan III Vasa, king of Sweden: 125–26, 180 n. 67

Johan Veldener: 415, 415 n. 14, 416, 416 n. 20, 425

Johann Agricola: 140

Johann Caspar Bencard: 395

Johann Eck, Lutheran theologian: 381 n. 56, 392 n. 104

Johann Fischart: 396 n. 119

Johann Knoblouch: 380, 391, 391 n. 98

Johann Prüss: 374

Johann Scheible: 395

Johann Spangenberg: 176 n. 50

Johann Ulrich Surgant: 56, 56 n. 26, 269

Johann von Venningen: 343 Figure 4

Johann Wild: 55

Johannes, parish priest in Brateiu: 204

Johannes Adolphus Muling: 377, 381, 381 n. 55, 383, 386, 392–93, 393 n. 106

Johannes Borquardi: 111

Johannes Busch: 421, 421 n. 35

Johannes Contractus: 322

Johannes de Budingen: 325–26

Johannes de Turrecremata: 35, 208, 266–69 *passim*

Johannes de Werdena: 326

Johannes Eck, Catholic theologian: 205, 207, 381 n. 56

Johannes Geiler von Kaysersberg: 28–30, 37–38, 40–41, 284, 341, 346, 346 n. 29, 349, 349 n. 35, 350, 356, 365–98 *passim*

Johannes Gritsch: 207, 323

Johannes Grossi: 322–23

Johannes Grüninger: 380 n. 53, 381 n. 56, 383, 385–86, 391 n. 98, 392, 392 n. 104, 393–94

Johannes Herolt: 18, 52–53, 53 n. 17, 55 n. 21, 73, 126 n. 56, 142, 207, 325–26

Johannes Hoochstraten: 139, 139 n. 27

Johannes Kreutzer: 29, 37, 40, 339–56 *passim*

Johannes Magnus: 142

Johannes Melber: 326

Johannes Meyer: 339–40, 344 n. 23, 345 n. 25, 346

Johannes Nider: 207, 326, 349

Johannes Pauli: 377, 379, 383–86 *passim*, 392–93, 393 n. 106, 398

Johannes Petri: 113

Johannes Schobser: 370

Johannes Schönsperger: 370

Johannes Schott: 373 n. 24, 386

Johannes Scutken: 412 n. 6, 421, 421 n. 35

Johannes Siberch: 81

Johannes Tauler: 30, 38–39, 445–68 *passim*

Johannes Vogele: 328

Johannes Zeckel: 29, 196, 209, 211

John Alcock: 31, 76–94 *passim*

John Baconthorpe: 317
John Bale: 73 n. 13
John Chrysostom: 25, 51, 54, 148, 420 n. 28
John Colet: 77, 79, 88 n. 38, 89, 90 n. 44, 91, 93, 93 n. 61
John Fisher: 40, 76–94 *passim*
John Folsham: 328 n. 74
John Foxe: 75, 84
John Gau: 139 n. 27
John Gipkyn: 81
John Longland: 76–77, 89, 89 n. 44, 93, 93 n. 57
John Lydgate: 87
John Mirk: 73 n. 12, 74, 74 n. 14, 77–92 *passim*
John Morton: 89, 93
John of Salisbury: 51
John of the Cross, saint: 330
John Pecham: 115
John Soreth: 320
John Stow: 82, 84
John Tuting: 60 n. 45
John Wyclif: 83
John Young: 92
John XXIII, pope: 289 n. 46
Jón Árason: 133 n. 1
Jöns Budde: 110 n. 8
Jordanus von Quedlinburg: 324–25
Jörg Preining: 377, 377 n. 38, 378, 387
Josedech, biblical figure: 85
Joseph of Arimathea: 30, 62–63
Joshua *alias* Nave, biblical figure: 85
Juan Unay: 227
Judas Tadeus, saint/apostle: 243
Julian Notary: 73, 75

Karl of Södermanland, duke *alias* Karl IX, king of Sweden: 125
Katharina Ingoldt: 347
Katharina Moleman: 486, 486 n. 33, 489–92

Katherine of Alexandria, saint: 268
Katherine of Aragon, consort of Henry VIII, king of England: 77, 80
Konrad Bitz: 119
Kristen Sørensen Testrup: 134

Laurence *alias* Lorenz, saint: 134 n. 2, 340 n. 8
Laurentius Andreae: 163
Laurentius Petri: 29, 33, 161–80 *passim*
Laurentius Surius: 39, 456
Lazarus, biblical figure: 294, 296, 302
Leo the Great, pope: 51
Léon Dacheux: 394–95
Leonardo da Udine: 204, 207, 321 n. 36
Leonardus, a priest in Sântana de Mureş: 205
Lilius Tifernas: 25
Loménie de Brienne: 269
Louis, king of France, saint: 287 n. 38
Louis XVI, king of France: 269
Lucas Vorsterman I: 475 Figure 12
Ludovica, a nun in San Michele sul Dosso: 286, 286 n. 31
Ludovico Pittorio *alias* Luigi Bigi: 29, 35, 40–41, 279–303 *passim*
Ludovico, Ser, probably connected to the Confraternity of San Ludovico: 287
Ludvig Holberg: 143
Ludwig I of Bavaria, king: 321 n. 36
Luigi Bigi *see* Ludovico Pittorio

Magnus Stjernkors: 114, 115, 115 n. 27
Marcantonio Guarini: 283 n. 18
Marcus Tullius Cicero: 178, 420 n. 28

Marcus Vigerius: 52

Margaret Beaufort, mother of Henry VII, king of England: 76, 90, 92

Margaret Tudor, daughter of Henry VII, king of England: 89

Maria, prioress in San Michele sul Dosso: 286 n. 31

Maria Magdalena Petrata: 284

Maria van Pee: 489 n. 38

Martin Luther: 19, 23, 23 n. 21, 24–26, 76, 79, 94, 122–23, 139, 162–63, 163 n. 12, 173–75, 296, 381 n. 56, 394, 445, 463

Martín Martínez de Ampiés: 227, 227 n. 17

Martin Morin: 75

Martin Schott: 373

Martinus, member of the parish clergy in Jelna [?]: 194

Martinus Huet: 204

Martinus Skytte: 122

Mary Magdalene, saint: 321

Mary of Alpheus: 243

Mary of Zebedeus: 243

Maternus Berler: 340, 342

Matheus of Rupea: 204

Matthias Hovius: 479, 481, 483, 493

Matthias Schürer: 284 n. 24, 380, 392, 393 n. 106

Maurelio, saint: 287 n. 38

Maurice de Provins: 258–59, 261, 263

Maximilian I, emperor: 373

Meffreth: 321 n. 39, 349, 349 n. 34

Melchior Lotter: 117, 117 nn. 17–19, 117 n. 21

Michael de Hungaria: 73

Michael Furter: 370

Michele Aiguiani: 317

Mikael Agricola: 122, 127

Moses, biblical figure: 292 n. 60

Muhammad, prophet: 144

Nave *see* Joshua

Nicholas V, pope: 117

Nicholaus, cleric of Yegerdorff: 195

Nicholaus, parish priest in Mojna: 195

Nicholaus de Dinkelsbühl: 207

Nicholaus de Graetz: 208

Nicolas Audet: 320, 328

Nicolas de Biard: 30, 35, 257–69 *passim*

Nicolas de Gorran: 142, 258–59, 263, 269

Nicolas Denyse: 52, 54–55

Nicolaus Benedicti: 162 n. 3

Nicolaus de Lyra: 118, 121 n. 43, 142, 168 n. 28, 207

Nicolaus Höniger: 394

Niklaus Manuel: 393 n. 108, 394

Nikolaj Frederik Severin Grundtvig: 145 n. 37

Nikolaus Lamparter: 37, 340, 346, 350, 355

Nikolaus Magni de Jauer: 322

Nils Rabenius: 161–62 n. 2

Olavus Magni: 112–13

Olavus Petri: 23, 29, 33, 161–80 *passim*

Olivier Maillard: 55

Oseas Schbadaeus: 342, 346

Osualdus de Lasko: 203 n. 63, 207

Ovid: 292 n. 37

Paola, a nun in San Michele sul Dosso: 286 n. 31

Paul III, pope: 39

Paulus Juusten: 107–08, 112, 112 n. 18, 122, 124, 126

Peder Laale: 138

Pelbartus de Temeswar: 203, 207, 326

Peregrinus de Oppeln: 117, 117 n. 31, 322

504 INDICES

Peter Attendorn: 370
Peter Schott the Elder: 373
Peter Schott the Younger: 372–74, 379
Peter van Dueren, pseudonym for Willem Gaillart: 459
Peter van Os van Breda: 425
Peter Wellen: 345
Peter Wickram: 379, 381, 381 n. 59, 383–84, 384 n. 67, 385 n. 72, 393, 393 n. 106, 397–98
Petrus Blesensis de Lutrea: 207
Petrus Canisius: 301, 301 n. 90, 302–03, 383–84, 384 n. 37, 385 n. 72, 448, 448 n. 9, 451, 452 n. 13
Petrus de Nieukerk: 324
Petrus de Palude: 207
Petrus Johannis Gothus: 164
Petrus Lombardus: 195
Petrus Mör: 344, 346, 346 n. 29
Petrus Noviomagus: 39, 448, 448 n. 8, 452 n. 13
Petrus Nowag: 196, 207
Petrus Särkilax: 122
Philip the Good, duke of Burgundy: 20 n. 10
Philipp de Lorenzi: 395
Philipp Melanchthon: 123
Piero del Pollaiolo: 298 n. 74
Pietro da Capua: 265
Pietro Ranzano: 245
Pietro Torrigiano: 89
Pius II, pope: 289 n. 46
Placita, a nun in San Michele sul Dosso: 286 n. 31
Pseudo-Albert: 349
Pseudo-Bonaventura: 354
Pseudo-Thomas Aquinas: 121 n. 43

Rafael de Mercatellis: 20 n. 10
Raymund Peñaforte: 121 n. 43
Richard Alkerton: 31, 81–84, passim, 93
Richard Fitzjames: 31, 76, 78, 80 n. 27, 76–94 passim
Richard Pace: 77, 80
Richard Pynson: 73, 75–77, 91 n. 51
Robert d'Anjou: 257
Robert Holcot: 121 n. 43, 196
Robert Mascall: 329 n. 78
Robert Redman: 77
Roberto Caracciolo da Lecce: 52, 55, 207–08, 280 n. 3, 289 n. 47

Samuel, rabbi: 227 n. 17
Saxo Grammaticus: 138
Sebastian Brant: 355, 371–74, 389–90, 390 n. 92, 396 n. 119, 394–95
Seneca: 178, 269
Sigismondo d'Este: 289
Sigismund, king of Sweden and grand duke of Finland: 125
Sigismundus, parish priest in Apoldul de Jos: 204
Simon, saint/apostle: 243
Simon Cardiaster: 120
Sirach, biblical figure: 85
Søren Aabye Kierkegaard: 145 n. 37
Stephan Fridolin: 356
Stephen Baron: 77
Stephen Douce: 92
Stephen Patrington: 329 n. 78
Susanne Hörwart: 373, 380
Symon Cock: 425, 457

Teresa de Ávila, saint: 330
Theodoric Rood: 75
Thomas Aquinas, saint: 118,
 121 n. 43, 268
Thomas a Kempis: 462
Thomsas Berthelet: 77
Thomas Betson: 75
Thomas Hunte: 75
Thomas Kempe: 91
Thomas Murner: 396 n. 119
Thomas Netter: 329 n. 78
Thomas Richard *or* Ricard/
 Richards: 90
Thomas Swalwell: 30, 49–66
 passim
Thomas Tempest: 53 n. 15, 56
Thomas Waleys: 54 n. 19
Thomas Wimbledon: 31, 75, 81–84
 passim
Tomás de Turrecremata: 266
Torsten Ståhlhandske: 116

Ugo da Prato: 125, 125 n. 56, 126, 142
Ulrich Zell: 25
Urs Graf the Elder: 391
Ursula Stingel: 373, 380

Valeriano da Soncino: 294
Veit Dietrich: 163
Veit Stoß: 327
Vicent Ferrer, saint: 27, 30, 34,
 36, 202–03, 207, 223–45 *passim*,
 296 n. 70, 326
Vincent de Beauvais: 204
Virgil: 292 n. 57

Walpurgis, saint: 193
Willem Gailliart *see* Peter van
 Dueren
Willem Vorsterman: 139, 424
William Caxton: 73, 74 n. 14, 75,
 91–92
William Durandus: 58
William Melton: 77, 79–80, 91
William Warham: 93, 93 n. 57
Wolfgang Hopyl: 75
Wynkyn de Worde: 73, 75–76

Zacharias, parish priest of Velţ and
 Senereuş: 205

506   INDICES

Index of Places

The Places index comprises locations, including sites of archival repositories from the medieval and early modern period, cathedrals, churches, educational institutions, friaries, monasteries, nunneries, preaching venues, printing centres, and so forth; it excludes editions known by the place-name such as 'the Emden edition'. Places of publication are only listed if they are found in the course of the discussion rather than as bibliographical entries. Places are rendered in the native and/or English form as necessary, for example, 'Milano/ Milan' and Finnish place-names in the diocese of Turku are additionally given in Swedish, for instance. 'Viipuri (Swe. Viborg)'.

Aarhus: 146
Åbo *see* Turku
Åland: 123
Alba Iulia: 197, 202–03
Albeşti: 197, 197 n. 38
Alemania inferior, Carmelite
    province: 36, 314, 314 n. 9
Alemania superior, Carmelite
    province: 36, 314, 314 n. 9
Alsace: 37, 340, 345, 350, 356
Antwerpen/Antwerp: 39, 139, 423,
    457, 462, 463 n. 34, 473, 475, 476
    nn. 6–7, 477
Apoldul de Jos: 204
Aquitaine: 317
Aragon: 223
Arnhem: 447 n. 6, 462
Arxiu de la Ciutat: 242
Augsburg: 198, 355, 367, 370–71,
    373–74, 377–78, 380–81, 387, 389,
    391, 395, 397
Auning: 134 n. 2
Avenches: 225
Aylesford: 318 n. 25

Bækkeskov/Bäckaskog: 136 n. 10
Barcelona: 242 n. 42
Barnwell: 78
Basel: 37, 198, 198 n. 41, 198 n. 43,
    262, 266, 269, 339–56 *passim*,

370, 372, 374, 374 n. 29, 381, 394,
    445, 453
Bavaria: 314 n. 9, 323 n. 52
Bern: 393 n. 108, 394
Bistriţa: 197 n. 38, 200–01
Bohemia: 27 n. 26
Boston, Lincolnshire: 318 n. 25
Braşov: 193, 196, 197 n. 38, 199 n. 43,
    202–03, 211
Brateiu: 204
Breda: 489 n. 38
Bristol: 88
Bruges: 73, 474, 476 n. 7
Brussel/Bruxelles/Brussels: 39, 41,
    324 n. 53, 476–77, 485, 489–90,
    490 n. 42, 491–93
Bury St Edmunds: 87

Cambridge: 72, 76–78, 81, 88, 91
Canterbury: 75, 89, 93
Cârţa: 195
Castile: 223
Cisnădie: 193, 195, 197 n. 38
Cluj-Mănăştur: 195
Cluj-Napoca: 195, 197 n. 38, 200–03
Codlea: 196
Colmar: 370, 387, 394
Copenhagen *see* København
Coventry: 78, 90
Crakow *see* Kraków

INDICES 507

Daia: 205
Dartford: 83
Dealul Frumos: 205
Delft: 414, 414 n. 11
Denmark: 23, 26–27, 27 n. 26,
  28 n. 31, 29, 32, 40, 71, 110, 133, 137,
  137 n.13, 138–40, 142, 145 n. 37,
  146, 146 n. 40, 156–57, 166 n. 20
Deventer: 262, 424
Dillingen: 395
Douai: 474
Durham: 30, 50–51, 53 n. 15, 56–57,
  61

Eindhoven: 457
Ely: 76, 78, 87
Emden: 39, 446, 459, 461–63
England: 21–22, 26–27, 27 n. 26,
  29–30, 50–51, 55, 55 n. 20, 56, 61,
  66, 71–94 *passim*, 111 n. 10, 115,
  317, 328 n. 74
Erfurt: 37, 136 n. 8, 340
Essex: 488 n. 38
Estruplund: 134 n. 2

Ferrara: 35, 40–41, 281, 281 nn.
  10–11, 282–87, 287 n. 38, 289,
  289 n. 46
Finland: 26–27, 29, 31–32, 71,
  105–28 *passim*, 165
Firenze/Florence: 284, 318
France: 22 n. 17, 26, 27 n. 26, 34–35,
  55, 72, 73 n. 10, 223, 259, 262, 317,
  474
Frankfurt am Main: 459
Frankfurt an der Oder: 370
Freiburg: 370, 372, 387, 394
Fribourg: 225

Geneva: 375 n. 33, 377
Gloucester: 88
Gørløse: 134 n. 2

Götaland: 126
Gouda: 414, 422–24
Gråsten: 153 n. 43
Greifswald: 117, 137
Groessen: 462
Guebwiller (Gebweiler): 37, 340,
  344, 344 n. 23, 345, 345 n. 25

Hamburg: 371 n. 18
Hämeenlinna: 125–26
Helsinge: 140
Helsingør: 137
Helsinki (Swe. Helsingfors): 106,
  116, 119, 121
Holy Land: 315–16
Holy Roman Empire: 73 n. 10, 198,
  314 n. 9
Horsens: 146 n. 40
Hulne: 318 n. 25
Hungary: 27 n. 26, 28 n. 31, 190–91,
  314 n. 9

Ireland: 28, 28 n. 31, 317
Italy: 22 n. 17, 23, 26–27,
  27 n. 26, 28, 34, 53, 54 n. 19, 55,
  72, 73 n. 10, 226 n. 14, 279, 281,
  284, 285 n. 29, 291 n. 52, 293 n. 62,
  298, 299 n. 80, 301 n. 90, 302,
  303 n. 92

Jelna: 194
Jerusalem: 58, 293, 315
Jutland: 134 n. 2, 153 n. 43

Kent: 83
Kiel: 188
Kirchheim: 355
København/Copenhagen: 133,
  135 n. 4, 137, 143, 145 n. 37, 146
Kökar: 109
Kokemäki (Swe. Kumo): 120, 122

INDICES

Köln/Cologne: 25, 34–35, 39, 51, 73, 138 n. 17, 198, 226, 244, 319, 328, 422, 425, 445–47, 447 n. 6, 450–51, 459, 474–76
Kraków/Crakow: 193, 196, 211, 327, 330
Kværs: 153 n. 43

Lechinţa: 196
Lecco: 299
Leipzig: 117, 138 nn. 17–19, 454
Liège: 474
Limburg: 474
Lincoln: 76, 318 n. 25
Linköping: 143, 162 n. 3
Lokalahti (Swe. Lokalax): 114
Lombardy: 317
London: 31, 40, 72, 74–78, 80–81, 81 n. 27, 82, 85–86, 91–93, 318 n. 25, 425 n. 49
Low Countries: 22 n. 17, 25–26, 27 n. 26, 29, 38–39, 73, 109, 138, 414, 427–28, 447, 473–76, 481–82
Lower Germany see Alemania inferior
Lübeck: 119 n. 40, 121, 163 n. 9
Lund: 137–38, 451
Lyon: 198, 199 n. 42, 226–27, 244, 323

Mainz: 36, 315, 319, 324–27, 329–30
Malmö: 139, 139 n. 27
Maribo: 136 n. 7
Mechelen: 473, 479
Mediaş: 193, 196–97, 203
Miercurea Ciuc: 197 n. 38, 198, 202
Milano/Milan: 279–80, 285, 299–300
Modena: 279, 286
Mojna: 205
Moldavia: 189
Moşna: 196
Mount Carmel: 36

München/Munich: 265, 301, 323, 323 n. 52
Murten: 225

Naantali (Swe. Nådental): 106, 109, 110 n. 8, 111, 113, 118 n. 34
Napoli/Naples: 245, 289 n. 47
Närke: 161
Netherlands: 26, 35, 73 n. 10, 259, 262, 314 n. 9, 459, 462
Normandy: 73
Norway: 32
Norwich: 318 n. 25
Nürnberg/Nuremberg: 53, 198, 198 n. 41, 227, 345

Odense: 146 n. 40
Örebro: 161, 163, 166, 175
Oslo: 146 n. 40, 323
Oxford: 57, 72, 75–76, 78, 80, 318 n. 25

Paris: 55 n. 21, 75, 79, 138, 138 n. 22, 195, 259–60, 262, 266, 269, 317
Payern: 225
Portugal: 28 n. 31
Pöytyä (Swe. Pöytis): 116, 116 n. 30, 117
Praha/Prague: 196, 211
Provence: 317

Rancio: 299, 300
Rauma (Swe. Raumo): 106, 109
Rendsburg: 166 n. 20
Reutlingen: 35, 198, 262
Rhineland see also Upper Rhineland: 447, 474
Ribe: 175 n. 45
Richmond: 89
Rochester: 76
Roma/Rome: 105, 113, 341–42, 345, 428, 474, 488
Romania: 26, 33–34, 187–212 passim

Roskilde: 137–38, 175 n. 45
Rostock: 164, 164 n. 13
Rottenburg: 327 n. 72
Ruși: 29, 196, 209
Rymättylä (Swe. Rimito): 113, 117,
    117 n. 32, 118, 118 n. 34, 119

Saffron Walden: 329 n. 78
Saint-Omer: 474
Sântana de Mureș: 205
Scandinavia: 22 n. 17, 25–26, 31,
    111 n. 10, 137
Scotland: 28 n. 31, 139 n. 27, 317
Sebeș: 195
Senereuș: 205
Shropshire: 91
Sibiu: 192–96, 198, 199 n. 43, 201,
    201 n. 53, 204, 207, 209
Sicily: 317
Sighișoara: 197 n. 38
Sinai: 292 n. 60
Sjælland: 134 n. 2, 137, 140
Skåne: 136 n. 10, 137, 139
Slesvig-Holsten: 166 n. 20
Spain: 24, 26–27, 27 n. 26, 34, 55,
    226, 266, 317
Speyer: 198, 370
St Albans: 72
Stavayer-le-Lac: 225
Stockholm: 146 n. 40, 161–62,
    163 n. 11, 178
Strängnäs: 162, 162 n. 3, 178
Strasbourg: 37–38, 51, 198, 198 n. 41,
    226–27, 244, 262, 284 n. 24,
    339–56 *passim*, 365–98 *passim*,
    445
Straubing: 36, 315, 320, 320 n. 33,
    322–23, 326–27, 329 n. 79, 330
Stuttgart: 146 n. 40
Sulsted: 157
Șumuleu-Ciuc: 201–02

Sweden: 23, 26, 28 n. 31, 31–33, 110
    nn. 8–9, 111 n. 10, 116, 120, 125–27,
    136, 142–43, 146 n. 40, 162–64,
    169–70, 451
Swiss Confederation: 27 n. 26,
    73 n. 10
Szeklerland: 200

Tammela: 121–22
Târgu Mureș: 197 n. 38, 203
Telemark: 143
Toledo: 266
Transylvania: 27, 29, 33, 187–212
    passim
Trier: 319, 325, 395
Trondheim: 143, 146 n. 40
Turku (Swe. Åbo): 29, 32, 105–28
    passim, 164
Tuscany: 317

Ulieș: 205
Ulm: 244, 370 n. 12
Ulvila (Swe. Ulfsby): 106
Upper Germany *see Alemania superior*
Upper Rhineland *see also*
    Rhineland: 376, 380, 383, 393, 398
Uppsala: 146 n. 40, 162, 168 n. 28
Utrecht: 328 n. 74, 415–16, 416 n. 20

Vadstena: 111, 113, 125, 174,
    174 n. 41, 179
Valencia: 223, 227 n. 19
Västerås: 33, 126, 164–66, 168, 175
Velț: 205
Venezia/Venice: 198, 199 n. 42, 227,
    259, 280, 286
Vic: 242 n. 42
Vienna *see* Wien
Vienne: 262
Viipuri (Swe. Viborg): 106, 109,
    134, 164

510 INDICES

Wallachia: 189
Westminster: 51, 72, 75, 89
Wien/Vienna: 196, 199 n. 43, 211, 319
Windesheim: 421
Wittenberg: 23, 122–23, 161 n. 1, 162
Worcester: 88

Wrocław: 196
Würzburg: 319

York: 77, 80, 91

Zaragoza: 227 n. 17

Index of Religious Institutions, Movements, and Orders

The Religious Institutions, Movements, and Orders index takes account of selected categories of material in the volume, including religious orders, educational establishments, and important religious movements. Of necessity, this index is confined to those entries that can be securely listed. For instance, while it is possible to index the few cathedrals and female religious houses as they are clearly specified, the same is not feasible for the frequent mention — sometimes in passing — of multiple churches/parishes and male religious houses or institutions (secular or monastic) that are best investigated under the Index to Places above and/or the various religious orders listed below.

Augustinian Order: 189, 196, 324
Augustinan/Austin canons: 74, 82
Augustinian Hermits *see*
  Wilhelmites
Benedictine Order: 30, 35, 41, 50,
  52, 57, 62, 188, 195, 285, 286 n. 31,
  289
Birgittine Order: 76, 109–10, 110
  nn. 7–8, 111–13, 136 n. 7, 136 n. 10
Brethren of the Common Life: 423
Büßerinnen *see* Reuerinnen
Calvinists *and* Calvinism: 23–24,
  187, 463, 473–74, 492
Canonesses regular of the Order of
  St Augustine: 477, 486, 488–89,
  489 n. 38, 492
Carmelite Order: 29, 36,
  73 n. 13, 284, 284 n. 26, 285,
  313–30 *passim*, 341
Carthusian Order: 39, 78, 136 n. 8,
  376 n. 35, 447–48, 451, 456

Cathedrals *and* Other Major
Religious Sites
  Basel, Cathedral: 341–42, 344
  Basel, Charterhouse: 349, 356,
    374 n. 29
  Coventry, Charterhouse: 90
  Durham, Priory: 30, 49–66
    passim
  Köln/Cologne, Charterhouse:
    447, 447 n. 6
  London, Hospital of St Mary
    Bishopgate *alias* St Mary
    Spital: 31, 81–89 *passim*
  London, St Paul's Cathedral: 31,
    40, 77, 78, 80–81, 83, 88, 91
  London, St Paul's Cathedral,
    Jesus Chapel: 88
  London, St Paul's Churchyard,
    St Paul's Cross: 31, 75, 77, 80,
    81–89 *passim*, 93
  Lund, Cathedral: 137–38

Lund, Cathedral, Altar of St
Christopher: 138
Lund, Cathedral, Altar of the
Three Kings: 138
Roskilde, Cathedral: 175 n. 45
Strängnäs, Cathedral: 162,
162 n. 3
Strasbourg, Cathedral: 37–38,
340, 340 n. 8, 367, 372, 376
Figure 6, 377 n. 38, 383, 393
Strasbourg, Cathedral, St.
Lorenzaltar: 37, 340, 340 n. 8
Trier, Cathedral: 395
Turku, Cathedral: 112
Viipuri/Viborg Cathedral: 134
Catholic Reformation *and*
Counter-Reformation: 21, 39,
190, 301–02, 447, 473
Churches *see* Index to Places *and/
or the individual religious orders*
Cistercian Order: 189, 195,
283 n. 17, 285, 286 n. 31, 325
Clarissan Order: 37, 40, 345, 347, 375
Confraternity *and* Fraternity
Ferrara, Confraternity of San
Ludovico: 35, 40, 286 n. 35,
287, 287 nn. 38–39, 290, 301–02
Genoa, Compagnia del Nome di
Gesù: 300
London, St Paul's Cathedral,
Jesus Chapel, Fraternity of the
Holy Name: 88
Council of Trent: 24, 38, 109,
243–44, 300–01, 428
Devotio moderna: 411, 412 n. 6, 421,
421 n. 36, 486 n. 36
Diet
Diet, of Kiel: 166 n. 20
Diet, of Rendsburg: 166 n. 20
Diet, of Västerås: 33, 126, 164–66,
168, 175

Dissolution of the Monasteries:
30, 56
Dominican Order: 17, 28, 34–35,
37–38, 40, 52, 54 n. 19, 83, 109–10,
113, 117–18, 125, 142, 189, 191,
194–95, 197 n. 38, 201, 201 n. 53,
202–04, 207, 211, 223–24, 241,
258–59, 266, 267, 313, 313 n. 2,
315, 318, 322, 325–26, 329, 344,
344 n. 23, 345, 345 n. 25, 346–47,
375, 375 n. 32, 445, 451, 489 n. 38
Evangelicals: 23, 94, 122–24, 126,
197 n. 38, 298, 447
Fifth Lateran Council: 25, 79
Franciscan Order *alias* Friars
Minor: 17, 28, 52, 55, 61, 66,
109–10, 118, 189, 191, 197, 197 n. 38,
201–03, 208, 208 n. 84, 209,
257–58, 283 n. 17, 313 n. 2, 314–15,
322–23, 326, 327 n. 72, 329, 379,
383–86, 398
Hermits of St Augustine *see*
Wilhelmite Order
Jesuit Order: 39, 41, 126, 190, 301,
451, 473–74, 474 n. 1, 475 n. 4,
476, 476 n. 6, 492
Lutherans and Lutheranism and
anti-Lutheranism: 18, 23, 23 n. 21,
24–25, 29–30, 32–33, 38–40, 55,
77, 81, 92, 94, 106–07, 107 n. 4,
108–09, 112, 122–26, 128, 133,
139–40, 143, 145 n. 37, 156–57,
161–62, 164–65, 167, 170, 173, 187,
193–95, 201–02, 285 n. 29, 342,
346, 368, 381 n. 56, 393, 393 n. 108,
394, 448, 451–52, 460, 462–64,
467–68, 473, 492
Magdalenerinnen *see* Reuerinnen
Mendicants: 17, 24, 27, 30, 36, 52,
54, 189, 191, 193, 200–01, 203, 206,
210–11, 313 n. 2, 313 n. 3, 316, 321,
329, 341, 372–73, 375, 384

512 INDICES

Mennonites: 463–64, 468,
468 n. 45
Observance and Observant
Reform: 28, 37, 344, 344 n. 23,
345, 350, 365, 373, 376, 394
Observance, Carmelites: 284
Observance, Clarissans: 375
Observance, Dominicans: 285, 339,
356, 375, 397
Observance, Franciscans *alias*
Friars Minor: 77, 203, 203 n. 63,
287 n. 38, 422–24
Orthodox Christianity: 105, 187
Ottomans: 187, 194, 199, 209
Premonstratensian Order: 136 n. 10
Protestant/s *and* Protestantism:
18, 21, 22–25, 27, 32, 38–39, 49,
52, 55, 73 n. 13, 76, 80, 83–84, 91,
94, 108–09, 133 n. 1, 137, 145–46,
153, 156, 187, 189, 191, 202, 365,
368, 393–95, 395 n. 113, 398, 428,
445–47, 456–57, 459, 461–63,
463 n. 34, 465, 468, 474, 482
Reformation/s: 19 n. 5, 21, 23,
23 nn. 21–22, 24–25, 27, 31–34,
52, 56, 61, 80, 83, 94, 94 n. 62,
106–08, 112, 120 n. 43, 122–28,
133–34, 134 n. 2, 135, 137, 139–40,
147, 149, 153, 156–57, 161–64, 168,
170, 170 n. 30, 175, 187, 189, 191,
195, 201–02, 207, 209–10, 320,
327–28, 356, 368, 393–94, 426,
447, 473, 476
Religious Houses (Female)
Arnhem, Sint-Agnes,
Canonesses regular of the
Order of St Augustine: 447
nn. 5–6
Augsburg, St. Ursula,
Dominican Order: 389
Barking, Barking Abbey,
Benedictine Order: 488 n. 28

Breda, Vredenberg, Canonesses
regular of the Order of St
Augustine: 489 n. 38
Brussel, Onze Lieve Vrouw ter
Rosen Gheplant in Jericho,
Canonesses regular of the
Order of St Augustine: 41,
477, 485–93 *passim*
Brussel, Sint-Elisabeth op de
berg Sion, Canonesses regular
of the Order of St Augustine:
486, 492
Ferrara, San Gabriele, Carmelite
Order: 284
Ferrara, Sant'Antonio in
Polesine, Benedictine Order:
35, 285, 289
Ferrara, Santa Caterina Martire,
Dominican Order: 286
Guebwiller, Engelporten,
Dominican Order: 344,
344 n. 23, 345
Maribo, Birgittine Order (of
nuns and brothers): 136 n. 7
Milano/Milan, San Michele
sul Dosso, Cistercian Order:
285–86
Naantali, Birgittine Order (of
nuns and brothers): 109,
110 n. 8, 111, 113
Pfullingen, Clarissan Order: 37,
345, 347, 350
Strasbourg, St. Clara im grünen
Wörd, Clarissan Order: 375
Strasbourg, St. Katharina,
Dominican Order: 375
Strasbourg, St. Magdalena,
Reuerinnen *alias* Büßerinnen
alias Magdalenerinnen *alias*
Sorores poenitentes: 37, 340 n. 5,
345–47, 350, 373, 375, 379–80,
383, 387, 389

Strasbourg, St. Margareta und Agnes, Dominican Order: 373, 375, 385 n. 72

Strasbourg, St. Nikolaus in undis, Dominican Order: 37, 345–48, 375, 385 n. 72, 389, 397

Syon, Birgittine Order (of nuns and brothers): 51, 76, 88

Toledo, Dominican Order: 489 n. 38

Vadstena, Vadstena Abbey, Birgittine Order (of nuns and brothers): 111, 113, 125, 174, 174 n. 41, 179

Religious Houses (Male) *see* Index of Places *and/or the individual religious orders*

Reuerinnen *alias* Büßerinnen *alias* Magdalenerinnen *alias Sorores poenitentes*: 37, 345–46, 373, 375

Servite Order: 283, 283 n. 18, 313 n. 2

Sorores poenitentes see Reuerinnen

Unitarians: 187

Universities/Other Educational Institutions

Basel, University: 37, 260, 339, 343 Figure 4, 344, 372

Braşov, Lutheran Gymnasium: 201–02

Bruges, Jesuit College: 474

Cambridge University: 76, 91

Cambridge University, Christ's College: 76

Cambridge University, Jesus College: 91

Cambridge University, St John's College: 76

Douai, Jesuit College: 474

Erfurt, University: 37, 340

Freiburg, University: 372

Greifswald, University: 117, 137

Heidelberg, University: 322, 341–42, 344

Leuven, University: 473

Köln/Cologne, Gymnasium Tricoronatum: 474, 474 n. 3

Kráków, University: 211

Oxford University, Merton College: 76

Paris, University: 195, 266, 269, 317

Praha/Prague, University: 196, 211

Roma/Rome, Collegium Romanum: 474

Saint-Omer, College: 474

Turku, Cathedral School: 127

Valladolid, University: 266

Whittington, College: 92

Wien/Vienna, University: 196, 211

Wittenberg University: 23, 122–23, 162

Wilhelmite Order *alias* Hermits of St Augustine: 313 n. 2, 376

SERMO

All volumes in this series are evaluated by an Editorial Board, strictly on academic grounds, based on reports prepared by referees who have been commissioned by virtue of their specialism in the appropriate field. The Board ensures that the screening is done independently and without conflicts of interest. The definitive texts supplied by authors are also subject to review by the Board before being approved for publication. Further, the volumes are copyedited to conform to the publisher's stylebook and to the best international academic standards in the field.

Titles in Series

Ruth Horie, *Perceptions of Ecclesia: Church and Soul in Medieval Dedication Sermons* (2006)

Veronica O'Mara and Suzanne Paul, *A Repertorium of Middle English Prose Sermons*, 4 vols (2007)

Constructing the Medieval Sermon, ed. by Roger Andersson (2008)

Alan John Fletcher, *Late Medieval Popular Preaching in Britain and Ireland: Texts, Studies, and Interpretations* (2009)

Kimberly A. Rivers, *Preaching the Memory of Virtue and Vice: Memory, Images, and Preaching in the Late Middle Ages* (2010)

Holly Johnson, *The Grammar of Good Friday: Macaronic Sermons of Late Medieval England* (2012)

The Last Judgement in Medieval Preaching, ed. by Thom Mertens, Maria Sherwood-Smith, Michael Mecklenburg, and Hans-Jochen Schiewer (2013)

Preaching the Word in Manuscript and Print in Late Medieval England: Essays in Honour of Susan Powell, ed. by Martha W. Driver and Veronica O'Mara (2013)

Preaching and Political Society: From Late Antiquity to the End of the Middle Ages / Depuis l'Antiquité tardive jusqu'à la fin du Moyen Âge, ed. by Franco Morenzoni (2013)

Sermo Doctorum: Compilers, Preachers, and their Audiences in the Early Medieval West, ed. by Maximilian Diesenberger, Yitzhak Hen, and Marianne Pollheimer (2013)

From Words to Deeds: The Effectiveness of Preaching in the Late Middle Ages, ed. by Maria Giuseppina Muzzarelli (2014)

Yuichi Akae, *A Mendicant Sermon Collection from Composition to Reception: The* Novum opus dominicale *of John Waldeby, OESA* (2015)

Siegfried Wenzel, *The Sermons of William Peraldus: An Appraisal* (2017)

Miikka Tamminen, *Crusade Preaching and the Ideal Crusader* (2018)

Christian, Jewish, and Muslim Preaching in the Mediterranean and Europe: Identities and Interfaith Encounters, ed. by Linda G. Jones and Adrienne Dupont-Hamy (2019)

Zachary Guiliano, *The Homiliary of Paul the Deacon: Religious and Cultural Reform in Carolingian Europe* (2021)

In Preparation

Christoph Galle, *Predigen im Karolingerreich: Die homiletischen Sammlungen von Paulus Diaconus, Lanthpertus von Mondsee, Rabanus Maurus und Haymo von Auxerre*